Beyond Misbehaving

By the same author:

Money Matters: A Keynesian Approach to Monetary Economics (with Sheila C. Dow, 1982, Martin Robertson)

The Economic Imagination: Towards a Behavioural Theory of Choice (1983, Wheatsheaf Books)

The Corporate Imagination: How Big Companies Make Mistakes (1984, Wheatsheaf Books)

Lifestyle Economics: Consumer Behaviour in a Turbulent World (1986, Wheatsheaf Books)

Monetary Scenarios: A Modern Approach to Financial Systems (1990, Edward Elgar Publishing)

Microeconomics for Business and Marketin: Lectures, Case and Worked Essays (1995, Edward Elgar Publishing).

Information, Opportunism and Economic Coordination (2002, Edward Elgar Publishing)

Business Economics: A Contemporary Approach (with Tim Wakeley, 2005, McGraw-Hill UK)

G. L. S. Shackle (Great Thinkers in Economics Series) (with Bruce Littleboy, 2014, Palgrave)

Principles of Behavioral Economics: Bringing Together Old, Newe and Evolutionary Approaches (2022, Cambridge University Press)

Toward a Wider Vision of Behavioral Economics (2024, PE:AT Publishing, second editin 2026)

Fiction, under the penname Darcy Crick:

Dealbreakers: Sex, Quiz, and Rock 'n' Roll (2025, Darcy Crick Books)

BEYOND MISBEHAVING

Changing Universities, Pluralism, and the Evolution of a Heterodox Behavioural Economist

(Second Edition)

Peter E. Earl

Honorary Associate Professor of Economics
University of Queensland

FOREWORD BY JOHN CREEDY

Available in eBook and soft cover print editions.
PE:AT Publishing, Westlake, QLD, Australia
Distribution to major online retail platforms via Draft2Digital

Table of Contents

List of Tables

Foreword

In this impressive book the author sets himself the difficult task of simultaneously meeting several different challenges. First, it is 'an intellectual autobiography addressed primarily to those who think of themselves as "heterodox" economists,' Second, in telling this story, he provides valuable background information, and judgements on, the vast changes that have taken place within universities over the last fifty years. This is informed by his wide-ranging experience. Third, and importantly, he extracts many valuable lessons for academics trying to navigate their own path through the academic maze. Indeed, Peter Earl takes the reader on an introspective journey that has a far broader interest, through his ability to recognise and communicate the 'universal in the particular', or what Alfred Marshall (following Plato) would call the 'one in the many, and the many in the one'. Essentially, we see a behavioural economist candidly and dispassionately evaluating his own behaviour. Even the clever title has several meanings.

This book, written by one who was not prepared to play the 'academic game' by the (ever changing) rules, illustrates 'what it is like to have an academic career that entails decades of operating without giving due thought to dominant ways of doing things or knowingly defying them.' Of course, a major 'rule change' has been the evaluation of 'research quality' by judges who do not read a single word of the research, and take a narrow view governed by arbitrary metrics. The book has the substantial advantage of being written in a lively and engaging style, displaying broad sympathies, a sense of humour and a lack of rancour. It will appeal to a very wide readership – indeed anyone who thinks seriously about what it means to be a university researcher and teacher. I can recommend it heartily without qualification.

John Creedy
Professorial Fellow
University of Melbourne

Preface

This book presents an account of my life as a heterodox economist, from which I draw career lessons for those who follow me down the less-travelled road in which economising activity is not reduced to acts of constrained optimisation by socially isolated, utility-seeking agents with 'given' preferences and 'rational expectations'. The idea for the book came to me in December 2020, almost exactly a year before I started writing it. I was about to retire and was therefore getting ready to vacate my office at the University of Queensland. The task of emptying my filing cabinets was akin to an archaeological exercise, as I uncovered documents that in some cases dated back to the late 1970s. Among the items that surfaced was a 2002 contract from the University of Michigan Press (UMP) for a book that would have been called 'Survival Strategies for Heterodox Economists'.

I had put together the proposal for the UMP book after being approached by the late, great heterodox economics activist, Fred Lee, who was advising on a series of books for the heterodox economics market. The proposal file was still on my computer, and it revealed that I had introduced the book's rationale as follows:

> Many academics embark on their careers on the basis of intrinsic motivation, a belief that they have something worthwhile to offer to their subjects, rather than out of a desire for fame and fortune, which, for economists, can be far more readily achieved in the corporate sector. Such motivation seems particularly likely to drive the efforts of heterodox economists. Unfortunately, it is ultimately rather difficult to have a satisfying career without job security, a work environment conducive to doing research on the things about which one feels passionate, and prospects of a good pension, possibly one that might permit early retirement if continued faculty membership becomes too frustrating or exhausting. Achieving such a situation has become increasingly difficult over the past couple of decades for academics in general but particularly so for heterodox economists, as the processes of increasing resource pressure in academic environments have worked in favour of the mainstream. As well as policy-driven pressures, such as research and teaching audits, there are more subtle hurdles for the heterodox economist to surmount,

such as the commodification of business education and the related McDonaldisation of teaching processes.

Would-be academic heterodox economists may be poorly aware of the hazardous environment they are getting into, whilst established ones may, like slowly boiled frogs, be struggling to survive without a clear appreciation of the subtleties of how things have gradually changed since they embarked on their careers. Those heterodox economists, both young and mature, who are already wise to the fact that things are now tough, may have trouble seeing what to do in the face of it. All could benefit from the proposed book.

However, I had not signed the contract due to the demands of the role that I then had as co-editor of the *Journal of Economic Psychology* and because, by the time the proposal was accepted, I was also planning a radical pluralistic business economics textbook with Tim Wakeley (published as Earl and Wakeley, 2005).

Digging up the unsigned UMP contract gave me pause for thought on two fronts. First, I wondered whether I should have written the book to which it referred, rather than the one with Tim, for although the latter yielded us some useful career lessons, its sales had been very disappointing. Secondly, there was the question of whether I had been qualified to write the survival strategies book back then and/or whether I would be qualified to write such a book two decades later, as heterodox economists faced an even more challenging academic environment. How well had I survived in my own career as a heterodox economist, and insofar as I had survived, was my knowledge of how to survive relevant for upcoming generations of heterodox economists?

Certainly, in material terms, my career had eventually turned out beyond the wildest dreams that I had in the early 1980s. This came largely because of my decision in 1984 to leave the UK and move to Australia. Yet that move was not without consequences for where I had got to academically. At the time that I was clearing my office, I was not about to transition to an emeritus chair in the way that I anticipated decades earlier. Instead, I was merely an associate professor and had been required by my head of school to provide a set of key performance indicators (KPIs) for him to use in the process of making a case for me to be offered a three-year post as an honorary associate professor, with my performance in terms of these KPIs potentially to be used in deciding whether the post would be renewed. How had it come to this, especially since I had started out seemingly with a bright academic future after I had achieved a double-first in economics at Cambridge, had been offered my first academic position early in the second year of my PhD studies, and had concentrated in a field – behavioural economics – that was struggling to gain traction at the time I started out but had become very popular over the course of my career? Compared with Richard Thaler – who had started working on a behavioural approach to economics around the same time as me but who went on to a chair at the University of Chicago and to be awarded the 2017 Nobel Memorial Prise in Economic Sciences, despite his PhD supervisor Sherwin Rosen not expecting much of him reportedly (see Thaler, 2015, loc. 254) – I appeared largely to have 'blown it' in career terms.

As I read what I had proposed to do in the book for UMP, I realised that, given what had happened in academic economics in the ensuing two decades, the project had probably become even more worthwhile to bring to fruition. In retirement, I would have time to write such a book once I had finished work on projects to which I was already committed. However, although uncovering the UMP contract rekindled my interest in writing a career self-help book for heterodox economists, I decided that I would write something different from what I had proposed in 2002. It would be a much more substantial, much more confessional kind of work and would be my equivalent of Herbert Simon's (1991) *Models of My Life* and Richard Thaler's (2015) *Misbehaving*. However, it needed to be written in a very different way from the intellectual autobiographies of Simon and Thaler so that it could yield career lessons as well as explaining how I came to develop my ideas and what these ideas are. I decided to call the book *Beyond Misbehaving* in the hope of signalling that I had worked on a much more radical vision of behavioural economics than the one that Thaler had developed. Despite it being the work of an academic also-ran who some might view as having frittered away a bright future, I hope this book will prove to be an interesting read and give younger generations of readers a sense of how much has changed in academic economics in the past half-century.

Unlike the book proposed in the UMP contract, the first edition of this book was not intended purely for those who view themselves as heterodox economists. I wrote the first edition in a way that I hoped might also make it interesting to mainstream behavioural economists, who face rather smaller career challenges than those that afflict their heterodox counterparts. I hoped that the former would see that the less-travelled road in behavioural economics that I travelled complements the one with which they are familiar and provides new avenues for analysis.

The first edition of *Beyond Misbehaving* was published early in January 2024. However, within a few weeks of publishing it, I concluded that I had probably positioned it in a way that put it in danger of 'falling between two stools.' On the one hand, the 'heterodox behavioural' phrase in its subtitle might deter heterodox economists from reading it if they have reservations about behavioural economics of the kind for which Thaler is known. There was a significant risk that they would not know that the kind of behavioural economics that I have practised has its roots in my pluralistic Cambridge education in the mid-1970s and weaves in ideas from institutional, Post Keynesian and neo-Schumpeterian/ evolutionary economics, as well as from marketing, organisation studies and psychology. On the other hand, the phrase 'heterodox behavioural' might be viewed with alarm by mainstream behavioural economists.

I therefore decided to prepare, in US English, a second, shorter memoir book addressed purely to mainstream behavioural economists, under the title *Toward a Wider Vision of Behavioral Economics*. That book focuses on the development of my behavioural perspective and does not include a chapter on career lessons. Because I was retired and operating as an independent publisher, I was able to produce and publish that book within six months. With that version done, an obvious future step was to prepare a second edition of the original book, adapting it purely for heterodox economists. I began work on that task in January 2026, after completing several other projects (including a heterodox economics novel published under the gender-neutral penname of Darcy Crick, 2025). However, I decided not to make any changes to the subtitle, despite my concerns with how heterodox economists might see the phrase 'heterodox behavioural economist', for it is the most succinct phrase for branding the kind of economist that I have been for the past fifty years.

Changes for the second edition go beyond reworking some parts of the book to reposition it as a 'heterodox-only' work, The biggest change for the second edition is the addition of a new final chapter, adapted from the final chapter of *Toward a Wider Vision of Behavioral Economics*. This chapter summarises my current vision of how behavioural economics should be practised and how that vision differs from the dominant approach. I have also been able to improve the accuracy and precision of the account in Section 4.7 of the 'revise and resubmit' stage of my PhD. The original account was largely accurate but purely memory-based, whereas the revision draws on the relevant documents that I could not locate when writing the original. The rediscovery of these documents was unknowingly facilitated by my brother-in-law, Andrew Gay, a few months after the first edition was published, when he arranged to ship to me several boxes of things that I had left with my parents almost forty years earlier when I emigrated to Tasmania. To my surprise and delight, it included a folder of PhD-related correspondence.

The page count and pagination of the print version of the second edition also differ considerably from the original because I decided to increase the inside margin sizes to make the book more comfortable to use. The bindings of the original soft cover versions were far more robust than a typical paperback, making it hard to flatten the pages when the book was open. This added about 45 pages to the print version before the new final chapter was incorporated and required a major reworking of the index. But it seemed all the more necessary once I decided to add the extra chapter.

While writing the original book and/or preparing this version, I had useful discussions with and/or received encouragement, helpful information, or comments on draft chapters, from John Austin, Ingrid Bailey, Harry Campbell, Greg Clydesdale, Alistair Dow, Sheila Dow, Glyn Kearley, Steve Kidd, John King, Alex Millmow, Charles Normand, Jason Potts, and Daniel Zizzo. John Creedy was especially helpful and provided swift and very thought-provoking feedback on chapter after chapter, along with the book's foreword. Geoff Hodgson read the original draft of *Beyond Misbehaving* and provided both encouragement and some very helpful suggestions about how it might be pruned to make it more viable as a publishing proposition. Much of what I removed after considering Geoff's suggestions (which amounted to nearly 30,000 words) is available, along with unpublished documents and papers referred to in this book, as 'supplementary material' at my personal website (see https://shredecon.wordpress.com/beyond-misbehaving). I also received helpful feedback from participants at a Zoom presentation that I gave in October 2023 to the University of Witwatersrand's workshop series on economic methodology. My reference in Section 10.9 to Pixar's way of promoting constructive criticism was the result of my wonderful team of high-achieving behavioural economics tutors – Jessica Downing-Ide, Ryan Palfrey, Lillian Rangiah and Edward Watson – giving me a copy of Ed Catmull's (2014) book *Creativity, Inc.* as a memento of our working relationship, after they had the insight to notice how it intersected with what we had been teaching.

I am most grateful for all the help and encouragement from those mentioned in the previous two paragraphs, and to Marc Lavoie (2024) and Jerry Courvisanos (2025) for their encouraging reviews of the original book, though I take full responsibility for any errors and omissions in this edition. However, my greatest debt is to Annabelle Taylor, my partner since 2005. Annabelle's love, support, and willingness to tolerate my distractedness during the writing of this book have contributed greatly to me being able to complete it rapidly despite it being a much larger and more complex undertaking than I initially imagined it would be. Her comments on the draft chapters have also been helpful in giving me a sense of whether I was succeeding in making it interesting to a wider audience and of the horror that some aspects of the Cambridge approach to teaching can generate in the mind of an experienced teacher who has been formally trained about pedagogy.

Introduction

This book is an unusual contribution to the literature on economic method and the history of economic thought. It is an intellectual autobiography addressed to those who think of themselves as 'heterodox' economists. However, it may also be of interest to students of economics and academic economists in general because of the insights it offers about how academia has changed over the past half-century. It should also help to satisfy any curiosity they might have about what it is like to have an academic career that entails decades of operating without giving due thought to dominant ways of doing things or knowingly defying them. In writing this book, I am continuing to misbehave: I am well aware that intellectual autobiographies are normally the preserve of those who have had outstanding careers and become very well-known and very extensively cited. My career did not come into these categories. But it might have done if I had played the academic game differently, and that is the point of writing this book.

To set the scene for what follows, it is probably best not to begin at the beginning but on Monday 2 July 2001. It was a typical, gloriously sunny, pleasantly warm winter's day in Brisbane, Australia, and it was the day that I started work as a senior lecturer in the School of Economics at the University of Queensland, the institution at which I spent the rest of my career. Taken in isolation, this might seem rather unremarkable. Set in context, it had greater significance. On that day, I was less than two months from turning 46. Almost exactly 22 years earlier, I had started my first lecturing position on a cooler summer's day at the University of Stirling in Scotland. I first became a senior lecturer at the start of 1987, at the University of Tasmania, Australia, and I was first offered a senior lectureship at the University of Queensland at the end of that year. On that occasion, I declined the offer, in no small part because I discovered during the interview visit that Brisbane's summer weather was far too hot and humid for me to enjoy. So why had I moved to Brisbane in July 2001? Given my age and climatic preferences, why was

I not moving to a much better job in a city with a more temperate climate? And why did I stay there, hankering for a different climate, for the rest of my career, despite not being promoted beyond the associate professor grade at the University of Queensland?

It was not that I was lazy, had a mental illness or allowed addictive forms of consumption to hold back my achievements. Nor did I lack the brains to do better: I graduated from Cambridge in 1977 with a double-first in the Economics Tripos and went on to complete my PhD there. Such qualifications usually open the door to a stellar career. Yet in early 2002, when my former PhD student Jason Potts and I applied for an Australian Research Council Discovery Grant, one of the referees questioned whether I was a worthy applicant since I had 'failed to live up to [my] initial promise'. I had been embarrassed to be a liability to Jason, and I doubted that the referee knew what had gone on in my career beyond the details provided in our application. But I knew that the referee's assessment of my achievements was well aimed. Eight years later, I succeeded in winning an ARC Discovery Grant, sharing the Chief Investigator role with my colleague Lana Friesen, and during the decade that ensued my work would have seemed much more consistent with the promise I had originally shown. The trouble was that what I did between 55 and 65 years of age was what I should have done when I was between 35 and 45 years of age and should have continued to do in the ensuing two decades.

It is precisely because of my failure to have the kind of career success and impact that I might have had that I decided to write this intellectual autobiography. I hope that, by sharing the secrets of my under-achievement, I may help some academic economists to limit the extent to which they fail to achieve as much as they might be capable of achieving in their careers. What follows is the tale of an unusual career from which I have been able to extract many lessons. I hope it will encourage readers to reflect during the rest of their careers on why they are doing what they are doing and whether they could be doing something better. It will become apparent that such reflection can be done not merely in relation to one's choice of economic method and where to apply it but also in relation to how one's mind works and the impact that this may be having on how one behaves – or misbehaves.

Three topics surface repeatedly in the chapters that follow. The first is that the environment in which I worked changed considerably during my career. This was partly because I moved between universities that had different operating systems and organisational cultures. As I learned the hard way, these differences can be surprising and perplexing. However, I also had to learn how to deal with changes in some of the things that universities have in common. Early- and mid-career academics may not realise how much universities in many countries have changed over the past half-century or the extent to which the career success and satisfaction of academics is contingent on their awareness of the nature of the system in which they are operating and how well they keep abreast of changes in that system. Much of what follows is a cautionary tale that illustrates how the context in which we choose affects the consequences of our behaviour and the extent to which we can 'get away with' not behaving in line with established norms. When the context in which we are behaving changes, actions that had once been career-enhancing may become problematic. However, I hope that the 'changing universities' theme will be stimulating in another way. I will show how changes to how the university system operates have made some aspects of academic life better but in other respects they have made academic careers much less attractive than they used to be. I hope that this book may thereby prompt readers to reflect on what might be done to recapture some of the desirable things that have been lost.

The second recurring topic in this book is the pursuit of pluralism in the teaching of economics. In many chapters of this book, I consider diverse ways in which students can develop their expertise in economics by being exposed to contending perspectives on the discipline and by having to get used to dealing with open-ended problems to which definitive answers are not possible but for which actions need to be recommended. It is challenging to teach in this way, rather than from a bible-like textbook and with closed problems that have definite answers, and it has become increasingly difficult to ensure that students receive a pluralistic learning experience. Despite this, I managed to operate as a pluralistic teacher throughout my career. Writing this book provides me with an opportunity to share how I did this, so that others may have a more straightforward time as pluralistic teachers than I sometimes did.

Last, but certainly not least, a recurring topic in this book is what it means to be a 'behavioural' economist and how I developed the behavioural perspective that, along with pluralism, became core to my identity as an economist. Like Geoff Hodgson (2019), I believe that taking a behavioural turn is key if heterodox approaches are to survive and their proponents are to thrive in an environment that has become increasingly challenging for them. However, Hodgson and I see the behavioural approach differently from how mainstream economists view it today. When I started out on my behavioural economics odyssey in the mid 1970s, the field had none of the popularity that it has today. But when it became a hot research area, I was puzzled to discover that Richard Thaler (the winner of the 2017 Nobel Memorial Prise in Economic Sciences) and others who called themselves behavioural economists were operating in a different way from me and seemed rarely to refer to sources that had informed my early work. In other words, I had developed a 'heterodox' approach to behavioural economics, and behavioural economics was itself a field amenable to teaching in a pluralistic manner. My approach includes some elements from what has become accepted as 'the' behavioural approach to economics, but I position them differently and offer a more extensive and more radical agenda that focuses on the processes by which knowledge grows rather than on departures from an idealised static view of what constitutes 'rational' behaviour.

With Thaler and his followers having redefined 'behavioural economics', some readers might think that it is time for me to admit defeat and cease describing myself as a behavioural economist. But it is difficult to find a simple alternative form of branding to describe what I do. In 2009, when I created my personal website, I did so under the banner *Eclectic Real-World Economics: Bringing together Austrian, Behavioural, Evolutionary, Institutional and Post Keynesian Economics*. This is an accurate description of what I spent my career doing, especially if it is qualified so that its amplifying clause reads as *Bringing together Compatible Elements of Austrian, Behavioural, Evolutionary, Institutional and Post Keynesian Economics* to capture the fact that I work with an underlying set of unifying principles. However, the best short-form characterisation of myself as an economist that may leave me with some hope of conversing with orthodox economists remains 'behavioural' and I hope that heterodox economists will keep in mind the extended banner as denoting what I really mean when I refer to my work in 'behavioural' terms in the pages that follow.

I have set out my alternative vision of behavioural economics elsewhere, both at length (Earl, 2022) and as a Lakatosian research programme (Earl, 2023a), but its key elements also figure in the chapters that follow, with the background to how I arrived at them, and in this book's final chapter. My career pursuing the kind of behavioural economics that I advocate did not bring me academic glory, but it did provide a very comfortable living without requiring me to sell out from heterodox ways of thinking. The journey along this less-travelled road left me with lessons about 'do' and 'don't' things that other heterodox economists might find it useful to know, especially if they are at an early stage in their careers and have only a fuzzy picture of the challenges of academic life.

If heterodox economists practise what I advocate, *and if they do so without branding it as 'heterodox'*, they have a good chance of enhancing their career prospects without compromising their core academic beliefs. They should also feel less besieged by practitioners of orthodox economics, and they may have a bigger chance of being able to succeed in winning over those from mainstream backgrounds who have been looking for new ways forward. Some of the latter may view the dominant behavioural economics as potentially leading to a dead end in terms of scope for novel research contributions, yet they may be concerned about the potential career damage of openly practising economics that is tagged as 'heterodox'.

The rest of this book is divided into ten chapters. The first two chapters explore how my pre-university experiences affected the kind of economist that I became. Chapter 1 covers childhood and teenage experiences that gave me an early sense that people do not always take wise decisions, along with a sense of how innovation and imitation are central to how the competitive process works. This came because I tended to pay close attention to what my parents did and because of the hobbies that I had when I was young. I was thereby primed to resist abstract, equilibrium-focused approaches to economics and to be interested in how people deal with the challenges of everyday life and why they differ in the lifestyles that they build for themselves. Chapter 2 covers my pre-university education in economics, which was historically grounded, pluralistic, and greatly dependent on experiences that I had at school.

Chapters 3 and 4 deal, respectively, with my undergraduate and postgraduate years as a student at the University of Cambridge. In writing the account in Chapter 3, I have tried to give a sense of the form that a pluralistic economics education can take when it is being delivered without the budgetary constraints that afflict the academic world of the twenty-first century. During Chapter 3, I set out my first encounters with behavioural economics and the Post Keynesian training that I received in macroeconomics, and how I started envisaging the two approaches as complementing each other.

The key theme of Chapter 4 is the difference between the experience that I had as a research student trying to get a Cambridge PhD and the kinds of experiences that deans of today's graduate schools hope that their research students will enjoy. My pathway to a PhD was very problematic, lasting almost seven years. Yet I was in residence in Cambridge as a research student for only the first two years, as the difficulties I was having set in motion events that led me to move on to an academic position elsewhere without even having achieved confirmation of candidature as a PhD student. Indeed, I ended up in the unusual position of having achieved tenure as a lecturer before I was confirmed as a PhD student. However, in many respects, my postgraduate experience entailed struggles that were common in the late 1970s in the UK doctoral system. Modern PhD programmes are designed to preclude the kinds of difficulties that I experienced. Amid these challenges, I was nonetheless able to form some key ideas that have stayed with me, though I also failed to spot important intellectual opportunities that seem, with hindsight, to have been lying there for the taking.

Chapters 5 to 8 cover my experiences in the period from July 1979, when I commenced my first academic position, to my retirement from paid, full-time academic work at the end of 2020. During this period, I worked at four universities that all were very different from Cambridge and differed from each other in ways that often came as a surprise to me as I moved between them. These chapters have identical overall structures, as follows:

1. An introductory overview of the institution in question, in time and space.
2. Reflections on my teaching experiences, the extent to which the curriculum was conducive to pluralistic and open-ended teaching, and the forces that constrained my efforts to implement teaching methods that made it possible for students to experience something as close as I could engineer to what I had enjoyed in Cambridge. The reflections on teaching often include material on my writing activities, for what I learned while teaching fed into several of my most important publications, some of which were also written to facilitate the kind of teaching that I was trying to do.

3. Reflections on the administrative and service roles that I experienced. These roles grew progressively as time passed, with consequences for the research that I was able to undertake.
4. An account of how my thinking as a behavioural economist evolved.
5. An account of my experiences as a conference participant, with critical reflections on the value of conference participation.
6. An audit of the published output that I achieved by working at the institution in question. Here, I provide commentary on how some works originated (where they have not been discussed in earlier sections), and I reflect critically on the (lack of) value of some of the publications that I achieved and what I might have been wiser to produce instead. Early career researchers should find plenty of food for thought here about how to manage their own research activities.
7. A reflective account of the process by which I came to leave my job at the institution in question and move on to the next stage in my life. In each case, it was not job insecurity that led me to want to move on: the moves were self-inflicted crucial experiments, from which I hope others may get food for thought about how they seek to run their own careers.

I adopted this section structure for these chapters mindful of the possibility that some readers will be interested only in particular topics (for example, pluralism and teaching, or how my behavioural perspective evolved). The standardised structure of Chapters 5 to 8 makes it easy for readers to navigate through the book if they want only to focus on a particular area.

Chapter 5 is devoted to my time at the University of Stirling in Scotland from mid-1979 to mid-1984. When I commenced work there, the University of Stirling was a small institution that had been running for barely a dozen years. During my time there, Brian Loasby was my intellectual mentor. I also worked closely with Sheila Dow, who is now rightly regarded as one of the world's top heterodox economists. It was a formative time for Sheila and me in terms of developing our thinking on monetary economics and economic method, and we both managed to complete our PhDs and write books and papers while we were doing so. However, Sheila spent the rest of her career at Stirling, whereas I moved 'Down Under'. An obvious question is whether my career strategy was a mistake. Chapters 6 to 8 provide some food for thought for answering this question.

Chapter 6 covers my seven years at the University of Tasmania, Australia, from mid-1984 to mid-1991. This period was not blighted by the kinds of resource constraints that I had experienced in Scotland, but there were two major challenges that I had to address. One was how to teach non-mainstream economics within a curriculum that was the most conservative I had yet encountered. The other issue was what to do as a researcher now that I no longer had to worry about getting a PhD but was geographically remote from researchers who were on a similar wavelength to me when it came to thinking about economics. What I opted to do delivered rewards rapidly in terms of academic advancement, earning me promotion to senior lecturer at age 31. Multiple interviews for more senior positions followed and the process culminated in me being offered the position of Professor of Economics at Lincoln University, near Christchurch in New Zealand. I accepted the offer, not merely because it seemed to be a better job but also because it would enable me to live in Christchurch, which I viewed as one of the most attractive cities in Australasia. I was only 35 when I took up the position in mid-1991.

Chapter 7 reveals how, in the decade that I held the chair at Lincoln, my career ran into difficulties that were compounded by some of the decisions that I made as I tried to deal with the problems I encountered. However, working there gave me my first experiences in PhD supervision, with evolutionary economist Jason Potts (who is now Distinguished Professor of Economics at RMIT University in Melbourne) as my first start-to-finish doctoral student. Working with Jason was a joy, in sharp contrast to the challenges that Lincoln posed for me in relation to maintaining teaching standards, cultivating a commitment to pluralism among my colleagues, and for keeping my research going even as communicating with far-off scholars became easy due to the spread of email and growth of the Internet. It proved to be a challenging environment from which to escape, too. I eventually bailed out by moving to the senior lectureship at the University of Queensland (UQ) that I mentioned earlier. With this shift to a very large, well-ranked institution, I felt I had a very clear idea about what I was getting into in academic and lifestyle terms, as I had spent the second half of 1999 at UQ as a visiting professor.

However, as Chapter 8 reveals, my time at UQ from mid-2001 to the end of 2020 came with another set of challenges. I had hoped that, during my career, I would get a chance to test my ability to deal with pretty much all the kinds of tasks that an academic economist might undertake. Two boxes remained for me to tick when I took up my position at UQ, namely serving as head of department (which I had mistakenly expected to get to do at Lincoln but which I correctly anticipated I would not be likely to do while at UQ) and being a principal investigator in a large grant-funded project. The latter box was indeed ticked while I worked at UQ, with an expensive study of how, and how well, people were dealing with the difficult task of not wasting money on connection service plans for their mobile phones. This project was very much in the territory of behavioural economics, as well as of obvious interest to heterodox economists concerned with the extent to which corporations can succeed in, as Akerlof and Shiller (2015) put it, 'phishing for phools', but the project also left me with knowledge, shared in this chapter, about the challenges of this kind of work.

The period covered in Chapter 8 was long enough also for me to do the following:

- Witness the processes by which pluralism can wither away as an economics department evolves in the face of changing external pressures.
- Have a major role in PhD administration and participate in systems designed to prevent students from suffering the kind of protracted experience that I had gone through with my Cambridge PhD.
- Clarify my vision of behavioural economics and its relationship with heterodox economics.
- Experience the challenges of trying to pursue a Cambridge-style teaching philosophy as resourcing levels and the norms of colleagues evolved and as teaching transitioned towards online methods.

All these areas are covered during Chapter 8, after which Chapter 9 brings together the wide variety of career lessons that were scattered through the book, along with some that are not covered in earlier chapters. Finally, Chapter 10 summarises my vision of how behavioural economics should be practised, why it is not being practised along these lines, and why heterodox economists should not be afraid of adopting the approach that I advocate. Chapters 9 and 10 can both be viewed as offering concluding reflections, but they have both been written as self-contained units, full of take-home messages for the convenience of those who are too busy to read the entire book.

1 Beginnings

I was born in 1955, the year of publication of a couple of the first economic journal articles that were harbingers for Richard Cyert and James March's (1963) *Behavioral Theory of the Firm*. One was Herbert Simon's (1955) formal model of choice under conditions of bounded rationality. The other was Cyert and March's (1955) analysis of how the responsiveness of large firms to changed market conditions could be affected by their organisational structures due to the need for information to be relayed from the initial recipient to the relevant decision-maker, after which the new price would in turn need to be relayed to customers. The year of my birth also coincided with the publication of George Kelly's (1955) magnum opus, *The Psychology of Personal Constructs*, in which people are viewed not as hedonistic utility-seekers but as if they are scientists seeking to predict and control what happens in their lives. The work of Cyert, March, Simon and Kelly would later have a major impact on my life. But in 1955, nothing in my family background would have served as a pointer to where my future lay.

My parents both came from working-class families in the St Pancras/Camden Town and Islington areas of London. They married on Christmas Day, 1945, when my father Eric, at twenty-one, was a private in the Royal Army Medical Corps. He had been drafted after spending most of the war making parts for Spitfire fighter aircraft and had met Julia, my mother, at a dance class. She had only turned eighteen a few weeks before their wedding and had been working in a confectionery factory. Both had qualified for 'central school' (i.e., middle ability) but Eric's father could not afford to keep him there beyond fourteen, while Julia, too, had ended her education very early due to not going back to school after returning to London following a brief evacuation at the start of the war. Julia's evacuation had taken her to live with a middle-class family in Hitchin, 35 miles north of London, and it gave her a short taste of the kind of life that she ultimately went on to have.

Unlike many in their generation, my parents delayed starting a family. Soon after they married, my father broke his leg badly in a motorcycle accident in his army camp at Tidworth in Wiltshire: he told me that it happened because an army truck unexpectedly turned out in front of him, and he had ridden his army motorcycle straight into it rather than swerving into a group of marching soldiers. To make matters worse, his leg had to be re-broken after being poorly set. After his slow recovery and demobbing, my parents were allocated a modern council flat not far from where they had grown up, and my father returned to working in a machine shop. However, my mother caught tuberculosis, probably from her father (who eventually succumbed to it, aged only 49). She was admitted to Grove Park Hospital in Lewisham, which had been a workhouse prior to World War I and had been acquired by the Metropolitan Asylums Board in 1918 for use as a specialist hospital for tuberculosis patients. At that time, tuberculosis had no drug-based cure and long-term resting in bed was the best hope for surviving it. On seeing how many fellow patients were succumbing to the disease, my mother decided to discharge herself and try to recover at home. With my father caring for her, she lived to tell the tale, but even once she had recovered, they delayed starting a family as she remained weak. Shortly after I was born, while she was pregnant with my sister, she caught tuberculosis again; this time, newly developed drugs provided the cure.

My mother's periods of illness had financial consequences, too, not merely by keeping her out of the workforce but also because my father's pride limited the extent to which he was willing to claim 'national assistance' when he took periods of unpaid leave while she was ill. As a result, they lived on their savings. When they told me about this in the late 1960s, as they belatedly began to accumulate a house deposit, it was my first lesson on principles-based behaviour.

At the time that I was born, no one in my family had been educated beyond age fifteen. If I had followed in my father's footsteps, I would have become an engineer by working my way up from teaboy in a small engineering works, becoming a skilled machine-tool operator and eventually being promoted to a junior management role in a large factory. However, my parents were keen not merely to take their own lives up into post-war Britain's middle class; they expected that my sister and I should both get the best educations that we could and have much better careers than themselves.

1.2   THE TOWN THAT MADE ME

Two years before I was born, my parents marked their aspirations for a better life by moving to Stevenage, about 30 miles north of London and 30 miles south-west of Cambridge. Stevenage was one of the rapidly expanding satellite towns that were being built about thirty miles from London under the 1946 New Towns Act, as part of the post-war planning and reconstruction process. When I was about ten years old, my parents investigated the possibility of emigrating to Australia, but they decided against doing so because they feared that what they viewed as a dusty land would exacerbate my problems with asthma. Otherwise, they showed no sign of considering moving elsewhere while I was growing up. Stevenage was thus the only town in which I lived before going to university, and it was in Stevenage that I got hooked on economics. These days, it is not a town that is seen as a great place to live, but in the early post-war period, it was seen very differently.

The decision of my parents to move to Stevenage was the result of a conversation between my father and a workplace colleague who was about to leave to take up another job. The colleague said that he was going to work in a factory in a new town that was being built in the countryside with clean air (unlike smog-prone London) and plenty of new houses to rent at reasonable rates. My father made inquiries about what might be available and, within weeks, he and my mother followed suit. Instead of being socially embedded in living close to the rest of their families, my parents had been very keen to move away.

As I grew up, I witnessed with great interest a ten-fold growth in my hometown's population. This experience helped me to get a sense not merely of the payoffs to planning but also of how planners could get things wrong due to deficient foresight. What particularly struck me was how the planners seemed to envisage that, if they equipped the town with an extensive set of cycle tracks, the residents of Stevenage would make great use of them for commuting. The planners seemed to fail to appreciate the extent of the motorisation that would take place in the post-war decades, with people (including my father) switching to commuting by car as they became more affluent. Motorisation resulted in suburban streets becoming increasingly clogged by parked cars – partly because most houses were not built with off-street parking, let alone their own garages, but also because vehicle ownership spread to spouses and then to teenagers. In Stevenage's main industrial area, there was a long period of disruption as the key arterial road was remodelled to cope with the volume of traffic. But at least Stevenage will not suffer the disruption that other cities face in attempting to retrofit cycle tracks into their transport systems to enable people to take a greener and fitter approach to commuting.

My parents' decision to move to Stevenage, coupled with the cohort into which I was born, gave me the educational opportunities that enabled me to achieve a place at the University of Cambridge amid students who mostly came from non-state schools. I had the good fortune to be in one of the last cohorts of school children whose academic abilities determined which high schools they were able to attend. Because of this, as a very weedy-looking, bespectacled eleven-year-old, I was one of a handfull boys from my junior primary school who started their high school education in the autumn term of 1966 at what was then known as Alleyne's Grammar School. Located at the northern end of old Stevenage, Alleyne's had been founded in 1558, the year that Elizabeth I became Queen of England, and it had a proud academic heritage, often recruiting teachers with Oxbridge credentials. It is now known as The Thomas Alleyne Academy. In Chapter 2, I will explain the role that Alleyne's played in starting me on the road that I took as an economist. But first, in the rest of this chapter, I offer a reflection on the non-academic side of my personal development and how it fed into the economics that I went on to do.

1.3   FORMATIVE EXAMPLES OF QUESTIONABLE CONSUMER BEHAVIOUR

I have a very rich set of memories about the evolution of the lifestyle of my parents while I was growing up in Stevenage. The vividness of these memories is a result of the fact that from a very early age I watched closely what my parents did and listened intently to what they told me or what I heard them saying to each other about their choices. What I observed primed me to be sceptical about rational economic agent models when I encountered them as an undergraduate. Later, these memories contributed significantly to my openness to the idea of taking a psychological approach to consumer behaviour, particularly in relation to the role of emotions and the management of cognitive dissonance. They also helped make me receptive to the work of Thaler and others whom Mehta (2013) has accused of 'pathologizing' consumers, even though I never accepted that what an 'econ' would be expected to do in terms of rational choice theory should be the reference point for thinking about rationality. However, my 'case study' of my parents' behaviour played no role at all in stirring my interest in the challenges that consumers face in dealing with complexity and how they try to cope with them.

My father was almost 47 when we moved, early in January 1971, into a five-year-old semi-detached chalet bungalow on a small private estate near the northern end of Stevenage old town, very close to my high school. Although my parents said that taking so long to get a foot on the property ownership ladder was a consequence of the impact of my mother's bouts of tuberculosis on their ability to save up a house deposit, I have often wondered whether, in the first couple of decades of their marriage, they had even seriously entertained the idea of becoming homeowners. Their track record in spending suggested their priorities lay elsewhere. This was not surprising, given that before they moved to Stevenage the only time either of them had entered an owner-occupied home had been when my mother was evacuated; on moving to Stevenage, they had ready access to affordable modern rental housing provided by the Stevenage Development Corporation that the government had set up to administer the creation of the new town. In 1957, when my sister was born, they upgraded from a two-bedroom house to a much more spacious three-bedroom house. Moreover, at that stage, inflation rates were low and there was no sense that delaying getting on to the property ladder could be a regret-inducing error.

While failing to save a house deposit, my parents did manage to save up for modern consumer durables, rather than using emerging hire purchase opportunities to get these products sooner. By the time they moved to Stevenage, they already had not merely a standalone radio (in a huge wooden cabinet) and a radiogram but also the television that made it possible for them and their neighbours to watch the coronation of Queen Elizabeth II in June 1953. Around the time that I was born, my father acquired a 1932 Austin Seven car and was trying, unsuccessfully, to pass his driving test. The Austin was sold after he failed the test a second time, which was around the time that my mother was again diagnosed with tuberculosis. He was also learning to play the piano and had replaced his original, old-fashioned Brinsmead (which had candlestick holders and must have been bought second-hand) with a brand-new Zender. Around 1960, a refrigerator was purchased, and my mother started to shop at the new supermarkets in the town centre (using my sister's stroller as the means to transport the shopping home) instead of making near-daily trips to the local shops.

Even though I was then very young, it was hard for me not to notice this sudden transformation and the exciting new environment of Sainsbury's supermarket, whose shopping trolleys I so keenly wanted to push. The following year, my parents had a telephone installed but they cancelled the service within a matter of months after repeatedly getting misdialled calls intended for a restaurant whose number was quite similar. They found this first telephonic experience so disconcerting that they did not have a telephone service again until they retired to Polperro in Cornwall in 1987, even though there was already a wall-mounted phone in the entrance hall of the house they purchased in 1971. Because of this, all telephone calls had to be made from a payphone and were only made when absolutely necessary. I thus grew up without developing any skills in handling telephone calls.

The first instance where I wondered about the quality of my parents' decision-making was in respect of what they did when the sales of domestic tape recorders started to take off in the early 1960s. I had barely been at school a year when my parents joined the tape-recording bandwagon and recorded me reciting the child's poem about how 'Incy wincy spider climbed up the spout'. However, they did not do this by purchasing the kind of reel-to-reel recorder that we had seen on a visit to London to see some of my mother's relatives, who keenly showed off their new toy. Instead, they economised by buying a 'Gramdeck'. It was the first grown-ups' product whose packaging grabbed my attention, as the various modules each came in a bright red box with an embossed brassy label that contributed to the product's air of quality despite it being targeted at those who wanted to reduce the cost of experimenting with tape recording.

As can be seen from videos posted on YouTube by collectors of vintage electronics products, a Gramdeck did not have an electric motor for driving the tape and the tape reel spindles. Instead, it piggybacked on the motor of a record player's turntable, over whose spindle it was mounted. It also lacked a power amplifier and loudspeaker, with the signal from its pre-amplifier module being fed into the power amplifier of the record player or radiogram whose turntable power it was using. It delivered comparable sound quality to a typical tape recorder of its time but inevitably was hardly ever used in households that primarily wanted to listen to records rather than tape recordings. It might not take long to unbox and set up, but a behavioural economist would today view this hurdle as enough to be a deterrent to its use by consumers who are naturally prone to suffer from availability bias and to engage in quasi-hyperbolic discounting. My parents' choice seemed crazy to me at the time, even though I was only six years old: it seemed obvious that the Gramdeck was hopelessly cumbersome to use and would be what I later learned to call a 'white elephant'. This unwise purchase resulted from a visit by a door-to-door salesperson and was my first lesson in the value of having the confidence to say 'No' and to think carefully about products before buying them. The experience of seeing my uncle's tape recorder and the Gramdeck led to a memorable case of confusion some months later, when I turned seven and moved from my infants' school to the adjacent junior school: my teacher, Miss Claxton told the class that, if we wanted, we would be able to start learning to play the recorder, but of course it was the wind instrument, which I had not encountered before, not what I thought she meant.

A year or so before the Gramdeck was purchased, my father had given me what was probably the first demonstration I received of technological progress: he had the original 78-rpm record turntable in the radiogram replaced by one that could play a stack of 45-rpm singles or 33-rpm albums. The first 45-rpm single that he purchased was one of my first tastes of something Australian, namely Slim Dusty's hit, 'A Pub with No Beer'. The song's lyrics puzzled me at one point, for without any notion of a dingo in my memory, the best I could make of the phrase 'wild dingoes call' was 'wilding goes cool'! I imagined that 'wilding' referred to what I latter came to know an Australian refers to as 'the bush'. Little did I know then, or subsequently with my confusion about 'recorder', that I would later spend a lot of my time dealing with the significance of our views of the world being personally constructed (Kelly, 1955) and memory-dependent (Hayek, 1952), as this instance neatly illustrates. Nor did I anticipate that, on a road-trip vacation over half a century later, my partner Annabelle and I would find ourselves disappointed that we could not eat at the hotel in Ingham, Queensland whose beer shortage story inspired the song. This time, the pub had plenty of beer, but it offered neither gluten-free nor vegan food.

Around 1967, my father decided to upgrade from the radiogram to a stereo system (without any form of tape recorder). Again, he seemed to make a mistake, despite this time being prepared to say 'No' to a salesperson. He arranged a home demonstration of a Bush Arena component hi-fi system by the local hi-fi store, Stevenage Record Centre. However, he decided against it under some pressure from my mother. Her concerns that the Bush system did not function as a piece of furniture were then addressed via the purchase of an elegant but sonically less capable stereogram from another store.

I was very disappointed, as it was clear to me that stereograms were becoming obsolete and that the component system that my parents had rejected would be easier to upgrade and, in any case, already sounded better. The upgrading issue was on my mind because it was clear that when the radiogram's turntable had been replaced, this had very obviously entailed replacing some of the elegant, polished wood in the cabinet with a sheet of plywood to accommodate the new turntable's mounting requirements. Any such transplant looked like it would be very problematic on the stereogram due to its very different cabinet configuration. It was also clear that the stereogram's integral speakers resulted in a less than ideal sonic experience because of where it had to be put to fit in the lounge, whereas separate speakers would have given the flexibility to get the best stereo separation. It was not clear that my mother really understood what stereophonic sound was all about, but she saw the teak stereogram as a nice piece of furniture that included storage space for their growing collection of records.

The stereogram served them well for a decade before it was given away and replaced by a Rotel component hi-fi system that included a cassette deck. This time, my mother could not veto a component system by questioning where it, and the LPs that had been stored in the stereogram, might be put: my father had already built a set of low cupboards that also served as a modern-looking stand. This was one of several rather IKEA-like items of furniture that he made using second-hand melamine-faced panels that he purchased from a stall in Hitchin market that sold parts of kitchen units that had been salvaged rather than simply being tossed into skips when homes were being renovated.

All in all, the stereo saga seemed to be blighted by short-term thinking. If they had bought the Bush Arena system, they could readily have upgraded the turntable (and added a stereo FM radio tuner) without any custom installation being needed, and the amplifier and speakers of the system would probably have served them for many decades. The saga was my first practical lesson on why it could matter whether systems were integrated or modular, an issue that would later become one of my enduring interests via Simon's (1962, 1969) work on the evolutionary significance of system architecture.

My parents' car choices provided other food for my thinking on consumer behaviour. After selling the Austin Seven, my father continued cycling to work until early 1964, when he bought a 1954 Standard Eight from a colleague, who also taught him to drive well enough to pass the test this time around. Never again did family holidays necessitate travelling by coach or train. However, at the end of 1964, the Standard Eight was replaced by a brand-new Monaco-red Ford Anglia Deluxe. I was disappointed that my father did not buy from the same dealer the one-year-old Anglia Super that he also considered. The latter had a bigger engine and a sportier look, as it was finished in white with a dark green roof and side stripes. However, my mother vetoed it on the basis that 'Bottle green is unlucky'. This superstition-based decision rule left me wondering about her sanity, but she is not a lone example of someone having this affliction, particularly in relation to cars – as is readily evident if one Googles <dark green unlucky> and examines the search results.

Unlike the blue Ford Anglia of the Weasley family in the Harry Potter movies, my father's red Anglia did not fly. Indeed, it suffered from terrible stalling and juddering when he took delivery of it from Zenith Motors in Stevenage, and it continued to operate as if it were powered by what my father called 'kangaroo petrol' until its woeful one-year warranty had expired. At that point, Zenith's mechanics seemed finally able to diagnose what was causing the problem, namely a porous carburettor casting. This was the first situation I encountered that looked like it was an example of what Williamson (1975) labelled as 'opportunism' – i.e., a possible case of guileful, self-serving behaviour by Ford's dealer, exploiting my father's lack of knowledge about their previous 'efforts' at diagnosing the problem.

It is to be hoped that these days Zenith Stevenage (which went on to become a local institution and is still the town's Ford dealer) would operate in a more Marshallian manner and treat its customers with what are now referred to as post-warranty 'goodwill gestures', and fix problems without charge if they become evident shortly after the expiry of vehicle warranties. However, the earlier failures to diagnose the carburettor problem may have been a case of incompetence, for other encounters with Zenith's service department drove my father to start to service the Anglia himself.

The last straw was when legislation was introduced requiring all new cars to have front seat belts (from 1 January 1968) and my father wisely decided to have some retrofitted even though the Anglia's December 1964 registration meant that it fell short of the compulsory retrofitting for cars made from 1965 to 1968. He asked Zenith to install the belts that he had purchased via a mail-order offer he had seen in *The Sun* (which had become our daily newspaper when it succeeded *The Daily Herald*, whose last year or so of output provided my first experiences as a newspaper reader). However, pre-fitted seatbelt mounts had not been made compulsory until the year after my father's car had been manufactured, and Zenith's staff clearly had no idea about where to mount the seatbelts: when my father collected the car, he found that they had anchored what should have been the door-pillar mount to the rear floor so that, as my father put it 'Even a deformed dwarf wouldn't have been able to use them'.

But although my father sought to overcome the risk of opportunism and incompetence by servicing the Anglia himself, he was over-confident about his own capacity to do the job. As a result, one Monday morning, my father and I had to push the Anglia to a local garage due to his service efforts the previous afternoon leaving it unwilling to fire properly. He was late for work that morning but fortuitously I was offered a lift by my form teacher who happened to be passing as we reached the garage. The Anglia thus provided my first experience of the economics of outsourcing versus do-it-yourself.

Despite not having accumulated a particularly high mileage, the Anglia was replaced around Easter 1970 by a brand-new Morris 1300. By this time, my mother had at last re-joined the labour force, greatly improving our family finances. However, trading up to the Morris had all the signs of being an unduly panicked reaction to the first signs of rust on the Ford. The Morris was purchased only eight months before they bought their first house and it chewed up a significant part of the house deposit that they were trying to accumulate. As a result, their first couple of years as homeowners involved needless mortgage stress. But they were happy to leave the house they had rented for the past thirteen year. They felt they had got out in the nick of time. This was not simply because of the increase in inflation of housing prices, but also because of their racial prejudices: they were concerned that, as the oldest part of the new town, the area in which we had lived was absorbing a disproportionate number of 'immigrants' as those who had been there longer moved on to newer public rental homes further from the town centre or, like us, became homebuyers in a private estate.

With front-wheel drive and a 'hydrolastic' suspension system, the Morris 1300 was mechanically much more complex than the Anglia and my father outsourced its servicing. However, he opted to have it serviced by an independent local garage close to where we lived, rather than by the authorised dealer from whom he had purchased it. This strategy also left us wondering about service quality. The most spectacular case was when one side of the front suspension collapsed one evening when my father was driving into our estate. More costly was the fact that the engine and gearbox wore out unexpectedly quickly, with my father having a reconditioned engine and gearbox installed when the car was barely six years old. His decision to authorise this rather than scrap the car was probably another mistake, for two years later he got a terrible trade-in deal due to the major rust problems that had emerged. But perhaps he was misled about the prospective costs of attending to the rust problem, for, a year or so later, he spotted the car running, with new sills. At that point, I had not yet come across the classic article on credence goods by Darby and Karni (1973), but my father's experiences with motoring ensured that I was very conscious of both the importance of trust for the functioning of markets and the problem of knowing when a supplier was trustworthy.

My father's behaviour in respect of the car with which he replaced the Morris provided my first experience of a factor that rational choice theory would view as irrelevant in choice, namely, a product's country of origin. (Note that, for all her racial prejudices, my mother was willing to buy and eat fruit that people of colour had grown and harvested.) The car in question was a brand-new Honda Civic, which my father sold, after only two years, in as-new condition (without even having removed the clear plastic film that covered the doors' interior trim) and with a very low mileage. Soon after selling the Civic, he told me that this was because he just didn't feel comfortable having a car that came from Japan, 'given what the Japs did to our forces in World War II'. He felt that he really should have bought a British car and hence traded the Civic against a brand-new Ford Fiesta. I was rather peeved he had done so without offering me the chance to buy the Civic from him. Given the maintenance costs I had run into on my first car, I would have been interested in such an opportunity. Even so, I refrained from immediately telling him that his 'British' Ford was actually made in Spain. His behaviour left me wondering how many people allow the country of origin to affect their choices. I subsequently encountered many other instances of this sort of behaviour (most recently in relation to people using a 'nothing from China' rule) and noted examples of it in some of David Lodge's novels (see Earl, 2011a). However, I have never sought to investigate it via a systematic empirical study.

The choices that my father made in relation to getting his cars serviced seemed, over-confidence aside, to have far more reasonable foundations than those that he and my mother made in relation to house maintenance. There, they displayed a dysfunctional reluctance to have tradespeople come to fix things that needed to be fixed. My father would instead do his best, as with bodged work on replacing rotting windowsills and the garden gate on the house they bought. If that strategy failed, the problem would be left as it was if they felt they could 'live with it'. An example of the latter was their willingness to keep flushing the upstairs toilet by taking the cistern lid off and fiddling with the mechanism: they never showed me or my sister the knack for doing this and they lived with this situation from the day they moved in until the day they moved out over sixteen years later following my father's retirement.

Their move to a brand-new bungalow in Cornwall left them without such problems for a while, but gradually more and more issues became evident each time I or my sister visited, such as a sagging kitchen ceiling and failed bathroom taps. At one point, the failure of the sound on the lounge TV was addressed by purchasing a cheap portable black and white TV and sitting it on top of the problematic TV as a source of sound, rather than by calling a TV repairer to see if the problem could be fixed.

Whenever I or my sister commented to them about things that they were neglecting to get fixed, their replies revealed that the issue did not seem to entail concerns about the risk of opportunistic over- or under-servicing that they might reasonably have had after their vehicle maintenance experiences, and they did not seem to have an exaggerated view of my father's capacities as a handyman (as opposed to his engineering expertise being applicable to servicing a car). Rather, both my parents were wary of having outsiders come to the house to do any work, as they suspected that those who came might gather information that might later be used for house-breaking and theft. How they came to hold such fears was not clear; however, if it were the result of having seen a news report about an instance of such behaviour, we might wonder about their skills in forming probability estimates or whether they were grossly overweighting the significance of very low probability events as they worked out their strategy, consistent with Kahneman and Tversky's (1979) prospect theory.

Fear also underpinned my parents' reluctance to outsource food preparation: they completely resisted any idea of eating out, except for getting fish and chip takeaways when we went on vacations. My father would try to dispose of any suggestion that they might dine out by questioning the point of doing so on the basis that my mother was a wonderful cook (which was not the case), without any recognition that she might deserve to be treated to some 'chef's relief' from time to time (since he did none of the cooking). However, persistent probing revealed that the real issue was their concern with kitchen hygiene where someone else was preparing food out of sight, unlike the case in fish and chip shops. This concern had nothing to do with my father's wartime duties in the Royal Army Medical Corps having been focused on hygiene in army camps. Rather, my mother explained that in one of their early holidays she had discovered cigarette ash in a café sandwich and had no intention of having an experience like that ever again.

1.4   THE SOCIAL SIDE OF CHOICE

Formative experiences in my life also came in relation to my parents' behaviour in social settings and via things they told me about their workplace experiences. Although they were quite early adopters of many consumer durables of the early post-World War II era, I never got a sense of them being keen to 'show off' how well they were doing by engaging in conspicuous consumption. They socialised very little, visits by relatives were rare, and I can only recall a handful of non-relatives ever being invited into the house. Even so, they seemed concerned about how others might view them when they were out in public. My mother was always determined to be well-presented and this, combined with her good looks, did not endear her to her female colleagues when she returned to the workforce. I rather got the impression that my initial academic success was their main status symbol with their acquaintances. Whenever I visited them after they retired to Cornwall, I would often go walking on the coastal path with them and was always embarrassed by the way that they introduced me when they encountered people that they knew.

Mostly, my parents preferred not to attract attention. I remember a tense evening when I was about fifteen and away on vacation with them at a caravan site near Polperro in Cornwall, minutes away from where they eventually ended up living. On the occasion in question, I probed them about why, not for the first time, they were not taking to the venue's empty dance floor despite their love of ballroom dancing. They would wait, and wait, until another couple did so. In replying, they explained that they did not want to have everyone looking at them and thinking they were showing off. The incident marked the start of my teenage rebelliousness: I found their attitude very strange and vowed never to be concerned about what strangers thought of me.

However, the dance floor episode contrasted sharply with my mother's workplace behaviour, which was characterised by a pride in doing her job well regardless of social pressures to conform to workplace norms. I became aware of such pressures via one of my father's bedtime stories about his early workplace experiences in Stevenage. He told of the retaliation meted out to a colleague who was both conspicuously productive and who – unlike almost everyone else – already had a car. The poor fellow sometimes had to contend with sabotage that took the form of sugar being poured into the car's fuel tank. What happened in the case of my mother was very different. When she returned to the workforce, she readily got a job as an assembler of industrial instruments at a US-owned company called Taylor Instruments. She proved to be very good in this role, often being used as a rate setter by her managers. After about six years, she was promoted to the role of instructress. She soon discovered that she hated this more socially interactive role and asked if she could return to her former role. As with her glamorous presentation, her productivity had not endeared her to her colleagues, and her request provided them with an opportunity for payback: she did get to 'go back on the bench' but the union dictated that she could only do this if classed as a new employee. When the firm put this proposal to her, she accepted it, little realising that it would soon prove costly. The firm's US parent company decided to close the factory a year or so later. Because she was formally a 'new' member of staff, my mother received a much smaller redundancy pay-out than her actual years of service would normally have yielded.

1.5   INSIGHTS FROM TEENAGE HOBBIES

The three hobbies that I pursued in my high-school years were ones that I pursued seriously, and they could have led me to take career directions that were very different from economics. They each had consequences for my economic thinking.

One was ornithology, which I picked up purely because my first-form desk partner at Alleyne's was a member of the Young Ornithologists' Club (YOC), the junior offshoot of the Royal Society for the Protection of Birds. I pursued ornithology very seriously for about five years, but I ultimately realised that my eyesight was a major constraint on how adept I was at identifying birds in the field.

Four decades later, my limitations as a birdwatcher had an impact on my contributions to behavioural economics, for they primed me to be receptive to Hayek's (1952) book *The Sensory Order*, in which he sets out a theory of how the mind works, and to appreciate the relationship between Hayek's theory and Kelly's (1955) *Psychology of Personal Constructs*. As a young birdwatcher, I was certainly fitting Kelly's notion that people may usefully be viewed 'as if' they are scientists, for birdwatching entailed a set of expeditions in which I tested my capacity to spot birds, especially ones that I had never seen before, either at all or in the environment in question.

To do this successfully, one needs two things. The first is the capacity to spot birds as patterns against the background of their environment; the second is to have a set of memorised templates of bird types and specific bird species to test for their match with the pattern that one has inferred. In other words, cognition is an active process that involves finding a pattern and then finding a match between it and patterns stored in one's memory: the birds that one is trying to observe do not tell us directly what species they are, and after going through this process we are left with conjectures (in Kelly's terms, 'personal constructs') about what we have seen.

Hayek's analysis of cognition brings out the first stage more explicitly than Kelly, who is clearer on the second. As a short-sighted, somewhat colour-blind birdwatcher, I would often not be able to spot a bird quickly enough or clearly enough, that others had noticed and whose features they had registered. If I did spot a bird that was available only for a fleeting glimpse, I would, other things equal, have a smaller chance of identifying it correctly. However, because I had spent a lot of time reading field guides for birdwatchers and memorised the templates for many birds, I would have a good chance of identifying birds if I got more than a fleeting glimpse and could confirm with others whether, say, the wading bird that I was looking at had red or green legs.

On occasions when I did get a 'good enough look' at a bird, I sometimes had the experience of being able to narrow down the range of possibilities very quickly based on what ornithologists refer to as a bird's 'jizz' (or 'gizz'), i.e., a simplified pattern comprised of its silhouette and style of behaviour or movement that serves as a kind of signature. I picked up the 'jizz' notion very early in my time as an avid birdwatcher, but three decades were to pass before I started to think about it in relation to economics and marketing (see Section 7.4), a decade before I at last read *The Sensory Order* (see Section 8.4).

My second formative hobby was slot-car racing, which I pursued from Christmas 1965, when my parents gave me a Scalextric set, until mid 1977, though it was very sporadic in the last four years of this period due to me and my enthusiast friends being away at university. It grew out of my long-standing childhood fascination with cars, that as a child I could only address in a hands-on manner via models, and, as with birdwatching, I went on to take it very seriously. Here, too, it primed me to become the kind of economist that I became, but it could readily have led me to a career in the automotive sector or at least in engineering if I had not become captivated by economics.

In my third year at high school, I moved beyond ready-to-go Scalextric slot-cars and small tracks at home, up to the club level. This entailed transitioning to much faster slot-cars and racing on very large 4–6-lane tracks. My first club-level cars were kits from the USA, but they were soon followed by my own creations with elaborate chassis frames made from soldered-together brass and piano wire. The bodies were purchased in clear-plastic form and then painted in one's chosen colours on the inside of the shell.

The market for the clear plastic bodyshells provided my first lesson about the role of product cloning in the competitive process. The bodyshells were mainly purchased by mail-order and I had read that they were made by a vacuum-forming process whereby heated sheets of thin plastic were sucked on to a mould. From the mid-1960s to the mid-1970s, the leading firm was a company called GT Models, whose name reflected not Grand Touring but the fact that its proprietor was Gordon Tapsell, a leading figure in the Electric Car Racing Association (ECRA) (of which

I became a member). I noticed that, when GT Models released new bodyshells, a raceway store in Southend-on-Sea often followed rapidly with its own-brand equivalents. The latter were slightly cheaper, and their shut-lines and window frames were sometimes not quite so sharp, but otherwise they looked identical to those from GT Models.

The idea that product piracy was happening came when, with my classmate and fellow slot-car enthusiast, Ian Reid, I compared the rival firms' versions of the Buick Riviera bodyshell, a popular choice in the large sedan class. It was evident that the one from Southend-on-Sea even replicated the rather poorly executed rear bumper in the GT Models version. From this, we deduced that the store in Southend-on-Sea might be making its products via moulds made from the original GT Models products. This led us to run an experiment to see if we could do likewise and even go as far as making a bodyshell. Ian's father made a surprisingly accurate cast from the inside of one of our Buick Riviera bodyshells by using concrete rather than plaster, after which Ian and I made a very primitive vacuum moulding system that entailed a small electric heater, a vacuum cleaner, and a large metal biscuit tin. We punched holes in the top of the tin and cut a larger hole in its side for the vacuum cleaner hose. The concrete mould was placed on the top, followed by a sheet of plastic that we melted with the electric heater from above. As it got softer, we started to pull it down, around the mould, on to the biscuit tin until the suction through the holes around the mould pulled the plastic tightly on to the mould. The quality of definition that we achieved was not as good as on the clone from Southend-on-Sea, but our crude system was a proof-of-concept indication of how easy it would be to enter this market via product piracy if the leading firm did not, or could not, attempt to sue for breach of copyright.

Slot-car racing was booming as an adult leisure activity in the second half of the 1960s. In the USA, the bowling alley equipment manufacturer AMF took note of this and got into the business of producing huge six- or eight-lane model raceways at commercial venues, A few AMF tracks were even installed in the UK, but serious slot-car racing in the UK mostly took place on large hand-built tracks at community centres or corporate social clubs. Stevenage was no exception: it had two slot-car racing clubs, one at Pin Green Community Centre and the other at the local Kodak factory's sportsground. Nearby, Hatfield had one (at what was then the Hawker Siddeley aircraft factory, previously de Havilland) and Luton had two (at the Vauxhall car factory and the Electrolux appliance factory, at both of which my team-mates and I would do our best, as early teenagers, to compete against adult teams in six-hour endurance races).

It was via competing in club-level slot-car racing that I learnt how 'creative destruction' worked, long before I heard of the term and the work of Schumpeter (1943) – and I am not referring here to the destruction, in high-speed crashes, of the models that we created. The pace of innovation was intense, just as in the full-size world of carmakers and racing teams, and those who took part eagerly awaited the latest magazine issues to find out what was being tried and how well it worked. I funded the parts for my first creation, a 1:32-scale Oldsmobile Tornado, by selling my model railway equipment to one of my father's workmates, for model trains had none of the allure of model cars. The Tornado consisted entirely of my choice of state-of-the-art, off-the-shelf parts and was a huge step up from the kit models that I already had. But within a few months its chassis design (which had an inline motor at a right angle to the rear-drive axle) had been rendered obsolete by what was called an 'anglewinder' design, which had the motor mounted as transversely as possible to the rear axle, permitting much more stable cornering. I took the Tornado to pieces and built my first own-design chassis, reusing all the other parts except for the main drive gear. Within a few months, the next chassis innovation came in: hinged chassis sides known as 'bat-pans', so I again set to work with the soldering iron. The process continued relentlessly in all areas of the models. Keeping up to date was made more challenging because most people raced in three or four different classes. Those of us who were relying on pocket money or newspaper delivery earnings to pay for our upgrades found it difficult to keep up with the adults who had bigger budgets to play with, and we tried to save money by recycling parts in new combinations as far as we could, or sometimes by buying second-hand cars from adults.

Eventually, ECRA decided to make things fairer in competitive terms by introducing a standard 'Formula 32' class for models with identical off-the-peg chassis and motors. The regulated competition of the Formula 32 standard was successful in enabling youngsters to compete with older players but, by the time that my cohort finished our A-Level examinations at high school, it started to seem that slot-car racing at the club level faced an existential threat from another kind of innovation: affordable, larger-scale radio-controlled model cars that could be raced on outdoor tracks. I could hardly have wished for a more compelling case study than this to get me thinking about competition as an evolving, dynamic process.

From 1970 onward, I added a new area of interest to my leisure commitments, namely music. It rapidly became, and remains, the dominant leisure activity in my life, but in embarking on it I had absolutely no idea how important it would become or where it would take me. My parents had not encouraged me to take music lessons, even though there was a good piano at home that was rarely used (due to my father giving up taking piano lessons not long after my sister was born). I had the good fortune to learn at junior primary school how to read music, but I soon gave up the recorder. There was a school orchestra at Alleyne's but few of my classmates seemed to be in it or taking lessons on an instrument of any kind. Alleyne's provided a weekly class in which we were introduced to classical music via recordings and by the teacher, George Partridge (who also taught me architecture and English literature) playing the piano, but these, too, included no attempt to nudge students into taking up an instrument. Otherwise, for most of my childhood and early adolescence, I had little involvement with music beyond listening to whatever my parents listened to, which tended to include what was in the singles charts at the time. In 1970, however, curiosity and social demonstrations led me to start listening to the album-focused rock music of that time, and to decide that I wanted to see if I could learn to play the guitar.

Classmates started bringing LPs to school to lend to each other; this was followed by acoustic guitars that were played during break times. I then discovered that BBC Radio 1 had started a weekday early evening programme called 'Sounds of the Seventies' that was devoted to albums, and I set out to use it to get some knowledge of what lay beyond the singles charts. Without even having touched a guitar or really knowing anything much about any guitarists, I announced to my parents that it was a guitar that I would like for my fifteenth birthday. They must have been very surprised but nonetheless gave me £10 to get one. On the morning of my birthday, I headed off to the Stevenage Record Centre, which offered a small stock of acoustic guitars and was at the time the only place in Stevenage where a guitar could be purchased. My budget constraint was enough to buy the cheapest steel-string guitar but not a nylon-string guitar of the kind my classmates played, which started at £12. It would prove a tougher way to start but probably accounts for the fact that I went on to become focused on rock and jazz guitar rather than folk or classical. As with my other leisure pursuits, I built my knowledge in a proto-academic manner via library books and, from September 1970, I became an eager reader of the weekly music newspaper *Melody Maker*.

In August 1971, my parents allowed me to purchase an electric guitar for my sixteenth birthday, with a much bigger budget that may have reflected both the evidence that my interest in the guitar was no passing curiosity and the swag of good O-Level results that I had achieved. The guitar was a second-hand, mint-condition Watkins Rapier 33 that came with a five-watt amplifier that was likewise a product of the British firm Watkins Electronic Music (WEM). Before the 1970s came to an end, events in the global electronic musical instrument industry would help to inform my understanding of the dynamics of the competitive process, just as slot-car racing had done, and decades later I would write a teaching case study on these events, including what happened to WEM. What I observed during the 1970s was a growth of knowledge process that transformed the guitar market. Japanese luthiers shamelessly copied classic US guitar designs and forced lower-tier firms such as WEM out of the market by undercutting their prices. The US firms sued, to keep the Japanese copies out of the USA, but the Japanese firms kept selling their 'lawsuit' models in other markets, with their quality coming to match those of the originals. The Japanese firms then moved up-market by creating their own designs and selling them at premium prices, competing head-on with the US firms.

A few weeks after starting my half-century-plus journey into the world of electric guitars, I was back at school, engrossed in my first classes in economics.

2 From School to University

   AN A-GRADE LEARNING EXPERIENCE WITH A-LEVEL ECONOMICS

The event that most aroused my interest in economics was seeing on television on 18 November 1967 the address in which Harold Wilson, the UK Prime Minister announced the devaluation of Sterling but claimed rather unconvincingly that it would not reduce the value of the pound in one's pocket. However, despite thereafter taking an avid interest in news reports about the struggles of the UK economy, I did not initially take any other steps to learn more about economics. At the time of Wilson's address, I was then in the second year of my high-school education at what was then known as Alleyne's Grammar School but which in 1969 became a comprehensive school and started admitting students of all abilities. Economics was only offered as a subject in the sixth form.

In 1971, at the end of my fifth form at Alleyne's, I has no hesitation in deciding that I was going to work toward A-Levels in economics, geography, and history when I went into the sixth form. Although I greatly enjoyed chemistry and biology, with the latter, like geography, being one of my top subjects, I did not for a moment consider taking A-Levels in any of the sciences. I also gave hardly any thought to the idea of doing mathematics at A-Level instead of history, despite having not done poorly with maths up to that point; I just opted to study what interested me most and presumed that if I needed more mathematics to accompany economics, I would be able to pick it up from courses at university or by teaching myself from textbooks. I have never regretted that decision.

Those of us who intended to take A-Level Economics were encouraged to get a sense of the subject over the summer vacation between the fifth form and lower-sixth by reading Michael Stewart's (1967) *Keynes and After*, and G. C. Allen's ([1939] 1970) *British Industries and Their Organisation* and/or Allen's (1968) *Monopoly and Restrictive Practices*. These books had a major impact on the kind of economist that I became. Stewart's account of the context in which Keynes's ideas emerged, what they were, and the impact that they had, was essentially a Post Keynesian view: as a member of the Department of Economics at University College London, Stewart was an enthusiastic

Keynesian and at the time his book appeared he was a senior economic advisor to the Cabinet Office of the Labour Government led by Harold Wilson. Allen's books gave me empirical foundations for an evolutionary view of firms and industries and an interest in structural change.

The A-Level Economics training that I received covered far more material than a typical first year of a university degree in economics, and I supplemented what we did in class by reading extensively from the impressive economics section in Stevenage Central Library. This collection included many publications by a right-wing think tank, The Institute of Economic Affairs (IEA), that provided plenty of material for generating classroom debate with the senior of my two economics teachers, Les Ransley. Les was a graduate of the University of Birmingham and was clearly a Labour voter. At that stage, in the UK's climate of terrible industrial relations, my microeconomic inclinations were very much in the Conservative direction, and they remained that way until Margaret Thatcher was elected and showed just how dogmatically neoliberal her party had become. As far as macroeconomics was concerned, however, nothing in the IEA's pamphlets shook my admiration for Keynes's ideas. Baiting Les Ransley with IEA-style policy ideas was one of my responses to comments by teachers in my Autumn 1971 school report about me being 'quiet' and 'reticent' in class despite displaying promise in my written work. Les took it all in good spirit and thereby provided me with my first role model in pluralistic teaching.

The other economics teacher was a recent London School of Economics graduate, John Rushton. He provided a role model of how to behave with humility if someone points out that one has made a mistake or not spotted something that is obvious to those that one is trying to teach. One day, he referred to the supply curve of an imperfectly competitive firm, which I knew from one of my textbooks was a mistake: such a firm's supply choice depended on both its marginal costs and marginal revenues, unlike a price-taking firm in a perfectly competitive market. When I pointed this out, he made no attempt to conceal that it was a lapse, as many might have done (e.g., by saying 'I was just testing whether you were awake and up to date with your reading'). Instead, he acknowledged his slip and congratulated me for raising the issue to the benefit of everyone. I have always tried to behave in this way if my own students pointed out that I had made a mistake in class.

John Rushton strongly encouraged my wider reading. This was especially the case at the end of the lower-sixth year. At that time my class had been required not merely to attempt to add O-Level Economics to our credentials; we were also required to sit a multiple-choice examination as part of a project being undertaken by a team at Heriot-Watt University in Edinburgh on the performance of high-school students of economics versus those taking first-year university courses in economics. I was one of two students in my class who scored exceptionally well in the Heriot-Watt test, and John was advised of the results just before the end of the school year. As I walked back to the sixth-form building from the final school assembly of the academic year, he came up to me and said, 'You've got something here, so don't waste the summer'. So, while many of my classmates found themselves a source of income via a summer job, I spent much of the time continuing to work through the economics section in Stevenage Central Library.

Messrs Ransley and Rushton were not the only sixth-form teachers who played a formative role in my life as an academic economist. Much credit is also due to one of my geography teachers, Roger Luxton, a Cambridge graduate. It was through his economic geography classes that I began to get interested in development economics and it was he who introduced me to Myrdal's work on cumulative causation and the relevance of the idea for regional policies. The classes in which this occurred were just before the entire sixth form was treated to a 'general studies' class at which the guest speaker was Professor Peter Bauer (who would become Lord Bauer during the Thatcher years). In essence, he presented the core of the arguments in his then-new (1971) book *Dissent on Development*, which presented a conservative critique of Myrdal's (1957) view that poor countries needed foreign aid in order to develop, since they were trapped in a vicious circle whereby their low incomes prevented them from restraining consumption and accumulating capital. Bauer maintained that the failures to develop were due to motivational shortcomings, which handouts from overseas would only made worse. In effect, his contention seemed to be that economic systems in poor countries contained enough slack for their populations to improve themselves if they were determined to do so. He argued that even a poor natural resource endowment can be overcome if attitudes are conducive to doing so, and he pointed to Hong Kong as an example of this.

In the ensuing weeks, Bauer's presentation sparked heated but inconclusive debates in class. For me, this was not merely a wonderful early experience of pluralism; the clash between a mechanical feedback system generating vicious circles versus potential to find an escape route via some form of slack if one were sufficiently motivated (as embodied in the maxim 'Where there's a will, there's a way') also became a key theme in my thinking. However, at that stage, it did not occur to me that one might apply it to industrial dynamics; five years later, I would discover this application, via Downie's (1958) analysis of the competitive process.

Towards the end of my lower-sixth year there was another formative experience, namely an 'industrial tour' for my economics cohort. It was not my first opportunity to view the internal workings of production systems, for there had previously been a school trip to the Fidelity Radio factory in Stevenage's industrial area. However, the industrial tour proved to be my equivalent of the industrial tour that Ronald Coase took while visiting the USA on a study scholarship to the University of Chicago in 1931–1932. In my case, the tour to which our class was treated visited memorable sites in the West of England and South Wales, with our accommodation being at the University of Bristol's Churchill Hall. Three of the sites that we visited were especially thought-provoking. The first was the W. D. & H. O. Wills cigarette factory in Bristol, an example of ethically challenged private enterprise, whereas the others were at the time parts of state-run industries.

The Wills factory overlooked the bonded warehouses where its tobacco supplies were stored. Inside, the aroma of tobacco was pervasive, and I found it nauseating. I suspect that my strong anti-smoking sentiments and new-found non-reticent mode of operating led me to ask something about business ethics in the question-and-answer session at the end, but I cannot recall this with certainty. However, what really hit me was the sight of the cigarette-rolling machines, which we were told were made by the Molins Machine Company, one of only a few in the world that had the capacity to make this type of machinery. The machines were astonishingly quick at what they did but it was the only thing that they could do. They provided a perfect example of what I would come, via Williamson (1985), to know as 'asset specificity'. I later realised that the challenge of making such machines would be a useful ingredient in a situation such as the German hyperinflation of 1923 in which cigarettes became a better store of value than the German currency, for if the supply of such machines could not be increased rapidly, neither could the supply of cigarettes.

Later in the tour, after a morning talking with town planners in Cwmbran, the Welsh equivalent to Stevenage new town, we spent an afternoon at the British Steel Corporation's Ebbw Vale steelworks. We observed the steelmaking process from start to finish. This, too, was replete with asset specificity, this time of a heavy-metal variety. Our guide stressed that the key to keeping costs under control was to keep the process running without interruption so that the in-process steel did not get a chance to cool down. However, disaster struck as we were walking the length of the final stage, the rolling and coiling process that turned slabs of hot steel into coils of sheet steel ready for car factories. The long sheets of thin steel that emerged from the rolling mill hurtled down a conveyor system before being coiled on reaching the end, but we witnessed an instance where the leading edge of the tongue of steel got stuck as it entered the coiling equipment. The jamming of the coiler caused the rest of the steel to concertina to a noisy halt. What then happened was remarkable: men immediately appeared, like ants, seemingly out of nowhere, to clear the wrecked new sheet of steel and unjam the coiler. Everybody performed their emergency roles as if they had been drilled for such an occasion. Shortly after, during refreshments, a somewhat embarrassed manager told us that although they had succeeded in sorting out the problem rapidly, it would probably have cost a six-figure sum in terms of the cost of keeping steel hot at earlier stages. What my classmates and I had witnessed was an example of internalised economic coordination that was a wonderful preparation for getting to grips with the transaction cost approach to industrial organisation that future Nobel Laureate Oliver Williamson was working on around this time.

The third memorable segment of the industrial tour was a visit to the huge British Rail engineering workshops at Swindon. This left me wondering about the extent of overstaffing in large organisations. Whereas the British Steel Corporation's emergency response team seemed to appear from nowhere and could justify their annual salaries in an hour or two, there seemed to be many men in the railway workshop who were conspicuously not doing much at all, and I remember noting the latter in a report on the industrial tour that I wrote for the school magazine. The spectacle did not align well with the idea of cost minimisation.

2.2   THE UNIVERSITY ENTRANCE PROCESS

Early in the upper-sixth year, I had to decide what to do about applying for university entrance. In the UK this necessitated applying through a central clearing house system (managed by a body known as UCCA) on a form that allowed applicants to nominate specific degree programmes at five institutions. My success by the end of the lower-sixth year led me to be advised to consider trying for Oxford or Cambridge. However, since at that time it was rare for Oxbridge colleges to make offers subject to the attainment of a particular set of A-Level grades, the best strategy was viewed as to delay an Oxbridge application until the 1973 round and stay on at school for the Autumn 1973 term to study for, and take, the Oxbridge entrance exams, even if by that point I was already armed with a stellar set of A-Level grades. In the meantime, I should apply for 1973 university entry to other institutions, so that I would have a fall-back position if the A-Levels did not go so well as hoped. It was also emphasised that placing high-ranking universities below the second preference would probably result in them sending an immediate rejection. Which five universities should I select, and which should be my top two preferences?

In the pre-Internet era, this could have been my first taste of choice overload in the context of quality uncertainty. Had I tried to make the choice purely on my own, I would have had to do so via the hard-copy prospectuses in my school's careers room, with no obvious means of ranking rival institutions. But the task was simplified because my teachers advised me that the next best universities to Oxford or Cambridge were Durham, Bristol or one of the best University of London colleges. Given this, the top two emerged readily. The University of Bristol was eliminated despite being in a city that I found appealing and whose Churchill Hall student accommodation had been a very pleasant base for my school's industrial tour. The problem was that Bristol required A-Level Mathematics for entry to economics. With Bristol eliminated, I needed to eliminate one from Durham, University College London, and the London School of Economics. UCL appealed to me because of Michael Stewart's presence, whereas the LSE had recently been getting a lot of publicity for demonstrations led by left-wing student activists, so I felt it would not be a good choice given the political views that I held at the time. Durham and UCL thus became my top two, with the remaining three being Birmingham, Aberystwyth, and Sussex for no particular academic reasons and without me really having thought I might need offers from them anyway.

I duly received invitations to interviews at UCL and Durham on adjacent days. This was very exciting, as it was my first trip away from home on my own and involved staying overnight in Durham. The UCL experience was very straightforward, and began with a presentation to interviewees by Malcolm Sawyer, who was then just 27 years of age and later became one of the UK's major figures in heterodox economics. To my disappointment, my interview was not with Michael Stewart but with Professor John Spraos, with whose work I was completely unfamiliar. We talked more about current affairs, particularly the Northern Ireland troubles, than about economics, but he explained that what UCL typically did with someone who looked likely to be an Oxbridge contender was to take the pressure off them by making the lowest offer that was possible, i.e., two E-grade passes at A-Level. Clearly, I had a very strong reference letter from my school, and precisely this offer was what I received a few days later, and I reciprocated by making UCL my back up option the following year.

After the UCL interview, I caught a late-afternoon train to Durham, to stay in Grey College overnight. The following morning, I was interviewed by John Creedy, who is now well known as a remarkably prolific scholar, mainly in labour and public economics. He was then only 23 and on a one-year lecturer contract at Durham; he returned to Durham as a fukk professor of economics shortly before he turned 30. Unfortunately, we did not hit it off together, and my subsequent interview at Grey College did not go well either. At the start of the following week, my bemused headmaster summoned me to his office and asked me to explain why, whereas UCL had immediately made the two-Es offer, Durham had equally rapidly rejected me outright, saying that I appeared to be arrogant and that my knowledge of economics did not match up with the reference my school had provided.

At the time, the heart of the problem seemed to me to be that John Creedy simply did not believe that I had been doing the amount of reading on economics that I said that I had been doing. He then seemed to decide to test my economic knowledge by asking me to 'draw the diagram of the theory of the firm.' His request completely flummoxed me. I did not think of the firm as something that could be reduced to a diagram. The picture that I had picked up of the economics of the firm was multifaceted. It included elements such as the idea that firms might grow via merger activity as part of a process of industrial restructuring (as I had learned from reading G. C. Allen's account of the industrial consolidation that produced the UK chemicals giant, ICI). I explained to him that I had never seen a diagram with such a name. He then said that what he wanted was the diagram for a perfectly competitive firm, which I duly drew despite merely viewing it as a diagram showing the theory of how a firm in a competitive market chooses its output. But I felt that, by then, the damage was done. Years later, it occurred to me that he had probably been hoping to see instant recall of thinking in the tradition of Edgeworth (on whom he became a leading authority) and Walras, whereas I was on the track that led from Marshall to Penrose and Chandler. In time, I would eventually have my own favorite diagram of how a firm addressed competitive challenges, but it would be the one offered by P. W. S. Andrews in his (1949) book *Manufacturing Business*, a diagram that came with a very different backstory from the one that John Creedy expected me to draw.

Nearly fifty years later, John Creedy sent me a long, pleasant, and helpful email after enjoying a paper I had co-authored to mark the fiftieth anniversary of the publication of Duncan Ironmonger's (1972) book *New Commodities and Consumer Behaviour* (Earl, Markey-Towler and Coutts, 2022). At the end of the email, he wrote "To change the subject ... didn't we meet once in Hobart ... when you reminded me that we met even earlier ... in Durham?" John's memory was spot-on, for he had visited the University of Tasmania to present a seminar at the time I worked there, shortly after he had taken up the Truby Williams Chair of Economics at the University of Melbourne. Before his seminar, I was a member of the group that took him to lunch at the staff club. On the way back to the department, I quietly told him that he had interviewed me at Durham and that despite Durham not being impressed with me I had ended up getting a double-first in Cambridge. On hearing this, he looked as though he remembered interviewing me, but we did not have any time to talk further.

It turned out that John Creedy had indeed remembered that interview in Durham. When I replied to his email, I confirmed his memory about our previous encounters. The following morning there was a further email from him, which included the following:

Perhaps I could add a few comments on my perspective of your Durham experience. One reason I remember it is that it was unique. My attitude was that I didn't really care how people interviewed. I felt that, in that situation, I would be very nervous and would not come over well (I never did have any interviews to get to Bristol or Oxford, and was terrified during my first-ever interview, for an ESRC grant). So, I always thought it was fairest just to recommend a 'standard offer' – if they got the grades, that was sufficient and one shouldn't really ask for more. During your interview, you certainly did not seem nervous at all, but even though I took my usual approach (no 'trick questions' … basic things to get going …), we could not somehow get 'on the same wavelength'. Then when the college telephoned (and they always took interviews much more seriously), it was immediately clear that they wanted to reject (Creedy, email to Earl, 2 September, 2022).

If Durham's standard offer to economics students was pitched at the right level to achieve a balance between available places and candidates who would go on to meet the required set of grades and want to study at Durham, Creedy's empathy-based heuristic for viewing interviews seems perfectly reasonable as well as fair.

Apart from the disconcerting experience at Durham, the second year of my A-Level studies went smoothly, and I duly achieved the three A-grade outcomes that my teachers had expected. As with other potential Oxbridge applicants in my cohort, I also sat two, more difficult, S-Level papers. (Only two were allowed and, of my three A-Level subjects, I opted not to take S-Level in history.) The S-Level papers had originally been designated Scholarship Level, for their role in the 1950s in allocating university scholarships but by the 1970s they were simply referred to as Special Papers and provided candidates with the opportunity to demonstrate how they fared with more challenging, unexpected questions based on the same curricula as their corresponding A-Levels. As such, they should indeed have assisted Oxbridge admissions assessors, for this was precisely the style of assessment that was core to the Oxbridge approach. Those who passed at S-Level could receive a 1 (as I received for geography) or a 2 (as I received for economics).

The results that I received probably reflected the fact that, paradoxically, I felt much better prepared for the economics paper and ran into a problem of choice overload. Normally, when faced with papers that gave a free choice of four essays from 10–12 questions, I did not scan the entire question menu before choosing what to do; rather, I simply worked down the menu until I encountered a question that I anticipated being able to do well and got to work on it, finished it, returned to the menu and continued down the list, and so on, only returning to the top of the menu at a later stage if I got to the end of the menu without finding four questions that instantly grabbed my attention and about which I felt confident.

Though this approach may seem unwise in terms of a view of choice that sees rationality in terms of taking account of all available options, it served me well, as I was usually able to spend almost the entire examination time writing my answers. I never made notes mapping out my answers in the way that many students do; rather, I formed an overall vision of how a good answer might work and got swiftly into the 'flow' (cf. Csikszentmihalyi, 1990) or 'the zone' of writing. It was a way of choosing that Gigerenzer and his colleagues (Gigerenzer and Goldstein, 1996; Gigerenzer, Todd and the ABC Research Group, 1999) would categorise as a 'fast and frugal' decision heuristic. But in the S-Level economics paper I felt I ought to be careful about my choice of questions to attempt, given that they were supposedly more difficult. I therefore gave the overall paper my attention before choosing. The trouble was that I realised, somewhat to my surprise, that I could do pretty-well any question on the paper, and I then delayed my start on my first answer by trying to think which would be the best one to do first. The issue of how I would choose the others then loomed as I wrote.

Armed with these results, I faced a different choice problem from the previous year when I came to make my serious university application in autumn 1973 while most of my classmates headed off to begin their university experiences based on the fit between their A-Level grades and the offers they had received after their 1972 applications. There were three issues to resolve.

First, I had to decide whether I was going to apply for Oxford or Cambridge: both would be oversubscribed with well-qualified applicants, so only one's first preference between these rival institutions would be taken seriously. My second preference on my UCCA form would therefore be my UCL fallback plan. I had no trouble deciding that I would try for Cambridge, and the choice had nothing to do with the convenience of its location, a direct one-hour rail trip from Stevenage. Rather, I knew it was where Keynes had written his (1936) *General Theory of*

Employment, Interest and Money and I therefore presumed his legacy there would be something that Oxford could not offer. This presumption was largely because I had become aware, via the biographical note in her *Economic Philosophy* (which I had seen in Stevenage Central Library), that Joan Robinson had worked in Cambridge in the 1930s and was still there. Fortunately, my presumption proved to be well-founded.

The second issue was which college I should apply to enter, for although Cambridge was part of the UCCA clearing house system, prospective students also had to apply directly to Cambridge and indicate their preferred college, and they would then be interviewed for admission to their preferred college by fellows of that college. This was a matter that my teachers knew had to be addressed very carefully. Each year, Alleyne's usually managed, from its pre-comprehensive intakes, to place a handful or so of its top students with Oxford or Cambridge, so it had a track record relationship with some colleges that might help its latest applicants to be taken seriously. The reason that I ended up applying to Queens' College – a choice that I believe was pivotal in getting me started along the behavioural economics track – came about because of this concern about these relationships but this was despite there being *no* recollection at my school of anyone having been sent previously to Queens'.

My destiny was determined by the fact that I loved geography as well as economics and, on looking for a way of studying in Cambridge that might enable me to do economics without altogether abandoning geography, I came across the possibility of following Part I of the Economics Tripos with a Part II in Land Economy. Because the number of students who studied land economy was much smaller than for economics, not all colleges had fellows who were members of the Department of Land Economy. My school arranged for me to go to Cambridge to talk about the land economy programme with Mike Turner, who was the Director of Studies for students in land economy at both Emmanuel (where the school had a track record) and Queens'. The meeting with Turner was very pleasant, rather as though we were gently interviewing each other, and at the end I asked him how Emmanuel and Queens' compared. His reply was frank and accurate: 'If you go to Emmanuel, you'll probably have to live in lodgings in the second year, whereas Queens' undergraduates usually get rooms in college for all three years, but the food in hall at Queens' isn't very good.' I was prepared to put up with poor food to avoid the isolation of living outside college (and the greater distance from lecture theatres and libraries that would likely come with it). My mentors at Alleyne's thought that it would probably be safe, now that the seeds of a new connection had been sown, for me to make Queens' my preferred college.

The third issue was which two subjects I should take for the Cambridge entrance examination. In addition to economics, I chose history rather than geography as it seemed likely to be easier to figure out what additional material I needed to study to cope with very wide ranges of questions that were set to accommodate applicants who had studied different syllabuses. I returned to Alleyne's for an additional term during which I studied an extra century's worth of British and European history and read further in economics. This did not entail going into school every day and, when combined with one-on-one meetings with teachers, it was very like studying as a university student. In addition to the November examinations, the selection process included college interviews. Because I had already met with Mike Turner, I was not required to be interviewed by either of the economics fellows at Queens', but my experience at Durham resulted in me being very cautious when I had my general interview, which was with tax lawyer John Tiley.

In the event, I won a place at Queens'. My next puzzle was what I might do with the first eight months of 1974. I soon found myself in a role that at the time was not uncommon for those in my situation: I was given what was formally a 'student teacher' role, initially to fill a one-term gap between the departure of one of the geography teachers at Barclay School (a former 'secondary modern' high school adjacent to Alleyne's) and the arrival of his successor. After teaching geography to second- to fourth-form classes and teaching fourth-form geology, I was then retained for a second term to teach CSE Economics (i.e., basic economics for students of low academic ability, which included a visit to the Vauxhall car factory in Luton) and remedial reading. Finally, during the summer vacation, I was hired to help oversee use of the school's swimming pool.

During the summer of 1974, my view of the world became larger and much clearer. This was due to my short-sightedness having become bad enough to enable me to have contact lenses fitted via the National Health Service, for a mere £9. Wearing contact lenses instead of thick-lensed spectacles seemed to slow the progression of my myopia as well as greatly improving how well I could see. My improved vision soon proved to be vital for dealing with distant blackboards in large lecture theatres.

3 Cambridge Economics, 1974–1979

3.1   INTRODUCTION

The University of Cambridge (to which I will henceforth usually refer simply as Cambridge) was founded in 1209. It is the third oldest continuously operating university in the world, the oldest being the University of Bologna, followed by the University of Oxford. Cambridge was almost 700 years old by the time the Economics Tripos, a three-year undergraduate degree programme, was established in 1903. However, as is evident from the two-volume study of Cambridge economics edited by Cord (2017), Cambridge's connections with economics date from a century before the Tripos. The Cord volumes are a remarkable resource, for they provide biographies of 53 key contributors to in Cambridge economics, along with surveys on key themes that link their contributions. They are well complemented by Saith's (2022) detailed account of the withering of heterodox economics at Cambridge after the years covered in this chapter.

Cambridge is a public, collegiate institution that today has 31 colleges. My college, formally known as The Queen's College of St Margaret and St Bernard, is one of the oldest colleges, having been founded by Margaret of Anjou, the wife of King Henry VI, in 1448. It is usually referred to as Queens' College, the plural apostrophe being used because it was re-founded in 1465 by Elizabeth Woodville, the wife of King Edward IV. Here, I shall usually refer to it simply as Queens'. Famous Queens' alumni include Stephen Fry and, I was disappointed to discover, Sue-Ellen ('Suella') Braverman, the Conservative MP who became well-known for her penchant for heartless policies in her role as the UK Home Secretary. When I went up to Cambridge in October 1974, Queens' was still an all-male college and I was one of eleven new students that it had admitted to study economics.

Along with St John's College, Queens' is one of two Cambridge colleges that occupy land on both sides of the River Cam. Its oldest and most picturesque buildings are all on the east bank, and its famous Mathematical Bridge provides a means of crossing within the grounds of the college to the 20th-century buildings on the west bank. Except for my first year as a research student, when I lived in the modernist Erasmus Building (designed by Sir Basil Spence, and opened in 1961), I lived on the west bank, spending my undergraduate years as a resident of the then-new Cripps Court, and having rooms in the 1930s Fisher Building in my final year in residence.

The modern buildings lacked the charm of the old ones on the east bank but were rather better endowed with bathroom facilities. Unlike my parents' house in Stevenage, where the inadequacies of the central heating system were never addressed, my rooms in Queens' were always well heated. This provided a benchmark for winter comfort that I was unable to match for most of my life after Cambridge. However, the fire-safety measures in the older buildings left me feeling nervous: the bedroom in my suite in the Fisher Building had a rope harness that I would need to wear to escape by lowering myself from the window in the event of a fire on the staircase. All the rooms were cleaned, and their linen was changed, by usually elderly women known as bedmakers or bedders. Many of them were very reminiscent of how female cleaners were portrayed in the TV comedy *Monty Python's Flying Circus* (except that they did not display any knowledge of philosophy) and it often seemed as though their role was mainly to check whether students were alive, well, and adhering to rules regarding how many nights they could spend away from their rooms during term or whether they had unregistered overnight guests. The bedmaker for my room in Erasmus was so bad at cleaning that one day I noticed a visitor to my room had written in the thick dust on top of the cover of my record turntable the words, 'Do not disturb. Wheat planted!'

My first-year room in Cripps Court was inward-facing, which ensured that it provided excellent opportunities to watch the construction of the remainder of the court, including the new Queens' dining hall. The noise was a big inducement to spend office hours at the Sidgwick Site, a collection of modernist buildings where the economics lectures were held and where the Austin Robinson Building housed the Faculty of Economics and Politics (nowadays merely the Faculty of Economics), which I shall henceforth usually refer to simply as the Faculty. This building also housed the Department of Applied Economics (henceforth, the DAE), the Marshall Library of Economics, the Marshall lecture room and, for refreshments, The Buttery. Occasionally, Austin Robinson (1897–1993) himself might be seen entering or leaving the building, and a very frail-looking Piero Sraffa (1898–1983) sometimes came into the Marshall Library via its staff entrance to seek help from Mr Finkel, the head librarian. A sprightlier legendary figure, who continued to lecture in her seventies, was Joan Robinson (1903–1983). She did not dress as others of her age dressed; instead, she typically was to be seen wearing a colourful poncho and wooden sandals.

The Marshall Library was usually quite empty in the evenings but was often busy on Saturday afternoons. Lectures did not take place in the evening, unlike in many universities today, but Nicholas Kaldor's lectures for Part II of the Tripos were held on Saturday mornings (in the Little Hall); it was said that, on weekdays, he was busy in London, advising the UK Treasury on what to do with the UK economy. (I attended these lectures during my Part I year, as I had worked out that Kaldor [1908–1986] was about to arrive at Cambridge's statutory retirement age of 67.) Many lecturers wore gowns while they performed, thereby limiting the extent to which their other clothes got covered in chalk dust; very few lecturers used overhead projectors and those who did so (such as David Champernowne [1912–2000]) generally wrote notes on rolls of transparent film as they lectured, rather than using previously prepared slides.

The Director of Studies in Economics at Queens' was Ajit Singh (1940–2015), whose life and place in Cambridge economics have been chronicled in detail by Saith (2019) and more briefly by Harcourt *et al.* (2016) and Scherer (2017)). Ajit was a significant contributor to industrial economics and development economics, and a leader of the far-left faction within the Faculty. He was a very colourful character, especially when he wore his 'traffic light' outfit: a red turban, orange sweater and green trousers. His capacity to work was extraordinary, so much so that, after he was diagnosed with Parkinson's disease (while only in his forties), a succession of assistants found it difficult to maintain the pace that he set. There was always a mischievous twinkle in his eye, but he provided a role-model for pluralistic teaching: he did not leave his students in the dark about his own position, but he was determined that they should understand and appreciate both the strengths and limitations of other economic perspectives. Ajit remained a fellow at Queens' for the rest of his life.

At the time that I became a student at Queens', the college's other economics fellowship holder was Brian Van Arkadie, a development economist with wide experience of working as an advisor in East Africa. Brian was my main supervisor during my first year. I recall that in one of the first supervisions he glanced over to a cabinet that was topped by large tray of wine and sherry bottles and asked me and my supervision partner, John Austin, if we would care for a drink. It was quite late in the afternoon, and Brian's strategy of running five supervisions back-to-back must have been exhausting. He looked rather disappointed to discover that neither I nor John drank alcohol, and he therefore refrained from pouring himself a glass. Apparently, he fared better with the group that followed, but I did not hear whether this became a standard feature of the late afternoon supervisions, and I did not make it a practice of my own when I became a supervisor three years later, on commencing as a research student.

After my first year at Queens', Brian Van Arkadie moved to a position at the International Institute of Social Studies in The Hague, and a junior fellowship was offered to Andy Cosh. Andy had just finished his PhD (on executive remuneration) at Queens' and supervised papers on economic statistics. Andy spent the rest of his career at Queens' and became the college's bursar. However, he found a lecturing role not at the Faculty but among a group that taught economics and management to engineering students. This group eventually grew into the Judge Business School. In later decades, the Judge Business School also proved to be a place where three of my other Cambridge teachers could prosper: John Eatwell, the main Post Keynesian lecturer, became its Professor of Financial Policy (while he was also the President of Queens'); Geoff Meeks, who was one of my main supervisors in my final undergraduate year, became its Professor of Management Accounting; and Alan Hughes, whose lectures on industrial economics had a major impact on my thinking, became its first Margaret Thatcher Professor of Enterprise Studies.

3.2 THE CAMBRIDGE TEACHING SYSTEM

There is much about the 1970s Cambridge undergraduate teaching system that would horrify students in the 2020s, for it favoured students who were self-motivated, who did not doubt their intellectual capabilities, and who had a high tolerance of uncertainty and ambiguity. This made it a good starting point for doing a Cambridge PhD, for as will become evident from Chapter 4, research students could receive very little supervision or guidance about what was expected of them. There was none of what we nowadays call 'dumbing down' or 'spoon-feeding' along the way to a Cambridge BA, but the high bar that one needed to get over to enter ensured this was not usually a problem. In Cambridge terminology, students were not 'studying for a BA in Economics'; rather, they were 'reading for the Economics Tripos', and the pathway to the graduation ceremony at the Senate House (which was conducted in Latin, with photography prohibited) involved reading and writing on a scale that modern students in a run-of-the-mill university would find hard to imagine.

The Tripos System
The word 'tripos' does not denote a three-part degree programme. Rather, it is believed to refer to the three-legged stool that early Cambridge students would sit on when undertaking oral examinations. The story of how Alfred Marshall established the Economics Tripos in 1903 and how it evolved in its first half century has been told by Tribe (2002, 2022, chapter 5), who explains that Marshall's original structure had a two-year Part I and a one-year Part II. However, in 1930, Part I was switched to one year and Part II was extended to two years. This format remained in place for 90 years. From the 2020 intake onwards, the Cambridge Economics Tripos has three components: Part I, Part IIA and Part IIB, with the final grades based only on performance in Part IIA (with a 30 percent weight) and Part IIB (with a 70 percent weight), though students must also pass Part I to qualify for an honours final class. This was a radical change, even though the number of 'papers' (the Cambridge term for a subject or course) has hardly changed: at the time that I was a student, honours classes were awarded separately for Parts I and II. The second year of the Tripos/first year of Part II was known as the Prelims year. There were Prelims examinations, but they had no bearing on one's Part II outcome.

In some other disciplines, as in the original Economics Tripos prior to 1930, Part I lasted two years and Part II only one year. Some students graduated after taking very different subjects for the different parts of their Tripos: for example, my next-door neighbour in my first year at Queens' read Natural Sciences Part I and then switched to Law Part II. Such switches were facilitated via studies during the 'long vacation'. As noted in the previous chapter, my original plan was to switch to Land Economy for my Part II, and I would have had to stick to it if I had not performed satisfactorily in the Elementary Qualifying Examination in Mathematics that I had to take in lieu of A-Level Mathematics as a requirement for entry to Part II Economics. Today, admission to Part I is not possible without having passed A-Level Mathematics or an equivalent.

The way that 1970s Cambridge students discovered how well they had performed in each part of their Tripos was very different from the way that many of today's students get their results. In the 2020s, the process is typically very private, either via an email generated automatically by the student records system of their university at a pre-announced time or by logging into that system. With no email available in the 1970s, Cambridge students were sent a postcard to advise them of the class of their result. In the case of my Part II result, the card only arrived at my parents' letterbox on the day of my graduation ceremony, just before we set off to drive from Stevenage to Cambridge. But I already knew the result, for I had received messages of congratulation from some of those who had taught me, and the results had been posted publicly in *The Times* newspaper (whose lists also mentioned one's high school), after initially being posted on one of the noticeboards on the outside of the Senate House.

Tripos outcomes were graded from first-class honours, down through upper- and lower-second-class honours, to third-class honours, with everyone enrolling as honours students. For those who, for whatever reason, 'bombed out' there was an 'ordinary' tier below a third, which was euphemistically referred to as a 'special'. However, the published Tripos results revealed nothing beyond the class of the outcome, and the Cambridge degree certificates did not even list the class of one's degree. The only way to discover how well one had performed within an honours class and on individual examination papers was via a private chat with someone who had this information.

In the mid-1970s, Cambridge admitted around 170 students each year to study for the Economics Tripos, and typically about 12–15 of them were awarded a first. To my surprise, at the start of my Prelims year, Ajit Singh congratulated me not merely for getting a first in Part I but also for getting the second-highest first. He said that he presumed that I had now abandoned any thoughts of taking Land Economy for my Part II, adding the comment that 'Land Economy is really for those who have a very rich father who has an estate for them to manage'. He was right about how I had changed my plans, but I doubt that he foresaw that the Department of Land Economy would become (like the Judge Business School) a place of refuge for heterodox economists in Cambridge, from which they could conduct research in areas such as ecological economics and property speculation. I did not foresee this either; my mind was coming to terms with a sense that the pressure was now on me to get a first in Part II as well, to prove that my Part I outcome was not some kind of fluke result that depended on the absence of technique-driven subjects. I managed to meet this aspiration in Part II, but was never given any precise ranking score, merely the impression that I had performed well within that class.

In Cambridge, a student could achieve a 'double-first' either by getting first-class honours in two different fields or, as I did, by doing so in both parts of a given field. I have long felt that the former achievement was more deserving of that term. This is possibly because the person who always comes to my mind as a stellar contemporary example is Adair Turner (now Baron Turner of Ecchinswell, and Chairman of the Institute for New Economic Thinking), He managed to achieve his double-first in History and Economics during his four years at Gonville and Caius College (the extra year being due to History having a two-year Part I) despite the diversions of his presidential roles in the Cambridge Union Society and Cambridge University Conservative Association. I had no expectations of having the kind of stellar career that Turner predictably had, but I know that Ajit Singh expected me to do better than I did: when I caught up with Ajit during the 2003 conference that the *Cambridge Journal of Economics* held to mark the centenary of the Cambridge Economics Tripos, he was most surprised to learn that my position was then merely that of a senior lecturer, just as it had been in 1990, the previous time that I had seen him.

Assessment

Unless students elected to do a dissertation in Part II, the classes of their outcomes in the Economics Tripos depended entirely on their overall performance in final examinations held at the end of May/start of June. There was no coursework component whatsoever, and, with one exception, none of my supervisors ever put a grade on the work that I did. That exception was James Trevithick, who had recently arrived from the University of Glasgow and hence may not have understood the value that Cambridge seemed to place on leaving its undergraduates uncertain about the quality of their work. (Trevithick supervised my final-year studies on monetary economics; he only rated one of the essays that I did for him as a first, scoring the others as of upper-second standard.) Moreover, in contrast to the 2020s, where best-practice 'electronic course profiles' typically include a section outlining what a student needs to do to achieve each class level of attainment, no advice was provided about how the performance of a mid-1970s student would be assessed in the Economics Tripos. Since all of my cohort at Queens' had similar, top-notch sets of A-Level grades, it was very hard to form expectations about how well we would each do in Part I. The only one of us who looked like he might stand out (as he indeed went on to do) was Andrew Goudie, whose performance in the entrance examinations had earned him a Queens' scholarship.

To most students in the 2020s, this uncertainty and reliance on final examinations would probably seem an unreasonable imposition, any prospect of which would be terrifying. Many of them might wonder why students working in such a system would bother to put much work into assignments that 'counted for nothing' or bother showing up to tutorials in which they would receive a grilling yet get no reward in terms of marks. In 1970s Cambridge, such thoughts were never entertained. We worked away at writing a relentless stream of assignments and it was rare for students to fail to submit an assignment or not attend a supervision (the Cambridge term for a tutorial). Work for supervisions, and attendance at them, was all seen as part of the process of preparing for the final examinations. At Queens', the process was treated rather as if we were getting trained up for a sporting event, for regular supervisions stopped halfway through the third (Easter) term and we were then expected to spend our time doing remaining reading and attempting practice examination papers under the time limits that we would face in the actual examinations.

The sense of getting trained up for a big event was enhanced by Ajit Singh's evident desire for the Queens' economists to ensure that the college was well-placed in the inter-college league table of degree outcomes. We were told that we were expected to keep the college near the top of the list for economics, with our main rivals being viewed as those at Clare College. (In my year, the Clare economists included Martin Weale, who in 1995 became the Director of the National Institute for Economic and Social Research.) Somehow, word seemed to get round about who some of the students from other colleges were who were expected to do well, so we recognised the Clare students in lectures despite not getting to know them. With Tripos results publicly available, we could see what we were up against after Part I and how well Queens' then fared against its rivals in Part II. The motivational impact of inter-college rivalry is difficult to assess, but students in universities that lack the college system would not get any sense of being part of a team in such a way.

The fact that essays written for supervisions counted for nothing in the assessment process was conducive to taking an experimental, creative approach to writing them. One might thereby find out what the supervisor thought of one's ideas and get a sense of whether they might be fit to deploy in an examination. In Section 3.4, I provide an illustration of this approach to writing supervision essays.

Examinations

Except for the Part II Applied Economic and Social Statistics paper, which required students to take both three-hour and four-hour examinations, the end-of-year examinations for each paper lasted for three hours. All the non-quantitative papers were based around essay questions, typically with an unrestricted choice of about thirteen from which one had to attempt four. Even the Part II economic theory paper could be addressed purely by writing essays. However, this is not to say that I never included mathematical content in my answers. I did not do so in the theory paper, but I recall that in one of my Prelims examinations, I wrote an answer that included a derivation of Kaldor's model of income distribution, with something rather similar for another answer in the same paper. I never did such a thing again: I felt it had not been a wise move as it probably looked like a case of 'parrot-learning' and it diverted me from doing something more creative and experimental.

Answers were not written in examination answer booklets that consisted of a particular number of pages; rather, the system used the more economical approach of providing a stack of sheets of lined paper, with students using only as many as they needed and then tying them to a cover sheet. Cambridge was ahead of many universities in ensuring the anonymity of examinees, for students only wrote on their exam coversheets the examinee number that they had been assigned and their desk number (the latter was presumably for checking on any cases where it seemed possible that one student had managed to copy the work of another).[1] I was told that all answers were marked by a pair of examiners

---

[1] This anonymous marking system had only just been introduced, having been one of the issues for reform explored by a staff-student committee of the Faculty prior to a large sit-in by several hundred students at the Cambridge registry in the Old Schools building on

whose scores were usually simply averaged, and that it was sometimes possible to get a first overall even if one got very high upper-second scores on all papers.

With such an assessment system, there was clear potential for students to be disadvantaged if they fell ill during the examination period, got into a panic in an exam or simply did not perform at their best for any other reason. Yet there was no sign of anything like modern-day routines in other universities (but not modern-day Cambridge) for offering 'deferred ordinary' and 'supplementary' examinations if things went awry. Instead, it appeared that in extreme cases an unclassed grade of 'honours in exceptional circumstances' might be awarded.

No opportunities were provided to 'view' one's examination papers and/or to try to negotiate a better grade with one's examiners in the way that some modern students seem to feel entitled to do. The examination process largely felt like sitting A-Levels, where scripts were marked remotely by nameless assessors. The best clue about who might have been involved in setting a paper and be marking it would be who showed up as an invigilator, but given the double-marking process, that was at best only half of what we might have liked to know. However, the Cambridge system did provide a form of general feedback that deserves to be more widely used even today. It took the form of 'Examiners' Reports' for each of the papers in the Tripos, which students could access in their discipline's library. I recall looking at the previous year's set of reports for Part I while armed with a copy of that year's question papers in the hope that there might be clues about the kinds of things that the examiners liked or found disappointing. The only thing that has stuck in my mind from it was that one of the politics lecturers had commented that, when it came to knowledge of Marx, that year's class would probably have been able to demonstrate much more knowledge of the ideas of Groucho than they had shown regarding those of Karl.

Organisation
Given how the performance of students in the Economics Tripos was assessed, the division of labour between the colleges and the Faculty was

---

3–5 February 1972. I was completely unaware of the sit-in, the Devlin Inquiry that followed it, and the role that Ajit Singh played, until I read Saith (2019, pp. 70–77). It helped me to appreciate why Robert Neild had commented, in one of his 1977 Part II lectures, that we seemed to be a passive bunch compared with students only a few years before.

potentially problematic. Lectures and the examination process were the responsibility of the Faculty, while the colleges decided which students they wanted to admit and then ensured that their students received supervisions to prepare them for the examinations. However, the system did not function like a franchise system. The curriculum of the Economics Tripos was only sketched out briefly and those who assigned work for college supervisions decided how to flesh out and teach what each paper was broadly supposed to cover. Hence, the teaching that students received could vary considerably between colleges. Some students might thus be advantaged because they received supervisions from college fellows who contributed questions to the examination papers and thus did not have to guess where they needed to focus the attention of those that they supervised.

Scope for coordination failures in teaching was enhanced by the way the lecture programme was organised. The lecture timetable, listing the lecturers, times, and locations, was published at the start of each term in Cambridge's gazette, *The Reporter*. It is possible that college fellows who were also Faculty members were given advance notice of the lecture timetable, but no such notice was provided for other supervisors, such as PhD students. Hence, some supervisors could find it necessary to prepare their lists of assignments and readings for an upcoming term without knowing who would be lecturing for the paper in question, let alone what they planned to cover in their lectures. Devising and handing out assignments week by week as term progressed was a way of buying time to find out what was going to be covered in lectures, but from a student standpoint it seemed as though supervisors mainly just 'did their own thing' and hoped that the wide range of questions on the examination paper would provide enough opportunities for their students to shine based on what they had covered in supervisions plus their own interpretations of other things that they had only encountered in lectures or via their wider reading.

Lectures

The lecture programme for each paper was very conducive to students receiving a pluralistic view of the area in question, for it was common for a paper to have three or four lecturers over the course of the academic year. There were also weekly lecture slots in some papers that were known as 'circuses', with a different lecturer each week giving a sense of the work that they were doing (as with some members of the DAE) or giving their perspective on the state of the UK economy and what policy interventions it needed.

Such an abundance of lectures per paper stands in sharp contrast with practice in the 2020s, where a typical one-semester subject commonly has only one lecturer, who delivers, say, two hours of lectures per week for twelve or thirteen weeks, and where there is sometimes an aversion even to dividing a subject's lectures between a couple of staff for fear that the students will experience 'difficulties in adjusting to changes in the lecturers' styles'. At first sight, this contrast might appear to reflect the squeeze in per-student funding that has taken place over the past five decades. However, it is important to note that much of the change in per-student funding has had its impact in relation to the variable costs of degree factories and manifests itself in rising tutorial sises, whereas the provision of lectures entails incurring fixed costs that fall per student as class sises increase.

Hence, we should not overlook differences between the Cambridge system and modern-day systems in the number of papers/subjects taught and the number of programmes offered. For example, the School of Economics at the University of Queensland, at which I ended my career, is rather similar in size to the Faculty in 1970s Cambridge, but it offers around 80 subjects. It is thereby able to provide a wide range of choice to students enrolled for three-year non-honours degrees, an honours year, a variety of coursework-only master's degrees, and several very low-enrolment PhD-only subjects. By contrast, the Faculty in Cambridge originally offered merely the Economics Tripos and taught, at most, just 26 papers (5 in Part I, the Elementary Qualifying Examination in Mathematics, 5 in Prelims, and up to 15 in Part II) until the MPhil programme resulted in a few more having to be offered. There were no papers for PhD students, but the level at which undergraduate courses were taught enabled PhD students to develop their capabilities by attending Prelims and (less commonly) Part II lectures. Cambridge-style pluralism would be possible in large-scale modern degree factories if they could engage in drastic pruning of their product ranges, with their non-core subjects then having greatly increased class sises. But the risk of major losses in enrolments stands in the way of doing this; hence, if their students are to be able to enjoy a pluralistic learning experience, these universities must provide it in other ways.

The small number of papers relative to the number of academic staff in the Faculty ensured that there were multiple staff who could lecture on each paper without having to lecture on topics that were not aligned with their research interests. Generally, those who lectured in an area were therefore lecturing based on extensive expertise in that area, and this was reflected in the comprehensiveness of the reading lists that they provided and in handouts that demonstrated their knowledge of data sources for areas in which they lectured. This was especially evident in the teaching of papers on economic history and development economics. In the former, I attended sets of lectures by Phyllis Deane, Charles Feinstein, Iain Macpherson, B. R. Mitchell, Donald Moggridge, Clive Trebilcock and G. N. Von Tunzelmann, all of whom were specialists in the areas on which they lectured. The same was true with economic development lectures from Valpy Fitzgerald, Michael Kuczynski, Suzy Paine, Brian Reddaway, Ajit Singh and John Wells. When it came to teaching the Elementary Qualifying Examination in Mathematics, Cambridge did not stint in putting an expert at the lectern for my cohort, for the lectures were delivered by David Champernowne, a gifted mathematician. The only set of lectures that I recall being given by someone who seemed not to be a specialist in the area in question were those for Part I macroeconomics: they were delivered by Robin Marris (1924–2012), whom I had hoped to see lecturing on his work on managerial capitalism (Marris, 1964). Given what we were doing for our supervisions, it looked as though his lectures were there mainly as a safety net, though at that time Cambridge was rather short of non-retired lecturing staff who specialised in macroeconomics. His role made a lot more sense if one knew that he had derived his strongly Keynesian views from his own Cambridge education in the 1940s at the feet of those who had been in Keynes's circle during the writing of the *General Theory.*

Beyond Cambridge, by contrast, it was common for lectures to be assigned to staff who did not have research- and/or application-based backgrounds in the areas in question. For example, in my own lecturing career I had to teach economic history (at the University of Stirling and the University of Queensland), economic development (at the University of Tasmania and Lincoln University) and introductory mathematics for commerce and economics (at the University of Tasmania). This was sometimes done quite deliberately as a means of ensuring that the lecturer did not offer research-based material that was far too advanced for the students: being only a few weeks ahead of one's class is certainly conducive to having empathy with the challenges that a subject entails.

Occasionally, students would be treated to college-only invited presentations. Part I Queens' students received one of these at an evening session in Ajit Singh's room, where Martin Fetherston from the Cambridge Economic Policy Group explained what became known as the 'New Cambridge' view of the UK economy (see further, Section 3.3). Very occasionally, lecturers would run additional classes for everyone who was taking the paper for which they were lecturing, with the presentation being made by students who had (been) volunteered to do so. Alan Hughes and Ajit Singh tried this for the Part II paper on the Modern Business Enterprise and Social Structure, with the first presentation, on the financing of investment by UK enterprises, given by me and Andrew Goudie.

Supervisions

Supervisions were conducted by fellows from one's own college or other colleges, research students, and research staff from the DAE. The traditional format of a Cambridge supervision entailed an hour-long meeting between the supervisor and just two students, in which each student would, in turn, read their essays aloud and from time to time be challenged by the supervisor and be required to defend what they had written. In this supervision mode, the supervisor might provide no written feedback and the student would be expected to add notes at the points where the interjections had occurred, either before moving on with reading the essay or on completing its reading. (In the latter case, this would be while the other student commenced reading, if one had been first to read.) Ajit Singh often employed the traditional mode and sometimes seemed to have a disconcerting capacity to keep processing arguments from the first essay while listening to the second one, for sometimes the first reader might be hit with a further question as an interjection during the reading of the second essay. Unlike a modern-day tutorial with many students, there was nowhere to hide and plenty of scope for embarrassment if one had made a glaring omission or logical error or could not reply to a question.

Sometimes, the supervision groups contained as many as four students, too many for the essay-reading approach to be used. Here, and sometimes with smaller groups, supervisors would operate in the manner of tutors in other universities, making written comments on essays and then using the supervision as a forum for discussing the issues raised by the question at hand. This was the more common approach of the supervisors that I had, and it was the one that I adopted when I got the chance to become a supervisor on returning to Queens' for my first term as a research student.

Even when using the traditional mode, Ajit Singh tended to signal at the start what we should focus on in any supervision. He would say, 'So, what's the point about this week's question? What important analytical issues does it raise?' This message was so thoroughly drummed into us that it was hard to resist the temptation to begin every essay with the words, 'This question raises the following important analytical issues ...' Thus, we knew better than to begin essays, as so many students do, with a waffling restatement of the question and instead we showed that we had, in effect, decoded the question and we then went straight into answering it. To convey further that we should be direct in our writing and write in a critical, constructive, and pluralistic way, we were invited to imagine that we were public servants who were writing briefings for a government minister to use in preparation for handling parliamentary question time: we had to anticipate alternative points of view and supplementary questions that might be asked.

The assignments that provided the focus for supervisions did not entail technical exercises of the kind that became common in the teaching of mainstream economics in more recent decades. In the latter, the student's appreciation of a theoretical tool is tested via an artificial, abstract puzzle to which there is one correct answer. To illustrate what the Cambridge approach entailed, I will reflect on the following question, which I had to address in my first Prelims essay for Ajit Singh:

'The Hicks–Allen model of consumer behaviour is utterly useless because it yields no testable hypotheses.' Discuss.

This question appears to have been inspired by the introduction to the article in which Lancaster (1966) sets out his 'characteristics-based' approach to consumer behaviour, an article that ends with an attempt to provide some testable implications of his 'new' approach. Ajit did not tell us this at the time and saved Lancaster's theory until a Part II supervision in which we were discussing the notion that 'non-price factors' lay behind the UK's declining performance relative to international trading partners such as Germany and Japan. But even without knowing the background to the contention that we were required to discuss, there were plenty of issues to raise, such as:

- Is the statement correct in relation to the theory having 'no testable hypotheses' and, if so, why? (One could begin by showing why the theory does not predict that a reduction in a commodity's relative price will necessarily result in an increase in its sales, as income effects may be either positive or negative without violating the assumptions about preferences, and a positive income effect might be large enough to outweigh the substitution effect. However, one might then argue that the theory does predict that the sign of the substitution effect is always negative. Ajit conceded this, but he then told us that, empirically, substitution effects at the level of the product category were small relative to income effects, as shown in Houthakker and Taylor, 1970.)
- Can a theory be useful even if it has no testable hypotheses, and, if so, how? (For example, can the Hicks-Allen theory be used as a foundation for statistical analysis of patterns of demand or for analysing the welfare impacts of rival economic policy proposals?)
- Can the Hicks-Allen theory be viewed as useless for reasons other than its (limited) ability to offer testable hypotheses? (For example, could it be misleading due to being based on unrealistic assumptions, or does the way it is constructed limit its domain and preclude it from being used to frame important real-world issues, such as how new products come to be adopted?)

Picking apart the question word by word may seem redolent of how members of a debating society go about constructing their speeches, but it is great for developing analytical skills. Having to contend with these types of questions and address them in this way promotes a much deeper kind of learning than one would get from undertaking a technical exercise built around the same piece of theory. It is as much a question about economic method as a test of how well one has grasped the theory and can explain how it was arrived at and where its strengths and weaknesses originate.

Library Resources and Reading
Students in today's world of online library catalogues with advanced search capabilities probably have far less respect for their instructors' reading suggestions than I had as a student. I regarded lectures and supervisors as mentors who had expertise that resulted in them providing

more relevant sets of sources than I might discover by myself in the time that I had available. The reading suggestions that supervisors and lecturers dispensed mostly referred to the research literature, for the teaching system was not built around working through textbooks a chapter at a time. This made life very challenging for students – not because the original sources were usually too hard to fathom but because of problems in getting access to readings when one wanted them.

On paper, the library facilities were wonderful: Queens' had a good economics collection in its own library; the catalogue of the Marshall Library of Economics usually listed all the items on reading lists; and the enormous Cambridge University Library[2] was one of the UK's few copyright libraries, whose catalogue was said at that time to list over three million works. In practice, however, the libraries were not well geared to serving the volume of students who were, literally, 'reading' economics.

The problem was that there simply were not enough copies of works that were in high demand. This issue could arise simply because a dozen students in a single college were working on the same supervision essay within a particular week, but insufficient multiple copies of in-demand works could be especially acute if students from many colleges were trying to access a common set of sources. A lot of time could be wasted queuing for copies of items in the Marshall's short-loan reserve collection or on fruitless trips to try to find them in other libraries from which they had already been borrowed.

Two issues exacerbated this problem. One was the decentralised nature of the college-based teaching system, with supervisors setting their own sets of readings and quite commonly not even handing out reading lists at the start of term and instead offering the essay topic and associated readings for the upcoming supervision at the end of the preceding supervision. There was no equivalent to the typical modern system in which each subject has a single set of readings and the course coordinator is required to submit the list of readings to the subject librarian a month or so before teaching commences. The staff in the Marshall Library must have felt as if they were repeatedly being

---

[2] The 'UL', as everyone called it, was built in the 1930s to a design by the great British architect Giles Gilbert Scott, who had previously designed the nearby Georgian-style Memorial Court of Clare College. However, the UL completely dwarfs Memorial Court and in some respects is rather like a hybrud between Scott's two most famous works: Liverpool Cathedral and Battersea Power Station.

ambushed due to unexpected short surges in demand for items that may have already escaped as non-reserve loans to the first students that went in search of them. Secondly, photocopying was not readily available to enable students to make their own copies and rapidly return the original. Not allowing undergraduates to borrow journals did not ensure that the sought-after articles at least stayed in the library, for it was not unknown for articles to be ripped (or cut via razorblades) from bound journals, causing great inconvenience to the library as well as to other would-be users. The modern world of downloadable articles and eBooks available to multiple users was beyond our wildest dreams.

So, how did I cope when making a serious attempt each week to treat each supervision essay as a research assignment? My approach was multi-pronged:

- Remind myself that no marks were attached to a supervision essay and that the recommended readings might have been suggested as substitutes, so it was OK to put an answer together without having read some sources – I could read later anything that seemed to be important but had been impossible to obtain within the window within which the essay for which it had been recommended had to be written.
- Not be afraid to look at seemingly related books close to where the sought-after book should have been shelved.
- Use what had been said about the work in a lecture as likely to be enough of a basis for taking account of it in an essay.
- Take careful note of references and footnotes in the sources that *could* be accessed, to find alternatives by the same author (for example, articles on which a book had been based).
- Look for a book review in the *Economic Journal* for a book that seemed important but was proving elusive.
- If there existed a 'Penguin Readings' collection of reprinted articles in an area that I was studying, purchase it; these were very cheap and often had superb introductions as well as key sources (as with Archibald, ed., 1971, and Sen, ed., 1970).
- Go to Heffers Bookshop and see if the book was in stock there; if it was, glean key ideas by browsing, or even buy it if it looked likely to be of enduring use and had a reasonable price.

But I probably should have had the confidence to take advantage of situations in which I could get by without even bothering to treat a supervision essay as requiring fresh research. Sometimes, it was possible to write supervision essays purely based on previous learning, one's general capacity to 'think like an economist', and one's capacities to pull questions apart and engage in critical and constructive thinking. This was essentially what we had to do in the examinations and was memorably demonstrated one day by my supervision partner, Steve Kidd. I called at his room shortly after midday to see whether he wanted to join me for lunch before our 2:00 pm lecture. However, he asked me to come back at 1:45 pm, as he had two supervision essays to write before the lecture. Steve was a seriously capable intuitive economist with a water polo team to organise, not someone who was running late due to procrastination. Hence, I wasn't really surprised that, by the time that I returned, he had completed writing both essays from scratch.

Workload, Health, and Safety
The Cambridge workload was far greater than that faced by the students that I taught in the two decades prior to my retirement. The latter typically had eight hours of lectures and four hours of tutorials per week and would have to complete up to three written assignments for each of the eight semester-long subjects for which they studied each year, i.e., up to 72 assignments in three years. (The actual figure might often be much less than this, due to lecturers commonly setting just a mid-semester exam and one other piece of written work for a single subject.) In Cambridge, about twice as many lecture hours per week were offered for the first two and a half terms, though I only averaged a couple of supervisions per week. However, the assignment tally was much greater, with about 35 for Part I, 28 for Prelims, and 36 for Part II, i.e., a total of about 99, not counting two practice exam papers each year or, during the first two terms of Part I, work on exercises for the qualifying paper in mathematics. This is not to say that 1970s Cambridge students were more stressed than university students in the 2020s, for the widening of access to tertiary education that has taken place since the 1980s has been accompanied by reduced per-capita government support of university students. A 1970s Cambridge workload would be impossible for a 2020s student who needs to find time to do a part-time job to avoid accumulating a huge student debt, something that 1970s UK university students did not have to worry about due to receiving generous study grants.

Studying for the Cambridge Economics Tripos was certainly a relentless process if one approached supervision tasks as research exercises and wrote, as I typically did, essays that averaged about 2,200 words, twice the length of a 45-minute examination answer. Once sources had been obtained and read, a typical supervision essay tended to take a couple of hours to write. There seemed to be no expectation that we should include formal reference lists or submit typed essays, merely that we should at least refer briefly to our sources at appropriate points and write legibly. When compared with what students submit today, these essays (of which I still have over 70 of those that I wrote) look completely unprofessional in their presentation. Yet they read more like real academic writing: they are not blighted by what I think of as the 'reference at the end of every sentence' style by which modern students often try to safeguard themselves against being accused of plagiarism when submitting written work where virtually every sentence is a paraphrase of a sentence in the work referred to at the end of that sentence.

Working nine-to-five, Monday to Friday, was not quite enough to get everything done if one attended most of the lectures as well as working industriously for supervisions. Hence, I usually found myself working some evenings and/or at the weekend. I did not particularly mind the total number of hours, but there was a feeling of being on a treadmill due to the way that as soon as one supervision assignment was finished, it was necessary to start the next one. The breaks between terms came as welcome relief, and it was probably a good thing that the system was built around three, nine-week terms rather than two, thirteen-week semesters per year.

Female students had an additional source of stress during my Part I year: from October 1974 to June 1975, there was the risk of becoming a victim of 'The Cambridge Rapist'. The perpetrator was Peter Samuel Cook, a very experienced burglar who broke into flats and bedsits. His modus operandi included wearing a leather hood, though he was wearing a long blond wig when arrested after a failed break-in at a nurses' hostel. Cook received two life sentences and died in Winchester jail in 2004.

Aside from walking to classes or when shopping, I took absolutely no exercise as an undergraduate, unlike those of my peers who were involved in sports teams. But, unlike probably a quarter of my peers, I did not actively smoke. Passive smoking could be hard to avoid, not merely from one's peers in social situations but also from those supervisors who smoked throughout supervisions. Some staff even smoked while lecturing, though the risk of passive smoking was much less in a lecture room than in a supervision in an office with a low ceiling in the DAE. One of the academics who smoked while giving lectures seemed to have a performance anxiety problem and smoked to calm his nerves. As the term progressed, it became apparent that he was lighting up earlier and earlier, so we would try to see how well we could anticipate how far he could get before starting to smoke. As the end of term approached, the consensus was that he would be smoking when he walked into the Marshall Room to deliver his final lecture. Instead, Len Warren. the custodian of the Austin Robinson Building, came in and announced that the lecturer was indisposed.

Given the pace of work, my lack of exercise, and the fact that I also tried to have a life beyond studying, it is perhaps not surprising that I did not make it to the end of Part II without getting sick. I spent the 1976 Christmas break at home in Stevenage trying to fight off what initially seemed to be a heavy cold that hit me at the end of a late-night gig at the architecture students' Christmas party. Foolishly, because I was now registered under the National Health Service with a doctor in Cambridge, I tried to get through it without taking medical advice. After several weeks, I coughed up some blood and it became apparent that I had a nasty dose of bronchitis. Fortunately, it soon cleared up after I belatedly went to see the doctor as soon as I returned to Cambridge.

3.3   PART I OF THE ECONOMICS TRIPOS

The Cambridge Economics Tripos in the 1970s was designed very differently from an economics programme in a typical 2020s university that advertises itself as being 'student centred' and offers considerable flexibility to its customers both in terms of the set of subjects taken and when they might be taken. Part I of the Economics Tripos was designed to ensure that students developed a specific set of foundations for Part II and for life beyond Cambridge. It consisted of five papers, with absolutely no choice and no chance of delaying taking a worrisome paper. This practice continues in Cambridge in the 2020s, for the great luxury of being an elite university that is hard to enter is that degree programmes can be designed from a 'merit good' standpoint rather than to give choice to customers who do not know what will be good for them in the long run.

Clearly, a paper on the Practice and Principles of Politics in Modern Britain would be a valuable foundation for students who were likely to end up in policymaking roles as politicians, advisors, and civil servants, or as business leaders who would need to lobby governments. Hence, Part I included precisely such a paper. The supervision tasks included an essay on pressure groups and a question that asked, 'Why was steel nationalised in 1949 and how has the subsequent history of this industry differed from that of the coal industry?' The 2020s Economics Part I still has this paper (now called Political and Social Aspects of Economics), but it now seems to have a usefully larger dose of material on institutions to enhance appreciation of the interface between political activity and the economy.

Knowledge of the economic history of the UK economy was also viewed as crucial, so there was a paper (which then carried the rather parochial title English Economic History) that charted British economic development from the industrial revolution, with emphasis on changes in Britain's significance and role within the global economy. That paper remains in Part I today, but it now has a half-century of more recent economic history and globalisation to consider.

Those who continued to Part II and into the world of business and government policy also needed to be comfortable about dealing with economic data and adept not merely at knowing how to use official statistics to analyse economic problems but also to be able to think critically about the quality and use of such data. Hence, there was a paper called Elementary Quantitative Economics that was built around the October 1974 issue of the *Monthly Digest of Statistics*. The name of this paper seemed appropriate, for it was not primarily an introductory course on statistics and focused at least as much on using published data as on knowledge of statistical techniques. It thus felt more like training in a junior research role as an advisor to a minister via its focus on practical problems. A memorable task for one of the supervisions for this paper included calculating an index of the real price of oil in the decades leading up to the 1973 OPEC oil price hikes: I initially thought I was doing something wrong when my calculations revealed that the real price of oil had been on a downward trend in the post-war period despite the massive growth in the use of oil. The fact that the paper in those days showed no signs of being an introduction to econometrics, in contrast to its 2020s counterpart (which is called Quantitative Methods in Economics), is especially easy to understand as soon as one recognises that what students could be asked to do in the examination was limited by the fact that they only had slide rules at their disposal. My cohort was the final one to which that constraint applied.

As in the 2020s Part I, the other two papers of the 1970s Part I of the Cambridge Economics Tripos were devoted purely to economics. However, what I experienced was radically different from what a 2020s Part I student experiences. One difference is that, in 1974, the economics papers were Macro-Economic Theory 1 and Macro-Economic Theory II – i.e., there was no microeconomics at all in Part I, whereas Paper 1 for a 2020s student is Microeconomics, with Varian's (2014) *Intermediate Microeconomics* as the key source. A lecture series on microeconomics was nonetheless offered in the 1970s. It was aimed at those who had not previously studied economics, with Alister Sutherland delivering the material to an audience whose size shrank rapidly after those who initially attended despite having previously done economics concluded (as I did) that they would learn nothing from it. The second key difference was that the teaching of macroeconomics in Queens' was not based around textbooks. Instead of being asked to master a potted 'state of the art' version of macroeconomics, the approach that was taken focused on the evolution of macroeconomic thinking and we had to contend with essay tasks that we were expected to address with reference to key original sources in the development of macroeconomics. In the rest of this section, I will try to convey what this entailed.

The first sign that Part I of the Economics Tripos was going to be very different indeed from A-Level Economics came at my Queens' cohort's first meeting with our supervisor, Brian Van Arkadie. Brian's room was above the original main entrance to the college in Old Court. Reaching it entailed going up a steep spiral staircase that offered a long rope instead of a banister on which to hold. A quick poll revealed that only one student, Simon Lewis, had not studied economics at A-Level. Simon looked a bit nervous on discovering this, but Brian then announced that there was no need for him to be worried since he was 'unencumbered by books and knowledge' in the area of economics. It was as if we were being told that we would be starting economics afresh. That impression was then confirmed when Brian told us that we would each need to go and buy a copy of Keynes's *General Theory*, as that was what we would be spending most of the first term trying to understand, assisted by the other reading suggestions that he gave us. He particularly recommended a little book by Joan Robinson (1937) that did indeed prove very helpful as a 'guide to Keynes'.

The next seven weeks were spent trying to get to grips with Keynes's own words rather than presuming that we already knew his economics via the 'income–expenditure' model of macroeconomics that we had all, except for Simon, covered at A-Level. That we had been given a very simplified picture became especially apparent with the essay topics for the supervisions in weeks 6 and 7, which were as follows:

'For Keynes, the rate of interest was a reward for lending; for "the classics" it was a reward for abstinence. But for both it was the cost of investment.' Discuss.

'If wages and prices were perfectly flexible, there would not be any problem for long with unemployment or over-full employment.' Discuss.

The first of these two questions resulted in much discussion about potential for hoarding money instead of lending it. These discussions would have been much more enlightening if we had not been thinking of hoarding cash 'under a mattress' as ordinary folk might have done in Keynes's time, instead of thinking about potential for hoarding money in a bank account, as modern consumers would do. The latter form of hoarding does not increase the ability of banks to lend if we simply fail to spend income payments that have been transferred to our bank accounts from the accounts of our employers. In failing to spend it, we hold up the circulation of money and the flow of demand for output, possibly even receiving interest while we exercise a preference for liquidity. The second question took us into chapters 17–19 of the *General Theory*, where Keynes wrestles with the dependence of aggregate spending on aggregate income and offers a vision of the price level chasing changes in the wage level unless the amount of money that people want to hold rather than spend changes in the direction that wages and prices are moving. It seemed rather unlikely that, if the price level were falling (rising), people would become more (less) willing to spend and thereby help to close a deflationary (inflationary) gap, as goods would become cheaper (more expensive) if one delayed spending.

By the end of the seventh week, we had 'read Keynes' and could move on to look at what happened in macroeconomics after the *General Theory* was published. The penultimate essay for our first term thus asked, 'What led economists in the 1930s and 1940s to believe that it would be difficult to achieve stable growth?' Answering it was much aided by a small investment in the Penguin book of readings edited by Sen (1970), after which we had an essay for which we familiarised ourselves with the alternative theories of the consumption function that emerged in the early post-war period. Here, as well as suggesting that we should read the survey article by Farrell (1959), Brian Van Arkadie told us that the textbook by Ackley (1961) had a very good survey chapter on the consumption function, and I therefore added the book to my rapidly growing collection. Brian was right about the chapter in Ackley's book (which, unlike Farrell's article, included the social psychology-inspired 'relative income hypothesis' proposed by Duesenberry, 1949). However, because I had purchased the book, I decided to read it from cover to cover during the Christmas vacation. This foray into the textbook literature proved to be a very disconcerting experience.

In contrast to the *General Theory*, Ackley sought to reduce Keynes's ideas to sets of multi-panel graphs. This led him to conclude that flexible wages would prevent an unemployment equilibrium from occurring because, as the price level followed wages downward, the transaction demand for money would fall, too, leading to a fall in the rate of interest and a rise in investment spending. The only things that he saw as standing in the way of a return to full employment in a world of flexible wages were an investment function that required a negative rate of interest to induce the requisite amount of investment, or the presence of a 'liquidity trap' whereby inelastic expectations prevented the rate of interest from falling to the (positive) level needed to induce enough investment. I could see all this via Ackley's graphs and his clear accompanying text, but it seemed not to capture properly what I had read Keynes as saying: Keynes's own words pointed to flexible money wages as being a destabilizing force, not a means towards macroeconomic equilibrium. What Keynes was saying did not align well with Ackley's mechanical graphs and their fixed functions that seemed to take no account of what might happen to expectations in the event of major changes in the levels of wages and prices.

I became even more puzzled on returning to Cambridge for the start of the 1975 Lent term, where the first supervision question was as follows:

'The crucial difference between Keynes and "the classics" related to periods of prolonged unemployment; in treating periods of sustained boom, the analysis offered by the models is essentially similar.' Discuss.

The reading that was recommended for this essay included the original article in which Hicks (1937) first set out the IS–LM model, bringing together the determination of the rate of interest and the rate of output in a static equilibrium framework. I did not warm to the IS–LM model, despite its simplicity compared with Ackley's attempt at a graphical perspective on the *General Theory*. There was no sign of the income multiplier working through as an out-of-equilibrium process that might result in further disturbances due to its impact on expectations and thereby on investment spending. But there was something of a recognition by Hicks that the supply of money might be affected by the level of economic activity, for he noted that, 'Instead of assuming ... that the supply of money is given, we can assume that there is a given monetary system – that up to a point, but only up to a point, monetary authorities will prefer to create new money rather than allow interest rates to rise' (Hicks, 1937, p. 157).

I did not pay particularly close attention to these words at the time, but a few weeks later the possibility that the money supply might be endogenous came to the fore as the focus of our supervisions turned to inflation and monetary policy via the contrasting views of Friedman (1968) and Kaldor (1970) about the role of excessive monetary growth as the cause of inflation: Friedman's monetarism presumed the central bank controls the stock of money and that monetary growth, rather than the wage bargaining activities of trade unions, determines the general rate of increase in prices and wages, whereas Kaldor saw monetary growth as normally driven by the level of economic activity. Kaldor's perspective seemed to offer scope for inflation to be much more of a political process whereby, as suggested by Cambridge's Jackson, Turner and Wilkinson (1972), a spiral of wages and prices was a manifestation of incompatible claims for wage and profit shares in the national income.

Such distributional issues had started to become apparent in the weeks between reading Hicks and reading Friedman and Kaldor when we looked at the early attempts to understand how balance of payments deficits could be addressed in the Bretton Woods era. Here, Sidney Alexander's (1952) analysis of the conditions required for a devaluation to work was a key reading, not merely for understanding potential limits to the effects that devaluing Sterling might have on the UK's situation but also for appreciating problems faced by developing countries: a devaluation will fail to improve a country's net exports if its economy lacks spare capacity and/or its employed population is not prepared to tolerate a fall in living standards or save more.

As the revision period approached, our tour through the preceding four decades of macroeconomic theory arrived at a radical new idea of such significance for macroeconomic policy that it was being discussed publicly without yet having been published in a journal article. It provided the basis for the final Part I macroeconomics supervision assignment:

'I did not repeat the Keynesian orthodoxy that the budget deficit should be used to determine the level of employment and the exchange rate to regulate the foreign balance. I said the opposite. The budget should be used to determine the foreign balance and the exchange rate the level of activity' (Robert Neild, letter to *The Times*, 26 February 1974). Discuss.

This way of thinking about macroeconomic targets and policy instruments was what became known as 'The New Cambridge Approach'. Although Neild was a leading proponent of the approach, the modelling work was being conducted in the DAE by the Cambridge Economic Policy Group (CEPG), led by Wynne Godley and Francis Cripps. It arrived in advanced UK textbook literature quite rapidly, in Chrystal (1979, chapter 6) and Cuthbertson (1979, chapter 3), but in 1974–1975 it was difficult to find information about it beyond the letters page of *The Times* and in the first issue of the CEPG's *Economic Policy Review* (published in February 1975). This led to the CEPG's Martin Fetherston being invited to give a talk about it to the Part I Queens' economists.

Fetherston explained that the central proposition was that the propensity of the UK private sector to purchase financial assets each year from the public sector or from overseas had been modelled as being stable, predictable, and close to zero. In other words, the annual net saving by the UK private sector was negligible. Hence, if the public sector was running a deficit and issuing financial assets, there would necessarily be a foreign trade deficit of a similar magnitude to the public sector deficit, offset by an inflow of foreign capital, as the 'net acquisition of financial assets' (NAFA) values for each sector of the economy must sum to zero. This being the case, attempts to reduce unemployment by running a bigger public sector deficit would result in a corresponding worsening of the foreign trade balance. Any devaluation of Sterling would fail to reduce the foreign trade deficit so long as the public sector deficit was not reduced. However, insofar as the UK's relative price competitiveness was enhanced by devaluing, rather than being wiped out by real-wage resistance, devaluation provided a means for reducing unemployment.

It was easy enough to appreciate the CEPG's point of view so long as one accepted the proposition that the UK private sector's NAFA tended to be close to zero, but why should this be the case? One might imagine, say, that the corporate sector had inelastic expectations about demand and simply absorbed any rise in household saving by engaging in corporate dissaving as receipts fell, but that line of thinking (which seemed unlikely across a prolonged downturn in consumer spending) could only account for the aggregate private sector saving level not changing, as opposed to it being prone to be close to zero. Would the latter depend on a particular demographic mix of savers and dis-savers at different points in their lifecycles?

We were left with the impression that the CEPG had found a statistical relationship but were yet to arrive at a theory to explain it. This all seemed rather odd at the time, but the CEPG's 'measurement without theory' approach was not without precedent: it was rather like the work on business cycles in the USA that was undertaken in the 1940s by institutionalist economists such as Arthur Burns and Wesley Clair Mitchell at the National Bureau of Economic Research. Such work had fallen out of fashion after the NBER research had been savagely attacked by economists at the Cowles Commission, most notably Tjalling Koopmans, who wanted economics to follow the theory-first methods of physical sciences (for an account of that controversy, see Mirowski, 1989).

A further source of material on the CEPG's analysis and then-current macroeconomic policy debates was recommended to us in time to prove a valuable revision resource, namely the *Ninth Report from the Expenditure Committee* (House of Commons, 1974). It contained memoranda submitted by Cripps, Godley and Fetherston on the CEPG model, by Laidler on the monetarist model, by Kahn and Posner on the Keynesian approach, by Worswick on the National Institute of Economic and Social Research's perspective, and by the UK Treasury, along with transcriptions of their replies to questions raised by members of the Expenditure Committee. As with the CEPG's *Economic Policy Review*, it was a very unusual thing for a first-year undergraduate economist to purchase, but by this stage, it just seemed to me to be a natural investment for me to make as part of the Cambridge way of learning in a pluralistic manner from primary documents rather than learning via bible-like textbooks.

3.4   THE PART II PRELIMS YEAR

The Prelims year only entailed four papers, and it left time for wider reading. There were two compulsory Economic Principles papers (with no division between microeconomics and macroeconomics, unlike in the 2020s Part IIA) and a compulsory paper on Economic and Social Statistics. There was a very limited choice for the fourth paper, and I chose Comparative Economic Development (an economic history paper that covered Japan, the United States, and Western Europe, with more development theory than there had been in the Part I economic history paper) rather than the alternative, a paper on sociology and political science.

Although the Prelims statistics paper was a major step-up from Part I, it was in technical terms way below the 2020s Part IIA equivalent, Theory and Practice of Econometrics. Much of what was being examined again seemed to be one's skills in selecting and looking at statistics with an economist's eye, and this time the required purchase was a copy of the latest *Blue Book* of the UK's national income accounts. Basic regression analysis was introduced and our capacity to apply it effectively was facilitated by the sudden switch from using slide rules to scientific pocket calculators. There was one problem, though: these early scientific calculators ran on nine-volt batteries that did not always last long enough to perform a second regression, so inputting data even for a single regression was a nerve-wracking experience due to the possibility that input errors might necessitate a second attempt. If that proved necessary, it was wise to insert a fresh battery.

The lectures for the two principles papers took the pluralistic experience of the Economics Tripos even further than in Part I, for there were rival sets of lectures by Frank Hahn (on mainstream microeconomics), John Eatwell (on Post Keynesian and Neo-Ricardian economics) and Bob Rowthorn (on Marxian economics), supplemented by lectures from Joan Robinson in which she gave her current perspective (essentially, an extended version of what was later published as Robinson, 1977) on what was going on in economics, and by lectures on paradigms and change in economics, delivered by Phyllis Deane and based on the book (Deane, 1978) that she was writing in that area. There were also lectures by David Newbery, on welfare economics, and from Luigi Pasinetti and Malcolm Fisher.

Hahn and Eatwell also gave some debate-style lectures together. These joint lectures were supposed to be only for Prelims undergraduates, but postgraduates ignored this after the first one. Joan Robinson complied with the rule in the sense that she did not enter the lecture theatre. However, she had her say at the second lecture by standing by the entrance and offering a handout to those who attended. The handout was a single typed sheet in which she explained how she expected Hahn and Eatwell to set out their views of how economics should be done, and her predictions for how they would end up talking through each other. Her expectations proved to be remarkably accurate.

During my time in Cambridge, there were no student evaluations of lectures. I enjoyed the lectures of Eatwell and Robinson enough to revisit them while I was a research student. There was nothing about Rowthorn's lectures that irritated me. But, when it came to learning about Marxian economics, I found it more illuminating to read books by Maurice Dobb or Paul Sweezy and always to keep in mind Joan Robinson's view that one could take the class struggle idea seriously without needing to bother with Marxian notions such as the 'transformation problem'. By contrast, Frank Hahn's lectures are memorable both for his mastery of his field and his sometimes-unprofessional mode of operating.

Hahn lectured with clarity and great confidence, completely without notes. He covered the Lady Mitchell Hall's blackboards with both mathematical script and graphs and generally was much more sensitive than I had expected to the needs of those of us whose mathematical skills were relatively limited. However, he exuded arrogance, and quite often would question members of his audience, without warning, to see if they understood the point he had just been making. If the response was poor, he would let rip with comments such as 'What are you doing here? You should be at the University of Bath!' But although this was a deterrent to making eye-contact with him, let alone ask a question, it became apparent that he usually picked on postgraduates when doing this. His humour was sometimes directed at other Faculty members. On one occasion, he sought to illustrate the notion of a Pareto improvement (i.e., a change that makes at least one person better off without leaving anyone worse off) via the following hypothetical example: 'Ajit Singh moves to the University of East Anglia and Cambridge hires no one to replace him.'

For the first (Michaelmas) term, Ajit Singh ran our supervisions and I armed myself with both Hicks's ([1939] 1946) *Value and Capital* and Scitovsky's ([1951] 1971) *Welfare and Competition,* the latter being Hahn's suggested fall-back source for those who preferred graphs to mathematical notation. When I mentioned Scitovsky's book to Ajit, he said that it was vital to read it mindful that the original edition, unlike my later paperback version, carried the subtitle *The Economics of a Fully Employed Economy.* Scitovsky's textbook was more illuminating than *Value and Capital* in relation to the functioning of real-world markets, but I found the latter much better for getting a sense of why Hicks came to theorise as he did. We spent the term looking critically at Hicksian theory and its welfare implications, concluding by working through the superb 'Simple analytics of welfare maximisation' paper by Bator (1957) that brings all the key elements together in a graphical analysis. Along the way, we studied production theory and the economics of profit maximisation. Here, Ajit recommended some critical readings that proved to be rather important, for they provided my first encounter with the field of behavioural economics. This aspect of my Prelims year is set out in more detail during Section 3.6.

The second (Lent) term of Prelims had a much wider range of content and, as I explain during Section 3.6, it played a key role in the development of my view that behavioural economics and Post Keynesian economics complement each other. During this term, my main supervisor was Vladimir Brailovsky, who worked in the DAE. Two of his supervisions were especially memorable.

The first entailed a discussion of the ideas of Axel Leijonhufvud, whose book *On Keynesian Economics and the Economics of Keynes* I duly purchased and spent a week working through. It was a very long book, and it helped me to appreciate better what I had experienced in Part I, after forming my own view of the economics of Keynes by reading the *General Theory* at first hand, when I read the portraits that Ackley (1961) and Hicks (1937) had offered. Yet in drawing the distinction between 'Keynesian economics' and what Keynes actually wrote, Leijonhufvud appeared to have ended up with yet another view as he sought to make sense of Keynes's ideas from a Walrasian standpoint. This led him to view unemployment as the result of uncertainty and information problems causing prices (especially the rate of interest and labour costs) to fail to adjust as rapidly as was necessary to prevent reductions in current spending from leading to workers being laid off. Steve Kidd, my supervision partner, demonstrated that sometimes less can be more when doing research, for instead of reading the huge tome, he simply read the very short volume that Leijonhufvud (1969) had written subsequently for the Institute of Economic Affairs: it was much clearer and it added something that seemed very useful, namely the idea that the size of the income multiplier that results from an initial change in spending depends on how much financial slack there is in the system in the form of liquid reserves that enable people to keep spending if their incomes fall.

Leijonhufvud's work focused my attention on economic coordination problems that underpin macroeconomic issues, though I felt he did not give enough attention to Keynes's argument that effective demand failures arise due to decisions to save not being accompanied by advance purchase orders for anything in particular to be delivered in future. This problem of people not signalling what their future patterns of demand are going to be resurfaced at the end of the term with more of a structural focus in a supervision essay that required discussion of the claim that 'The reason for creating a planned economy is that the market cannot give effect to individual preferences.' In exploring arguments for economic planning, I came across the work of Vera Lutz (1969) about 'indicative' planning methods used in market-based economies as means of dealing with the coordination problems that central planners in socialist systems tried to circumvent. Lutz examined the French planning system in which government planners get together with industry representatives to work out how much capacity growth is needed in each sector to deliver desired rates of growth of final outputs. In contrast to the Soviet system in which enterprise managers were given directives about how much to produce, indicative planning systems left it up to individual firms to take their investment decisions mindful of the targets that had been worked out for their sector. As Lutz realised, unless everyone attempted to expand at the rates that had been announced for their sectors, there could be problems if too much or too little capacity was created via the plans that the firms arrived at without knowing what their competitors were going to do.

My concern with coordination problems then led me to write a very different essay from what I knew I was expected to write for one of two supervisions that Ajit Singh arranged for Ken Coutts to provide on Sraffian economics. The essay task involved discussing a quotation from Ricardo about the significance of commodities being in some cases produced and in other cases being non-reproducible. This was a task for the Easter vacation, so I wrote it not in my room in Queens' but in Stevenage Central Library, armed with my copies of Sraffa (1960) and Sraffa's edition of Ricardo's *Principles* (Ricardo, 1951). However, despite having invested in these books, I did not allow sunk-cost bias to drive me to write the Sraffa-focused essay that I knew I was expected to deliver. Instead, I approached it mindful of something that Joan Robinson had said in one of her Prelims lectures. She had started the lecture by brandishing a letter that she had just received from Robert Clower and saying that it was clear that his way of trying to rewrite Keynes's thinking in Walrasian terms meant that he ended up missing much of what made a production economy different from a pure exchange economy.

As I reflected on what she had said, it occurred to me that those who invest in systems to produce goods and services face a wider range of uncertainty than those who try to make a profit by purchasing and reselling non-reproducible assets. The latter's returns depend on what others turn out to be prepared to pay to get control over those assets, whereas the profits that the former make depend not merely on the demand for the output of the product to which their investment contributes but also on the extent to which others invest in the same supply chain or in producing the same type of output. This is because the investment that others make will determine the costs of inputs that they need and, depending on how much capacity gets created, the price that their output will fetch, given the demand for the product in question. As entrepreneurs consider adding to production capacity by investing in reproducible goods, they must contend with the fact that their payoffs are mutually interdependent, as in Lutz's concerns about the limitations of indicative planning. To eliminate such uncertainty, they would need to be able to make forward purchases of their inputs and forward sales of their output over the lifespans of their investments. But I could see good reasons why, in the real world, comprehensive futures markets are conspicuously absent – such as the difficulty of handling products that have not yet been invented.

From there, my mind moved to scope for coordination failures of the kind encapsulated in the 'cobweb diagram' analysis of price and output instability that I had discovered during A-Level Economics. In the cobweb diagram, firms were portrayed as ignoring the mutual interdependence of their returns and as if they made their supply decisions by assuming that the price realised in the current period would be the price next period. Reflection about this led me to a further concern: if there were no entry or exit barriers in product and factor markets, there was potential for the economy to operate completely chaotically in real time as investors and workers tried to chase opportunities based on current prices.

The implication seemed to be that some so-called 'market imperfections' are necessary to enable orderly adjustment of supply to changes in patterns of demand in a production system. I made this the basis for the essay that I wrote for Ken Coutts, who found it 'very interesting' and suggested that I might enjoy the Marshallian view of market processes that he had recently seen in a University of Stirling discussion paper by Brian Loasby (later published formally as Loasby, 1978). I took a look at the paper but did not follow up any of its references at the time. Hence, I failed to discover that I had just reinvented ideas that are central to George Richardson's (1960) book *Information and Investment*. During the 1976 long vacation between Prelims and Part II, I expanded the ideas from my essay into an article-length entry for Cambridge's Adam Smith Essay Competition. My entry came third (with my supervision partner Steve Kidd submitting an empirical piece that shared first place), earning me an 'honourable mention'.

3.5   PART II OF THE ECONOMICS TRIPOS

The first two papers on the Part II list were a compulsory pair on Economic Principles and Problems. This was the same as in Part IIB of the 2020s Economics Tripos except that, in Part IIB, Paper 1 is on microeconomics and Paper 2 is on macroeconomics. In the 1970s there was no such distinction and the examination questions ranged very widely across both kinds of problems in both papers. The questions often contained half a dozen, or more, lines of text, and sometimes included tables of data to analyse. They generally seemed to be testing whether students were ready to graduate into real-world policy-making or advisory roles in public service or corporate head offices. Such questions could be done well even by those whose reading had not been extensive, so long as they had paid attention in supervisions, were familiar with current policy debates, and had developed the capacity to dissect questions with the eye of an economist. Michael Posner's entertaining lectures showed Part II students how to analyse policy issues effectively by creatively and critically applying core ideas. He would start with a topical issue – such as whether the UK government should provide financial support to struggling Merseyside manufacturers of telecommunications equipment – and then kick it around for an hour, rather like a jazz musician improvising around a theme. There was no pretence of high theory being deployed but Posner always left his audience with a sense of how economists could earn their keep many times over by applying ideas that ordinary folk did not have at their disposal.

Beyond Papers 1 and 2, Part II offered a much wider range of choice than Prelims, but this came at the cost of more papers having to be taken, or at the cost of writing a dissertation. In the 2020s, Part IIB students are required to choose two papers from a list and must write a dissertation, whereas 1970s students were also required to take at least one of either Labour or The Modern Business Enterprise and Social Structure, plus at least three elective papers or one elective paper plus a dissertation. I chose the latter of the either/or compulsory papers and, as is explained in the second half of Section 3.6, it had a major impact on my development as a behavioural economist. It also provided very useful material for Papers 1 and 2.

At the end of the Prelims year, I elected to do a Part II dissertation on development economics and Ajit Singh tentatively arranged for Suzy

Paine to supervise me. However, during the 1976 long vacation, I bailed out of the dissertation strategy after deciding that I would rather get a wider grounding in my knowledge of economics. This move also enabled me to avoid worrying about whether I could develop the statistical skills that I might need if I were to produce a first-class empirically based dissertation. Indeed, I eliminated statistical concerns altogether by simply choosing the papers that I thought would interest me most. However, with hindsight, I think that one of the papers that I chose was a big mistake.

The two papers that I was especially keen to do proved to be very worthwhile. One was Banking, Credit and Public Finance: via Tony Cramp's lectures on the financial system, my emerging Post Keynesian view of macroeconomics was greatly enhanced, but it was also a delight to attend the lectures on public finance delivered by Mervyn King (now Baron King of Lothbury), who was then a very dapper 29-year-old. King's lectures have stuck in my mind far more than most of those that I attended; he examined with great clarity the key budgetary reform issues that politicians consistently are too afraid to address. I also had a strong intrinsic interest in taking the paper on The Economics of Underdeveloped Countries. It played a significant role in establishing my structuralist and institutionalist sensibilities, as it led me to read extensively on the problems of Latin American economies. It also provided a foundation for me to teach a few times in the area that it covered.

The paper that I should not have chosen was Economic Theory. The problem was not that it involved a step-up in terms of its mathematical demands, for its mathematical content was generally less challenging than that in Hahn's Prelims lectures; rather, the issue was that it did not add much of value to the theoretical perspectives that I had developed in Prelims. John Eatwell was my main supervisor for this paper, as well as one of its lecturers. The essay questions that he set for the supervisions give a good indication of how different Economic Theory was from similarly titled papers in the 2020s:

1. Explain the economic basis of the transformation problem. What is its relation to Ricardo's search for a 'standard of value'?
2. What role is the concept of the quantity of capital supposed to play in the neoclassical theory of profit? Illustrate your answer with reference to either Walras or Wicksell.

3. Is it possible to develop a theory of a general rate of interest on the basis of intertemporal choice?
4. To what extent is it possible to reproduce Keynes's analysis within the framework of neoclassical general equilibrium theory?

I was also given a few supervisions by Oliver Hart, a future Nobel Laureate. I have not been able to unearth any written work that I wrote for him, but I recall that we did not see eye to eye on the distinction between risk and fundamental uncertainty. Hart was very dismissive of Keynes's (1937) view that, in respect of many issues that may affect us in the future, we have no basis for calculating probabilities and 'simply do not know' how likely it is that events will unfold in particular ways. Hart argued that, if presented with any 'fundamentally uncertain' situation in which a gamble might need to be taken, he would always be able to identify a monetary bet whose odds he viewed as equivalent to the 'uncertain' gamble.

John Eatwell was not sure how I would fare with Economic Theory, so Ajit Singh advised me to take a fourth elective paper in case Economic Theory proved unduly challenging in technical terms. I therefore added an extra paper that would enable me to play to my strengths in economic history, namely The Economic Development of Russia Since 1860. The best three of my four elective papers would then be used in working out my honours class. To this day, I do not know which three papers were counted, but I suspect that the Russia paper trumped Economic Theory even though I had no trouble finding four questions on the latter than I felt confident I could answer well.

In fact, it was the examination for the Russia paper that came with some drama. I wrote no essays and had no supervisions ahead of sitting the examination. Instead, I prepared for it purely by attending lectures and reading extensively from the reading lists that were handed out at the lectures. The examination was held on Monday 30 May 1977 and was my last-ever written examination. It was clear to me that I was getting exhausted by this stage. After sitting The Economics of Underdeveloped Countries on the afternoon of Friday 27 May, I had felt too tired to do much final revision for Banking, Credit and Public Finance on the Saturday morning and Economic Theory on the Saturday afternoon. I planned to get up very early that Saturday to complete my revision but did not wake up until nearly 8:00 am and could do no more than have a quick re-read of my essays before heading off to the first examination.

By the end of the Economic Theory examination, I again felt too tired to do much revision about Russia and therefore retired early to bed. By Sunday evening, I still had a long way to go in my Russia folder. A very early start on Monday morning was vital.

This time, I succeeded in getting up at 3:00 am and had a very productive final revision session. However, just as I was starting my first answer in the examination, students around me started talking in distress. Phyllis Deane was invigilating and said, 'What seems to be the problem?' Because I had followed my usual strategy of starting to write an answer for the first question that I read that I felt I could do well, I had not yet turned to see any of the questions on the back of the examination paper. Those around me had done so and the consternation was because the questions were on American economic history. There had been a mix-up when the paper was being printed, but fortunately, the paper from which the offending questions came had been sat already. Phyllis Deane told us all to get on with the examination as best we could while she arranged for the correct paper to be printed, and she allowed an extra quarter of an hour in case anyone was disrupted by the late arrival of the remaining questions. The extra time proved very useful to me, for I continued writing right to the end.

I am glad that I sat the Russia paper, but I should have let it serve as a safety net for a different paper: instead of Economic Theory, I should have taken Applied Economic and Social Statistics. This would have meant that I had the same set of papers as my Queens' classmate, Glyn Kearley, who also achieved a first in Part II. Glyn remembers the day of the Russia examination paper somewhat differently, for after sitting the Russia paper and having some lunch, he then had to sit the four-hour second paper for Applied Economic and Social Statistics, i.e., seven-and-a-quarter hours of examinations in one day. But the prospect of the additional four-hour examination was not the reason why I had not chosen the latter paper.

I had avoided signing up for Applied Economic and Social Statistics because I knew, from what Ajit had told me, that I had not achieved a first on the statistics papers that I had taken in Part I and Prelims. I now realise that it would have done me good to take the paper while simply viewing it as potentially disposable because of taking four electives. But back then I told myself that I would be able to learn more statistical techniques later in my career if the need arose. Such a need never arose. For many years, my research was non-quantitative, and I realised that, if

I ever needed to work on a project that needed statistical or econometric skills, it would make more sense to work with someone who had them already but who was keen to work with me because of my creative, critical, and writing skills and my distinctive knowledge base.

The latter presumption turned out to be correct: as is explained in Section 8.4, I did end up doing applied behavioural economics with a colleague who provided the quantitative capabilities that I lacked, via a large grant-funded project on which we were both chief investigators. However, on reflection, I think that my avoidance of quantitative work in Part II was probably a career-cramping mistake, for it resulted in me not trying for most of my career to use quantitative empirical work as a means of raising the profile of the kind of behavioural economics that I ended up doing. It probably also contributed to my failure to develop a publications list that was dominated by well-ranked journal articles.

3.6 EVOLUTION OF A HETERODOX BEHAVIOURAL ECONOMIST (1)

The Seeds of a Behavioural/Schumpeterian/Post Keynesian Synthesis
My first encounter with behavioural economics came towards the end of the first (Michaelmas) term of my Prelims year when I was reading for an assignment that Ajit Singh had set on alternatives to the profit-maximising approach to theorising about firms. That week's reading focused on the 'new theories of the firm' that proliferated in the period from 1958 to 1964. It included Machlup's (1967) critical methodological reflection on these contributions, the Marshall Library copy of which had been defaced with the phrase 'sexist pig' (or other words to that effect). This was at the point where Machlup (1967, p. 21) was considering Williamson's (1964) model of top managers who use their discretionary control over resources to maximise their utility at the expense of shareholder returns. They could do this by pursuing 'pet projects' and/or enjoying perks that might include, as Machlup put it, a 'lovely secretary'. That issue aside, Machlup's paper stands up well as a thoughtful defence of 'as if' profit-maximising models; it was a very helpful introduction to alternatives to such models, with careful reflection on the contexts in which they might be useful. I also read some of the contributions reprinted in Archibald (ed.) (1971), which included a list of 'non-maximising' approaches to the firm but reprinted none of them. Finally,

I read Simon's (1959) survey on models of decision-making, which included his aspirations-driven 'satisficing' view of search and choice.

Those who advocated the behavioural approach built models based on what was known about real-world behaviour. Machlup suggested they were succumbing to the 'fallacy of misplaced concreteness' because their research programme produced more complex models from which it could be difficult to glean predictions. I could accept that any model must be a simplification, but I was wary of the idea of building models based on assumptions which are clearly false. Hence, I thought I should remain open to Simon's attempt to take account of the realities of managerial decision-making even though I did not yet have a sense of where I might use his satisficing perspective.

Ajit Singh noticed my interest in Simon's work and, more generally, my growing resistance to the sets of assumptions that lay behind orthodox economics. But I also made it clear to him that I was disappointed with what I had seen of the microeconomic content of the Marxian and Neo-Ricardian alternatives. As a result, he suggested that I should read Janos Kornai's (1971) book *Anti-Equilibrium* during the Christmas vacation as something that might appeal to me more. This was a very important suggestion, for although I have not referred frequently to Kornai's book over the course of my career, it had a big impact on my view of economics. Kornai is best known for his work as an economic planner in Hungary, but *Anti-Equilibrium* appeared to be an attempt to challenge static equilibrium analysis and build a framework for understanding how an economic system evolves as product lifecycles unfold when innovation happens and decision-makers use norms and simplifying rules to cope with the complexities of their changing environments. Kornai seemed to be signalling that economists should build a synthesis between the behavioural approach of Simon (1947, 1959) (and of Cyert and March, 1963, whose approach to the theory of the firm was one of those considered in Machlup, 1967) and the evolutionary approach of Schumpeter (1943). This was, in effect, what Nelson and Winter (1982) later delivered in their remarkably influential book *An Evolutionary Theory of Economic Change*, with no reference to Kornai as a precursor to their work.

In the rest of the Prelims year my focus shifted from the limitations of the equilibrium-centred, constrained optimisation view of microeconomics to the impact that uncertainty and problems of knowledge have on the functioning of the economic system as a whole.

As should be evident from what I have said previously about the Prelims year, this shift in my focus was partly the result of where the supervision tasks took me (i.e., in relation to thinking about the case for planning, having to read Leijonhufvud's work, and the 'very interesting' experimental essay that I wrote for Ken Coutts). However, the spring of 1976 was also important in my development because I found time to read George Shackle's (1967) book *The Years of High Theory*. It had been listed for some of Brian Van Arkadie's Part I supervisions and though I had not read it at the time I remembered the title and it occurred to me that it might be relevant for Prelims, especially now that I had seen what Leijonhufvud had said about Keynes's *General Theory*. It led me to read many of Shackle's other works and turned my growing interest in problems of knowledge and uncertainty into my focal concern in relation to how the economic system works.

Shackle presented the essence of Keynes's theory of employment in terms of material from chapters 12 and 17 of the *General Theory* and from Keynes's (1937) article in the *Quarterly Journal of Economics*. He also used ideas from Townshend (1937) to build his view of the radical departure that Keynes's work represented. The level of employment at any moment depends on the extent to which entrepreneurs see potential for generating profits by hiring workers to produce new output rather than exercising liquidity preference and holding on to, or switching their wealth into, money or other stores of value that cannot be reproduced by employing workers. Investment is risky partly due to scope for misjudging the relative mix of supply and demand for different types of products. But producing output ahead of making sales to customers also entails the risk of losses due to potential purchasers of output opting to exercise liquidity preference, which may include being reluctant to use their capacities to borrow to spend more than their existing financial balances permit. This preference for liquidity results from uncertainty about what the future entails, which is significant if one is considering investing in durable assets and production systems that can generate flows of services for many years. Such durability is a characteristic not merely of buildings, plant and equipment used by firms but also of consumer durables, as Townshend acknowledged via an allusion to a contemporary advertisement in which the Austin car company declared that those who bought its cars were making an investment. Of course, durable physical assets, or shares in firms that own them, can be sold, if one's circumstances or expectations of yields change, but the prices they will fetch depend on the expectations held by others. Employment is thus contingent on how people form expectations or otherwise seek to deal with uncertainty.

This view of the economic system posed an even bigger challenge to the notion of rational decision-making than what I had picked up from Simon's (1959) survey. For Simon, 'bounded rationality' is essentially due to finite cognitive processing capacities that force people to find ways of arriving at decisions without being able to get as far as gathering and processing all the information needed to arrive at optimal solutions. But liquidity preference arises due to inherent gaps in information and knowledge of the future because the future depends to some degree on events that have not yet taken place and choices that have not yet been made. There is no guarantee that there will be no structural change as the future unfolds, or that structural change will not take surprising forms, so one cannot confidently infer probabilities in an inductive manner by looking at past evidence of the frequencies of particular classes of events.

Decision-makers with this 'fundamental' kind of uncertainty are faced with open-ended choice problems, for which it is not possible to specify optimal solutions. All they can do – and this is where Simon's focus on the use of decision rules and heuristic devices such as setting adjustable aspiration levels lines up with Keynes's perspective – is to adopt a heuristic device, a 'way' of dealing with the problem. For Keynes, these ways of coping could in some cases entail following conventions, but in other cases they might entail taking cues from other people. There was potential for resource allocation patterns to be shaped by questionable relative values that were being distorted by whirlpools of speculation. But it was problematic to say what the right set of values was, given that the potential for structural change called into question the notion that there is an ideal set to be inferred by modelling based on what are commonly referred to as 'market fundamentals' that reflect past conditions and behaviour. Townshend summed up his interpretation of the implication of Keynes's analysis in a way that I found memorable and useful: he asked his readers to consider the difficulties of knowing what relative values ought to be if everyone woke up one day with no memories of what relative prices had been, and he suggested that, in essence, the market system is held up by its own bootstraps, with prices generally being anchored by conventions but with scope for speculation sometimes to dislodge them from established reference points.

Next, I read Minsky's (1975) book *John Maynard Keynes* after seeing it on display in Heffers Bookshop following its 1976 UK publication by Macmillan. It added weight to the signals that Keynes offered about the importance of being mindful of the psychological drivers of behaviour in financial markets, introducing the idea that market bubbles could be associated with speculators starting to experience feelings of euphoria – i.e., widespread over-confidence and a misplaced belief that 'the sky's the limit'. Minsky seemed implicitly to be suggesting that, from time to time, the norms that Townshend's paper had seen as playing key roles in enabling the economic system to work in an orderly manner could cease to apply as system-wide reductions in liquidity preference took hold. I got a better sense of Minsky's view during Part II, via Tony Cramp's lectures on money and banking, where emphasis was given to the tendency of financial systems to become increasingly fragile as people moved from their familiar financial market habitats into unfamiliar areas that had started to seem less risky, and as complex multi-layered structures of interconnected balance sheets emerged. This seemed fertile territory in which to keep in mind Simon's emphasis on the limited information processing capacities of decision-makers in relation to fathoming complex problems, especially where people are short of what we now call 'financial literacy'. But the role that shifts in expectations and risk assessments played in Minsky's analysis also seemed related to how fundamental uncertainty leads to an absence of firm foundations for expectations that people form about prospective asset yields.

The Significance of Slack in Firms
Much of the focus of the Part II Principles and Problems papers was on the policy challenges associated with the UK's slow rate of per-capita income growth and its declining economic performance relative to countries such as Germany and Japan. However, the initial supervision tasks for these papers required us to explore the nature of the problem from a macroeconomic standpoint. This was done primarily by contrasting Denison's (1967) neoclassical empirical analysis of growth as being constrained by growth in supplies of factors of production, and Cripps and Tarling's (1973) Keynesian view that the UK's problems resulted from the absence of consistently strong effective demand needed to stimulate the investment that was required to raise output capacity and productivity.

Denison's approach was not convincing, for it was based on an aggregate production function with constant returns to scale and assumed that factors of production received their marginal revenue products. The relative contributions of growth in supplies of capital and labour were weighted according to their shares in national income. It was here that the seeds of my scepticism about the wisdom of always assuming the possibility of substitution were sown, for Denison's use of the relative shares of profits and wages in national income to measure marginal products of capital and labour assigned capital growth a far less important role than it gave to growth in the supply of labour. Worse still, it implied that if there were no new capital equipment there would still be economic growth if the supply of labour grew, with more workers somehow making use of the existing capital stock. That issue aside, there was also the problem that the residuals in Denison's regressions were substantial, with this being ascribed to the significance of factors such as technical progress as a source of productivity growth. This was something that the neoclassical approach was not well equipped to handle, and it begged the question of why nations might differ in the technological dynamism of their firms, or in whatever else it was about their firms that affected productivity and was buried in Denison's residuals.

The behavioural view of firms offered a way of understanding this, for it did not presume that firms necessarily behave in the same way even in a particular market context, let alone in different countries. Differences in how aspiration levels were set and adjusted in response to attainments could affect the effort that went into searching for better ways of doing things and the kinds of quality control standards that were pursued. With marginal products being hard to identify, returns to stakeholders could vary depending on how bold staff were and on how pushy people were during organisational bargaining, or in making contracts for the supply of inputs. The returns potentially available to the various stakeholders would differ not merely due to differences in the quality of equipment or scale of production but also due to the sets of rules and routines that firms used. Furthermore, the ways in which, as a rule, managers and other personnel in a firm saw external threats and opportunities could affect how they reacted: for example, if hubris has taken hold, we would be unwise to assume that potentially grave long-term threats will be recognised as such or that new ways of doing things that have been devised in other organisations will be taken as seriously as in-house proposals or routines that have hitherto served the firm well.

None of the Part II lecturers systematically set out such a view, but it was where I had broadly arrived by the end of Part II. I then got a clearer vision of it during my first year as a research student, especially after discovering the 'Japanese way' of doing business via Adams and Kobayashi (1969). Key ingredients came from the lectures that Alan Hughes contributed to the Modern Business Enterprise and Social Structure. Three sources from his reading lists proved to be especially formative.

The first was Silberston's (1970) superb survey article on the price behaviour of firms, which emphasised the diversity of economic perspectives on how firms behave as competitive conditions change. It offered a bigger view than I had got from Machlup (1967) of what a behavioural approach constituted, for it included analysis of behavioural studies on pricing (that pointed towards a rule-based view of pricing in which prices were set by adding a mark-up to 'normal costs') as well as considering the essence of Cyert and March's (1963) *Behavioral Theory of the Firm*. I found their notion of 'organisational slack' especially interesting. Their idea was that the various stakeholders in a firm could not be sure how far they could improve their positions at the expense of other stakeholders but were aware of the risk of ending up worse off if they pushed their luck too far and caused some other, hard-to-replace stakeholders to exit for better deals elsewhere. Given this risk, the hypothesis was that they would not push their luck so long as they were meeting their aspirations regarding what they got from their membership of the coalition that made up the firm. If they raised their aspirations less rapidly than their attainments, it would become possible for other stakeholders to capture the surplus from them by bargaining more assertively. There could thus be a buffer that would enable some stakeholders to get back to achieving satisfactory returns if they bargained harder after finding they were unable to meet their aspirations.

In relation to pricing, this could mean, for example, that managers might find they could get away with passing increased costs on to their customers, despite not having dared to charge higher prices before their costs increased. But it seemed also to point to scope for managers to keep a firm going in the face of tougher external competition by cutting their mark-ups and reducing dividends to shareholders and/or squeezing the real wages of their employees, so long as these parties had been getting more than their 'transfer earnings', i.e., more than the minimum that they would tolerate rather than move elsewhere. For a time, then, it might be possible for the firm to keep going in the face of tougher competitive conditions without doing anything more fundamental, such as developing new production methods or better products.

The second formative source was Salter's (1966) analysis of how competition worked in industries where firms operated with different 'vintages' of equipment. Even though investments in new technologies with lower average total cost would depress market prices as output from them came on-stream, it would not necessarily force the overnight abandonment of all the older, less productive technologies, only those whose average non-sunk costs per unit exceeded the market price. Of course, when production systems with historic average total costs per unit greater than the market price eventually wore out, they would get replaced by more modern technologies, but the process whereby old technology vintages were retired could take many years. There seemed to be even more potential for processes of structural change to be protracted if one took account of Cyert and March's ideas about the uptake of organisational slack, as managers of older production systems could have potential to push per-unit operating costs down if they could get away with bargaining more aggressively with their employees and other suppliers of inputs.

Thirdly, there was Downie's (1958) book, *The Competitive Process*, which is a precursor to Salter's analysis but in some respects goes beyond it (and in doing so is a precursor to Nelson and Winter, 1982 – see further Nightingale, 1997, 1998) by taking account of the feedback relationship between profits and productivity, with an emphasis on the relationship between market share and unit costs. Downie was concerned about the future of competition if a 'transfer mechanism' was operating, whereby firms with bigger market shares enjoyed lower unit costs than their smaller rivals and could plough back more into investing in new products and processes that would enable them to take even more market share and further squeeze the smaller players. However, he acknowledged that this feedback process might be held in check by an 'innovation mechanism', whereby existential threats concentrated wonderfully the minds of staff in firms whose profit margins were being squeezed, with the result that they were able to come up with innovative production methods or products. Implementing such innovations would require them to be able to invest enough, despite facing a squeeze on their retained profits.

If the innovation mechanism had enough power, Downie's thinking pointed towards a view of industries as operating rather like sporting leagues whose teams occupy changing rankings as the years go by, rather than becoming dominated by a single team that is able always to hire the best players. However, in light of Salter and of Cyert and March's notion of organisational slack, it seemed to me that it was an open question whether potential existential threats were perceived as such and did produce this sort of pattern: on the one hand, if such threats provoked creative thinking, then taking up organisational slack might facilitate getting the resources necessary to put new ideas into practice; on the other hand, as noted earlier, taking up organisational slack might simply provide a means of keeping afloat temporarily without making any fundamental changes. The compounding effects of feedback processes could mean that denying the gravity of a competitive threat could result in delays in making changes that, if implemented earlier, could have prevented the crossing of tipping points beyond which a firm's demise becomes inevitable.

These lines of thought were amplified in my mind when Ajit Singh encouraged me to read Leibenstein's (1966) first paper on the notion of '*X*-inefficiency', a paper to whose empirical content Ajit had contributed as a doctoral student at Berkeley while working as Leibenstein's research assistant. Leibenstein argued that, due to their habit of assuming that firms maximise profits, economists had limited themselves to talking about inefficiency only in relation to deadweight losses associated with market imperfections that distorted relative prices. Moreover, in assuming that production costs were as low as they could be given the prevailing set of prices, economists ended up underestimating the efficiency impacts of market imperfections. In Leibenstein's terms, firms whose unit costs were needlessly high were suffering from '*X*-inefficiency'. He saw considerable potential for firms to achieve lower costs and higher productivity if they were better managed and under stronger competitive pressure. As he saw it, firms were often failing to use best-practice methods and managers often allowed workers to make the most of vagueness in employment contracts and get away with less industrious behaviour than they would be prepared to offer if pushed harder or given tighter job specifications.

It seemed to me that there was a good deal of overlap between Leibenstein's *X*-inefficiency notion and Cyert and March's idea of organisational slack. Leibenstein seemed to be recognizing potential for applying better knowledge to improve or bolster returns to stakeholders, and to be taking the view that this knowledge would be found and applied if there were external pressure to find ways of reducing unit costs and/or if more capable managers with higher performance aspirations were appointed by firms that were underperforming. However, he seemed to be oblivious to the distributional consequences of his arguments: he seemed to focus purely on scope for cutting costs, without any concern for the impact that this might have on employee welfare via rationalisations that led to workers being retrenched or workers having to work harder. By contrast, distributional issues were central to Cyert and March's view that returns to stakeholders depended on their success in bargaining, although Cyert and March seemed to be underplaying the potential for raising productivity by applying better knowledge as opposed simply to working harder (if one kept one's job).

Leibenstein's vision of workers guilefully exploiting vagueness in their job descriptions and inadequate monitoring by managers pointed toward efficiency-enhancing policies based on tightening up employment contracts and investing in more supervisors to monitor compliance with these contracts. Such policies did indeed become part of managerialist thinking during the 1980s, but I could see that a more carefully considered behavioural approach was necessary. This was partly because during Part II I read Coase's (1937) analysis of the nature of the firm, which Gordon Hughes had mentioned in his lectures for the Economic Theory paper and which I had seen referred to by Goodhart (1975) around the same time. As Goodhart noted, Coase had shown that firms emerge as means of reducing transaction costs that arise when people are beset with uncertainty. Instead of trying to organise production by complex labour-hire contracts to cover all possible contingencies, or by negotiating successive short-term contracts to deal with contingencies as they arise, entrepreneurs or managers hire workers via incomplete employment contracts and, as contingencies arise, they provide instructions about what the workers need to do and try to ensure that it gets done. In a world based around contracts that specify precisely what workers deliver, there would be no need to incur the costs of having managers, but there could be major costs of forming contracts and litigating over alleged failures in their implementation. Having managers plus loosely specified employment contracts is a cheaper way of getting things done in a world of surprises that require adaptive behaviour. Leibenstein seemed oblivious of this, whereas anyone familiar with what happened when trade union members 'worked to rule' would be able to appreciate the hazards of trying to organise production via contracts with clauses that preclude flexible behaviour that managers might prefer to see from their workers as a means of keeping output flowing amid unexpected problems.

My doubts about the wisdom of using more detailed job contracts and more supervision as means of raising productivity also came partly from D. K. Lee, the final figure who played a key formative role in my interest in how aspects of internal organisation affect the productivity and resilience of firms in changing environments. Lee lectured on the 'sociology of organisations' for The Modern Business Enterprise and Social Structure paper. He was something of a mystery figure: I cannot recall his first name (if indeed he supplied it) and I have not been able to find any trace of him during research for this book. If I recall correctly, he said he drove up from Colchester to give his lectures, so he may have been from the University of Essex. I did not feel that we were being short-changed by lectures on this topic being outsourced, for it showed that those who designed the Economics Tripos had a clear vision of the lecture content that we needed to be provided with, recognised a gap in local expertise, and were not unwilling to seek assistance from someone who had the requisite knowledge. I found Lee's lectures fascinating.

I appreciated the behavioural theory of the firm better via what Lee said about March and Simon's (1958) book *Organisations*, with its detailed analysis of the impact of individuals' sub-goals and its emphasis on organisations having 'persistence' tendencies (which most behavioural economists would nowadays call 'sunk cost bias') that resulted in them failing to abandon projects in the face of unexpectedly poor performance or dramatic cost over-runs. More importantly, via what he said about the work of Selznick (1957), I started to develop a sense of the importance of organisational cultures that could shape how members of an organisation viewed the external environment and in turn shape the organisation's internal modes of operation, for good or ill, sometimes keeping it within a predictable behavioural 'groove' for decades. It was from here that I started to see that the cultures of business organisations are rather like scientific paradigms in the way they affect how the world is seen and the kinds of changes to which people are open.

I do not recall learning anything from Lee (or anyone else, at that stage) about Chester Barnard's (1938) emphasis on managerial authority being granted by those who are being managed, rather than coming automatically via being given a specific managerial role. That Lee did not cover Barnard is not surprising, for Barnard had written his analysis based on decades of experience as a practising executive, not as an academic sociologist. Nor do I recall being introduced to Herbert Simon's (1947) extension of Barnard's thinking via the notion that the 'docility' of workers is necessary for organisations to run smoothly and adapt to changing conditions. However, I picked up these notions via Lee's exposition of what Gouldner (1954) observed in an ethnographic study of a gypsum mine where attempts by a new manager to run a tighter operation to deal with health and safety issues were resisted by the workforce whose behavioural norms were being challenged, with this resistance increasing as even more supervisors were put in place to try to ensure compliance.

At the end of his series of lectures, Lee discussed Joan Woodward's (1965) work on the importance of firms aligning their preferred type of organisational system with the type of operating environment they face. This helped me to appreciate better the difference between Leibenstein and Coase in relation to contractual incompleteness, and it reinforced my sense that Leibenstein's view was rather simplistic. Woodward saw a formal, bureaucratic organisation as well suited to a surprise-free environment in which jobs entail limited sets of operations (as with, say, workstations on a production line). Such a situation might indeed be one where the more tightly specified contracts that Leibenstein seemed to view as desirable might raise productivity by keeping workers better focused on their jobs; moreover, if the attention of managers was not frequently being arrested by surprises, they could focus on monitoring whether workers were doing their jobs in the ways that they were supposed to do them. By contrast, Woodward saw the need for workers to be given the right to use their expertise as they saw fit, without first getting permission from higher authorities, if they were working in environments in which surprises could have very expensive consequences if they were not attended to promptly (as in, say, a nuclear power plant or in the cockpit of an airliner). Trusting professionals to do the right thing and hiring them via vague contracts that left them with considerable discretion seemed to align well with Coase's way of thinking about the nature of the firm.

Yet, in a sense, the way that Lee presented Woodward's vision of trusted professionals implied that we might extend Coase's notion of the firm as a loosely specified pool of resources to be allocated contingently, for it admitted the possibility that workers could be left to figure out for themselves in what ways to change what they were doing as their situations changed, without managers needing to be present to decide what needed to be done and give them the corresponding instructions. A workforce of intrinsically motivated professionals could function effectively with minimal need for managers so long as everyone was careful to consult with their colleagues to avoid coordination problems. That possibility seemed to get ignored in the era of managerialist organisational reforms that commenced soon after I left Cambridge. Instead of accepting the presence of a few slackers as the price of getting the benefits of trusting everyone with professional capabilities to use their skills with pride, managers have applied simplistic views of organisations and slack as a basis for treating everyone as if they are not trustworthy and work in demotivating roles.

Such managerialism has been particularly evident in the university sector (for a study in the Australian context, see Lafferty and Fleming, 2000), which historically had operated with minimal spending on managers and little monitoring of the performance of academic staff. From the 1980s, universities commonly turned increasingly into untrusting bureaucratic systems with more and more layers of management and massive manuals of policies and procedures to keep everyone in line and thereby supposedly increase their productivity. The productivity of academics working 'at the coalface' has thereby increased according to some measures, but we may wonder what percentage of the gains has been captured by the additional layers of managerial staff.

3.7   SUPERVISING CAMBRIDGE UNDERGRADUATES

My three years as an Economics Tripos student were followed by two years during which I served as a supervisor of undergraduates in addition to working as a research student. I did not need to do any teaching to get by financially, as my Social Science Research Council (SSRC) scholarship was perfectly adequate, but I was rightly confident that I would enjoy the experience of being a supervisor. The extra income was probably a mixed blessing: on the one hand, it enabled me rapidly to build up savings that I used for upgrading my music gear and to buy (and then rectify problems with) my first car. However, if I had not enjoyed such a financial experience, I might not have felt as financially frustrated as I did when I moved to Stirling and had to contend with the costs of running a non-college lifestyle.

I began by co-teaching Queens' Prelims students with Andy Vickerman, who had likewise decided to stay on at Queens' to study for a PhD without realizing how protracted the process of getting it was going to be. My teaching grew to include supervising students from other colleges and for Part II. Some of this was due to word getting round among students after I informally helped some that I got to know when attending lectures by Joan Robinson and John Eatwell for a second time. Those students were struggling with poor supervision and asked their directors of studies if they could switch to me for the following term. However, as will become apparent in Chapter 4, my popularity as a supervisor was not one of the things that caused my PhD saga to drag on as long as it did. Rather, the buzz that came from feeling that I was doing a good job in the role and the social interaction that came via supervisions contributed to the ultimate success of my quest for a PhD, for it helped me maintain the gumption that I needed to keep going during my first two years as a research student.

Ajit Singh must have had great confidence in Andy Vickerman and me when he assigned us the task of supervising the Queens' Prelims year. This was probably a result of him having seen how we performed as Prelims students and hence believing that we would be able to replicate what we had experienced under the guidance of himself and our other supervisors. However, we were left essentially to teach as we saw fit each term and were allowed to draw up our own sets of essay topics and readings. All this was in sharp contrast to modern systems in which tutors operate essentially as franchisees and have weekly meetings with course coordinators who provide them with tutorial notes and discuss strategies for running upcoming tutorials. We were probably wise initially simply to set the same set of essay topics and readings that we had been given two years earlier, but things did not stay this way: filing cabinet archaeology revealed that I made significant changes the following year, when I was supervising Prelims on my own. However, as I personalised what I taught, my goal remained to be pluralistic, to teach the students better thinking strategies rather than what they should think.

4 A Difficult Pathway to a Cambridge PhD, 1977–1984

4.1   INTRODUCTION

A doctorate in economics is now a prerequisite for an academic career that goes beyond the misery of casual teaching positions. It can also serve as a credential to fast-track a career as a professional economist in the corporate sector or public service. Some doctorates result simply because students enjoy researching in a particular area, like the idea of having a doctoral title, and wish to maintain a student lifestyle for as long as possible, even though they may intend to pursue a career in an entirely different field. But whatever the motivation for commencing their doctorates, research students are unlikely to complete their dissertations and graduate unless they have personalities that will keep them motivated and focused on the task.

Resilience is a key requirement, as doctoral projects typically run into major hurdles at various points, such as major technical or data-related problems, difficulties in getting ethical approval where human subjects are involved, and issues with one's supervisor(s) or opposition to one's work from those who are called upon to assess its potential, progress, or eventual quality. A related requirement is to be the kind of person who is not driven by the prospect of the 'buzz' of a rapid sense of accomplishment. Those who crave such a 'buzz' probably should avoid doctoral programmes and any thoughts of pursuing academic careers, even if they are clearly very bright and highly capable when it comes to the economic way of thinking: they are likely to be much happier, and very successful, as economic advisors in government service or working in consultancy firms.

Over the course of my career, I have seen traditional British-style monograph-based PhDs evolve towards much more US-style papers-based PhDs in the UK, Australia and New Zealand, and the associated evolution of PhD programmes from relatively informal to managerialist modes of operation. As will become clear in Chapter 8, this change occupied much of my time and energy toward the end of my career during stints as a PhD programme administrator. However, my appreciation of the pros and cons of the changes that were taking place owed much to what I had experienced as a research student enrolled in Cambridge from 1977 to 1984. In this chapter, I recount the story of my PhD in the hope that it will serve as a cautionary tale that may help readers appreciate the risks that students face if they are producing monograph-style PhDs while working in an informal relationship with a single supervisor, rather than producing a set of papers under the guidance of a team of advisors. Along the way, I explain how modern best-practice systems of administering research higher degrees are designed to try to ensure that research students do not have the kind of experience that I and many others had in the bad old days. The chapter also provides material on the early evolution of my ideas that complements the analysis set out in later chapters and may serve as food for thought for future research topics.

4.2   BECOMING A RESEARCH STUDENT

In the Lent term of 1977, I decided that I wanted to continue studying economics after completing my Cambridge BA, rather than move on to a graduate-entry job in the corporate sector or public service. This decision had the advantage of greatly simplifying my life as I concentrated on consolidating my knowledge ahead of the Part II examinations. Unlike many of my peers, I did not have my time chewed up by preparing job applications and attending interviews. I filled in just four application forms and only had to attend one interview. There was no requirement to send a detailed research proposal with any of the forms; at most, I just had to give an indicative topic and write a paragraph about what I had in mind. I applied to enter the Cambridge PhD programme and, for a back-up, to one-year coursework master's programmes at the LSE, UCL and the University of York, each of which could lead to doctoral studies at these institutions.

I was aware that, from the standpoint of the behavioural economics that I had so far encountered, what I was doing might seem to be a case of satisficing with needlessly low aspirations and local search. I knew that if I got a first in Part II, I probably had a chance of winning a postgraduate scholarship wherever in the world I wanted to study: John Eatwell provided a role model for such a pathway, for after studying as an undergraduate at Queens' he had done his PhD at Harvard. Taking that route would require me first to take a GMAT examination, and a typical modern behavioural economist would no doubt see my reluctance to follow in Eatwell's footsteps in terms of hyperbolic discounting and present bias regarding the hassle of meeting the GMAT requirement. But there were two, more basic, dealbreaker issues when it came to the idea of applying to a top-tier US university. One was that I had, and still have, a complete aversion to spending time in a land where gun culture rules and corrupts the political process. The other issue was the kind of programme that would be entailed. All I really wanted to do was to get straight into research, with the aid of world-leading library facilities, without any further coursework.

Cambridge ticked those boxes. I did not want to go to a top-tier department in the USA to take courses that would improve my technical skills for doing mainstream economics; rather, I simply wanted to get on with doing the kind of economics that excited me, a mixture of behavioural, evolutionary, and Post Keynesian economics. I had no plan to get a PhD as a stepping-stone to an academic career, or to any other career; I just wanted to get a better understanding of how the economic system worked. It was as simple as that. Working out what career I wanted to pursue was something I could do later.

My attitude toward US postgraduate economics would probably be viewed by mainstream economists as presumptuous. It was not based on careful research, merely on Ajit Singh's assertion that what my classmates and I had learned even in the Cambridge Prelims year went conceptually way beyond what one would do in a well-ranked US postgraduate programme before being allowed to advance to the PhD. This was the great advantage of focusing on methods and concepts, often via primary sources, rather than on mastering techniques required for solving closed problems set out in advanced textbooks. My position was, and remains, that rigorous economic thinking does not have to be based on formal models, and formal models may be precise on their own terms yet be built on logically flawed foundations. The Cambridge capital controversies that Geoff Harcourt (1972) surveyed with clarity and wit, and which were part of my Cambridge undergraduate experience, epitomise this. Decades later, I would cringe each time I found US-trained economists teaching models based on aggregate production functions to students who remained as oblivious as their instructors to the logical problems that lie beneath such technical analysis.

When I asked Ajit what an economics PhD entailed, his answer was simple. In essence, he said, 'You spend three years writing a book in which you make an original contribution to economic knowledge.' I imagined that, before I came to write my thesis, I would spend a lot of time reading critically what others had written and looking for clues about the kind of contribution I could make. However, I had not ruled out the idea of doing empirical work as a major part of my thesis and I presumed that I would be able to pick up relevant empirical techniques if the need arose.

Clearly, I needed a fallback position in case I failed to do well enough to get a scholarship to stay on in Cambridge. As with my undergraduate applications, I viewed UCL as my preferred fallback position. I knew that not only was Michael Stewart still there but that the UCL economics staff now included Vicky Chick, whose (1973) book *Theory of Monetary Policy* I had been finding very useful during Part II. This time, Michael Stewart interviewed me and once again UCL was willing to serve as my fallback; I do not recall pursuing the LSE or York applications any further once the UCL offer arrived.

In the end, I got my hoped-for finals result. On graduation day, I returned to my former room at Queens' and found a note pinned to the armchair instructing me to ring John Llewellyn immediately. John held the position of Assistant Director of Research, which meant that he managed the Cambridge PhD programme in economics. I went down to the porters' lodge and phoned him. It was a very short conversation. He told me that he had one fewer Social Science Research Council PhD scholarship than he had suitable candidates. (The number of scholarships was either three or four, rather fewer than I had imagined Cambridge would get.) He then asked, 'Do you want one of these scholarships? Yes or no, now!' I said 'Yes', thanked him and went back to my room to continue getting ready for the graduation procession.

4.3   STARTING OUT AS A RESEARCH STUDENT

Today, students who enter a well-run research higher degrees programme will be provided with induction resources to ensure that they understand what is expected of them and to assist them in delivering it. The programme coordinator will deliver a PowerPoint presentation, followed by refreshments; there is likely to be a detailed pdf manual to download, plus an online hub of other downloadable resources – such as John Creedy's (2007) very useful guide, 'A PhD thesis without tears' – and courses will be available at the library about the online resources that are available and how to use them. The programme coordinator may follow the induction session with monthly 'catch-up' sessions in which the research students report on how things are going and raise any issues of concern. Social events such as morning teas and pizza lunches will also be laid on as means of ensuring that research students develop a sense of esprit de corps and do not feel isolated.

All this is designed to enable research students to begin and continue working with focus, confidence, and a sense of what their thesis advisors will be trying to ensure that they do. Moreover, as part of the application process, they will have been required to secure support from at least a prospective principal supervisor/advisor, if not also one or more associate advisors. This is a significant part of the application process in terms of risk management, especially where the track records of advisors are part of the scoring process when scholarship applicants are being ranked: if students cannot enlist experienced advisors, it is inferred they will be at higher risk of running into problems. Taking account of advisors' track records also reduces risks because it pushes would-be advisors to seek to generate suitable track records by serving their apprenticeships as associate advisors with experienced principal advisors, rather than by offering to be principal advisors despite having no experience. The research profile webpages of academic staff will include details of their current and past advisory roles to enable applicants to find advisors with expertise in the right area and to gauge their experience in advisory roles. A regime of regular meetings between research students and advisors (typically fortnightly) is established from the outset so that progress can be monitored and problems can be detected at an early stage.

Requiring students to have at least two advisors reduces the risks that the research students face, as do requirements that advisors attend training sessions before they are allowed to serve in such roles (especially as principal advisors) and that they periodically attend refresher training sessions. By having 'advisors' rather than 'supervisors', the modern process attempts to nudge research students into following up on suggestions and feedback, as well as into taking responsibility for their own progress. The modern terminology also reflects the absence of any ultimate judgemental role for the 'advisors', in contrast to what is connoted by the more hierarchical 'supervisor' notion: advisors dispense wisdom, having demonstrated their competence to do so. However, although they may also advise those who assess the student's progress and how it is being affected by the willingness of the student to take advice, they do not control the outcomes of assessments.

Back in 1977, Cambridge offered its new research students in economics very little initial guidance – though I do recall there was a morning tea for my cohort. My first task was to find myself a supervisor (note the singular), for the application process did not require applicants to have enlisted support from a supervisor prior to submitting the application. Given the size of Cambridge's Faculty of Economics and Politics, it was reasonable to expect that finding a suitable supervisor should not be a problem. In my case, however, the difficulties I had in getting supervision set the tone for the rest of my experience as a research student.

At the time that I applied for a place in the PhD programme, my tentative project title was 'A Keynesian Approach to Structural Change'. What I wanted to study was how an economy achieves coordination at the sectoral level as patterns of demand change and as innovations occur. I was concerned that the price system had shortcomings as a signalling mechanism (as I had explained in my entry for the Adam Smith Essay competition) and that, given what I knew from behavioural economics and organisation theory, firms might not be as responsive or adaptable as the proponents of the market mechanism seemed to presume. I called it a 'Keynesian' approach because it was related to what Keynes had addressed at the macroeconomic level via a focus on the saving-and-investment coordination problem and possible failures in market signalling mechanisms.

In my 'Keynesian' vision of the challenges that structural changes pose, the possible failure of firms to respond effectively and in an orderly manner to changing conditions played a role that was analogous to how Keynes saw the possible failure of money markets to prevent macro-level deflationary or inflationary gaps in his analysis of the problem of avoiding unemployment and/or inflation. Moreover, as Goodhart (1975) had pointed out via Coase (1937), firms and money were institutions that emerged due to transaction cost problems: both exist to provide cost-effective ways of dealing with contingencies as they arise and for taking advantage of better knowledge if and when it becomes available. Neither firms nor money have any role in the idealised static, transaction cost-free world of general equilibrium theory, in which there are no macroeconomic problems or problems of structural adjustment because production does not commence until contingent claims contracts that address all possible states of the world have been concluded for the purchase of inputs and outputs.

Given that my thinking about structural change and coordination had been triggered by the roles that Ajit Singh, Ken Coutts and Alan Hughes had played in my undergraduate studies, it might appear that I was spoilt for choice when it came to finding a supervisor. But this was not the case. Ajit had not volunteered to be my supervisor and I would have been wise not to ask him to serve in the role given that one of my key ideas clashed with his claims about the policy implications of his work on de-industrialisation (Singh, 1977). The issue harked back to the clash to which I had been introduced at high school between Myrdal's view of cumulative causation and Bauer's view that vicious circles can be broken, given determination to do so, because systems usually have some slack. Ajit was very much in the Myrdal camp and hence saw a strong case for import controls and other government intervention to help firms in the UK recover lost ground against their overseas rivals, particularly firms in Germany and Japan. I was less sure what was needed, for I recognised that although slack provides a basis from which recovery or development may be possible without assistance, it may instead be used as a means of carrying on with outmoded ways until it is too late to recover.

Given this, Alan Hughes seemed a better choice as a potential supervisor, for it was he who had introduced me to the industrial economics equivalent of Myrdal versus Bauer, namely Downie's (1958) analysis of the 'transfer mechanism' versus the 'innovation mechanism'. But Alan was still enrolled for a PhD himself, which meant that he was precluded from being a PhD supervisor. The same applied for Ken Coutts. I think it was John Llewellyn who then suggested that Richard Goodwin might be interested, given his work on economic dynamics and because he had supervised Paul Stoneman's PhD on the uptake of computers in the UK (published in slightly revised form as Stoneman, 1976). I went to see Goodwin, but he was not interested.

The only other person who was suggested to me was James Trevithick, my monetary economics supervisor for Part II. He did not have a PhD and had not been in Cambridge very long, but he seemed to be gaining some traction as a Keynes scholar as well as for his work on inflation: my Part II supervisions had entailed traipsing out to

Fitzwilliam College, but now he was a fellow at King's with a room in the magnificent Palladian-style Gibbs Building. Although much of what I intended to do was not in his zone at all, the 'Keynesian' tag was enough for him to agree to take on the role. It is possible that I was his first research student and that he felt some pressure to accept the role as part of the process of getting a firm foothold in Cambridge.

Aside from finding a supervisor, the only initial formal task was an interview with senior members of the Faculty of Economics and Politics. A few weeks after term started, John Llewellyn's secretary asked if I would be able to come in for a Saturday morning chat with some of the staff. She did not give any indication that when I was shown into the room, I would be the only research student present and would find myself facing David Champernowne, Phyllis Deane and Frank Hahn, along with John Llewellyn (and one or two others that I do not recall with certainty). Very soon it became clear that this was not a welcome but an interview. I was asked to explain what my research topic was and my key ideas, and John then invited the senior staff to question me in turn. I have no recollection of the questions or my replies, but what I do recall is that when it was Frank Hahn's turn, he declined to ask me anything and said, to the others, 'He's clearly an economics poet.'

Hahn's arrogant put-down seemed less insulting after I heard him used the same phrase on my next encounter with him. The latter occasion was about a year later at a meeting of the Political Economy Club (for high-flying undergraduates) held one evening at Hahn's house. I attended it to support Chris Chaloner, the star Queens' undergraduate, who was giving a paper about the role of slack in economic systems. The paper was based on sources on the behavioural theory of the firm and economic coordination that I had fed to him during Prelims supervisions. This time, 'economics poet' was applied to Brian Loasby, whose thinking figured in Chris's paper. So, I was in good company when it came to being an 'economics poet'! I also warmed to Hahn on that occasion because it was clear that he was listening with interest and knew of the behavioural theory of the firm and the notion of X-inefficiency: when Oliver Hart was having trouble getting his head around what Chris was saying about the nature of organisational slack, Hahn cut in and said, 'No, he's perfectly right on this.'

As my first term as a research student progressed, I began to wonder whether I should have continued searching rather than agreeing to have Trevithick as my supervisor. On the rare occasions that we met, his focus seemed to be on me fitting in with his research activities rather that serving as a mentor to me in relation to what I was proposing to do. I realised that I was probably going to have to fend for myself when he suggested I should read a recent neo-Keynesian book by Barro and Grossman (1976): it had nothing to do with what I was proposing to do but it was one of two books that were the subject of a review article he was preparing (published as Trevithick, 1978). My next task was to comment on his draft, which he probably viewed as a good research training activity, something that I would not have had to do as an undergraduate. However, I now think that the key issue underlying our failure to develop an effective, regular working relationship was probably that neither of us had a clear sense of how we should be interacting, especially given that I was concentrating on reading things that mostly were in fields outside his comfort zone.

The feeling of isolation that my supervisory situation produced was compounded by a decision that I made in the first week: I was not going to work in the research students' room below the Marshall Library and would instead carry on working in the library itself, just as I had as an undergraduate. I realised that it would limit my chances of getting to know other research students in economics, but using the room came at the price of having to put up with cigarette smoke, whereas the library was a smoke-free zone. I thus had no idea about the supervision experiences my peers were having. At one point, I went to see Ian Gosling, one of my Alleyne's classmates, who had returned to Emmanuel College after getting a double-first in maths and physics, to see how he was faring as a research student in electrical engineering. Sadly, his situation was rather like mine.

It might seem that another reference point would have been my Queens' contemporary, Andy Vickerman, but I did not get a sense of how he was faring. Unlike me, Andy lived out of college, so it had been decided that he would use my room as a venue for holding his supervisions of Queens' Prelims students. Andy was a smoker, as were some of his students. Each time I returned to my room after they had been there, it reeked of tobacco smoke, despite the 'No Smoking' reminder I had chalked on my blackboard before heading off to the Marshall Library. Never very close as undergraduates, Andy and I were now barely on speaking terms.

My first day in the Marshall Library in my research student role had also been very disconcerting. I had planned to begin by reading Brian

Loasby's (1976) *Choice, Complexity and Ignorance*. I had seen it on display in Heffers Bookshop during Part II, and I had sensed that it might bring the perspectives of Shackle and Simon together. However, I had decided to delay reading it until I was free from the essay-writing treadmill. A minor surprise was that the Marshall did not have a copy listed in its card catalogue. That was easily remedied: I pointed out the gap to Mr Finkel, the librarian, and he said he would get a copy from Heffers right away. But there was a big shock at the point in the catalogue where I had expected to find Loasby's book, namely a card that referred to a recent discussion paper that he had written. Its title was 'On imperfections and adjustments' (Loasby, 1977, which eventually led to chapter 6 of Loasby, 1989). My heart sank: I correctly surmised that I was going to learn from it that what I had argued in my Adam Smith Essay about the coordination problem and the beneficial aspects of so-called 'market imperfections' as facilitators of orderly structural adjustments had already been argued by someone else. Day one of my PhD thereby became the day that I discovered George Richardson's neglected (1960) book *Information and Investment* and that I had reinvented what is now known, by those who know about its origins, as 'the Richardson problem'.

The discovery that I had reinvented Richardson's core idea meant that one aspect of what I hoped to write about in making my 'original contribution to knowledge' had evaporated. But on seeing that Richardson had developed his analysis of the investment coordination problem into a PhD-length book, I got a sense of confidence about my critical and creative thinking capacities: it showed what I might have been able to do if he had not done it already. There was also a sense of relief that I was not alone in worrying about the standard view of how the market mechanism works. But it was also a lesson that I should proceed very carefully in developing my knowledge of the literature to ensure that the ideas that I had for my thesis were original.

In the absence of online citation tracking tools or the kind of powerful search engine that a modern academic library offers, this was a much more challenging task than it is for today's doctoral students. I realised that I was going to have to be vigilant in following up sources from reference lists and footnotes.[3] The task was going to be like that of a

---

[3] For example, it soon became apparent that I could have discovered Richardson in my Prelims year, for on re-reading the section of Leijonhufvud (1968, pp. 69–70) that had

detective, always on the lookout for new leads and clues. I soon saw the significance of self-citations for nudging readers to explore the genealogy of one's ideas, and that, by publishing in a restricted set of journals, one could make it easier for others to find one's more recent contributions if they latched on to one's earlier publications. Further clues about relevant sources could come from carefully reading prefaces to books and acknowledgments footnotes in articles. But the whole process could be accelerated if one had a supervisor who had extensive knowledge of the area in which one had chosen to conduct research.

As I did not have such a supervisor, the foundations for my first year of research came from the reference lists in Loasby's *Choice, Complexity and Ignorance* and Williamson's (1975) *Markets and Hierarchies*, and – as had happened in my discovery of the latter – by delving into books that were adjacent on the library shelves to works that Loasby and Williamson cited. I also came to see the need to be determined to track down sources that were missing from the Marshall's shelves (as was the case with Richardson's *Information and Investment* whenever I tried to find it there), even if this meant making a trip to the University Library. It could be hazardous to tell myself that 'I'll get to it later' because of the risk of forgetting to do so. Trying to make do with a review of an absent book could be hazardous, too, if the reviewer failed to convey the key messages correctly.

4.4   CONFIRMATION OF CANDIDATURE

Today's students in well-designed research higher degree programmes are commonly required to survive a set of milestone tests held at roughly twelve-month intervals on the way to submitting their dissertations for examination: confirmation of candidature, mid-term review, and thesis review. Each milestone may require written work to be submitted, a presentation to be delivered, and an interview with members of a milestone committee that includes the student's advisory team and an

---

triggered my interest in the impact of uncertainty on market coordination, I discovered footnote references to Richardson. Moreover, on looking through my notes from Alan Hughes's Part II lectures on industrial organisation, I discovered that *Information and Investment* was on his reading list. Alan had been one of the assessors for the Adam Smith Essay competition, so this discovery left me with the uneasy thought that he might have wondered whether I had plagiarised Richardson's analysis.

independent assessor, and which is chaired by the programme coordinator or a milestone coordinator. The interview section may comprise three segments: (a) the student is interviewed by the full milestone committee, (b) a discussion between members of the milestone committee, with the student not present, and (c) the student is interviewed by the independent assessor and the committee chair. Ideally, the verdict is reached by consensus in stage (b); if not, the independent assessor and chair may over-rule the advisory team. Stage (b) provides the independent assessor and chair with the opportunity to find out whether the advisors view the student as having the capabilities needed to complete the project and whether the student is open to taking their advice, and usually successful in applying it, rather than operating like a prima donna. Stage (c) provides an in-confidence opportunity for the student to provide a view of how things are working out with the advisors.

In such a system, a detailed template is provided to help candidates prepare their written submissions for the confirmation of candidature milestone. In essence, the candidate's task is to demonstrate that he or she has worked out a project – to be written up in the form of several related article-style 'essays' or as a traditional monograph-style thesis – that is coherent, has the potential to result in a sufficiently substantial and original contribution to knowledge to earn a doctorate, and is feasible within the required timeframe, given the available resources. The template for the 'confirmation document' will typically require it to do the following, within a maximum of, say, 15,000 words or 45 pages:

1. Identify a knowledge gap via a review of the literature in a particular area, a review that shows how the literature in the area has evolved and pins down significant unresolved or unexplored issues.
2. Specify the researcher's primary goal in relation to going some way toward closing the knowledge gap.
3. Specify the main research questions that the researcher will attempt to answer to meet the primary goal.
4. Specify the things that the researcher plans to do (in managerial terms, the research objectives) in order to answer the research questions and justify choosing them in preference to alternative potential ways of answering the questions (i.e., set out the methodological basis of the project, including, where applicable, an explanation of how data will be collected and analysed).

5. Specify the expected outputs of the project, in terms of the types of findings, areas of potential policy implications, and the kinds of publications that are envisaged for disseminating them.
6. Discuss ethical issues associated with the project and how they will be addressed.
7. Set out the budget plan for the project, including costs for software, data collection, payments to subjects in economics experiments, and conference travel
8. Set out and explain the timelines for the rest of the project in relation to the dates by which the remaining milestones would need to be completed and the date by which the finished dissertation must be submitted for examination.

This sequence is expected even if the student begins the research with a proposition – a 'thesis' in its briefest sense – or wants to build a project around a novel modelling or empirical technique. The document will gradually come together via successive meetings with the advisory team. The initial focus of these meetings will be on how the student has drafted a fresh section of the confirmation document, and it will be fine-tuned to ensure that all the parts line up coherently. Students will be encouraged to have a 'dress rehearsal' in which they deliver their oral presentation to their advisors, with the slides then being revised for final delivery.

If the student has fortnightly sessions with the advisory team prior to the confirmation milestone, it is possible that as many as 25 hours of these meetings will have taken place before the milestone is held. Given this, the modern system may superficially appear to be one in which relationships between advisors and students entail spoon-feeding and rescuing via the advisory team providing suggestions about what to do next, with rather little happening via the student's own initiative. It certainly may begin like this if the student does not initially seem to have a sense of how research projects are devised and undertaken. However, another vital part of the research training process entails subjecting the work of research students to criticism and getting them used to having to defend their work so that they learn how to become better self-critics. Here, members of advisory teams may seem to operate rather like a 'good cop, bad cop' police partnership. Given that research students typically will have been used to being high achievers, such criticism is likely to come as a painful surprise, but they need to go through the experience to get their confirmation document – and, eventually, their thesis – as bulletproof as possible and reduce the risk that they will have to deal with unexpected challenges during the oral section of the confirmation process – particularly from the chair of the confirmation panel and the 'external' assessor. Experiencing brutally frank criticism is also vital training for what lies ahead in the business of getting research papers published.

The system that I experienced in Cambridge required students to go through a confirmation process, too, but there were no mid-term or thesis review milestones. Confirmation recommendations were made to the Board of Graduate Studies by an independent committee but understanding what the committee expected had to be arrived at without any downloadable resources or templates. The confirmation process was based purely on a piece of written work, the 'thesis proposal'; there were no milestone presentations by other students that one might attend as a means of getting an idea of what was expected. This amplified the need for an experienced and committed supervisor. The only things that were made clear at the outset were that one did not officially become a PhD candidate until one received a letter from the Board of Graduate Studies saying that one's thesis proposal had been approved, and that this normally occurred around the end of one's first year as a research student. I do not recall being given any instructions on what a thesis proposal should look like or the criteria in terms of which it would be assessed. But before getting to that stage there was another fuzzy requirement: one had to submit, by the end of April, 'a substantial piece of work' as evidence of what one had been doing. In the absence of effective guidance, my path to confirmation of candidature as a PhD student proved to be far longer and more troubled than that which a modern student is allowed to experience.[4]

---

[4] After reading the first edition of this book, my former Stirling colleague, Peter Bird contacted me about his Cambridge PhD experience. He was several years ahead of me and had no recollection of having to submit a 'substantial piece of work' or get confirmed as a PhD student. This seems to imply that the system I experienced had only been in place for a couple of years. Peter's experience may have been even more harrowing than mine would turn out to be. Like me, it took him around seven years to get his Cambridge PhD, but this involved a succession of half a dozen supervisors, each of whom failed to provide him with advice. The absence of the confirmation process also meant that he got no feedback from confirmation assessors, either. Peter's thesis on commodity speculation thus ended up being almost entirely a do-it-yourself project; the only significant input he recalls having was from Tony Cramp (who was not one of his succession of supervisors), who introduced him to Minsky's work on financial instability.

Attempt 1 (1978): A Keynesian Approach to Structural Change
Towards the end of March 1978, after six months of reading, I began to type my 'substantial piece of work' on a manual Smith Corona typewriter. The ensuing five weeks were hard going for my fingers and for the typewriter. The latter had hardly been used in the decade or so since my mother had purchased it to see whether she could learn to type. After four weeks, the machine was showing signs that it was not an office-grade tool, for the paper roller was giving trouble, but it had enabled me to produce a 147-page document (and a carbon copy) entitled 'A Keynesian approach to structural change'. I was happy with it, but in the absence of any guidelines, I had produced a piece of work that was far too substantial. By this stage, John Llewellyn had left to take up a position in Paris as a senior economist at the OECD. His replacement as Assistant Director of Research was one of my Part II supervisors, Geoff Meeks. Just before I finished my tome, I saw Geoff and reported on where I had got to. He was alarmed to hear how substantial it was, and he said that he would never be able to get anyone to agree to read it at that length. He therefore directed me to spend the remaining week before the submission deadline writing a version of it that was no more than about thirty pages in length.

I managed to deliver it on time. However, given that the typing experience left me fearing that I might damage my fingers, it was the last thing I ever typed on a manual typewriter. As luck would have it, an Adler electric typewriter came my way in time to use a couple of months later when I was preparing my thesis proposal: a fellow Queens' postgraduate asked me to mind it for him while he took a year out from his studies.

The feedback on my 'substantial piece of work' was not extensive and I cannot recall that it proved to be of great use when I wrote my thesis proposal document. Again, there was little advice on what was required beyond a summary of what one had done during the first year of research and what one planned if one achieved confirmation. The document that I submitted consisted of ten, single-space pages, the first six and a half of which summarised and neatly categorised the reading that I had been doing. My thoughts on what I might do next amounted to slightly less than two pages, and the remainder of the document consisted of the list of references. I suggested two possible research projects as sequels to what I had done so far.

The first project would have been reasonably straightforward to undertake, namely a study of the impact that switching to an organisational structure based on mini-firms-within-the-firm 'profit centres' had on the performance of firms in the UK context. In a PhD-based book, Channon (1973) had detailed how firms in the UK had adopted this 'M-form' kind of structure, often in the process of following advice from the McKinsey consulting group, but he had not explored the effect that the change had on their financial performance or productivity. The fact that it seemed an obvious opportunity made me nervous that it might not be substantial enough for a PhD and that other researchers might also be attempting to do it. My caution turned out to be justified, for very soon after, in the September 1978 issue of the *Journal of Industrial Economics*, Steer and Cable published a paper that reported the results of a study that did something akin to what I had envisaged. It was indeed useful to be mindful of the Richardson investment coordination problem in the market for contributions to economic knowledge.[5]

My second project proposal was spelt out at much greater length. It was essentially an extension of my original 'Keynesian approach to structural change' idea, presented with a closing emphasis on Leijonhufvud's (1969, 1973) urging of economists to study why multiplier processes usually do not work explosively, and what role system buffering plays in damping these processes. However, this time it was framed explicitly as aiming to test Ajit Singh's contention that unorthodox policy measures were necessary to prevent the further de-industrialisation of the UK economy that was otherwise inevitable because of cumulative causation processes having taken hold (Singh, 1977). Rather than framing my thinking in terms of Downie's transfer mechanism versus his innovation mechanism, I stressed the need to study the different learning curves that UK firms and their overseas rivals were on, and the responsiveness of UK firms to growing existential threats: the slower their responses, the more challenging their performance turnarounds would be insofar as differences between them and their overseas rivals became amplified by differences in their learning curves.

To conduct the latter empirical investigation, I would need firm-level data, and therein lay the key problem, for unlike Downie, I was not a public servant who could get access to raw data from the Census of Production. I therefore tentatively suggested that I might be able to get

---

[5] Many years later, I wrote a paper (Earl, 1995d) about the relevance of Richardson's idea in relation to academic work, which was presented at a colloquium held at St John's College, Oxford in Richardson's honour.

data via bodies such as the Business Ratios organisation that enable firms to learn where they stand in the pecking order for their line of business, and from industry-level development agencies such as those whose reports on structural change I had read.

My attempt at confirmation was not successful. In looking at it from the standpoint of my later PhD administrator roles, I have no hesitation in saying that Phyllis Deane and her committee were entirely right in deciding not to recommend my confirmation of candidature as a PhD student, even though the process did not provide any opportunity for me to discuss my proposal with them, defend my position by addressing any questions they might have, or discuss any ideas they might have about how to extend what I had been doing into a viable study. In a well-run modern system, a student would get all of these opportunities.

With hindsight, I think that there were two kinds of things that I could have been encouraged to consider on structural change and corporate responses to increasingly challenging external conditions. One possibility would have been a more case study-based approach in which I examined differences between firms that managed to 'dig themselves out of a hole', versus competitors that 'went to the wall'. This would have been a precursor to works such as Erica Schoenberger's (1997) book *The Cultural Crisis of the Firm* and Clayton Christensen's (1997) PhD-based book *The Innovator's Dilemma*. In a sense, my 1984 book *The Corporate Imagination: How Big Companies Make Mistakes* went in this direction: it used much of the reading on which this attempt at confirmation was based, supplemented by case study work taken from business history. That book took a scientific paradigms-/research programmes-based view of firms and the difficulties that they often have in adapting to change, which was very much a precursor to Schoenberger's analysis. However, I did not arrive at that view of the firm until the Michaelmas 1978 term.

The other possibility that I can now see probably would not have been feasible at the time, due to limited computing resources: there was scope for developing a multi-firm simulation model to explore how an industry evolves when firms experience different rates of learning-by-doing and differ in their responsiveness to falling attainments.

The failure of my first attempt at confirmation led me to reflect seriously on my future as a research student. Given that I was not focusing on macroeconomics, it was clear that James Trevithick was not the right supervisor for me. Perhaps we might have developed an effective working relationship if I had opted to go down the road of mining Keynes's *Collected Writings*. I readily could have done this, given that I had already read (and referred to in my first confirmation attempt) a loose-leaf draft of what was then catalogued in the Marshall Library as 'Volume 14b' but which eventually appeared as Volume 29 (Keynes, 1979). Indeed, between October 1978 and February 1979, I wrote three papers on Keynes, money, and unemployment, the first of which used ideas from that loose-leaf volume. These papers were never submitted for publication but ideas from them were eventually used in Dow and Earl (1982, especially chapter 8) and Earl (1990c).

My concerns about the Richardson problem applying with academic research investments seemed relevant in this area, too, and once again they were justified: Roy Rotheim soon went down the track that I imagined taking via a 'Keynes (1936) chapter 17' view of the theory of value, augmented via material from Volume 29 of Keynes's *Collected Writings*, and he did so to very good effect (see especially Rotheim, 1981). But a more fundamental reason why I did not become a Keynes scholar was that I felt I had got enough out of Keynes already and that my biggest interests centred on structural adjustments and the efficiency and evolution of firms. Given this, I felt that I needed either to get a new supervisor or to call it quits as far as a PhD was concerned and pursue my interests in the more hands-on world of management consulting. I decided to arrange a meeting to put this to Geoff Meeks before heading off to spend my summer break back at home in Stevenage.

Geoff immediately signalled that he would do whatever was necessary to deter me from pulling out. He did not start thinking aloud about whether he might himself be the supervisor I was looking for. This was despite the fact that he might have been a potential supervisor, given that I had liked his recently published PhD-based book on the impact of mergers on corporate performance (Meeks, 1977). Nor did he ask why I was not suggesting having Ajit Singh as my supervisor. Instead, he said that it was possible to arrange an external supervisor if an appropriate case could be made. He then asked me to name the person I would like to have, given that possibility. Without hesitation, I said, 'Professor Brian Loasby, of the University of Stirling.' Geoff told me to leave the matter with him and he would see if this could be arranged.

A few weeks later, I was reading *The Economist* in Stevenage Central Library and noticed an advertisement for a teaching assistant, two lecturers and a senior lecturer at the University of Stirling. I contacted Geoff to see whether he thought it would be appropriate for me to apply for the teaching assistant position or even for a lectureship as a means of working alongside Loasby if he became my supervisor. Geoff advised me only to apply for a lectureship and pointed out that even if I did not get the job I might at least get an expenses-paid trip to Stirling for an interview and thereby get to meet Loasby. I took his advice and did indeed get an interview – despite sending only a very brief application letter in which I named my referees, mentioned what my potential areas of interest in teaching were and that I was a research student, without even saying how well I had performed as an undergraduate.

The interview at Stirling did not take place until late October or early November 1978. In the meantime, I ploughed on without any supervision or sense of where I should be trying to go as far as the PhD was concerned. I decided that it might be useful to get my thoughts clear on the intersection between unemployment associated with deficient aggregate demand and unemployment associated with coordination failures as the structure of aggregate demand changed and new technologies were introduced. This was the first of my three Keynes-related papers, and much of it sought to confront Keynes's views with those of Hayek, mindful of material in the 'Volume 14b' draft about the distinction between a monetary economy and a barter/entrepreneur system. The technology side of the paper was inspired by Michael Posner's Part II lecture on whether it made sense to provide financial support to factories on Merseyside that made telephone exchange switchgear that had been rendered obsolete. After consulting with Geoff Meeks, I sent the paper to Brian Loasby so that he could get a sense of what I could do. His reaction to the paper turned out to be a sign of how things were going to be with him as my supervisor.

I spent the morning before my Stirling job interview talking to Loasby. After explaining that he was on sabbatical and therefore was not part of the hiring process, he turned to my paper, saying that, coincidentally, he, too, had recently been reading some of the Hayek works to which I had referred. He then launched into his thoughts on Hayek and, after also noting my interest in system buffering, he started drawing connections with some of his favourite sources. It was like being treated to a live improvisation in the broad area of *Choice, Complexity and Ignorance*. But I never received feedback on the paper that I had sent to him, and I ended up simply filing it away. On re-reading it during the research for this chapter, I realised that I probably should have submitted it to the just-established *Journal of Post Keynesian Economics* to see what feedback I got, as it was by no means a terrible paper despite being my first attempt to write something in the journal article format.

Unlike my Saturday morning grilling by the senior Cambridge economists a year earlier, my Stirling job interview was an enjoyable experience. Indeed, I was so relaxed that (as is detailed early in Section 5.2) I even dared at one point to offer a reply that would initially have seemed very flippant. Within a couple of weeks, I was offered a tenurable lectureship, with only a two-year probationary period. However, I did not immediately accept the offer, as a salary at the bottom of the scale did not look particularly enticing given my current income from my SSRC scholarship and from supervising undergraduates. Furthermore, as one of two Munro Scholars at Queens', I now enjoyed spacious, rent-free accommodation and the right to dine free at high table once a week. The Munro Scholarship had been awarded to me based on the reputation I had rapidly built for my teaching in my first year as a research student (and it was the only teaching award I received in my entire career), but it only lasted for two years, and it was not clear that I would then be able to move up to the next step, a college research fellowship, to see me through to the completion of my PhD.

My delay in reaching a decision resulted in a message in my pigeonhole at Queens' porters' lodge asking me to call Professor Chuck Brown, chair of the Stirling interview panel. Because my application letter had been so brief, he had no idea of what the Munro Scholarship entailed, and once I explained the details to him, he revised the offer two points up the salary scale. He also said that, if I performed well, there were good prospects for me to be given accelerated promotion up the lecturer scale (which had 14 levels beyond that of the revised offer). I accepted this revised offer, but it turned out initially to leave me feeling poorer than I had been in Cambridge.

Attempt 2 (1979): Progressive and Degenerating Research
Programmes in Economics: A Lakatosian Appraisal While Applying
Lakatos's Methodology of Scientific Research Programmes to the
History of Economic Thought
Although I accepted the job at Stirling and Brian Loasby became my external supervisor, I had to complete two years of full-term residence in Cambridge as a research student before I could move to Scotland and take up the position. This kept me in Cambridge until June 1979 and in March I submitted my second attempt at getting confirmed as a PhD

candidate. This time, my proposal focused on economic method: I abandoned any thoughts of an empirical study of the competitive performance of UK firms. I proposed instead to study whether Lakatos's (1970) methodology of scientific research programmes could be used to make sense of the preference of economists for continuing to employ the deterministic, equilibrium-focused approach to economics despite the existence of a body of economic thought that took seriously the open-ended nature of problems that real-world decision makers have to address. To make this project work, I would need to construct a picture of the latter as a scientific research programme and then compare its empirical content with that of the orthodox approach. This proposal can to some extent be viewed as intending to go from the first attempt to apply Lakatos's thinking to economics, namely Latsis (1972), to the reappraisal of it eventually offered by Nightingale (1994), while dealing with thorny questions about the kinds of useful empirical content that economists can generate and the problems of specifying what constitutes efficiency in a world in which slack in systems can be welfare-enhancing.

The proposal was partly a consequence of a few letters that Brian Loasby and I exchanged, which resulted in me taking my reading on methodology beyond the work of Kuhn (1962). The proposal is dated 3 March 1979, which was several weeks before the purchase dates that I wrote on my copies of Lakatos (1970) and books on economic method by Hutchison (1938, 1977) and Latsis (ed.) (1976) that I expected to use frequently if the project gained approval. However, I do not recall any detailed discussion with Loasby about the proposal. Given that it was not until 5 February 1979 that I finished the third of my three papers organizing my thoughts on Keynes, money and unemployment, the obvious inference is that this second proposal was cobbled together in haste, possibly to meet a submission deadline. That is not the way to prepare this kind of document.

Late in the afternoon on the day before my candidacy was due to be considered, an envelope was posted under the door of my room at Queens'. It contained a card that read, 'Good Luck with the Philistine!' The card was from a student in one of my Part II supervision groups. The members of this group were not from Queens', and we had all become good friends. I had mentioned to them my upcoming milestone and my concern that my progress might once again be thwarted by Phyllis Deane and her committee. The greeting raised an interesting cognitive puzzle: should I view it as indicating wit or as the result of the sender trying (with

English as her fourth language) to make sense of what I was saying, without her having ever encountered Deane as a lecturer?

Once again, however, my proposal was rejected. I have been unable to find any written record advising me of the outcome, and it is possible that I simply received verbal notification from Geoff Meeks. My recollection was that I was advised that a methodological thesis would be challenging to present as a contribution to knowledge, and that Phyllis Deane was not convinced that I would be able to demonstrate the existence of a coherent alternative scientific research programme in economics along the lines that I outlined. This recollection was confirmed when I discovered in my files a carbon copy of a letter that I had written to Professor Elizabeth Brunner at the University of Lancaster, dated 29 January 1980, seeking clarification about several aspects of her work with P. W. S. Andrews. I explained that I was attempting to piece together what I called a 'disequilibrium' approach to economics using elements from 'Post-Marshallian industrial economists' (specifically, Andrews, Brunner, Downie, Lamfalussy, Penrose and Richardson), 'subjectivists' (here I mentioned Austrians, Keynes, Shackle, and practitioners of the LSE approach to costs epitomised by the papers in Buchanan and Thirlby, eds, 1973), along with American institutionalists and behavioural economists. I mentioned the difficulties I was having with my PhD confirmation and noted that:

The reaction was that:

(a) A methodological work, even one attempting to operate on the additional level of appraising Lakatos's theory of the growth of knowledge as applied to economics, would not contribute [enough] to knowledge given the high standard required in Cambridge.

(b) Phyllis Deane took an unreasonably narrow interpretation of Lakatos and said that because some of the disequilibrium economists attacked each other their work could not conceivably belong to the same research programme.

On revisiting my proposal with the benefit of over four decades more experience, I think that the committee rejected the proposal for the wrong reasons but was nonetheless right to force me to have a further rethink. To say that economists cannot be thought of as members of a group because they do not agree on every aspect of how to view the economy is rather like saying that a particular political party is a sham because it is made up of several factions. The key issue for the coherence of a group is whether its members' views of the world intersect in core areas. In the case of the group that I had in mind, these core areas entailed the recognition of uncertainty, that people use rules to cope with the challenges of real-world decision-making, that economising activity takes place amid events that unfold in historical time, and so on. The real problem was that the proposal was far too ambitious for a PhD, as it was promising to get into challenging territory in terms of comparing the empirical content of research programmes that have very different implications about the kinds of predictions that are valuable, and it would have entailed a major effort (not just one major chapter) to stitch together and justify the synthesis comprising the alternative research programme that I envisaged. Therein lay the basis for my third attempt at confirmation.

Attempt 3 (1981): A Behavioural/Post Keynesian Micro/Macro Synthesis

By the time I wrote my third proposal, I was in my second year of working at Stirling and my ideas had developed considerably, partly via suggestions that Brian Loasby had made about things that I should read, but also partly because of other events. That process is charted in the next chapter during Section 5.4. Archaeological activities in my filing cabinets failed to unearth any documents pertaining to my third attempt at winning confirmation, and even the title that is listed above is an approximation. It was, in effect, my response to the reported basis for the verdict on my second attempt: it took the research programme idea even further and was based on a book proposal that I had put together after realising that there was potential for integrating the work I had been doing on consumer behaviour (Earl, 1980a) and wage stickiness (Earl and Glaister, 1979) since arriving at Stirling (see Chapter 5) with the behavioural theory of the firm, Post-Marshallian theories of price, investment and firm growth, and Post Keynesian perspectives on money and employment.

In its book proposal version, this project had failed to generate much enthusiasm when it was sent to Oxford University Press. It also failed as a PhD proposal. Again, Phyllis Deane proved to be immovable. However, Geoff Meeks relayed to me a comment that she had made about it that has stayed in my mind ever since: she had said that it was not suitable for a PhD dissertation since it was 'either trivial or a lifetime's work'. With hindsight, it seems to me that she was spot-on in her judgment. I still had a long way to go in developing the consumer behaviour side of my work, and I had not yet given much attention to the theory of the banking firm. In a sense, my 1990 book *Monetary Scenarios* was my first attempt to do what this proposal had envisaged, but it was well over the length of a PhD. It would indeed be something like a 'lifetime's work' before I got closer to where this proposal had envisaged going, namely my (2022) *Principles of Behavioral Economics*, a book that – despite being light on the monetary side – is nearly three and a half times the length allowed for a Cambridge PhD.

Looking back, one might say that my thesis ideas in 1978 were closer to raising the kind of 'research question' that I should have used as a basis for a PhD than they had become with my third attempt at confirmation. At the start, my implicit underlying question was an empirical one: 'To what extent can non-optimising theories of business decision-making explain evolving patterns of relative national competitiveness?' Where I had got to with my third proposal was a much more conceptual question, where the value of an answer would be harder to demonstrate: 'Is it possible to construct a coherent, unifying approach to economics that takes due account of complexity and fundamental uncertainty?'

The implicit message in Phyllis Deane's comment was that I needed to come up with something that was tightly focused and had depth. However, nothing was coming my way in terms of advice about what a prospective 'contribution to knowledge' had to look like to win confirmation of candidature. By the time that the third thumbs-down was delivered, there was a potential research question that I might have considered based on where I had got to, and it would have provided the basis for a well-defined empirical project: 'What role are non-compensatory decision rules and personal principles playing as determinants of penetration of the UK's car market by imported products?' This could have been anchored to Stout's (1977) report on non-price factors in international trade. It could have been based on surveys or focus group-based research with car buyers and could have included interviews with car dealers and marketing executives of carmakers to determine whether they were aware of the possibility that consumers were using intolerant decision rules. The ingredients were there – Stout's paper had piqued my interest in non-price factors, the potentially catastrophic effects of a single shortcoming for sales of a product were very much 'on my radar' via media attention given to catastrophic early rust problems with Lancia Beta cars in the UK shortly after I had started to view choice as a process of 'characteristic filtering' and discovered the marketing literature on non-compensatory decision rules (see Section 5.4), and the story of my father's Honda Civic had got me wondering about principles-based choices – but I failed at that time to make the connection in terms of potential for a research project of this kind. However, even if I had seen the potential of such a project, I would have had little hope of completing it by 30 September 1982, the deadline by which I needed to submit my thesis.

Attempt 4 (1982): A Behavioural Analysis of Choice
The deadline got much closer before I ended up with a more tightly focused project than my third proposal, albeit one that was not focused on an empirical research question. Instead, it focused on why people choose as they do. It came about purely by happenstance rather than any deep reflection on how I might be able to win over Phyllis Deane. Here is the story of how it emerged.

One afternoon, towards the end of the first semester of 1981, I went with some colleagues to the University of Edinburgh to attend a seminar. This gave me my first opportunity to meet Gavin Reid, whom I had been hoping to thank for passing to Fred Lee (who had studied with him before shifting to Rutgers University) a discussion paper that I had written (Earl 1980b) about economists' behaviour. This collegial act kindled what turned out to be a long-term connection between Fred and myself. After I thanked Gavin, he told me about his new book, *The Kinked Demand Curve Analysis of Oligopoly* (Reid, 1981). This was naturally of interest to me, given its connection with the Oxford Economists' Research Group. Soon after, I acquired a copy of Gavin's book. It appeared to have been written as a side-project from his PhD and was a short, single-issue book that dealt well with its topic. I found it very useful when teaching second-year microeconomics, but it was its form that got me thinking about whether I might write a short book of my own, a book on the alternative view of consumer behaviour that I had been putting together over the past eighteen months.

The book that I decided to write ended up quite a bit longer than Gavin's one. I gave it the working title 'A Behavioural/Post Keynesian Analysis of Choice' but it was published as *The Economic Imagination:*

Towards a Behavioural Analysis of Choice (Earl, 1983a), by Wheatsheaf Books, a new economics imprint of the Harvester Press. The main title was the idea of Wheatsheaf's managing editor, Edward Elgar. Edward had conceived it as ideal for a book that had a strongly subjectivist flavour, as mine had, that he had thought he might one day be able to get someone such as Jack Wiseman to write. By the end of 1981, I had a contract with Wheatsheaf and – despite some of my research time being diverted late in the summer by the need to work with Sheila Dow on the final version of our book *Money Matters – The Economic Imagination* was well on its way. However, the same still could not be said for my PhD.

I had not been giving the PhD much thought while I worked on *The Economic Imagination*, and the pressure to get a PhD seemed rather diminished since I had completed my two-year probationary period at the University of Stirling and was now a tenured lecturer. I was enjoying writing books and I wondered if I might be able to be as productive on that front as John Hey and Mark Casson, whose new books I kept seeing, along with signs of their career progress, in publishers' catalogues. Had I known at that time that Casson had been a casualty of the Cambridge PhD system and that Hey, too, did not have a doctorate, their role-model impacts might have cemented further the idea that one did not need to complete a doctorate to enjoy a successful academic career, even in the 1980s.

My decision to have a further shot at getting my PhD candidature confirmed was triggered on 23 January 1982. This was the day that George Shackle came to Stirling to deliver the Scottish Economic Society's annual Shell Lecture. I was tasked with being his minder for the day, which included picking him and Catherine Shackle up from Stirling station and the disconcerting experience of seeing that there had been no warning that George was on a special diet and that there was virtually nothing that Catherine deemed he could safely eat. However, my minder role did not prevent me from spending some time catching up with Neil Kay, and we talked about PhDs. Neil had been one of the very first economics students when the University of Stirling was established, after which he completed his PhD there. His thesis had been published in revised form as *The Innovating Firm: A Behavioural Theory of Corporate R&D* (Kay, 1979). I had bought the book in March 1979, and it had a major influence on my thinking (see Section 5.4). After listening to where I had got in my PhD saga, Neil urged me not to give up on getting a doctorate. 'It's your travel ticket', he said. I took his advice.

My fourth proposal necessarily had to be quickly assembled and quick to complete, as Cambridge required PhD dissertations to be submitted within five years of commencement of candidature and I was already into the second quarter of my fifth year. What I proposed to submit as 'A Behavioural Analysis of Choice' consisted essentially of *The Economic Imagination*, minus the second chapter 'Pricing Choices', with an extended 60-page version of my discussion paper 'A behavioural theory of economists' behaviour and the lack of success of behavioural economics' (Earl, 1980b) added at the end as a case study of decision-making involving a rule- and template-based filtering process. The case study paper had already benefited from comments by referees whose reports resulted in it being given a 'revise and resubmit' verdict by *History of Political Economy*, but I had not resubmitted the article despite having prepared a revised version that addressed all the comments that the referees had made. This was because, after Gavin Reid had sent the Stirling discussion paper version to Fred Lee, Fred had shown it to Alfred Eichner, triggering the latter's idea for the edited volume *Why Economics is Not Yet a Science* (Eichner, ed, 1983); I was thus waiting to see whether Eichner's book was going to happen with my paper included in it. This time, Phyllis Deane would not be a potential impediment, as Geoff Harcourt had replaced her on the committee.

Late in May 1982, over four and a half years after commencing as a research student, I received a letter (date 24 May) from the Board of Graduate Studies informing me that my candidature as a PhD student had been confirmed. The letter included the unsurprising reminder that my candidacy would be terminated if I failed to submit my thesis by 30 September 1982.

4.5   PhD 'MUST-HAVES' AND THE FEEDBACK ISSUE

Given that PhD students are required to produce original contributions to knowledge, they need to be able to demonstrate the following three things:

(a) The existence of the research gap that their work seeks to fill – which is commonly done via a literature review section (in the confirmation document) or chapter (in the dissertation) that displays a comprehensive knowledge of the achievements and limitations of prior work in their proposed area of research.

(b) That they can succinctly articulate the nature of the contribution to knowledge that they intend to make or (in the finished dissertation) have made, the method they intend to use or have used to make their contribution, and the extent and limitations of their contribution. In a finished dissertation, this is commonly done via a concluding chapter that offers a summary and suggestions for further research.

(c) Why their contribution is of significance – which is commonly done via a section or chapter on the implications of the work for practitioners in the area in question or for policymaking more generally.

Advisory teams have a duty to remind their research students of these three 'must-have' features of the material that they submit for confirmation and of the dissertation they submit. A corollary of this is that advisory teams have a duty to give their research students a sense of how confirmation assessors or thesis examiners might be able to criticise the work that they are proposing to submit. The meetings between research students and their advisors provide venues for ensuring that research students end up doing the things they need to do in order to graduate with a doctorate. Via these meetings, they can be tutored about what they must do, given gentle nudges to keep them focused on doing it, or, if necessary, be told sternly that they are in danger of failing unless they start heeding the advice that is being provided to them. Today, many students are also encouraged by their advisors to participate in 'Three-Minute Thesis' competitions, which are good training venues for achieving clarity in the second and third areas.

The three 'must-have' ways of demonstrating the prospective contribution of a PhD project or achievements of a finished thesis seem obvious to me with hindsight and I have tried to ensure that my PhD students always deliver them.

However, the way that Brian Loasby and I interacted resulted in these issues never being given the attention they warranted before I made my revised confirmation attempts or submitted dissertation. Just as had been the case with James Trevithick, Brian Loasby did not hold regular meetings with me for critically discussing my progress and plans. This was despite me floundering in terms of the confirmation issue. Moreover, in my first couple of years at Stirling, it was difficult to extract signs of what he thought of the work that I had done or was proposing to do.[6] I often felt that I was providing more comments on his latest working papers than he provided on what I was doing.

Things improved somewhat after my candidature was confirmed. However, because the confirmation process had chewed up so much of the five years in which I was expected to produce my thesis, I did not get the opportunity to experience two or three post-confirmation years of the kind that PhD students normally get for receiving feedback on their attempts to implement the project that has been approved. Normally, this would include feedback on draft chapters and on revisions to them. The feedback that I received from Brian Loasby after my proposal had been confirmed ended up being confined essentially to brief comments pencilled in the margins of the draft thesis as the submission deadline approached, and it resulted in no substantive changes being made. Much the same thing happened the following year when I showed him the draft of *The Corporate Imagination.*

The fact that Brian pencilled rather little in the margins of these drafts did not particularly surprise me, as I felt that it may have resulted from the impact that his way of thinking and writing had had on how I thought and wrote. However, minor tweaking advice with a submission deadline looming was far less important to receive than much earlier advice on big-picture issues that I needed to address if I were to come up with a thesis proposal that would be viewed as sufficiently original and feasible to put together in the time I had left, or swift big-picture advice about where my draft thesis looked vulnerable to being criticised by its examiners.

It is important to note that, in principle, there can be good working relationships between research students and their supervisors even if the latter merely supply written comments on work that the former submit. All that is required is that the research student receives effective feedback and then beavers away addressing it and keeps supplying the supervisor with work to review. However, I suspect that the prevalence of

---

[6] This experience with Brian Loasby as my supervisor led me to wonder how Neil Kay had fared when doing his Stirling PhD. I thought I might find a clue if I looked in the acknowledgements section of his PhD-based book. He had indeed acknowledged Brian Loasby, but only for 'initial encouragement' (Kay, 1979, p. xiii). Richard Shaw then became his main mentor and played a key role in ensuring that he ended up with a viable thesis.

supervising almost entirely by providing marginal comments may have contributed significantly to how long my generation of research students were taking to complete their doctorates, why so many of them never got as far as submitting, and why those who got that far failed or had to revise and resubmit their dissertations – issues that were highlighted in reports by Rothschild (1982) and Swinnerton-Dyer (1982).

On the surface, the main limitations of this way of operating are that it lacks the rapid-fire interactive potential that meetings offer, plus there is the risk that the absence of meeting-related deadlines will result in one or both parties being slow to play their respective roles. But there is a deeper issue that deserves attention, namely that this kind of supervision is prone to result in research students receiving comments that will mainly pertain to the quality of the exposition in the draft, technical mistakes, or potential connections or implications that they have failed to spot. Perhaps unsurprisingly, given the way that Brian's own contributions work, it was the last of these three kinds of comments that he mainly provided on my thesis draft. All three of these kinds of comments facilitate polishing one's draft but they do not address whether the work aligns with the sets of 'must-have' requirements that are likely to be used by those who assess it.

In my case, it would have been possible for Brian to have observed, in marginal comments on drafts that I gave him, that I had failed to include a systematic literature review as a means of establishing wherein lay the originality of what I was planning to do or had done. However, this shortcoming (spoiler alert: it was a key issue with the dissertation that I submitted) was likely to be overlooked in comments-based supervision by a scholar whose own writing did not follow the now-common formulaic approach of having a literature review immediately after any introduction. If research students are to receive comments about key things that they *are failing to do* rather than about the limitations of what they *have done* in the work that they have asked their supervisors to review, their supervisors must review their work with the former in mind and be capable of anticipating with sufficient accuracy the judgmental templates that third-party assessors are going to apply and how the assessors are likely to construe the work in question.

It is also possible for PhD supervisors to use marginal comments to congratulate research students on the quality of a chunk of what they have done, even if they are issuing serious warnings elsewhere. The positive comments would be likely to ensure that students reacted better to negative comments and did not waste time trying to improve work that was already good enough. But I never got much of a sense of how favourably Brian viewed my work: even when he came to review my post-PhD book *Lifestyle Economics* (Earl, 1986b), he did not explicitly commend my work at all; he simply described very incisively what I had done and how it differed from conventional thinking about consumer behaviour, made a couple of minor criticisms, and ended by suggesting that the book's own arguments implied that it might have difficulty winning converts (see Loasby, 1987).

The difficulty of extracting significant feedback from Brian about what he thought of my ideas or what I wrote appeared to be more the result of his social idiosyncrasies and limitations in how he construed his supervisory role than due to him being too short of time to discuss my work with me. Brian quite often would poke his head into my office and then talk about economics in the way that he had done at our first meeting. It was always interesting to hear what he had to say, but sometimes the timing was not ideal. I soon realised that if Brian came into my office and sat on one of my low-level filing cabinets near the door, as he seemed particularly prone to do late in the afternoon, I would not be able to end the interaction by using normal social cues if I needed to get away.

On one occasion this happened when I needed to leave to drive to Glasgow for a performance by Scottish Opera. Because I planned to drive there straight from work and had decided to be dressed for the occasion, I had worn my suit to work that day and had endured a seemingly endless stream of 'Where's the job interview?' quips from colleagues. However, until I cut in and said that I really had to go, and why, Brian seemed completely oblivious of what I was wearing and that it, and my other non-verbal cues, signified that he should wind up what he was saying.

I was not the only one to be treated to this, but I probably benefited more than my colleagues did. One, who shall remain nameless, explained to me that he had tried to make his office 'Brian-proof' by moving his filing cabinets away from the door, making it difficult for Brian to lean on anything, let alone sit down. The colleague advised me that I had the worst possible arrangement: low-level filing cabinets close to the door.

On one of these occasions, I managed to get Brian on to the question of my PhD and the challenge of knowing what to do to get confirmation. As I did so, I raised a question that had puzzled me ever since I first saw the departmental letterhead, which listed the titles and degrees of the department's professors: I said that I had noticed that he had taken an MLitt in Cambridge rather than a PhD and that I had no idea what an MLitt was. Brian looked very sheepish and said, 'It's a failed PhD.' He then explained that his thesis had been a study of the economic history of the Northamptonshire town of Kettering from 1850 to 1914 and that his examiners felt that it should have included a model of industrial transformation, given that his focus was on how Kettering became a major producer of boots and shoes. I looked at his dissertation in the University Library on my next trip to Cambridge: it was a meticulous piece of economic history research, with an implicitly Marshallian feel, but there was indeed no explicit model being used as an organizing framework.

Many years later, Brian told me more about his Cambridge experience. This was during an interview he gave me to help Sheila Dow and I put together the introductions to the pair of volumes that we edited in his honour (Dow and Earl, eds, 1999a, 1999b). He said that he had chosen to do a thesis on economic history because he felt he did not know how to do one in economics. He then had a succession of supervisors, all of whom must have failed to push the idea that an economic history thesis should have strong and explicit economic underpinnings. Given that two of the three supervisors that he named were economists (Austin Robinson and Kenneth Berrill), this is surprising. His experience of life as a research student in Cambridge does not sound like a very promising basis from which he could develop the skills necessary in the role of a PhD supervisor (for a more detailed examination of Loasby's career and lessons that can be drawn from it, see Cañibano, Earl and Muñoz, 2025).

Inexperienced supervisors in the system that I faced in Cambridge were little better placed than their students when it came to construing what the latter needed to deliver. As noted earlier, in contrast to a best-practice modern PhD management system, those who administered the Cambridge system provided little initial guidance. Given this, supervisors should have been offering advice about what needed to be done or, at least, warnings if key things were not being done. However, supervisors were not involved in their students' confirmation or thesis examination processes. With these processes being conducted behind closed doors by third parties, the Cambridge system was admirably insulated from any pressure that supervisors might want to exert. However, this made it very hard to learn how the game was played and advise students accordingly. Moreover, because the system entailed having only one supervisor per student, rather than a team of supervisors or advisors, it was not possible for inexperienced supervisor to learn, rather like an apprentice, from an experienced team member how the game worked and how to offer effective supervision. It would have been especially difficult for an external supervisor to obtain intelligence about what was expected of students.

The best hope for being able to infer the rules of the game seemed to come from looking at successful PhDs that had been published as monographs. I probably should have looked more closely at more of these than I did, but Brian did not suggest in any comments or conversations that I should do this – though he did encourage me to read the PhD by Juli Irving (1978) on P. W. S. Andrews that he been given by A. W. (Bob) Coats, one of its examiners. A deterrent to investing time in trying to infer from past PhDs what would tick the right boxes was the fact that the Cambridge PhDs that were published as DAE monographs did not look like role models for mine, as they tended to be dominated by empirical work.

4.6   SUBMISSION AND ORAL EXAMINATION

The short window between the confirmation of my candidature and the date by which I needed to submit the finished dissertation did not seem to me to be a problem, even allowing for several weeks of exam marking, a few weeks of vacation, and a week or two for getting the copies bound and delivered, for what I intended to submit was essentially ready to go aside from some editing and splicing. By the time of my oral examination, its ingredients were 'in press' as accepted publications: *The Economic Imagination* had been refereed for Wheatsheaf Books by Mark Blaug and Stephen Littlechild, and endorsed by Shackle, and Eichner had confirmed that he had got a contract for the book that he had built around my paper. Given that economists of some note had liked my work, there was potential for me to be over-confident about my chances. However, I was mindful that a doctoral thesis is assessed in terms of different criteria from those used for monographs and chapters in edited books. The trouble was, I still did not know which criteria my examiners might use, to assess whether my work was a sufficiently big contribution to knowledge to be worth a doctoral degree from the University of

Cambridge. It really was a case of wondering 'What could possibly go wrong?'

My oral examination in November 1982 was held at the Master's Lodge, Clare College, as my internal examiner was R. C. O. (Robin) Matthews, who was the Master of Clare as well as Professor of Political Economy. Geoff Meeks told me that Matthews seemed a good fit for the task since he was 'getting into institutional economics.' I had been to the Master's Lodge at Clare once before, to a function that Matthews held to celebrate James Meade's success in being awarded the 1977 Nobel Prise in Economic Sciences. Otherwise, my only interaction with Matthews was when he contacted me because of my reputation as an undergraduate supervisor (all eighteen months of it!) to see whether I would be willing to take on a Clare student whom he felt was at risk of failing Part II due to over-indulging in student politics. He was probably impressed by what I did after taking on the task, for the student in question ended up with a lower-second. But I had no idea how my research would fare with him. Had I realised that Matthews was, with Hahn, engaged in making Cambridge economics more orthodox, I would have been very nervous indeed.

My external examiner was Professor John Pickering of the University of Manchester Institute of Science and Technology. He was one of very few suggestions that I had offered to Geoff Meeks about someone who might be right for the role. Pickering was a man of high integrity whose career (as his Wikipedia entry explains at some length) was later blighted by what happened when he acted as a whistle-blower against the Vice-Chancellor of the University of Portsmouth while serving as the latter's deputy. He was the only British economist that I could think of who was familiar with behavioural approaches to the firm as well as being interested in consumer behaviour. In the latter context, his work focused on the demand for consumer durables with a Katona-like emphasis on the role of consumer sentiment. However, although I had suggested Pickering, the thesis that I had submitted without knowing he would be my external examiner was not one that set out to cultivate his approval. It had two Pickering-related issues that had potential to have the reverse effect. One was that in my chapter on economists' choices I had critically commented on Pickering's (1976) contention that Andrews and Brunner's view of pricing was not 'sufficiently general' in terms of the industries to which it might be applied. The other was that although my awareness of Pickering's work on consumer behaviour came from seeing a review of his book *The Acquisition of Consumer Durables: A Cross-Sectional Investigation* (Pickering, 1977), I had forgotten to check it out and see how it related to my thesis. Although I doubt that either Pickering-related issue was decisive, my advice to PhD students has always been to take careful account of the work of those that one nominates as potential examiners, and to be very careful not to get on the wrong side of them by challenging their work: not all academics will have the kind of integrity for which Pickering came to be known.

The hour-long grilling that Matthews and Pickering dispensed was very disconcerting, for they raised no issues about my original contributions; indeed, they barely commented on what I offered. Instead, it seemed as if all they were checking was my awareness of what they viewed as classic non-mainstream contributions on consumer behaviour that might relate to what I was offering. These included Houthakker and Taylor (1970) (which I knew about from Ajit Singh mentioning it in my first Prelims supervision – in relation to the great importance of income effects relative to substitution effects as drivers of changes in the pattern of demand – but which I had never read) and the British market research pioneer Harry Henry's (1958) critique of linear demand functions. In asking about possible similarities between Andrews' methods and those of Wesley Clair Mitchell, Matthews provided evidence of his research direction that was consistent with what Geoff Meeks had said but also exposed a gap in my knowledge. My examiners thereby found my Achilles' heel: a lack of due diligence in developing my knowledge of the literature relevant to the thesis I had ended up submitting, a thesis on a very different topic from the areas on which I had read prodigiously and with scholarly determination in my first two years as a research student. I made no attempt to feign knowledge that I did not possess and eventually left Matthews's study without a strong sense of what the outcome would be.

4.7   REVISE AND RESUBMIT

Modern-day doctoral candidates are usually advised, at least informally, of the outcome of their thesis examination process on the day of their oral examination or within a few days of it. Detailed examiners' reports that include specific suggestions of any changes that should be made follow within a couple of weeks. In my case, by contrast, over two months passed before I received notification from Dr N. J. B. A. Branson, the Secretary of the Board of Graduate Studies in a form letter dated 1 February 1983. The letter explained that the Board had decided not to award me a PhD but to allow me to choose between revising and resubmitting my dissertation by 1 January 1985 or not doing that and instead being awarded the degree of MSc forthwith. The letter did not include any reports from my examiners to indicate the basis for the decision, but it informed me that if I replied to confirm that I was going to revise and resubmit, or that I was having difficulty deciding whether to do so, then my examiners would be contacted to ascertain which sections of their reports should be provided to me (though they would be sent to my supervisor) to assist me with the revision or my decision about whether to revise my dissertation. The letter then informed me, rather ominously, that I should not assume that I would be granted a PhD if I revised my dissertation along the lines suggested in the extracts from the examiners' reports, for a fresh examination process would begin when I resubmitted my dissertation and it would not necessarily involve the same examiners. The letter thus left me completely unclear about how much revision I might need to do and what my chances of success might be if I submitted a revised version of my dissertation. Yet it was clear that I needed to revise and resubmit, for as Neil Kay had said a year earlier, a PhD was my 'travel ticket'.

Finding out what the examiners thought of my work was not something that I needed to do with urgency. This was not merely because of the generous resubmission deadline but also because I knew that I was not going to be able to start work on the revision until the middle of the year. This was because I was about to begin my first sabbatical, the goal of which was to write *The Corporate Imagination*, which Edward Elgar had commissioned for Wheatsheaf Books in January 1982, only seven weeks after commissioning *The Economic Imagination*. At the time that the contract was drawn up, the plan was for me to deliver it at the end of the sabbatical that I expected to get, and I was determined to stick to this plan.

A week after the notification letter from Branson, I received a more positively worded letter from Geoff Meeks, dated 8 February 1983. In contrast to the bureaucratic tone of the one from the Board of Graduate Studies, Geoff's letter showed concern about the impact such news might have on the morale of a research student. It read as follows:

Dear Peter,

I am sorry that your PhD was not completely straightforward. But I can confirm that both examiners said that you should be encouraged to resubmit and that the extra work should not be enormous. They also said many enthusiastic things.

They make the following suggestions:

'The things we should like to see are as follows. In the first place, more thorough treatment should be incorporated of the relevant empirical findings in the literature; this could be done either by means of a new chapter or by making insertions at appropriate places in the text. In the second place, a new chapter should be added giving a synoptic view of the theory of consumers' choice which the author is putting forward. In addition to these changes, the author will no doubt himself wish to make a number of alterations in the light of the evolution of his own thought.'

The examiners would also be willing for you to consult them informally if you need further clarification.

Although the resubmission is a minor inconvenience, therefore, there is no reason to be depressed about it.

With best wishes,

Yours sincerely,

G. Meeks

The examiners' request in relation to relevant empirical literature were not at all surprising, given what had happened in the oral examination, and I realised that a synoptic chapter would be a good means for demonstrating my interpretation of my contribution to knowledge. It would also provide a means for ensuring that my examiners 'got' what I had done. Seen thus, the examiners' two specific requests did indeed not look particularly onerous, so long as I could find a way of liberating space to implement them without breaching the 80,000-word constraint into which I had shoehorned the original thesis. However, about six weeks later, when the extracts from the examiners' reports arrived, I inferred that I would be wise to do a quite major rewrite and try to extract further economic implications from the clinical psychology perspectives that I had used. This seemed particularly necessary from the report of 'Examiner A', whom I inferred to be Pickering – both from the greater length of his report (of which I was sent more than four pages) and from him saying that he felt the structure of the arguments needed to be clearer to be readily grasped, for he had found the writing challenging despite the fact that he, 'at least, [had] considerable sympathy [with the behavioural approach].' In the extracts that I was sent, my examiners essentially described what I had done or had failed to do; they gave me little sense of whether they thought my departures from mainstream thinking were significant and had potential for empirical applications. I therefore felt I should find ways of developing my contribution in case they had not really warmed to what I was saying.

While working on *The Corporate Imagination*, I had many ideas about how I could improve my analysis and began to envisage what I wrote as *Lifestyle Economics* (Earl, 1986b) a couple of years later (see Section 6.4). With *The Corporate Imagination* finished on schedule, I began what I intended to be a major revision of my original dissertation. If I removed the chapter on the behaviour of economists (a shorter version of which was now available in published form as Earl, 1983b), it would give me enough space to incorporate my new theoretical ideas and demonstrate their policy implications, as well as for adding the synoptic chapter and covering the literature that I had failed to review in the original version.

After I had been working on the revision for about three months, I was confident that I was writing a much more mature and carefully considered work than *The Economic Imagination*, whose subtitle *Towards a Behavioural Analysis of Choice* now seemed to have personal connotations, especially via its first word. But I then had to go down to Cambridge for an offshore interview for a job that I had applied for at the University of Tasmania (see Section 5.7). Naturally, I called in to see Geoff Meeks to assure him that I was well into the revision. When I told him that I was building in many new ideas that greatly improved my analysis, he almost seemed to levitate from his chair with alarm. He said, 'No, don't do this; they might not like the new material. All you really need to do is add a standard literature review chapter at the front and a conventional summary and conclusions chapter at the end. That's all they wanted; they liked your original work!' So, *that* was what he had been trying to convey in his letter of 8 February 1983, whereas I had thought I needed to do more, to be on the safe side, because of what I had read in the extracts in the examiners' reports.

As a result of this chain of events, the revised dissertation ended up as a kind of half-way house between *The Economic Imagination* and *Lifestyle Economics*. I told Geoff that one of the things I really wanted to include in the revision was a section in which I critically discussed text from motoring magazines in which the motoring journalists gave their summary rankings in multi-vehicle test reports. This was not merely an unusual empirical technique; it also provided a way of showing how non-compensatory decision heuristics could sometimes be readily identified as being used in practice. Geoff encouraged me first to write to Robin Matthews about this idea to see whether he approved of it. I did so on 14 November 1983; three days later, Matthews replied, encouraging ment to proceed on this basis, and to remove the chapter on economists' behaviour.

In the end, it was fortuitous that I switched to the more modest revision plan, for early in January 1984 I accepted the job that, following the interview, I had been offered at the University of Tasmania, with a starting date in early June. To give the examiners time to read the revised dissertation and, if necessary, also to run a further oral examination, I estimated that I needed to be ready to submit the revision around mid-March. On the morning that I accepted the Tasmanian job, it was snowing heavily in Stirling, so staff were advised to head home. Given the deadline that I now faced, I asked if I could take with me the departmental IBM golf-ball electric typewriter that I had been using. In the past, academic staff had not enjoyed a personal typewriter such as this, but I had been able to purloin it a few months earlier when word processors had been provided to more of the office staff. The weight of the typewriter made the journey out to my car rather hair-raising, as conditions had become very slippery by the time I set off into the snow.

I completed the revised dissertation on schedule and sent it to Cambridge on 20 March 1984. Soon after, my teaching timetable enabled me to take a few days' leave during which I visited music stores in London and Cambridge in search of a guitar that would serve as a suitable reward-to-self at the end of the PhD ordeal. In normal circumstances, I would have waited until I knew the outcome before doing this, but I was only a few weeks from having my possessions shipped to Hobart and I knew that guitars were much more expensive in

Australia due to import tariffs. In London, I decided to walk from Kings Cross station to the guitar stores in the Charing Cross Road area (an obvious retailing example of a Marshallian business district) via the LSE bookstore.

One of the books that I bought there was a heavily discounted copy of Pickering's (1977) *Acquisition of Consumer Durables*. I did not need it for the revised dissertation, as a library copy had already served me for that purpose, but it was a fitting memento for the end of the PhD saga. Given what happened in the examination of my thesis, readers who are familiar with Clive James's famous poem 'The Book of My Enemy Has Been Remaindered' may think it could provide a model for the kind of thoughts that were going through my head at the time I bought Pickering's book. Had I been buying the book a year or so earlier, such a conjecture might have been well-aimed. However, having gone through the revision process, I had a much more mature perspective and fully appreciated the earlier verdict. The residual frustrations that I felt concerned the paucity of advice and limited feedback that I had received along the way. A few weeks after I arrived in Tasmania, I received a letter in which Sheila Dow sent her congratulations, saying that she had heard via Geoff Harcourt that the revised dissertation had passed. A couple of weeks after that, I received the news formally from the ever-leisurely Board of Graduate Studies.

4.8 POSTSCRIPT

In the UK summer of 1987, I was a participant at the first Malvern Political Economy Conference. Geoff Harcourt was there, too, and during one of the breaks he found an opportunity to congratulate me privately on my post-PhD book *Lifestyle Economics*. He also told me about the just-published review of it in which John Hey (1987) commented very favourably on the progress that I had made in the three years since *The Economic Imagination* had appeared. Geoff then offered a one-line comment that seemed to pin down my academic character succinctly: he said that I was resistant to the disciplinary efforts of others but had enormous self-discipline, and that was how I had in the end gained my PhD and produced my new book. As should be clear from the present book, I certainly have a determination to do things 'my way' and a capacity to keep going when this makes progress difficult. However, I think that because Geoff became a player in my PhD saga when it was already well advanced, he may have misunderstood why the saga was happening. The root cause was not that I had a rigid idea of the dissertation that I wanted to write, for although my four proposals had areas of intersection, they had very major differences. Rather, the problem was that I had been feeling my way in the dark, with little counselling or feedback, trying to figure out what might work.

5 University of Stirling, Scotland, 1979–1984

5.1   INTRODUCTION

The University of Stirling (hereafter usually abbreviated to 'Stirling') was established in 1967, the last 'new university' of the group established following the publication in 1963 of the Report of the Committee on Higher Education. The chair of this committee was Lord (Lionel) Robbins (1898–1984), well known to economists for his work at the LSE. Robbins became the first Chancellor of the University of Stirling. The campus is one of the most beautiful in the UK, despite its buildings having been constructed cheaply from concrete, for it is located at the foot of the Ochil Hills on the estate of Airthrey Castle, a grand country house designed by the renowned architect Robert Adam. Airthrey Castle (built 1790–1791) overlooks the eastern end of a small loch, across which a bridge was built to link the students' halls of residence on the north side with the main academic buildings on the south side.

In mid-1979, when I started working at Stirling, it was a very small university, with little more than 3000 students, whereas today it claims to have around 14,000. Soon after I arrived, I was told that its ability to attract students was still being hampered by the reputational impact of the small but rowdy demonstration that had taken place during the visit of Queen Elizabeth II on 13 October 1972. A colleague showed me a copy of the cover of the satirical magazine *Private Eye* that appeared soon after. The main caption was 'Stirling Crisis', and four speech balloons had been added to a photograph of the event, in which one of the protesters was swilling from a bottle of alcohol. Two of the speech balloons depicted HM The Queen as asking, 'Who is this?' and being told, 'He's a pissed graduate, ma'am', with the other two raising the question, 'What's he studying?' and offering the answer, 'Meths'. A consequence of the reputational damage was said to be that Stirling was recruiting proportionately more students from England relative to other Scottish universities.

The early growth of Stirling's economics department had been overseen by Professor Andrew Bain when he was only in his thirties. I had first become aware of him via his Cambridge PhD-based book on the growth of TV ownership in the UK (Bain, 1964), but he is better known for his subsequent work on the financial system. However, Bain had moved to the University of Strathclyde in 1977 after a major falling out with his successor as head of department, Professor C. V. (Chuck) Brown, a very orthodox American microeconomist who specialised in public sector economics. When I arrived, Chuck was running a major project that aimed to discover, for the UK Treasury, the short-run elasticity of supply of labour. The project's timing was unfortunate, for although Margaret Thatcher's Conservative Government would have been interested to know the impact that cuts to income taxes might have on the supply of labour, its monetarist policies soon generated unemployment on such a scale that survey respondents saw little hope for working more in response to tax cuts.

Externally funded research projects were rare at that time. Unlike today, there was little publicity for annual competitive grant application rounds or pressure to apply within them. Aside from Chuck Brown, the only member of the department I was aware of who held a research grant was David King, a specialist in fiscal federalism who had done his undergraduate degree at Oxford and his DPhil at York. Prior to coming to Stirling, he had taught A-Level Economics at Winchester College, one of the UK's most prestigious 'public' schools. Like Sheila Dow, who joined the department a few months after me, David spent the rest of his career at Stirling and was eventually promoted to a personal chair.

The department that entered the 1980s was very different from a modern economics department in many other ways. It was Oxbridge-dominated. My arrival brought the number of Cambridge-educated staff back up to seven. Of these, only two had doctorates: Paul Hare, who became a pioneer of transition economics, had an Oxford DPhil, and Robin Ruffell, the econometric brains for Chuck's project, had a PhD from Bristol. Moreover, aside from Chuck, there was only one other American, George Evans, whose list of degrees included not merely degrees in mathematics and statistics from Berkeley but also an Oxford BA in Politics, Philosophy and Economics. All the other academic staff, except for Dipak Ghosh (who had a master's from Birmingham), were British. There were around 20 academic staff, four research staff, a secretary, and several typists. There were no casual staff and, aside from Dipak Ghosh, who had started his PhD after commencing as a lecturer, there was just one PhD student (who was from Greece and close to completion). Unlike a typical modern department, about two-thirds of its academic staff only held lecturer (assistant professor) positions, and aside from Chuck Brown, the only other professor was Brian Loasby, who had a personal chair in management economics. Then aged 49, Brian was the oldest member of the department.

The large percentage of lecturer-level staff had much to do with the fact that nine of us were at various stages of working on our doctorates: George Evans and his wife Pauline Andrews (whose undergraduate training was also at Oxford) were in the final stages of finishing Berkeley doctorates, with George's Berkeley thesis being the first one I knew of with the 'three essays' format that is now so popular; Alistair Dow was finishing his University of Manitoba doctorate and Sheila Dow, who had worked previously at the Bank of England and as an economic advisor to the government of Manitoba, was only a year into her Glasgow PhD; Dipak Ghosh was doing his internal Stirling PhD; Peter Bird was finishing the Cambridge PhD that he had been working on five years earlier when I commenced my undergraduate studies; Bob Hamilton, who (like Neil Kay) had been among Stirling's very first undergraduates, was finishing his London Business School PhD, while another Stirling alumnus Charles Normand was working on his York DPhil; and I was at an early stage in the tortuous process outlined in the previous chapter. I was not quite 24 when I arrived and was by far the youngest of the lecturing staff, with Charles, the next youngest, about three years older. Overall, it was a very youthful group of lecturers, most of whom were in the 28–33 age band.

Those were the days in which it was still quite easy to get an entry-level position even if armed merely with a master's degree, and where it was common for PhDs to run for far longer than the three years for which PhD scholarships lasted. Not having a PhD might be problematic if one wanted to work in North America, but it was not catastrophic for an academic career in the UK. Indeed, Richard Shaw and Sue Shaw both did exceptionally well just with Cambridge undergraduate degrees: Richard was a senior lecturer when I started at Stirling, and he went on to become Principal of the University of Paisley (now part of the University of the West of Scotland). His success in moving up to managerial roles was no surprise to me, for during my time at Stirling he had a stint as head of department and provided a great role model of 'management by walking about'. Sue became a professor of marketing and Vice-Principal of the University of Strathclyde.

Two other members of the department enjoyed ongoing academic careers despite not bothering to do PhDs after getting their master's degrees. One was Paul Tompkinson, who joined at the same time as me after working at the University of Tasmania. The first time I met him he said he found Stirling very flat compared with Hobart. His comment surprised me at the time, but it turned out to be well aimed. He left Stirling before I did, for a position at Victoria University in Wellington, New Zealand. The other was Ron Shone, who was promoted to senior lecture in the early 1980s and stayed at Stirling for the rest of his career. Like me, Ron enjoyed writing books, but his commercially most successful books were not on economics and came about because Ron suffered badly from back pain even though he was then only in his mid-30s. (This was, of course, before the health and safety consequences of sitting at one's desk for long periods were recognised and publicised via online training modules on 'workstation safety', and standing desks were nowhere to be seen.) Ron explored using autohypnosis as a means of dealing with his back pain. This led him to write books on autohypnosis and creative visualisation. They were well received and sold well, often via health-food stores. The cover of the first one (Shone, 1983) listed Ron's academic credentials below his name, without giving any hint that his degrees were in economics.

When I arrived at Stirling, I no longer had a typewriter, having returned to its owner the Adler electric typewriter that I had been minding. Not having a typewriter was not a problem, as the department's office staff were remarkably swift in getting everyone's typing done. Significant revisions were often handled via 'cut and tape' methods, with previously typed materials being held in place not with paste but by 'magic tape' that did not show up on photocopies. Of course, EndNote did not yet exist to speed up the compilation of lists of references, but there was an analogue substitute for it: we wrote citation details for each work on a separate index card and handed the relevant cards, in alphabetical order, to the office staff with our handwritten manuscripts. After the typing had been done, we then slotted the paper's reference cards (back) into our collections of index cards that we maintained in alphabetical order in plastic index card boxes.

From early 1983, word processor computers gradually started to replace the IBM golf-ball electric typewriters that the office staff had used, and it was one of the latter that I was able to purloin for working on the final version of my PhD. Fortunately, the long list of references was word processed for me by one of the office staff. During the transition, it was important to know whether one's work had been typed or word-processed: writing corrections on a typed document was not a good way to endear oneself to the office staff, as they would then have trouble implementing corrections without major retyping, in sharp contrast to the case with word-processed documents.

Almost all the academic departments were in the long Cottrell Building, which snakes along the slopes near the southern side of the loch. The Cottrell Building actually consists of two long parallel buildings on several levels, with short linking corridors between them. The short corridors contain the stairwells, a few offices, and toilet facilities. In the men's toilet closest to Economics, someone had written 'Sociology Degrees – Please Take One' on the paper towel dispenser. Economics was located on the third level on the outer building, so none of us had a view of the loch or the Ochil Hills. My first office looked out to offices in the inner building and to the narrow courtyard between the inner and outer buildings, but after I had worked there a couple of years several of us had to relocate to the other end of the department to enable more offices to be allocated to Psychology. Our relocation was made possible by staff in Sociology moving further along the building in a similar way. I never discovered what happened at the far end of the building, or how far back towards the other end the relocation process had started.

As I settled into having, for the first time, an office of my own, I went through much the same experience that Mark Casson (2006) has reported having had at the start of his career: I had the same allocation of bookshelves as my older colleagues, but my collection covered barely one of the metal shelves. The empty shelves were not conducive to feeling that I was in the same league as the others when it came to scholarly wisdom. This did not take me down the track of obsessive book collecting that it took Casson (who ended up with over 30,000 economics and economic history books), but by the time I left for Tasmania, I was quite a few shelves into having my own 'wall of books'. However, my collection of books was not yet at the stage where students who came into my office would ask, 'Have you read *all* these books?' with a look of disbelief and a lack of appreciation of the benefits of having instant access to one's own reference library. Nor was it a weighty enough collection to cause the hanging fasteners of its shelves to break free from the concrete-block wall and spill the books on to the floor, as had happened with part of Paul Hare's impressive collection during my interview trip to Stirling. But by the time I left Stirling, my office library was already a much bigger collection than one commonly sees nowadays in the offices of orthodox economists who rarely read anything except journal articles. It included a set of Kaldor's books that I had hoped one day to use, in conjunction with my notes on his lectures for Part II of the Cambridge Tripos, in writing a book on Kaldor's economics. However, three years after I left Stirling, when I was at last in a position to work on this project, Richardson's competitive investment problem reared its head once again: I discovered that, in a just-released book, Thirlwall (1987) had got there first. I felt relieved that I kept a watchful eye on publishers' catalogues, though Thirlwall's book proved not to be definitive: see, for example, King (2008).

Having an office also meant that, for the first time, I had a phone. However, the idea of receiving social calls while at work was nowhere in my mind when I answered an early caller to my office, who said, 'It's Jill here.' Having not yet met anyone called Jill at Stirling, I asked, 'Jill who?' The response, 'Your sister', had the tone of someone who felt disappointed to have been forgotten. Using my office phone externally, even for local calls, required going through the switchboard, whose operators were prone to refuse to connect calls if they suspected the calls were for personal reasons, such as in connection with having one's car serviced or booking a medical appointment. For such calls, one often had to traipse over to a public phone near the entrance to the library.

My original office was close to a kink in the corridor where the departmental coffee room and meeting room were located. The latter was normally the venue for weekly seminars by visiting speakers and for lunchtime workshops by members of the department, all of which were normally attended by virtually all the academic staff no matter what the topic was. Unlike today, when economics and econometrics seminars in very large departments may have topics so specialised that very few understand the seminar flier or care about the topic, seminars at Stirling were invariably accessible to a wide audience. Most of the speakers were well-known, senior figures. Several of us tried to run as many of our tutorials as possible on the day of the seminars, with the seminar providing an interesting break after a morning of tutorials, before we held our final tutorials later in the afternoon. For some reason, the seminar venue was changed one semester to a south facing tutorial room that was not well ventilated and received a lot of afternoon sun. This was a bad move for those of us who were not at our best in the couple of hours following lunch, for the room was one in which it proved very hard to keep awake even during an interesting presentation. When Michael Artis was the guest speaker, he had to contend with multiple members of the audience nodding off at various times, myself included.

5.2   TEACHING

When I went into the interview for the job at Stirling, I had no knowledge of its teaching system, for I had not sought to gather information about it at the social event that was held for candidates the previous evening and it did not occur to me that I might be wise to go into the library and look at a list of economic subjects and the rules of degree structures in the University Calendar. So, when Chuck Brown asked me during the interview how I would go about teaching a second-year macroeconomics subject, I confessed my ignorance of the programme and asked what the students would have covered in the first year. Having been told to assume they had experienced a standard course built around the top-selling texts by Lipsey or Samuelson, I had a ready answer. I said, 'In that case, I'd be inclined to start again from scratch.' Clearly, it was not the answer that Chuck expected, for he had the look of a stunned mullet when he asked me why I had given that answer. The atmosphere of the interview became more relaxed as I said that I thought that the standard income–expenditure model failed to capture much that I had picked up from Keynes's *General Theory* and that, like Leijonhufvud (1968), I drew a big distinction between what was taught as Keynesian economics and what Keynes was trying to convey – though I did not think Leijonhufvud had got the latter completely right, either. Although I got the job despite my flippant approach, I was never asked at Stirling to lecture on second-year macroeconomic theory. The only macroeconomics lecturing that came my way was in a new subject on how countries differed in their approaches to macroeconomic policy. This was towards the end of my time at Stirling, and the unit was part of a new degree programme in public policy that was one of Chuck's pet projects.

The next clue about how teaching worked came when I obtained the keys to my office and found that there was a stack of six chairs in the corner near the door. This was a sign that tutorials were often conducted by lecturers in their offices, rather than in tutorial rooms. Stirling would be my final university at which this was the norm. First-year tutorials were the usual exception, being held in groups of about ten in classrooms, but otherwise tutorials commonly consisted of groups of six students, sometimes on an alternating fortnightly basis. It was thus a system in which it was possible to get to know the students quite well, as in Cambridge. This was much more difficult where I worked in my post-Stirling career, especially as tutorial sises grew from 12 to 25 as the years went by. I can still picture and remember the names of many of my Stirling students.

Stirling was unusual among UK universities in the 1970s in conducting teaching in a pair of 12-week semesters rather than three, nine-week terms, and each subject ran for a single semester. However, unlike the semester-based systems that I later experienced Down Under, the standard load did not consist of four subjects per semester. A three-year 'general' (non-honours) degree consisted of only 15 subjects, with the division between 'general' and 'honours' students taking place at the end of the third semester, at which point students would have completed their eight-subject Part 1. The honours stream was a four-year programme that included a dissertation. Unlike the Australian and New Zealand systems, students taking Scottish honours degrees only graduated once, rather than graduating after three years and then taking the honours year, if they met the entry qualifications, as a separate degree. Because Scottish high schools typically did not follow the English A-Level system, the Scottish students often started their studies, like their counterparts Down Under, aged only 17, so the students that came to Stirling via the A-Level system were typically more mature than their local counterparts.

There is a lot that today's universities could learn from the 1970s Stirling system. Having fewer units per semester (three rather than four) and having some semesters where only a couple of units needed to be taken had benefits for both staff and students. It reduced the teaching load for staff while making smaller tutorial sises possible. It left the students with more time to read and made it easier for them to find time to play active roles in extra-curricular activities on campus and to catch up if they had to re-sit a subject. To some extent, we might view the Stirling system as closer to the Cambridge system that I experienced than to a modern semester-based system: in my three undergraduate years in Cambridge, I was required to take 15 papers, rather than the 24 that had to be taken by the students I taught after leaving Stirling. Moreover, as in Cambridge, final exam scripts were usually double-marked and external examiners (one of whom was Professor Mark Blaug) played an active role. In universities Down Under, both these quality assurance mechanisms seemed to be reserved for dissertations, with the latter only being used for PhDs.

However, a striking feature that set Stirling apart from the other four universities covered in this book was that no graduate students, full-time tutors, or sessional staff were involved in the teaching of economics. Except for a few first-year tutorial groups that were taken by full-time research assistants, all the tutorials were conducted by the lecturing staff. With subjects that had high enrolments, other lecturers shared with the subjects' lecturers the running of tutorials. Indeed, Brian Loasby once explained to me that in the early days at Stirling there had been an attempt to offer a compulsory subject to all first-year students across all disciplines, for which all staff from all disciplines were required to run tutorials. It was intended as a kind of bonding process where students learned about the thinking skills they would need, and the kinds of issues they would encounter regardless of their discipline. The textbook was written by Frank Bradbury (1969), who was still active as an emeritus professor of management by the time I joined the staff. The book was called *Words and Numbers: A Student's Guide to Intellectual Method*. Brian had a great respect for Frank Bradbury and obviously liked the concept, and so do I. However, he said that the subject had been abandoned due to resistance from staff, not from students.

Tutoring for subjects on which one did not lecture was very good preparation for serving as an examiner for those subjects, but it also was a means by which one could move into the lecturer role with minimal additional costs in tooling up. My approach to learning how the subjects on which I was tutoring were being presented was to attend the lectures and take notes, with these notes being the starting point for my own lecture notes if I inherited the subject. In the case of Brian Loasby's sixth-semester honours unit on the theory of the firm, I was able simply to walk in and deliver the subject just as Brian had delivered it, without writing a fresh set of notes from which to lecture.

On paper, the teaching load at Stirling was far heavier than in the universities at which I subsequently worked. Typically, I had 84 or 96 contact hours per semester. This usually comprised three or four lectures and four or five tutorials per week, though in my first year, much to my disappointment, I was given no lectures and was simply required to conduct six tutorials each week. The latter was by way of complying with a request from Cambridge that I should not be loaded up unduly as I was only in my third year of my PhD. However, even once I had a regular load, the amount of marking was limited by the tutorial sises, and I never felt the kind of stresses I felt toward the end of my career when I had to tool up for an unfamiliar subject on which I had not tutored. I never found it necessary to resort to teaching from a single textbook, one chapter per week, in the style that has become common. Thus, when I taught British Economic History Since 1939, I found there was plenty of time to research the subject with fresh reading, such as on the economics of wartime Britain, through to classic contributions on macroeconomic management in the UK, and recently published books on the de-industrialisation process. Despite my lack of experience, I was able to lecture with the confidence that I knew, from personal research, what I was talking about; I was not operating as a franchisee of a big textbook publisher.

The Writing of 'Money Matters: A Keynesian Approach to Monetary Economics' (Dow and Earl, 1982)

My first two sets of lecturing tasks, in the autumn 1980 semester, both involved team-teaching work. One was to share, with Sue Shaw, the teaching of Principles of Marketing. The other was to teach a master's-level subject on monetary economics with Sheila Dow. The latter task was somewhat unusual: we knew it was the last time that the subject was being offered, as it was part of a programme that was being discontinued, and there was going to be just one student. This put us in a situation rather like that of modern-day sessional teaching staff who have no sense of long-term ownership of the subjects that they teach and are not properly reimbursed for the hours of preparation that they put in: the incentive to make a serious investment in writing lectures did not seem strong. One way of dealing with the situation would have been to operate the subject by setting reading assignments for the sole student, but we did not take that route. On hearing of the status of the subject, I had an idea for how we might get a good return on investing in teaching it just once: we should write it up as a book while teaching it.

When I put the idea to Sheila, she was initially not enthusiastic about it, fearing it would get in the way of finishing her PhD. But I persisted, saying that if she gave the first block of lectures, I would be able to write near-verbatim lecture notes from them, which she could turn into chapters while I was writing and presenting my half of the material, before she returned to deliver the closing lectures, on which I would once again take near-verbatim notes. If all went according to my scenario, we would be able to have a complete manuscript ready to send to a publisher before we were very far into 1981. Today, it might seem like a vision based on misguided youthful exuberance, but back then we were not going to be chewing up our time by fussing over PowerPoint slides. We already felt we knew what we wanted to say, and so long as my handwriting turned out to be sufficiently legible, Sheila's lectures could be based, as lectures then often were, on quite skeletal notes. Sheila agreed to see if we could make it happen. She has reminded me that, at the end of the course, we asked the sole student how he had found it; he replied that he would have liked it to have been more mathematical!

Around the start of that semester, Philip Allan, the owner of an independent publisher of economics books, paid his annual visit to Stirling. When he came to my office, I mentioned to him that Sheila and I were thinking of writing a book on monetary economics. He indicated that he would be interested to look at the manuscript if it materialised, and I thought that his firm would be an interesting one to approach first as he worked closely with the well-known monetary economist David Laidler. If we could write our Keynesian view of monetary economics in a sufficiently pluralistic way to satisfy Laidler, that would be a good achievement, but even if Laidler did not like it, we might get some useful feedback from a monetarist perspective.

Writing the book went pretty much according to the scenario that I had presented to Sheila. Philip Allan was clearly quite surprised that by Easter 1981 we were able to send him a complete manuscript that ran to over 400 double-space pages of typing. For my part, the writing process was aided by two things. One was that the monetarist policies of Margaret Thatcher's government had entailed a sharp rise in mortgage interest rates, which limited my ability to pay to heat my flat as the Scottish winter encroached. Hence, I often spent my evenings in the library, writing chapters/lectures, thereby economising on my heating costs. This often involved eating at non-standard times – such as cooking and eating my evening meal as breakfast – to avoid the cost of dining on campus prior to my evening of writing. The other thing that made it possible to write the chapters so rapidly was, I suspect, that I was writing them by hand rather than word-processing them: I find that word-processing encourages one to engage more in time-consuming experimentation with improvements to sentence construction, whereas the costs of changing what one writes by hand and then has typed by someone else concentrate the mind wonderfully on getting an acceptable exposition at the outset.

Sheila and I were a little surprised by Laidler's reaction to the book, which resulted in it not ending up in Philip Allan's catalogue. I had been especially nervous about how he might react to my attempt to offer a sympathetic a picture of monetarist thinking as I could, before writing a critique of it, but it was the chapter I had written on schools of thought in monetary economics that seemed most to offend him. Laidler declared that he did not think it appropriate to have a chapter of this kind in a book for students, and that economic methodology was something that should be left for discussions in private between consenting adults. We then sent the manuscript to Martin Robertson, whose referees raised no such objections.

The version that was published in the summer of 1982 benefited from minor reworking during the summer of 1981, with chapters 8–16 having been written by me. The only major change was that I axed a chapter on the Friedman–Meiselman hypothesis and used material from it for a case study in the chapter on methodology. But otherwise, the changes were done on the original typed version. As the book was my very first publication, it was especially exciting to see the page proofs as it went through the production process. One major typesetting error was avoided at the last minute: our eyes tend to see what they expect to see, and initially neither of us spotted on the proof for the cover design that Sheila had been typed as Shelia. When I eventually noticed the spelling, I initially wondered whether I had been spelling Sheila incorrectly.

Writing *Money Matters* was a very important early-career experience for me. It gave me the confidence not merely to write other books but to believe that I could write books rapidly. But this came at the cost of me ending up failing to focus on building a portfolio of journal articles by going through the drudgery of accommodating journal referees and editors on every little issue they saw fit to raise. Sheila did not fall into this trap, though by the time I left Stirling she was well into writing her first solo book, *Macroeconomic Thought: A Methodological Approach* (Dow, 1985). Laidler would not have approved of it at all.

Pluralistic Pluralism
Economics students at Stirling received a pluralistic education, though how pluralistic it was depended on whether they went down the honours

track and on how they chose to specialise. Pluralism was evident both within and between subjects.

One way that students could experience pluralism was via their lecturers tutoring on each other's subjects, for this could work more like the college-based Cambridge system than a typical modern-day franchise system where the tutors – typically postgraduate students – and the lecturer are working through a textbook, aided by accompanying instructors' resources. David King was the main first-year lecturer, and he offered a mainstream coverage, privately lamenting how little he could cover compared with what he had taught to his A-Level students at Winchester. However, that did not stop me from providing a more pluralistic experience to the first-year students that I tutored. At the micro level, I used ideas from P. W. S. Andrews to try to ensure that conventional price theory did not go unchallenged. (An example of this is provided in Section 7.2 when I discuss in depth the challenges of teaching in a pluralistic manner.) At the macro level, I offered an extra tutorial to anyone from my tutorial groups who wanted to learn the economics of Keynes rather than the simplified textbook version of Keynesian economics. Though there was no obligation to attend, and no expectation that what I covered would be 'examinable', I regularly had an office full of students to whom I presented my interpretation of a chapter or two of Keynes's *General Theory* each week. The students received summary handouts typed by the office staff. I eventually turned the handouts into an A4-size booklet (Earl, 1981), a batch of which was printed for sale in the campus bookstore.

Secondly, pluralism was achieved by having more than one lecturer in a subject. The most significant case of this was the third-semester unit on intermediate microeconomics, where Chuck Brown presented a thoroughly orthodox treatment, with a focus on income and substitution effects, in the first half, and Alistair Dow presented a more institutional approach, with a focus on the work of Galbraith, in the second half. I inherited Alistair's half and retained much of what he had been covering (especially the material on Galbraith) but introduced a behavioural critique of neoclassical microeconomics, especially in relation to problems of uncertainty and information. Chuck was not happy to see the latter on the draft subject outline and tried to get me to remove it. Fortunately, by this time, Richard Shaw was the head of department, and he came to my office with some suggestions on how to change the wording to give Chuck the impression he had got his way, with me then doing rather more covertly pretty much what I had planned.

Toward the end of that semester, I attended a student comedy review at the Macrobert Arts Centre and was fascinated to see one of my students presenting a sketch that satirised the teaching of economics. Colin, the student in question, was the only one I ever taught who came from Bermuda, and he did a hilarious job, supposedly lecturing on decision-making under uncertainty. He seemed to be overlaying a probability distribution diagram with a wider, lower, upside-down version of a Shackle-style potential surprise curve. It gave the impression that he might be trying to reconcile what he had heard in class. The exposition was deliberately too fast to follow seriously, and it was all designed to culminate in a very phallic-looking diagram.

While Sheila Dow was developing her pluralistic approach to macroeconomics and bringing it to the honours students within a single subject, third-year honours microeconomics mainly provided between-subjects pluralism. It began with a more advanced treatment of mainstream theory and applications of it, presented by Ron Shone, but it then continued in the second semester with Brian Loasby's lectures on the evolution of the theory of the firm. However, although Ron had written a highly formal advanced microeconomics textbook before coming to Stirling (Shone, 1975), his lectures came to include non-standard content, such as X-efficiency and learning curves, which he included in a book that he built around this course (see Shone, 1981, applications A6 and A7).

Pluralism was also evident beyond the core units. For example, natural resource and environmental issues were taught in the second year by Alistair Dow and Peter Bird in a much less mainstream way than in the more advanced environmental economics subject taught by Mick Common. This may help explain how the department provided a starting point for ecological economist Clive Spash and environmental economist Nick Hanley, who were both undergraduates there in the early 1980s and returned as members of staff. Stirling's pluralism and openness to interdisciplinary work appears to have rubbed off on Mick Common, too. Mick had 'accidentally' become an academic after starting his career by joining the Merchant Navy rather than going to university (see McKenney *et al.*, 2019). He progressed rapidly and joined the department as a senior lecturer shortly before I arrived. Although he initially seemed very mainstream, he evolved into an ecological economist with an enthusiasm for interdisciplinary teaching and research.

Learning tasks and assessment methods were more diverse than I had experienced in Cambridge. To be sure, essay questions were commonly set for in-semester assessments and final examinations. However, multiple choice questions were introduced to the first-year units in the early 1980s, while open-ended case studies had a major role in the teaching of marketing and management economics. As I taught in both of the latter areas, I had to learn how business case studies were designed, with features such as the inclusion of 'red herrings' to snare the unwary. Sue Shaw and Richard Shaw were key in helping me to get into this way of teaching how theory could be applied, and I found it very exciting. Later, I included a couple of their case studies, with my own notes on how they might be addressed, in my 1995 pluralistic textbook *Microeconomics for Business and Marketing*. Honours students produced dissertations in their final semester, and there did not seem to be a general expectation that their projects should include econometric analysis.

The final dissertation of the few that I supervised was the only one that included any statistical work, and it had potential to yield a journal article. The student in question, Donald Shaw (who was not a relative of Richard and Sue), had carried out a hedonic pricing analysis of the crowded UK market for hi-fi cassette decks by extracting specification data from what I would now view as one of the institutions of this market, a special edition of one of the 'What Hi-Fi?'-style magazines. The fit between actual prices and the prices that Donald's regression analysis predicted, based on the specifications of the cassette decks, was generally very good. The big exceptions came at the thinly populated top end of the market, where the price premia were much greater than those predicted from their superior performance. Donald provided his original data source and all the printouts from his statistical endeavours in case I wanted to build a joint paper out of it. However, all the material lay in my filing cabinet right through to my retirement, provoking guilt each time I came across it. Because my statistical expertise was very rudimentary, I had shied away from the task, even though, as second author, I could have positioned Donald's findings very well in relation to normal cost approaches to pricing and my work on consumers' decision criteria.[7] To make the article happen, I should have enlisted, as a third author, a colleague who had experience in writing up applied economics papers.

My final teaching-related activity at Stirling provided me with a good picture of the range of dissertations that the honours students produced, for I was given the task of being one of the markers for all those that were submitted (aside from Donald's). This was part of the process of ensuring that everyone had a fair share of examination marking, for I needed to leave Stirling before the examination period was finished so that I could start my job in Tasmania at the beginning of the second term in the first week of June. The fact that I had been allocated the task proved to be fortuitous, for I discovered a case of plagiarism that none of my colleagues would probably have spotted. An international student had copied, without attribution, about four pages of the typescript of my in-press book *The Corporate Imagination*, a pre-production version of which I had provided to him and other members of the management economics unit that I had taught that year. I do not know what kind of penalty was imposed on the student following my departure. It was the first of many cases of plagiarism that I uncovered. and was by no means the worst. The most worrying case came a quarter of a century later, when Google helped me rapidly to confirm my suspicions and pin down a University of Wollongong discussion paper from which the bulk of a master's thesis had been copied, an issue that the other examiner completely failed to spot.

5.3   ADMINISTRATION AND SERVICE

There were very few administrative diversions to prevent junior staff at Stirling from getting on with their research. I was given the task of being the departmental representative on the library liaison committee, the

---

[7] Years later, I did get as far as extracting a paper from a statistically based master's thesis. The project in question was by Anders Moe, a Norwegian student, who had attempted to model the Norwegian pop singles charts based on a simple bandwagon model in which the peak chart position of a song was predicted based on the level at which it entered the chart and how far it jumped in the following week. I sent the paper (available from my personal website as Moe and Earl, 2009) to the *Journal of Cultural Economics*, whose referees confirmed what I had suspected: the front end that I had written was well received but the econometrics work was not sophisticated enough to earn it a 'revise and resubmit' verdict.

focus of which was mostly on dealing with cuts in the purchasing power of the library's budget – just at the time that the number of economics journals was starting to grow rapidly with the launch of specialised titles that began to spell the end of the era in which, via routine browsing, one could hope to keep in touch with what was happening in all the major generalist journals as well as all the 'field' journals, if there were any, in one's area of research. Trying to find journals whose subscriptions could be axed was both a depressing and illuminating task. After looking at the list of annual subscription charges for economics journals and reflecting on the interests of my colleagues, I concluded that the *Journal of Economic Theory* should be the prime target for discontinuation: it was a very expensive luxury for a department that had no mathematical economics specialists. By axing it, we could avoid axing several journals that were more likely to be used in departmental research activities. But when I put this suggestion to my colleagues, it turned out that, although it was hard to find any regular users of the *Journal of Economic Theory*, the view was that it was the sort of journal that the library needed to have to signal that Stirling had a serious contingent of economists.

My only other university-level administrative work was a short stint on the committee for academic staff training and development, to help organise and run the annual induction course for new academic staff at Stirling, St Andrews, Dundee, and Heriot-Watt University. Each year, in rotation, one of these four universities hosted the course. Sheila Dow and I had attended the 1979 version of it at the University of Dundee, from which I could remember gleaning rather little to share with the committee.

Three things stuck in my mind from Dundee. One was how the convenor of the course was probably the least inspiring and most monotonous performer I had ever seen. Secondly, I remembered that one of the activities included being videoed while giving a ten-minute 'lecturette' to a small group of one's peers and then discussing the playback of the recording. I think it was via my lecturette that Sheila got to know of the work of George Katona (1960) on the impact of consumer confidence on saving behaviour, which I presented as something that needed to be brought into Post Keynesian economics. Finally, for me, the most memorable of the training sessions at Dundee was one about reading for research. It had been presented by Frank Quinault, an educational psychologist from St Andrews University. Frank argued that one of the skills we would need to develop, and pass to our students, was that of being able to 'gut' books and papers, i.e., to be able to extract the key messages without normally reading our sources in full.

When Stirling ran the course, I contributed a module on the challenges of marking examination scripts. This was built around photocopies of answers that a sample of students had written to a question on problems faced by Soviet planners. Most, if not all, of the participants were not economists but they were soon pleasantly surprised to find that they were nonetheless able to discuss the quality of the answers that I supplied to them. There were major differences in the analytical skills that the sample of students applied when answering the question, even though they had picked up much the same sets of facts and concepts from class.

Within the department, there were usually no administrative demands on my time except for participation at monthly departmental meetings and, on the first day of each semester, discussing enrolment plans with a dozen or so students that I had been assigned to mentor. However, I do remember an unusual minor administrative task that I was given when Nobel Laureate Sir John Hicks (1904–1989) visited Stirling with his wife, fellow economist Lady Ursula Hicks (1896–1985). He had been invited to give the 1981 Robbins Lecture. The Department of Economics wanted to publish Hicks' lecture, which focused mainly on early theories of the trade cycle. However, the referencing in the version he supplied was terribly incomplete. Brian Loasby therefore assigned me the task of getting it into shape, which was not easy in a library that lacked the old original sources. I managed to undertake the task by finding other works on trade cycle theory that had also cited works that Hicks had referenced poorly. Alas, it was the original, not the Stirling version (Hicks, 1981), that Hicks included in one of his collected papers volumes, with all the sloppy incomplete references.

Hicks's delivery of his lecture is memorable, too, but not for the quality of his analysis. The event was a most uncomfortable experience. His presentation was intelligible so long as he read from his paper, but when dealing with questions, he seemed completely unable to assemble sentences that he could finish. I initially thought this was an issue specific to the public speaking context. However, Sheila Dow and I were invited to dine with Sir John and Lady Ursula after the presentation, at the impressive on-campus home of Stirling's Principal, Sir Kenneth Alexander (1922–2001), who was himself an economist and was a former chair of the Highlands and Islands Board. Ursula turned out to be the better one to converse with, whereas Sir John was little better than when he was off script in the lecture. He was amused when I showed him my copy of his book *A Contribution to the Theory of the Trade Cycle* (Hicks, 1950), which I had bought second-hand in a bookshop in York while attending the 1981 conference of the British Association for the Advancement of Science, for it is possibly unique in having been made with the wrong cover – that of Hicks's (1942) *The Social Framework*. Perhaps foolishly, I did not ask him to sign it.

The few external service roles that I played for the department all provided opportunities to foster pluralism by sharing some heterodox thinking with my audiences. They mostly entailed giving presentations (one of which yielded Earl and Dow, 1984) to groups of high-school economics students and/or their teachers, though my very first role in what is now often known as 'engagement' entailed participating in a BBC Radio Scotland discussion programme on economic method, in a series called 'Time to Talk', recorded at the BBC Scotland Kelvingrove studios in Glasgow in March 1980.

None of my research time was chewed up by refereeing papers for journals, whereas in my final two jobs I refereed 5–10 papers and a couple of book proposals and/or competitive research grant applications per year, typically spending a day on each of these tasks. Nor were there any PhDs to examine or books to review. In the 36 years after I worked at Stirling, I prepared 12 PhD examiner reports and reviewed 36 books, with each PhD or review consuming about a week of work. Overall, the absence of such external service tasks left me with about three to four weeks more per year for research than was, on average, available in my post-Stirling career.

5.4   EVOLUTION OF A HETERODOX BEHAVIOURAL ECONOMIST (2)

In my first three years at Stirling, I switched from focusing on industrial and corporate change to focusing on consumer behaviour from what I had come to call a behavioural/Post Keynesian standpoint. My work was 'behavioural' in the sense that it took ideas from the behavioural theory of the firm and blended them with psychological inputs. It was 'Post Keynesian' partly in the sense that it drew on Keynes's views on the significance of confidence and crowd behaviour in a world of uncertainty, as well as on related contributions by scholars that Coddington (1976) had called 'fundamentalist Keynesians'. But I also saw it as something that could help fill a gap that had become evident with the publication of Eichner's (1979) edited volume, *A Guide to Post-Keynesian Economics*, a book that lacked a chapter on consumer behaviour. Given my light teaching load and negligible administrative and service roles in my first year at Stirling, it should not be surprising that the period from July 1979 to August 1980 was the one in which I developed most of the key themes on which I have subsequently built most of my academic work. Indeed, by August 1982, I had already expanded some of them into my first solo book, *The Economic Imagination* (Earl, 1983a). In this section I explain what these key lines of thinking were, how I arrived at them, and opportunities related to them that I failed to grasp during my time working at Stirling.

Going Beyond Reductionism

When I started my lectureship at Stirling in July 1979, I was in the process of considering the implications of two books that I had been reading in my last few weeks in Cambridge. One was *The Innovating Firm*, by Stirling alumnus Neil Kay (1979); the other was *Beyond Reductionism*, a volume edited by Koestler and Smythies (1969) from what was known as the 1968 Alpbach Symposium. I discovered the latter book via a reference that Kay had made to one of its contributors. Kay's book was my first encounter with material on the theory of the firm that accused mainstream approaches of being reductionist and suggested that the way ahead for analysing how firms allocated resources to research and development was to view firms as hierarchical systems.

My first encounter with the concept of reductionism had been via Coddington's (1976) paper in which he used the term 'reconstituted reductionism' to characterise macroeconomists who tried to understand Keynes's insights in terms of models that entailed aggregating the choices of individuals modelled in an orthodox Walrasian manner. This was epitomised by the work of Clower (1965, 1967), who argued that macroeconomic coordination failures could arise due to workers being unwilling to spend if they did not have jobs, and employers being unwilling to hire more workers unless they could see excess demand for current output. On this way of thinking, macroeconomic outcomes are simply aggregates of what people attempt to do at the microeconomic level. To Post Keynesians, however, something more complex needs to be understood: reductionist economists typically succumb to a 'fallacy of composition' error when suggesting that unemployed workers can price themselves into jobs by offering to work for less than current hourly rates. They tend to miss a key ingredient in Keynes's analysis, namely, the idea that workers have a marginal propensity to consume of less than one. This matters in a monetary system because unspent income may simply be held as pre-existing bank deposits rather than cause an equal amount of extra lending to occur. Hence if firms do expand production in response to wage reductions, they may find that they gain less in revenue than they spend on expanding output. To appreciate the latter view, one needs to view the economy as a system of interacting components and be mindful of the operating rules of the institutions that facilitate these interactions: a monetary system works differently from a barter system in ways that go beyond the 'Catch 22'-like issue that Clower identified.

Within a firm, a reductionist approach to resource allocation would view all potential uses of its financial, physical, and human resources as mutually rivalrous, i.e., as substitutable for each other: a dollar not spent on one form of investment could be used in any number of alternative investments, or in alternative advertising strategies, staff training or recruitment programmes, and so on. But from Kay's standpoint, it is misleading to view resource allocation in terms of an all-embracing trade-off. For one thing, it is cognitively too challenging to do this, but there is also the problem of how one compares alternative uses of resources in the presence of radical uncertainty of the kind faced by, say, a pharmaceuticals corporation that must choose which new drugs to try to develop.

As a result, firms allocate resources in a top-down manner that begins by making allocations between broad generic categories and then gradually gets down to more detailed sub-categories. Thus, spending on advertising may be traded off against spending on research and development in general terms to derive budgets for the marketing and research departments, but subsequent choices of how these budgets get deployed do not involve comparisons of specific uses of resources on advertising against specific uses of resources on research and development. Similarly, competing uses of research and development budgets between 'research' and 'development' may be traded off to give separate budgets for these two categories, but once this has been done, specific research projects are not compared with specific development projects. On the way down to signing off specific projects, organisations may follow industry norms and/or apply rules that they have developed by experimentation.[8] In other words, just as firms have hierarchical organisational structures, they also allocate resources to departments and, ultimately, to individuals by hierarchical processes that refer to abstract notions before getting to the level of specific activities and projects.

The 1968 Alpbach Symposium volume opened a wider vista of the world as a system of systems that were usefully to be viewed as functioning holistically, with a focus on how outcomes depend on linkages between component parts. I had been introduced to this idea at high school in the context of biology via some classes on ecology, but I was now being introduced to notions such as systems having 'emergent properties' (for example, life, resilience, or the capacity to fly) that may only be present if specific sets of system elements are present, and the idea that cognitive processes could be based on 'gestalt' configurations. The latter reminded me of the notion of 'jizz' that I had encountered in ornithology.

This was not the kind of thinking that would be conducive to accepting Margaret Thatcher's famous reductionist claim that 'There is no such thing as society.' She was well into her time as prime minister when she made that claim (in an interview published in *Woman's Own*, 31 October 1987). However, in mid-1979 as I studied *Beyond Reductionism*, I had been intrigued to see that Thatcher's guru, Friedrich Hayek had been listed as one of the participants at the Alpbach Symposium. The book did not include a paper by him, leaving me wondering why he would have been there. My only idea was that it had something to do with his view of market systems producing spontaneous order as a kind of emergent phenomenon. (Years later, I had another idea about why Hayek was a participant: see Section 8.4.) However, Marshall's way of viewing the economic system seemed to have more obvious parallels than Hayek's had with anti-reductionist ecological thinking in biology.

---

[8] The allocation of research grants to academics can be viewed similarly, with rules being applied in relation to the track records of grant applicants and grant reviewers, as proxies for the probability that funds will be well spent if allocated to one project rather than another. However, track records in business and academica are not static, so the relative credibility of project advocates and critics will change through time. Two papers that I wrote much later with Jason Potts (Earl and Potts, 2013, 2016) explore the process of allocating resources to individual projects in relation to tidal shifts in the balance of power between 'creatives' and 'bean-counters'.

It gradually became apparent to me that the Marshall-inspired works of P. W. S. Andrews (1949, 1964, and papers by Andrews that were among those later reprinted in Lee and Earl, eds, 1993; Andrews and Brunner, 1951, 1975) that I had been trying to get to grips with for the past couple of years made a lot more sense if one thought about them as an interlinked set that had not been written from a reductionist standpoint. Andrews seemed to think holistically rather than in relation to equalisation at the margin. For example, in analysing investment in the steel sector, Andrews and Brunner (1951) did not present steelmakers as considering great arrays of projects with marginally different capital requirements. Rather, firms would consider very limited sets of specific proposals in terms of their prospective returns on the capital that would be invested in them. They would exclude dominated alternatives, rank the un-dominated projects in order of their respective overall rates of return, and then implement all the projects that seemed to offer a big enough return to cover the rate of interest required to finance them. In other words, an entire project whose *overall* return only just matched the required return would be 'marginal'; there would be no equalisation of the return on a marginal dollar of capital investment with the cost of obtaining a marginal dollar of funding in the way that reductionist thinking would presume.

Likewise, Andrews did not see pricing of manufactured products as entailing the equalisation of marginal costs and marginal revenues, with prices emerging and being adjusted according to the transactional interplay between individual producers and consumers who are all simply looking for the best spot deal at that moment and who would not think twice about dealing with someone else next time. Rather, he assigned major roles to long-term goodwill relationships between suppliers and their customers: he emphasised that customers were often other firms within a supply chain, not end-consumers. The existence of such relationships meant that trading was not about maximizing returns on individual transactions; what counted were the net returns that one enjoyed over the long run, with negative returns on some transactions being the price that was worth paying to achieve greater positive returns on others in the long run. The analysis of pricing therefore should not be reduced to the competitive interplay of those currently demanding and supplying the product in question, for in the long run suppliers would always need to be mindful of the threat of entry by those who are not currently competing for business but have the capacity to start doing so (including one's own colleagues/employees).

In respect of retailing, Andrews's non-reductionist way of thinking led him to focus on the importance of being competitive at the level of the 'basket' (in modern terms, the 'shopping trolley load') of goods that customers typically bought, because shopping was too complex and time-consuming if approached on a reductionist basis with a focus on getting each commodity from the cheapest supplier. He also recognised the structural complexity of purchasing and retailing processes that act to structure or generate demand, such as how the pressure of competition is increased by people's lives entailing mobility (so that having to travel to conduct some kinds of activities provides scope for shopping for other things on route, which limits market power of local suppliers) and how stocks of one kind of product may induce sales of other products to buyers drawn in by the prospect of finding the former product. A similar emphasis on the rich web of relationships that shapes how the competitive process works, including how coordination failures can be avoided, was evident in the work of Richardson (1972) and, much earlier, in Marshall (1890).

While I was reflecting on all this, I started to see that Neil Kay's 'top-down' view of corporate resource allocation could have parallels in terms of the budgeting of resources in households. The evolution of my thinking in that area is covered later in this section, but this was by no means the only impact of Neil Kay's systems-focused, non-reductionist way of looking at organisations on my own thinking.

Soon after I arrived at Stirling, Neil gave a presentation as a visiting speaker in which it became evident that the next stage of his non-reductionist thinking focused on the significance that complementarities between the things that firms developed, produced, and marketed had for the strength and vulnerability of firms. Sharing investments between products is great for spreading fixed costs, but linkages between activities can result in a problem with one activity also afflicting the other activities to which it is linked. Diversification limits the risk of corporate failure arising due to having 'too many eggs in the same basket', but it comes at the cost of sacrificing economies of scale or potential for synergy. He developed this structuralist view of corporate strategy in his next books (Kay, 1982, 1984), also emphasising the organisational challenges that linkages between activities pose as a firm grows: the cognitive limitations of managers necessitate the creation of organisational structures that compartmentalised activities.

I realised that these ideas, too, could be applied in the context of consumer behaviour, in relation both to how resilient different kinds of lifestyles are and to differences in the resilience of the ways that people organise their ways of looking at the world. I arrived at this line of thinking in early 1984 while revising my PhD but decided to limit the extent to which I included it in my thesis.

Just before leaving Stirling, with the thesis resubmitted, I began to pursue this theme in two ways, First, I spent a day in Edinburgh with Neil planning a joint paper (published as Earl and Kay, 1985) for a Shackle symposium in which we would explore the significance of strategic linkages for resilience in a world of disruptive surprises for both firms and their employees. Secondly, as a visiting seminar speaker at Birmingham Polytechnic, I signalled where my work was heading and alluded to the inspiration that I drew from Neil Kay's book *The Evolving Firm* by delivering a presentation entitled 'The evolving consumer'. The event in question was a double-header seminar that provided my first chance to meet the seminar convenor, John Pheby, with whom Sheila Dow and I had been corresponding about economic method, and the other speaker, Geoff Hodgson, whose 1982 book, *Capitalism, Value and Exploitation*, I had purchased a few months previously. It was clear from this book and his presentation that Geoff was moving in directions that complemented where my thinking was going. His subsequent work had a major influence on mine, even despite my inability to keep up with the extraordinary volume of his output.

People as Scientists

By the time that I took up my position at Stirling, I had become a member of the Scottish Economic Society and thereby a subscriber to the *Scottish Journal of Political Economy*. This resulted in me seeing a personally significant paper as soon as it was published, a paper that I otherwise might never have noticed. The paper in question was by Andrew Skinner (1979) from the University of Glasgow. Skinner was a leading Adam Smith scholar, whose work Brian Loasby greatly admired. The paper explored similarities between how Kuhn's (1962) paradigms-based view of the history of science, Shackle's (1967) *Years of High Theory* account of the imperfect competition and Keynesian revolutions, and Adam Smith's ([1795] 1980) posthumously published work on the history of astronomy. The last of these remains little known in economics despite Skinner's attempt to draw attention to it. But, for Brian Loasby and I, Smith's foray into astronomy is a remarkable contribution for what it says about how humans in general operate.

Smith saw human action in general, like that of astronomers, as a scientific activity: people marvel at things they cannot immediately fathom, and they give their attention to attempting to figure out what makes these things possible. On this view, life is a knowledge-generating process in which people construct frameworks for making sense of things that intrigue (or threaten) them, and they modify these frameworks to accommodate anomalies. As time passes and conditions change or people get data from a wider area, these modifications become more extensive, and they tend to be ad hoc when people find it difficult to accommodate new observations. These frameworks thereby become increasingly unwieldy. But new frameworks that offer different ways of understanding the phenomena in question tend to be resisted until existing frameworks become cognitively too cumbersome to use. At that point, people become willing to incur the upfront costs of getting to grips with a new way of making sense of things that may – once they have got used to using it – prove to be both more effective and easier to use.

At the time I read Skinner's article, I was in the process of getting to grips with a perspective very similar to that of Smith. This was a result of the first of two things – beyond inspiring me by what he wrote and what he said about economics – that Brian Loasby did in his role as my external PhD supervisor that had major positive impacts on my PhD and my career. He told me (if I recall correctly, in a letter he sent to me in Cambridge a few months before I moved to Stirling) that he had recently been reading George Kelly's (1963) book *A Theory of Personality*, which he had found very useful and strongly recommended that I, too, should read. The second thing he did, nearly two years later, was related to this: he asked me if I would like him to recommend me to Jack Wiseman for an opportunity to present a paper at the economics session (Section F) that Wiseman was putting together for the 1981 Conference of the British Association for the Advancement of Science (BAAS). Brian said he was going to present a paper that applied Kelly's work to problems of corporate change, which I might complement with one showing how I was applying Kelly's thinking to consumer behaviour. Here, I will focus on the impact that Kelly's work had on me; the significance of the invitation to participate in the BAAS conference is best saved until Section 5.5.

The fact that Brian applied Kelly's theory in relation to corporate behaviour is easy to appreciate, as he had learned of Kelly via Charles Suckling, an ICI executive who was an adjunct professor of management at Stirling. Suckling had said that he had found Kelly's ideas useful for understanding the behaviour of people in organisations. I sonn realized that Kelly's theory of personality has much in common with how Kuhn (1962) and Lakatos (1970) view the role that, respectively, scientific paradigms and scientific research programmes play in shaping how academics and research scientists go about their work: although their work entails creative thinking, it runs along established lines and uses established ways of thinking and unquestioned core assumptions and operating rules that limit the kinds of things they find worthy of investigation, which kinds of evidence they will take seriously when their theories are being challenged, and which of their theories they will be willing to modify or abandon when there are mismatches between predictions and evidence. Kelly arrived at a similar view of how people deal with problems of knowledge ahead of Kuhn and Lakatos, but not in the context of the history and philosophy of science; rather, Kelly (1955) presented his analysis in his two-volume magnum opus *The Psychology of Personal Constructs*, from which the opening three chapters were extracted as his *Theory of Personality*. The fact that Kelly's major contribution to psychology has much in common with Kuhn and Lakatos is hardly surprising, for Kelly's key idea is that to understand people, it is useful to view them as if they are scientists seeking to predict and control aspects of the world in which they find themselves.

Even before reading Kelly, Brian and I were both conscious of the value of thinking about the behaviour of firms as if the cognitive processes of their staff or prospective customers could be constrained by established ways of thinking. I first picked up this idea in autumn 1977 from Loasby's (1976) references to resistance to Halothane, a new anaesthetic; by late 1978, I had realised, as a result of reading Alfred Chandler's (1962) *Strategy and Structure*, that the process by which major new ways of doing business are taken up resemble those that Kuhn (1962) had emphasised in the history of science: like scientific revolutions, revolutionary change in the ways that firms operate may be resisted because existing ways of doing business have served managers well in the past and because established ways of thinking get in the way of appreciating the potential of new approaches. As Kelly had realised, the key problem for changing how we look at the world, whether in science, business, or in the ordinary business of everyday life, is that people can only assess alternative perspectives on what to do from the standpoint of their existing way of thinking. Until those who are trying to promote changes of behaviour can find a way of packaging how the alternatives should be viewed that will permeate the established mindset, those who need to change will stick to their old ways. In the meantime, the latter will keep operating in needlessly dysfunctional ways and squander resources.

This permeability problem was central to Brian's presentation to the 1981 BAAS conference, published as Loasby (1983). It was also the key idea behind my book *The Corporate Imagination: How Big Companies Make Mistakes*, that I wrote during the first half of 1983 in my first sabbatical (for which I stayed at Stirling). It also underlay how I was thinking when I wrote in my post-PhD book *Lifestyle Economics*, soon after leaving Stirling, about consumers who resist change and make mistakes. Ironically, however, these contributions have failed to permeate far into either heterodox or modern behavioural economics, let alone orthodoxy.

The fact that my early writing as a behavioural economist emphasises that people are prone to make systematic errors rather than achieve optimal outcomes might make me sound very much like a modern behavioural economist who portrays people as if they are, to use Thaler's (2015) term, 'misbehaving' in the sense that they fail to do what a 'fully rational' economic agent should do. This might result in heterodox economists misconstruing my work as being overly wedded to mainstream economics. The truth is that my 'way' of construing human fallibility is different from the 'way' that human fallibility is seen in the behavioural economics that Thaler has done so much to popularise. Also, I make no presumption that optimal choices are knowable; I merely focus on failures to opt for *better* strategies that could have been readily identified by using a different way of looking at the world.

Here, it is important to realise that the 'personal' aspect of personal construct psychology makes Kelly-inspired behavioural economics problematic for typical behavioural economists. Like conventional economists, the latter find it convenient to view economic agents as if they are all the same as each other. Failures to behave as an idealised 'econ' would supposedly behave are therefore analysed as arising due to the use of heuristics from a long list identified experimentally as being genetically programmed into humans. I had no problem with the idea of people in general having such tendencies, which I became familiar with via Hogarth and Makridakis (1981) and Nisbett and Ross (1980). However, these inherited heuristics are not the only means by which people cope with life: Kelly's message is that people develop hierarchically organised, rule-based personal systems for constructing models of parts of the world and deciding what to do. It is the uniqueness of our personal construct systems that makes us the individuals that we are.

Aspects of our personal operating systems *that are not part of our generic ways of being human* can play key roles in shaping how successfully we cope with life's challenges. Our personal 'ways' can amplify or over-ride our generic human 'ways' of behaving and can initiate behaviour. For example, people in general may be prone, as humans, to suffer from sunk-cost bias, but some of them may over-ride that tendency because they have been trained as economists or have otherwise come to see that there is no use in 'crying over spilt milk' and/or 'pouring good money after bad'. Emphasis on individuality clashes with the conventional 'representative agent' way of practising economics but it does not mean it is impossible to group people, as marketers do, based on similarities in their ways of thinking that produce similar values, just as economic methodologists group economists into schools of thought.

Although Kelly (1963) became one of Brian Loasby's frequent sources for understanding how people deal with problems of knowledge in economic systems, Brian did not seem interested in doing more with Kelly and did not engage with the wider literature on personal construct psychology to see what it implied for economics. By contrast, I became captivated with the idea of replacing the notion of utility maximisation with a Kellian view of human action in which life is about making sense of the world, increasing one's knowledge (including self-knowledge) and being in control rather than at the mercy of events. When I explored Kelly's (1955) magnum opus and some of the major secondary sources, I was particularly fascinated by the way that emotions were framed in relation to concerns about loss of control and/or scope for damage to one's self-construct if one ventured into unfamiliar territory or engaged in action that was 'out of character'. Clearly, one's knowledge and ability to control events is not going to advance if, in the process of testing hypotheses (or even in acquiring knowledge from others), one is unwilling to risk getting into situations that are difficult to make sense of and/or in which it is difficult to maintain control. When we recognise this, there seems to be a lot to be said for the heuristic that is commonly attributed to Sir Thomas Beecham, namely, 'Try anything once, except incest and folk dancing.' It helps to be open to experimenting with things that others view as perfectly normal, even if they are in a minority, rather than limiting oneself to what one already knows. However, how risky an experiment will seem is not determined by the experiment; it depends on the personal construct system that one has constructed, for this will determine the implications that one sees as potentially associated with one's options.

This way of looking at human action seemed to me to have enormous potential for understanding consumer behaviour, in ways that utility theory simply could not match. As I set out to see what I could do with it, my only concern was that my lack of life experience might result in me being oblivious to some of its applications. However, I hoped that I might compensate for this vicariously: here, I was encouraged by the new insights it gave me about my parents' behaviour and by the way in which some of the novels that I read seemed to resonate with Kelly's analysis.

Complex Decision Cycles versus Simplified Decision-Making
One of the surprising things that I discovered soon after arriving at Stirling was that being deprived of access to a copyright library (the Cambridge University Library) and a very well-resourced specialist economics library (the Marshall Library) had beneficial consequences for my development as a behavioural economist. This happened because I was able to discover things that I would not have been likely to notice when using the fabulous libraries in Cambridge. Within my first few months of using the library at Stirling, I stumbled upon an area of scholarship that was totally unfamiliar to me, namely, consumer behaviour research conducted by marketing specialists in business schools. I discovered books on consumer research purely by chance while walking past the shelves that housed them when I was making my way to something nearby related to the behavioural theory of the firm. Soon after, on the racks that displayed new issues of journals, I discovered the *Journal of Consumer Research*, and the other key marketing journals, near to the economics journals in which I routinely browsed. The two accidental encounters led me to recognise that there

was much scope for taking a pluralistic approach to the study of consumer behaviour, as well as adding further impetus to my pivot towards focusing on a behavioural analysis of choice.

The stroke of luck that I had in where my gaze landed among Stirling's library bookstacks was truly remarkable, for the first thing that caught my eye was Nicosia's (1966) *Consumer Decision Processes: Marketing and Advertising Implications*. This was a seminal contribution within the marketing literature, and it looked for all the world as though Nicosia had tried to write a consumer behaviour version of Cyert and March (1963). This impression was amplified by the fact the covers of the two books were almost identical. Nicosia presented a boxes-and-arrows version of consumer decision-making as a sequential process. It contrasted with orthodox economic analysis that reduces consumer choice to a single diagram, in just the same way that Cyert and March's view of the operations of a firm contrasts with the one-diagram orthodox approaches to the theory of the firm.

Close to Nicosia's book was a much bigger book, a research-based consumer behaviour textbook by Engel, Kollat and Blackwell (1968), in its third edition (Engel, Blackwell and Kollat, 1978), built around a different boxes-and-arrows model that was already well-established as simply 'the EKB model'. Just as Loasby (1976) had frequently referred to decision cycles in corporations, so the EKB team presented a problem-solving view of consumer behaviour built around the decision cycle concept. The EKB team's approach to consumer research was a sign that, contrary to how it is often viewed, marketing is not a 'Mickey Mouse' subject, for their text is a serious work of evidence-based scholarship. It led me to Dewey's (1910) pioneering statement of the decision cycle process that runs from problem recognition to search for possible solutions, evaluation of the contending potential solutions, choice, implementation, and hindsight review. I saw the EKB model not as something that could be readily tested but as a very useful organizing framework for initiating and considering the potential implications of fine-grained research related to its various modules. If one wanted to test the applicability, in a particular context, of something akin to a single-equation model in applied economics, there was, as Tuck (1976) argued, the model set out by psychologists Fishbein and Ajzen (1975) – which, of course, had rapidly found its way into more recent editions of the EKB team's text. If I had not started to believe that I might be able, via personal construct psychology, to make my own contributions to the analysis of consumer behaviour, I could readily have concluded that economists simply needed to look at the work marshalled by the EKB team if they wanted a behavioural view of consumer choice.

It was an article by Olshavsky and Granbois that I discovered in the just-arrived September 1979 issue of the *Journal of Consumer Research* that alerted me to the limitations of the EKB team's approach to consumer behaviour even before I had spent much time looking at their work. Olshavsky and Granbois argued that the EKB model and its rivals gave the misleading impression that all consumer behaviour entails extended problem-solving, whereas in reality a very large amount of consumption is selected via habits, simple decision rules, and social norms, with little search, evaluation, or consideration of rival offerings. Clearly, a pluralistic approach to consumer behaviour was needed, one that embraced both fast and drawn-out decision-making processes, and those between these extremes. I felt that it needed to be done mindful of the possibility that there could be great variety in how different people arrived at their choices in a given context, rather than merely focusing on how decision-making processes differed in a general way between different types of context – though I remained open to the idea that the context of a choice (for example, how big the range of choice is, how much uncertainty there is, how costly a bad choice might be) could play a major role in shaping how decisions get made.

The Olshavsky and Granbois perspective was challenging for consumer behaviour researchers, for what they were arguing reduces to barely a line of text that has much in common with the institutional economist's view that choice is primarily driven by habits, rules, and norms (as emphasised in Hodgson, 1997). Yet it leaves us with very little to say when teaching or writing about the theory of consumer behaviour. Instead, it implies that we should be focusing on conducting empirical work on the practices of consumers and the norms of everyday life and feeding these findings into what we write and teach. The latter is not the kind of thing that those who see themselves as heterodox consumer theorists are likely to be keen to do, for it seems rather like becoming a sociologist or social anthropologist. It is therefore easy to succumb to the temptation to focus on more complex decision processes about which more can be said from a theoretical standpoint.

Despite the impact that the Olshavsky and Granbois paper had on me at this formative stage, I struggled to write much in this vein when completing *The Economic Imagination* in 1982, though I was pleased that, in its sixth chapter ('Budgets, habits and behaviour dynamics'), I did at least attempt to draw attention to simple, rule-based choices. I referred to them as 'cybernetic' decisions, in light of the title and third chapter of the book by Steinbruner (1974) that Roland Clarke – one of the most impressive undergraduates that I had supervised in Cambridge – drew to my attention when he visited me in November 1979.[9] It was significant that Steinbruner chose to consider simplified ways of making decisions in the context of high-stakes political choices, not in relation to consumer behaviour: there should be no presumption that the more important a decision is, the greater the mental effort people will put into taking it. This point seemed not to have been registered when, in the wake of Olshavsky and Granbois' critique, established consumer behaviour texts in marketing – such as the fourth edition of the EKB text (Engel and Blackwell, 1982) – started to distinguish between 'high involvement' and 'low involvement' decision-making.

Toward a Hierarchical View of Decision-Making
Unlike all my subsequent work on consumer behaviour, my first attempt at devising an alternative to the dominant Hicksian indifference curve/budget line approach was framed in the goods space rather than focusing on choices made in characteristics space. It was inspired by Hicks's (1976) confession that he felt that the Marshallian approach that his analysis had displaced actually seemed the more realistic of the two. Marshall's (1890) view did not portray people as considering all feasible substitutions simultaneously. Rather, his idea was that people decided whether to buy something according to whether the marginal utility they derived from it was no less than the marginal utility of holding on to the money they would have to forgo to get it. It thus seemed to be a kind of liquidity preference approach to demand, which seemed applicable to situations such as where a consumer is deciding how expensive a product

---

[9] Roland Clarke also commended to me a remarkable new book by Hofstadter (1979), which proved to be very helpful for thinking about the challenges to reductionism that were already much on my mind. It also fostered my interest in infinite regress problems and gave me the idea of experimenting with the use of dialogues, one of the aspects of *The Economic Imagination* that readers seem most to remember. Roland's visit to Stirling sticks in my mind in relation to the struggle I was already having in finding enough from my pay to keep my little flat tolerably warm: he was visibly surprised by how low a temperature I was prepared to tolerate before I turned on the electric radiators, and he made his point by asking if he might take a hot bath as a means of getting a bit warmer.

to buy in a market crowded with products that differ both in price and how much value for money they offer.

However, the picture of demand that I had been getting from Andrews (1964) acknowledged a prior stage in the choice process, namely that the consumer would not look at all products within a particular category and would instead only attempt to equate the marginal utility of spending in the category and the marginal utility of money in respect of products whose prices fell within a particular range that had upper and lower bounds. This seemed to require a theory of budgeting that grappled with the sequential nature of attention to budgetary categories and uncertainty about how much would end up being spent within each range that was set for the various budgetary categories. I could see that perhaps (in line with Keynes's view of saving as a residual) the total of the set of upper budget ranges would be constrained not to exceed the consumer's total spending capacity, with any residue from spending somewhat less in some categories then being saved. But how would the lower bounds of budgets be set, and what determined the sequence in which budgets were used up?

I presented this perspective as my first departmental workshop, emphasizing that I had no idea whether there was any literature on household budgeting that looked anything like this, and I noted that this top-down way of allocating household resources was in some respects like Kay's (1979) non-reductionist view of the allocation of resources to research and development in firms. Ron Shone's feedback was especially helpful, for he introduced me to the 'utility tree' literature particularly associated with the work of Strotz (1957) that is sometimes presented as lying somewhere between good-space and characteristics-space modes of thinking due to budgetary categories ultimately being based on differences in the sets of characteristics that their respective products offer or the wants that they enable consumers to meet. However, I was not left with a sense that this literature captured the sequential aspect of spending processes or the idea of double-sided budget ranges.

Not long after presenting my workshop, I had a 'lightbulb moment' that led me to question a key idea in the orthodox theory of rational choice, namely, the 'axiom of Archimedes' or 'principle of gross substitution'. In the standard goods-space view of choice, indifference curves that slope downwards to the right at a decreasing rate guarantee that changes in relative prices always produce a substitution effect. Likewise, in Lancaster's (1966) characteristics-space analysis of choice, not only can substitution always be induced by a price change of some magnitude, but weaknesses of products in some areas may be offset by suitably strong performances in other areas.

I had experienced a sense that there might be some cases where this did not apply when I read Stout's (1977) report exhorting UK manufacturers to be mindful of the impact of 'non-price factors' in international trade, but Michael Posner argued soon after in his lectures (and in Posner, 1978) that 'If you can't sell good goods, sell cheap goods', i.e., that with an exchange rate depreciation and/or improvements in production efficiency, a country's firms should be able to survive competition from overseas rivals whose products they cannot match in terms of design and/or standards of quality. From Posner's standpoint, the key question was whether workers will accept real wage reductions of the size necessary to make possible price reductions that are big enough to offset non-price shortcomings.

My 'lightbulb moment' could readily have been the one that led me to resolve to become a vegetarian in the New Year of 1982, a resolution that I have not deviated from since then except by becoming a vegan a few months later. In that case, the lightbulb moment came in the departmental coffee room when I was having my lunch with several colleagues. The group included Sue Shaw, who was doing research on fish marketing and had just returned from visiting a salmon farm. She noticed that I winced as she described how the salmon were harvested via an electrocution tank, and she went on to add that it was a more humane process than what happens in an abattoir. Somehow, this had a much bigger impact on me than that generated by the posters about veganism on the door of Dr Enid Marshall, Stirling's Reader in Business Law, which I often passed as I came in from the car park. Indeed, what got me thinking that I might as well also give up eating eggs and dairy products was the hassle I soon encountered as a new vegetarian when trying to source cheese made with animal-free rennet (which was often out of stock in the local health-food store) and free-range eggs (which could more reliably be found in a butcher's store).

These dietary changes were clearly at odds with Lancaster's model, as they involved an ethical principle that ruled out consuming food from murdered or exploited animals, and a desire to prevent the process of shopping for food from becoming too fraught. But there was clearly also a growth-of-knowledge process going on as I changed my dietary constructs both in terms of what I was prepared to eat and what I knew how to prepare. Indeed, it was attending a talk about veganism by Eva Batt, a vegan cookery writer, at Stirling's vegetarian society, rather than lurking by Enid's door to read small print about 'What happens to the calf?', that sealed my decision to become a vegan. I had not really thought what the dairy business entails, especially because gender selection is not part of the process at the outset. However, while it was that conversation with Sue Shaw that set me thinking about how dietary choices could entail no-go zones, I was, at the time of that conversation, already about two years into thinking about choice in a way that clashed with the principle of gross substitution: it entailed setting priority rankings for characteristics and setting targets for how options must perform in respect of these characteristics in order to be deemed acceptable.

The actual 'lightbulb moment' came on a Saturday morning as I was reflecting on how tired I was, as I had been on quite a few previous Saturday mornings. On Friday nights, many members of the department and some of the postgraduate students usually went to one of the pubs or hotels close to the campus. Afterwards, most of the group would adjourn to someone's house nearby. Ron Shone's bungalow was a common post-pub venue, and much merriment was sometimes had as he tried out his skills as a hypnotist. On one occasion, the venue was a house that a rich Greek master's student had rented in Bridge of Allan, which had his very expensive Lancia Flavia Coupé in the garage and a video cassette recorder in the lounge. The latter was the first domestic VCR that any of the rest of us had encountered and it was duly demonstrated with a screening of the 1978 Joan Collins movie *The Stud*, while the host served copious amounts of ouzo.

These Friday nights were the main element of my social life in my early months at Stirling, but I was losing my enthusiasm for them. This was partly due to the inequities of the round-buying system when I was merely drinking orange juice, and on the lowest pay, while others drank expensive brands of whisky. But there was also the problem that I found myself sometimes getting to bed well after 2:00 am, partly due to first driving home, in the opposite direction, Stirling's sole politics lecturer, Kevin Featherstone (later Professor of Greek Politics at the LSE), who was nearly as young as myself and did not yet have a car. As I walked to the supermarket that Saturday morning, I was reflecting on my shortage of discretionary income and time and the problem of budgeting. Something had to go.

In concluding that I would rather spend money on LPs or petrol to drive out into the mountains, and that I would rather be able to enjoy a full Saturday of leisure without failing to get enough sleep, I realised that I was not thinking along the lines presumed in the utility tree view of budgeting. I was thinking in terms of priorities over separate goals and asking whether I was getting enough in top ranking goals before being willing to allocate resources to ones that I viewed as less important; I was not computing overall scores for rival strategies by weighing together how much I got on different dimensions. To get enough sleep, I must either get up later and lose my Saturday morning, or give up the social Friday nights, which would also leave me with more money to spend on things that I ranked higher than conversing with colleagues. Based on this, I stopped joining my colleagues on Friday nights.

It was a short step for me from starting to think about priority-based budgeting between activities to starting to think about choices between rival products in terms of priority-based tests of adequacy for expected performance in relation to targets for product characteristics. From this standpoint, the process of choosing looked rather like a hurdles race in which failure to clear a hurdle results in disqualification, with the product that survives the most tests, in priority order, being the one that gets selected, and with simple tie-breaker rules being used if more than one product is deemed adequate for all the characteristics on the buyer's checklist. I coined the phrase 'characteristic filtering' to denote this priority-based view of choosing.

I soon discovered that the idea that consumers might use checklists when choosing was known in the consumer behaviour literature in marketing as a 'conjunctive' way of choosing, to distinguish it from what was labelled a 'disjunctive' approach in which the consumer is obsessed with getting as much as possible of a single characteristic. However, the marketing literature did not seem to envisage a series of priority-ordered targets as being used to deal with situations in which no option 'ticked all the boxes'. Rather, reference was made to two other possibilities. One was the use of lexicographic rules that entail a hierarchical ranking of disjunctive wants, rather than targets, with a tie for the maximum offered on the top-priority want leading to a focus on which of the tied products performed best in terms of the next highest-ranking want, and so on; the second was Tversky's (1972) notion of 'elimination by aspects'. The latter does entail the use of characteristic targets, but they are not prioritised; instead, the order in which they are applied is probabilistically grounded and triggered by contextual factors.

These approaches were categorised in marketing as 'non-compensatory' ways of making decisions, in contrast to 'compensatory' or 'expectancy value' methods that were the marketing equivalent of Lancaster's (1966) analysis of choices in characteristics space. Some of the compensatory models that were popular in marketing seemed to go beyond Lancaster by (a) recognizing that cognitive constraints could limit the number of characteristics that were considered, (b) offering plausibly simple ways of incorporating uncertainty, and (c) recognizing that consumers may weigh their personal assessments against how they think their social referents would view them if they selected the products under consideration (most notably in the model offered by Fishbein and Ajzen, 1975). In contrast, the non-compensatory approaches seemed much less well developed, especially in relation to uncertainty about how products would perform for some or all characteristic axes. I set out to remedy this by integrating the basic characteristic filtering idea with ingredients from Simon and Shackle. By August 1980, I had written a discussion paper (Earl, 1980a) in which I set out where I had got to on this front, and in thinking about hierarchical budgeting in graphical terms. In the ensuing two years, these ideas and those that I had developed from reading about personal construct psychology grew into my first solo book, *The Economic Imagination* (Earl, 1983a).

What I did not know at this stage was that, in coming to view choices as based on hierarchically ranked, satiable wants, I had, in effect, arrived where Duncan Ironmonger had arrived almost twenty years earlier in his Cambridge PhD, belatedly published in slightly extended form as Ironmonger (1972). Ironmonger had used linear programming in his formal analysis. but this had entailed not addressing the question of how consumers handled uncertainty. Though I was oblivious of his analysis, I sensed that the graphs that I drew to understand household budgeting processes aligned somewhat with linear programming, for I had learned some of the basics of linear programming when I read Baumol (1972, chapter 5), during the 1975 long vacation, as part of my preparation for the Prelims year of Part II of the Cambridge Tripos. However, although I worked through all Baumol's exercise questions, I never went on to make any formal use of the technique. Indeed, although I included a graphical analysis of priority-based budgeting in my first solo discussion paper and developed it further in the original draft of chapter 6 of *The*

Economic Imagination, I deleted the graphs on budgeting just before the book went to press, without the publishers' reviewers having had any issues with them.

Issues in Budgeting

The reason that I ultimately did not even take a graphical approach to budgeting, let alone try to re-learn and then apply linear programming, was that I noticed that some of the budget lines might not be linear, due to complementarities or negative externalities between different activities that affected attainments for multiple targets. Drawing and explaining hierarchical budgeting with a mix of linear, concave and convex budget lines, and showing how they could move due to changes in income or relative prices was quite a challenge, even for budgeting between just two categories. I felt that I should limit what I wrote to what seemed simple enough to be plausible.

My experience in using graphs to conduct a hierarchical analysis of budgeting provides a good example of how traditional economic tools can lead one to miss what people really do in the area that one is analysing. If one wants to present such an analysis, the obvious strategy is to show budgeting between two categories on a graph whose axes show the amount allocated to the respective categories. A linear budget line with a 45-degree downward slope can be drawn from the maximum that can be spent in the category represented on the vertical axis to the maximum that can be spent in the category represented on the horizontal axis. One can then successively work down the hierarchy of wants, considering what are the cheapest sets of combinations of the two product categories that will enable the first-priority want to be met. In some cases, this will only entail spending in one of the product categories; if so, this can be represented by a line perpendicular to the spending axis for that category of product at the amount that needs to be spent to satisfy the want.

In other cases, where combinations of the two product types can serve a want, we may get an efficiency frontier that is a straight, convex, or concave line from one axis to the other. We can then show what happens to the efficiency frontier as the consumer moves on to consider combinations of spending that enable the second priority to be met without compromising the first, and so on for the third and subsequent priorities. As we stack on further layers of spending, the shape of the efficiency frontier may become a complex set of segments of lines and curves that moves progressively towards the budget line and eventually starts to cross it. Sooner or later, we will arrive at a point where the next priority cannot be met without the entire efficiency frontier being to the right of the budget line, so we then have to retreat to the efficiency frontier arrived at for the previous priority and examine the feasible set of allocations that remain, some of which may have a residual amount that can be used to get some way toward meeting the next priority. The allocation between the two product categories that will be selected is the one that will take the consumer closest to meeting the next priority.

Clearly, this is challenging to generalise beyond two dimensions, but the way the graph gets constructed even for two dimensions has a more fundamental problem. In the process just outlined, we began with a blank graph and worked towards the budget constraint by extending spending to cover successively less important wants. To derive the efficiency frontier for any set of n hierarchically ranked wants, we proceed as if the consumer explores all possible combinations beyond the frontier previously arrived at for n -1 wants, computing the total cost of each combination of spending in the two categories. However, real-world consumers seem more likely to reflect on budgetary allocations at points in historical time, after experiencing changes in prices or income, to address questions about how to limit the impact of tighter budget constraints or not miss opportunities presented by easier budget constraints. Given their starting point for budgeting, people will only consider a limited set of new allocation strategies, due to their cognitive constraints, and will stop devising and considering alternatives once they conclude they have found a good enough way of limiting attrition (or advancing, in the case of an easier budget constraint) in the priorities they expect to be able to meet in their current planning period. Instead of considering a comprehensive range of possibilities, people will operate rather like organisations do when budgeting, with routines for seeing where cuts might be possible without unnecessarily compromising the attainment of high priority wants, and with wish-list projects to implement if financial slack appears.

In other words, contrary to the impression that graphical analysis fosters, people who are considering what they can afford do not need to reflect on their options as if budgeting from scratch. Rather, they are typically considering an addition to what they consume, financed by running down their financial reserves and/or making a specific reduction in another area of spending. Hence, the key issue is, 'If I spend on what

I'm currently considering, to meet a goal that I am not currently meeting, will this prevent me from meeting any more important goals that I will be able to meet if I don't do the spending that I am contemplating?' They thus look back from less important to more important wants in an 'other things equal' manner, and if the way they are thinking of adding to the spending and financing that spending leads them to think of *any* presently-met wants that will be compromised, the idea of such spending is then ruled out. This is a kind of marginal adjustment, but it works in a hierarchical sense, not in terms of maximisation of an additive utility function.

However, a year before I decided to abandon my graphical analysis of budgeting, I had begun to have a different kind of concern about how people figure out what they can afford. I realised, via Steinbruner (1974, chapter 4) and from my own experience in wrestling with budgeting problems, that cognitive processes could limit how carefully consumers think through the implications of choices that were being driven by temptation associated with prospects of meeting hitherto unmet goals and/or desperation associated with difficulties in continuing to meet more basic priorities.

By March 1981, increases in my pay should have been helping me to restore my discretionary spending by offsetting the increased monthly mortgage payments that monetarist anti-inflation policies had triggered. Yet I was having trouble saving up for anything because I had experienced a string of expensive bills for my 1972 Ford Cortina. I thus began trying to figure out whether I might be better off if I took out a bank loan to buy a much newer car that would, at the cost of increasing my non-discretionary outgoings (i.e., via monthly payments to the bank) enable me to reduce or eliminate the risk of such bills, thereby making some saving possible as I repaid the loan even though the loan would finance a depreciating asset. After rejecting the idea of buying a new or very recent small car on the basis that I would lose the high-speed cruising capabilities that the two-litre Cortina provided, I ended up trading the Cortina against an ex-fleet Vauxhall Cavalier Coupé that was five years younger, a generation more modern, more luxurious, and more stylish. But I made the decision with little idea of the comparative probabilities of repair bills on the two vehicles: by that stage the Cortina had many new parts so it might then have given several years of trouble-free motoring, but there was still a lot that could go wrong and rust was starting to concern me; the Cavalier had a full service history and came with a one-year warranty that covered some major components (and was duly honoured when the Cavalier's water pump failed soon after I purchased it) but I had no knowledge of when maintenance might start getting expensive.

Amid that uncertainty, I could tell myself that upgrading the car was possibly a means to improving the predictability of my finances, and it did indeed prove much cheaper to maintain. However, a cynic might argue that, at the time I bought the Cavalier, it was more clearly a means to meet less-basic goals and thereby give me a sense that I was getting somewhere. As I reflected on my decision, I could appreciate Garfinkel's (1967, pp. 113–114) contention that the human mind attempts to provide an illusion of rationality by concocting convenient stories to justify actions that the mind has already decided upon by means that might not be clear to the person in question. For some, this might result in dangerously weak-willed behaviour in pursuing low priority goals, accompanied by an 'I'll cross that bridge if I come to it' attitude in relation to how they will pay bills related to more basic needs.

Failures of Imagination in Relation to the Non-Substitution Perspective
There were several things I could readily have realised if I had asked myself whether viewing choices as based on intolerant rules linked up with other parts of the work that I was doing and whether it had wider implications than those that I was seeing in relation to non-price competition. Looking back, I am surprised that I did not do a better job of integrating this view of choice with personal construct psychology. In essence, the characteristic filtering view of choice can be viewed in terms of a stack of performance targets on personal construct axes that are either binary or scalar. The complete stack can be viewed as the decision-maker's personal construct for his or her 'completely acceptable' vision of the product type to which it refers. As such, it is indeed a 'template' against which contending products are assessed for their fit. However, although Kelly spoke of personal constructs as akin to templates, I failed to arrive at such a visualisation until I read Grupp and Maital (2001) in 2006 in preparation for writing what was eventually published as Earl and Wakeley (2010a): their notion of a 'technometric scale' was, in effect, a 90-degree rotation of a stack of constructs. I did not refer to Kelly in that paper, but did explicitly make the connection, and give an illustration in stack form, in Earl (2022, p. 102).

Clearly, having stacks of separate wants makes it cognitively much easier to rethink one's preferences than would be the case with convex preference sets of the kind that Lancaster assumed consumers have. A stack-based view of what one is looking for in a particular area thus aligns better with Kelly's 'people are like scientists' perspective: such a stack can be viewed as a basis for experimentation; if the results of applying it seem problematic, one can then use these results as a basis for re-prioritizing it and see whether it generates a better capacity to predict and control events. Moreover, new construct axes, with their respective experimental targets, can readily be slotted into such stacks.

It was also not until 2006 that I started to think seriously about the relevance of intolerant choices to the production side of the economy. The idea that there might be technical and human capability prerequisites and co-requisites should be obvious to any academic who works in an institution whose degree programmes require students to satisfy prerequisites and/or co-requisites for sets of subjects that must be completed to qualify for graduation. Yet, around 1980–1981, as I failed to spot how mainstream production theory overlooks this kind of issue, my eventual partner, Annabelle Taylor, was studying to be a teacher and was taught about the prerequisites for learning to occur in a primary school classroom. Annabelle's education lecturers presented the idea in relation to Maslow's (1943, [1954] 1970) notion of a 'hierarchy of needs', stressing that learning is not going to happen, regardless of the teacher's knowledge and ability to articulate it, if (a) children have not had breakfast, and (b) there is no discipline in the classroom. I was not aware of this in 2006 when I wrote a paper about the significance of capability prerequisites and co-requisites in production systems. The paper was dismissed as 'merely an essay' by the referees of *Metroeconomica*, a journal that I had expected to be interested in this heterodox perspective. It seemed as if the themes of the paper would only be taken seriously if expressed as a formal model of production. Many years passed before I wrote about the issue again (in section 3.8 of Earl, 2022), this time in relation to contributions to development economics by Rostow (1960) and Schumacher (1973).

Missed Opportunities Due to Insufficiently Diligent Scholarship
During 1980, I discovered that Lutz and Lux (1979) and Bettman (1979) had recently analysed, respectively, budgeting and product choices in non-compensatory terms. The former was inspired by Maslow's

'hierarchy of needs'; the latter came from the marketing literature but was inspired by Simon's work on information processing with finite cognitive capacity. After the briefest of perusals, I made a mental note to read them one day. However, I then got diverted by the self-inflicted task of writing *Money Matters* with Sheila Dow after getting as far as buying a copy of Bettman's book on 26 September 1980. I did not bother to look at my copy of Bettman or at the library's copy of Lutz and Lux's book until at least three years later. This was when I was revising my Cambridge thesis, having failed to refer to them in *The Economic Imagination* or in the original version of my thesis. My PhD examiners did not pull me up for this, or for the other scholarly shortcomings that I detail below, but they were spot-on in realizing that I had not displayed the scholarly diligence necessary to construct a literature review that took adequate account of precursors to the contribution that I was making. In revising my thesis, and in the years that followed, I discovered more contributions to a hierarchical view of choice, though never as many as Stirling PhD alumnus Stavros Drakopoulos. Readers who are interested in this field should consult the surveys provided by Drakopous (1994; Drakopoulos and Karayiannis, 2004). Here, I will concentrate on the cases of my slack scholarship that I most regret and which I hope will motivate early-career economists to be much more tenacious as scholars than I was back then.

Very early in my time at Stirling, when I went to the library to consult further Kelly's (1955) *Psychology of Personal Constructs*, I happened to notice near to it a book called *The Sensory Order*. I was surprised to see that it had been written by Friedrich Hayek (1952). At the time, I took a brief look at it, suspecting that it might complement the subjectivist psychology that Kelly offered, but I soon reshelved it. It looked like it was going to be even harder to digest than the books by Hayek that I had consulted a year earlier and referred to in the paper that I had sent to Brian Loasby before my interview trip to Stirling. Reshelving *The Sensory Order* at that point in my career was a big mistake, for thirty years later I found that my original hunch that it complemented personal construct psychology was right (see Section 8.4). Loasby, too, seemed to know of the book's existence back then, but the first time I have found him citing it is in Loasby (1996), with his first paper focused on it being Loasby (2004).

Secondly, there was my failure to give due attention to Ironmonger's (1972) *New Commodities and Consumer Behaviour*. I do not recall reading Ironmonger's book until I was revising my PhD dissertation, after *The Economic Imagination* was published, even though the latter does refer (on pp. 52 and 63) to Ironmonger. There, I had relied on my memory of Ajit Singh having pointed me to the *Economic Journal* review by Prais (1973) of Ironmonger's book, around the time he introduced me to Lancaster's (1966) work. Ajit had said that in the review Prais had likened the spread of demand for new commodities to the process whereby a contagious disease spreads, and it was in that context that I had cited Ironmonger. What I had not remembered was that Prais had not said that Ironmonger had suggested the contagious disease parallel but that he *should* have raised it. Yet it turned out that my reference to Ironmonger in that context was correct because Prais had somehow failed to read Ironmonger's fourth chapter where the disease parallel is noted, along with relevant modelling methods. There is a lesson here about scholarship: always check your primary sources before you put anything into print, and, in case your memory lets you down, recheck them if you have already viewed them at first hand. It is possible that I did try to check what Ironmonger had written, for I can recall a couple of early attempts when I tried to find the library copy without success. I can also recall that when I did eventually get to look at it, the extent of mathematical content was rather intimidating, and I did little more than register that the diagrams presented a hierarchical, target-based view of wants and were similar to those that I had been drawing.

Despite having accidentally given the right impression in referring to Ironmonger without having checked his book, I really regret not having bothered to read Ironmonger's book before late 1983. By following his reference trail, I might have avoided having to revise and resubmit my PhD, and at the very least I could have referred to Ironmonger's failure to accommodate uncertainty in his hierarchical model as a gap that I was seeking to fill by integrating the priority-based view of choice with a satisficing version of Shackle's view of choice under uncertainty.

Ironmonger's emphasis on the role that the growth of knowledge played in the gradual adoption of new products also added weight to the case for my attempts to integrate personal construct psychology into the economic analysis of consumer behaviour. It was not until I was writing a retrospective assessment of Ironmonger's book after I retired (Earl, Markey-Towler and Coutts, 2022) that I looked carefully at the second part of it, where he sets out evidence on how long adoption processes can take before market saturation is reached. Much of his work entailed examining the adoption of new types of food and beverage products before World War II, many of which took three or more decades to achieve saturation, whereas I spent my career using the much shorter product lifecycles of modern electronics products as sources of inspiration. If I had been aware of the food-related analysis in Ironmonger's book when I was working in New Zealand during the 1990s, it might even have inspired me to consider potential for an agribusiness-related research grant application with some of my colleagues.

What Ironmonger discovered about the slow uptake of new types of food and beverage products seems also to apply to the spread of lifestyle practices, such as the uptake of vegetarian and vegan diets or 'green' practices more generally, yet when I came to write about lifestyles shortly after leaving Stirling, my failure to give due attention beyond the first, theoretical part of Ironmonger's book meant that I was not primed to give much attention to long-term processes of lifestyle change. When I at last came to write anything about this issue (in Earl, 2017a), the inspiration came via Hayek's *Sensory Order*, not Ironmonger, for I still had not carefully read the second half of Ironmonger's book; indeed, I had not looked at it at all since about 1985. Things might have been different if I had bought a copy of it early in my career rather than just before I retired: availability bias favours the use of books in one's personal library, the more so the more one works from home rather than on campus and keeps one's library at home.

The way that I came to incorporate Shackle's analysis also involved happenstance and scholarly deficiencies. The fact that I came to be reading Shackle's work in late 1979 was purely the result of the manager of the campus bookstore notifying me that he had received a copy of Shackle's (1979) book *Imagination and the Nature of Choice*, which he thought might be of interest to me. This was excellent service, to say the least, and (on 23 November 1979) I duly purchased the book. I then read earlier books in which Shackle (1949, 1958, 1969) had set out his theory in more detail and I began to see how it could be fitted into a hierarchical view of wants. I realised that people could be viewed as dealing with uncertainty about whether an option would meet their target for a particular characteristic by asking themselves (a) whether the options seemed to have any potential (or, in later versions, enough potential) to meet a 'gain aspiration', and (b) whether it did not seem to have any potential (or, in later versions, not have too much potential) to result in a loss that they viewed as too big relative to the target that they were uncertain the option could meet. If it seemed OK on both counts, the option would be deemed an acceptable gamble in respect of the characteristic in question, with the decision-maker then considering how it fared in terms of the next most important characteristic. This seemed cognitively simpler than the focusing process that Shackle set out in his books. Sure, Shackle's view did involve simplification in that the theory of attention embodied in his 'ascendancy function' generated a 'focus gain' and a 'focus loss' for each of the options that were under consideration, but it then entailed a convoluted process by which these focal pairings could be ranked for rival options: his view seemed less plausible when a decision-maker was dealing with many decision dimensions rather than merely financial returns.

The period in which I was exercising my imagination about ways of adapting Shackle's theory into a hierarchical context lasted until early March 1982 when, with extracts from letters that I received from Shackle, I finalised chapter 4 of *The Economic Imagination*. During this period, there were two areas where I should have been a better scholar. One was that I did not pursue the genealogy of Shackle's thinking in the way that I had pursued the genealogy of the ideas of other scholars whose work excited me. For example, when I discovered Richardson's (1960) *Information and Investment*, I made it my mission to find all the steps in his published work that led to it, and everything he published subsequently, even though there was no Google Scholar to speed up the process. In Shackle's case, I did not bother to see whether his 1949 book *Expectation in Economics* had been preceded by articles, and I only discovered one such article (Shackle, 1943). This discovery occurred purely by chance when I was looking for a paper by Alfred Schutz (his name spelt as Schuetz on this occasion) that I had seen referenced in Garfinkel (1967) and which happened to be in the same issue of *Economica*. But there were earlier papers, and they would have been easy to find.

If I had taken the trouble to do this, I would have discovered then, rather than 30 years later, that Shackle, too, had initially seen investment projects as being ranked using cut-off rules. First, he suggested that an entrepreneur would take the best outcome that seemed 'perfectly possible' as a 'working hypothesis' about what will actually eventuate and then choose the scheme with the largest prospective 'best' outcome 'so long as the worst is not too bad' (Shackle, 1940, p. 46). Shackle

(1941) then suggested that entrepreneurs might focus on whether their prospects of meeting an upside target if they chose a particular plan did not seem too difficult to believe, and their prospects of not falling below a tolerable downside target were not too difficult to disbelieve. In other words, where I arrived at was very similar to where Shackle had got to before developing his 'ascendancy function' view of how the attention of an entrepreneur gets focused. Shackle had made no reference to these early papers in our correspondence.

But I would have been wise also to look more carefully at how Shackle presented his critique of probabilistic thinking, how he engaged with probabilistic ideas after *Expectation in Economics* was published, and what adherents to probabilistic approaches themselves wrote. In my enthusiasm for Shackle's view that actuarial risks entail knowledge, whereas genuine uncertainty entails a lack of knowledge, I failed to notice for three decades that Shackle failed to engage with the subjective approach to probability that emerged while he was developing and launching his theory. Via his skills in the rhetorical use of prose and my failure to study seriously subjective probability analysis (or even Keynes's *Treatise on Probability*), I ended up accepting Shackle's view that a range of mutually exclusive outcomes for a scheme of action may be viewed as 'perfectly possible' with none of them being viewed as potential causes of surprise if they eventuate. This mattered, for it is the part of his analysis that causes problems if one tries to merge it with probabilistic approaches.

What Shackle had in mind as a 'perfect possibility' is an event that seems to have no credible barrier to prevent it from taking place. While it is easy to view outcomes that are seen as sources of astonishment as having zero probability, we clearly cannot assign probabilities of one to more than one imagined outcome, and if we assign a probability of one to any outcome, we must assign probabilities of zero to all other imagined outcomes. From Shackle's standpoint, zero potential surprise thus should not be viewed as equivalent to certainty, but his argument that *multiple* outcomes could seem perfectly possible becomes questionable if we take the view that it is illogical to view a set of rival events as perfectly possible, since acceptance of rivalry must entail accepting that causal processes that favour one outcome serve as barriers to the eventuation of others.

Rejecting the 'perfect possibility' aspect of Shackle's theory may make it legitimate to view Shackle's potential surprise scale as an inverted mapping to or from a subjective probability scale. This is the view that I have very belatedly come to take (see Earl, 2023b), but I think that it should not divert us from the merits of thinking about uncertainty in terms of the presence or absence of barriers to the eventuation of particular outcomes and thence to rate rival outcomes in terms of how surprised we would be if they occurred: it may be very useful to think about uncertainty by asking, 'What could possibly go wrong or (be made to go) right)?'

During my formative years in Stirling, I might have been more critical of Shackle, but also more able to use some of his ideas more constructively, if I had examined the relationship between Shackle's thinking and Kahneman and Tversky's (1979) prospect theory. I became aware of the latter at an early stage, via Thaler's (1980) pioneering use of it in the first issue of the *Journal of Economic Behavior and Organization*. An inspection copy of the first issue was circulated in the department as soon as it was published, and I greatly enjoyed much of Thaler's article, little realizing the impact it would ultimately have. However, I did not warm to prospect theory at that point. It seemed to me to be essentially a tweaked version of subjective expected utility theory, for although it portrayed decision-makers as considering separately the utility of gains and the disutility of losses, it remained a compensatory view of choice, with the net prospective change in utility being the criterion by which options are ranked. It had been developed in relation to choices between rival lotteries with simple payoff matrices, rather than via an attempt to find a plausible means of understanding how people deal with the cognitive challenges of choosing in situations where they face a wide range of choice between options that have many characteristics and uncertainty about what their options may deliver on some characteristic scales. Although Shackle's view of uncertainty had not been set out for such options, it seemed to be taking serious account of genuine uncertainty, and I had found a simple way of integrating it with a characteristics-space view of choice that took human cognitive limits seriously.

My failure to embrace prospect theory had a cascade of consequences for the contribution that I made to behavioural economics. I did not notice at this early stage that Shackle's theory can be viewed as a precursor to prospect theory, since both theories offer a reference-dependent view of risk-taking. Because of this, I failed to consider what benefits might come from seeing whether the two approaches could be blended. Had I attempted to do this, I would have had to address carefully which parts of Shackle's potential surprise approach to uncertainty could be reconciled with probabilistic thinking. Even if I had not ended up rejecting his perfect possibility notion, I might nonetheless have realised that, if one is willing to apply Shackle's analysis of focusing to a probabilistic view of rival outcomes, then one gets a view of how decision-makers might reduce choices over wide ranges of rival outcomes for rival schemes to the simple kinds of payoff matrices used in the experiments that underpinned prospect theory.

From there, I could have seen that, if one is applying the *S*-shaped utility function of prospect theory to situations where uncertainty is not an additional complicating factor (as Thaler was doing), then it might have much to offer for analysing behaviour where products are only viewed as presenting trade-offs between a pair of characteristics (instead of an overall gain and an overall loss), as opposed to a stack of many characteristics that would necessitate a non-compensatory approach or other means of simplifying decision-making. One implication of doing this would have been that, because of loss aversion, choices do not have the reversibility they seem to have, if changes in incentives are reversed, in Lancaster's (1966) characteristics-based model of choice. I also might have given the notion of 'loss aversion' more attention and, having realised that it can readily be incorporated in Shackle's view of choice, I might have given earlier attention to how it might be understood in terms of the cognitive underpinnings of resistance to change.

My missed opportunities in relation to Hayek, Ironmonger, Shackle, Thaler, and Kahneman and Tversky in the early 1980s seem amenable to being characterised in behavioural terms: Hayek looked insufficiently engaging/too difficult to digest; Ironmonger's book was disadvantaged by (un)availability bias because I did not have a personal copy to keep delving into and thereby keep noticing more in it; I was overawed by Shackle; and prospect theory seemed unsatisfactory in some ways without giving me cause to question the synthesis I had been constructing. But I think my scholarly shortcomings need to be viewed against the backdrop of the fact that, in the summer of 1980, I had started to find the process of writing, and the creative thinking that it led me to do, to be much more exciting than beavering away studying what others had written.

During my two years in Cambridge as a research student, I had been researching the literature on industrial change with a 'leave no stone unturned' mentality. But I lost this mentality in the excitement of my change of focus to consumer behaviour in my first year at Stirling. This switch was exacerbated by the excitement of being able to write my chapters of *Money Matters* simply by applying what I already knew. If I felt that I had enough ingredients for what I was intending to try to write, I got on with my writing; I did not anxiously keep reading to discover things that might derail my progress. My view was that, if I later discovered things that I could use to enhance my analysis, or if others drew them to my attention, then I could write a new edition or a sequel that was better (rather as Shackle did when he wrote *Decision, Order and Time* as a successor to *Expectation in Economics*). In other words, I accepted that academic research was a satisficing process and hence I did not view any of my work as definitive. The subtitle of *The Economic Imagination* captures this: *Towards a Behavioural Analysis of Choice*. Clearly, scholarship has to involve satisficing behaviour, for there is insufficient time to read everything that might be relevant to what one is considering writing, but I had allowed my standards to slip to a level that was preventing me from offering contributions of the kind that I could have produced if I had been less brash and more fastidious in my scholarly style.

Pluralism and Behavioural Economics

There is a rather inconsistent look to the way that I practised pluralism in relation to behavioural economics during my years at Stirling. On the one hand, I rejected a one-size-fits-all view of consumer behaviour in favour of a view that embraced both extended problem-solving and extreme simplification. Furthermore, in the original version of my Cambridge dissertation, I criticised Pickering (1976, p. 622) for suggesting, in his review of Andrews and Brunner's (1975) *Studies in Pricing*, that they had failed to offer a 'sufficiently general' theory of the behaviour of oligopolies, as though a theory should apply generally within the context it purports to address. But prior to 1983 (including in *The Economic Imagination*, which I had completed in 1982), I was prone to try to 'sell' my 'characteristic filtering' view of choice as a general way of viewing what people do when choosing between a wide range of options that offer many characteristics. This is especially evident in the dialogue that I wrote for section 4.9 of *The Economic Imagination*. Yet, in all honesty, I did not really believe it applied generally in that sort of situation. So, why did I write as though my approach was right and the marginal trade-off approach was wrong, rather than preach the need for pluralism?

My concern was that, if I accepted that people might differ in the ways that they take their decisions in a particular context and that some people's behaviour might align well with the received wisdom, then I would be unlikely to attract an audience for my heterodox perspective: allowing that there could be more than a grain of truth in the orthodox perspective could result in me getting no traction due to orthodox economists not being open to pluralistic thinking. If so, there was the risk that they would respond by asserting that their approach was 'sufficiently general' to use as 'the' way to view behaviour in that context. They would also be likely to present instances where their view does not seem implausible as means to dismiss the credibility of arguments that I raised to suggest their theory could not accommodate other instances. In other words, they might adopt the rhetorical strategy of saying that if one dug deeper, or bigger changes in incentives had been applied, then cases that I raised to illustrate non-substitution would be revealed as ultimately reducing to cases where 'everyone had their price', as in any instances where I accepted the substitution principle. Given the risk of such a reaction, it might be better simply to use strong-looking examples of non-substitution wherever possible and not mention examples where people do indeed seem to make trade-offs along the lines envisaged by Lancaster. Of course, orthodox economists might react by digging up such examples and accusing me of presenting a very one-sided view, but perhaps they might start to advocate the case for a pluralistic approach if, on reflection, my non-substitution examples seemed plausible.

In advocating a 'characteristic filtering' view of choice to the exclusion of both the conventional good-space view and Lancaster's characteristics-space view, I thus failed to be as pluralistic as I was in my later writing but naively hoped to promote pluralism in others, to which I would of course be able to accede. When Mark Blaug visited Stirling in his external examiner role a few months after *The Economic Imagination* was published (with his very supportive comments as one of the publisher's referees), he told me that he had greatly enjoyed the book and that, in writing it, I had been 'very courageous'. I had merely thought that I was doing what academics are supposed to do, i.e., facilitate the growth of knowledge by challenging the conventional wisdom. However, later in the 1980s, I was told that an external assessor for a job that I had applied for at the University of Auckland had dismissed my application by saying that I was 'a brash young man by all accounts'. My lack of life experience was certainly an issue when I wrote the book, for I had simply not done enough shopping or read enough product reviews, or talked enough with others about their purchasing decisions, to be able to offer copious illustrations of intolerant and/or checklist-based decision-making. I also should have made much more use of applications of Lakatos's (1970) methodology of scientific research programmes to economics (such as Latsis, 1972, and Remenyi, 1979), to highlight the intolerance of the 'positive heuristic' and 'negative heuristic' (i.e., the 'do' and 'don't' rules) of mainstream economics for specifying acceptable forms of behaviour within economics. In the event, although *The Economic Imagination* was reviewed quite widely and often more sympathetically than I had expected, no debate ensued about the relative applicability of substitution-based and non-substitution-based views of choice, and the book achieved virtually no citations in mainstream literature.

I would have had a better chance of gaining traction if I had been able to show economists, via empirical work in contrasting contexts, how propensities to choose in particular ways differ between contexts, why this is so, and why it matters for policy. By such work, I might have argued that a better way ahead for everyone is empirically-grounded pluralism, which accepts that rival ideas may each apply to some degree and attempts to study relative incidences of applicability in both a broad context (for example, how people decide whom to approach via online dating sites) and within variants of that context (for example, whether the applicability of a particular view of such choices varies according to how much information an online dating site displays on a page of search results – cf. Lenton and Stewart, 2008). Such empirical research could perhaps have provided me with a basis for a PhD if I had started working in this area back in 1977. However, a more realistic view is that it was something for which the role-model needed to be provided by a well-resourced team of researchers. This was eventually delivered by Payne, Bettman and Johnson (1993).

5.5   CONFERENCE PARTICIPATION

Academic conferences ideally provide good opportunities to do the following:

- Network with like-minded scholars and gather intelligence about job opportunities.
- Discover contributions to one's field before they are formally published.
- Publicise and stake claims of originality for one's latest ideas before they are formally published.
- Receive feedback on papers that one might not have written were it not for having made a precommitment to deliver them and wishing to avoid the embarrassment and possible reputational damage that would come from bailing out.
- Enjoy fine-dining and tourism experiences.

In practice, however, there may be a dearth of memorable presentations, few attendees at one's own session, and/or little useful feedback. One may get stuck talking with uninspiring participants rather than those that one had hoped to meet, and the dining experience may be very disappointing, especially if one has unusual dietary needs or preferences. As will become apparent in later chapters, my enthusiasm for conferences proved hard to sustain and the last one that I attended took place over seven years before I retired. But perhaps my gradual loss of enthusiasm was the result of my initial conference experiences leading me to have lofty expectations of what conferences can deliver.

The financial support that was provided at Stirling for attending conferences was very poor, barely enough to cover attendance at the annual conference of the Scottish Economic Society. Attending anything further afield required the shortfall to be self-funded unless the event was funded by a third party. I got a taste of an all-expenses-paid event in January 1984, near the end of my time at Stirling, when the Economic and Social Research Council funded a wonderful 'Workshop on Economic Beliefs' at the University of Bath. It brought together interdisciplinary researchers from all over the UK to present 'position papers' and discuss new research directions. Being invited to it gave me a great sense that *The Economic Imagination* had been noticed and I was being taken seriously. The workshop also was a way to get to know of the work of researchers such as Paul Mosley and Ronald Dore that has had an enduring impact on my thinking.

The two conferences that I attended while working at Stirling both took place in 1981, were small enough to be single session events, and focused on specialised themes. One was on 'The New Orthodoxy in

Economics' and was held in Sidney Sussex College, Cambridge and sponsored by the *Cambridge Journal of Economics*. The paper that Sheila Dow and I presented eventually proved to be my first journal article (Dow and Earl, 1984), albeit after several attempts and ultimately not in an easily accessible journal, after failing to attract sufficient enthusiasm from the sponsors. The highlight was the conference dinner, where Sheila and I had the good fortune to sit directly opposite Joan Robinson and Andre Gunder Frank, the last of whom was clearly surprised to be a lone Marxist against three Keynesians.

The other conference that I attended was the economics section of the BAAS that Brian Loasby has arranged for me to attend, whose theme was 'Beyond Positive Economics?' It was held at the University of York and provided a great opportunity to meet some senior figures who were interested in economic method, especially of a subjectivist variety. This was my first opportunity to meet George Shackle and his wife Catherine, but it was also where I got to know A. W. (Bob) Coats, John Hey and Stephen Littlechild, all three of whom later served as referees for me and contributed chapters to books that I edited. Indeed, I doubt that I would have become a professorial contender in 1990 were it not for John Hey later commissioning a major survey article from me (Earl, 1990a). The BAAS conference was also where I was impressed by the paper that the then-Chief Economist at Shell, Michael Jefferson, presented on the use of scenario planning as a technique for coping with non-probabilistic uncertainty. Michael's paper (Jefferson, 1983) had a huge impact on me, and over thirty years later it was a delight to be able to enlist him to contribute a chapter about the relationship between Shackle's work and Shell's scenarios to the book on Shackle that I wrote with Bruce Littleboy (Earl and Littleboy, 2014).

5.6   RESEARCH AUDIT

As is clear from the reflections of Creedy (2022) and as will become increasingly evident through the rest of this book, there have been major changes in the academic publishing environment over the past half century. Among the most significant is the explosion in the range of scholarly journals and the introduction of periodic audits of research quality whose results depend significantly on journal ranking scores. In the early 1980s, such audits were not even being discussed as possibly somewhere over the horizon. With hindsight, the absence of such discussion is somewhat surprising, for when the University Grants Committee (UGC) was working out the funding cuts that it imposed on UK universities in 1981, its decisions must have had a basis that included at least some kind of informal assessment of the quality of the research output being produced in the departments that it savaged or treated more generously.

At Stirling, these cuts were especially severe, in the region of 30 percent overall, despite Stirling's then-Principal, Sir Kenneth Alexander telling the 'Academic Assembly' (a meeting of most of the academic staff in one of the largest lecture theatres) that he was 'cautiously optimistic' after returning from a meeting with the UGC not long before the cuts were to be announced. Stirling's Department of Economics was hit particularly hard, being told it must downsise from 21 positions to just 12 (though fortunately, by the time the announcement was made, two academic staff had already departed). In the absence of published data from any formal audit as a basis for comparing Stirling's fate with rival institutions, it was very hard to make sense of the scale of the blow that had been dealt to the Department of Economics and the University as a whole. Rumours circulated about how the allocation of cuts could have been driven by the composition of the UGC itself and closeness of ties between UGC members and senior staff in departments at Stirling – if I recall correctly, mathematics was an area that was mentioned as having emerged suspiciously well compared with other departments Having experienced this episode, I think that, in principle, research audits are a good thing if they are based on transparent criteria and their findings are published. However, the big problem in practice is the choice of the assessment criteria and how they are weighed together or ranked by other means.

In this section, and in the corresponding sections in the three chapters that follow, I will attempt to provide some career lessons by reflecting on my research output from the standpoint of a modern-day faculty dean, with a focus on the 2019 iteration of the journals ranking list produced by the Australian Business Deans' Council (ABDC) – a list that seems to have become well-known beyond Australia. As well as reflecting on my output in terms of journal articles, I will also be listing other categories of scholarly output that I was required to list each year in my 'academic portfolio' for annual appraisals, confirmation of employment, and when applying for promotion, at the University of Queensland from 2002 onwards.

Table 5.1: A Dean's View of My University of Stirling Research Output

Type of Research Output	N	Reference Tag (and Name of Journal) in Reference List Order
A*-Ranked Articles	0	
A-Ranked Articles	0	
B-Ranked Articles	0	
C-Ranked Articles	0	
Unranked Articles	1	Dow and Earl (1984) *Economie Appliequée*
Refereed Conference Papers	0	
Research Monographs	3	Dow and Earl (1982), Earl (1983a, 1984)
Other Books	0	
Parts of Edited Books	3	Earl (1983b, 1983c), Earl and Dow (1984)
Review Articles	0	
Book Reviews	0	
Other	2	Earl (1980a), Earl and Glaister (1979)

Table 5.1 summarises my Stirling research output as seen from this kind of standpoint. All the items tagged here are included in this book's list of references. In this case, the category 'other' refers to departmental discussion papers that were not subsequently published, and 'other' was all I had to offer prior to the 1981 UGC cuts. To a modern-day dean, such a set of data would be most perplexing. It would be clear that I had been busy but also that I had been misbehaving, as I had not been producing high-ranking journal articles that would most clearly help to enhance my department's score. Books of the kinds that I had written are problematic to rate with the clarity accorded to journal articles, for although a book is much more substantial than a journal article, books are not refereed as closely as journal articles and publishers differ greatly in the rigour with which they assess book proposals and finished manuscripts. Even so, experienced academics will probably rank publishers informally in broadly similar ways. Moreover, unlike journal articles, books are often publicly reviewed by multiple reviewers, and reviewers differ in their standing. Within an internal tenure and promotion process, or in hiring processes, it is more feasible to argue carefully about the significance of books than it is possible to do when aggregated data are being considered

for entire departments. Hence, for external research audits, a dean will generally prefer that academic staff perform well in terms of their journal article trophies, unless, say, they have achieved acclaim for a book published by a top-tier university press.

The three books that dominate my Stirling research output would all be somewhat problematic to justify as being equivalent to upper-tier journal articles. My two solo books were published by a new, unknown imprint of a publisher that did not have a long track record, though *The Economic Imagination* could boast a foreword by Shackle and a very favourable publisher's review by Blaug. The problem with *Money Matters* is different. It concerns whether it should be listed as a monograph or in 'other books'. The latter category pertains to various kinds of edited books and to textbooks. Such works are assigned lower status because they are not the result of original research by the scholar(s) whose name they bear; rather, they result from applying existing knowledge of the field and capabilities such as those in project management, critical thinking, or pedagogical creativity. Some internal audit systems (such as the one that I later had to comply with at the University of Queensland when updating my academic portfolio) class these kinds of books as 'unrefereed'. This overlooks the fact that, when one produces a major anthology or reference book, the publisher may require the introduction and contents list to be signed off by referees who may first note gaps that should be filled, while, in the case of textbooks publishers may send manuscripts to many more referees than a journal article ever has. In some respects, *Money Matters* was like a research monograph but – not surprisingly given its origins – it was also seen by reviewers as suitable for use as an upper-level textbook.

A modern-day probationary lecturer would be strongly advised by his or her head of department and/or departmental supervisor against writing these kinds of books and would be told instead to aim for at least one A*-ranked and one or two A-ranked journal articles if (as in, for example, Australia's immigration visa-driven system) they are required to apply for confirmation of employment after three to five years. Given the lead time in economics between writing a paper and getting it accepted, the pressures of working in this kind of system may be far worse than those for which the seven-year US tenure track system was already notorious when I started my career. By contrast, no such expectations were set out to new recruits at Stirling at the time I was there. However, although there was no statement that it would be 'publish or perish' as per the US system, the department's active discussion paper series, and the circulation of such papers from other institutions, gave clear signals that research output was one of the things that members of staff were expected to produce.

The only nudge I can remember receiving about writing for journals came in a conversation with Richard Shaw in the coffee room. He said it would be wise to generate a mixed portfolio of outputs that included journal articles. He added that getting into the habit of writing articles and dealing with referees had benefits for the quality of work that one would discipline oneself to produce. By the time of that conversation, I had already been granted tenure: I had only a two-year probationary period and my job was confirmed without my PhD candidacy having been confirmed, though *Money Matters* may have passed the review stage by that point.

The apparent addiction to writing books that I may seem to have developed from late 1980 onward was not entirely due to my discovery of how much I enjoyed the excitement of trying to marshal ideas on a large scale. It also was a consequence of what I had experienced in my first attempts at getting papers published. The first paper that I wrote after arriving at Stirling was a joint piece with Keith Glaister, who was then working as a research fellow on Chuck Brown's labour supply project but who later had a stellar career as a UK business school academic. Our paper was called 'Wage stickiness from the demand side' and it owed much to our mutual interest in the work of P. W. S. Andrews and Elizabeth Brunner (Andrews, 1949, 1964; Andrews and Brunner, 1975). Whereas I had got interested in their work via reading Loasby (1976), Keith's familiarity with it was more direct: his first degree was from Lancaster, where Andrews and Brunner had both worked. However, infusing our paper with their way of viewing competition proved problematic. This was very ironic, since around the time we wrote it and were trying to find a home for it in a journal, I had been reading a recent University of Wollongong PhD entitled 'P. W. S. Andrews and the Unsuccessful Revolution' (Irving, 1978) and corresponding with both its author and with A. W. (Bob) Coats, who had been its external examiner and had sent his copy to Brian Loasby, whence it came to me.

I had the idea for the paper while Vicky Chick was presenting chapter 5 of her in-process book *Macroeconomics After Keynes* (published as Chick, 1983) at a departmental seminar. Her chapter addressed the microeconomic underpinnings of the aggregate supply function.

Naturally, it took account of the kinds of issues that Keynes had viewed as limiting the tendency of workers to try to preserve their jobs in times of falling labour demand by offering to work for less. It suddenly dawned on me that the usual presumption was that employers would wish to cut wages if demand fell, so that they could reduce their prices and thereby hope to maintain output and employment. Yet, here we were, in Margaret Thatcher's Britain, and employers did not seem to be trying to initiate wage cuts any more than trade unions were trying to do so. It occurred to me that this might be due to the employers having concerns that if they initiated wage cuts, there could be adverse consequences that went beyond unions retaliating with strike action. Perhaps they were afraid of losing their best workers and/or that productivity would suffer due to employees who had previously been very cooperative now merely doing the bare minimum within the terms of their fuzzy job contracts. I got talking with Keith as soon as the seminar finished, and we decided to write a joint paper about this issue. Before the year's end, a discussion paper (Earl and Glaister, 1979) was released, after our draft had been scrutinised by Paul Hare, who edited the discussion paper series.

We submitted the discussion paper to the *Bell Journal of Economics*, as that was where one of our most recent sources, Williamson, Wachter and Harris (1975), had been published, but the paper was rejected. In July 1980, before submitting the paper to the *Economic Journal*, we tweaked it slightly by adding a recent quotation from leading Conservative politician Sir Keith Joseph as an epigraph. His words epitomised the view that we were challenging, for he presumed that if workers were willing to work for less, they would be able to price themselves into jobs. The policy significance of the paper seemed to us to make it worth sending to the UK's top economics journal, but it was again rejected. We then wrote a less technical, graph-free version and sent it to the *British Journal of Industrial Relations*, where our work fared no better. At this point, we decided that we were getting nowhere and gave up trying to get the paper published. This was probably a mistake, for given the kind of feedback we were getting, we might have stood a better chance if we had submitted it to a heterodox journal such as the newly established *Journal of Post Keynesian Economics*, or the *Cambridge Journal of Economics*. However, the need to get the paper published in a journal seemed to evaporate once I had included the essence of its thinking in *Money Matters*.

My recollection of the feedback is that the referees were not as bemused by the idea that cutting wages could reduce profits due to productivity being adversely affected, as they were by the literature on which we based our analysis. They seemed to be puzzled as to why we had used sources that were not widely used in economics at that time.

We had stressed, via Coase (1937) that employment contracts do not set out in detail the tasks that workers will be asked to perform, and we drew on the behavioural theory of the firm and the recently published Williamson *et al.* (1975) paper (which I had been familiar with via its inclusion as chapter 4 of Williamson, 1975) to stress the discretionary nature of effort and responses to managerial requests, with workers in particular job categories not necessarily being assigned the same tasks or performing any given task with the same degree of efficiency. At the time of hiring workers, employers cannot be sure how well they will perform; once employed, workers are paid salaries rather than being rewarded based on their rate of output. Those who perform better than their colleagues in similar job slots do so in the hope of eventually getting promoted to jobs that have better salaries. Thus, we argued via Andrews (1958) that 'internal competition' normally has a major role in promoting industriousness even though outputs are not specified in detail in employment contracts. When demand drops, cutting output and retrenching the weaker performers provides a way for firms to get by without suffering from productivity reductions that could come from driving wages down and then losing better workers – workers that it may be impossible to rehire by restoring wages when demand recovers. We explored this in a pluralistic manner, both for firms that set their prices and outputs by applying conventional marginalist rules and for firms that are, as in Andrews's (1949) analysis, fearful of potential competition, and of wrecking goodwill relationships with customers, and which therefore base their prices on 'normal' costs and then supply as much as customers demand at those prices.

Our referees seemed puzzled by our pluralistic approach, given that the normal cost perspective was one that had not become standard fare in economics, and by our concern with the internal operations of firms. We were less surprised that our enthusiasm for Andrews's work seemed odd to them than that we were running into difficulties due to being ahead of the game in the belated uptake of Coase (1937) and in employing Williamson *et al.* (1975), and because we had failed to notice that interest in Cyert and March (1963) had collapsed. But what really bugged me

195

was that, in expecting us to argue from well-established sources, it was as if they doubted that arguments from elsewhere could be worth taking seriously and they were therefore not bothering to read and reflect on our analysis carefully. Our analysis was not crazy: all we had done was arrive too early and from left field with an idea that others marketed successfully a few years later as 'efficiency wages' (see Akerlof and Yellen, eds, 1986) without committing the sin of using unpopular foundations.

This experience helped to prepare me for the failure of my paper on characteristic filtering to get anywhere when I sent it to the newly launched *Journal of Economic Behavior and Organization*, for I had made the mistake of trying to build it around Kelly's psychology of personal constructs as an alternative to viewing economic agents as utility seekers. It resulted in a presentation of characteristic filtering that was viewed as far too wordy and difficult to understand, yet I do not recall the referees suggesting that I ought to have presented a formal model built around linear programming. Except for some references to Herbert Simon, it is likely that everything I referred to would have been unfamiliar to US-sourced referees if they were economists rather than consumer behaviour researchers in marketing. From these experiences, I concluded that I would need much more space to introduce and integrate unfamiliar ideas in a way that sustained the attention of readers.

The paper on characteristic filtering was written during the 1980 long vacation. After completing it, I decided that I would have some fun by writing a somewhat satirical paper, to which I gave the reflexive title 'A behavioural theory of economists' behaviour and the lack of success of behavioural economics.' It was inspired by reflection on my experience with the referee reactions to the paper I had written with Keith Glaister, how I had come to know about the sources that informed my work, and on the struggle that I had been through with some of these sources (especially with those by Andrews, which entailed multiple readings of them) until I felt confident that I really had 'got' what they were saying.

This reflection had left me feeling that the processes that determine the success of contributions to economic knowledge are rather like those that determine the sales of products offered in supermarkets. Like supermarkets, university libraries offer ranges of products so vast that it is impossible for their customers to become familiar with everything that is being offered that may be relevant to their research and teaching. Choices must therefore be simplified via rule- and routine-based filtering processes that are affected by social interactions. Books and journal articles may thus fail to enjoy the attention they deserve, and this shortage of attention will impact on refereeing processes partly via its impact on referees' knowledge of cited sources and partly via how much time they invest in trying to appreciate what authors are trying to do. However, as Irving had tried to demonstrate in her study of the fate of Andrews's work, the preconceptions of referees can result in them failing to draw the right inferences about what authors are trying to do. Furthermore, I felt it was unwise to assume that academics were single-mindedly operating as 'humble seekers after truth' as opposed to having multiple goals that might be hierarchically ordered, thereby making them intolerant of particular kinds of contributions. Some might be lazy, self-serving folk who prefer 'playing with models' to wading through complex prose. As referees, they may fail to give serious attention to works whose style is not to their taste, especially if they enjoy both the convenience and sense of power of performing a quick hatchet-job rather than ensuring that they 'get' what the author is trying to do and then offer constructive criticism. Whether, and where, academic ideas end up getting published and cited may thus have little to do with their benefits for society at large. With hindsight, I would have added that this makes the design of research audit systems very problematic, with the audits having potential to corrupt the ways in which academics operate, to the detriment of society at large.

Although written with satirical intent, my behavioural analysis of academic economics was released as a departmental discussion paper (Earl, 1980b) immediately following the one on characteristic filtering. I therefore decided to submit it to *History of Political Economy* to see whether it would be taken seriously. Somewhat to my surprise, it was. In contrast to the previous two papers, it received some very constructive feedback and an invitation to revise and resubmit. However, as noted in Section 4.4, I never resubmitted it due to Alfred Eichner asking if he could build an edited volume (Eichner, ed, 1983) around it. I realised that letting Eichner have the paper was not my best strategy for enhancing my CV, but I felt obliged, out of collegial duty, to allow him to use the paper: he had given me great encouragement and I felt that my paper could help the book's co-contributors get their related perspectives noticed if other scholars made their way to the book after seeing my contribution being cited. It was the first of many obligational publications that would limit the time that I spent enhancing my list of journal articles in the ensuing four decades.

5.7   EXIT

The cuts that the UGC imposed on Stirling did not inspire hope for accelerated movement up the lecturer's salary scale, but they certainly created a rather grim atmosphere even in the absence of any talk about compulsory redundancies of staff from the Department of Economics. I declined an invitation to consider moving into Stirling's fledgling Department of Business Studies, as I realised that my mission was to try to promote a more interdisciplinary way of doing economics, which I felt was best attempted from within the discipline. However, even in the absence of firm pressure to move elsewhere, there was little scope for applying for academic jobs in the UK as very few vacancies appeared in the first couple of years after the cuts were announced. As 1983 approached, a further constraint appeared, namely that I was scheduled to have my first sabbatical in the first half of 1983. Given that I would then need to serve at least a semester after the sabbatical, the earliest I could aim to move on would be early 1984. Hence, the best thing would be to enjoy the sabbatical and get *The Corporate Imagination* written, and see what vacancies started to appear toward the end of the sabbatical.

While I was on sabbatical, it became apparent that the UGC had realised that having a significant period with no prospects for doctoral students to move into entry-level jobs could damage the UK university system in the long run. Suddenly, some universities were allowed to offer 'new blood' lectureships. But the change came with a disconcerting catch: anyone who had already held a lectureship for three years or more was barred from applying for these positions. So, despite being some months short of turning 28 and with my PhD saga still in progress, I was too much of an old-timer to apply for any of these jobs in the hope of getting an offer nearer the top of the lecturer scale. The only way to improve my real income was to try to move up to a more senior position somewhere else in the UK, or to emigrate.

I doubted that I would be able to get shortlisted for a senior lectureship in a UK university while my PhD was still in progress, but it occurred to me that, with my track record in writing books, I might be able to get a principal lectureship within the polytechnic sector. I knew that the teaching loads and libraries would be worse, but I was also aware that a significant number of the UK's heterodox economists (such as Philip Arestis and Geoff Hodgson) worked in the polytechnic sector and were nonetheless able to be active as researchers. So, when Oxford Polytechnic (since 1992, Oxford Brookes University) advertised a principal lectureship in economics, I decided to apply, had a pleasant interview experience, and was offered the position. The increase in my take-home pay would have been spectacular, but I declined the offer without giving much thought to the academic challenges that I might run into or how I would feel about working in Oxford but not at Oxford University. There was a more basic problem: unless I opted to live a long way from Oxford and commute in (which I was not prepared to do), the cost of housing was so much greater that I doubted I would be any better off than if I stayed in Stirling. Leaving Thatcher's Britain seemed the best road toward a more positive future.

At no point did I consider the possibility of moving to the USA. This was not because my PhD was still in progress but rather, as when I was considering where to do my PhD, because of my aversion to its gun culture and political system. Nor did I investigate New Zealand, despite two of my colleagues, Paul Tompkinson and Bob Hamilton, moving to jobs there (in Bob's case, after a very protracted visa process), for my impression was that the New Zealand economy was not faring well. Australia seemed to be the obvious place to try, so I applied for two positions in Sydney and others at the Australian National University in Canberra and at the University of Tasmania in Hobart. I did so without doing any research on the institutions or cities beyond reading the little that came in the further particulars packs. In the pre-Internet, pre-videoconference era, one obtained further particulars packs and applied for such positions via the Association of Commonwealth Universities, which arranged for UK applicants to be interviewed by UK-based academics. The only position for which I was shortlisted was the one in Tasmania, which was for a three-year contract rather than a tenurable position.

The interview took place late in the autumn of 1983. As luck would have it, I was interviewed by the only Australian academic economist that I already knew, namely Geoff Harcourt. By chance, he was joined by the acting head of the University of Tasmania's economics department, Tony Hocking, who happened to be in the UK to attend his mother's wedding and who was in the process of pivoting his work from economics to marketing. The interview was held at Geoff's rooms in Jesus College at the time that Prince Edward was a Jesus student. I was slightly late arriving for it, having got stuck in traffic, and as I approached Geoff's staircase, his unmistakable voice greeted me cheerily from the window above, saying, 'Hurry up or you'll miss seeing the prince!' Edward had been in the court that was visible from the other side of Geoff's suite and had indeed vanished from sight by the time I entered. A very relaxed interview ensued.

It was only when a telegram arrived from the University of Tasmania informing me that an offer was on its way that I realised I had a big decision to take. I had very little idea about the cost of living in Hobart, but at the prevailing exchange rate the position I was offered on the lectureship scale seemed to pay about 70 percent more than I was getting at Stirling. The real worry was the three-year non-tenurable nature of the job: this made me feel that, if I took up the position, I would not really feel like I was emigrating, thereby also raising the issue of whether I should ship everything to Hobart or leave some of my possessions in the UK. As Christmas 1983 approached, I decided to decline the offer. This did not go down well with my then-partner, Sharon, who had applied for a scholarship to do the University of Tasmania's two-year Master of Clinical Psychology; when Christmas arrived, I received a present from her in the form of a jigsaw puzzle of an illustrated map of Tasmania (which these days hangs, framed, on a wall in my lounge). However, on my first morning back on campus in New Year 1984, I was invited to reconsider my decision.

The invitation came in a phone call from Professor Harry Campbell, who had just moved to the University of Tasmania and was calling as the new head of its department of economics, By this point, penny-pinching in relation to office telephones had gone a lot further due to the UGC's cuts to Stirling's funding: the office phones were removed unless staff were prepared to pay for them. Because I was not prepared to do so, any incoming call for me went to the departmental office and the secretary would then come to my office to tell me to go and answer it on her phone. Harry Campbell thus had to wait until I picked up the receiver after sprinting along the corridor. Stirling's telephonic poverty was a symbol of the madness of Thatcher's policies and rather conducive to my on-the-spot acceptance of the three-year position after Harry had explained that two staff were scheduled to retire in the next few years and that I should therefore be able to apply for a tenurable position before the contract came to an end. Sharon's Tasmanian application came good, too, and before the end of February she had headed off to start her master's programme in Hobart.

There are three important memories that I have from the end of my time at Stirling, aside from the stresses of leaving with my flat unsold, the challenges of my final few weeks living in the empty flat after international removalists had packed and taken away its contents, and the warmth of the ways in which my colleagues farewelled me. The first concerns the hassle in getting a visa and the surprise that the visa entailed. Such experiences are common for those who emigrate to Australia. I heard nothing for several months after I completed the paperwork and had my medical check with the doctor in Stirling that the Australian Consulate in Edinburgh required me to use. When I complained about the time it was taking, I was told that my chest X-ray had not been received, and I then had to have a fresh X-ray. When my passport at last came back, the three-year residence visa stamp noted that I was not allowed to apply for any jobs in Australia for the duration of the visa. If this condition were enforced, how would I apply for a tenurable job there? I was subsequently advised in Hobart that these conditions were not actually enforced for university staff.

The second important memory is that, when finalising my exit from Stirling, I discovered that in agreeing to start in Hobart at the beginning of June 1984, at the start of the second term, I had unwittingly imposed a significant cost on myself: the date of my exit meant that the total duration of my service at Stirling was four years and eleven months, one month too short to enable me to remain a member of the UK universities' pension scheme. I therefore received a refund of my personal contributions but lost the employer contributions and any future part-pension rights.

The third important memory is that when I visited Cambridge shortly before leaving Stirling, I visited Andrew Goudie, one of my Queens' contemporaries, who was then working in the DAE. Andrew had achieved the top first in Part II Economics and would go on to have a stellar career as a public service economist that culminated in a long spell as Director General Economy and Chief Economic Advisor to the Scottish Government. He always seemed not just very bright but very wise. He wished me well with my move Down Under, but he also said that it might not prove easy to return to work in the UK. As usual, he was right, though in this case possibly not for the right reasons.

6 University of Tasmania, Australia, 1984–1991

6.1 INTRODUCTION

The University of Tasmania (henceforth usually abbreviated to UTAS) was founded in Hobart in 1890 and is Australia's fourth oldest university. Today, it is a multi-campus institution that ranks around 300th globally and 20th in Australia. The main campus is in Sandy Bay, an up-market suburb, about 35 minutes by foot from Hobart's city centre. It dates from the early 1960s and nowadays hosts around 10,000 students, considerably more than when I started working there. The Sandy Bay campus has the spectacular vista of Mount Wellington as its backdrop and is on a sloping site that provides views of the Derwent estuary. Although it appeared far less starved of funds than Stirling during the 1980s and began its expansion into a multi-campus operation during that decade, the fact that UTAS had only advertised three-year contract lectureships in 1983 was a symptom of the Australian Federal Government imposing significant funding cutbacks during that decade. One of Professor Harry Campbell's main challenges as Head of the Department of Economics was to convince the Vice-Chancellor to allow tenurable positions to be advertised as the market for academic economists got tighter. Eventually, he succeeded, but modest growth ensured that the department remained smaller than the one at Stirling relative to the size of its enrolments. There was a sense that the Faculty of Commerce was being squeezed in its per-capita resources to cross-subsidise some of the other faculties.

When I arrived there in June 1984, Harry was the sole full professor in the UTAS Department of Economics, with the rest of the academic staff consisting of two tutors, five lecturers, three senior lecturers, and a reader. There were also several research staff in the department's consulting arm, the Centre for Regional Economic Analysis (CREA), and often, during my time there, some teaching was done by a visitor from overseas. More tutors were soon hired, and they played a key role in enabling the department to raise its research profile without letting teaching standards slip. With the tutors running most of the tutorials for large classes. the contact hours of the rest of the academic staff could be kept to levels lower than I had been used to at Stirling, though each tutorial normally had a dozen students.

The system was something of a precursor to the present-day Australian system in which undergraduate tutorials are largely conducted by fourth-year honours students. However, it entailed hiring full-time tutors who had recently completed master's degrees. They came mainly from Canada and did not enrol for PhDs; instead, their jobs were more like coming to Australia for a working vacation that lasted for two or three years, after which they moved elsewhere. Harry was able to recruit a succession of very capable tutors and the system thus worked very well as a means of limiting the impact of the funding situation. So, why did it not become the norm as academic labour markets became increasingly globalised?

From a trade unionist's perspective, such tutor positions looked like bad jobs because they did not offer any career development pathway from tutor to lecturer. It appears that to placate the National Tertiary Education Union and create such a pathway, the rank of assistant lecturer was added to the Australian academic hierarchy, with assistant lecturers having fewer contact hours than tutors had and working part-time on PhDs. In a sense, the Australian assistant lecturer role was like the role that the junior staff at Stirling were playing while finishing their PhDs on the lower rungs of the longer pay ladder that existed for UK lecturers. However, in the Australian context, the idea of replacing the kinds of tutors we had at UTAS with assistant lecturers completely ignored the implicit 'working vacation' appeal of the tutor role. Certainly, the assistant lecturer grade could be a useful means whereby a 'grow your own' strategy could be employed to deal with difficulties in attracting lecturers with PhDs but, in most disciplines, it would be more cost effective simply to hire lecturers with PhDs via global labour markets and pay honours students and other sessional staff to run tutorials and mark the bulk of assessed work for large classes.

Unlike the situation at Stirling, none of the lecturers were working on a PhD, and I was no longer the youngest lecturer: Ben Heijdra was two years younger, with a doctorate from Simon Fraser University in Canada; he, too, had accepted a three-year position. Until Harry Bloch joined the department, I was the only seriously heterodox person there, but I did not feel like I was an out-of-place lone wolf: it was possible to discuss different approaches to economics without being 'shut down', for this was before orthodox economists started asserting that non-orthodox ways of doing economics are 'not economics'. Closest to me in terms of background was Bob Rutherford, who was about three years older than me and had studied at Oxford. He seemed to have read widely and had a healthy interest in the history of economic thought as well as in economic policy. During my last couple of years in the department, the latter interest led him to go on secondment as an economic advisor to the Tasmanian State Government during the time of the Labor–Green Accord, and although he returned to the department not long after I departed, he ultimately opted to become a senior Tasmanian public servant.

During my job interview in Cambridge in 1983, Tony Hocking (the sole reader and at that time the acting head) had predicted that Bob and I would get on really well, and I did indeed greatly enjoy having Bob as a colleague. However, I correctly anticipated that my closest colleague would be Michael Brooks, who had initially studied at Monash University in Melbourne before moving to Virginia to do his doctorate under the supervision of James Buchanan. He took a serious interest in hierarchical approaches to decision-making after I introduced the field to him, and he was the only UTAS colleague with whom I collaborated on a publication (Brooks and Earl, 1987).

Moving to Tasmania was not conducive to joint research with my existing contacts. Airmail to the UK entailed at least a couple of weeks between sending a letter and receiving a reply. Mail contact with the USA was on average far worse, and far more unpredictable: Fred Lee and I continued our correspondence about P. W. S. Andrews and normal cost pricing, but the mail delays caused Fred to comment in one letter that he wondered whether the US postal service waited until it had a big enough sack of airmail for Tasmania before putting it on a flight. Matters were not helped by the lack of knowledge of Tasmania among US postal workers: when Roy Rotheim sent me his thesis so that we might better share our enthusiasm for chapter 17 of Keynes's (1936) *General Theory*, the long delay in its arrival turned out to have been partly due to it having initially been sent to Tanzania, despite Roy correctly addressing it.

In this environment, I only engaged in one international collaboration as an author aside from finishing the Shackle symposium paper that I was already working on with Neil Kay (Earl and Kay, 1985) at the time I arrived in Hobart. It entailed a minor role in a joint paper with Fred and other fans of the work of Andrews (Lee *et al.*,1986).[10] But distance did not prove a barrier to keeping in touch and working collaboratively in other ways, such as via my first role as a book editor. In fact, except for the area of the history of economic thought, I was better at maintaining and extending my overseas network than I was at developing a network of Australian contacts.

The period covered in this chapter saw rapid change in information technology. Very soon after arriving, I bought a Cannon Typestar portable electric typewriter. It had a prodigious appetite for ink cassettes but offered a one-line memory and two fonts. It only served me for two years. Soon after I bought the Typestar, Tony Hocking obtained an Apple Lisa (a precursor to the Macintosh, with a five-megabyte hard drive) and started using it to analyse spatial consumer census data. By 1986 academic staff were starting to do their own word processing using the UTAS mainframe computer from terminals in their offices, and the department then obtained some of the original IBM personal computers that ran on the MS-DOS operating system. It was via one of these that I was able to deliver my first edited book (Earl, 1988a) to its publisher as a set of non-WYSIWYG WordPerfect files. The non-WYWIWYG experience drove my decision to become a user of Apple computers.

When I got the chance to try the Macintosh and an Imagewriter printer that the department acquired just before I finished getting the edited book ready, I immediately realised how much easier the task would have been with its WYSIWYG screen. I was able to keep the Apple equipment, but I made a costly mistake when rearranging my office to accommodate it better. When I turned on the printer, its start-up seemed a bit lethargic, but I did not have the presence of mind to check the power cords to make sure I had plugged the one that had a 240v–110v transformer into the Macintosh. I soon realised my mistake, for when I turned on the Macintosh there was a sharp bang, which was the sound of the glass of its fuse breaking as the computer's power supply module got destroyed. The repair cost around AUD400. By mid-1987, I had purchased my own Macintosh (a 512k 'enhanced memory' model), an external disk drive (to

---

[10] This paper was not a good use of the time of any of its authors. The journal in which it was published, the *British Review of Economic Issues* (*BREI*), was published by the Association of Polytechnic Teachers of Economics and had seemed to be a promising outlet for heterodox economists. I used to browse the *BREI* in the library at Stirling but never saw it again after leaving the UK and – perhaps not surprisingly, given that UK polytechnics became 'new universities' from 1992 – it is hard to find any trace of it after 1995, and Google Scholar shows no sign of the Lee *et al.* paper having been cited.

make it easier to use, given that it had no hard-drive memory and only one in-built disk drive) and an Apple Imagewriter II printer for a total cost of (in 1987 prices) around AUD3000 to enable me to work at home on projects that I also worked on at the office. By early 1991, some staff started using email, and it achieved widespread adoption just after I left in the middle of that year. It was not until just before email started to take off that departmental fax machines came in as a means for fast international mail. even though there was a university-level 'facsimile' number on the UTAS letterhead right from the time I arrived.

6.2   TEACHING

In applying to UTAS, I had not given much thought to what its students might be like. I had been unaware that Tasmania has an unenviable but seemingly justified reputation for the insularity of its population and that this has consequences for tertiary education uptake. My first sign that I might need to know more about what I was getting into came when I went to say goodbye to Geoff Harcourt when I visited Cambridge shortly before moving to Hobart. Geoff was running an undergraduate supervision when I knocked on his door. He introduced me to his students by saying that I was about to take up a job in Tasmania and that, when I arrived, I would discover that I was the only person there without two heads. This was an allusion to the alleged tendency of Tasmanians to be overly inbred, a phenomenon particularly associated with its rural backwaters. Later, I would discover that tertiary education rates of Tasmanians were poor relative to their counterparts across the Bass Strait. This was sometimes explained as being due to Tasmanian parents being fearful that their children would move to the Australian mainland, or beyond, after graduating. Hence, they did not encourage their children to stay at school long enough to get university entrance qualifications.

Local tertiary education participation rates are important for universities in Australia as domestic students mostly enrol at universities in their home city or, at least, their home state, with many of them living at home until they graduate. This 'commuter university' culture was very different from the system in the UK when I was an undergraduate: in the UK, one could live comfortably away from home and thereby escape from parental strictures so long as one's parents topped up one's means-tested student grant or were poor enough (or rich enough to use ruses such as family trusts to give the illusion of incomes low enough) for their children to be eligible for 'the full grant'. UTAS thus had very few interstate students, but it also did not lose Tasmania's brightest students to mainland universities.

The proportion of exceptionally able students was thus much better than at Stirling. Three of those that I taught (Robert Mallick, Michael Buchanan, and Randall Weeks) had high-flying international careers after going on to Oxford as Rhodes Scholars. Others that I taught went on to senior positions in the financial sector or in the public service on the Australian mainland. One of my star students, Mardi Dungey, did eventually return to Hobart after getting her PhD at the Australian National University and making her mark there and in Cambridge as a financial economist. However, her time in the role of Professor and Head of the Department of Economics at UTAS was cut short when she succumbed to cancer at the age of only 52 (for a memorial article on her life, see Dempster and Gatheral, 2022).

As at Stirling, the international students in economics classes at UTAS in the 1980s came mainly from Malaysia. Many brought 'parrot-learning' techniques with them, which did not serve them well in my classes. But there were also some incredibly impressive international students, almost all of whom seemed to come from Singapore, often as public service scholars and with the advantage of having experienced UK-style teaching and acquiring A-Level credentials. The latter students tended also to be technically very capable, and I could see that, although they were adept at dealing with open-ended problems, they were rather sceptical about the attempts I made to foster a scenarios-based way of thinking about the future rather than one based on building deterministic or probabilistic predictive models. I was therefore delighted by the contents of a letter that I received from one of these students a couple of years after she graduated. She had achieved high distinction grades from me when she took Money and Banking in 1987 and Business and Government Policy in 1988. In her letter she explained that she was now working in what seemed to be Singapore's equivalent of the Australian Security Intelligence Organization. She said that she could not tell me anything about what she did but wanted me to know that she now appreciated much better what I had been attempting to do: the scenarios way of thinking – in which one focuses on trying to identify possible ways in which the future *could* unfold, and then analyses how seriously to take them to avoid being unpleasantly surprised or missing opportunities – was proving to be very useful in her work.

Throwing a Heterodox Spanner into the Works

When I arrived at UTAS, the teaching calendar consisted of three, nine-week terms with final examinations all taken at the end of the academic year. By the time I left, this traditional Cambridge-style system had been replaced by one based on two, thirteen-week semesters with final examinations at the end of each semester, similar to what I had become used to at Stirling. The term-based system gave students more time to absorb each subject. However, for those who were not deep learners, the long gap between the early material and final examinations made it more likely that early material would get forgotten, making it more difficult to understand later material that built upon it. For academic staff, the term-based system meant there were no examinations to mark in the between-term breaks, but the marking process at the end of the year was gruelling. With UTAS students taking eight subjects per year, the term-based system was built around each subject having a single lecture per week and fortnightly tutorials. In my first term, I only had one subject to teach, and its lectures were on Friday mornings. As I settled in and got over jet-lag, I wrestled with a dilemma about how I was going to teach it and what I would say to my class at the end of the week in my first lecture.

Given that I had co-authored *Money Matters* a few years earlier, it came as no surprise that Harry Campbell was keen for me to teach the second-year unit called Money and Banking when I arrived. The first term had been taught by Don Challen, who had gone to Canberra on three years' secondment to the Economic Policy Advisory Council (from which he did not return to UTAS). He had been teaching the subject via a textbook (Challen and Hagger, 1981) that he had written with Alf Hagger, who by the time that I arrived was a retired member of the department attached to CREA. I realised that I had a problem as soon as I obtained a copy of the textbook. The UTAS Bachelor of Economics programme did not include a second-year intermediate macroeconomics subject, but that was what Challen had, in effect, been teaching. Moreover, he had been teaching it in an extremely orthodox, technique-driven way based on developing a series of increasingly advanced models. If one wanted to teach that kind of macroeconomics, the Challen and Hagger approach had much to commend it. I therefore had to choose between finishing what he had started or actually teaching the subject with a focus on money and banking.

As the Friday lecture loomed, I realised that I could not bring myself to become a Challen and Hagger franchisee by teaching from the textbook in which the students had invested. I would start as I meant to go on in subsequent years when I taught the subject from the outset: I would begin with a revision of the IS–LM model and explain why Post Keynesian monetary economists do not base their work on it. Having done this, I would chart the alternative path that I planned to take. Clearly, it would be problematic to switch to using *Money Matters* as the subject's textbook, for even if copies could somehow be shipped rapidly to Hobart, there would doubtless be resistance from the class to having to buy another textbook. I decided to deal with this problem by writing detailed lecture summary handouts each week for the class as well as giving them a reading list of articles and books to which I would be referring.

The Money and Banking students looked rather shocked when I explained what I was going to do, and why. In fact, they seemed too shocked to start challenging me during that first lecture. However, I had not been back at my office for very long when three students, Paula, Terri and Brenda, came by to introduce themselves, welcome me and let me know that they and their classmates were rather alarmed by the unexpected turn the subject seemed to be taking. I tried to reassure them that they would be able to cope and that it would prove to be an interesting and enjoyable experience. A week or so later, the departmental secretary advised me that Harry Campbell wanted to have a chat with me. Harry, too, was concerned, for he had been visited in a more formal manner, by the students' representative. Fortunately, he seemed prepared to wait and see whether the class would settle into what I was trying to do, as indeed they did.

The students in the Money and Banking class were generally more technically adept than those I had taught at Stirling, so the main challenge that they faced was the switch to a teaching style that took them away from technical exercises to a discursive approach that required them to develop their critical thinking skills. However, the weekly lecture summaries may have limited the pressure that some of the international students should have felt to rethink their routines for learning and surviving assessment tasks. The problem was that the lecture summaries – which filled both sides of a sheet of A4 paper with single-spaced type – turned out to be short enough for them to parrot-learn. As a result, some of the international students attempted to deal with the final examination by trying to find a match between some of the words in a question and the words in a lecture summary, and then reproduced the lecture summary pretty much verbatim as their answer.

This behaviour helped me to appreciate the difference between having information and having knowledge, for what such students were doing was essentially uploading, storing, and downloading information without providing much of a demonstration that they understood its significance or that they could use it to construct arguments or reflect on the appropriateness of rival policies in a particular context. It was not until late 1991, shortly after I had left UTAS, that I was provided with a way of making sense of this sort of behaviour and trying to counter it – see Section 7.2. In the meantime, no matter what the tutors and I said about the importance of not trying to use such an approach, there would always be several students who behaved in this way when I provided lecture summary notes. These students condemned themselves to scraping a bare pass, if they were lucky.

Each of the four versions of Money and Banking that I delivered was pluralistic, but they differed in how they were pluralistic. Clearly, the 1984 version involved staff who did economics from different standpoints, whereas from 1985 to 1987 I was the sole lecturer. In the latter versions, I did not present a one-eyed Post Keynesian perspective, and toward the end I was working with a monetarist tutor, Tom Rohling, who had come from Calgary in Canada and went to work at the Reserve Bank of Australia after his stint at UTAS. Tom really got into running the tutorials in a pluralistic way and we decided to use one of the lecture slots to stage a Post Keynesian versus monetarist debate about monetary policy. It was well received by the class.

The 1987 iteration of Money and Banking particularly engaged the class due to real-world events providing some exciting case material. One of these was very local: the collapse and rescue of the Campus Credit Union (CCU) in the third quarter of the year. Shortly before the CCU collapsed, hints that something unusual was going on were provided to me by Bruce Felmingham, whose office was opposite mine and who was on the CCU's governing body. The auditors had found some irregularities in the accounts but could not figure out what was going awry. Bruce was evidently determined to use his local knowledge to solve this mystery. One day, without giving the game away, he told me that he thought he was getting there with his quest. A few days later, CCU members received letters advising them of the untimely death of the

CCU's manager. The letters also said that business would continue as normal, but I realised, given my conversations with Bruce, that this was unlikely.

It turned out that the deceased manager had taken his own life via a shotgun to his head after embezzling about a tenth of the CCU's assets to fund his gambling addiction at Hobart's Wrest Point Casino. He had been doing so in a way that would only be discovered by someone with local knowledge. The major accounting firm that audited the CCU had seen unexpected growth in problem debts that needed to be written off, but, as I was given to understand, the debts had been written in the names of past CCU members whose accounts had been dormant due to them having died or moved away. Local knowledge was the key to noticing this. I realised that it was only a matter of time before there was a run on the CCU's deposits, and I felt rather guilty about needing to withdraw money to pay for the Apple Macintosh bundle that I had ordered some weeks earlier. I shared my understanding of the situation with no one before heading off to the UK for most of August.

While I was away, rumours spread and the CCU inevitably had to impose limits on withdrawals to contain the run on its deposits. But, as I expected, the CCU's problems were soon addressed by merging it into a larger institution. The episode provided rather mixed messages about whether non-bank financial intermediaries like the CCU deserve to be allowed to operate under less demanding regulations than those that apply to banks. Clearly, an institution-based credit union potentially can enjoy a reduced risk of bad loans due to having better local knowledge of its customers than a bank can have, especially if long-standing employees serve on its governing board and decide which loan applications are approved. However, in the CCU case, the local knowledge was employed too late to thwart the manager's guileful behaviour.

Financial drama on a much larger scale was provided on 19 October 1987 by the 'Black Monday' global stock-market collapse. I had covered Minsky's financial instability hypothesis in class in some detail a few weeks earlier (via Minsky, 1975, 1982a, 1982b) and discovered that some of the students were especially interested because they were active speculators. These students were not the first I encountered who operated like this: at Stirling, I had first learned of speculation in financial options from a student who watched the financial markets via the library's teletext screen and, if necessary, called his broker via the payphone near the library entrance. But the UTAS students were the first I had who decided to rein in their speculative activities after comparing material on Minsky with what they were observing in the markets. An American exchange student told me at the end of the last lecture before Black Monday that he had offloaded everything as he was convinced that the markets would tumble at the start of the following week. Of course, I had made no attempts to predict when the turning point would be, as I saw Minsky's analysis, coupled with lessons from financial history, as a great vehicle for showing how a scenarios-based approach to monetary economics can usefully inform policy even though it does not attempt to predict the future.

Although the initial resistance from students to the way I taught Money and Banking soon faded away, objections to how I taught the subject started to come from colleagues such as Ben Heijdra who discovered that it did not provide third-year macroeconomics students with the kind of foundations that normally could be taken for granted. In other words, providing students with a Post Keynesian view of the financial system posed a barrier to covering what it was normal to cover in a conventional third-year macroeconomics class, with potential collateral effects for what the honours students might be able to achieve in the fourth year. From that standpoint, it seemed that I was being selfish rather than collegial in offering students a wider range of perspectives and viewing monetary aggregates as endogenously determined rather than as being determined by reserve bank policy.

The obvious solution was to replace Money and Banking in the core of the Bachelor of Economics by a conventional intermediate macroeconomics subject, with Money and Banking then becoming a complementary elective subject. This is what happened, but when I ceased to be the Money and Banking lecturer at the end of my 1987 iteration of the subject, it ceased to be taught from a Post Keynesian perspective despite events having just demonstrated the value of taking Minsky seriously. It was the first time I really had a sense of how hard it is to have an enduring impact after investing a lot of effort into infusing heterodox ways of thinking into an economics curriculum.

Other Pluralistic Teaching
The unit on Money and Banking was by no means the only one that gave me an opportunity to provide UTAS students with a taste of alternatives to mainstream economic thinking. For example, in the final term of 1984,

I also had one-off stints lecturing for the second-year subject Theory of the Firm (which was shortly to be replaced by a conventional intermediate microeconomics unit) and third-year macroeconomics. The former provided a venue for introducing the behavioural theory of the firm and Andrews's 'normal cost' approach to pricing, while I built my lectures for the latter around Coddington's (1976) contention that there were three kinds of 'Keynesian economics' in the literature, which he characterised as 'hydraulic' (mechanistic model-based), 'reconstituted reductionist' (based on Walrasian microeconomic foundations) and 'fundamentalist' (emphasizing crowd behaviour, the fragility of expectations and the significance of speculation). Later, there were opportunities to offer different approaches from my colleagues when I co-taught subjects on Industrial Organization and on Trade and Development, and when I got the chance to teach part of Honours Microeconomics I did so by basing each class around a key heterodox book, such as Kornai's (1971) *Anti-Equilibrium* and Nelson and Winter's (1982) *An Evolutionary Theory of Economic Change*.

However, my most significant opportunity for teaching in a pluralistic manner came via the first-year subject Australian Political Economy, for which I was the sole lecturer from 1985 to 1987. This subject was designed primarily for Bachelor of Arts students but was also available as an elective to Bachelor of Economics students. It was a great opportunity to cover contemporary topics on economic policy from contending standpoints (so there were lectures covering key ideas from Friedman, Marx, Keynes, and Galbraith) and with a view to different ways of organizing economic systems. As when teaching Money and Banking, I provided detailed lecture summaries (a complete package of material for the 1987 version of Australian Political Economy is available at my personal website in scanned form), but there was no parrot-learning problem in the final examinations. Virtually no international students enrolled for this subject; instead, I was rather conscious that the class list seemed to include the children of quite a few Tasmanian politicians.

Opportunities for me to teach heterodox material to economics students dried up towards the end of my time at UTAS. In one case, this was due to Harry Campbell remembering that I had once said to him that, because I had not done any mathematics since my first year in Cambridge, it might do me some good if one day I had a go at teaching a first-year mathematics course for economics and commerce students;

doing so would enable me both to refresh my knowledge of the mathematics of constrained optimisation and motivate me to get some knowledge of things that I had never covered, notably matrices and financial mathematics. This task eventually came my way in 1990, and I am glad that it did, for it had precisely the benefits that I hoped it would. However, despite the effort that I put into tooling up for it by getting to grips with the material and devising assignments, I was relieved not to have to repeat it the following year. The final grades worked out fine, possibly because the weaker end of the class benefited from their lecturer having a sense of what they might be going through, but it was not the kind of lecturing that I enjoyed.

In the other cases, it was subjects normally taught in business schools that kept me away from teaching economics subjects. Sometimes, as I taught Principles of Marketing, Strategic Marketing, and Organisational Behaviour, I wondered whether it had been decided that I was too much of a loose cannon to allow to teach core economics units, but I also recognised that my background and interest in cross-disciplinary work meant that I was the obvious choice in these areas. In teaching Strategic Marketing (which I resisted separating from strategic management), I used a leading business school text by Wheelen and Hunger (1986, 1990) as a source of case studies. The instructor's manual was hopeless, for the notes for running the case studies seemed to be nothing more than summaries of the case study material with little analytical content, and the theory chapters from the book seemed very lightweight. It was no wonder that industrial economist Michael Porter (1980, 1985) and his protégé Kathryn Harrigan (1980, 1983) had attracted so much interest in business schools, for their work showed much more sophisticated and penetrating thinking than such textbooks had been offering. Although Porter and Harrigan offered their personal frameworks for organizing strategic thinking, these frameworks operated in a pluralistic manner by emphasizing how appropriate strategies varied according to context, so the ability to dissect contexts was a crucial skill to develop.

It was clear to me that the work of Porter and Harrigan should figure in my lectures for Strategic Marketing. But when I started reading some of the case studies, I realised that they also provided much scope for analysis using economic perspectives of the kind that I had used in my book *The Corporate Imagination*, along with Williamson's (1985) extension of his transaction cost view of industrial organization. The latter had informed my lectures in Business and Government Policy, the subject that Strategic Marketing had replaced. Williamson's work would make the subject more pluralistic, for his view of the choice between vertical integration and outsourcing had a different focus from that of Harrigan, who did not display his obsession with potential for opportunism (i.e., self-serving, guileful behaviour) on the part of external contractors or employees). However, while teaching Williamson's ideas suited my scenarios-based approach with its emphasis on thinking about what could go wrong with deals that firms make, it did make me wonder whether I was cultivating the capacities of my students as devious strategists when I encouraged them to try to think what opportunistic ploys might be tried in particular contexts.

There was also scope for considering how Andrews's (1949, 1964; Andrews and Brunner, 1975) views on competition and pricing fared against Chamberlin's (1933) *Theory of Monopolistic Competition* in different product contexts. In doing this, I saw another area for non-reductionist thinking: just as Andrews had emphasised the need for supermarkets to match their rivals in terms of the overall pricing of a typical 'basket' of groceries while experimenting with different relative prices for individual products (as with 'weekly specials'), so we should also recognise that, when potential entrants are judging whether incumbent players are being greedy in their pricing, the issue they should be looking at is what the profit margins are for entire ranges of products within which the mark-ups for individual variants may differ considerably. Thus, there might appear to be Chamberlin-style discretionary pricing at the level of the product but Andrews-style entry-deterring pricing at the level of the product range.

The investment that I made in bringing such ingredients together to teach Strategic Marketing from an economic standpoint had payoffs in publications, beginning with a paper taking a behavioural view of normal cost pricing for a symposium organised by Fred Lee (Earl, 1991a) and later providing ideas and material for parts of my (1995a) textbook *Microeconomics for Business and Marketing*. Another non-economics teaching assignment was to co-teach Organisational Behaviour in my final two years at UTAS. This had some publication outcomes, too, but aside from a case study that I wrote about the events that resulted in an Air New Zealand airliner crashing into Mount Erebus on an Antarctic sightseeing flight (Earl, 1992g), they came many years later when I fed material on corporate culture into sections 10.10 and 10.11 of Earl (2022).

215

6.3   ADMINISTRATION AND SERVICE

I was not surprised to see my administrative duties grow as my experience increased, especially after I was promoted to senior lecturer. The most demanding role was serving as 'sub-dean' in 1989. This was substantial enough to allow some relief from teaching: as well as entailing membership of the standing committee of the Faculty of Commerce and Economics, it required me to advise on, and check, all the economics enrolments. By contrast, when I first started at UTAS, I was, once again, merely given the role of departmental library liaison officer. As at Stirling, there was pressure to find areas in which expenditure could be cut. Initially this seemed to be a means for accommodating new journals rather than due to cuts in funding. However, in May 1986, the library faced an external shock: the Australian dollar fell sharply against major currencies after the Federal Treasurer, Paul Keating expressed his concern that, if Australia could not contain wage increases and revitalise its manufacturing sector, its over-dependence on commodity exports was in danger of leading it to become 'a third-rate economy, a banana republic'. Prices of imported books and journals thus increase sharply, for they were denominated in foreign currencies. Even so, the need for cuts never felt so dire as at Stirling.

From 1985 to 1990, Harry Campbell assigned me the task of compiling the department's annual research report. In this pre-Internet era, such reports tended to be sent out to institutions that were on the mailing lists for departmental working papers. They thus helped to promote a department's achievements in a way that would both increase the chances of its publications being read and give prospective job applicants a sense of its relative standing. However, copies were also provided to members of the department, so it is possible that collating research achievements into such reports also impacted upon productivity levels by making it easy to establish a sense of performance relativities and performance norms.

In an era without email, those who failed to supply any details of research output before the deadline expired would receive a visit from the report's compiler and be asked whether this reflected tardiness or not having any output to report. Having to confess the latter and then have this displayed in the report could be embarrassing. Today's automated systems for compiling staff research profiles may be less effective at imposing such social pressures to deliver research output, especially if data from, individual staff profiles are not displayed publicly in aggregated form to show departmental output in each category. Automated systems may be less accurate, too: for example, I was surprised to discover that my University of Queensland colleague John Foster's staff profile included at the top of his list of books a 2014 Indiana University Press book about ancient sea life in North America during the Cambrian era. John was surprised, too, when I asked him if this was the result of him having a side interest in fossils, about which I had not previously know.

During my time at UTAS I also started having to deal with invitations to provide external collegial inputs in the form of referee reports and book reviews for journals. At first, these invitations are likely to seem somewhat flattering signs that others are acknowledging one's expertise in a particular area, but if one performs these tasks well, the invitations become increasingly frequent, to a point where it is wise to start declining some of them. It is therefore important to develop appropriate rules for deciding how to respond. During the last two decades of my career, I decided that refereeing up to eight papers per year is probably a reasonable collegial contribution, based on the assumption that research-active academics on average get a couple of papers accepted each year and experience a couple of rejections of papers that get as far as being refereed, with each paper having two referees. Fortunately, I did not need to employ this kind of rule while I was at UTAS, and I generally accepted refereeing invitations unless the papers appeared to go beyond my technical competence. With refereeing requests arriving by airmail with hard copies of the papers to which they pertained, declining requests was more costly than in today's online systems: it involved writing a letter and sending the paper back. Moreover, when given the paper at the outset, rather than merely an abstract, it was hard not to sink some time into skimming through it before deciding whether one was a suitable referee. Having done this, it became cognitively harder to decline the task if one felt competent to referee the paper and had started to get an idea of the kind of report that it might warrant.

While I was working at UTAS, I wrote twelve book reviews and one review article. This was a much bigger reviewing rate than later in my career: these reviews were produced in a five-year period, whereas my average rate of writing reviews from my first one in 1986 to my retirement was just one per year. But I did not feel that I was having trouble finding the time that these tasks entailed; instead, I appreciated the opportunity that reviewing provided to add expensive books to my personal library, the great majority of which I ended up citing and would have wanted to read even if I had not been asked to review them.

6.4 EVOLUTION OF A HETERODOX BEHAVIOURAL ECONOMIST (3)

The philosophy that underlaid much of my teaching at UTAS and the research that I produced while working there came from a joint paper that I wrote with Neil Kay at the request of Frank Stephen. Frank was then working at the University of Strathclyde, from where he edited the *Journal of Economic Studies*. He sometimes initiated symposia or special issues of invited contributions as a means of raising the profile of this journal and getting contributions from authors of higher standing. Neil and I were on a contributor list for a special issue on G. L. S. Shackle that included Professors John Hey, Brian Loasby, Jim Ford and Andrew Skinner. Neil and I mapped out our paper shortly before I left Stirling. Then, during my first term at UTAS, Neil's section arrived by airmail for me to stitch into what I had written. Our paper (Earl and Kay, 1985) was offered as a riposte to Coddington (1982) and Cross (1982), who had argued that adopting a Shacklean approach to economics has nihilistic implications for economics as a discipline since emphasizing potential for surprise and kaleidic change (as in Shackle, 1974) raises doubts about the value of building models aimed at predicting future economic outcomes.

Our defence of Shackle's view of the economic system was constructed mindful of Jefferson's (1983) account of why and how the Shell energy company engaged in scenario planning. We argued that a scenarios-based approach to dealing with uncertainty permits economists to offer policy insights even if the prediction of behaviour is problematic due to its susceptibility to being affected by changes in the state of the news and by the tendency of people to take cues from each other when trying to deal with surprises and uncertainty.

Our contention was that the key thing that policymakers and individual decision-makers need to focus on is ensuring that they create systems that will be resilient if hit by shocks. However, we recognised that making systems shock-proof has costs, such as tying up resources in reserves and foregoing benefits from specialization and creating synergy links between activities. In other words: it can be dangerous to 'put all one's eggs in the same basket' and not invest in buffering and crumple zones if one inhabits a turbulent environment; but it can also be a mistake to hedge one's bets and invest heavily in shock-proofing if one is operating in an environment that is not susceptible to shocks and one is trying to compete with other players who enjoy lower costs and/or can produce better products because they sacrifice flexibility and concentrate on being very good at doing a narrow range of things. The latter may be more able to survive rare shocks that force less committed players out of the game. Hence, as practitioners of scenario planning recognise, the key strategic issues to address are:

- How shock-prone are the environments between which one is choosing?
- What is the range of possible outcomes that warrant serious consideration for each variable of interest?
- Is it possible to implement a strategy that offers adequate shock-proofing as well as offering good prospects for survival and growth if present trends are maintained yet is flexible enough to enable one to grasp opportunities that one cannot yet imagine?

In other words, even if economic predictions are inherently unreliable, economists can contribute usefully to (a) assessing the costs and benefits of (not) being prepared for rival possible outcomes, and (b) imagining possible situations that could arise and assessing how seriously they deserve to be taken.

Lifestyle Economics
As soon as the paper with Neil Kay was finished, I began substantially reworking my PhD into the book that was published as *Lifestyle Economics: Consumer Behaviour in a Turbulent World* (Earl, 1986b). I suggested this title to Edward Elgar (who was still running the Wheatsheaf Books imprint of Harvester Press) in a letter that I wrote to him on 14 September 1984. Two weeks earlier, he had written to me about my proposal, saying that he did not think that 'The Evolving Consumer' did justice to what I was trying to do in the book. The phrase 'The Evolving Consumer' was thus relegated, with a bracketed numerical suffix, to a section header role in three chapters where parallels between business strategies and lifestyle choices were being discussed.

The way that I was using 'The Evolving Consumer' idea was inspired by Neil Kay's (1982) *The Evolving Firm*, i.e., with a focus on the significance of linkages between activities, products, and personal expectations. Consumers who specialise in developing their knowledge and capabilities in a few areas of interest, seek to make the most of complementarities between the things they buy or do, and build close ties with select bunches of social contacts, may enjoy deeply fulfilling lives, making the most of their resources without running into decreasing marginal returns. However, their narrow ranges of commitments also make them vulnerable if their key assumptions, assets or relationships fail. More diversified lifestyle strategies provide a way of insuring against this risk. However, the more diversified a person's life is, the more there is the risk of it proving unfulfilling due to superficiality that comes from a lack of in-depth commitment to anything or anyone, the result being that nothing seems to matter.

This view of lifestyles was not inspired merely by Neil Kay's work on corporate strategies. It also drew on things that I had picked up from my research on personal construct psychology and from my then-partner Sharon's clinical psychology books. The latter sources led me to argue that life is likely to prove problematic for those who try to cope with the world by building ways of life and ways of thinking that are so full of linkages that small disappointments tend to turn into cascades of difficulties (exemplified in the extremes of those afflicted by the obsessive–compulsive disorder), or who largely fail to build their lives around any organizing principles (the extreme clinical case of which is thought-disordered schizophrenia). Viewing lifestyles with a focus on complementarities, specialization and linkage structures was very different from the conventional reductionist approach to the economics of consumer behaviour that emphasised substitution at the margin and assumed linear household production functions and diminishing marginal utility, thereby excluding potential for patterns of spending to be affected by economies of scale or scope in consumption. My perspective complemented but went beyond the way that lifestyles were seen in marketing as sets of similar values that groups of people shared (see Wells, 1975).

Given the novelty of the lifestyle concept, I could readily have focused the next stage of my career on work related to it, rather than leaving it merely as an aspect of a book that, despite its title, was mostly addressing the area of its subtitle by exploring – in a much more pluralistic way than in *The Economic Imagination* – ways of understanding how consumers cope with the decision-making challenges of a world of information overload, complexity, rapid change and uncertainty. A good first move, when I completed writing *Lifestyle Economics* in October 1985, would have been to write a theoretical article that focused on the lifestyle concept and its implications (including testable hypotheses) for research on the economics of consumer behaviour. Empirical work could have followed, taking me into areas such as the economics of happiness, health and ageing, regional and urban development, the uptake of new technologies and transitions to sustainable living. But this was not what I wanted to do; after devoting about two-thirds of my research over the past six years to consumer behaviour, I wanted to shift my research focus elsewhere, and I naively thought that *Lifestyle Economics* might be enough to trigger research on lifestyle-related issues by people whose applied research skills were already much better developed than mine.

Two (Potentially) Significant Extensions of the Personal Constructs View of Choice
While writing *Lifestyle Economics*, I wrote a related paper that also could have provided the basis for a research programme. It was called 'A behavioural analysis of demand elasticities' and was written rather in haste in March 1985 for the 14th Australian Conference of Economists. What I attempted to provide in it was a way of understanding why, in some cases, people switch to other products in response to very small changes in relative prices whereas, in other cases, they continue to buy products whose prices have increased sharply relative to other products. The key idea in the paper was that how attached people are to an established way of behaving depends on the net total of the number of positive and negative 'implications' that they view as being associated with switching to something else. Having or not having a particular feature in a product matters to consumers because of the implications they see as contingent on its presence or absence. Furthermore, how much any individual implication matters depends on the net total of desired and undesired subsidiary implications that it is viewed as having.

On the surface, this may sound like nothing more than a Lancaster-style compensatory view of choice in which losses in respect of some characteristics are weighed against gains in respect of others. But it offers something deeper: a unit of analysis for which data can readily be obtained and which removes any need to refer to the more nebulous notion of utility. My thinking was inspired by the work of Dennis Hinkle ([1965] 2010), one of George Kelly's graduate students. Hinkle studied resistance to change with the aid of some new empirical techniques that he added to the 'repertory grid technique' that Kelly had developed for eliciting the sets of construct axes that people employ to characterise particular kinds of events. In trying to understand resistance to change, Hinkle had focused on the significance of hierarchical relationships between construct axes.

While I was working on my PhD, one of Hinkle's novel techniques, 'construct laddering', had been picked up by scholars in marketing (see, for example, Gutman, 1982, Reynolds and Gutman, 1984) as a means for digging deeper into the minds of consumers: by asking which pole of a construct axis (for example, 'exciting' versus 'bland') a consumer prefers, one may elicit a new layer of constructs (for example, 'I prefer 'exciting' because...'), to which the same process can be applied, and so on, until one gets to the stage at which the consumer says, 'I prefer this because I do, period.' But the marketing scholars had not taken up Hinkle's idea of an 'implication' as being a change between the poles of a construct axis that a person's construct system requires if there is a polar change on another axis. Depending on the hierarchical rules that structure a person's construct system, switching to a different form of behaviour might have few implications overall, or there could be many implications, skewed heavily in one direction. Sometimes, it would seem 'crazy' not to switch, because of the net balance of negative implications of not switching, whereas in other cases there might be a wide range of negative implications and few implications that were viewed positively, so change would be resisted. If constructs are viewed in simple dichotomous terms, an implication of change on one construct for where one will be on another construct is like throwing a switch, but one could do a somewhat more complex analysis for scalar constructs, in terms of how much movement on other constructs would be implied if a consumer moved between specific points on, say, a 1–10 scale.

In short, the desire or unwillingness of consumers to change their behaviour will depend on how the features of the alternative forms of behaviour matter due to the hierarchical webs of implications that they carry. We can get a sense of this if we reflect upon how, if something goes awry with our plans, we experience a cascade of mental images of what this enforced switch means in terms of shattered expectations and new challenges. Hinkle had made a start in showing how patterns of implications and associated resistance to change can be mapped and measured empirically with the aid of what he called 'implication grids' and 'resistance to change grids'. However, although his construct laddering technique revealed that people typically end up at the 'I prefer this construct pole because I do, period' stage within six or fewer construct layers, Hinkle had only reported analysis via his innovative grids in terms of the initial set of constructs that he elicited from each of his subjects and a single layer of constructs laddered from them.

The implications of going down a Hinkle-style route in consumer research are, of course, dramatic, for researchers will need to engage closely with research subjects to peel back their layers of systems of personal constructs instead of focusing on differences between products in their 'objective' characteristics in the way that Lancaster (1966) envisaged. I wrote my paper without taking the time to develop a detailed example to illustrate what I had in mind and how a multi-level implications map could look, let alone waiting until I had an empirically based 'proof of concept' demonstration to offer, and I never got as far as doing these things. The complexity entailed in developing the idea further led me to appreciate the challenges that people could have in computing the overall implications of choices involving many dimensions of surface-level constructs that might affect constructs up to half a dozen layers away. Hence, I ended the paper on a pluralistic note by noting these computational issues and arguing that, when the mind runs into them, we should expect it to switch to non-compensatory ways of choosing.

Given the conceptual challenges that the implications-based view of choice entails and the limitations of my paper, it is not surprising that it failed to generate any feedback from my small audience at the conference, and it failed to generate any enthusiasm soon after when I submitted it to a marketing journal. Rather than filing it for future attention, I found an easy route to get it published as it stood. I had refereed a paper for the *Journal of Economic Studies* and when the editor, Frank Stephen wrote to thank me for my report, he mentioned that he would be interested to know what I had been working on after writing the invited paper with Neil Kay (Earl and Kay, 1985) for the Shackle symposium that he had organised a year earlier. I sent him a copy of the paper and, rather as I anticipated, he said he would like to take it for the *Journal* (where it was published as Earl, 1986a). I should have declined

Frank's offer of publication and should instead have worked further on the paper and then submitted it to the *Journal of Economic Psychology* or the *Journal of Economic Behavior and Organization*; that way, I might at least have got some decent feedback and been prodded to invest even more time in improving it. Instead, following Frank's acceptance of the paper, I did not return to its central idea until 35 years later when I was writing chapter 7 of my *Principles of Behavioral Economics* (Earl, 2022). At that point, I explored it further in theoretical terms, but it *still* awaits empirical investigation.

It was not until 1990 that I had any other fresh ideas in relation to personal construct psychology. I returned to this area when writing a paper for the 1990 conference of the International Association for Research in Economic Psychology (IAREP). The conference appealed to me because it was to take place at the University of Exeter, the main UK centre for economic psychology aside from Bath and not far from where my parents now lived. The paper that I wrote was published in revised form (Earl, 1992c) in a volume of papers selected from those that were presented at the conference, but it probably would have been much more widely read if I had declined to make it available for that book and instead found a place for it in a journal.

The Exeter paper explored the relationship between George Kelly's ideas and the famous theory of cognitive dissonance that Leon Festinger (1957) proposed shortly after Kelly's (1955) magnum opus appeared. These two works seemed potential complements because Festinger's theory essentially proposes that when people discover that their initial way of construing a situation results in a pair of constructs that clash, they resolve this dissonance by changing one of the constructs to make it compatible with the other one, with the change being justified by telling themselves a story about why the change is reasonable. For example, suppose that a person who construes himself to be a diligent scholar is considering reshelving a library book that he had initially construed as potentially relevant to the research that he is doing. The act that he is contemplating clashes with his self-construct. From a Kellian standpoint, the unease that this person feels is a manifestation of guilt, for the person is contemplating acting out of character. The person can remove the cognitive dissonance and guilt by relaxing somewhat how he construes what being a scholar entails, or by changing how he construes the potential value of the book to the research that he is doing.

To me, this kind of scenario begs the question of which construct will be twisted or, if both are modified to some degree, what determines the extent to which they are modified. This question seemed not to be addressed by those who appealed to cognitive dissonance theory to make sense of behaviour, and it was difficult to find an answer when I read Festinger's book. From the standpoint of personal construct psychology, the obvious place to look for an answer was structural relationships between constructs and the idea that some constructs are assigned more of a 'core' role than others in the predictive systems that people construct for coping with life. Hinkle's extension of Kelly's ideas seemed to be relevant once again: in his terms, it may not be possible to bend one construct without having collateral implications for the viability of other constructs and hence for one's prospective capacity to predict and control events. This pointed to the conclusion that the processes that remove cognitive dissonance entail our minds selecting the way of re-construing the constructs in question that is least costly in terms of the cognitive effort that is required to deal with the wider implications of changing any of these constructs. In general, dissonance will be removed by changing the more peripheral construct while leaving unchanged the construct that is closer to the core of the person's way of thinking. In other words, I ended up viewing the mind as an economizing entity: changing how one sees things chews up mental energy but different ways of making changes differ in how burdensome they are because they entail different patterns of cognitive implications.

In the scenario above, we would expect the person to change how he sees the potential relevance of the book, rather than change his self-construct as a scholar and how he construes the nature of scholarly activities, for changing the latter is more likely to raise all manner of questions about the kind of person he really is and how he is going to behave in future as a researcher. The cognitive effort of addressing these questions can be avoided by downplaying the significance of not bothering to read the book (such as by telling himself that, 'Surely, others would be citing it in this area if it were worth taking seriously').

However, we should note that the scenario begs the question of why the person is considering not bothering to read the book in question, if the initial impression is that it warrants attention. The answer could be that the idea of reading the book clashes with other constructs in his system (for example, due to the book looking too difficult), so reshelving it is a way of removing this dissonance, but it comes at the cost of creating other dissonance. For example, the person may already have written or planned a piece of work that seems to hold together perfectly well without needing to draw on the book in question, whereas reading the book and taking account of relevant material may delay publication of what is already seen as a prospective career-enhancing contribution that seems unlikely to be criticised for failing to take account of the book in question if no one in the field seems to refer to this book. With its potential relevance downplayed, the book ends up being reshelved without any admission that lust for career progression has trumped scholarship. The scholarly self-construct can even be buttressed, by making a mental note to look carefully at the book – 'just in case it has undeservedly been overlooked by others' – at some future point if one can find the time, despite denying its importance today. I did not use this scenario in the cognitive dissonance paper, but it seemed worth including here as a way of making sense of some of my own scholarly lapses, including one that figures later in this section.

An Experiment with Psychological Economics
Before I had got very far into writing *Lifestyle Economics*, I received an invitation from Warren Samuels to edit a book for Kluwer Academic Publishers (now part of the Springer group) under the title *Psychological Economics: Development, Tensions, Prospects*. It was an interesting concept: rather than aiming to offer a set of chapters that sought to present new research findings about economic issues that had been arrived at by applying concepts and methods from psychology, it would set out to identify areas with potential for economists to learn by employing psychological concepts and research methods, It would then explore the challenges that such an approach presented, mindful of the way that mainstream economics had distanced itself from psychology over the preceding half-century. I accepted the invitation after only a brief reflection on the kinds of chapters I might commission and whom to approach to write them, and after giving even less thought to how much of my time the book would consume.

All except for one scholar that I approached agreed to write a chapter for the book. The only psychologist among the contributors was Alan Lewis, whom I had got to know at the 1984 ESRC Workshop on Economic Beliefs and who provided a chapter on research methods that economists might borrow from psychology. I did not invite any other psychologists because I decided to see what would happen if I invited contributions from authors who largely had no experience at all of engaging with psychology but whose areas of interest appeared to have potential to benefit from infusions of psychology. There was also a pluralistic agenda, for as well as getting John Hey to write a chapter about prospects for mathematical economic psychology, as a contrast to what Alan Lewis covered, I set out to see how economists from different schools of thought saw the potential for engaging with psychology. My three favourite chapters from the book were those by Malcolm Rutherford (an institutional economist, who examined differences between economists' and psychologists' views on expectation formation and rationality and the methodological challenges implied therein), my colleague Michael Brooks (who examined how psychologically-informed economics could help shed light on areas such as voting behaviour and bargaining over resources) and Jochen Runde (who examined the compatibility of Austrian subjectivism and psychological methods).

The chapter that I wrote as the conclusion to the volume had rather similar intentions to the present book. Its title was 'On being a psychological economist and winning the games economists play'. It applied psychological perspectives on resistance to change, and ideas from business strategy, to illustrate why taking a psychological approach to economics was likely to be an uphill battle and how the career risks of taking such an approach might be managed. I also used experiences from the process of producing the book to illustrate some of the difficulties experienced by the contributors, such as the problems they faced in knowing how to get started with an unfamiliar discipline that, unlike economics, did not have a dominant unifying core.

The effort that I put into editing *Psychological Economics* (Earl, ed., 1988a) had only a small impact on my thinking as a behavioural economist. It is mainly evident via my use (in Earl, 1995a, pp.128–130) of Michael Brooks's (1988, pp. 171–2) adaptation of an Edgeworth box diagram into a principles-based satisficing view of bargaining, which I call the 'Brooks box'. Of all the papers in the book, Malcolm Rutherford's displayed the greatest willingness to go where economists had not previously gone in the literature of psychology. His impressive paper considered not only differences in the implications of the Kahneman and Tversky style of work on heuristics versus Simon's research programme, but also drew on what he had gleaned from examining attribution theory. The contrasts that he drew between the fields that he surveyed led to a powerful discussion of methodological issues whose clarity of thought contrasts sharply with the methodological incoherence that is often evident in modern behavioural economics due to its use of the traditional economic view of rationality as a reference point. Sadly, his paper has not received the attention it deserves, not merely in terms of its methodological insights but also in terms of signalling the relevance of attribution theory.

Editing the book enabled me to assuage a little the guilt I felt about not reading Hayek's *Sensory Order*. I achieved this by asking Jochen Runde to write a synopsis of it as an appendix to his chapter, given that Hayek is the only Austrian economist to have contributed to psychology. Runde's synopsis conveys how challenging the book is, while stressing the non-reductionist, context-based vision that Hayek has of the nature of cognition. However, the synopsis did not trigger the impact that Hayek's book had on me when I at last read it over two decades later (see Section 8.4). By the time that I read *The Sensory Order*, I had completely forgotten that I had commissioned the synopsis and what Runde had written for it, and hence I had to make my own sense of Hayek's theory. I only remembered the Runde appendix when reflecting on the process of editing the book for which he wrote it and the impact that the editorial role had on my research, with my failure to read Hayek's book at Stirling already drawn back to my mind. This forgetting and remembering is, ironically, entirely consistent with Hayek's theory of the mind.

Behavioural Economics as a School of Thought

With *Psychological Economics* well into its production phase, I received an invitation to edit a different kind of book, a two-volume anthology of articles on behavioural economics for the 'Schools of Thought in Economics' series that Edward Elgar planned to publish via the company that he had set up after leaving Harvester–Wheatsheaf. I was flattered to receive this invitation, for the general editor of the series was Mark Blaug and this was further confirmation that he took my work seriously. Obviously, if the series were taken seriously, too, it would help establish my reputation as a behavioural economist. If so, editing *Behavioural Economics* (Earl, ed., 1988b) could warrant an intensive investment of my time, both to establish my expertise and to try to steer the field in directions where it could have significant impacts. But how seriously would the series be taken?

The series was one of the first of several that Elgar has produced that publish reprints of articles (and occasionally, book chapters), and the editors of these books have usually been far more eminent that I was at that time. However, I suspect that many economists who are familiar with these Elgar series view them as 'rip-off' products, little more than very expensive bound sets of photocopies. Cynics might also wonder whether producing 'collections' as a steady stream of books through time was a means for achieving subscription-based sales that continued because of institutional inertia rather than because the later volumes would be as valuable as the initial ones. My own view is much more positive, and I will share it here before I reflect critically on what I did in my editorial role.

First, we need to recognise that these collections largely date from before publishers digitised their back catalogues and took their journals online. We would be wise to consider the reprint license charges that Elgar might have had to pay for each collection, the costs in staff time for arranging these licences, and the costs of ensuring a reliable supply of pristine photocopies. Regarding the last of these, we might imagine an arrangement between the publisher and the library of an elite university, whereby the former services the lease payments on a very expensive photocopier that can scan side-by-side pages without any issues at their bound edges because it allows open bound volumes to be placed on it at right angles, with the library in question supplying the requested photocopies but also being able to use the photocopier for its own activities.

Secondly, it should be noted that, compared with the 'rip-off' prices that journal publishers might set for their back catalogues of bound volumes, the prices of each collection would probably seem far less of a 'rip-off' to a new university, or an established university in a non-English-speaking country. If we think of such universities as the main markets, at a time before journal articles could be accessed online, then we would be wise to recall that most journal articles are read by very few researchers, so collections of classic sources also reduce the costs of storing entire runs of bound journals just in case someone will one day want articles from them. The institutions that purchase the Elgar collections may also hope that they will raise the productivity of their academic staff and students because the editors of the volumes reduce the users' search costs and provide authoritative introductory overviews.

Finally, we might be wise to note that, if these collections left Elgar with a very healthy net margin, despite the production costs not being as trivial as critics may believe, this may have enabled Elgar to take more risks in signing up a disproportionately large number of books by heterodox economists for its catalogue.

When one is preparing such a collection, the key question that must be addressed is the extent to which one should treat it as a research task versus the extent to which one should make selections based on the knowledge that one already has about the field in question. Nowadays, with Internet search engines, online databases, and Google Scholar to call upon, it would be both presumptuous and remiss of an editor simply to rely on his or her existing knowledge, for these technologies make it possible to check rapidly for significant contributions that one has not been aware of or considered including. Back in 1987, editing such a collection was much more a matter of considering whether one had a compelling enough list of sources already at hand from which to make the selection. If this were not the case, then one might spend time looking in likely journals to see if there were any papers that could fill the gaps that one had identified. This was how I put my proposed contents lists together for the two volumes, and I hoped that I could rely on Mark Blaug's legendary encyclopaedic knowledge of the economics literature to kick in if there were any glaring omissions. I do not recall feeling that I did not have enough papers to give a good sense of what behavioural economics entailed and examples of where it had been employed. I knew that I had not read extensively in the US literature from psychology and management science on judgement and uncertainty to which some of the contributors to *Psychological Economics* had referred. However, this did not seem to matter since I included the superb survey of this field by Hogarth and Makridakis (1981) that organises the findings in this literature around the various stages of a decision cycle.

With hindsight, I wish that I had included papers that Thaler had published between his seminal contribution on consumer choice (Thaler, 1980), which I did include, and the time I edited the book, such as his economic theory of self-control (Thaler and Shefrin, 1981) (which I had referred to in *Lifestyle Economics*), his paper on mental accounting (Thaler, 1985) (which I had noticed soon after it appeared but had forgotten to follow up) and the paper on fairness and profit-seeking behaviour that Kahneman, Knetsch and Thaler (1986) had just published (but which I had not yet seen). I also regret not including Leff's (1985) paper on the realities of decision-making for planners in developing countries: he sent me a copy of it at some point in the late 1980s, and it is possible that this was before I was working on the collection and that I had at that time simply forgotten about it because I originally filed it with the letter that Leff had sent, rather than in the box files in which I kept photocopies of my favourite behavioural contributions. There are lessons here about giving better thought than I was in those days giving to the organisation of one's filing system (for example, file copies in multiple places – something that, on environmental grounds, I had been reluctant to do in the days of hard copies) and developing routines about creating 'to read' lists and working through them.

The introduction that I wrote has been a much bigger source of regret to me than deficiencies in the sets of articles that I included. I felt that anything I said about the nature of behavioural economics needed to be said in both volumes, for it was possible that prospective users of library copies would find that one of the volumes was out on loan. To stop the length of my introduction from ballooning out in either volume, I limited the extent of my commentaries on the papers in each volume more than I perhaps should have done, especially insofar as the volumes had a role to play in helping their readers make connections between the papers. However, my serious failure lies in the methodological analysis that the two volumes share. I suggested that there were four main sub-schools of thought within behavioural economics, and I tagged them as follows: via the institutions whose contributors exemplified them:

1. *The Carnegie School* – led by Cyert, March and Simon, drawing heavily on organisational analysis and simulation methods, and emphasising finite human information processing capacities and the role of satisficing as a means for dealing with uncertainty and complexity.
2. *The Oxford School* – epitomised by the Oxford Economists Research Group (especially the work of P. W. S. Andrews), Richardson and their graduate students, who studied actual business practices and were keen to understand how complex business processes were coordinated in the real world.
3. *The Michigan School* – led by Katona, that focused on the psychology of consumer behaviour, especially the macroeconomic significance of shifting consumer sentiment.

4. *The Stirling School* – led by Loasby, that took a highly eclectic and inter-disciplinary approach that embraced elements from the other three approaches and focused on how decision-makers, in households as well as firms and other organizations, cope with problems of knowledge.

Significantly, I also drew attention to what I called 'pseudo-behaviouralists' and raised the possibility that contributions by these kinds of economists might lead to behavioural economics being absorbed into mainstream economics in a way that led to key insights being lost, rather in the way that Post Keynesian economists view as having happened with Keynes's ideas via the 'neoclassical synthesis' that reduced Keynes's *General Theory* to the IS–LM diagram.

What I meant by the 'pseudo-behavioural' approach was research that accepted some genuine behavioural lines of thinking but incorporated them into modes of analysis that were in other respects highly orthodox. I used the work of Kenneth Arrow (1974) and Oliver Williamson (1964, 1975, 1985) to illustrate what I had in mind. These eminent scholars accepted that the economics of organisation and the organisation of the economy were linked to human cognitive limitations, but their natural inclinations were to view choices in terms of constrained optimisation with cognitive limitations coming in as an additional constraint.

I used Williamson's chapter in the original edition of Cyert and March's (1963) book *A Behavioral Theory of the Firm* as an illustration of pseudo-behavioural economic analysis. Williamson's chapter is in essence a potted version of his (1964) PhD-based book, and I argued that although it might seem to be behavioural, as it originated with the PhD that Williamson had done under the guidance of the Carnegie team, it was at odds with the methodology of the behavioural theory of the firm. Williamson saw managers as able to get away with operating in self-serving ways due to the bounded rationality of other corporate stakeholders, yet he used a constrained optimisation model of how managers maximise their utility by only pursuing profits to a limited degree and making trade-offs between the pursuit of 'pet projects' and perquisites. He did not offer a satisficing model and treated the rest of the firm's employees as if they perform in a way that minimises the costs of doing what the managers ask them to do. Cyert and March (1992) seem implicitly to agree with this assessment, for they omitted Williamson's contribution from the second edition of their book.

My 'pseudo-behavioural' label was perhaps too harsh when applied to Williamson's (1975, 1985) work, where he is rather vague about how managers and their subordinates take decisions. There, his focus is simply on how choices of transactions and organisational arrangements are likely to be affected by concerns that the other transacting party will behave guilefully if they enjoy an information advantage and believe that the reputational risk of being revealed as opportunists is worth taking. Such risks will seem small if, in the event of their opportunism being discovered, it will be difficult to replace them with a less devious trading partner.

Williamson's analysis of how people deal with these risks can be read from a satisficing standpoint or envisaged in terms of transactors attempting to maximise utility under uncertainty. However, my concerns about where the contributions of Arrow and Williamson on the economics of organisation might lead seem to have been well aimed, for the field did become dominated by the work of those who approached the problem from a constrained optimisation standpoint. This was signalled by the award of the 2016 Nobel Memorial Prise in Economic Sciences to Bengt Holmström and Oliver Hart. Given what I had seen of Hart's way of thinking in my days as a Cambridge student, it was no surprise to me that he sought to offer an optimising analysis of the design of incomplete contracts to deal with the contracting issues associated with the impossibility of specifying every possible eventuality in a contract.

The main cause of my regret in this area is that I failed to give enough thought to what, at the time, was only a small 'elephant in the room' problem for my characterisation of behavioural economics: where did Kahneman and Tversky (1979) and Thaler (1980) fit into my taxonomy? In hindsight, it seems obvious that I should have suggested that their work marked the beginning of a fifth behavioural school. I could also have noted, in my discussion of pseudo-behavioural contributions, that there was a risk that the kind of work they were doing could end up getting absorbed by the mainstream, since it seemed to entail ad hoc modifications to the mainstream rational choice model without setting out to offer a fundamentally different view of economics. I could have likened the situation to what happened in astronomy when the Ptolemaic view encountered empirical anomalies and was initially rescued via the ad hoc inclusion of orbital epicycles rather than by switching to the radically different Copernican view.

Before deciding how to position the work of Kahneman, Tversky and Thaler, I should have devoted more time to (a) carefully re-reading both papers, (b) working back along the genealogy of the works that they cited, and (c) checking via the Social Sciences Citation Index to discover where they were being cited and how they were being employed by their early adopters. In the case of Kahneman and Tversky's prospect theory article, serious reflection might have had a bigger payoff for me than merely putting me in a position to write a better introduction to the nature of behavioural economics: it could have resulted in me noticing what I had so far missed and did not notice until a quarter of a century later about areas of overlap between prospect theory and Shackle's potential surprise model of choice under uncertainty (see Earl and Littleboy, 2014, chapter 8), which would have provided the basis for a good journal article.

But I did none of these things. Instead, I simply did not give special attention to these two contributions. The issue that led me to do this was the organising framework that I was using: there was no single geographical location to use as a tag: Kahneman and Tversky were West Coast psychologists, whereas Thaler seemed to be a lone-wolf East Coast economist who was, like me, trying to take a bounded rationality view of consumer behaviour.

Thaler (1980, p. 40) had quoted Simon's (1957, p. 398) definition of bounded rationality in the introduction to his paper and seemed somehow to have latched on to Kahneman and Tversky's new heuristics-based prospect theory model as a fruitful way to make sense of what consumers do. Little did I then realise that, unlike me, Thaler was referring to Simon merely as an anchor for his paper; it was not a sign that he was an avid follower of Simon's perspective. In the absence of the story that Thaler (2015) tells of how he hooked up with Kahneman and Tversky, and with Thaler not using their theory with a focus on risk-taking and instead making novel use of its S-shaped utility function in a more general manner, I did not see what their connection was and was not thinking of them as a research group. I had run into a similar issue when considering where to place Leibenstein's work on X-inefficiency, which he had commenced at Berkeley and continued at Harvard in what appeared to be a lone-wolf manner without connections to the Carnegie group.

I should have realised, from these classificatory problems, that perhaps I should not have been using a research centres-based way of identifying different behavioural approaches and should instead have grouped behavioural economists based on how they operated. I had got on to the centres-based organizing framework because I had already been tagged geographically by Cross (1984, p. 108) as being, with Brian Loasby, part of 'the Stirling school'. If I had been focusing on methods rather than centres, I might have identified a 'heuristics and biases'-focused method there and then, and presented the papers by Kahneman and Tversky, and Thaler, as extensions of the research on judgment and decision-making that was surveyed in the Hogarth and Makridakis (1981) paper that I had included in the same section as Kahneman and Tversky's paper. I might then have used, say, 'satisficing and simulations', 'survey-driven', 'growth of knowledge-focused' and 'information processing' as my other categories instead of the four centres-based ones that I chose. If I had done this, I might even have tried to draw a Venn diagram to consider how researchers whose work was included in the collection could be located on it, with some of them working at the intersection of several of these approaches. Had I done this, the collection might have had a different and more substantial impact, and my own work on behavioural economics would have taken a rather different pathway.

There is an obvious irony here: I was very familiar with the idea that how people view things is constrained and shaped by the cognitive frames they employ for making sense of the world, yet I was not reflecting on how the frame that *I* was using was limiting the effectiveness of my characterisation of behavioural economics. Nor was I arguing the case for considering the intersection between my 'personal construct systems' view of cognition, the 'attribution theory' view that Rutherford (1988) had included in his chapter in my *Psychological Economics* collection, and the heuristics-based view evident in the work of Hogarth, Makridakis, Kahneman and Tversky. But the shortcomings of my work on the introduction to *Behavioural Economics* were also the result of me believing that what I had put together was good enough and my desire to focus on my goal of writing my solo follow-up to *Money Matters*.

Integrating Behavioural and Post Keynesian Economics
With my work on the two edited books complete, I would have been able to work on the book on Kaldor that I had envisaged at Stirling as a good post-PhD project. However, the publication of Thirlwall's (1987) Kaldor book scuppered that idea and left me free to begin writing another book

that I had been hankering to write, namely, *Monetary Scenarios: A Modern Approach to Financial Systems* (Earl, 1990c). I had raised the possibility of a book on banking and the theory of the firm with Edward Elgar even before signing the contract for *Lifestyle Economics* in October 1984, but the scope of the project grew as I kept polishing my teaching on Money and Banking and expanded my reading in that area to keep abreast of what was happening in financial markets that were being deregulated and populated by players who took a 'greed is good' approach to their work. At the end of my fourth and final stint teaching Money and Banking I had a clear idea of what I wanted to write, a thick wad of lecture summaries on which to build, and the prospect of a sabbatical in the second half of 1988 that would give me the opportunity to make rapid progress. I started to write it in March 1988. Nothing unexpected occurred to delay my writing and the book was finished around Easter 1989.

The manuscript was then reviewed for Edward Elgar by Mark Blaug and Vicky Chick, one of whom commented that its length might be a deterrent to publication but that it was hard to see how it could be pruned due to the lack of padding in how it had been written. Despite the book being written in an accessible style and based on what I had taught, Elgar decided only to release it as a hardback.

The reason why I am including the work that I did for *Monetary Scenarios* as part of the story of how I evolved as a behavioural economist is that one of my main objectives in writing the book was to integrate, in a non-reductionist way, the kind of behavioural microeconomics that I had been doing for the past decade with Post Keynesian macroeconomics. In 1987, I had argued the case for doing this in the paper that I wrote for the first Malvern political economy conference (published as Earl 1989a). However, when I attempted to undertake such an integration in the book, I did not choose a title such as 'Modern Monetary Economics: A Behavioural/Post Keynesian Synthesis' that would have made this goal evident. So, why did I fail to give the book a title that signalled that this was what I was trying to do?

The title and subtitle that I chose reflected two other things that I was trying to do in writing it. The key words in this respect were 'scenarios' and 'systems', but their significance would have eluded the great majority of those that I hoped would find the book interesting. To have any sense of what I was trying to signal with this title, prospective readers would need to be familiar with the defence of 'fundamentalist

Keynesianism' that Neil Kay and I had offered in our invited joint paper (Earl and Kay, 1985) for the Shackle special issue in the *Journal of Economic Studies* – a journal not noted as an outlet for work by Post Keynesian or behavioural economists. From a scenarios standpoint, getting creative and critical in thinking about what could go wrong or could present opportunities that others fail to consider is central to designing policies. In the case of financial systems, policymakers need to ensure that the rules of the game (a) do not inhibit socially (and environmentally) desirable investments, and (b) limit systemic risks that come from the interlinked nature of individuals' balance sheets and limitations on the capacity of individual players to appreciate how their fortunes are linked to those of others.

From this standpoint, it seemed to me that there was an obvious link between the bounded rationality perspective of behavioural economics and the view of tidal shifts in systemic risk that is central to how Minsky extended Keynes's analysis to embrace the complex modern world of multi-layered financial structures and financial innovations. Here, a key issue is what can happen when new financial opportunities become available to those whose expertise and ways of taking financial decisions are not conducive to seeing the risks that come with seizing these opportunities. Bringing the two approaches together implies major roles for policies that entail prudential supervision of financial institutions and include measures aimed at improving financial literacy. Unfortunately, I failed to illustrate the potential significance of these policies by presenting a scenario designed to show how some of the new financial instruments to which I referred, such as options and securitisation, could be increasing systemic risk if they were being layered together in hard-to-fathom ways that gave the illusion that all risks were being insured against despite there being no guarantee that those at the end of the chain would be able to honour their commitments. Hence, I cannot say, 'I told you so' ahead of the 2008 Global Financial Crisis.

I did a better job in applying my interest in slack and limits to substitution within firms or by consumers to the performance of the economy as a whole: the book's penultimate chapter is on 'bottlenecks, slack and macroeconomic dynamics'. Over three decades before the global economy was disrupted by the COVID-19 pandemic and Russia's invasion of Ukraine, my concern was with how the resilience of the supply side of the economic system to shocks depends on the extent to which the matrix of production is decomposable into modules (which also matters for the resilience of the nexus of financial balance sheets) rather than depending on supplies of what Sraffa (1960) called 'basic commodities', i.e., commodities that are prerequisites for the production of everything. This perspective was inspired by Simon's (1962, 1969) writings on the evolutionary significance of system architecture for system resilience.

As with my failure at Stirling to read Hayek's (1952) book *The Sensory Order* despite briefly looking at it, I wrote *Monetary Scenarios* without reading a book that I believed might be relevant for the kind of work that I was doing. On this occasion, the book that I looked at briefly but then reshelved was Godley and Cripps's (1983) *Macroeconomics*, nowadays recognised as a bold pioneering contribution to 'stock–flow–consistent' methods of macroeconomic modelling and the precursor to Godley and Lavoie's (2007) influential book *Monetary Economics: An Integrated Analysis of Credit, Money, Income, Production and Wealth*. I decided not to read the Godley and Cripps book even though my brief examination of it revealed that, as I suspected, it might complement what I intended to write. I told myself that this scholarly shortcoming was acceptable because I knew that what I already had mapped out offered enough originality and was going to result in a significantly longer book than those that I had written before; moreover, I wanted to focus more on the role and impact of financial institutions than they seemed to be doing and to write a much less technical book than theirs. Godley and Cripps had tried to make their book accessible, too, by putting the more difficult mathematical material into appendices, but I could see that, despite having been published as an innocuous-looking Fontana paperback, it remained hard-going and that mastering it would hold me up significantly. (For an account of that book's background and its reception, see Shipman, 2010, chapter 11.)

My failure to read the Godley and Cripps book may look most peculiar, given that my attempt to conduct monetary and macroeconomic analysis in a non-reductionist manner (despite building on realistic micro-level foundations) was influenced by their earlier work with the CEPG. In chapter 7 of *Monetary Scenarios*, I brought together the household, business, government, and overseas sectors that I had analysed in the four preceding chapters in terms of a blend of behavioural and Post Keynesian ideas. In chapter 7 I examined how the sectors were interconnected in terms of their sources and uses of funds, and what I wrote was inspired mainly by what I had learned as a Cambridge undergraduate from studying the CEPG's view of the UK economy with frequent reference to the 'NAFA identity' which says that the sum of sectoral totals for net acquisitions of financial assets is necessarily equal to zero. When used in a flow of funds chart, the NAFA identity provided me with a means to highlight how the borrowing and (dis)saving decisions made in the various sectors intersect. This was useful for making sense of, for example, how low rates of domestic saving are connected to growing foreign indebtedness and growth in the monetary base and public sector borrowing. But it also raised the question that I explored in the next chapter, namely what is the significance of the banking sector if, like its component financial institutions, it has a NAFA of zero? Once I had explored the economics of financial institutions (in chapter 8) and shown how they could make it problematic for reserve banks to control the size of monetary aggregates (in chapter 9), the impacts of financial institutions on sectoral NAFA compositions and totals seemed to require analysis in relation to how changes in lending by financial institutions impacted on output and employment and thereby generated multiplier effects. The latter were explored in chapter 10 of *Monetary Scenarios*, ahead of chapters on unemployment and inflation and financial instability.

In chapter 10 of *Monetary Scenarios*, I arrived at issues that I was only able to explore in terms of an unfolding process via a scenario with a simple numerical illustration, and I realised that I would need to make a major investment in developing my technical skills if I were to go any further. Getting to grips with Godley and Cripps (1983) would only have been the start of what I would have needed to do. In essence, the view that I had formed of what Post Keynesian economists needed to do was very similar to that which led Godley and Lavoie (2007) to produce their remarkable book.

After completing *Monetary Scenarios*, I did not go any further because I sensed from my brief look at Godley and Cripps's book that they were already 'on the case'. With modern computers, there seems enormous potential to model the macroeconomy in terms of micro-level behaviour based on simple behavioural rules regarding levels of spending, speculation, lending, borrowing, and saving, and how these levels are affected by the operating rules that financial institutions and foreign currency traders use and that impact on the availability of loans and on interest rates and exchange rates. One can then apply a scenarios-based standpoint and explore how such a simulation model behaves in response to changes in the behavioural rules that are assumed to apply and in the rules of the game that constrain offers that can be made to potential borrowers.

The *Monetary Scenarios* project was very disappointing in terms of the ratio of hours invested in it to the number of citations that the book achieved. Very few people other than close contacts of mine have cited it. Furthermore, the fact that it was not released in paperback ensured that no one would ever build a course around it even though I wrote it with students in mind, hoping that it would be released as a paperback a couple of years after being published. Wherever possible, I illustrated my arguments with real-world examples and the result was that it often veered too far in the direction of financial journalism instead of presenting tightly written abstract analysis in the academic style. With hindsight, I think that I should have written a shorter book in the latter style, that was aimed squarely at my academic peers and set out my mission and methodological stance more carefully.

Marc Lavoie's name often comes to mind when I think about *Monetary Scenarios*. This is not merely in relation to his 2007 book with Wynne Godley but also because of two earlier connections. The first is that one of the reasons for wanting to write a sequel to *Money Matters* was that Lavoie (1985) had noted that book's lack of attention to the notion of endogenous money. This criticism was entirely justified and the embarrassment that I felt about it led me to be determined to show that I had developed a useful perspective on how monetary endogeneity arises. Secondly, the failure of *Monetary Scenarios* contrasts with the deservedly great success of Lavoie's (1992) *Foundations of Post-Keynesian Economic Analysis*. Lavoie's book is a far more substantial and thoroughly academic work that in many respects tries to do rather similar things to mine and generally does them better. Unlike me, he had taken the trouble to read Godley and Cripps (1983).

6.5   CONFERENCE PARTICIPATION

The resourcing of conference travel that UTAS provided seemed to be totally off the scale when compared to what had been available at Stirling. Soon after I arrived in Hobart, Harry Campbell encouraged me to spend part of the break before the final 1984 teaching term attending the 13th Australian Conference of Economists at what was then known as

WAIT (the Western Australian Institute of Technology, which later became Curtin University). Funding for the long flight to Perth, accommodation and registration fee was available even if I did not offer a paper, as the conference was seen as a means for getting a sense of who was who and what was what in Australian economics. It was the first large, general, parallel-session conference that I attended, and it did not lead me to become a fan of the genre. It also left me thinking that many Australian economists essentially were local in their focus and that many of the big names had an air of what I latter came to think of (after I became familiar with the 'World famous in New Zealand' marketing slogan of the New Zealand 'Lemon and Paeroa' soft drink) as 'world famous in Australia'.

A significant proportion of the policy-related papers at the WAIT conference were attempts at applying to Australian industries the theory of contestable markets that had recently been proposed by Baumol, Panzar and Willig (1982). This theory challenged the previously dominant structure–conduct–performance approach to monopoly and competition policy by focusing on the significance of potential competition as a deterrent to the abuse of monopoly power in markets that can be entered without incurring significant sunk costs. As devotees of Andrews's work such as myself had realised (see also Davies and Lee, 1988), the Baumol *et al.* analysis is superficially similar to Andrews's 'normal cost' view of pricing because both approaches assign a major role to the power of potential competition. However, the theory of contestable markets lacks the Marshallian elements that underpin Andrews's work, particularly the role of the accumulation of customer goodwill in determining market share. There were blank looks when I asked questions from an Andrews-style standpoint to presenters of papers who had written them based on Baumol *et al.*'s analysis. Nor could other members of their audiences 'get where I was coming from' if I tried to talk with them about such presentations in the breaks that followed.

I had a similar experience the following year with I attended the 14th Conference of Australian Economists, at the University of New South Wales in Sydney. My paper applying personal construct psychology to analysing responses to changes in prices was paired with one on expectations and savings behaviour. My paper pretty much generated a bewildered silence whereas the other one attracted plenty of interest on minor econometric issues. I was puzzled by the latter paper's failure to mention Katona's work on consumer confidence or to make any use of an index of consumer sentiment, but questions closed without me getting the chance to ask about this from the floor. After the session closed, a short chat with the speaker revealed that he had simply assumed that consumers formed 'rational expectations' and that he had no desire to learn about Katona's perspective.

After these two conferences, I pretty much decided never to attend such conferences again, and I stuck to this policy for the rest of my career, with just three exceptions. The first was when I attended the 1989 Australian Conference of Economists. It was in Adelaide and its timing intersected perfectly with the return leg of a Hobart-to-Darwin road-trip that I took with my then-partner Sharon for our winter vacation, but none of the presentations was memorable. The other two came shortly after the end of my stint in Tasmania. Lincoln University, the institution to which I moved, hosted the 1991 New Zealand Conference of Economists and as the new professor in the host institution, I felt under an obligation to present a paper and be visible. My paper was an extension of the permits-based view of monetary management that I set out in the final chapter of *Monetary Scenarios*. It did not draw much of an audience or any usable feedback, and I cannot recall any of the other presentations. Finally, I attended the 1992 Australian Conference of Economists. It was held in Melbourne and again was mainly forgettable, aside from providing a pleasant chance to catch up with some historians of economic thought via the session to which my paper on the challenges of teaching economics in a non-deterministic way (see Section 7.2) had been allocated.

Otherwise, I opted only to attend conferences that were small, single-session events (the 1986 Australasian Personal Construct Psychology Conference, the 1987 History of Economic Thought Society of Australia Conference, the 1987 and 1988 Malvern political economy conferences, and a conference at UNSW in 1988 on Post Keynesian economics) or, if they were one a larger scale, were in my core area, as with the 1990 IAREP conference at Exeter. By far the most significant of these events for me was the 1987 Malvern conference, not because it yielded two publications (Earl, 1989a, 1990b) but because it led to the setting up of *Review of Political Economy*. Inevitably, as a founding member of its editorial board, I went on to receive a steady stream of refereeing requests from this journal, but it has been a delight to see the *Review* become a major forum for research in heterodox economics.

With my growing experience of participating in conferences, I also started having rather mixed feelings about the impacts that writing conference papers can have on one's work. Making a commitment to give a conference paper is often an effective self-control device for those who are otherwise prone to allow procrastination or laziness to get in the way of turning their ideas into outputs. But if one does not have such afflictions, 'coming up with something' for a conference can be a diversion from staying focused on more important work that is not suitable, or is a long way from being ready, for presentation at a conference. Moreover, insufficient assertiveness in the presence of obligational pressure may result in conference presenters accepting requests from conference organisers to allow their work to be included in an edited volume of papers from the conference, even though their papers had bigger chances of making an impact if they went through the more arduous process of getting them accepted by a well-ranked journal. Indeed, although (if one is lucky) the number of people who comment on one's paper at a conference may be greater than the number of referees from whom one gets comments if one sends it to a journal, the latter may provide a much better set of comments if they are well-chosen and do their work thoroughly and constructively. So, one might end up with a better paper by simply sending it straight to a journal and not even offering it for presentation at a conference.

6.6   RESEARCH AUDIT

My growing body of publications was enough to enable me to be shortlisted for senior lectureships from late 1985 and, from late 1989, for some of the professorial positions for which I applied. But this was in the era before research audits, and the kind of research output profile that I was generating was not of the kind that would have enabled me to garner such shortlistings if the rules of today's research audit-driven hiring and promotion processes had applied back then.

Tables 6.1 and 6.2 summarise, respectively, the outputs that I produced and how my journal articles came to be published. Taken together, these tables show that (a) I was publishing mostly in output categories that a modern-day dean would not view as indicating that I was engaging in high-quality original research, and (b) much of my work had been getting into print via patronage relationships, often without going through rigorous refereeing processes, after being initiated by others. From a modern-day dean's perspective, I would be viewed as having been badly misbehaving by failing to try to contribute as much as possible to enhancing the reputation of the institution that employed me.

Table 6.1: A Dean's View of My University of Tasmania Research Output

Type of Research Output	N	Reference Tag (and Name of Journal) in Reference List Order
A*-Ranked Articles	2	Brooks and Earl (1987) *Journal of Consumer Research* Earl (1990a) *Economic Journal*
A-Ranked Articles	0	0
B-Ranked Articles	6	Earl (1986a) *Journal of Economic Studies* Earl (1987a) *HETSA Bulletin* (now *History of Economics Review*) Earl (1990b) *Review of Political Economy* Earl (1991a) *Journal of Post Keynesian Economics* Earl (1991b) *Prometheus* Earl and Kay (1985) *Journal of Economic Studies*
C-Ranked Articles (0)	0	
Unranked Articles	1	Lee, Irving-Lessman, Davies and Earl (1986) *British Review of Economic Issues*
Refereed Conference Papers	0	
Research Monographs	2	Earl (1986b, 1990c)
Other Books	2	Earl (ed.) (1988a, 1988b)
Parts of Edited Books	4	Earl (1987b, 1989a, 1993c, 1992d)
Review Articles	1	Earl (1988c)
Book Reviews	12	Earl (1986c, 1987c, 1987d), 1988d, 1988e, 1989b, 1989c, 1990d, 1990e, 1990f, 1990g, 1991c)
Other	3	Earl (1987e, 1988f, 1992g)

Two other concerns would arise if a dean or an appointment panel were to go beyond categories of output and examine the nature of the outputs. A minor one is that, although the Brooks and Earl (1987) paper was fully refereed, it is actually little more than an extension to a paper by Coursey (1985): it exposes a gap in Coursey's analysis and fills it. Most authors who write such papers give themselves away by including the phrase 'a comment' somewhere in their title. So, would this paper really qualify as of A* quality? The second concern that a modern-day dean would have about where I had got to by 1991 is much more important: careful examination of the titles of the outputs from my time in Tasmania calls into question my potential to deliver original research.

Table 6.2: Origins and Refereeing of My University of Tasmania Research Articles

Type of Article	N	Reference Tag and [ABDC Ranking Category] (in Reference List Order)
Journal articles that were unsolicited submissions and were fully refereed	2	Brooks and Earl (1987 [A*]) Lee, Irving-Lessman, Davies and Earl (1986 [unramked]).
Invited submissions accepted after being revised in response to referee comments	1	Earl (1990a [A*])
Articles written for 'special issues', or as invited contributions to symposium sections	2	Earl. (1991a [B]). Earl and Kay (1985 [B[)
Articles that were invited submissions and/or were accepted by journal editor without referee reports being supplied or revisions requested	4	Earl (1986a [B], 1987a [B[, 1989b [B], 1991b [B])

To be sure, I was developing a reputation as someone who sought to integrate economics and psychology and had a command of the literature of psychological and behavioural economics not merely via my own research but also via my contributions as a reviewer and survey writer. But this is not the same as focusing on two or three tightly defined ongoing programmes of original research that will yield high-quality publications. (More than three would run the risk of running into difficulties in keeping up with leading-edge research in each programme area.) I had only generated a couple of extensions to my personal constructs approach to consumer behaviour and had shown no inclination to do any empirical work relating to personal construct theory or hierarchical/non-compensatory decision-making processes. Meanwhile, my interests in industrial organisation and Post Keynesian monetary economics were mainly feeding into my teaching, not into steady flows of original research output based on sets of connecting principles. Nor was I showing a determination to establish myself as a key figure in economic method or the history of economic thought. I was developing an unusually wide range of knowledge and contributing across a wide range of areas, but I lacked the depth and focus that is needed to become a big player in any area.

Yet although my research record by 1991 may seem to be devoid of the kinds of focused research programmes that one can discern in the careers of heterodox economics stars such as Sheila Dow, Geoff Hodgson and Marc Lavoie, my apparent dabbling in a wide range of areas (and, it must be added, my willingness to engage with the work of heterodox scholars from across an unusually wide political spectrum) belies the deeper kind of research programme that I was pursuing. I was trying to find connecting principles between the fields in which I worked that might provide the basis for a coherent alternative to orthodox optimisation- and equilibrium-focused ways of doing economics. This was a Loasby-inspired way of operating; its mission could be summed up as an attempt to build a 'growth of knowledge' approach to economics but, for want of that phrase, I was still thinking of it as a 'behavioural/Post Keynesian' approach even as I absorbed compatible themes from Austrian, evolutionary and institutional economics.

This wider mission meant that I simply was not operating with the mindset that is nowadays expected of an academic economist a few years on from being awarded a doctorate. To make the progress that would satisfy a modern-day dean, I should have sought to obtain research funding for empirical work on applying the personal constructs approach in economics. If I failed to win funds from a research council, I should have plodded away for as long as it took to do the empirical work without any research assistance. (Given that the research methods of personal construct psychology entail working with small samples of subjects but involve long sessions with each subject, time was the issue; I did not need to fund a major research questionnaire.) Either way, I should then have written up the research meticulously, for submission to high-ranking journals. This was the road that Richard Thaler took with his approach to behavioural economics and in taking it he demonstrated that mainstream journals are much more open than heterodox economists seem to think to empirical work that challenges accepted ideas. I simply was not thinking of going down that road, and in the mid-1980s there was no pressure to do so or guidance of the kind that research-oriented universities in the 2020s offer their staff about how best to chase research funds.

A neat illustration of my failure to chase empirical opportunities concerns the issue of 'rip-offs' in pricing. Most behavioural economists are aware of Richard Thaler's work on bargains and rip-offs and his notion that people derive or lose utility when making transactions depending on where the price that they pay sits relative to what they have in mind as a reference price. A famous aspect of his work in this area is the 'beer at the beach' study in which the research subjects were typically willing to pay significantly higher prices for beer brought to them at the beach by a friend if it were purchased at an upmarket beachside hotel than if it were purchased from a run-down convenience store nearby (Thaler, 1985, p. 206). Although the beer is consumed on the beach in both scenarios, the idea is that paying a higher price at the hotel is not a rip-off since the hotel supplies it with ambience-related advantages that could be enjoyed by consuming it at the point of purchase. Around the time that Thaler was developing his ideas about pricing, I, too, wrote (Earl, 1986b, pp. 260–1) about the rip-off concept, arguing that consumers may resist buying things, despite wanting them and being able to pay the asking price, because they believe that the supplier has set a price that is unacceptably greater than the cost of producing the product and offering it in the market. Consumers may not know the full details of the production process, but we might think of them 'as if' they can compute a hedonic price equation that predicts what relative prices should be based on knowledge of the products' features and quality of construction. This was a perfectly testable proposition (that I based on introspection) but I didn't think for a moment of investigating it systematically and building journal papers around it.

During my time at UTAS, my broad long-term hope was not to produce articles within a narrowly defined field for high-quality journals but to keep abreast of relevant literature across a broad front by successively coming back to consumer behaviour, the theory of the firm, and monetary theory/macroeconomics as each decade passed, and in the process gradually build a better and better alternative way of doing economics. Each circuit would involve writing a new book in each of these fields. In a sense, my research strategy was rather like that of a carmaker that offers three product lines that are synergistically related and successively revised, each of which has a decade-long product lifecycle. With *Lifestyle Economics* finished, I hoped next to make my second foray on the monetary theory/macroeconomics front before then spending several years working towards a sequel to *The Corporate*

Imagination (rather in the way that Michael Porter followed his 1980 book *Competitive Strategy* in 1985 with *Competitive Advantage*). After that, I would return to consumer behaviour for three or four years, and so on. The teaching that I was assigned had complemented this plan very well and, despite being diverted by work on the edited books, I got my money book finished by mid-1989 with four years of research and writing time remaining to produce my second theory of the firm book before I hit the tenth anniversary of completing *The Corporate Imagination*. However, sticking to the plan came at the cost of the money book being short-changed in terms of the research that went into it, which in turn affected how I wrote it. This would not have been obvious to selection committees in 1990 who saw *Monetary Scenarios* listed on my CV.

Impacts of Patrons on Research Output and Reputation

The role that patrons played in this phase of my career warrants careful consideration. Some of the writing or editing invitations that I received would have served me well as endorsements of the quality of my previous work, for they came from senior figures, and I was careful to note them when listing publications in my CV. However, I did not appreciate at the time the extent to which having eminent patrons can be a mixed blessing.

To illustrate this, let us first reflect on the wider impact on my career of the book editing projects that I had undertaken for Warren Samuels (Earl, 1988a) and Mark Blaug (Earl 1988b). These edited books certainly would have helped to establish my reputation in behavioural and psychological economics. In time, they would be reasonably successful in terms of citations scores relative to my solo contributions. But they were major distractions and diversions from my own research, and they had psychological consequences that affected the choices that I made as a scholar.

The invitation from Warren Samuels to edit *Psychological Economics* came less than six months after I arrived in Tasmania, and the contract to proceed with it is dated 17 December 1984. My work on it ended late in August 1987 with indexing and proof corrections while I was in the UK on recreation and conference leave. By the time that work on the volume that Samuels had commissioned was coming to an end, I was beginning work on the Elgar anthology on behavioural economics that Mark Blaug had invited me to edit. While working on these volumes I also started receiving, and accepted, invitations to write book reviews and, from John Eatwell, invitations to write three short biographical entries (Earl, 1987b) for *The New Palgrave* dictionary of economics.[11] In early 1987 I also found myself feeling obliged to come up with a paper (Earl, 1987e) for yet another patron, Don Lamberton, whose place in my career I will explore shortly. Soon after writing the paper for Lamberton, I wrote a paper (Earl, 1987a) for the *HETSA Bulletin*, published by the History of Economic Thought Society of Australia. I felt obliged to write this one, too, having been encouraged to do this after attending the 1987 HETSA conference.[12]

Taken together, these activities make it very easy to understand what happened to my own original research between 1985 and 1989. I managed to finish *Lifestyle Economics* by October 1985 despite also working on getting contributors lined up for *Psychological Economics*. This was pretty much on schedule, but in the process, I did not give

---

[11] It was very magnanimous of John Eatwell to invite me to contribute the entries to *The New Palgrave*. In 1979, shortly before I moved from Cambridge to Stirling, I had been asked to write a piece for the student-run newsletter for Cambridge's economics students, and the piece that I wrote included criticism of Eatwell's Prelims lectures for, among other things, ignoring the work of Andrews (1949) when he talked about mark-up pricing. His invitation had a useful payoff for how I came to think about the resilience of economic systems, for in addition to asking me to write entries on Andrews and Shackle, he asked me to write one on Albert Hart, whose work I had seen referred to but had not previously read (and perhaps Eatwell was giving me a subtle hint that I needed to read it). As a result of looking at Hart's work, I learned to be mindful of two things: (a) the strategic benefits of production systems that enable rates of output to be adjusted over a wide band without sharp increases in average costs per unit, even if average costs are somewhat higher than those that can be achieved at the most likely level of sales by production systems that are optimised for that level of output; and (b) if buffering or reserves are absent, one minor problem can trigger a series of increasingly dramatic problems.

[12] In 1991, *The HETSA Bulltein* became the *History of Economics Review*. The short paper that I wrote explored potential for using citation statistics and network analysis to understand better the history of economic thought, It was ahead of its time, but has not been cited. Having had the idea, I should have spent some time on a 'proof of concept' application of it in a context of interest and written it up as a paper for *History of Political Economy*. But at that time I did not view myself as a serious historian of economic thought and my focus was on getting my editorial tasks finished so that I could get on to writing *Monetary Scenarios*. Nowadays, computer apps are available that make it easy to do the sort of analysis that I wrote about in the paper: see for example, Citation Chaser (which allows forward and backward citation searches: see https://estech.shinyapps.io/citationchaser/), Connected Papers (which offers network mapping of references: see https://www.connectedpapers.com/) and Citation Gecko (which does similar thinks to Connected Papers, though is different in some respects: see https://www.citationgecko.com/).

enough attention to developing my paper about the relevance of personal construct psychology for understanding how people respond to changes in relative prices. In taking an easy route to publishing it in its original, written-in-haste form (as Earl, 1986a), I escaped from having to worry about when I was going to find time to improve it and how I would do so. With that paper and *Lifestyle Economics* out of the way, I would have been able, in the absence of patronage-related diversions, to shift my research focus to the next book that I wanted to write – either the Kaldor book that I had envisaged at Stirling), or my solo sequel to *Money Matters*. Instead, I spent the next couple of years disposing of my editorial tasks and other diversions while hankering for the time when I would be able to write either of these books.

The diversions did, of course, have a couple of important benefits in relation to my 'next solo book'. Without them, I might have started work on the Kaldor project in 1985, only to discover a year or two from its completion that Thirlwall (1987) had been ahead of me. The diversions also ensured that I came to write *Monetary Scenarios* after the 1987 financial collapse had occurred. However, if I had been able to move straight on to the Kaldor book in 1985, I probably would have followed the scholarly lessons that I applied to revising my PhD and writing *Lifestyle Economics*, for I could not have written it without immersing myself in the collection of Kaldor's books that I had accumulated. I might then have been in a position at least to write some Kaldor-related articles after Thirlwall's book appeared. But when the publication of Thirlwall's book ensured that my next solo book would be *Monetary Scenarios*, the two years of hankering affected how I went about writing it. Despite the improvements in my knowledge that had come via reading I had done in preparing material to teach Money and Banking, I really should have taken a break from writing and done some serious reading within the scholarly literature before I wrote *Monetary Scenarios* and, where necessary, while writing it.

But I did not take such breaks and I viewed my 1988 study leave mainly as time for writing. I mostly skipped the research phase aside from reading material in books by financial journalists in relation to financial innovations, financial deregulation, and the October 1987 financial crisis. I did not bother to study the finance literature to see if any behavioural contributions were being made there or whether/how ideas from new institutional economics were being used in theorizing about financial institutions. Similarly, when, partway into writing

Monetary Scenarios, I discovered Basil Moore's (1988) major new work *Horizontalists and Verticalists* by attending lectures he gave at the University of New South Wales (as part of a short Post Keynesian economics conference there in October 1988), I wove in some of his ideas simply by relying upon my notes from these lectures rather than by being a true scholar and carefully reading his book at first hand. Chapters that I should have written with their own critical literature reviews, more in the style of journal articles, ended up remaining too close to the lecture material that I had written for my undergraduates. I have no doubt that I would have made better creative contributions if I had given myself more opportunities to reflect critically on what others had done.

Underlying this post-hankering behaviour was the problem that I was too much of a 'young man in a hurry'. This problem would probably have let *Monetary Scenarios* dominate over the Kaldor book even if Thirlwall (1987) had not appeared and a choice had been necessary about which one to work on first, for the Kaldor book would have seemed likely to take a year or two longer to produce. I was fearful that having periods of zero new publications in my CV would give the impression that I was unable to sustain the rate of output that I had previously generated. If I had been in less of a hurry and not trying to get my solo book writing 'back on track', it is possible that I would have delivered a more systematic, more substantial but more abstract analysis instead of a rather 'thinking aloud'-style of book that was rather overly peppered with financial journalist-style case material.

If I had not been writing *Monetary Scenarios* as a 'young man in a hurry', I might even have invested time in getting to grips with Godley and Cripps (1983) and then invested more time in seeing if I could figure out a better way of using a sequence of charts for flows of funds and national income to present a process-based view of how changes in the willingness to spend and take financial risks change incomes and financial fragility. Because I recognised that academic works are not going to be definitive contributions, the question when writing a book was whether I had enough of an improvement to offer by the time I wrote it, rather than whether it was the best book that it could be. At the time I wrote *Monetary Scenarios,* I was in no doubt that it embodied much knowledge that I had not possessed at the time that I wrote my chapters for *Money Matters*, and it seemed 'sufficiently original'.

Although having Professors Samuels and Blaug as patrons impacted on my self-initiated research, it at least led to research outputs that usefully raised my international profile in the short term. By contrast, I believe that allowing Don Lamberton (1927–2014) to become one of my patrons was a bad mistake in career terms, even though›, for reasons that will shortly become evident, the results were not quite as bad as they could have been. At the time I arrived in Australia, Lamberton held a chair at the University of Queensland, where, I was later told, he had proved to be a highly divisive head of department. I was already aware of his interest in the economics of information and knowledge via the book of readings that he had edited in this area (Lamberton, ed., 1971). But there was another reason why it was rather inevitable that I would get to know him after moving to Australia, namely, that he had completed his Oxford DPhil (published as Lamberton, 1965) under the supervision of P. W. S. Andrews. Sure enough, early in 1987, he invited me to write a paper for his Information Research Unit (IRU) and present it as a visiting speaker. Thus began, with my (1987e) paper, my association with the University of Queensland. During that visit, he gave me copies of *Prometheus*, a journal on information and technological change that he had established in 1983 and edited until 2009 – much of the time while also editing *Information Economics and Policy*. I soon provided a second IRU Occasional Paper (Earl, 1988f) and accepted his invitations to write a book review (Earl, 1988e) and a review article (Earl, 1988c) for *Prometheus*. In the years that followed, five of my papers were published in Lamberton's journals (Earl, 1991b, 1994a, 1998a. 2009; Earl and Mandeville, 2009) and I also felt obliged to produce a paper (Earl, 1999) for a festschrift volume in his honour.

Each of my papers in Lamberton's journals were accepted by him without being refereed. By the end of 2023, none of the Lamberton-related works had achieved double digit citation counts on Google Scholar. From a modern dean's standpoint, the list of publications on my CV would have looked better without these papers. As it was, they gave the impression that I was not trying hard enough, or was unable, to achieve higher-status publications: in the research audit game, less can be more.

Having Lamberton as a patron also posed a problem once I had let him release my 1987 seminar paper as an IRU Occasional Paper: I was not sure whether it would irk him if I then tried to get it published as a regular journal article, as the fact that I was from a different institution made it seem unlike a regular departmental working paper that one has no qualms about sending to a journal. On that occasion, I was in any case too busy on other projects to think which journals might be appropriate for it. Hence, the paper languished in my filing cabinet for over four years without being sent anywhere and I came to view it as too old to send to a journal of high standing. (It was eventually published in revised form, after being properly refereed, in a very obscure journal, as Earl, 1992b.) I was less conscious of this issue with my second IRU Occasional Paper, as I reworked material from it into a chapter of *Monetary Scenarios.*

In the case of my (1991b) paper, the opportunity cost in terms of my time was not significant as I had originally written it as a presentation to deliver as part of the process of being interviewed (without success) for a chair in marketing at Griffith University early in 1990.[13] But the context of the story of how it ended up in *Prometheus* is worth recording, as it reveals another aspect of how one needs to be careful about getting too close to an academic patron.

I refined the paper before presenting it about a year later for another seminar that Lamberton invited me to deliver. This time, it was held at the Centre for International Research on Communication and Information Technology (CIRCIT) in Melbourne, for Lamberton had left the University of Queensland in 1989 to help set up CIRCIT and become its deputy-director. He had also tried to get me to join the ranks of CIRCIT staff, as a senior research fellow. However, I had resisted this opportunity for a research-only position due to not wanting to be confined to a particular research area. This proved to be a fortuitously wise move. CIRCIT had been set up following promises of major funding from the Victorian State Government and occupied premium-grade riverside offices in the centre of Melbourne. However, it had not been operating long before its funding was cut as the State Government's finances came under pressure following the collapse of the Pyramid Building Society. As a result, CIRCIT had to shift to consultancy work and there was a major falling out between Lamberton and CIRCIT's director, Bill Melody, not long after my visit. If I recall correctly, CIRCIT was eventually absorbed into La Trobe University on a much-reduced scale.

---

[13] This was the first of half a dozen or so applications that I made during my career for business school-style positions, for almost all of which I was shortlisted. But I never pursued this career direction with determination, for I viewed myself ultimately as an economist and feared that holding such positions would both prevent me from contributing to areas to which I might wish to contribute and limit how seriously my work was viewed in economics.

The only case in which having a patron had unambiguously beneficial consequences for me was the impact that John Hey had. It was at his invitation that I wrote the only paper (Earl, 1990a) among my Tasmanian output that was of the kind that would delight a modern-day dean. It would have been instrumental, along with references from Hey, in getting me shortlisted for professorial positions in 1990.

Early in November 1989, I received a letter from Hey, who was then the editor of the *Economic Journal*, informing me that he had both good and bad news for me. The good news was that he wanted me to write a long survey article on economics and psychology; the bad news was that I would need to deliver my draft by the end of January 1990 and that I would also need to expect to have to find time in March to address referee reports, so that it could then be published in the September 1990 issue of the *Economic Journal* as one of the distinctive contributions Hey had in mind for its centenary year. Clearly, this was the one invitation from this period that I could not decline, and it had come my way despite me having shocked Hey by my sartorial misbehaviour when I visited him at the University of York on an unusually hot August day in 1988. On that occasion, I showed up at his office, at the time we had arranged for a chat about his latest research, in bright yellow shorts and a 'Viva La Wombat' T-shirt, looking as if I had just come from an Australian beach. Although produced under time pressure, the resulting paper was properly researched – for example, I worked through all the extant issues of the *Journal of Economic Psychology* before writing it – and relatively few changes were required by the referees. It was the first time I had advanced my knowledge of the area beyond where I had arrived at while writing *Lifestyle Economics*.

According to Google Scholar, the paper is my third most-cited work, behind *The Economic Imagination* and *Lifestyle Economics*. However, analysis of the citations reveals a cautionary message about what a heterodox economist can achieve by publishing in a UK-based journal, even if it is the top-ranked UK-based journal. The contrast with Matthew Rabin's (1998) *Journal of Economic Literature* survey on economics and psychology is stark. As of 19 January 2026, Rabin's paper had 4720 Google Scholar citation hits, including many citing articles that are in top-tier mainstream journals that have been cited thousands of times. Whereas, my paper had a mere 306, barely a handful of which are in top-tier mainstream journals, with the most-cited works scoring citations in the hundreds rather than the thousands. Those who cite my paper are predominately heterodox economists (especially in evolutionary and institutional economics), economic psychologists and applied researchers (for example, in areas such as tourism); it has not found an audience among the modern behavioural economists whose eyes I had hoped it might open to a far wider psychology-related literature than they usually employ.

The timing of John Hey's invitation to write the survey was perfect, for it came at the start of the summer research period, after I had finished writing *Monetary Scenarios*. The high-pressure deadline it entailed meant that it was not an ongoing distraction or diversion from research that I had been hoping to do; it merely delayed by a few months the start of my return to making my own original contributions to behavioural economics. When the survey was finished, I got back into doing work of my own for the rest of 1990 via my attempt to integrate personal construct psychology and cognitive dissonance theory (eventually published as Earl, 1992c) and by using a symposium invitation from Fred Lee as an opportunity to write a pluralistic paper that I had been wanting to write about pricing (Earl, 1991a). It felt as if I was picking up where I had left off during 1985. But I then failed to maintain this way of operating.

In mid-1990, Warren Samuels invited me to write a chapter on Tibor Scitovsky (Earl, 1992d) for a volume he was editing on leading economists who tried to take economics in new directions. However, in career terms, the Scitovsky chapter was not a good use of my time. It consumed all my research time from November 1990 to April 1991, for this was not a chapter that I could 'come up with' merely by employing my existing knowledge of Scitovsky's work. That research did not have a significant impact on my subsequent work and the chapter only generated a few citations, albeit more than have been achieved by almost all the chapters that I have contributed to edited volumes. The chapter on Scitovsky would turn out to be the last work until 1999 that I based largely on fresh research as opposed to writing things that had been in my mind for a long while or 'coming up with something' to serve a request from someone else.

6.7   EXIT

My years at UTAS were those in which I made my most frequent forays into the academic labour market, for although I enjoyed living in Tasmania and usually experienced less daily stress at UTAS than anywhere else that I worked, I never felt very settled there. My then-partner Sharon did not put down roots there, either, despite readily finding a position as a clinical psychologist after finishing her UTAS master's. However, as may be common with dual-career households, the fact that we both had 'itchy feet' did not mean that we wanted to move in the same direction.

The thing that first unsettled me was the astonishment I felt, shortly before the end of the 1984 academic year, when a colleague showed me the letter that he had received informing him that he was being promoted to senior lecturer. Given how little he had published, this was a complete shock to me, even though I rated his abilities very highly; he, too, seemed somewhat surprised that his application for promotion had been successful. It made me wonder about the kind of university that I had joined. Here I was, with several books to my name and (unlike him) a PhD, yet I was unable to apply for promotion so long as I was on my three-year contract.

What I did not realise was that I was looking at a phenomenon of the Australasian tertiary education sector at that time known as a 'career grade' promotion. In other words, the norm was that, unless an academic staff member was caught behaving in a disreputable manner (for example, a case of 'gross moral turpitude'), he or she would be promoted at least as far as senior lecturer even without having developed a strong track record in research; promotion to senior lecturer was just a matter of 'keeping one's nose clean' and serving enough time in the role of lecturer. However, those who continued to achieve little in terms of publications would then stay at the senior lecturer level for the rest of their time at the institution in question.

With no appreciation of 'career grade' promotion norms, I started keeping an eye on Australasian academic vacancies. About six months later, I applied for a couple of positions in New Zealand. Victoria University in Wellington offered me a senior lectureship without even calling me for interview, and the University of Auckland flew me over for interview for a senior lecturer/associate professor position and offered me a position some way up the senior lecturer scale. I liked the people that I met at Auckland, and I was impressed with the thoroughness of their interview process, my first experience of having to give what is now called a 'job market paper', and spend several days meeting members of the department, as well as having the formal interview. It set the benchmark for how I expected I should be appraised whenever I applied for jobs in future. But I realised that I must be a bit more patient, for given the prices of houses in Auckland and Wellington, and interest rates that were well into double digits, either position would be a backward step in financial terms.

Soon after this foray into the New Zealand job market, the two retirement-related lectureship vacancies that Harry Campbell had foreshadowed nearly two years earlier were advertised. One of them was offered to me, and the other went to Ben Heijdra, the other three-year contract lecturer. (Ben moved from UTAS to Monash University in 1990 and has held chairs at the University of Groningen since 1998.) However, I then discovered that another colleague had not been successful in his first attempt at getting promotion despite having a steadily growing pile of articles. What happened to him made me nervous about my chances of getting promotion at the end of 1986, given that the system did not seem very consistent, and I would not quite be at the top of the lecturer scale. Hence, I applied for a senior lectureship at the University of Adelaide: I liked the city on my interview visit and would probably have been a better fit there than in Hobart, but I was not offered a position.

When a senior lectureship in economics was advertised at UTAS, I thought that it was worth applying as it might give me further interview practice and send some useful signals, even though it seemed very likely that it would go, as it did, to Harry Bloch, who had been visiting from Denver. I did get the interview practice, but I subsequently got something far more valuable: a member of the selection panel said to me, in the strongest terms, 'Do not use Loasby as a referee again.' Later, I discovered that I was not the only former member of Stirling's Department of Economics to have been given that advice. I never discovered precisely what kind of unhelpful reference Loasby had written, but the following year he wrote a rather unenthusiastic review of my *Lifestyle Economics* (see Loasby, 1987; I did my best not to let this affect my mood when I reviewed his book *The Mind and Method of the Economist*, see Earl, 1990g).

Promotion to senior lecturer did come my way with effect from the start of 1987. However, toward the end of that year I applied for a similar position at the University of Queensland, where I had earlier given a seminar at the invitation of Don Lamberton. It seemed a potential way of getting into a larger department, on the Australian mainland, in a city whose house prices were (in those days) very affordable. Sharon was increasingly hoping to move to Queensland for its warmth and sunshine, and among her Tasmanian mental health colleagues emigrating to the Sunshine State was commonly known as 'the geographical cure' for patients who were depressed. However, neither of us had so far visited Brisbane in the summer and my discovery of how hot and humid it was there in December became a deal-breaker when I realised that the School of Economics was, at that time, located in a building that lacked air conditioning.

Soon after that interview trip, we flew to Christchurch for a vacation of touring around New Zealand's South Island, and I immediately felt glad that I had declined the offer that I had received from the University of Queensland. Christchurch was a delightfully elegant city, rather like a scaled down version of Adelaide without the latter's ferocious dry summer heat. It looked like it would be a good place to live if I could get a chair there one day, but the chances of doing this seemed slim given the thoroughly orthodox reputation of the University of Canterbury's economics department. At the end of our vacation, we met up with my former Stirling colleague, Bob Hamilton, who now worked in the University of Canterbury's department of management. When we asked what Christchurch's climate was like in winter, he said that although it was cool at night, the winter sun rapidly raised the morning temperatures. Since he had not mentioned that the east-coast city had a surprisingly continental climate, with frequent frosts and a temperature inversion that trapped smoke from wood-heaters, we got the impression that its winters were like those in Hobart.

The trips that I made back to the UK in its 1987 and 1988 summers left me puzzled about whether I really wanted to stay Down Under even though, after getting the permanent job, I had been granted permanent residence (a process that took seven months). Life in the UK seemed to have got less bleak in the time since I had left Stirling and my trips back had given me a sense of how hard it was to combine recreation leave, conference leave and catching up with family and friends via fleeting visits. Matters were not helped by my parents having chosen to retire to Polperro in Cornwall, which was almost as far as possible from where many of my friends lived. Hence, when I saw an advertisement for a fellowship in economics at Worcester College, Oxford, I decided to apply and thereby see how hard it would be to get interviewed and what I would feel if I received an offer. I felt rather guilty about submitting the application as I was also in the process of applying for Australian citisenship.

Somewhat to my surprise, I was invited to an all-expenses paid interview. Since I was on sabbatical at the time, there was no barrier to attending it, so I flew to the UK for the second time that year. The trip provided a reminder of how frosty the UK climate could be even before the depths of winter arrived, and how long the shadows could be. By the time I had my interview, my enthusiasm had been diminished by the discovery that, five years on from my Oxford Polytechnic interview visit, housing affordability in Oxford had got even worse.

I have hardly any recollections of the interview. Much more memorable was that, after dining in hall, the candidates were taken to the senior common room. I had a good conversation with Dick Smethurst, a management scholar who had a joint fellowship with Worcester College and Templeton College. Wilfred Beckerman was there, too, even though he was a fellow at Balliol College; presumably his involvement in the interview panel, was as a representative of Oxford's Department of Economics. After I had been chatting with Beckerman for a while, Smethurst returned with a tray on which there was a small box. He just about managed to keep a straight face as he said, 'I don't suppose this will be your scene, but would you care for some snuff?'

Although I did not get the job, Beckerman contacted me shortly after I got back to Hobart. He wanted to let me know that another position was going to be advertised, this time at St Anne's College, and he encouraged me to apply for it. In the event, I was not able to attend an interview as its timing clashed with my need to be in Hobart in the run-up to the start of the 1989 academic year to fulfil my duties as sub-dean during the enrolment period. It was probably a good thing that I did not get an economics fellowship at Oxford, for I would not have enjoyed the college tutor role after economics at Oxford, as elsewhere, became increasingly narrow and driven by technique.

Being taken seriously in Oxford led me to decide to focus on applying for chairs. This decision was reinforced when, within weeks, I was interviewed for a chair at Deakin University in Geelong, west of Melbourne. I was not asked to give a seminar presentation or meet any of the staff; it was just an interview, and I had a sense that they were not seriously interested in my application. But at least it was a start in that direction. After the interview was over, I took the rental car they had provided for me at Melbourne airport for a long drive along the Great Ocean Road to see the spectacular coastal scenery.

Eighteen months passed before I was invited to another professorial interview in economics, this time at University College North Wales, nowadays known as the University of Bangor. With its beautiful location, Bangor seemed to be something of a Welsh equivalent of Stirling, though the town itself was much smaller and much further from any large cities. However, it was an area where Welsh was commonly spoken, and my minder helpfully advised that I would need to be careful with the local 'Taffia' council representative on the interview panel. He was not kidding.

It was the kind of interview visit that I had experienced in Auckland, where I had to make a presentation and could meet prospective colleagues prior to the interview. There was also a social event for candidates at which the external assessors were present. One was David Ulph, who had been at Stirling before I was there and had occasionally visited during my time at Stirling. The other was John Hey, who clearly had not forgotten our previous meeting. He greeted me by saying, 'What, no shorts?' Much of the interview focused on where I hoped to take the curriculum if I got the job and came to Bangor. David and John seemed genuinely interested in my hopes for running a pluralistic microeconomics sequence in which the standard neoclassical tools were taught alongside material from behavioural and evolutionary economics. But then it came to the 'Taffia' representative, who was concerned about the kind of education his daughter might receive if she came to Bangor under my watch. With his heavy Welsh accent, he put it to me that I was claiming that I could squeeze a quart into a pint pot, which surely would result in a lowering of the quality of what was taught.

Not getting the job thus came as no surprise to me, and it meant that I did not get to find out whether Sharon had been calling my bluff when she said that if I got the job and accepted it, she would not be coming to Bangor with me. But my Bangor interview led me to resolve that one day I would write a scholarly pluralistic microeconomics textbook that demonstrated that what I had in mind was indeed feasible. I did not realise that barely eighteen months later I would start writing such a book (which was published as Earl, 1995a).

My final batch of professorial applications in 1990 led me to be invited to interviews at the University of Sheffield, Massey University (at Palmerston North, New Zealand) and Lincoln University (near Christchurch, New Zealand), but rather disappointingly, not at the University of Auckland. The Sheffield and Lincoln interviews clashed and the personnel section at Sheffield advised me that their timing was immovable since their vice-chancellor was retiring at the end of the year and, before leaving, wanted to determine who got the economics chair. I could imagine finding it difficult to warm to such a vice-chancellor during an interview, as I felt that he should have let his successor make the choice. I therefore decided to decline the Sheffield interview and attend the one at Lincoln instead. Given that Sheffield's outgoing vice-chancellor, Geoffrey Sims, was a physicist, I would probably have been unable to outperform the successful candidate, Sean Holly, a much more technically skilled economist than me.

Ultimately, I declined the Massey interview, too. Before its scheduled date, I had been offered the Lincoln job, and the choice between the city of Christchurch and the country town of Palmerston North was a no-brainer. However, Massey's personnel selection processes were interesting to observe up to that point. It was emphasised that the successful applicant would soon be expected to assume the departmental headship, a job that required 'being willing to accept frequent task changes with equanimity'. This was a remarkably frank signal that the job might not suit a research-focused academic as opposed to someone who wanted to steer the department in a particular direction. I sensed that I had hoped to be able to play both roles and might have been a bit short in the area of equanimity. This is probably why, when I did a Myers–Briggs personality type identifier test as part of Massey's pre-interview process, I seemed to be on the cusp between an INTJ 'mastermind' (i.e., someone who is keen to figure out how systems work and devise ways of improving them, which the material that Massey sent labelled as a 'scientist') and an ENTJ 'field-marshal'.

The Lincoln interview process consumed almost a week. Prior to applying, I had been largely ignorant of Lincoln University, aside from what I had heard from a fellow musician in Hobart's Adult Education Concert Band (in which I played bass guitar) who had completed his biological science PhD at Lincoln prior to moving to Hobart. He had said that the head of the Department of Economics and Marketing, Tony Zwart was only about 40 years of age and was the Professor of

261

Marketing. Tony Zwart seemed pleasant, and I was pleased to discover that, via his focus on agricultural marketing systems, he had got interested in Williamson-style transaction cost approaches to the choice between markets and hierarchies. My minder, senior lecturer Rod St Hill had recently completed his PhD at Lincoln and was a Post Keynesian, as was the rising young star, senior lecturer Paul Dalziel, who would later succeed me as holder of the established chair in economics (which he held from 2002 to 2024). With Lincoln University set to grow, as evidenced by the building site where the new commerce building was being constructed, the chances of building a pluralistic group of economists and fostering cross-disciplinary work seemed good, despite some of the longer-established staff lacking PhDs and having track records of delivering little research. Moreover, the Lincoln campus was in the countryside, an easy short drive from Christchurch.

My Lincoln presentation and interview both went well. At the start of the interview, the chair of the interview panel remarked that I hadn't been dressed quite as they anticipated I might be. I had been wearing a summer suit for most of that week and then went to the interview in my formal three-piece suit despite it being about 30 degrees due to a 'nor-wester' blowing in hot air from Australia, so I smiled and said, 'I'll get John Hey for that!' Laughter ensued around the interview table. Otherwise, though, it was great to have John as one of my referees. A week later, Professor Bruce Ross, the Vice-Chancellor of Lincoln University, phoned to say that they were going to offer me the job.

After the call finished, I went to Harry Campbell's office to see his reaction to this news. Harry said, 'Great. If you can get the offer in writing, it should help you get a readership in next year's promotion round.' I suspected that Harry's reaction reflected two things. One was the fact that, at the prevailing exchange rate, the recently upgraded New Zealand academic pay scale still left a New Zealand full professor only with the equivalent of what a reader (associate professor) received in Australia. (My own view, which was confirmed when I moved to Christchurch, was that the actual purchasing power of academic salaries in New Zealand was much better than was implied by such calculations, for New Zealand had become a more open economy than Australia and academics were better paid relative to the rest of the population.) I also suspected that Harry had a justifiable sense that, under his direction, the UTAS Department of Economics had made great progress and had many advantages over its Lincoln counterpart. If he had shown he was keen to keep me and had told me to defer my decision until he had seen whether he could get the UTAS vice-chancellor to offer me a readership there and then, I would have been prepared to wait and see what happened. Harry seemed to be signalling that he did not believe such a counteroffer would be forthcoming and I felt, as did Sharon, that it was time to move on from Hobart anyway. Despite my enthusiasm for scenario planning techniques, I did not reflect on the key question that I should have reflected upon *before* the Lincoln interview trip, to yield issues about which to gather intelligence while I was there, namely, 'What could possibly go wrong?' I made the mistake of presuming that Lincoln University would be much more like the universities I was familiar with than it turned out to be.

7 Lincoln University, New Zealand, 1991–2001

7.1   INTRODUCTION

Lincoln University is located on the Canterbury Plains near the township of Lincoln, 15 kilometres west of Christchurch, the largest city in the South Island of New Zealand. Its campus dates from 1878, when it was established as the school of agriculture of what was then Canterbury University College. In fact, it was the first agricultural college to be established in the southern hemisphere. Lincoln University – hereafter usually referred to simply as 'Lincoln', as was the standard practice of its staff – was created in 1990 by separating Lincoln College, Canterbury from the University of Canterbury. By that point, activities at the Lincoln campus had expanded well beyond agriculture, with the Department of Economics and Marketing having grown out of the teaching of agricultural economics and the study of the operation of agricultural markets.

In its early years with university status, Lincoln was New Zealand's smallest public university, with enrolments of around 2000 on an equivalent-full-time student (EFTS) basis. But it seemed set to grow. With the arrival of university status came impressive new lecture theatre blocks with state-of-the-art audio-visual equipment, and, just before I arrived, the Department of Economics and Marketing moved to a brand-new building. A promised extension to the latter was constructed a few years later to accommodate the growing number of staff. However, little long-term growth took place: by 2018 (the most recent year for which I have been able to find data), its enrolments on an EFTS basis were only 2695. It has struggled financially, leading many to wonder whether it should be absorbed back into the University of Canterbury.

When I arrived in mid-1991 to take up Lincoln's established chair in economics, the Department of Economics and Marketing also taught business management but not the other areas of commerce that were represented at Lincoln, namely, farm management, accounting and finance, and property studies. During the decade that I worked there, all these activities were merged into Lincoln's Commerce Division, with the directorship of commerce teaching programmes being in the hands of a Lincoln stalwart who had not been in the Department of Economics and Marketing. He took an agriculture-centred view of what needed to be offered. This had consequences for my attempts to keep alive the pluralistic approach that I introduced to the teaching of economics and for my attempts to embed behavioural and evolutionary approaches in the curriculum.

Although my interest in marketing and management might seem to have made me especially suitable for contributing to these areas at Lincoln, the signals that I detected after I arrived seemed to imply that the Vice-Chancellor, Professor Bruce Ross, had hired me more with a view to my potential role in developing social science activities. Lincoln's social scientists were mainly based in the Department of Landscape Architecture, or the Department of Tourism and Recreation Management. They made themselves known to me soon after I arrived, and they proved to be the colleagues with whom I was happiest to work.

The smallness of the institution gave the impression that it might be able to adapt in a nimble way, and I soon was on first-name terms with staff from a wide range of departments, as well as senior administrators. Unfortunately, it had an operating system that was at odds with the principles that I wanted to apply. Those who had spent their careers at Lincoln and were comfortable with the established system did not welcome the 'breath of fresh air' that I represented. 'Out-group' members such as myself privately referred to the former as 'the Lincoln Mafia'. I soon realised that there were many things that ought to be changed, but I was never offered the position of head of department, a position I had anticipated would come my way when the marketing professor's term as head expired.

Lincoln's culture and 'mafia' problems applied at levels higher than that of individual departments or, later, divisions. When a deputy vice-chancellor was hired, there was considerable surprise that the job went to Professor Trevor Bryce, an eminent Australian scholar of the Hittites and near-eastern history. This seemed further to signal that Bruce Ross wanted to diversify from Lincoln's focus on agriculture, However, to the great disappointment of myself and the other social scientists, things did not work out well for Trevor. As he put it to me during a break at a weekend retreat for senior staff, 'I just can't get the V-C to see that it's the Registrar who's really running the show'. He was finding it impossible to action changes that he hoped to make. Soon after this, he resigned.

Within Economics and Marketing, the ratio of staff to full-time-equivalent students was not particularly terrible. Contact hours per year were typically fewer than those I had been used to at the University of Stirling, as fewer hours went into tutorials. However, long-serving lecturers and senior lecturers without PhDs produced little or no research output year after year. Their performance contrasted sharply with that of Paul Dalziel and Ross Cullen, who had PhDs and had joined recently from other New Zealand universities. Paul and Ross cranked out good research by making the most of the lecture-oriented teaching system while the research non-performers were not required to switch to teaching-focused contracts or develop their research skills.

There was little sign that an equitable workload allocation model was being applied: for example, I found myself with about four times as many examination scripts to mark as Ralph Lattimore, who had a personal chair in economics. However, when I suggested, at a departmental meeting, that a system for making marking loads more equitable was needed, it appeared that a gerrymander prevented reform on this front. After I had been there a couple of years, I used the opportunity of a week as acting head of department to prepare a 'discussion document' that was a draft teaching plan for the coming year, showing how a Stirling-style system could be applied fairly with the existing resources. I knew that, on his return, the head of department would regard it as misbehaving, as indeed it was – he accused me of trying to undermine his authority – and of course it was never discussed in a departmental meeting.

Lincoln's library was another problem area. I rather liked it as a building and appreciated the efforts of its staff. Unfortunately, I had been kept so busy during my interview visit that I had not been able to undertake due diligence in respect of the library's collection in the way that one can now do remotely by using online catalogues. Alas, the collection was poor and funding for filling gaps was very limited. The library did agree to get a subscription to the *Journal of Economic Behavior and Organization*, which I judged would be key for me to keep up with developments in behavioural and evolutionary economics, but that was it as far as new journals were concerned. The cost of that subscription was such that I soon felt guilty about not getting time to look at what it was paying for. But then it became apparent that we had been fooled about the cost: it was three times as bad as it had seemed, since Elsevier published three volumes per year, whereas the library and I had mistakenly assumed the per-volume prices covered the annual cost. Given this, I said that the subscription should be cancelled and that I would use the much larger collection at the University of Canterbury when I ran into gaps in Lincoln's collection. This was my first experience of what I would now view as a form of 'confusopoly'-style pricing, which two decades later would become a focus of my research.

So far, this introduction to my Lincoln University experience may have given the impression of a very insular institution in which I was surrounded by parochial colleagues and somewhat cut off from the latest literature. However, I had an email account from day one at Lincoln, so my ability to communicate internationally without using fax machines depended on the uptake of email overseas rather than any problem of technological backwardness in New Zealand. It also needs to be emphasised that, despite its geographical isolation, New Zealand was not short of international academic visitors. Those that did not come to Lincoln often came at least as far as the University of Canterbury, as in the case of Stephen Lea, leader of the economic psychology group at the University of Exeter. I got to know Stephen well while sharing guest lecturer roles with him on the University of Canterbury's master's subject in economic psychology. Visitors to Christchurch from the ranks of heterodox economics during my time at Lincoln included Paul Davidson (who, to my disappointment, had been unaware of my *Monetary Scenarios*), Warren Samuels and John King, while in 1993 Lincoln simultaneously hosted John Pheby and Clive Spash as sabbatical visitors.

7.2   TEACHING

My decade in New Zealand enabled me greatly to add to my range of teaching experiences, particularly in relation to the challenges of delivering subjects in a pluralistic manner and focusing on open-ended problems, and in postgraduate thesis supervision. These areas will be the focus of this section. But it will probably be useful to note first some of the things that I was surprised to discover about teaching at Lincoln – things about which I might have been able to gather intelligence during my interview week had I not falsely assumed that Lincoln's modus operandi would be pretty much the same as what I had got accustomed to at the University of Tasmania.

A key unexpected issue was the impact that Lincoln's agricultural college heritage had on its timetable system, rather in the way that, in the UK, one could be taken by surprise by contact hours for subjects in some universities that started life as colleges of higher education or as polytechnics. Avoiding surprises in this area is vital because of the potential consequences for one's capacity to find time to conduct research effectively, and for the extent of reading that one might expect students to be able to do. Lincoln's heritage had resulted in subjects in commerce and social science disciplines being timetabled rather as if they were taught by lab-based classes, with five contact hours per week of lectures for each of the four subjects that students took per semester. Moreover, each of the five hours would be timetable on different days, unless one had a subject with a two-hour lecture block, in which case the subject would be taught on four days per week. It was thus practically impossible to get teaching-free days for research during semester.

The mindset and resourcing favoured lecturing to students rather than having tutorials in which open-ended problems or debates were explored. For large classes, the tutoring budget for hours of assistance from postgraduate tutors amounted to about one hour per student in each subject, to cover contact hours and marking, and the supply of rooms in which to hold tutorials was rather limited. My colleagues generally seemed not to regard small-group tutorials as important and they usually set deterministic assignments for large classes, which could be marked quickly within the tutoring budget. But I wanted my students to develop their capacities to think for themselves about open-ended problems and develop their writing skills.

Given the budget, providing my large class with small group tutorials, office-hour consultations and good feedback on written work was problematic unless I took a significant share of tutorials and their associated marking. This is what I did initially, but I eventually concluded that the way to deal with the situation was to give up running small-group tutorials altogether for my large second-year microeconomics class and switch to using one of the five lecture slots for whole-class tutorials in which students worked in small groups in the large lecture theatre and the tutor (by this point, Jason Potts) and I raced between groups fielding queries and monitoring discussions. This freed up enough of the tutoring budget to cover the marking, with students being instructed to come to my office hours with other queries rather than taking them to the tutor. To cut the time it took to mark each assignment, I provided the tutor with 'feedback sheets' in which I had tried to anticipate and list in detail the likely mistakes, omissions, and areas of confusion. Each item on the list was given a letter or number that could be ringed by the tutor, who would then attach the sheet to the assignment, add further comments if necessary, and then return it to the student. Of course, such sheets could also list things that the student may have done well, but I left it to the tutor to add brief comments in this area as well as to note problems that I had not anticipated. It was a woefully low-budget system compared with what I had been used to, and the hourly rate that the tutor(s) received was similarly woeful.

Pluralistic Microeconomics

This sub-section is a cautionary tale of what can happen, even to a full professor with no probationary worries, if one dares to abandon teaching norms and teach in a pluralistic manner. It has some similarities with what happened during my stint at the University of Tasmania in relation to monetary and macroeconomics. However, it was a much more frustrating experience. Along the way, I developed a better appreciation of the challenges that are entailed even if one demonstrates willingness to teach orthodox economics alongside heterodox material and to be as positive as possible about the former rather than attempting to reject it altogether and merely teach the latter.

From my arrival in 1991, until 1999, my large class was the second-year subject ECON201 Microeconomics for Business and Marketing, which had previously been taught from standard US textbooks on intermediate microeconomics. This seemed to be an excellent opportunity for me to design a subject that was, indeed, 'for business and marketing' students, the great bulk of whom would not take a further microeconomics subject. Since the subject was not called 'intermediate microeconomics', I did not feel obliged to follow the usual approach of teaching second-year students in a needlessly narrow, abstract, and technique-driven manner, 'as if' most of them would then take a third-year advanced microeconomics subject and progress from there to honours- and graduate-level studies. My view was, and remains, that if one insists on providing the latter kind of training, the way to do it is not at the expense of denying terminating business and marketing students a view of economics that goes beyond constrained optimisation and closed problems. Rather, economics majors should be required to take not merely a second-year microeconomics subject geared for terminating students but also a mathematical economics unit ahead of, or alongside, an advanced third-year microeconomics subject. (Moreover, in such a major, constrained optimisation would be taught in a pluralistic manner, covering linear programming as well as calculus-based approaches.)

On arriving and discovering how the timetable system worked, I decided that the unexpectedly large number of lectures would make it easy to teach the subject in a pluralistic manner, even in the absence of a textbook that covered the material that I wanted to add from behavioural, evolutionary and institutional economics. I set Douglas (1987) as the required reading, as its coverage included material better suited to business and marketing students, and I hoped that my lectures and some recommended readings would be enough to cover the non-neoclassical material that I wanted to introduce. To help the students to appreciate the pluralistic approach, I decided to present the material with reference to the evolution of the history of economic thought and thus covered Marshall's view of the firm before moving on to perfect, imperfect and monopolistic competition, kinked demand curves, normal cost pricing, and so on.

After a couple of weeks, it became clear that there was strong opposition to this way of presenting microeconomics. The students were used to the idea of economics textbooks as bibles whose graphs they had to learn; they were not interested in attaching ideas to the names of those who had coined them or what problems these economists had been trying to address. Instead, they simply wanted to know 'the' way to look at how the economy worked at the micro level, not unresolved rival perspectives on how one might view it. They also seemed not to be used to being expected to think for themselves or even to constructing their own lecture notes in words rather than merely transcribing diagrams.

It was clear that they would have been far happier with a subject that merely covered orthodox microeconomics, even if it gave them a perspective that often would be of limited use. It was also clear that the two master's students who had been allocated to the subject as tutors were nervous about where things were heading, for they, too, only had an orthodox economics training. I knew that the tutor problem was one that I would have to weather by putting time into pre-tutorial training sessions for the first few years. Thereafter, I would be able to select tutors from the ranks of students who had studied with me (ideally in my own tutorial groups), and thus knew the subject content and how it worked. But how was I going to be able to keep my students from being restive for the rest of the semester and in future years?

The first thing that I decided to do was to start writing support material that summarised what had been covered in lectures and tutorials, much as I had done at the University of Tasmania. When this material began to appear, the mood of the class became much less restive. We survived to the end of the semester and by then I had decided that I was going to develop material from the subject into an innovative textbook that was not merely pluralistic but also brought together lecture material, tutorial cases and discussions of open-ended assignments or exam questions. The book was going to need these examples of how to apply the material and debate theoretical issues, for without this material, anyone who built a subject around the lectures would be likely to face an endless stream of students, each expecting a personal tutorial on how to do their assignments. I knew this from the experience I was having with my 250-strong class, few of whom seemed to have any experience of thinking for themselves in relation to the subjects they were studying, though some did tell me that, at last, they were experiencing what they had imagined studying at a university might be like.

The next three cohorts of students were able to buy versions of the in-progress textbook, at cost, that had been produced by Lincoln's printery. Having one's textbook produced only metres down the road proved fortuitous when enrolments shot up, for supplies could be expanded rapidly. One year, a total of 400 copies had to be produced, while I contemplated with dread what this was going to do to my workload, but numbers trended down thereafter.[14] Until it was finished in mid-1994, writing the text (published as Earl, 1995a) consumed pretty much all my research time and a lot of my leisure time, with the manuscript being finished on a winter vacation at a motel in Arrowtown while my then-partner enjoyed the nearby ski-fields.

The students clearly enjoyed having 'their own textbook'. The production process meant that the published version was not available in time for the class of 1995, but Edward Elgar Publishing let me use the camera-ready copy in a final Lincoln printery version, which seemed to sustain the students' sense of ownership. When the class of 1996 were able to use the published version, some of the local students told me how delighted they were that its cover even had the black and red colours of

---

[14] To ensure quality control in marking the final examination, I did most or all the marking rather than having a lot of it done by the tutors. This made large enrolments especially terrifying, for the practice when timetabling examinations at Lincoln was to put the large classes at the end of the examination period in the hope of reducing the likelihood of students having parties in the halls of residence while others were still trying to study. The consequences of this policy for those who had to mark the scripts seemed to have been ignored.

the Canterbury rugby team, though the credit for this was due to Elgar's cover designer rather than any suggestion that I had made.

I kept refining the subject after the textbook was finished, increasingly structuring it around problems of knowledge that impinge on resource allocation decisions. One year, as I lectured about the kinds of knowledge that are relevant in economic systems, I was interrupted by a sceptical student in the back row of the lecture theatre. He seemed unhappy, as he felt he was being given a philosophy lecture and he said, 'What has any of this got to do with economics?' I replied that I had been just about to move on to show how what I had been saying was central to understanding the economics of McDonald's. I then proceed to do this, as the first case study in the subject.

Not long after, I discovered a recent article by Holbrook (1995a) about the commodification of marketing education, which helped me appreciate part of what I was up against in trying to bring to such students an approach to teaching that was different from the approach of what Holbrook called the 'big textbook publishers'. Holbrook contended that these publishers have fostered a 'banausic' approach to education, i.e., one that is craft-oriented, focused on providing students with tools to use after they graduate. This is what students such as the one at the back row of my lecture had come to expect, and Lincoln's mindset was particularly banausic due to not having many staff with connections to the humanities and social sciences. Like other heterodox economists, my approach takes, in Holbrook's terms, a more 'ludic' view of tertiary education, i.e., it presents some knowledge as if it is worth having 'for its own sake', to appreciate better the nature of the world even if it does not immediately represent an obvious addition to students' mental toolkits. However, much of what those who do not think deeply would regard as ludic teaching is conducive to becoming more adept at appreciating the strengths and limitations of the tools that one acquires. The lecturer's challenge is to cultivate openness to deeper learning, for example, by leaving students with a sense that knowing how and where particular analytical tools emerged is not necessarily to be viewed as ludic padding. Giving a sense that context matters is a vital aspect of being a pluralistic teacher.

The second thing that I started to do, with effect from 1992, was to include, in the first lecture of any subject that I was going to teach in a pluralistic manner, a simplified introduction to William G. Perry's (1970) schema of the progression by which college students change how they view the learning process and the nature of knowledge. Perry's schema has nine stages, but the essence of it can be conveyed in five steps, and this was how it had been introduced to me by Neil Fleming, the director of Lincoln's education centre, when we were talking about the students' initial reaction to my non-deterministic way of teaching. Neil gave me several papers about Perry's work and, on reading them, I concluded that anyone who wants to run subjects in a pluralistic way should be mindful of the 'Perry Progression' and should talk about it with their students. I also decided to write about Perry's work in the introduction to my microeconomics textbook.

Perry was a Harvard educational psychologist who sometimes had to counsel students who had been used to being high achievers at high school but were struggling with their university studies despite working hard. By the sound of it, these Harvard students had a modus operandi rather like that of some of the international students who had tried to cope with my classes at the University of Tasmania by parrot-learning my lecture handouts and 'regurgitating' them verbatim when they could find matches with key words in final examination questions. Perry formed the view that the students who were having trouble coping at Harvard, despite putting a lot of effort into their studies, had been used to teaching systems in which they were presented with facts, and they had been rewarded for demonstrating the facts that they had learned, which they did by downloading them in their assignments and examinations.

To Perry, the problem was that these students were operating with a dualistic, black-and-white view of knowledge and of how classrooms function. To these students, claims about the nature of the world could be divided into two piles: genuine knowledge/truth and old, discredited ideas or quackery. Good teachers knew what was true and dispensed it to the students, whose role was to absorb it. Students with this view of the world would struggle with open-ended questions and would be reluctant to contribute verbally during class unless they could respond to a specific question with what they knew to be 'the right answer'.

From Perry's standpoint, the challenge for teachers was to help students toward less dualistic ways of thinking and help them to develop their capacities to make creative connections and construct arguments about the pros and cons of rival points of view in the contexts with which they had to deal. I realised that the parrot-learner international students in my classes at UTAS probably had not advanced beyond dualistic thinking, unlike other international students (notably those from

Singapore) who had been through the British A-Level system and typically did very well in my classes. (I am focusing on 'international' students here because the extreme memory feats of learning detailed lecture notes verbatim were never displayed by local students who regurgitated subject content rather than displaying any creative or critical thinking skills when answering questions.) As I reflected further on this, I recalled that, twenty years previously, in the first few weeks of taking A-Level History, my classmates and I had initially struggled to go beyond what we had been doing in O-Level History, where the focus had been on learning facts about what led to what. I recalled that Chris Wright, my A-Level teacher for European history, had then tried to explain what we were now being expected to do. I cannot recall precisely what he said, but the result was that I rapidly changed my modus operandi and became adept at dealing with 'discuss the contention that …'-style essays and applied these skills in all my subjects. This equipped me very well for the pluralistic, non-deterministic teaching experience that I enjoyed in Cambridge. But it also resulted in me unwittingly assuming that, on commencing tertiary education, students are usually aware that what is known, whether about the past or how things work today, can be just as debatable as what will happen in the future.

The second stage in the simplified version of the Perry Progression is where students notice, among other things, that some of the academics that they believe they have reason to take seriously disagree about how to look at the world. Early in my time at Stirling, I had encountered an example of a student who, unexpectedly, had just found himself in this situation. It was at the end of a first-year microeconomics tutorial during which I had challenged the textbook analysis of the shut-down condition for a firm in perfect competition. I had argued, via Andrews and Brunner (1975) that a firm needs to cover more than just its average variable costs if production is to be worthwhile; it needs also to be able to generate enough revenue to cover other 'paying-out costs', such as local authority rates and its managerial overheads. Mr Tan, a very industrious Malaysian student, came up to me at the end of the tutorial and was clearly very perplexed. He had understood my argument and wanted to know why the writer of the textbook did not take the same view. He respected the textbook as an economics bible but also respected me as his tutor (as was evident, at the end of semester, when he asked to be photographed with me).

Such an awakening to the co-existence of rival ways of looking at aspects of the world is not typically followed by acceptance that even that knowledge that experts in a field possess is inherently conjectural. Rather, the third stage is to see debate in an area as a sign that, in effect, not enough data have yet been gathered to enable controversial issues to be resolved one way or the other. Today we may have to put up with multiplicity, but we may tell ourselves that this cognitively uncomfortable situation is only going to be temporary. Eventually, experts will agree on what the truth is. Lecturers may add support to this view if they attempt to show how contending perspectives can be seen in terms of a single modelling framework, with the uncertainty reducing to the sises of key parameters, as with the use of the IS–LM framework in orthodox intermediate macroeconomics classes to frame differences between monetarists and Keynesians.

The fourth stage in this simplified version of Perry's progression of 'intellectual and ethical development' commences where students start realizing that many debates in the fields that they are studying have been around for many years without being resolved. This can lead to a sense that 'anything goes', with academics carrying on operating along particular lines regardless of challenges being mounted against their ways of thinking. From there, it is a short step to concern about grading processes, for if experts do not agree on the nature of things, what entitles them to pronounce on the quality of claims that students make? Students may thus start taking the view that their own ideas are at least as good as those of their teachers, especially if their teachers disagree with one another as well as reporting ongoing controversies in their areas of expertise.

It is possible that I was at this fourth stage when I was baiting my left-leaning teacher Les Ransley with right-wing conservative ideas in my A-Level Economics class. Certainly, I have encountered quite a few 'know it all' students over the years, whom I would now view as being at this fourth stage in the Perry Progression.

Lecturers have an incentive to try to help their students move beyond the fourth stage, namely the possible pain of having to deal with appeals against their marking if they dare to penalise students who have failed to consider subject material that could have been used to argue against a monist point of view that the student has presented as 'the' answer. Setting questions or tasks in ways that explicitly require contending perspectives to be considered is a way of limiting appeals against 'unfair' grading, or at least of being able rapidly to dispose of such appeals. But what the pluralistic economics lecturer really needs to promote is recognition that (a) even if one ends up with a preferred way of viewing the workings of the economy, being aware of alternative perspectives may help in recognizing contexts where one's preferred way could be misleading and an alternative might be more applicable, and (b) that the wise student does not jump to conclusions about what their favoured perspective is going to be without first having done some serious exploration of contending perspectives. Students who have the intellectual maturity to think in this kind of way have reached the final stage in the Perry Progression.

The 'know it all' student will normally need to recognise that his or her lecturers have spent a lot more time getting to know about rival perspectives and can therefore help them avoid the pitfalls of jumping to conclusions based on superficial knowledge. It is important for pluralistic lecturers to stress that any perspective has limitations that its rivals may not have in some contexts, and hence that the aim of a pluralistic subject is not to provide a menu from which students will find one perspective that they like best and which they will then use in a one-eyed manner, in effect, reverting to a dualistic mode of thought. Lecturers who take pluralism seriously should be demonstrating, by their behaviour, that they are not trying to impose their favoured view and that students should view them as mentors who can provide ways of getting to deeper insights about the strengths and limitations of a variety of perspectives and who are interested in hearing their students talk about how their ideas are developing.

Perry's perspective on the stages that students may go through in developing their views of the nature of knowledge and the process of acquiring knowledge and wisdom needs to be used mindful that students will differ in the speed at which they move along the Perry Progression and in how far they will ultimately progress. It may be possible to help some of them speed up their progress by talking with them, as I have done in my classes, about Perry's thinking and how it relates to what is going on in class. Getting the message across may be easier if one talks about how, outside the classroom, students will probably find themselves open to multiple points of view and be able to engage in critical discussions with each other. But even if one does this, it is likely that one's pluralistic classroom will still contain students at different stages in their intellectual development.

Perry's work gave me much pause for thought about what I should do when designing assessment tasks. Suppose all the tasks that I set were either open-ended case studies or discussion-type questions that required the capacity to argue about the merits of contentious claims. If so, the prospects of passing could be bleak for students who were unable to progress from dualistic thinking and a regurgitation-based approach to written work, even if they worked industriously and understood the material. But it was equally clear to me that I should not be giving high grades to students who had an impressive capacity to parrot-learn and regurgitate subject material but no ability to think for themselves about how to apply it and about the pros and cons of using rival theoretical tools. In the worst cases of verbatim regurgitation, students might even just be dispensing information, without having acquired any insights that could be said to constitute knowledge. The way that I sought to resolve this dilemma was to design my assessment systems so that they included enough scope for using regurgitation-style methods to get a basic pass, with the rest of the tasks providing opportunities for students to demonstrate not merely how much work they had done but also how adept they had become at thinking critically and making creative connections.

The effort that I put into making my pluralistic microeconomics subject work may have helped me stay at its helm for nine iterations, but it yielded no enduring legacy at Lincoln. As the years went by, my 'for business and marketing' focus was staunchly opposed by the other professor of economics, Ralph Lattimore, who claimed that what I was doing was wrecking Lincoln's reputation in relation to the quality of its economics majors, the best of whom might hope to get jobs at the New Zealand Treasury or the Reserve Bank of New Zealand. This did not seem to be an evidence-based claim, for Lincoln's top students were now able to graduate not merely with the technical skills that were expected of them but also with much better skills in critical and creative thinking. Indeed, the reports that I received (e.g., when providing references over the phone) were that the latter skills were valued highly. However, Lattimore and others who took the orthodox line found a way to keep an orthodox subject in intermediate microeconomics alive that would work well politically. This entailed having a second-year subject, Agricultural Economics, that was, in essence, intermediate microeconomics with agricultural examples and was usually taught via a standard microeconomics text.

Agricultural Economics played a major role in ensuring that my approach to teaching microeconomics had no legacy at Lincoln. Initially, it provided the benefit of reducing my teaching load in the second half of my decade at Lincoln, for as its enrolments grew, enrolments in Microeconomics for Business and Marketing decreased significantly where degree rules enabled substitution. The lesson seemed to be that risk-averse students will stick to dualistic subjects whose assignments have 'right' answers that they may hope to arrive at, so pluralistic subjects may need to be compulsory to ensure students graduate with the 'merit good' benefits for their critical thinking. However, in 2000, my time running Microeconomics for Business and Marketing came to an end, as I was assigned a subject on economic development.

Microeconomics for Business and Marketing was allocated to Lana Friesen, who was fresh from a mainstream PhD programme at Simon Fraser University in Canada. Faced with the challenge of tooling up at Lincoln, Lana predictably decided to turn the subject into a standard intermediate microeconomics subject and teach what she knew, rather than get herself familiar with my textbook and the material that I had been teaching. This meant that, in all but name, there were now two orthodox intermediate microeconomics subjects at Lincoln, and no heterodox microeconomics.

Given this situation, I decided to push for a different approach to pluralism in microeconomics. To me, the obvious thing to do was to come clean about what Lana had done and revamp the Lincoln University Calendar entry for ECON201 from 'Microeconomics for Business and Marketing' to 'Intermediate Microeconomics'. With Agricultural Economics now offered with dual codes as Agricultural/Forestry Economics, the sensible thing to do would then be to offer a single set of intermediate microeconomics lectures under three different codes and offer tutorial streams for 'economics', 'agriculture' and 'forestry'. I was therefore happy to do the paperwork to address Lana's de-pluralisation of the subject that I had taught, for rationalisation of orthodox intermediate microeconomics teaching would then make it easier to argue that case for a new third-year subject on Behavioural and Evolutionary Economics to be offered. It would not displace the advanced microeconomics subject.

However, although my proposed new subject was approved for the 2001 Lincoln University Calendar, it did not get taught. Its approval had come without acceptance of what I envisaged for intermediate microeconomics, agricultural economics, and forestry economics. This proved problematic at the start of 2001 when pressures to cut costs led to a search for subjects to axe. Because of the political influence of the farm management group at Lincoln, any rationalization that entailed no longer offering a (supposedly) dedicated subject in agricultural economics was ruled out as if that subject were a kind of sacred cow. Instead, it was decided that behavioural and evolutionary economics could be canned. Given that I was soon to leave, there would have been no one to teach it from 2002.

When I reflect on this experience, I am left wondering where my colleagues should be seen in terms of the Perry Progression if they genuinely thought they were doing a good job by merely teaching orthodox economics and assessing students via deterministic multiple-choice questions, 'problem sets' and/or requiring students to describe or explain orthodox economic concepts. It is possible that they had not advanced beyond stage-one dualism themselves due to their own educational experiences being much like what they were providing for their students. I doubt that my nemesis, Ralph Lattimore, or others who went along with him in supporting the orthodox ways of teaching, really had much idea of the alternative theoretical perspectives that I was bringing into my classes, for unlike the case with Brian Loasby's lectures at Stirling, none of my colleagues ever audited my lectures.

But if I dare to apply a Perry-style perspective to my colleagues, then I probably should apply it to myself, not merely as a student, as I did earlier in this section, but also to myself as an academic. When I first became familiar with the Perry Progression, it seemed clear to me that, during Part II of the Cambridge Economics Tripos, I was thinking about alternative perspectives in the manner characterised above as Perry's fifth stage, for I was exploring behavioural and evolutionary thinking carefully due to feeling somewhat disappointed with aspects of Post Keynesian/neo-Ricardian material that John Eatwell had covered, as well as with the neoclassical/general equilibrium and Marxian approaches. However, I now realise that *The Economic Imagination* might be characterised – despite me having used dialogues as a pluralistic device in that book – as the product of someone who was operating rather like a student at stage four in the five-stage version of the Perry Progression that I have described above. At that time, I was challenging the mainstream via knowledge of the field of consumer behaviour that was nowhere near as deep as that which I employed when I wrote *Lifestyle*

Economics, and the tone of the latter was much more mature, as John Hey (1987) signalled in his review.

Getting Started as a PhD Supervisor
My first experiences in supervising a PhD in economics came at Lincoln, a decade after I finished my own PhD. Given my difficult road to a doctorate, there was obviously potential for history to repeat itself when I began to supervise research students – rather in the way that those who grow up in families beset by abusive relationships are prone to create similar kinds of families when they become parents. However, although I had not experienced styles of thesis supervision that I regarded as good role-models, I had at least emerged from the process with a PhD and a sense of the kinds of mentoring that might have speeded up the process.

Jason Potts was my first start-to-finish doctoral student in economics. He had studied economics at the University of Otago and approached me after an economist at the University of Canterbury declined to be his PhD supervisor and suggested that, given his area of interest, he might try me instead. However, when Jason approached me to ask if I would be willing to supervise him for a PhD that would develop an evolutionary analysis of entrepreneurship, my initial suggestion was that if he wanted to do a PhD in evolutionary economics, it would be better for him to do it at the University of Queensland in Australia, under the guidance of Professor John Foster. As luck would have it, some weeks later Jason came to my office to say that he *really* would like to work on his PhD under my supervision. The thesis that he eventually produced was a remarkably original piece of work, contributing to evolutionary economics in ways that went beyond the area of entrepreneurship. It was published, with an additional chapter, as *The New Evolutionary Microeconomics* (Potts, 2000) and it shared the 2000 J. A. Schumpeter Prise with Loasby's (1999) *Knowledge, Institutions and Evolution in Economics*.

Jason's PhD is a work that it is hard to envisage being produced via a doctoral programme that is run along today's best-practice, managerialist lines with an emphasis on risk management and the expectation that students will produce, and be able to defend, rather tightly specified plans for what they are going to do. Jason was required to make a presentation and answer questions about it for his confirmation of candidature, but his proposal was far less thoroughly spelt out than today's best-practice demands. Even so, he recalls that the day of his confirmation, about eight months after his commencement, was one of high anxiety:

It was basically a staff seminar type session, where rather a lot of people turned up. It was in a lecture theatre, and I presented my proposal and initial theory and ideas for about 30-40 minutes, then [there was a] discussion.

I know all of this because it was the first time I had ever done a public scholarly talk, and I have never been more nervous in my entire career. Not doing live TV, not giving keynotes in front of 500 people, nothing. I also had a huge snafu, when I arrived at Lincoln about 2 hours early to print off my talk, and it was the first time I'd tried to use Lincoln printers and networks for this, and of course nothing worked. So I had to do a mad dash into Christchurch (in my car that I'd bought for $280 and was 50/50 whether it would start or not overheat on any given day) to print notes because doing my first ever academic talk in front of many people to determine whether I'd proceed with my PhD was the single most terrifying thing imaginable.

After all that, I gave my talk, and then you asked the first question, giving thoughtful feedback about how I could proceed. I've never been more relieved in my life. (Potts, email to Earl, 8 March 2022).

The central ideas of Jason's thesis only came together much later, after I had given the thumbs-down to a succession of things that he had written, and after he had taken some time out having an overseas experience. Yet, before he arrived at the core of his thesis, it was clear to me that he was seriously bright and a very hard worker who had what it would take to get a PhD, so I was happy to sign off any progress reports. Then, one day, he came to my office and said, 'I've got it: Graph Theory!' He proceeded to explain what Graph Theory was and its relevance to evolutionary economics and economics more generally.

Jason's central proposition was that conventional economics differs fundamentally from heterodox approaches in how it sees relationships between elements of the economy. The conventional approach is premised on a mathematical perspective that views every element as connected, to some degree, to every other element. In other words, the economic system is viewed much as the Universe is seen from the standpoint of Newtonian physics, where it is envisaged as a force field in which stars, planets, moons and asteroids exert different degrees of gravitational pull on each other. General equilibrium models of economic systems are perhaps the most obvious parallel to the Newtonian view of how heavenly bodies all interact with each other to some degree, even if in many instances their pull on each other is tiny. In the general equilibrium view, a shock to the system in one market can trigger changes in relative prices, outputs and quantities consumed, to a greater or lesser degree, across the entire economy, as everything is seen as ultimately substitutable, to some degree, for everything else.

What Jason had picked up via Graph Theory was that an alternative to viewing the economy as if it is a force-field is to view it as a 'complex system' whose elements only have connections with *some* other elements. Taking the latter view opens possibilities that heterodox economists view as significant even though mainstream economists seem oblivious of them, such as:

- Purposive activities of entrepreneurs and consumers entail the creation of systems – such as new products, production systems and consumption lifestyles – with specific architectures of connections for how their elements go together.
- 'Structural change' can occur, whereby innovations lead to changes in the connective architecture of the economy, with new patterns of economic connections being established and old ones ceasing to apply, rather than there being merely changes in relative prices and quantities via established links.
- The economic system may display 'breaks in chains of substitution' that limit the effectiveness of policies designed to work by triggering a cascade of relative price changes, for there may be areas in which people are completely unwilling or unable to change their behaviour in response to changes in relative prices.
- Some kinds of economic activities will not occur unless specific connections can be made; in other words, production or consumption may not be possible without complementary prerequisite or corequisite assets or inputs.
- The strategic vulnerability of the economic system, or sub-systems within it, depends on the structure of linkages within the system or between systems.

In short, system architecture is a key concern if one does not employ the 'field' perspective. Policymakers may need to focus on non-price drivers of economic behaviour and performance, and policy interventions may need to focus on ensuring that necessary connections can be made and dangerous connective structures do not emerge.

This system-based view was an appealing way by which I could bring together the approaches to economics that appealed to me and get a clearer sense of what made my overall approach to economics different from that of the mainstream. It is a way of bringing together heterodox ideas as diverse as Keynes's 'Chapter 17' view of money, institutional perspectives on the significance of social rules, and the significance of patronage networks and discrimination in labour markets – as well as my long-standing interest in the significance of non-compensatory decision rules and the effects that the ways that people think have on their openness to change. However, it took me a while before I habitually thought explicitly from a connectionist perspective.

On that key day, I tried to soak up Jason's abstract thesis by trying to relate it to concrete examples from economic systems and asking if I was getting the message correctly. This way of operating continued in successive meetings and the dissertation then started to come together quite rapidly. However, in 1997, well over a year before he submitted the thesis, I was nervous about what kind of reception his work might get. To ensure that Jason's ideas did not get examined without having been tried out on leading evolutionary economists, and to help his employment prospects, I told him that he should write a paper based on his key proposition and use his entire research fund allowance to buy a return ticket to attend a conference at the University of Stirling that I was organising with Sheila Dow in honour of Brian Loasby, and that I would pay for his conference fee and accommodation.

On the final morning of the conference, Jason began his presentation by saying, 'What I'm going to talk about may be important for evolutionary economics or may be mistaken, and I'm hoping you will be able to tell me which it is'. His paper (published as Potts, 1999) rather stole the show, with Richard Day, co-founding editor of the *Journal of Economic Behavior and Organization*, leading the very positive reaction. John Foster was also in the audience, and he resolved that he was going to hire Jason, who duly joined the School of Economics at the University of Queensland at the start of 1999.

Although Jason Potts was my first start-to-finish PhD student, he was not the first PhD student that I worked with at Lincoln. At the time Jason commenced his work, I was already getting some experience as an associate supervisor for an interdisciplinary farm management doctorate by Ngenang Jangu (1997), who was studying how farmers made their decisions to adopt an innovative milking shed design. In a sense, this was a case study in evolutionary agricultural economics, but I was invited to get involved because Ngenang's principal advisor knew of, and shared, my interest in personal construct psychology (PCP) and Ngenang was using research tools from PCP to uncover differences in how adopters and non-adopters saw the innovation. Since he was probing towards the cores of his subjects' belief systems, this project had an ethical dimension that went beyond basic concerns about preserving the anonymity of his subjects: he had to be careful not to anger his subjects by trying to get them to articulate bases for things they said they believed 'because I do, period'.

Lincoln's PhD system ran in a way that had elements of both the Cambridge system that I had experienced and modern best-practice systems. As is already evident from Jason's recollections, students were required to give, and defend, an oral presentation as part of the process of having their PhD candidature confirmed; however, there seemed to be no other formal milestones prior to the submission of the thesis. If students failed to submit within eight years from commencing, their candidacy was terminated. In contrast to the rather casual approach to monitoring progress, the examination process was much more rigorous than the systems used in Australian universities for which I had served as an external examiner, where there was no oral examination and examiners simply submitted their reports and outcome recommendations. Lincoln required its PhD students to be orally examined by a committee consisting of an external examiner from another New Zealand university, an overseas external examiner, and members of the student's advisory team. However, examiners submitted their reports and outcome recommendations prior to the oral. In the event of a dispute about the outcome, a further external examiner's opinion would be sought.[15] I felt that having the supervisors involved in the oral

---

[15] In late 2009, over eight years after leaving Lincoln, I was invited to arbitrate in this way for an adventurous thesis on ecological economics. I attended the oral examination in person in January 2010 while on vacation in New Zealand. My next visit to this part of New Zealand was about six months after the February 2011 earthquake that caused major damage in Christchurch and the surrounding area, and significant aftershocks were still happening (there were three between 4.2 and 4.8 on the Richter scale on my final day there), Lincoln University has fared well during the earthquake, whereas. at the University of Canterbury, the Commerce Building was closed and a large marquee had been erected

exam provided a good way for them (me included) to get some benchmarking experience relative to external assessors.

In Jason's case, the overseas external examiner, Stan Metcalfe, did not attend the oral and instead provided a set of questions to be asked on his behalf. This seemed to be the normal practice. However, in Ngenang's case a video conference was organised. The most obvious overseas expert for the task was Roy Murray-Prior, in Western Australia, another farm management scholar who had used PCP in his work. Although this was at an early time in the development of video-conferencing technology, the video link worked surprisingly well; indeed, it provided an effective illustration of Herbert Simon's (1991, p. 306) 'travel theorem' whereby it is argued that if the only point of travelling is to gather information, then there should be no need to undertake the journey, since it should be possible to obtain the information locally via a good public library or remotely via telecommunications technology.

Ngenang's doctorate was not the only interdisciplinary project in which I began to get experience as a PhD supervisor. While supervising Jason's work I had another enjoyable associate supervisor role in a study by one of Lincoln's tourism lecturers, David Fisher (2000). David's project was an ethnographic study of differences between how tourism providers and tourists in a South Pacific destination viewed the attractiveness of that destination. This, too, could have involved the research tools of PCP, but David decided to adopt the anthropologist's approach of embedding himself in the local community – one of the kinds of information gathering that Simon acknowledged as an exception to his travel theorem, which he only claimed to apply for visits to a destination of less than six months.

The early phase of David's project provided a lesson that is relevant for all PhD confirmations, namely the need to have a 'Plan B' in case the proposed project turns out not to be feasible. David's original plan was to do his research in Vanuatu, but the local volcano erupted, and we were not sure how long volcanic ash would continue to be a problem. He therefore decided instead to base himself in Levuka, the first western-style town to be built in the Pacific islands and the original capital of Fiji. It transpired that whereas its visitors were attracted by Levuka's antiquity, local entrepreneurs tended not to appreciate this and viewed

---

nearby. The devastation in the centre of Christchurch was horrific, with so many buildings having been removed that it was hard to get a sense of what one was looking at, through the cordon of steel fencing.

modern development projects as the means to increase visitor numbers. Levuka was designated as a World Heritage site in 2013.

Lincoln University also provided the venue for my second role in supervising a PhD in economics, though, in this case, the project was not quite finished by the time I moved back to Australia. The PhD in question was by Greg Clydesdale, for whom it opened the door to an academic career in entrepreneurial studies and a base from which to contribute across a wide range of areas that intersect with behavioural and evolutionary economics. These areas have included the creative industries (Clydesdale, 2006, 2015) and the impact of culture on motivation (Clydesdale, 2021). At the time that Greg started his PhD, he had a very clear vision of what he wanted to do: he wanted to write a book about the long-term dynamics of national rivalry and leadership in the shipping industry and its impact on economic growth. It was an ambitious idea, effectively an evolutionary and institutional analysis spanning many centuries. He already knew a lot of the relevant history, especially in relation to the rise and fall of India and China as leaders in shipping. After getting started, he showed great determination and resilience. But there was a problem that he had to overcome and which he is happy for me to share here, namely the fact that he wanted to write a book on this topic. Greg enjoys writing and writes very well but, in the early years of his work on the project, there was a clear danger that he would end up writing a book for a much wider audience, rather than the relentlessly analytical thesis that he needed to write for his PhD examiners. In a sense, he was in a zone that combined elements of where I had been in the period 1981–1982, and where Loasby's model-free research project in economic history was heading in the 1950s.

For a long while, almost all my effort as Greg's supervisor seemed to go into trying, repeatedly, to get across the message that the book would not work as a PhD. It was a frustrating but necessary experience for both of us, but in the end, Greg got the message and wrote a well-received PhD dissertation in the area of his chosen topic; it was only after his academic career was well established that a version aimed at a much wider audience was published (see Clydesdale, 2016).

7.3   ADMINISTRATION AND SERVICE

The effort that I invested in writing the microeconomics textbook in my early years at Lincoln did not leave me with time for research once the book was finished. As I got under control the time that teaching-related matters consumed, there were growing demands on my time for administrative inputs. Departmental administration included matters to do with teaching, recruitment, inducting new staff, and annual 'retreats' that seemed to achieve nothing but were all the rage in New Zealand organisations at that time. This was also the time when Lincoln, like many other universities, started experimenting with offshore teaching, which in Lincoln's case involved an arrangement with a Malaysian electricity utility. I was on the working party that put in a successful bid to run commerce programmes. My second-year microeconomics subject ended up being part of a franchise arrangement in Malaysia, too. However, when I was asked to moderate the offshore examination paper, I discovered that it was simply being taught as a mainstream subject with conventional deterministic assessment tasks. It was, of course, too late to do anything to rectify the situation.

In the case of Lincoln's domestic activities, my role as moderator of departmental examination papers became rather fraught when one of the recently hired management strategy lecturers took exception to my calmly delivered critical comments about the paper he had set: he got up from his desk and threw me out of his office. By this time (around 1995–6), Ross Cullen had been given the head of department role that I had once thought would come my way, and I immediately reported the event to him. Ross was visibly astonished, but I knew that taking the matter further would have meant a lot of paperwork for Ross as well as for me, and his expression turned to one of relief when I told him that I did not wish to take the matter further. An apology was soon offered, and I accepted it.

Within the wider university, mornings, afternoons, or entire days were consumed on administrative matters with relentless frequency by tasks such as attending academic board and board of studies meetings, convening PhD oral examinations, serving on appointment panels, scenario writing for a Lincoln 'management futures' exercise, and membership of a working party on designing a new organisational structure for the university (which was an enjoyable task, given my knowledge of the economics of organisation, but frustrating when the structure of a rival team was favoured).

Two other working party roles made particularly large demands on my time. One entailed co-chairing a group to design bachelor and master of social science degree programmes, within a very tight remit for the number of new subjects that could be included. This was a very enjoyable task and I then had to devise and teach (1997–1999) a capstone subject for the 'society and business' stream of this programme. It was a way of getting more heterodox economics into Lincoln's curriculum. However, this capstone unit was replaced by the never-offered subject on behavioural and evolutionary economics that was mentioned in the previous section. Given the limited range of subjects that could be allocated to the Bachelor of Social Science, I was not surprised to find that, two decades later, there was no trace of the degree on Lincoln's website.

The second of these bigger administrative roles entailed chairing a working party to propose a system to ensure ethical issues were handled properly in social science research at Lincoln, where previously there had been only an ethics committee for research involving non-human animals. Inevitably, I then became the founding chair of Lincoln's human subjects' ethics committee. It was a role that lasted for about five years, until shortly before I began my ninth year at Lincoln by taking a six-month period of study leave at the University of Queensland.

Amid the pressures of teaching and administration, I made external collegial contributions by organizing the 1997 conference in honour of Brian Loasby, writing nine book reviews and a review article on three Shackle-related books, greatly increasing the number of articles that I refereed and, from 2000, becoming co-editor of the *Journal of Economic Psychology*. Given the difficulties I was having in making my own original research contributions, these service activities could be construed as things that I should not have agreed to do. I was not oblivious of the opportunity costs of my time, so why did I take on these tasks?

In the case of the Loasby conference, it was a case of feeling a sense of obligation, rather more to Sheila Dow than to Loasby himself. The idea of a festschrift for Loasby had first been suggested to me by Edward Elgar at a social event held at John Pheby's house at one of the Malvern conferences. On that occasion, my reaction was that, while Loasby's contribution to economics deserved such an honour, I was mindful of the impact that his approach to being my external PhD supervisor had on my time at Stirling, and of the unhelpful references that I had been told he had written. However, as the thirtieth anniversary of Loasby's arrival at Stirling approached, Sheila raised the idea of hosting a conference at Stirling to celebrate his work. I could see that it would be somewhat challenging for Sheila to have sole responsibility, given that most of those who would be interested in attending and contributing to the post-conference festschrift volume would be scholars of the theory of the firm and industrial organisation, not methodology and monetary economics. Hence, I decided to put my history with Loasby to the back of my mind and agreed to help make the event and book (or, as it turned out, books) happen.

Book reviewing was no longer something that I thought might help to establish my scholarly standing while helping me to limit the costs of building my personal reference library. Instead, I increasingly saw myself as doing it for two other reasons. The first was obligational: given that I was writing, editing and contributing to books that others would end up reviewing, I would have felt guilty if I were not, in return, reviewing books that others produced. Those who concentrate on writing journal articles and rarely, or never, write book reviews might decline invitations to write book reviews because of the opportunity costs that this entails for the production of articles that will better establish their career standing. However, they would be unlikely to experience the sense of obligational pressure to accept such invitations. My second reason for agreeing to review books was as a self-control device for ensuring that I read books that I needed to read to keep up with recent developments in the areas in which I hoped to maintain my research expertise. Without a deadline to meet, there was a risk that I would not conjure up time to read books that book review editors had rightly realised would be of interest to me.

Refereeing journal articles, or editing a journal, can likewise be a means for avoiding losing touch with developments in one's fields of interest. However, refereeing a paper takes more time than if one were just reading the paper, and the papers that one referees will usually need to be refereed a couple of times before they achieve publication or will not be good enough to publish. Given this, should a career-obsessed academic decline refereeing requests and attempt to devise an alternative self-control strategy for giving time instead to high-quality articles that others have had to referee? Possibly not, since (a) refereeing tasks typically pertain to more recent research than is reported in papers that have already been published, not all of which can be found in working papers, (b) refereeing can provide opportunities for the referee to steer authors into taking account of the referee's own work (where this is appropriate), and (c) those who repeatedly decline to assist a particular journal as a referee risk alienating that journal's editors and having their own papers denied scarce space in the journal unless their papers are clearly exceptional contributions. I probably could have declined more refereeing invitations than I did, without running into the third consideration, for I provided editors with evidence that, when I accepted invitations to referee, I rapidly produced detailed reports. But much of my service to journals was the result of simply wanting to help the journals in question (for example, *Review of Political Economy* and the *Journal of Economic Psychology*) develop good reputations in fields to which I expected to contribute in the long run.

When University of Canterbury psychologist Simon Kemp suggested that he and I would be a credible team if we put in a bid to become editors of the *Journal of Economic Psychology* for the period 2000–2005, part of the reason that I agreed was that, by this stage, I had decided that one of the things I wanted to do in my academic career was experience as many of the different things that academics did, and thereby find out what each kind of task entailed and whether I was capable of performing them successfully. My teaching and administrative loads at Lincoln had lately become much less demanding, so I felt that editing a journal, especially jointly with Simon and with a team of associate editors, would be feasible without preventing me from getting my own original research happening again. However, Simon and I soon found that the task was initially going to consume a lot more of our time than we had imagined.

The key thing that an incoming journal editor needs, in order to begin as intended in terms of his or her quality aspirations, is a buffer of accepted papers to fill the first few issues – ideally, the first volume. However, with the previous editorial team having overseen the switch from four issues per year to six issues per year, the buffer had ended up being rather limited. This was despite the growing interest in behavioural economics, for the *Journal* still seemed mainly to be attracting papers from those in the old European tradition in economic psychology. To rebuild such a buffer without lowering one's sights for the quality of regular articles, one needs to generate papers rapidly, via calling for papers for special issues and/or commissioning survey papers or obituary articles or using particular articles as bases for creating symposia by inviting responses or complementary papers from scholars whom one believes are likely to be able rapidly to deliver good copy. Some further pages to meet the publisher's required annual total can also be achieved by running more book reviews.

By these kinds of measures, we managed to satisfy Elsevier and create a buffer. But it was very challenging initially, for we had to find a couple of replacement associate editors and engage in damage control after analysing the progress on getting submissions refereed and discovering that some of the associate editors that we had inherited had been allowing turnaround times to drag badly. We also had to look for a new book review editor (with me taking over the role in the interim), after discovering that this section of the journal was on the verge of collapsing, and that publishers were not amused by how few of the books they sent actually got reviewed in a timely manner, or at all. Amid these recovery activities, we sought to signal openness to behavioural economics papers from North American authors by enlisting some big-name US behavioural economists for the editorial board, making clear that their duties would be very limited. To our delight, Richard Thaler accepted, whereas Matthew Rabin declined, saying that if he got involved with the *Journal* it might have adverse consequences for his mission to get psychology into the core generalist economic journals. The fact that Rabin had been succeeding in his mission should have provided a signal to me to take a close look at the kind of behavioural economics that was proving acceptable in these journals, but I was too busy in my editorial role, and in getting back into my own work, for this to register at the time.

7.4   EVOLUTION OF A HETERODOX BEHAVIOURAL ECONOMIST (4)

As a result of my administrative load and the challenges of trying to teach at Lincoln in a pluralistic, non-deterministic manner, I produced very little original output as a behavioural economist from mid-1991 until I had settled into my study leave as a visiting professor at the University of Queensland in the second half of 1999. Even so, there were two senses in which my thinking evolved during those eight years.

One was that I started to bring together the birdwatcher's notion of 'jizz', and Kelly's view of personal constructs as templates for characterizing things, in relation to a term that I had often seen motoring journalists use, namely the idea that car brands or car models often had 'signature' aspects of their designs that remained rather stable across successive generations of products. The trigger for this came via another area in which the 'signature' phenomenon is also common, namely music, where it enables us to have a good chance of identifying composers or performers. Inspiration on this front came after a mutual friend introduced me to Chris Hann, a superb young pianist and drummer. However, although I went on to make multi-track recordings of him playing music that he had written, it was not his music that got me thinking about the signature features of objects and how they ease the process of cognition.

These days, Chris is an associate professor of engineering at the University of Canterbury, but at the time I first knew him he was just about to reach the confirmation stage of his Canterbury PhD in mathematics. He explained to me that the title of his confirmation presentation was going to be 'When is a cat a cat?' and that he was exploring how object-recognition systems in engineering could employ mathematical characterisations of objects as simple configurations of lines, curves and/or circles. The question was how simplified these characterisations could be and yet still capture the essence of the target object. I immediately realised that he was doing the mathematics of jizz and product signatures. At the time, I thought that one day I might pursue these ideas in relation to marketing theory and try to study how the performance of firms is affected by the extent to which they employ product signatures. To date, I have not taken that research idea further, but thoughts about the intersection of the jizz notion and the challenge of programming object recognition systems would later prove very instructive when I was trying to get to grips with Hayek's (1952) book *The Sensory Order*, and I referred to some of Chris Hann's work in the first piece that I wrote in relation to this area of Hayek's work (Earl, 2010b).

The other senses in which my approach to behavioural economics evolved entailed methodological experimentation by seeing what behavioural insights I could get by taking my use of published text beyond material from product reviews, and by going much further in getting ideas via introspection.

The former was a belated result of meeting Charlotte Phelps at the 1990 IAREP conference, where I seemed to be about the only person at her session who appreciated her bold effort (Phelps, 1990) to explore labour supply choices by examining how Arthur Miller had presented such choices in his play *The Price* (Miller, 1972). One idea that I had was to explore the view of human behaviour offered by Marcel Proust in his seven-volume novel *À la Recherche du Temps Perdu* (Proust, 1913–1927; in English: *Remembrance of Things Past*, or *In Search of Lost Time*), which I suspected would be fertile territory for a view of behaviour that largely reflected habits and social norms. But the scale of such a study ruled it out, given how pressed I was for time. Instead, I tried something much more modest, in a book chapter on 'Consumer goals as journeys into the unknown' (Earl 1998b).

This paper was written in late 1995, a few weeks after I attended a performance of the Stephen Sondheim and James Lapine musical *Into the Woods* at Christchurch Town Hall. It seemed fitting to begin the paper by referring to the musical before proceeding to explore why bold ventures are prone to go awry. Some of my paper's analysis of 'the problem of arriving' drew from the autobiography of a New Zealand property developer who made and lost a fortune in New Zealand's Minsky-style mid-1980s episode of financial instability, but the paper also drew implicitly on my own reflections about how, by giving too much attention to the task of winning the job at Lincoln, I had failed to glean enough intelligence about what I could be getting into. However, four years elapsed before I found time to write a paper that was entirely and explicitly based on introspective methods.

The work that contains the classic discussion of the use that economists can legitimately make of introspection is Hutchison's (1938) *The Significance and Basic Postulates of Economic Theory*. I had a copy of this book, and I knew of its relevance in this area, but it was not what led me to make a serious and explicit effort to bring introspective methods into behavioural economics, for I had barely looked inside since purchasing it in April 1979. Rather, the inspiration for my introspective turn came from the work of Morris Holbrook, a professor of marketing at Columbia University who has often allowed his love of jazz into his writing on consumer behaviour. I have referred earlier in this chapter to Holbrook's (1995a) paper on the commodification of marketing education, and it was this paper's reference to the difficulty that he had experienced trying to publish an unorthodox book on consumer behaviour via a 'big textbook publisher' that led me to discover that he had written an entire book on introspective consumer research (Holbrook, 1995b). I obtained a copy of it in late 1997 and read it during the ensuing summer vacation. If I could think of a way of doing something similar in economics, it would certainly be at risk of being viewed as misbehaving by those who conflated introspection and *a priorism* and who, like Hutchison, wanted economics to be an empirical science based on applying statistics to falsifiable hypotheses. However, I discovered that Hutchison had not made such a conflation and that he did acknowledge a role for introspection in economics, namely as a disruptive tool for questioning empirical claims and suggesting alternative lines of theorizing that might yield testable hypotheses.

The challenge was to find an area in which I could use introspective methods in this way, and toward the end of my 1999 study leave I found a perfect opportunity. Like Holbrook's examples, it involved music, though in my case it was not jazz but the question of whether I should attend a concert by the classically-influence Swedish heavy-metal guitar virtuoso Yngwie J. Malmsteen. His playing had been inspirational to me during the preceding two years. However, for several weeks after discovering he was going to be performing in Brisbane, I reminded myself why I had given up going to rock concerts and that if I took Simon's travel theorem seriously, there was no point in going since I already had all of Malmsteen's albums, along with several videos of him playing live, and note-by-note transcriptions of much of his music. My then-partner Sharon could not believe I was resisting getting a ticket on this basis. Ultimately, I felt I really should go, and we got some tickets. Sure enough, the concert made no sense in terms of gathering information about Malmsteen's playing, and it came with downsides, most notably the dangerously loud volume level (even though I was armed with shooters' earplugs), exactly as I had anticipated. But it did not refute Simon's travel theorem, for via introspection, I realised that a recorded concert does not enable one to meet some objectives that a fan may be able to meet by attending a live show. One such motivation is to pay homage to a performer that one admires, the musical equivalent of making a religious pilgrimage to Mecca.

After drafting my Holbrook-inspired paper on the demand for live music (eventually published in revised form, including some feedback from Holbrook, as Earl, 2001a), I spent the last couple of weeks of my study leave writing an autobiographical account of my car-buying decisions over the preceding twenty years. This was an exploration in a more Proustian style of introspective economics, but I then put it aside until 2010, when I updated it and found myself with a 'much too long' 50,000-word tale of 'Remembrance of Cars Past' that set out thirty years of learning about what I really wanted in a car and the limits to what I was prepared to pay to get it, with intolerant decision criteria repeatedly shaping the choices that I made. I attempted to capture the essence of this experiential analysis of automotive consumption in Earl (2012a), my contribution to a dual special issue of the *Journal of Business Research* on introspective methods.

The business plan for my study leave at the University of Queensland did not foreshadow these introspective efforts. Rather, it concentrated on my need for a world-class research library in order to extend my expertise in behavioural economics by editing, for Edward Elgar Publishing, a two-volume anthology of reprinted papers that would demonstrate the intellectual legacy of Herbert Simon in economics. This was to be a much more intensive exercise than my previous Elgar anthology on behavioural economics (Earl, ed., 1988b), for I intended to compile it with the aid of the Social Sciences Citation Index (SSCI). I had previously used the University of Queensland's hardcopy version of the SSCI when preparing my paper for the festschrift volume for George Richardson (Earl, 1998c) while visiting to attend the 1995 HETSA conference, but by July 1999 the online Web of Science version was available there. In the introduction that I wrote for the Simon volumes (Earl, ed., 2001b). I used the experience of trying to work with the SSCI as a way of introducing Simon's challenge to the notion of optimisation: Simon's work was so extensively cited that I faced information overload when trying to consider which were the most significant economics-related works that cited his contributions – and this was despite Web of Science running into difficulties displaying beyond about the top 400 citing works.

To deal with the information overload, I had to figure out a system of rules for deciding which papers to include. This entailed working with a plan for the structure of the two volumes and concentrating on recent papers unless I had other reasons for including somewhat earlier work. The focus on recent contributions seemed to be the best way – given the 'legacy' theme – of getting a sense of where mainstream and behavioural views of bounded rationality had got to and of the range of applications of Simon-inspired analysis. In less than five months, I managed to decide which papers to include and to write detailed introductions to both volumes. I was very happy with the outcome: Simon-inspired behavioural economics seemed to have been making great progress over the past decade and Simon's legacy in economics seemed secure and significant.

This confident assessment was shattered a little over a year later, after Elgar had obtained all of the reprint permissions and the Simon Legacy volumes were about to go into production. Herbert Simon died unexpectedly on 9 February 2001. That news was bad enough, but two days later the *New York Times* published a pair of articles about the emergence of a new field called behavioural economics, one of which focused on the work of Richard Thaler (Lowenstein, 2001), with the other spotlighting David Laibson, a younger rising star of whom I had not previously been aware (Uchitelle, 2001). Neither article mentioned the work of Simon, let alone his passing, or the work of Cyert and March on the behavioural theory of the firm. I was bewildered by this turn of events: it was as if Simon and others who had pioneered the behavioural approach before Thaler's (1980) initial contribution – indeed, even before Laibson's birth in 1966 – had been airbrushed from the history of economic thought at precisely the time when Simon's impact in economics ought to have been acknowledged. Six years would pass before I came to understand what was happening to behavioural economics (see Section 8.4).

But at least things had been looking up in terms of my ability to make original contributions to behavioural economics. When I returned to Lincoln at the start of 2000, my teaching and administrative loads turned out to be much lower than I had ever experienced there. By the time of Simon's passing, and as the result of a couple of trips back to the University of Queensland to maintain contact with Jason Potts, I had a pair of related papers in process. The first (published as Earl and Potts, 2000, though it did not appear until well into 2001) examined how shopping malls are designed to promote browsing behaviour rather than to minimise the search costs of busy shoppers. A significant volume of purchasing decisions may thus arise contingently depending on the success of attempts to manage the attention of shoppers, rather than emerging as shoppers find what they went out to purchase or solving the problems they went out hoping to solve. Some years later, we discovered that what we had been writing about is known in marketing as 'The

Gruen Transfer', after Victor Gruen, the pioneering designer of modern shopping malls.

The second paper (eventually published, after a typically leisurely *Cambridge Journal of Economics* refereeing process, as Earl and Potts, 2004) was the last that I worked on in my decade at Lincoln, and the most significant. It takes a less cynical view of the role of shopping malls, viewing retailers as one category among a variety of types of market institutions that enable inexperienced, boundedly rational consumers to outsource their preferences to those who have specialist knowledge about the sets of product characteristics that it is wise to obtain in a particular context, and which products match these templates. This view of consumer behaviour entails a multi-level view of preferences, for when another party (e.g., a salesperson at a retail site, an online recommendation, suggestions from an interior designer or other service consultant, or members of one's social network who appear to have the requisite expertise) suggests what we should want or buy, we are not obliged to 'buy' their suggestion.

Jason and I coined the term 'the market for preferences' to denote the set of institutions that make it possible partially to outsource one's preferences. Clearly, it is not a market in which transactions necessarily involve payments for the preferences that one takes on board. Sometimes we do pay money for our outsourced preferences, as when we pay a premium price if we choose to shop at a full-service retailer, or purchase something to give to a social contact as a token of our appreciation for their help in discovering what we need. But sometimes we spend less money by using the market for preferences, as when we, in effect, let Aldi shop for groceries for us by presenting us with a very limited range of choice of products that offer excellent value for money due to Aldi concentrating its buying power on products whose attribute mixes will serve most customers well.

7.5   CONFERENCE PARTICIPATION

One area in which Lincoln did not disappoint was in relation to conference travel and facilitating periods of study leave that involved overseas travel. By these means, in my decade at Lincoln, I was able to attend three conferences in Australia (1992, 1995, 1999), and make five conference visits to the UK (1993, 1994, 1995, 1996, 1997). Funding such travel is probably a wise investment for Australasian universities insofar as these opportunities make it easier for them to attract and retain high-calibre staff from overseas.

These trips certainly enabled me to maintain overseas contacts (for example, by attending two more Malvern political economy conferences) and to meet for the first time those whose work I had long admired (especially George Richardson, at the colloquium held in his honour at Oxford in 1995)) or had corresponded with for a long time (such as Fred Lee, whom I did not meet in person until the 1993 Post Keynesian conference at Leeds, shortly after we had finished editing the collected papers of P. W. S. Andrews, over twelve years after we first started exchanging letters). They also enabled me to visit friends and family. However, as the decade passed, I began to consider whether I would continue making such trips. This was partly because I had found Simon's travel theorem persuasive when reviewing (Earl, 1993c) his autobiography (Simon, 1991). But there was also the dread and actuality of making journeys that usually took over thirty hours each way, and sometimes involved ten or more hours of turbulence when I flew to London via Los Angeles. Moreover, although aircraft cabins were now much more pleasant during the flight due to smoking no longer being allowed, I increasingly found that I was picking up northern hemisphere bugs (probably partly due to the cabin air no longer being refreshed so frequently) that would tend to kick in just as I got over the jetlag after arriving back in Christchurch and needed to be in good shape to start a new semester.

7.6   RESEARCH AUDIT

The research outputs that I produced at Lincoln were mostly at odds with what I knew I needed to produce to look appealing in terms of the research audits that came to dominate academic life in the UK in the 1990s and would inevitably get mimicked Down Under. A world in which one gets judged largely on one's output of journal articles in the past three to five years was going to be inherently difficult for heterodox economists with limited chances of publishing in high-ranking journals. But, as can be seen from Table 7.1 (which, like Table 6.1, uses the 2019 Australian Business Deans' Council's list of journal rankings), I was badly misbehaving even in terms of what a good heterodox economist might be able to achieve.

Table 7.1: A Dean's View of My Lincoln University Research Output

Type of Research Output	N June1991to June 1996	N July1996 to June 2001	Reference Tag (and Name of Journal) in Reference List Order
A*-Ranked Articles	0	0	
A-Ranked Articles	0	2	Earl (1998a) *Information Economics and Policy*[A] Earl (2001a) *Journal of Economic Psychology*[B]
B-Ranked Articles	1	1	Earl (1994a) *Prometheus*[C] Earl and Potts (2000) *Managerial and Decision Economics*[D]
C-Ranked Articles	1	0	Earl (1992a) *Human Systems Management*[E]
Unranked Articles	1	0	Earl (1992b) *Cyprus Journal of Economicss*[F]
Refereed Conference Papers	0	0	
Research Monographs	0	0	
Other Books	3	5	Dow and Earl (eds) (1999a, 1999b) Earl (1995a) Earl (ed.) (1996a, 2001b) Earl and Frowen (eds) (2000) Earl and Kemp (eds) (1999) Lee and Earl (eds) (1993)
Parts of Edited Books	5	4	Earl (1992e, 1992d, 1992e, 1994b, 1995b, 1996b, 1998b, 1998c. 1999a, 1999b)
Review Article	1	0	Earl (1993)
Book Reviews	6	4	Earl (1992f, 1993b, 1993c, 1995c, 1996c, 1998d, 1999c, 2000, 2001c)
Other	0	0	

Notes to Table 7.1

[A] I wrote this paper at the request of *Prometheus* editor, Don Lamberton, who also edited *Information Economics and Policy*. However, the reason that I found time to write it was that Lamberton wanted to raise the profile of informational perspectives on economics by putting together a set of papers for the recently established 'Controversies' section in the *Economic Journal*. He said that he had been given the go-ahead for this from the section editor, Huw Dixon (who had been one of the referees of my textbook). One of the papers would be written by Joseph Stiglitz so it seemed too good an opportunity to let slip away. Alas, Lamberton's plan fell over, as Stiglitz was unable to write his paper due to his work chairing the US Council of Economic Advisers. The papers that did get written thereby ended up in *Information Economics and Policy*, despite the journal mainly publishing papers on telecommunications economics.

[B] This was accepted, subject to some changes, before I became co-editor of the *Journal*, and thereafter it continued to go through the normal refereeing process.

[C] I now regret not trying to place it with an economics journal; Don Lamberton was keen to have it for *Prometheus* when he heard about it, and the fit, in principle, seemed OK, but it has gone almost completely unnoticed.

[D] In a special issue on the behavioural economics of consumption.

[E] In a special issue on information economics and the design of organizations.

[F] I had been encouraged to submit to this short-lived journal after doing some refereeing for it. I felt it was a journal that showed promise and was surprisingly pluralistic: the sample issue that I was sent included a paper by Frank Hahn, and previous issues included papers by noted heterodox economists Philip Arestis and Ben Fine. The paper that I submitted went through a full refereeing process, and the editor, George Georgiou, made some astute choices of referees who suggested some useful improvements via papers that were unfamiliar to me.

However, my behaviour was not a sign that I was rebelling against the new world of academic research audits. It was the result of how I sought to keep my publications output going amid the challenges of doing research at Lincoln. In hindsight, it is clear that I should have declined many of the publication opportunities that I accepted and that I should have instead concentrated on producing works of the 'right' kind, even if there were far fewer of them.

Absent from Table 7.1 is an entry for a work that would have been of the 'right' kind, if only it had made it into print. This was 'Economics and marketing: A survey', which I wrote in mid-1996 at the request of the A-ranked *Cambridge Journal of Economics*. Although it was written around the mid-point of my decade at Lincoln, it was the first thing that I wrote at Lincoln that was based on extensive new reading. Finding the time to do this was not easy and because the library's collection of marketing journals was essentially confined to the 'core' titles, I fully expected that the refereeing process would suggest that I considered papers that I had not come across.

However, despite being invited to revise the paper, I never did so. This was because one of the referees (who also claimed that my paper was written in a boring way) gave few clues to support his or her claim that there were many relevant marketing publications that I had neglected to consider. Trying to second-guess what this referee meant was not an attractive task, and no help was forthcoming when I asked the journal's managing editor to try to get the referee to be more specific. In this sort of situation, one might reasonably expect a third referee to be invited into the process – especially with an invited paper that crossed disciplinary boundaries. Given that I had spent a good chunk of vacation leave in the UK writing the paper rather than relaxing, the waste of my time was especially annoying.

The disaster with this paper was something that I knew I could ill afford in the new research audit-centred environment if I were to have any hope of escaping to the UK or, when research audits arrived Down Under, to another Australasian university. Yet, although Lincoln had adopted annual appraisal systems for its staff, its senior managers seemed to be asleep at the wheel in the face of the looming possibility that research audits would soon be introduced in New Zealand.

There was no effort to alert staff to the publication pressures that they could be facing in the future. No signals were provided about the volume and kinds of research output expected from staff in the Department of Economics and Marketing (later part of the Commerce Division). If concerns were raised, during my annual performance appraisal meetings, about the volume of original research that I was producing, it was me who raised them. No one pulled me up for failing to publish output that embodied new ideas and fresh scholarship. In contrast to my ill-fated survey on the relationship between economics and marketing, the research output that I produced in my first eight years at Lincoln arose almost entirely with minimal new reading and entailed either writing up ideas that had been on my 'to do' list for a long time or editing the work of others. At annual appraisals, I emphasised that this situation was not sustainable, and that building up new intellectual capital was hampered by the difficulties of finding big enough blocks of time to get immersed in research and by the limitations of Lincoln's library collection, which had to be worked around by finding worthwhile blocks of time to visit the library at the University of Canterbury.

My early sense that senior management were not very fussy about the kind of output that was produced, so long as one did publish regularly, was reinforced in 1995 when the publication of my textbook *Microeconomics for Business and Marketing* was followed by me being given one of Lincoln's annual research awards. Yes, the book was innovative, unusually scholarly for a textbook, and had earned terrific pre-publication praise from Richard Cyert, Paul Ormerod and Herbert Simon. But it was not what I viewed as an original contribution to knowledge. The textbook aside, in my first four years at Lincoln, I had published the following:

- Three articles in obscure journals: Earl (1992a) was based on a guest lecture I had given to MBA students at the University of Canterbury, employing my existing knowledge of the car industry; Earl (1992b) was slightly modified from an old working paper (Earl, 1987e); and Earl (1994a) was the inaugural lecture that I had been asked to give after I had been at Lincoln for two years, where I explored the institutions and operation of the market for tertiary education services from the standpoint of the analysis of the nature of the firm proposed by Coase (1937).
- A co-edited collection of papers by P. W. S. Andrews (Lee and Earl, eds., 1993) to which my only scholarly input (as distinct from turning Fred Lee's digitised versions of Andrews's papers into typeset format) was the epilogue chapter (pp. 402–427) entitled 'Whatever happened to P. W. S. Andrews' industrial economics?', originally written in 1985 as a job market paper for an interview at the University of Auckland and subsequently presented at the 1987 HETSA conference.
- Five book chapters, of which the best two (Earl, 1992c, 1992d) had already been in press at the end of my time in Hobart.
- A review article, and three book reviews.

To me, this publication record did not warrant an award for research achievements.

In the year that followed the award for my 'research', the struggle of trying to do the research for the economics and marketing survey helped to crystalise my sense that I needed to initiate action that would get me time to do genuine research rather than just 'coming up with' publications based on my existing knowledge. Even before I started to write up the survey, I decided that my best hope for delivering the kind of research output that I knew I ought to be producing lay with a change in my employment arrangements. I therefore arranged a meeting with Paul Bradley, Lincoln's head of human resources, and the Vice-Chancellor, Professor Bruce Ross, at which I set out the difficulties I was having and what I had in mind. I requested a new contract in which I would work, and be paid, based on a 70 per cent load, with all of my coursework teaching to take place in one semester each year, leaving me to spend the second semester as if I were on sabbatical and with no requirement to be resident in New Zealand and able to visit the Lincoln campus during that semester, though I would supervise PhD students remotely as necessary. With my then-partner Sharon talking with increasing determination of her desire to move to Brisbane, such a contract would have made it possible for me each year to spend a semester there, too, and conduct my research with much better library facilities, possibly with a fractional appointment there.

The proposal went down well and a contract embodying it was drawn up before I set off for the UK to attend the tenth Malvern Political Economy Conference, spend a week in Scotland visiting the Dows and Neil Kay, and take some leave visiting my parents/writing the economics and marketing survey. By this point, however, it had been announced that Bruce Ross was moving on, to become New Zealand's Director-General of Agriculture. Bradley assured me that he would get Professor Ross to sign the contract before he left. Unfortunately, this did not happen, and I returned to discover that the Acting Vice-Chancellor, Professor Roger Field, refused to sign it. Field explained that Lincoln could not afford to have 'another airport professor'. He went on to explain that a similar kind of arrangement had been made with (if I recall correctly) a professor of agricultural engineering, who had then essentially used his university title to enable him to operate pretty much as a full-time consultant. Field was not prepared to saddle the next vice-chancellor with the risk that I would morph into that kind of operator – despite the fact that I had shown no interest in consultancy work. He did not show any inclination to renegotiate the contract so that it could be terminated if I failed to meet specific research performance targets. So, I either had to move elsewhere, or find a way of making my job work. But with the rise of research audits, it had begun to appear that I would only be able to move to a chair elsewhere if I could first make my existing job work well enough to enable me to produce research outputs that ticked the right boxes. To succeed at that would probably be a five-year task, even if I were resolute in not allowing my time to be diverted into producing things that ticked the wrong boxes.

In the ensuing three years, up to my study leave at the University of Queensland, I failed to show such resolve. Almost all the research time that I could muster went into four edited books (Dow and Earl, eds., 1999a, 1999b; Earl and Kemp, eds., 1999; Earl and Frowen, eds., 2000). Working on these edited volumes was much less challenging than trying to do original research of my own would have been, as I could make progress with them by snatching a few hours here and there between teaching and administrative tasks; they did not require entire days to be regularly available to ensure that momentum was maintained. They also had the potential advantage of keeping me internationally visible and well-networked. Even so, I worked long hours on them, knowing that a research audit game player would not have got involved in any of them. So, why did I not play the game and single-mindedly seek to crank out at least one well-ranked paper per year instead? The answer lies in the nature of these books.

These four edited books were very different projects from *Management, Marketing and the Competitive Process* (Earl, ed., 1996a), which had been 'in press' at the time of my attempt to obtain the fractional contract. That volume was completely initiated by me and consisted mainly of papers that others had sent to me and which I knew had not yet been placed elsewhere (including one that David Harper had cut from his PhD and which I reworked somewhat into a joint paper), plus a few that I commissioned from close contacts, and one that I had been planning to write since 1989. It did not chew up a lot of time and was something I wanted to put together as an interdisciplinary book on business as an exemplar of what a journal that brought economics, marketing and management together might look like. During my interview for the Lincoln chair, I had indicated that one of the things I hoped eventually to do was to set up such a journal. I never delivered on this, not just because I did not have the time to do so but also because *Industrial and Corporate Change*, first published in 1992, went a long way in the direction that I envisaged. With hindsight, I would have done better if I had not assembled this volume and had instead used my time simply to write my solo and joint chapters from it and place them with appropriate journals, where they would be more likely to be discovered by those who would find them interesting. (In the case of my solo paper 'Contracts, coordination and the construction industry', the appropriate place might have been in a project management journal.) In terms of citations, the book had a very poor impact. Its main benefit to me seemed to be that it contributed to me being invited to become a founding member of the editorial board of a new journal, *Marketing Theory*, which would hardly help my career in economics, though it might have helped facilitate an escape into a marketing department.

The two volumes that I edited with Sheila Dow were a consequence of my visit to Scotland in the UK summer of 1996, when Sheila and I discussed the idea of organizing a conference to honour Brian Loasby's contributions and celebrate his thirty-year association with the University of Stirling. These two volumes were based on papers from the conference, after I had put a lot of time into providing constructive feedback to their authors. However, as is normally the case with festschrifts (including the ones for George Richardson and Don Lamberton to which I contributed chapters – respectively, Earl, 1998a, 1999a), the papers in these two volumes have not had much impact in terms of citations. With hindsight, Sheila and I would have been wiser to try to get them (or the best of them) published as a (couple of) special issue(s) of a journal. The publication of festschrift papers as books may well reflect over-confidence bias on the part of editors and publishers, who know that the odds of high sales and impact are not good but who take the view that they have a much better chance than usual due to the status of the person being honoured and of many contributors, and/or the quality of the contributions.

While Sheila and I worked on the Loasby festschrift books, I was also working, with Simon Kemp, a psychologist at the University of Canterbury, on a much bigger task, namely getting around 100 authors to contribute to a reference book covering the intersection between consumer research in marketing, behavioural economics and economic psychology. When Edward Elgar floated the idea, I knew it would be crazy for me to edit it alone, but with Simon sharing the task, I enjoyed working on it as an experience in project management and in the hope that it would provide a way for me to get back up to speed with the literature in this area. Although it did not help tick the right boxes in terms of a research audit, it left Simon and I in a strong position to pitch successfully for the role of editors of the *Journal of Economic Psychology*, to commence in 2000. I knew that this could be viewed as misbehaving, but I hoped that the role might at least signal that I was well in touch with the latest literature in this area and hence that I was capable of getting back to making my own original contributions.

In late 1998, as soon as I had finished editing the books with Sheila and Simon, I began work editing *Economics as an Art of Thought: Essays in Memory of G. L. S. Shackle* (Earl and Frowen, eds, 2000). I took on this task at my own initiative purely for obligational reasons, with the hope of ensuring that the book would be published while George Shackle's widow, Catherine, was still alive. In that respect, it was a great success, as Catherine, then in her 91st year, was clearly delighted when she attended an event that was held at UCL in the summer of 2000 to mark the book's publication.

The Shackle volume had a long and very odd history. It was originally set in motion around 1991, by John Pheby, Stefan Boehm and Stephen Frowen, as a volume to be presented to George Shackle on his 90th birthday in July 1993 but was turned into a memorial volume following Shackle's death at the age of 88 in March 1992. I had written a chapter on 'Indeterminacy in the economics classroom' in which I used Shackle's inaugural lecture at the University of Liverpool, 'What makes an economist?' (Shackle, 1953) as the starting point for a reflection on the challenges of teaching in a pluralistic manner and focusing on open-ended problems. I then examined the lessons that Perry (1970) offered for those wishing to embrace these challenges. It had been a good means of organising my thoughts after Neil Fleming had introduced Perry to me, and it turned out neatly to complement Brian Loasby's contribution, 'How do we know?' I had submitted it on schedule, before using it as my presentation to the 1992 Australian Conference of Economists.[16] But things then went very quiet with the editorial process.

---

[16] I went on to present this paper in March and April 1993 as a visiting speaker at the University of Lancaster, Leeds University Business School, Victoria University of Wellington, and the Department of Management at the University of Canterbury. The last of these could have been a disaster, and I hope that, in explaining why, I will not cause readers to have nightmares. So frantic had things been at Lincoln that I had forgotten all about the seminar until the day before, when I noticed in my diary a note saying 'seminar, Canterbury'. However, I thought that it referred to a seminar by someone else, as Alan Singer, a member of Canterbury's Department of Management had become a good friend after I got to know him via being an examiner of his PhD, and he sometimes invited me to seminars there. When I arrived and found the seminar room, it was fortuitous that, before going in and taking a seat, I decided to look at the notice on the door, to see who the speaker was going to be. I was shocked to find that it was me, and I realised that I would have to deliver it without any slides. Afterwards, Bob Hamilton – who had been a

Routledge's representatives gave vague answers about its progress when I raised the issue with them at the 1994 and 1996 Malvern conferences, eventually advising me that the manuscript had been lost in transit to their London office, and that Stefan Boehm was going to reconstruct it. But there continued to be no sign that the book was going to go into production. Brian Loasby was clearly as disappointed as I was about the situation, referring to the volume, in one of his dinner talks at the conference in his honour, as something which he hoped might be published in his own lifetime. I therefore asked him whether it might be a good idea if, with due consultation with Routledge, I hijacked the project and attempted to reconstruct the book. He supported the idea and hence that is what I did, after Routledge had explained my proposal to Boehm and given him a final deadline to deliver the completed manuscript.

After the manuscript again failed to arrive, I set to work on reconstructing the book. All I had to go on was the original tentative list of contributors, not all of whom I could locate. During the process of getting a copy of Vicky Chick's paper, she put me in touch with Stephen Frowen (1923–2007), who had, by this stage, become an honorary research fellow at UCL. Stephen's knowledge of how the original editorial team had failed to produce the volume was sketchy. In his own case, the story was especially bizarre: it involved him being diverted by having to nurse his wife after they had been lucky to escape alive from a house fire in Germany that resulted from a faulty Christmas tree light. He was keen to help me revive the project and I accepted his offer despite initially being somewhat nervous about how things might go, as I had noticed that the volume that he had edited based on a 1983 conference celebrating Shackle's 80th birthday had taken seven years to be published (Frowen, ed., 1990). He then played a key role in getting Stephen Littlechild to supply a brand-new chapter about the Shackle papers in Cambridge University Library. I enjoyed working with Stephen Frowen via many faxes and emails before eventually meeting him at the book's launch. However, I wish he had prevented me from a very embarrassing and out-of-character slip with the book. I will now end this section by recounting what it entailed.

---

colleague at Stirling and was now a professor of management at Canterbury – came up to me and said, 'That was a very good presentation, with no notes at all!' I then told him why I had not been using any notes.

The original sheet of paper that listed prospective contributors included a joint chapter by James Buchanan and Viktor Vanberg, but as Christmas 1998 approached, I had not been able to find email addresses for either of them, (It probably did not help that I was a few months away from discovering the wonders of Google.) I made a mental note to write an airmail letter to Buchanan in the New Year – which I then forgot to do amid other tasks on returning to campus in January 1999. The book was thus completed without a chapter by Buchanan and Vanberg, as Stephen Frowen did not remind me that there should have been one and neither did Routledge after I sent the typescript to them in camera-ready form, early in 2000. But, despite having provided me with no copies of early correspondence about the book, Routledge clearly did know that Buchanan was supposed to be one of the contributors, for soon after the book appeared, Buchanan wrote to me to say that Routledge had sent him a copy and he had been surprised to find that it did not contain his chapter with Vanberg. He was very pleasant about the matter when I explained what had happened, and he said he doubted there would be any difficulty publishing the paper elsewhere, even almost a decade after they had written it. Given that he was a Nobel Laureate, I had no reason to doubt his conjecture.

7.7   EXIT

It is quite likely that I would have been able to bail out from Lincoln soon after I had discovered the reality of working there. In early 1990, I had applied for a chair at the University of Manchester Institute of Science and Technology (UMIST, which, from 2004, became part of the University of Manchester). I had not been called to interview for the position and thus was surprised to discover later that year, via Ajit Singh, that I had been ranked near the top of the list of applicants. This information was confirmed during my first year at Lincoln, when I received a letter from UMIST informing me that the successful candidate for their chair had resigned for personal reasons; it went on to ask if I would like to be considered again for the position. I decided against this, thinking that I had not yet established whether I could make a success of working at Lincoln. Bur by the end of 1992, I had decided that I really should consider making an early exit and I found that I could still get as far as being interviewed for an economics chair.

However, I was very mindful of the risk of 'jumping from the frying pan into the fire'. One of the interviews that I achieved was at the University of New England (UNE), in Armidale, New South Wales. UNE offered its degrees remotely as well as on campus and, like Lincoln, it had a strong agricultural focus, as befitted its rural location. The pre-interview meetings and reaction to my paper on Perry and pluralistic teaching did not leave me feeling enthusiastic, and although Armidale's facilities were not terrible for a small country town, it was no match for Christchurch. Moreover, UNE appeared to be facing some challenges and after discovering at the candidates' dinner the identities of my rivals, I felt that I was unlikely to be ranked at the top. It was thus with rather limited enthusiasm that I went into the interview, where I could not resist an opportunity to misbehave when responding to the external assessor's question. I knew that the assessor was the person who, some years earlier, had dismissed me as 'a brash young man by all accounts' when he was serving in a similar role at the University of Auckland. When his voice came remotely from Melbourne via a loudspeaker, his question was, 'What do you regard as your most important research contributions?' I began my reply by saying that 'My best-known work is my book *The Economic Imagination*, written when I was a brash young man, but my later book *Lifestyle Economics* is much better, since ....'

After my failed attempt to switch to a part-time contract at Lincoln, I returned to the professorial job market. Given the new obsession with the Research Assessment Exercise (RAE) in the UK, I was less surprised that I got nowhere with economics chairs there than with the fact that I did achieve an interview for a chair in business strategy at the University of Bath around October 1998. My shortlisting at Bath might have had something to do with the fact that John Pickering, the external examiner of my PhD, was now working there in a similar role and was on the interview panel. The interview visit provided me with my first opportunity to meet Tim Wakeley, one of my future co-authors, but it left me wondering why Bath had invested in the cost of flying me in for the interview: there was no request for me to give a presentation, and aside from meeting Tim (which we arranged ourselves, having been corresponding for the previous couple of years), there would have been no discussions with anyone had I not requested to have a chat with the head of the School of Management. In the interview, Pickering looked affable and asked me a question about links between Shackle's work and scenario planning; there was little attempt at inquisition about my research plans. After the interview, I spent a few days in Stirling, where I caught up with Sheila Dow and interviewed Brian Loasby to fill in some of his biographical details for the introductions to the two volumes in his honour. Of course, as with the interview at Bath, it would have been far more efficient to do this remotely, and no jet lag would have been involved.

A few weeks later, I flew to Australia to be interviewed for a chair in economics at the University of Newcastle, New South Wales. It was this interview that crystalised the disastrous impact of my time at Lincoln for my career prospects. The interview was organised along modern managerialist lines in which members of the interview panel attempt to ensure equal treatment by asking each candidate to answer an identical set of questions. On this occasion, the set of questions gave the farcical impression that no one on the panel had read my CV. I was asked to talk about the standing of the journal articles I had published, and I responded by saying that the research environment had been such that I had mostly not been writing articles but had instead been doing a lot of book-editing as a way of maintaining an international profile given the difficulties that I faced in doing research. I was then asked what research funds I had raised, and I responded pretty much by repeating the previous answer, for I was not in a space where I could come up with original proposals for research funding: my only venture into that territory had been a rushed and inevitably unsuccessful attempt as part of a multidisciplinary bid in the UK (with economic psychologist Alan Lewis, from Bath, and management lecturer Anthony Beckett, from the University of the West of England) shortly after I arrived at Lincoln. I managed to resist the temptation to say that it was economically questionable to judge research based on funding inputs, for all I needed was time and a good library. There may next have been a question about consulting income, to which I again repeated my earlier answer about how, and why, I had been spending my time at Lincoln. I was left with a strong sense that the only way I was going to escape from Lincoln was if someone who knew me well had a job to offer and had no trouble believing that I would deliver original research if given the opportunity to work in the right environment.

The person who did precisely that was one of Newcastle's external assessors, namely John Foster, the new head of the School of Economics at the University of Queensland (UQ). He had looked on sympathetically during that interview. I had first met John when I was working at the

University of Stirling, when he was working at the University of Glasgow. We had kept in touch over the next fifteen years, during which he became a leading figure in evolutionary economics. A few weeks after the Newcastle interview, he was able to hire Jason Potts by using his discretionary capacity to create a one-year position, but for the moment, there were no established positions that he could advertise. He was delighted to host me as a visiting professor at UQ in the second half of 1999 and was able to retain Jason for 2000 via another one-year contract. He was determined to give Jason a more secure future and it was clear that he hoped to hire me, too. However, I returned to Christchurch at the start of 2000 still wondering how long it would be before any positions were advertised at UQ and at what level they would be offered.

The period of study leave in Brisbane left me with mixed feelings about the idea of moving there permanently. UQ had not been a disappointment: the library was indeed world-class, members of the School of Economics had made me feel very welcome, and the students in the Philosophy of Economic Thought unit at which I had taken a guest slot had impressed me. But, as when I declined an offer at UQ in late 1987, I really did not like Brisbane's summer heat and humidity, which seemed a high price to pay for sunny, mild winters, The kind of commuting that life in Brisbane would entail was also something that I preferred to avoid. Given that my teaching and administrative loads at Lincoln were now much less worrying than they had been prior to my study leave, I began the new millennium with an open mind about whether I might at last be able to enjoy working at Lincoln and thus get to make the most of life in Christchurch. This could be facilitated via the University of Canterbury's library and by making a few trips to UQ each year.

In August 2000, I visited Brisbane as a stopover on the way back to Christchurch from recreation leave in the UK that had enabled me to visit UCL and give a presentation at the event that Stephen Frowen organised to launch the Shackle memorial book. During that stopover I saw John Foster and he told me that approval had been given to advertise four lecturer/senior lecturer positions in the near future. A position at the top of the senior lecturer scale would, in effect, take me back to where I was at the end of my time at the University of Tasmania. However, with Australian academic pay having grown significantly while my real income in New Zealand had stagnated, such a position now readily matched what I was currently getting, at least in terms of a simple exchange rate conversion.

It seemed possible that, if I took the unusual step of moving down to a senior lectureship, I might never have a professorial title again. But, having 'been there and done that' on the professorial front, that possibility did not really concern me. The choice thus reduced to other lifestyle and workplace differences. By the time the advertisements had appeared and the closing date for applications was approaching, it had become clear to me that work trumped lifestyle and that I should apply to UQ. I had, by that point, run into the sacred cow of the agricultural economics subject and concluded that the director of commerce programmes was impossible to deal with (and this was before I discovered that the new behavioural and evolutionary economics subject would not be offered). Moreover, it was difficult to forget the difference that a brilliant library made to the research process. But I also realised that student quality really mattered to me.

Lincoln did have some very good students, but, as Christchurch's lower-status university in business-related areas, grade distributions tended to have a long tail of poor achievers. Because final grades were based on distributions rather than being criteria-based. I usually found that I was expected to award marks that averaged about five percent more than I felt was warranted by demonstrated attainments. Lincoln's academic registrar, Roger Smyth, had in recent years been sending end-of-semester letters and forms to examiners that set out the circumstances in which grade distributions could differ from those that were expected, but there were no boxes to tick pertaining to deficiencies in the ability or studiousness of one's students. I was tired of feeling ethically challenged by the pressure to pass students whose attainments seemed to warrant failing grades, and I imagined that the situation at UQ would be nowhere nearly so bad, even in an age in which the dumbing-down of higher education seemed to be widespread. To get my research back on track, continue with my pluralistic teaching mission and maintain my principles as an examiner, I was going to have to say goodbye to Christchurch.

The interview entailed a conference call between me, John Foster and Ian Zimmer, the faculty dean, and it had the air of a mere formality. In June 2001, after completing a semester of notice, I drove home from Lincoln for the last time. On this occasion, it was to the music of the movie soundtrack of Pete Townsend's rock opera *Tommy*, which I had cued to start with the track entitled 'I'm Free!' I had just become an ex-professor.

8 University of Queensland, Australia, 2001–2020

8.1   INTRODUCTION

The University of Queensland (hereafter usually referred to simply as UQ) was founded in 1909 and now operates on a scale that completely dwarfs the other universities on which this book has focused. By 2019, before the COVID-19 pandemic impacted on enrolments of international students, the number of enrolled students exceeded 55,000. During the years that I was working at UQ, its research standing increased, taking it to second place nationally and to the middle of the top-100 in its overall ranking globally. The very attractive main campus is a few kilometres south-west of the central business district of Brisbane, adjacent to the Brisbane River, with many impressive modern buildings. Older sandstone buildings ring its magnificent heritage-listed Great Court. Everything about the main campus exudes its big-league status, and there are frequent reminders that UQ's mission is to enable students to 'create change'. Major addresses have been delivered at the UQ Centre by US President Barack Obama and Nobel Laureate Joseph Stiglitz.

Yet UQ's big-league status is relatively recent, its transition having commenced from the late 1990s under the vice-chancellorship of the late Professor John Hay, AC. Its growth in size and standing has followed that of Brisbane as a city. Back in the 1970s, Brisbane was commonly viewed as an oversised country town, but in 1982 it hosted the Commonwealth Games, followed six years later by World Expo 88. It went on to host the 2014 G20 World Leaders' Summit and is to host the 2032 Summer Olympic Games. In the mid-1980s, when I first visited Brisbane, UQ had the air of a rather grand provincial university, and its economics department seemed to be focused on applied economics, not theory – though one should not forget that, in the mid 1950s, its staff had included John Harsanyi, who later shared the 1994 Nobel Memorial Prise in Economics Science with John Nash and Reinhard Selten.

The rise of UQ's School of Economics (to which I will henceforth refer simply as the SOE) dates from 1989, when Clem Tisdell (1939–2022) joined as its new head. Clem was an extraordinarily prolific contributor across an implausibly wide range of fields of the literature of

314

economics. During his decade as head, the staff that he hired continued mostly to be focused on applied issues, but they did so with more outward looking perspectives. The school's capabilities most noticeably grew in the areas of development and the environment. However, Clem's most significant act of recruitment, soon after he arrived, was the bold step of hiring John Foster to a chair in applied macroeconomics. I say 'bold' here because, a few years earlier, John Foster (1987) signalled via his book *Evolutionary Macroeconomics* that he was no ordinary macroeconomist. John's appointment, from a senior lectureship at the University of Glasgow, would surely have mystified the Australian macroeconomics establishment, but it did not prove to be a mistake. In addition to becoming a major figure in evolutionary economics (culminating in his presidency of the International J. A. Schumpeter Society), John accelerated the SOE's upward trajectory on succeeding Clem as its head. Somehow, like Clem, he managed to keep his research flourishing during the decade of the UQ SOE's growth that he oversaw.

The SOE expanded and changed with surprising rapidity, bankrolled in part via a strategic early move into the market for coursework master's degrees aimed at domestic graduates seeking to make a 'knight's move' into economics from other disciplines (the flagship programme for economics graduates being the more challenging Bachelor of Economics (Honours)), and international students seeking simultaneously to up-skill and obtain, in an English language environment, a credential from a well-established institution. Just before I arrived, one of the key recommendations of a routine seven-year review of the SOE was that two chairs in microeconomic theory should be created. But senior-level expertise in orthodox economic theory soon grew by much more than this, due to some Australian Research Council Professorial Fellows opting to hold their fellowships at UQ. Meanwhile, an instant, state-of-the-art centre for research on productivity and efficiency analysis was created by hiring, from the University of New England, two professors and two senior lecturers in econometrics, who specialised in this area.

John Foster's successors as head of the SOE augmented this surge in senior-level recruitment by hiring high-calibre entry-level staff through the academic labour market based around the American Economic Association's annual conferences. Via these processes, the SOE became increasingly dominated by orthodox economists and able to rank among the top three economics departments in Australia for research. It now has around 50 full-time established academic positions, as well as many casual staff, active honorary or adjunct staff, and support staff. This scale of operations for a single discipline is about as big it can be without its staff becoming unable to know all their colleagues, let alone get to know those in other schools within the Faculty of Business, Law and Economics (which also includes a significant group of tourism academics). Although my only collaborative research with UQ colleagues outside the SOE was with members of other faculties (on health policy: see Foster, Earl, Haines, and Mitchell, 2010), I did get to know a few staff in the business school, who shared my interest in complex systems and the growth of firms. It was good to know that, if ever things became impossibly orthodox within the SOE, I might be able to shift into the Business School and get to work alongside them. But such a shift did not prove to be necessary.

The building that houses the SOE is named in memory of Colin Clark (1905–1989), who started his career as a Cambridge contemporary of Keynes, pioneered the use of the term 'Gross National Product', and held major positions as a public service economist in Australia. In retirement, he remained active as an applied economist, holding an honorary position at UQ. (I remember seeing him in the departmental coffee room during my first visit to UQ in 1987; for an intellectual biography of Colin Clark, see Millmow, 2021.) His grandson, Joseph Clark, was a high-flying economics undergraduate when I took up my position at UQ. Joseph then became my first start-to-finish UQ doctoral student. He thereby introduced me to the notion of a 'confusopoly', via his thesis project, which used online experimental methods to show that even professionals in the market for superannuation products struggled to make good choices about switching between rival superannuation funds with complex fee structures (see Clark, 2007). As will be shown in Section 8.4, the confusopoly theme later became a focus for my own research.

Because I worked at UQ for almost 20 years, this is a very long, chapter despite being short relative to the previous three chapters on a pages-per-year basis. The chapter's length is the price of employing the same sectional structure as the previous three chapters. By adhering to this structure, it is possible to get a much better sense of how my UQ experience evolved as the years went by. Although life was different working under John Foster's headship from working under his successors, having a chapter break on that basis at the end of 2008 would have detracted from the emphasis that I wish to give to the role that changing long-term *external* conditions played in shaping internal changes and the flow of this stage of my career.

8.2   TEACHING

As I had hoped, the UQ grading system proved to be criteria-based, without pressures to conform to a particular grade distribution. Better still, very few students failed my subjects under criteria-based grading. On average, the UQ students were impressive, and the best were extraordinarily good. They were also expected to put in the kind of effort that meant that studying was a full-time job: according to UQ policies, which we were expected to draw to the attention of our classes in our introductory lectures, students were expected to put in 9–10 hours of work per week for each of the four subjects they took each semester on a full-time load. After deducting the two-hour lecture and one-hour tutorial, this left my students with at least six hours per week for reading and writing. However, it was not quite a return to Cambridge-style expectations. Requiring students to submit four essays for each subject would have been roughly equivalent, given a four-subject semester load, to the regime that I had experienced. But this would have generated an impossible marking load, given that tutorial groups consisted of up to 25 students, so subjects that involved written assignments typically had only a pair of in-semester essays (three, at the very most) or reports. Most weeks, then, students would have time to do about six hours of reading. The challenge was to get them to use their time this way.

To signal that I wanted my first cohort of second-year business economics students to start thinking for themselves and do more than merely rely on their lecture notes, I constructed a traditional reading list based around classic articles reprinted in readers edited by Buckley and Michie (1996) and Foss (1997), whose publisher, Oxford University Press, bundled together for a special price. However, some of my students reacted aggressively to this attempt to get them to 'read' for their degrees. Several weeks into the subject, these students began a 'trolling' campaign against me by sending abusive emails about the course, and my teaching and expertise, with the worst messages coming from untraceable Hotmail addresses. Many of these emails were copied to John Foster. John replied individually to them, pointing out that I had been hired for my expertise in the area and was not harbouring unreasonable expectations about what they should be capable of doing.

When I talked with my tutors and with students in my own tutorial groups about what was going on, it was clear that most of the class knew of the campaign against me and were not happy that it was taking place. What I did not initially know was that one of my colleagues was experiencing something similar with his second-year microeconomics subject, where there were fears about how difficult its upcoming mid-semester examination was going to be. (Mid-semester examinations were a common alternative to essay-based assignments.) The experience was extremely stressful. My sleep was so badly disrupted that, on two occasions, I experienced 'micro-sleep' incidents while driving. It seemed like a re-run of my initial difficulties with the Lincoln students, only far worse. Eventually, as I stood firm and it became clear that John was not going to replace me with someone who would dumb down the subject, the trolling stopped, and I was very happy with the final achievements of the class.

As I reflected on that first semester, I concluded that my mistake had been that I had not commenced my lectures by introducing the class to the Perry Progression. I had not though that this would be necessary, as I was now working in an elite institution with stiff entry requirements compared with those at Lincoln. I wrote a short piece about the experience for the *Post-Autistic Economics Review* (which later was more formally published as Earl, 2003a) and vowed always to introduce Perry whenever I taught subjects that involved contending perspectives and required open-ended problem-solving. The trolling never occurred again in my classes. However, I later discovered, from a student's comments on an evaluation form, just how careful one must be in talking about Perry. The student in question had misconstrued my five-stage version of the Perry Progression as being about what students were expected to experience in five years of university studies, with each year being designed to take them one stage further. Based on this, the student claimed that I was teaching the class as though they were in the second year of a master's degree (stage five), rather than second-year undergraduates.

The Withering of 'Big Menu Pluralism'

The SOE offered a huge range of subjects, about 80 in all. When I started working there, the list included subjects on economic history and the philosophy of economic thought. Economics departments that operate on this kind of scale have scope for enabling their students to experience what we might call 'big menu pluralism' even if individual subjects are mostly not taught in a pluralistic manner and mostly do not involve open-ended problem-solving tasks. If enough of the subjects that are offered are presented from diverse perspectives, students can assemble something akin to what the 1970s Cambridge Economics Tripos provided via a rather limited choice of subjects that often were taught by multiple staff who presented different perspectives. When I arrived at UQ, the SOE operated via 'big menu pluralism'.

John Foster ensured that the menu of subjects became better and better for providing such a learning experience, even though the notion of pluralism barely seemed to be explicitly articulated when changes were being made. In 2007, toward the end of his decade as head of school, John asked me to design and prepare the paperwork for a new second-year undergraduate unit. Like the stillborn subject I had devised at Lincoln, it was to be called Behavioural and Evolutionary Economics. Finally in 2008, he asked me to co-design Evolution of Economic Systems with two other heterodox staff. This was to be a third-year undergraduate unit, also to be offered at the master's level, that would use evolutionary economics to analyse processes of development, structural change, and economic growth. By the time that these subjects were going through the approvals process, the SOE's executive committee included recently hired senior staff who were orthodox theorists, but the latter did not try to thwart the proposals.

In the ensuing decade, there was no sign of a concerted effort to eliminate non-mainstream economics from the curriculum. Indeed, when behavioural/experimental economist Daniel Zizzo joined UQ SOE as its new head in late 2018, I was excited to see him use the word 'pluralistic' within the first few sentences of his address at the morning tea that marked his arrival. Not long after he arrived, Daniel asked me to work with a heterodox colleague to design a new subject called Ethics in Economics. It received Faculty approval based on the paperwork and indicative outline that we prepared. However, by 2023 it had not yet been offered. Its repeatedly rescheduled launch will be significant: since 2012, scope for undergraduates to enjoy 'big menu pluralism' has undergone steady attrition and the UQ SOE has become the very model of a modern orthodox economics department. How did this happen?

In posing and addressing this question, I want to make it clear that I am not criticizing UQ or any of its officers, despite my commitment to pluralistic economics education. To understand the withering of pluralism at the UQ SOE and to learn lessons for both the future of heterodox economics and the pluralistic teaching of economics, it is helpful to think in terms of a path-dependent evolutionary process that was largely the result of external pressures, rather than ascribing the withering of pluralism to any kind of attempt by orthodox economists to eliminate dissidents and cleanse the subject menu of non-standard material.

To be sustainable, the kind of pluralism that prevailed when I arrived at UQ requires the following conditions to be maintained:

(a) Appropriate staff must be hired and retained

The success of a non-mainstream subject is not likely to be assisted if it is taught by someone who is not a specialist in the area in question. Without depth of expertise, a lecturer is unlikely to feel comfortable in the classroom, for it will be hard to deliver material with the confident air of authority that he or she displays in other classes. I was especially conscious of this when I became the instructor for International Economy in the Twentieth Century, a subject that requires a mass of institutional and historical knowledge: there simply was not enough time to do all the reading I wanted to do to be sure of what I was saying, let alone add more spice to it to keep my audience attentive. Teaching and subject ratings will suffer in this sort of situation, and word will get around that the subject is rather dull.

A large department in a well-ranked institution should have a bigger chance of avoiding this, compared with smaller rivals that will have greater trouble attracting staff and be more likely only to have, at the best of times, one person who has deep knowledge per specialist area. However, as is evident from the fact that I ended up teaching International Economy in the Twentieth Century, even an institution like UQ can find it challenging to manage succession problems caused by resignations or retirement of staff who have specialist expertise. This makes heterodox kinds of subjects especially vulnerable.

Economic history is an especially challenging area to maintain. When I first visited UQ in the 1980s, economic history seemed to be one of its strong areas, with two readers (associate professors) who specialised in international economic history. Both retired some years before I joined

UQ's staff, and soon after I arrived, the remaining economic historian also retired. John Foster managed to hire two replacement staff in succession, both of whom blended interests in economic history with interests in other areas of economics, but neither stayed for more than a few years. No new staff with backgrounds in economic history were hired for established positions in the field between 2008 and the cessation of teaching in this area at the end of 2020, despite occasional applications from economic historians among the many hundreds received each year after UQ began recruiting via the academic hiring rounds that are attached to the annual conferences of the American Economic Association.

It is not hard to see why this is so. When regular research audits were introduced in Australia, universities were put under pressure to be ranked as high as possible, to signal their credibility both globally and to national funding bodies. In this environment, heads of economics departments would be doing their institutions a disservice if they ignored the journals ranking list of the Australian Business Deans' Council. The two key economic history journals on successive iterations of this list are both well ranked: *The Economic History Review* is A-ranked, and *The Journal of Economic History* is an A* journal. However, unless one is a labour historian or business historian, there are no other A-ranked economic history journals to target on the list. So, from a dean's perspective, economic historians will tend to look much more risky than mainstream economists to hire. When economic historians retire or resign from established positions, the hiring incentives favour filling the vacant positions by hiring orthodox economic theorists and applied economists/econometricians who have demonstrated the capacity or potential to publish in the A*-ranked journals on the ABDC list. The same applies when vacancies arise due to resignations or retirements of heterodox economists of any kind, for there are very few heterodox economics-friendly A*-ranked journals on the ABDC list, and the list of A-ranked heterodox journals is also very restricted.

When universities face this kind of external environment, pluralistic teaching and heterodox research face a bleak future even if departmental policymaking and hiring is not controlled by orthodox economists who take the view that non-orthodox approaches to economics are 'not really economics' at all. But it should be noted that these processes also work against the hiring of orthodox applied economists if their work is viewed as less likely than that of theorists to enhance departmental ratings. In one of its first forays into the annual 'AEA hiring rounds', UQ's SOE interviewed a minerals economist who made a very favourable impact among staff and was clearly attracted by the idea of working at the best university in Queensland, a state whose economy depends heavily on its mining sector. However, a theorist was hired instead, leaving the SOE without anyone in this area.

These hiring incentives result in non-mainstream/non-core subjects being taught by shrinking ranks of ageing staff that students may regard as less 'student friendly' or 'approachable' than those who teach the mainstream subjects. UQ's unit on Australian Economic History survived until 2020 partly because its enrolments were protected by its status as the capstone unit for those taking an economics major in the Bachelor of Arts. But in 2020 it was dealt a death blow via a 'BA Reset' that gave greater choice to final-year students. Its demise solved the economic history succession problem that would have arisen with the retirement of its 2018–2020 coordinator, who had picked up the course after the death of the previous coordinator, a long-serving casual lecturer. In retiring at the end of 2020, the final coordinator of Australian Economic History contributed, as I did, to what was nearly a complete loss of the SOE's non-sessional, non-mainstream human capital, for our exits coincided with those of three other staff with heterodox backgrounds. It was not quite a complete wipe-out: monetary endogeneity would still be taught, as it is one of the interests of one of the continuing teaching-focused staff.

The subjects for which I was the final coordinator and lecturer came to me via this process of replacing staff who had non-core capabilities with staff with orthodox skills in core areas: I inherited Philosophy of Economic Thought, as well as Political Economy and Comparative Systems, due to the retirement of their instructor; International Economy in the Twentieth Century came my way when Jason Potts moved to RMIT (having himself been given the subject after the abandonment of attempts to find a specialist in the area) and, when it was canned, the gap in my teaching load was filled by Evolution of Economic Systems becoming vacant due to John Foster's retirement. I continued the master's-level version of Evolution of Economic Systems in my final, pandemic-disrupted semester of teaching. After this, the master's-level Evolution of Economic Systems passed for 2021 to one of the heterodox sessional staff, who had previously picked up Economics of Innovation and Entrepreneurship (and invested a lot of time in revamping it, with great success in terms of enrolments). The latter subject had long been taught by his former PhD supervisor, who had retired with his position then filled by a freshly minted orthodox economist with expertise in other areas. Then, in 2022 and 2023, Evolution of Economic Systems fell into the 'not offered' category.

The career prospects for heterodox sessional staff look very bleak in this environment, even when such staff invest unpaid hours in ensuring they are in command of the material and succeed in growing the enrolments for their subjects. The externally driven logic of the hiring process prevents them from getting shortlisted for established teaching and research positions, and their teaching loads prevent them from finding time to extract publications from their PhDs.

(b) Staff who inherit subjects that have previously been taught in accordance with faculty-approved heterodox subject specifications must be willing to conform to the spirit of the approved specifications rather than flouting heterodox clauses or merely paying lip-service to them.

As in Coase's (1937) characterisation of employment contracts in his analysis of the nature of the firm, academic employment contracts are loosely specified, typically with only a few vaguely worded lines setting out the duties that each position entails. This ensures that the institution can readily adapt by changing what is asked of staff as conditions change, as well as leaving room for staff to make original contributions to knowledge. Academics hope eventually to be rewarded for the latter via promotion rather than by performance-based pay, though the latter has become more common recently (cf. also the analysis of employment contracts offered by Simon, 1951). Such employment contracts help to account for why the task of the head of an academic department is often viewed as being akin to 'herding cats', as academics typically seem to want to teach *as they see fit* the subjects that they are allocated. The bigger the department in which they work, the harder it will be for the departmental head, or his or her delegate(s), to monitor how they operate. So long as students do not complain about what is being taught, lecturers may enjoy considerable scope for taking subjects in new directions without running into issues with the departmental head – at least until there is a departmental or programme review in which subject outlines get scrutinised.

Academic staff can use such wriggle-room in two ways. On the one hand, it can enable orthodox subjects to be transformed by infusions of heterodox material, open-ended assessment tasks and an emphasis on pluralism. This was what I did, even despite initial student opposition, when teaching Money and Banking at UTAS, Microeconomics for Business and Marketing at Lincoln, and Business Economics at UQ. On the other hand, wriggle-room may allow orthodox economists to remove heterodox content even where outgoing heterodox coordinators have attempted to future-proof 'their' subjects by getting the approved descriptions modified to refer explicitly to non-mainstream content. Incoming subject coordinators can thereby avoid the costs of learning how to run the subjects in the ways that their predecessors had been running them. My experience has been that this happens even if one indicates to the new coordinator that one is happy to supply all the teaching and learning resources that one has developed. Given this wriggle-room, the hiring of orthodox staff as heterodox staff retired or moved elsewhere was largely guaranteed to ensure the withering of pluralism in the UQ SOE.

It was no surprise to me that this issue arose when I ceased to be the coordinator of subjects that had long been taught in heterodox ways. It first happened to a limited degree with the pluralistic MBA Business Economics unit that I had taught between 2003 and 2009, sometimes with contributions from visitors Tim Wakeley and Neil Kay. The MBA unit had provided the basis for the pluralistic business economics textbook that I wrote with Tim for McGraw-Hill (Earl and Wakeley, 2005). Tim and I had tried to make our book as easy as possible for instructors to use by providing most of the usual 'big textbook publisher' suite of support materials, and McGraw-Hill outsourced some further material without telling us they had done so. Between 2005 and 2009, I had developed further teaching resources for that unit, as well as making audio recordings of classes. However, the colleague who inherited this course – one of the SOE's star teachers – already had other plans and set an orthodox 'essentials of economics' text as the required reading. I was, however, pleased to see that the subject retained its emphasis on critical thinking about choices made by real-world firms.

In the case of Behavioural and Evolutionary Economics, much more drastic departures from what had originally been approved took place after my 2008–2010 and 2013–2019 stints as the coordinator of this subject. First, in 2011 and 2012, it was taught in what appeared to have been a very interesting but highly idiosyncratic way by Paul Frijters (based on Frijters and Foster, 2013). Following Paul's departure to the LSE, it returned to me, and to the original format until 2019.[17] Then, in 2020, to the surprise of some who enrolled, it suddenly became a conventional behavioural economics subject, taught in the modern US-style way with assessments focused on weekly exercises rather than essays and authentic report-writing tasks. Again, the incoming coordinator made the changes despite all my teaching resources being readily available. I was not at all surprised to watch this happen, for the new coordinator's training in behavioural economics had come at Berkeley as a student of Matthew Rabin.

After seeing that students were not going to have the kind of behavioural economics unit that I had provided, I acted collegially to help ensure that students would not be surprised by the changes and to give them as much value as possible for their investments in the subject. I proactively filled out the paperwork to rename Behavioural and Evolutionary Economics as, simply, Behavioural Economics – much as I had done the paperwork to turn Microeconomics for Business and Marketing into Intermediate Microeconomics a decade earlier following a rather similar fait accompli at Lincoln. Perhaps, in the best interests of UQ students, I should have changed the subject's name even during my time as coordinator of the subject. Towards the end of my time as the course's coordinator, I discovered that the student records system abbreviated the original title to Evolutionary Economics on student transcripts, which probably made them seem a bit less valuable to prospective employers than they might have done when behavioural economics became widely known as a field of study. But the point of the long title had been to ensure that the subject included a significant amount of evolutionary economics in the tradition of Veblen, Marshall, Nelson and Winter.

(c) If students are required to take a set of orthodox 'core' subjects but are not required to take subjects that cover a variety of economic perspectives, there must be enough voluntary demand for subjects

---

[17] The teaching and learning resources that I have made available at https://shredecon.wordpress.com/principles-of-behavioral-economics/teaching-and-learning-resources-to-accompany-principles-of-behavioral-economics/ to supplement my *Principles of Behavioral Economics* are based on those that I developed during this period.

*based on heterodox, methodological, or historical material to ensure
the viability of the latter subjects.*

Today's fee-paying students often seem to take the view that, if they are paying for their degrees, they should have considerable freedom to customise what they get. (Underlying their thinking might be the fact that they are being asked to invest as much for a degree as it costs to buy a luxury car, and that manufacturers of such vehicles usually offer a huge range of options rather than supplying them on a take-it-or-leave-it basis.) In most cases, they know nothing of the concept of a 'merit good' and presume that they are competent enough to choose elective units or that they can choose with the aid of study advisors. Their desire to have a good range of choice of subjects may seem rather at odds with the reaction of students when one presents them with reading lists and invites them to select two or three sources from each week's recommendations, for in the latter case, they seem to expect that the lecturer should know the best set to read and they thus resent being given the chance to select the suggestions that look most appealing. However, such resentment may have the same fee-payer origins: they may feel that they are paying for, among other things, the service of not having to figure out the best set of things to read.

In today's tertiary education environment, such attitudes can make it dangerous to offer degrees with compulsory cores that leave little room for choice: to do so may give the impression of a paternalistic operating mode that is not 'student centred'. Meanwhile, very large institutions, such as UQ, can obtain a competitive advantage by being able to offer a wider range of choice than their smaller counterparts, and this enhances their scope for setting more demanding entry requirements.

When the compulsory core of an economics programme is restricted to permit a wide range of electives, heterodox material is inevitably confined to the elective units. This is because the compulsory core must contain enough orthodox subjects to ensure that the programme in question does not run into reputational issues – such as having its graduates blacklisted by employers' lobby groups – or harming the ranking of the department that delivers it. During an external review, such issues will lead to the department in question being advised to fall into line with conventional practice. For a head of department who is trying to foster 'big menu pluralism', keeping all the core courses orthodox also has advantages of the 'let sleeping dogs lie' kind in terms of relations with orthodox colleagues.

The success of an attempt to pursue 'big menu pluralism' thus depends on students knowing, or being advised, that they should choose electives that will give them a range of contending perspectives on economics and diverse learning experiences. They also need to be willing to take that advice. Unfortunately, in the UQ context, these conditions did not apply to a sufficient degree. Students failed to favour heterodox, non-quantitative subjects on a big enough scale to keep them viable. As a result, in my time at UQ, I had the dispiriting experience of being the last person to lecture on four subjects that had helped to make it possible for students to achieve a well-rounded pluralistic experience, namely, Philosophy of Economic Thought (last taught in 2012), Political Economy and Comparative Systems (last taught in 2015), International Economy in the Twentieth Century (last taught in 2015) and the undergraduate version of Evolution of Economic Systems (last taught in 2019). In each case, the problem was that the subject struggled to attract more than about 25 students, in sharp contrast to orthodox electives.

It is possible that the students were operating with a banausic view of what they should be getting from their courses and viewed these subjects as unlikely to add to their sets of tools that could be useful after they graduated. If so, they were choosing their electives oblivious to the potential benefits that these subjects might offer for their critical and creative thinking skills – for example, by enabling them to employ lessons from history in designing economic scenarios. However, there are reasons to believe that this was not the only driver of the failure of students to choose such electives.

One issue is that students are likely to view such subjects as peripheral to the bulk of what they are studying, and orthodox instructors in the latter are unlikely to see reasons to promote the former to students who take their classes. Students may be wise to take such a view, for electives that are based on mainstream thinking may provide synergy benefits with compulsory units. The mainstream electives often involve applying core ideas in particular contexts, whereas taking heterodox courses may seem more of a leap in the dark that could harm their grade-point averages. If students are nervous enough not to experiment with a heterodox elective in one semester, they will not learn how well they could have handled it, and hence will run into the same issue the following semester, and so on, rather than ending up taking multiple heterodox units and finding synergies between them. Moreover, if heterodox courses are deleted due to inadequate demand and are replaced on lists of electives by new orthodox courses (for example, in game theory), the result may not be that the remaining heterodox courses become more viable; instead, the reverse may happen, due to the remaining heterodox electives having fewer opportunities to be used as prerequisites or recommended preparation for other heterodox electives.

We also need to be mindful of the impact that differences in assessment systems have on relative enrolments of orthodox and heterodox electives. These differences became increasingly striking in my second decade at UQ as retirements, resignations and new hiring led to a great increase in the proportion of staff with orthodox North American doctoral educations. The impact of this change in staff backgrounds on assessment practices was glaringly obvious when I compared subject outlines and final examination papers for 2010 and 2018 in preparing for the process of reviewing the economics major in UQ's Bachelor of Arts programme: in 2010, assessment tasks in orthodox courses were much less mechanistic and more focused on real-world issues than in 2018. By 2018, final examinations followed North American standard practice and had substantial sections of multiple-choice and short-answer questions, with a focus on abstract problems like those in the 'problem sets' that dominated in-semester assessments. During that decade, the heterodox courses had maintained assessment systems based on open-ended tasks that entailed writing essays, reports or annotated bibliographies.

Clearly, the old-fashioned heterodox approach to assessment entails spending more time on marking assignments than would be consumed by marking deterministic exercises. But ample tutorial and examination-marking assistance was available in the SOE for those who wanted to use assessment methods that involved substantial written work: as enrolments soared on Behavioural and Evolutionary Economics, I ceased doing all the marking and running all the tutorial groups myself. Instead, I delegated a growing proportion of the tutorial groups and marking to wonderful teams of tutors of the highest calibre, all of whom were alumni of the course – and this was in the context of a subject in which, by this stage, the tutorials were timetable, and often ran, for two hours. Had they wished to do so, orthodox colleagues could have set more authentic assignment tasks of the kind that were being set in 2010. That they did not do so seemed to result from operating with different mindsets from their predecessors, fostered by their education in North American universities. I do not think that what my recently recruited orthodox UQ colleagues were doing was at all unusual.

The difference between the assessment systems of orthodox and heterodox subjects had significant impacts on which kinds of students elected to take heterodox subjects. In essence, non-European international students rarely elected to take subjects that entailed open-ended tasks, written work, and creative and critical thinking. Such subjects would naturally also scare off domestic students who still had a long way to go along the Perry Progression; they could also seem unattractive to technically gifted students who were aiming to maximise their grade-point averages and felt that this would be easier to do via subjects whose assessment tasks were technical in nature. The impact that freedom of choice had on the kind of students that I got was nowhere clearer than with Evolution of Economic Systems, which was an elective for third-year Bachelor of Economics undergraduates but compulsory in the Master of Development Economics. The latter included many students from China, whereas the former had virtually none.

Differences between orthodox and heterodox approaches to assessment modes become increasingly significant as the number of subjects that involve open-ended problems and writing tasks falls. Although some students will be delighted to discover that not all subjects operate in the modern orthodox manner, a heterodox instructor will tend to find that fewer of those who enrol have any other experience of pluralism and writing-based assessments. With fewer students having got very far along the Perry Progression, it is likely to become harder to generate final grade statistics with higher grade proportions on a par with those achieved by one's orthodox colleagues. Insofar as word gets around that it is harder to score highly on heterodox-style courses, enrolments will tend to suffer further.

It is possible that economics is not the only discipline in which a drift toward artificial, deterministic assessment tasks has been taking place. By the time that I conducted my comparison between 2010 and 2018 assessment methods, senior management at UQ were already several years into trying to ensure that staff across the university appreciated the importance of 'authentic' assessment tasks as means for preparing UQ students to be able to 'create change' after they graduated. Messages from the Deputy Vice-Chancellor (Academic) were amplified within the Faculty of Business, Economics and Law by the Deputy Dean (Academic), and a hitherto-unfamiliar breed of support staff called 'learning designers' were brought in to help ensure that students did indeed get to experience 'authentic' assessment tasks.

When Daniel Zizzo arrived at UQ as the SOE's new head in October 2018, I sent him a memo that I had written in relation to the challenges that the drift away from open-ended, real-world-focused assessment tasks posed for the economics major in the BA programme, and I found that he, too, already saw the cultivation of 'authentic' assessments as a significant part of his mission. He then ensured that the issue received discussion at some of the major planning meetings held in 2019. These meetings were attended not merely by all academic staff but also by 'learning designers' from the Faculty. Around the time that I retired, the SOE hired its own 'learning designer' and, while this book was being written, a workshop programme for sharing expertise on the design of 'authentic' assessment tasks was established. No doubt, achieving the desired transition is also part of the remit of the Director of Education position that Daniel Zizzo established in the SOE soon after his arrival, an office that, within a couple of years, was given added weight by being put in the hands of a senior member of academic staff with a strong record of commitment to teaching excellence.

This scale of commitment to 'authentic' assessments is something that institutions that are smaller and less resource-rich than UQ might have trouble affording, and I have every hope that the mission will be successful in the long run. But we need to be mindful that, in the context of economics, this kind of mission is aimed at changing the dominant culture of the discipline, where mainstream staff operate within a research programme that does not readily accommodate fuzzy, open-ended resource allocation problems. As UQ's senior managers appear to recognise, this is not something that can be addressed successfully by taking a heavy-handed 'micro-management' approach of tightening academic job specifications and zealously monitoring staff to ensure they comply with directives and formally approved subject specifications. This is because staff who resent being denied the freedom that they expected to have to 'do their own thing' as teachers may be readily able to move elsewhere, the more so, the higher their calibre. When university managers are in the business of 'herding cats', they have to play the long game. While they are playing it, heterodox staff who never went down the road of setting abstract, deterministic assessment tasks, and who will be the most open to making their assessments even more 'authentic' (for example, by moving from essays to role-play report-writing tasks) will be the odd ones out and most at risk of losing students who prefer to avoid the challenges of open-ended problem-solving.

Pluralistic PhD Projects

In my time at UQ, I served as an advisor to ten PhD students, but only six of them stayed the distance and graduated (in one case, at Bond University rather than UQ, due to the principal advisor moving to a law chair at Bond). One gave up within a year, whereas three others withdrew as the mid-term review approached. The comments that I made at the start of Chapter 4 about the kind of person who may be wise not to enrol in a PhD programme in economics were informed by my experiences with these four research students. In each case, they went on to careers in consulting and/or teaching. The projects of those who completed were all unusual by mainstream standards. I will end this section on my UQ teaching experiences by commenting about what these research students did, as this may provide food for thought about the kinds of pluralistic and heterodox PhDs that can be undertaken.

I have already mentioned my first start-to-finish role with Joseph Clark's (2007) experimental analysis of retirement savings services as a confusopoly. This could readily have opened the door to a career as an academic or industry regulator, but instead he has become a professional in the industry that he focused on in his thesis. Working with Joseph was not my first UQ role as a PhD advisor. That opportunity came with a project by Lauchlan Mackinnon (2006) that was already underway when I arrived. It was a study of the social construction of economic man. It had started out as a philosophy and economics project with a philosopher as the principal advisor, but it evolved more into a contribution to the history of economic thought. Lauchlan seemed to be taking his PhD as a purely ludic experience, for his career interests were in change management. His thesis was the last that I supervised that was submitted in hard copy, but it has since been digitised by UQ Library, making his contribution readily available even though he did not attempt to publish any papers from it.

A very different cross-disciplinary PhD was the one that was completed at Bond University, by Peter Macmillan (2015). It was a law and economics thesis that used verbal protocol analysis to study differences in the thinking styles of experienced and recently qualified competition lawyers. I had no doubts that it was going to be the impressive piece of work that it turned out to be, as Peter had performed very well as one of my students at the University of Tasmania and had gone on to have a very successful career as a Hong Kong-based competition lawyer. His success as a lawyer had enabled him to retire in his forties and his PhD was his way of beginning to put something back into the legal profession to help with the training of competition lawyers. There were indeed significant differences between seasoned and rookie competition lawyers in how they thought aloud as they each spent 45 minutes perusing summaries of several in-process cases that were before the Australian Competition and Consumer Commission and considered which of them would be likely to be taken to court.

Both the projects on which I advised to completion between those of Joseph Clark and Peter Macmillan were pluralistic empirical contributions, but they were set in different contexts. The first was by Ti-Ching Peng (2009), who is now a professor in the Department of Real Estate and Built Environment at Taiwan's National Taipei University. She originally came to UQ to study for a coursework master's degree, the thesis component of which Jason Potts and I supervised. After this, she stayed to work on her PhD with me as her principal advisor and Jason – in his first PhD advisor role – as her associate advisor. Her master's thesis was on the dynamics of housing prices in Brisbane (Peng 2004). While Ti-Ching was working on her PhD, the three of us published a paper that emerged from talking about how the decision rules that buyers of investment properties used could get degraded as they spread socially. To me, this 'decision rule cascade' perspective complemented Minsky's (1975) analysis of financial instability, so we initially sent the paper to the *Journal of Post Keynesian Economics*. However, we had omitted to anchor it to any contributions by the then-editor, Paul Davidson. It was rejected, and we then sent it to the *Journal of Economic Psychology* (where it was published as Earl, Peng and Potts, 2007) – an outlet more highly ranked on the ABDC list but where it was less likely to be noticed by Post Keynesian economists.

In her master's thesis, Ti-Ching analysed the processes by which increases in residential property prices spread across Brisbane between 1998 and 2003. She did so by following my suggestion that she could put the quarterly data she had for median house prices in Brisbane's 190 suburbs into an approximate map consisting of cells in an Excel spreadsheet, with the Brisbane River being marked as a bold line at the boundary of the cells representing suburbs that bordered it. For each quarter for which she had data, she produced a separate sheet, which she then turned into a colourful three-dimensional map on a PowerPoint slide by colour-coding the cells according to their median property values. If one worked rapidly through the set of these slides in sequence, it was like viewing a movie of how prices rose through time. In effect, it was an exercise in what one might call institutionalist economic geography, whereby the focus was on spotting patterns rather than formal testing of hypotheses that had been formed deductively. But it was difficult at that time to see how it might be turned into a journal article.

In today's world, where journals permit supplementary material to be made available online with published articles, the Excel and PowerPoint files could be submitted as well as the text that explained the method and analysed what was going on, and one could even upload a video of the process by recording a screen-capture movie of the slides in rapid succession. However, a complementary approach to using the data would have been to employ spatial econometrics to test hypotheses about the relationship between a suburb's median price and price movements in previous periods in adjacent suburbs. We discovered the potential for the latter when Michelle Baddeley, a UQ psychology and economics alumnus, gave a seminar as a visiting speaker and presented work of the latter kind that she had been conducting in Cambridge using UK data.

Ti-Ching chose a different kind of real estate-related project for her PhD, namely a study of the decisions of property renovators in Brisbane (Peng, 2009). This was heterodox and pluralist in multiple ways: it used primary data from a large-sample mailed questionnaire; it explored the empirical payoffs to adding proxies for psychological factors when modelling over-capitalisation and choices to renovate via do-it-yourself versus hiring contractors; and, in attempting to apply ideas from the literature on vertical integration by firms to DIY and outsourcing by households, it did so via both Williamson's (1975, 1985) neo-institutionalist and Richardson's (1972) capabilities-based perspectives. Ti-Ching and I later (Earl and Peng, 2012) labelled this kind of work as 'Trojan horse pluralism': at first sight it can look like conventional applied econometric analysis, but it has potential to draw orthodox economists (and journal referees) into being open to heterodox lines of thinking.

The second pluralistic applied economics PhD on which I served as the principal advisor was by Mary Hedges (2010), a teaching-focused economics lecturer from Auckland. Like Peter Macmillan, she mostly worked remotely on her PhD. She wanted to enrol at an Australian university because she had discovered something that I had known for a long time, namely that New Zealand citisens, like Australians, were not required to pay tuition fees for their PhDs, whereas they would have to pay tuition fees if they were research students at New Zealand universities. Unlike one of my non-completing students, who was likewise a teaching-focused academic, Mary was not being pushed to do a PhD by the university for which she worked. Rather, she was keen to understand how students in New Zealand made their tertiary education choices, and she saw this as an opportunity to conduct a pluralistic study that explored both the rational choice, human capital perspective and behavioural ideas that took account of social pressures, norms, and social embeddedness. Her study employed primary data from a questionnaire and, unusually in economics, made use of factor analysis. Like Ti-Ching, Mary showed the value of adding behavioural proxy variables to orthodox models.

The final research student whom I advised all the way to his doctorate was Brendan Markey-Towler. Brendan had produced a remarkable UQ Bachelor of Economics (Honours) dissertation under John Foster's supervision after getting hooked on evolutionary economics via John's authoritative version of Evolution of Economic Systems. Formally, John was the principal advisor of Brendan's PhD, even though we both served on a 50-percent basis. Both John (playing 'good cop') and myself (playing 'bad cop') often met separately with Brendan, but we met as a trio for rehearsals of Brendan's progress review presentations. Brendan produced his PhD thesis on schedule despite also publishing journal articles based on side projects at a faster pace than I could make time to read them. His thesis (Markey-Towler, 2017) attempted to follow, in a highly mathematical way, the adaptive complex systems track that Jason Potts (2000) had mapped for evolutionary economics in his prise-winning PhD-based book. John and I had high hopes that Brendan would be 'another Jason' in terms of academic achievement but instead of taking up the academic opportunities that he was offered, he initially opted to work in Brisbane in the private sector despite already having had papers published in the *Cambridge Journal of Economics*, the *Journal of Evolutionary Economics* (twice) and the *Journal of Institutional Economics* (twice).

8.3   ADMINISTRATION AND SERVICE

When an established academic joins a very large department, the news about administrative duties can be good or bad. The scale of the department makes it possible for the departmental head to spread administrative duties around so that many people have minor regular duties or irregular bursts of more intensive activity. But some tasks may be on a large scale because of the scale of the department's operations and may not be easily divisible. This may make it very difficult for the officeholder to get much research done even if the department has a workload allocation formula that is designed to ensure that staff have similar scope for conducting research. This is due to a problem that Shackle would have appreciated: it is very difficult for designers of such formulae to imagine all the things that an officeholder may have to address.

In my time at UQ, my administrative duties were generally interesting, and on average the load seemed fair and reasonable, but its variance did affect significantly the flow of my research.

When I began at UQ, the news on the administrative front was unexpectedly good: John Foster was able to give me virtually no internal administration because of my external service role at co-editor of the *Journal of Economic Psychology*. Even after I stepped down from that role in early 2004, I enjoyed nearly three years of negligible administrative duties. But at the start of 2007, when I had got my research on a roll, I was given the role of coordinator of the SOE's PhD programme. This put a brake on my research until the next head, Flavio Menezes, relieved me of that role in mid-2009. My research then picked up again as my administrative duties were again very low until part of the PhD coordination role came back to me from 2013 to 2016, and very low again in 2017 and 2018. But in 2019, the PhD coordination role came back in full. In 2018, before that role came back to me, I had begun a stint as the SOE's representative at the Faculty of Human and Social Sciences board that oversees UQ's Bachelor of Arts programme. Work in relation to this stepped up, too, for 2019–2020 via the 'BA Reset' that aimed to standardise the BA format across its many disciplines and give more choice to students. So, in 2019, my research again pretty much ground to a halt. Daniel Zizzo, who joined as head in October 2018, attempted to compensate for this in 2020 by relieving me of Behavioural and Evolutionary Economics but it then proved necessary to allocate to me half of a new fourth-year Bachelor of Politics, Philosophy and Economics honours unit on 'wicked problems' and policymaking. I was glad that I had not signed a contract for the behavioural economics magnum opus that I had started writing in mid-2017, for I made virtually no progress on it between February 2019 and July 2020.

In this section, I reflect on the two periods of PhD administration, which provide a sense of how PhD processes evolved and of the difficulties of importing US-style economics PhD structures into Australia.

PhD Administration (1): Improving Completion Rates
In 2007, when I became the SOE's 'RHD coordinator', the SOE had about 40 research students. The RHD aspect of the title referred to 'research higher degrees' because it was possible to enrol in either an MPhil or a PhD, though the former were very rare indeed. I soon discovered that PhD confirmations could be stressful experiences not merely for research students but also for PhD administrators. At that time, RHD students were assessed by their respective supervisory teams and the RHD coordinator, who reported their confirmation recommendations on a form that was sent to the Graduate School for approval. This could be an uncomfortable process for the RHD coordinator if the student's project seemed rather unoriginal but was being endorsed by the advisory team.

As a non-mainstream economist in the RHD coordinator role, I felt that if I refused to sign confirmation forms for mainstream projects, the supervisory team would probably complain to the head of school that I was insufficiently well versed in the field to be able to make such an important judgment. Yet if I did not resist projects whose methods seemed to be of dubious value in the chosen context, I suspected that the completed theses might end up getting externally examined by assessors who would be as blind as the supervisors to heterodox perspectives on their value. In these kinds of situations, I did not hold back from raising critical perspectives in the feedback that I wrote for the students, and I did have some tense situations with supervisory teams. However, I ended up signing off projects that the supervisory teams insisted were OK. In these sorts of cases, challenging the nature of the projects was tantamount to challenging my colleagues at least as much as their research students. I suppose that putting my objections on record, while signing off the project, was a kind of pluralism, but it left me very uneasy.

Back then, the system for monitoring and speeding up the post-confirmation progress of the SOE's research students also seemed problematic. It centred on the completion of annual report forms that were signed by the student, the supervisors and the RHD coordinator before being sent to the UQ Graduate School. I soon realised that these forms might help to explain why the SOE's research students were in many cases taking far too long to reach the thesis submission stage. Often, they only got there after switching to part-time study or withdrawing temporarily to buy themselves more time. The problem was that the forms were not conducive to students or their supervisors being frank about each other's performance. If students used the annual review forms to register their dissatisfaction with their supervisors, this could affect the kind of report that the supervisors wrote and which the student was required to read before signing the form. But if the supervisors made adverse comments about the quality and/or quantity of the student's work, or about the student's willingness to respond to the supervisors' feedback, the student could then use the process to demand a new supervisor or a new supervisory team. Most of the time, both sides avoided starting a fight, even where the pace of progress seemed to me to imply that things that should have been said were not being said on the forms.

Soon, it became apparent that the Graduate School's new dean had a similar view of the limitations of this long-established process and was on a mission to introduce a better system. It would operate along the lines set out at the start of Section 4.4, i.e., supervisors would become merely advisors; students would be required to pass confirmation, mid-term and thesis review milestones that each entailed the submission of written work, an oral presentation, and an interview with closed, in-confidence components; and, at these milestones, the progress of the students would be assessed by staff who had appropriate expertise but were not members of the advisory team.

It fell to me to 'sell' the proposed milestone process to the SOE. Things did not go well when I gave a presentation on what it entailed: there were strong objections that it was going to chew up the time of many staff in assessor roles. Most of my audience seemed to think that they should be trusted to operate as professionals within the existing system and that I was failing to defend the SOE against the Graduate School. A few weeks later, after two and a half years at RHD coordinator, I was relieved of the role, but my successor did not escape the task of overseeing the implementation of the Graduate School's milestone system. A few years later, the RHD coordinator role was divided between two members of the SOE: the RHD coordinator now handled admissions and the SOE's role in the scholarship allocation process, while the progress of students was overseas by the SOE's 'milestone convenor'. For the period 2013–2016, the latter became my role, usually consuming a Friday morning or afternoon each week.

As I expected, the milestone system was a major improvement on the system that it replaced, but no students ever made any critical comments about the quality of advisory inputs, not even in a few cases where advisors acted as if they were largely unfamiliar with the documents their students had submitted: during the oral presentation, they asked really basic questions whose answers they should have known via past meetings with the students or from reading earlier drafts of the confirmation documents. Perhaps these advisors were indeed 'acting' that way as a means of forcing the students to offer verbal explanations of what they were doing. But perhaps not. What was clear in such cases was that the students had not been put through the kind of dress rehearsal process that some advisory teams required of their students. At dress rehearsals with my PhD students, my 'bad cop' act included not merely critiquing the presentation slides and delivery but also trying to present the student with questions that orthodox colleagues might raise. The latter was important, for the withering of pluralism could make it difficult to come up with milestone assessors who were familiar with heterodox approaches but were not members of the advisory team.

PhD Administration (2): Back to Pluralism

The milestone convenor role ensured that I was on the SOE Research Committee at the time an attempt was made to remodel the SOE's PhD programme along US lines. My orthodox colleagues were strongly opposed to the UK model that Australia had followed, whereby advanced coursework was not compulsory (though many of the SOE's PhD students did follow suggestions from their advisors that they should take advanced core subjects from the Bachelor of Economics (Honours) year), and where the thesis was essentially a monograph. John Quiggin, the SOE's most senior professor, kicked off this process by arguing that advanced coursework was necessary since, 'Doing a PhD in economics isn't like, say, doing one in English literature where you spend three years among the library bookstacks and emerge with a thesis about Jane Austen.'

In saying this, John Quiggin neatly captured the modern mainstream view. However, it seemed to me that, from a pluralist standpoint, we might be wise to recognise that some kinds of economics PhDs do indeed need (some) advanced formal coursework and/or cutting-edge training in econometrics but that other PhDs might make valuable contributions based on years spent 'among the bookstacks'. To heterodox economists, requiring all PhD students to take a standard US-style set of courses that only cover the dominant approach smacks of a kind of initiation rite to enable entry to a cult, supports the cult's succession and growth processes, and excludes those who do not see two years of investment in receiving the initiation as a worthwhile way to spend their time. But it does offer two clear benefits to those who do not intend to employ the material they are forced to master: one is that if they decide that being heterodox is too hard in terms of its career implications, or they later opt to work in contexts where mainstream tools seem to have advantages, they can reinvent themselves as mainstream economists; the other benefit is that they will end up in a stronger position to offer critiques of mainstream thinking and thus have a better chance of getting their non-mainstream perspectives taken seriously. Indeed, Quiggin himself has been able to stray from extreme orthodoxy without losing credibility because his orthodox colleagues know that, whenever he wishes, he can do their kind of work.

But the author of *Zombie Economics: How Dead Ideas Still Walk Among Us* (Quiggin, 2012) also wanted to enhance the SOE's global credibility. He was concerned that the SOE would find it difficult to attract top-grade research students and staff if it did not offer a US-style PhD programme. However, the SOE would have to think carefully about the cost of getting these benefits, for the Australian rules regarding tuition fees and study visas did not align with the US system of offering teaching assistant roles to enable PhD students to pay their way: requiring PhD students to take a longer programme would get nowhere unless longer scholarships were offered.

It was evident from this meeting, and from subsequent ones, that my orthodox colleagues had a clear idea of the kind of programme that they wanted. But there was a problem to be surmounted: their vision was for a two-year advanced master's, followed by three years of writing a thesis consisting of papers fit for high-ranking journals, whereas Australia's

Federal Government had a PhD funding model built on the idea that PhD scholarships were for programmes in which dissertations would be submitted for examination around the middle of the fourth year, with the examination process being completed by the end of the fourth year. As a result, it was decided that the prerequisite for entering the SOE's PhD programme would be the completion, to a satisfactory standard, of a *one-year* Master of Advanced Economics (which everyone called the 'MAE') that consisted of eight compulsory subjects. The second year of advanced coursework would take up much of the first year of the PhD. It would consist of a further three papers in the first semester, followed in the second semester by a 'PhD colloquium' of weekly seminars at which the research students would, in effect, offer role-play presentations of recent cutting-edge papers by leading economists, as if the students themselves had been the authors.

One year of MAE plus four years of a PhD whose first year consistent mainly of further coursework certainly added up to the desired five years of graduate-level study. But it begged some big questions. The first was whether the SOE would be wise to fund the MAE year, given the risk that those whom it funded might not succeed in winning PhD scholarships within the competitive pool of disciplines to which economics scholarship applicants were assigned. This might also mean that the SOE would have trouble securing research students who found they could win five-year scholarships from rival institutions. Another issue was the compatibility of the proposed programme with the Graduate School's milestone schedule: with very demanding coursework in the first semester of the PhD, and the colloquium to contend with in the second semester, would students be able to get a good enough idea of their thesis projects to enable them to pass the confirmation milestone at the end of that year or, at the latest, by March in the second year?

I was left unclear about how these questions were going to be addressed. Initially, when the programme went ahead, I did not have to worry about them, as I was relieved of the position of milestone convenor at the end of 2016. The role was folded back into that of the RHD coordinator, who would now also oversee the new MAE programme. I indicated that I would, at the very least, be perfectly happy to continue as convenor for the remaining milestones of the existing students, but it seemed that I was surplus to requirements. In the following two years, there ceased to be signs that the milestone process was continuing: the flow of emails inviting academic staff to attend milestone seminars ceased. This led me to suspect, correctly, that wriggle-room was being exploited: it turned out that, in effect, the clock had been turned back to circa-2007 for the PhD progress review system in the SOE, except that the current milestone forms were being filled out for the Graduate School. The wriggle-room came because the forms did not have to be signed by the external milestone assessors, which would have been problematic once assessors from outside the advisory team ceased to be used.

By the start of 2019, when the SOE's new head, Daniel Zizzo, put me back into the coordinator role, 'research higher degrees' had become 'higher degrees by research' in Graduate School parlance. This time, therefore, I was the HDR coordinator and needed to get to know the latest Dean of the Graduate School, Professor Alastair McEwan. He turned out not to be a fan of the MAE-based PhD. Though his own field was in the biological sciences, he seemed to take a social science view of economics – indeed, he pleasantly surprised me by saying that he had been reading Skidelsky's (2013) biography of Keynes. From the perspective of heterodox economics, this was very encouraging, but it also seemed not to be conducive to him entertaining any long-term idea for bundling PhD scholarships with the SOE's MAE scholarships.

During 2019, a key part of my HDR coordinator role was to prepare the paperwork for Daniel Zizzo's vision of a pluralistic PhD programme and help him 'sell' it to the SOE. I liked what he had in mind, namely a 'dual pathway PhD' in which students would take either the US-style version with the MAE prerequisite, or a PhD with a 'tailored' (possibly even empty) set of coursework units recommended by their advisory team. But, once I discovered what had happened to the progress review process, I realised that it was also going to be necessary to complete the paperwork setting out how the SOE was in future going to follow the Graduate School's milestone process, 'sell' it to the SOE Executive Committee, get it approved by the Graduate School and then ensure that colleagues in the SOE implemented what had been approved.

It wasn't quite Groundhog Day with the milestone process, for matters went much more smoothly with academic colleagues this time around; they had enough information overload already in terms of getting their heads round the pluralistic/dual-pathway PhD. The biggest challenge concerned the problem of getting an acceptable return on the SOE's investment in MAE scholarships and attracting students to the

MAE pathway when we could not say that success in the MAE guaranteed a PhD scholarship.

As I have foreshadowed, the HDR coordinator role resulted in an eighteen-month halt in progress on my behavioural magnum opus. This had much to do with the scholarship allocation process. This had become the key determinant of the SOE's intake of PhD students, for we were no longer in a world in which scholarships from the Federal Government were freely available to Australian citisens and permanent residents who attained first-class honours at the bachelor level and where overseas students were either self-funded or sponsored by their employers. The schools where scholarship recipients would be based had to rank the applicants that they hoped to host, but they were not each given a quota of scholarships to allocate (based on, say, how much revenue they generated). Rather, it was a Graduate School-run committee, on which the SOE had no representation, that decided which applicants were successful. Under the prevailing system, the SOE was getting fewer research students than it had when I was the RHD coordinator, and the dual pathways for entering the SOE's PhD programme meant that, from the 2020 intake onward, those applying via the MAE pathway, with SOE scholarships for the MAE, would henceforth also have to compete against those trying to enter on the non-MAE pathway.

There was much drama at the end of 2019 when the much-feared scenario of good MAE graduates not winning PhD scholarships turned into reality. Consoling and advising the distraught students consumed the time that I had hoped to have for writing before UQ shut for the Christmas/New Year break. In January 2020, I was again diverted from writing by the process whereby the SOE and Graduate School came up with further scholarships outside the regular allocation round, and then by trying to ensure that the students in question could return in time to start their PhD coursework or what could be done if they were delayed. At the end of 2020, I was glad to be packing up my office ahead of retiring, rather than facing scope for a re-run of that scenario with the added complications associated with pandemic-related travel restrictions. I wrote a detailed set of handover notes to help reduce the burden my successor faced.

8.4   EVOLUTION OF A HETERODOX BEHAVIOURAL ECONOMIST (5)

Despite my move to the much better research environment that UQ offered, my early years at UQ did not entail any major advances in my thinking as a behavioural economist. Initially, aside from getting the 'market for preferences' paper (Earl and Potts, 2004) through the refereeing process, my focus was on consolidating what I had started trying to do towards the end of my time at Lincoln University. One area, which I pursued with Tim Wakeley, entailed trying to develop Jason Potts's (2000) very abstract Graph Theory-inspired connectionist perspective on heterodox economics into something that was more accessible. We sought to do this by finding examples of its practical significance. Our pluralistic business economics textbook (Earl and Wakeley, 2005) provided a venue for this, as did a couple of papers (Earl, 2003, and Earl and Wakeley, 2010b) from this perspective. Tim moved from the University of Bath to a senior lectureship at Griffith University in Queensland in 2006 and we hoped that we would do a lot of collaborative work. Unfortunately, Tim had a more challenging teaching load, spread between three campuses on the Gold Coast and in Brisbane, and I then began my first major stint in PhD administration. As a result, we achieved fewer joint outputs than we had hoped and our best papers were published with long delays, compounded by slow refereeing processes: the first version of our 2010 connectionist paper was written early in 2006, as was the original version of our paper showing the significance of non-compensatory decision rules for product development strategies. The latter was published as Earl and Wakeley (2010a).

Old and New Behavioural Economics
One of the papers in which I sought to clarify where I had got to in my view of behavioural economics was 'Economics and psychology in the twenty-first century', written for a plenary presentation at the September 2003 conference organised by the *Cambridge Journal of Economics* to celebrate the centenary of the Cambridge Economics Tripos. However, this was very much my personal, normative view of how economics should embrace psychology. I devoted the third section of this paper to an attempt to characterise psychological economics as a Lakatos (1970)-inspired scientific research programme consisting of sets of hard-core

axioms and 'do' and 'don't' heuristics for conducting research. Until 2007, I remained as bemused about what was going on in behavioural economics as I had been in February 2001 on seeing behavioural economics being hailed in the *New York Times* as a new field without any reference to Herbert Simon's contributions and Nobel award.

In 2007, I started to realise that my work as a behavioural economist, and the work that inspired it, was heterodox in a way that the contributions that were gaining traction were not. Coming to this realisation was an unexpected consequence of Bruce Littleboy and I organising the annual conference of the History of Economic Thought Society of Australia (HETSA), whose proceedings are available as Earl and Littleboy (eds) (2008). Rather than offering a regular paper, I used a gap in the programme to give a short, unscripted talk about the need to be careful with search terms when using Google in work on the history of economic thought. I illustrated my theme by noting that, if one were studying behavioural economics, the search results that Google displayed differed considerably depending on whether one typed in 'behavioural' or 'behavioral'. I then wondered aloud about whether the lack of impact of my work among the latest generation of behavioural economists was because it was written in UK English rather than US English and was therefore being disadvantaged in Google searches conducted by those who used the US spelling of 'behavioural'. My argument was part of my bigger concern about the consequences of US academics operating in a parochial manner when consulting journal articles, for virtually none of them had cited my *Economic Journal* survey article on economics and psychology (Earl, 1990a): if they were happy to rely on Rabin's (1998) survey in the *Journal of Economic Literature*, they would fail to discover the different sources that I had considered.

In other words, I was trying to make sense of how behavioural economics was evolving based on cumulating satisficing processes driven by differences in the search rules that scholars were using. The discussion that my talk provoked led a participant from Western Australia (Greg Moore, if I recall correctly) to ask if I had come across Esther-Mirjam Sent's (2004) article in *History of Political Economy* on how psychology was being readmitted to economics in a rather limited way. Although Sent and I had been corresponding a few years before she wrote her (2004) paper, we had then fallen out of touch and I had not previously known of this paper. As soon as the conference was over, I read Sent's article and realised that I was working in the tradition of what she called an 'old' behavioural economist, whereas those whom she labelled as 'new' behavioural economists had a different approach to behavioural economics.

My view of how the economy functions began with the problems of information and knowledge that real-world agents have to deal with, and I considered how people operate when facing these problems. Such ways of operating range from highly effective systems of rules and shortcuts, through to operating systems that can lead decision-makers to end up with outcomes that are much worse than they might readily have obtained if they were using different rules. What fascinated me were the differences in functionality of the rule systems that people use, how people come to use the systems of rules that make them the individuals they are, and why they differ in their willingness to embrace new rules if their existing ones are no longer serving them well or new kinds of behaviour become possible. I saw some rules as being inherited as part of human nature, some as being acquired socially, and others as being personal creations, with the structural relationships that people assign between the rules they have in their repertoires determining how clashes between rules are resolved and the admissibility they assign to potential additions to their repertoires of rules.

This rule-based view of human action applies to what people believe, to the processes by which people go about gathering information, and to how they choose given the information they have obtained. It implies a growth of knowledge view of human action, in which the quality of choices is limited by what the decision-maker currently knows but can improve as the decision-maker's knowledge grows via the formation of new connections and/or as the decision-maker acquires better-functioning heuristics for handling complex situations. Mindful of this, I had come to focus on current best-practice in the context in question as the benchmark by which one should assess the decision-making competence of consumers, much in the way that Leibenstein (1966, 1976) seemed to think about the efficiency of firms. Indeed, in a training session on behavioural economics that I provided in Wellington for the New Zealand Ministry of Economic Development and Ministry of Consumer Affairs in September 2005, I explored parallels between the reasons that Leibenstein identified for the failure of firms to attain best-practice levels of productivity and efficiency, and reasons why consumers may under-achieve. In other words, Leibenstein's '*X*-

inefficiency' concept should be extended to the analysis of consumer welfare (see Earl, 2005c, 2007).

With this way of doing behavioural economics, I had essentially abandoned the orthodox normative view of rational choice: after noting its inapplicability in many situations, I began afresh, employing psychology that began with the problem of coping with a problematic world rather than by assuming that people were trying to optimise in terms of a given objective function. From my vantage point, real-world choice problems were usually open-ended and had to be closed by applying rules to avoid decision paralysis.

Via Sent's (2004) paper, I came to realise that 'new' behavioural economics was essentially a set of ad hoc modifications to the established view of choice in closed settings. The modifications had been derived by studying behaviour experimentally in close-choice settings (such as lottery choice experiments). These experiments had been used to infer that humans have evolved to use a set of heuristics to cope with real-world cognitive challenges – heuristics that a 'fully rational' economic agent would not need to use. Real people therefore are predicted to behave in systematically different ways from how rational choice theory says they should behave. In other words, the heuristics that are part of human nature 'bias' behaviour away from what an 'econ' would do, with the 'bias' being conceptualised with reference to 'fully rational' behaviour, given a pre-specified view of the situation being analysed, rather than using current best-practice behaviour as the point of reference.

I thereby realised the 'new' behavioural economics is much more conservative than the 'old'. My kind of behavioural economics readily embraces heuristics that appear to be part of human nature and capable of driving predictable departures of behaviour from best-practice ways that some people have figured out by going beyond human nature, whereas adherents to the 'new' behavioural economics would have to give up the full-rationality reference point to embrace the perspective that has driven the work of 'old' behavioural economists such as myself. With its focus on a repertoire of heuristics that are part of human nature, the 'new' approach also does not clash with the orthodox economists' preference for building models based on representative agents, whereas in the 'old' approach, as in marketing, one is interested in individuals or, at least, groups of individuals with similar ways of operating. It is thus not surprising that the 'new' behavioural economics has been much easier to sell to orthodox economists, especially by those armed, as Thaler and his colleagues have been, with evidence of 'anomalies' (in terms of orthodoxy) that could be explained with reference to specific heuristics.

The Mobile Phone Connection Plan Choice Project

Toward the end of 2008, Lana Friesen and I started discussing ideas for possible grant-funded projects. This might surprise readers who remember me referring in Section 7.2 to Lana as the person who inherited Microeconomics for Business and Marketing from me at Lincoln University and proceeded to turn it into a mainstream intermediate microeconomics subject. However, Lana had evolved from specialising in environmental economics into a 'new' behavioural economist and had developed expertise in experimental economics. In 2007 she left Lincoln and joined the UQ SOE, giving up a Lincoln senior lectureship for a UQ lectureship and a much-improved teaching and research environment. We reckoned that we could make a good research team for a project in applied behavioural economics, with my wider knowledge of behavioural economics and its research methods being complemented by Lana's knowledge of conventional experimental economics methods and her statistical expertise. The key challenge was to find an original project for which we could readily make a case to the Australian Research Council (ARC) and its referees.

My initial suggestion was that we might study resistance of commuters to switching to transport modes that would enhance their physical fitness and reduce their environmental impacts. I could readily imagine exploring this area via a large-sample survey and a small-sample application of repertory grid and construct laddering methods from personal construct psychology. However, this field was already well-researched, and it did not seem to be well suited for applying experimental methods. We therefore decided to go with Lana's suggestion, namely a study of how, and how well, consumers cope with the challenges of trying to choose connection service plans for their mobile (cell) phones without ending up wasting money and having nasty 'bill shock' surprises. The risk of error seemed enormous as there were many providers, most of whom offered a wide range of plans that came with contractual 'fine print'. The market for mobile phone connection services plans thus appeared to be a 'confusopoly'.

We then set about the task of writing our research proposal as if we were conducting research for an article to submit to a top journal. It was crucial that we could demonstrate we knew the existing literature, had identified a significant gap to fill, and were familiar with best practice in terms of the research methods that we intended to employ. The process of researching the project consumed much of the 2008–2009 summer. To me, it seemed rather like getting a PhD project into shape to sail through a confirmation process, whereas unsuccessful ARC Discovery Grant applications that Jason Potts and I had made in my first few years at UQ were assembled without such rigour. I hoped that this time around, unlike with the first effort with Jason, I would not be written off by referees as 'someone who has not lived up to his initial promise'.

It was an easy project to justify based on its prospective benefits to the Australian population: the project would pay for itself even if it only resulted in the average Australian resident saving a few cents on their spending on mobile phone connection services. Late in 2009, we were informed that our application had been successful and that we had been awarded AUD394,000 over the period 2010–2013. However, it took much longer than this to deploy the funds that we had been awarded.

It is possible that the project has had a positive return based purely on consumers reading the three blog posts that I wrote about mobile phone service contracts while we were working on it. By September 2022, these blog posts had only had a total of 2773 views. Yet, if each viewer had on average saved about AUD125.00, they would have matched the ARC's AUD349,000 investment in the project. It is not inconceivable that this could have happened, for such savings could accumulate in just two years, even if the viewers of the blog posts on average only saved AUD5.00 per month by taking note of what I had written about how to calculate the costs of using one's phone, how different kinds of contracts arrive at their monthly charges in different ways, and on the economics of buying an iPhone outright versus via a monthly mobile phone service contract.

These calculations make me feel rather happier about the returns to the project than I felt at the time we realised that the first phase of the project had largely failed after consuming over a third of our research budget. We had hoped to find out how much Australian consumers were spending on their mobile phone service contracts beyond what they needed to spend to get the services that they used. To do this, we used our research resources in two ways.

First, we designed a questionnaire that was completed online by a representative sample of over 1000 mobile phone users. This was administered by a market research company, and to reduce the risk of respondent fatigue, we followed the company's advice to limit our questionnaire to what could be answered in about 25 minutes. The questionnaire sought responses about which connection service offers our respondents were using, their rates of use of the various services (calls, SMS, data) and how they had chosen the offers they had taken up. We also asked respondents to answer several call-cost and bill-cost calculation questions, and to supply standard demographic information.

Secondly, we employed a full-time research assistant for two years, with her primary task being the construction of an Excel database covering the mobile phone plans that were offered in Australia at the time the online survey was conducted (which numbered over 800, from over 50 providers, even without also taking account of plans that included handsets). This was to be programmed to serve as a calculating engine to find the least-cost way of obtaining each respondent's mix of service usage. In our research proposal we suggested that, once constructed and working reliably, our Excel spreadsheet and calculating engine could be made publicly available to help consumers make more cost-effective choices of mobile phone service offers. We indicated that we hoped to keep the spreadsheet and calculating engine up to date as the project progressed and that, on completion of the project, it might then be handed over to a public agency for ongoing updating.

The ARC's referees did not suggest that our hopes of ongoing updating were wildly optimistic, but we soon realised that this was the case: the mobile phone service sector was characterised by frequent changes in the menu of offers, and we happened to be running our investigation of the sector at the time at which the adoption of smartphones led to a major shift of service plans toward a focus on data. That shift eventually made choices of mobile phone service plans rather more straightforward for many customers, with even the offers that only included a few gigabytes of data commonly allowing unlimited national calls and SMS usage. In a sense, then, our study was a contribution to economic history.

However, the failure of our attempt to use the survey and calculating engine to find out how much money Australian consumers were wasting on their mobile phone connection service contracts had nothing to do with whether we could keep updating the information we had about the set of available service offers. We were only trying to answer that question in respect of a point in time (late 2010) and we had archived all the relevant pages from the 50+ providers' websites while the online survey was running. Rather, our attempt to answer this question arose from the problem of bounded rationality that provided the study's rationale. It impinged on both the online survey and the Excel programming.

The programming involved different challenges for 'pre-paid' and 'post-paid' types of service offers. The former often caused complications by having credit expiry periods that were not based on calendar months, or by having credit carry-forward between months due to credit top-ups needing to be purchased part-way through a month, whereas the latter entailed monthly bills but multi-tier pricing. When our first research assistant resigned (without notice, on the day she was scheduled to move to a part-time contract after two years on a full-time contract), the Excel programming remained incomplete. However, enough of it had been completed and tested for Lana to begin to use it to test the quality of the usage data that our online respondents had supplied. She discovered that, in many cases, the responses given for usage rates and typical monthly outlays for the offers that our subjects claimed to have taken up were significantly at odds with the amounts the Excel calculating engine said they should have been having to spend per month. The implication was that, if our survey respondents had recalled correctly which plan they were using, many of them had a poor idea of their usage patterns and/or monthly outlays.

Clearly, we could have continued this part of the project after removing the roughly two-thirds of subjects whose data seemed to be blighted by defective recall, but there remained the problem of getting the programming completed and we were not clear how much more of the budget this might consume. Computing the per-capita needless overspending of Australians on mobile phone service contracts seemed less important to study than which types of plans were especially problematic for consumers to assess, how the ways that consumers took these kinds of decisions affected the quality of the outcomes, and the relative effectiveness of feasible policies aimed at ensuring consumers reduce the extent to which they waste money on needlessly expensive mobile phone service plans.

These were issues that we had proposed to study in the second and third phases of the project, via very different research methods. The second phase employed a pair of conventional multi-treatment economic experiments, both of which used stylised mobile phone service contracts in computer laboratory settings. Both experiments went largely as originally envisaged. The only problem was that we had significant delays in getting to run them. The delay started because the programme that the original research assistant had written for the lab failed to save the data and there was a significant hiatus before we were able to find a new research assistant on whom we felt we could rely.

The first experiment, reported in Friesen and Earl (2015), explored the impact that service plan formats and usage uncertainty had on the quality of plan choices. The choice environment was artificial, with probabilistic usage variability, easy switching between plans, and only seven plans between which to choose, but it showed the significant adverse impact that two-tier pricing schemes had on the costs that our subjects incurred, especially for those who had to contend periodically with usage spikes, even if they were free to experiment and learn by switching between service offers as the experimental 'months' passed. The second experiment, written up in Friesen and Earl (2020), tested the impact of a variety of policies – something that it is difficult for regulatory authorities to do via randomised or geographically segmented trials where products are being purchased online.

We designed the mobile phone service plans in these experiments with a view to seeing whether initial choices could be explained in terms of the use of plausible simple rules, such as 'try first the plan with the lowest cost for a two-minute call'. Otherwise, however, we deferred until the third phase the task of studying how research subjects went about choosing among rival plans.

In the grant application, we had envisaged that the project's third phase would employ the MOUSELAB software developed for research by Payne, Bettman and Johnson (1993) whereby subjects are presented with a multi-layered search environment that provides opportunities for them to click for different kinds of information. MOUSELAB automatically records the clicks that they make as they search within this environment. However, when the project was underway, I devised a much more naturalistic way of gathering information: we would set our research subjects the task of finding, among real plans, the cheapest pre-paid phone plan to service a particular usage remit, with our subjects each being given an hour to undertake the task and being required to think aloud as they did so. As in a conventional economics experiment, subjects would be rewarded according to how well they performed.

The third phase was thus an application of the verbal protocol analysis method set out in Ericsson and Simon (1993), but with some original twists. First, instead of working with short and relatively simple tasks, we would use a complicated, hour-long task that was very likely to prove cognitively exhausting. Our subjects did indeed become cognitively exhausted, and it was at times difficult to keep prodding them to 'keep talking' without seeming to harass them. Fortunately, I had realised that, if we were prepared to invest time in dealing with non-automated data collection, we could supplement verbal data with a screen-capture movie that recorded everything each subject did on the computer screen: Apple's Quicktime app made this very easy to do, and it made it much easier to understand how decisions were arrived at and to see how mistakes were made (for example, when scrolling too fast to notice information that was being sought, or failing, while slowly studying a screen, to acknowledge cues that should have been useful). But with 41 subjects, transcribing nearly 41 hours of 'thinking aloud' soundtracks and forensically analysing and categorising what happened on the screen in our Quicktime movies took a *very* long time.

The subjects in the third-phase experiment were divided into offline and online groups. The offline subjects searched within clones of provider websites that we had created from the webpages that we had archived at the end of 2010, whereas the online subjects were allowed to operate like real consumers. Subjects in the offline group were provided with a home page that contained an alphabetical list of links to each archived provider website, whereas the online subjects were simply given a Google search page as their starting point. The offline setting was clearly unusual, despite entailing real service contract offers, but the point of using it was to see how well subjects were able to choose, and how they went about the task, if forced to operate in a totally self-reliant manner (aside from us having provided the homepage list of links and letting subjects use the Apple laptop's calculator). This enabled us to get a picture of the difference that online market institutions – i.e., Google, discussion boards and product comparison websites – made to the quality of choices and how decisions were reached. The difference between what I decided to call 'self-reliant choices' and 'market-assisted choices' was the focus of the first paper from this part of the study (Earl, Friesen and Shadforth, 2017).

A second paper (Earl, Friesen and Shadforth, 2019) used the data from the Quicktime movies of the online subjects to explore what constituted 'procedural rationality', i.e., 'appropriate deliberation' (Simon, 1976) in this setting. This was done by compiling a list of 51 types of behaviour (divided into five groups) that we had observed some subjects to engage in and which we hypothesised were procedurally rational to use. We noted the incidence of each of these kinds of behaviour among our sample, and the cost of the plan that each subject selected, and then explored the relationship between them via non-parametric statistics. This was thus a statistical, practice-based analysis of procedural rationality. It was much more likely to yield useful lessons about how to cope in this kind of environment than we would have obtained by simply trying to generalise from the behaviour of those who selected the cheapest or second-cheapest plan for serving the specific remit that we had presented to our subjects. Even those who had performed very well in the experiment had achieved their rewards partly by luck, after making mistakes that could have produced very different results if the remit or set of available plans had been somewhat different.

We thought that we were being methodologically radical by (a) using a statistical approach to uncover what constituted 'appropriate deliberation' in this kind of context and (b) focusing on procedural rationality in a situation in which we had been able, via many hours of work, to uncover the least-cost plan. To my surprise, the editors of the *Cambridge Journal of Economics* decided to reject the paper as being far too orthodox. I suppose its editors might feel vindicated by the fact that the *Journal of Economic Behaviour and Organization* later accepted it, but I still regard it as a very heterodox paper. This experience reinforced a view that I had been developing as I pondered on why I seemed to be a rather lone wolf in taking a very eclectic approach to heterodox economics: some heterodox economists appear to have a rather specific view of what constitutes heterodox economics, which results, via dualistic thinking, in them viewing other heterodox approaches as coming from the orthodox camp.

Hayek's Theory of the Mind
While Lana and I were beginning the collaboration just described, I took my solo research into territory that I should have ventured into thirty years earlier, namely finding out what I could learn from Hayek's (1952) book *The Sensory Order*. I soon realised that, if I had read it in 1979, I

would have had a different view of why Hayek had been a participant at the 1968 Alpbach Symposium that had yielded the volume *Beyond Reductionism* (Koestler and Smythies, 1969) that did not include a paper by him. Hayek presents in *The Sensory Order* his theory of how the mind works. He had originally worked out its core ideas in the early 1920s and it complements his subjectivist view of economic action. Hayek's theory does indeed go 'beyond reductionism', for it sees cognitive processes as working by finding *patterns* in incoming stimuli that match events that we have previously encountered, and which have been stored by our brains as memories in terms of networks of neural connections. As Hayek emphasises, it is not by registering in our minds the individual tesserae in a Roman mosaic that we figure out what kind of mosaic it is; rather, it is the overall configuration of the tesserae – the structure of the relationship between the tesserae – that is of interest to us. If a set of tesserae has been laid out in a way that matches the configuration we have memorised as 'a swan', then we know we are looking at a mosaic 'of a swan'.

I found Hayek's theory very helpful in understanding how people deal with unfamiliar products and situations (Earl, 2010b, 2013b). On these occasions, we may struggle to find any patterns in incoming stimuli that match something we have memorised. To avoid cognitive paralysis, we must ignore, dismiss, or remove the incomprehensible stimuli. or we must be able to arrive at an interpretation that we view as a satisfactory basis for going forward. We may be able to do the latter by finding sub-patterns within the flow of stimuli that each match a different item in our memory. If we can do this, we can then classify the situation as a hybrid construct and store it as a new set of neural connections. These connections will be activated next time we think about that situation or next time we are in a situation where we find that the incoming stimuli have the same pattern.

However, in some situations we may end up making dysfunctional or comical categorizations because the stimuli are incomplete or somewhat scrambled. Thus, for example, if I talk about Phyllis Deane to someone who is unfamiliar with the female first name Phyllis, I run the risk of be viewed as talking about someone who operates like a Philistine. I might even be viewed as if I am referring, with rather poor diction, to someone who is known via an unfortunate nickname as 'Syphilis Deane'. This is, of course, the kind of process that results in 'mondegreen' misinterpretations of song lyrics, as when a person hears Jimi Hendrix as singing 'Excuse me while I kiss this guy' in his song 'Purple Haze' and ABBA as opening their song 'Chiquitita' by singing 'Take your teeth out, tickle my toes'.

Sometimes, we may get completely the wrong match initially, but then find the right one seconds later. I vividly recall experiencing this in Sydney in 1987 when I met up with one of my Cambridge friends (coincidentally, another member of the supervision group that included the friend who sent me the 'Philistine' card). Before she introduced me to her fiancé, she took me aside and said, 'Please don't tell him about my 2:2'. Initially, I was bewildered, as what I thought she had said was, 'Please don't tell him about my tutu' and I had no recollection of having ever talked about ballet with her. But then I realised what she meant: I now remembered that, to my surprise and her disappointment, she had only achieved a lower second in the Part II of the Cambridge Economics Tripos, and I could see that, as a merchant banker with a well-known economist/banker as her fiancé, she might be embarrassed if this came up in conversation. I had not thought about her degree class in the intervening years: she always came to mind as someone whose career was going really well, not as someone whose degree class had been a bit disappointing. But, if I recall correctly, ballet had been on the agenda when my then-partner Sharon and I met up with her in Sydney a year earlier, for on that trip we saw the ballet version of 'The Sentimental Bloke' at Sydney Opera House.

When I read *The Sensory* Order, it brought to mind my disconcerting 'tutu' cognitive experience, and the memories that I associate with it, for they aligned well with another key aspect of Hayek's analysis. To appreciate this aspect, it us helpful to recognise that the brain's problem when forming cognitions is rather like that of a locksmith who has a vast collection of keys and is trying to open a lock: the brain has a huge array of memories to try as templates to find a pattern in each set of stimuli. Hayek's theory of how the mind does this does not presume it tries all memories at once (hence the 'tutu' experience). Instead, his analysis complements Herbert Simon's view of how cognition works.

Simon emphasises the scope for hierarchical filtering to narrow down the set of conjectures about what we are looking at: i.e., we begin by defining a context, which puts boundaries on the set of things we may normally expect to find; we keep adding more detail and reducing the set of contending possibilities until we arrive at a position where one option seems a good enough solution. In Hayek's analysis, our brains examine how good a fit we get with the first memory that comes to mind, moving on to a second if the first seems problematic, and so on. He argues that the probability of a memory being used to try to find a match with incoming stimuli is a joint function of how frequently and how recently we have called that memory to mind in that context.

This implies that our minds are dynamic entities: the set of neural connections that is first used as a template to find a pattern in a new set of stimuli will have an increased probability of being used in that kind of context in future, relative to other stored sets of connections that might have been fired up. When memories that have been most recently/frequently activated do not lead to the discovery of a matching pattern, we 'wrack our brains', successively trying other memories that come to mind until we get a satisfactory fit. In the latter case, things we have not thought about for ages and/or rarely think about at all will become more likely to come to mind in future, as they have now been 'recently activated'. What we expect to see in a particular context can thus change as we accumulate a changing set of memories of what we have encountered. Over time, then, things that we once viewed as normal and acceptable can come to seem abnormal and unacceptable, and vice versa. However, if we do not operate in environments that involve diversity in the sets of stimuli that we need to make sense of, we are unlikely to develop new sets of neural connections, with the result that our thinking appears to be close-minded and driven by a limited range of stereotypes.

Hayek's *Sensory* Order is a remarkably prescient book that now comes to my mind any time that I am thinking about problems of coordination and change. His memory-based view of how cognition works prefigures Kahneman's (2011) view of the role of 'associative memory' and tacit pattern recognition in what is commonly referred to as 'expert intuition'. Hayek's probabilistic analysis of the process of using memories as means for categorising things is also a precursor to the modern neuroscience notion of 'brain plasticity', whereby each act of thinking changes how we think (see further Doidge, 2007). As such, it points towards a path-dependent view of consumer preferences insofar as consumers reflect on their consumption experiences and observe each other's behaviour.

Revisiting Shackle's Theory of Choice Under Uncertainty
Soon after Kahneman's (2011) *Thinking, Fast and Slow* appeared, Stuart Macdonald[18], the new editor of *Prometheus*, invited me to write a review article giving an economist's view of the book. The similarities of some of Kahneman's analysis with Hayek's *Sensory Order* were not the only areas of the book that grabbed my attention in relation to earlier contributions. It was evident that Kahneman had a tendency to use endnotes as a means of both showing he was aware of, and burying, major contributions that some might view as challenging his work. He did this with Simon's work, which he only highlighted in respect to what Simon had done on the behaviour of expert chess players, and with Gigerenzer's positive view of the role that heuristics can play as 'fast and frugal' means for reaching smart decisions. But what he said about how he and Tversky (1979) had arrived at their prospect theory view of risk-taking called to mind the 'potential surprise' theory of choice under uncertainty that Shackle had devised three decades ahead of prospect theory.

Kahneman emphasised that, when he and Tversky started to consider the implications of their experiments for the theory of risk-taking, they realised that it was much easier for people to focus on prospective gains and losses relative to a reference point rather than in relation to the impacts that rival outcomes might have on their total wealth. Hence, they built their theory around a reference-dependent view of utility. Shackle's (1949, 1969) theory had already offered a view of choice centred on gains and losses relative to a reference point – which he called the 'neutral outcome' – but in his case, he was thinking of the reference point as the entrepreneur's view of the safest alternative to undertaking an

---

[18] Don Lamberton, the founding editor of *Prometheus* stepped down as editor at the end of 2009 at the age of 82. Stuart Macdonald had been part of Lamberton's Information Research Unit at UQ in the early 1980s and later became Professor of Information Management at the University of Sheffield. It has been good to see that Stuart has taken a very rigorous approach to refereeing *Prometheus*, including with invited papers such as the one he asked me to write (Earl, 2010a) about the state of economics in the light of the Global Financial Crisis. On Christmas Day 2020, he wrote to let me know that referees of a submission to *Prometheus* by Chidambaran Iyer had found that Iyer had plagiarised material from one of my papers (Earl, 2003). Further investigation had led to the discovery that Iyer had previously got away with doing the same thing with another journal. Stuart's message included a copy of the letter he had sent to Iyer's head of department about this misconduct.

investment, against which prospective gains would provide hope and prospective losses would seem worrying.

Shackle's model predicts that, for each scheme of action that is under consideration, the decision-maker will focus on the most attention-arresting prospective gain and the most attention-arresting loss, via an 'ascendancy function' in which the attention-arresting power of an imagined outcome is an increasing function of its distance from the reference point and a decreasing function of how potentially surprising it seems in prospect. Focusing on these pairs of possible outcomes reduces the cognitive demands of weighing up one's options, thereby sidestepping an issue that prospect theory runs into if applied to choices that involve payoff matrices that are more complex than those that Kahneman and Tversky employed in their experiments. In Shackle's analysis, rival schemes are viewed as if they are ranked via the decision-maker's 'gambler preference map' on which each focal gain/loss pair reduces to a single point on an indifference map whose axes essentially represent the degree of excitement/hope that the decision-maker associates with focal gains, versus the degree of nervousness/fear associated with focal losses. (I say 'essentially' because Shackle's own way of explaining how focal gains and losses are weighed up removes the psychology of hope and fear and instead is needlessly convoluted and entails the conversion of 'primary' focus gains/losses into 'standardised' focus gains/losses – i.e., gains/losses that would be just as attention-arresting as their 'primary' counterparts if they were viewed as perfectly possible – with gambler preferences being expressed in terms of the latter.)

Rather than merely writing my review article (Earl 2012c) on *Thinking, Fast and Slow*, I also wrote a paper entitled 'Kahneman's *Thinking, Fast and Slow* from the standpoint of old behavioural economics', which I presented at the HETSA conference held in Melbourne in July 2012 (Earl, 2012e). In the HETSA paper, I explored the relationship between Kahneman's views and the work of Simon and Shackle. However, I never turned the paper into a journal article. Instead, I developed ideas from it into a chapter on Shackle and behavioural economics for a book about Shackle that I had started to write with my UQ colleague Bruce Littleboy (published as Earl and Littleboy, 2014).

This was not a book that I had planned to write, but I was not surprised to find myself working on it. I had encouraged Bruce, in my role as his supervisor, to try to build a study leave plan around spending time in

Cambridge as a Shackle Fellow at St Edmund's College and exploring the Shackle papers in Cambridge University Library. He followed my suggestion and had a very productive study leave in Cambridge, so writing a book on Shackle for Palgrave's 'Great Thinkers in Economics' series seemed the logical next step. He had been keen to take that step, so long as he could concentrate on Shackle's philosophical perspective and approach to macroeconomics, with me coming in as co-author to write the chapters on Shackle's potential surprise view of choice. I was happy to do this, since there seemed to be time to get the book finished before I had to focus on the data from the third phase of the mobile phone service contracts project and write papers based on that data. We also managed to get Michael Jefferson, whom I had not seen since the British Association conference at York in 1981, to write a chapter about the relationship between Shackle's work and the use of scenario planning at Shell. As Shell's former chief economist, Michael was far better placed to do this than Bruce or myself.

The Shackle book project was a very enjoyable task, marred only by the painful process of getting our manuscript turned into the published book. I produced the manuscript in 'camera-ready' form to Palgrave's style, but Palgrave insisted that we submit it in the old-fashioned double-spaced mode with minimal formatting. The manuscript was then sent to India for copy-editing, whereby many errors were added while quite a few of our typos and occasional stylistic inconsistencies did not receive attention. After we had spotted and noted both what the copyeditor should have spotted and the mistakes that had been introduced, the manuscript was typeset and ended up looking almost identical to my original 'camera-ready' version. One key difference was that Palgrave would not allow us to include a photograph that I had taken of Shackle's gravestone during a pilgrimage to Aldeburgh in 2013. We were told that the photograph could not be included unless we had written permission from the 'owner of the grave'. Since the authority that administered the cemetery could not advise us whom we needed to contact, we had to make do with a typed transcription of the words on the gravestone.

As far as my own research was concerned, it would likely have been better if I had merely written the chapter on 'Shackle and Behavioural Economics' as an article for a well-ranked journal, for that would probably have attracted the attention of a wider audience and chewed up much less time. This chapter went beyond the HETSA paper by showing that, if excitement/hope and nervousness/fear are viewed, respectively as proxies for prospective utility and disutility, then some versions of Shackle's theory imply an *S*-shaped utility function, while he sometimes drew the gambler preference map in a way that implies loss aversion, as well as with a limit to acceptable levels of risk.

My main regret about the Shackle book was that, yet again, I had not invested time in developing my knowledge of Keynes's (1921) *Treatise on Probability* and the emergence of subjective expected utility theory. In a sense, this meant that I repeated Shackle's own shortcomings by failing adequately to consider (a) how decision-makers make inductive use of evidence in forming conjectures, rather than operating in a purely deductive manner, and (b) the extent to which the subjective probability perspective is immune to Shackle's critique of probabilistic thinking in the context of individual decision-makers who are taking one-off decisions. To some degree, I have attempted to make amends in this area in Earl (2023b).

Principles of Behavioural Economics
As the thirtieth anniversary of the publication of my (1983a) book *The Economic Imagination* approached, Edward Elgar began to encourage me to think about writing a new edition of it to take account of how my thinking as a behavioural economist had evolved in the interim. To facilitate this, he secured the return to me of the book's copyright and, for good measure, the copyrights of *The Corporate Imagination* and *Lifestyle Economics* from Pearson Publishing, into whose ownership they had come following a series of acquisitions in the publishing sector. With the commencement of the mobile phone service contracts project, I thought it more realistic to aim to mark instead the thirtieth anniversary of the 1986 publication of *Lifestyle Economics* by preparing a combined update of it and *The Economic Imagination*, under the title of *Consumer Lifestyles and the Economic Imagination*. To get this project started, I obtained a scanned copy of *Lifestyle Economics* that was made using an optical character recognition app, but I soon realised that I really wanted to write the book from scratch rather than by word-processing material from the old books. Given the need to prioritise writing up and publishing findings from the mobile phone project, it was clear that I was not going to be able to get the book ready for publication in 2016 even though, by the end of 2013, the Shackle book was out of the way. Having held off from getting as far as a contract with Edward Elgar, I decided to put the book on hold until I was free from other commitments.

The publication of Richard Thaler's *Misbehaving* in 2015 left me with very mixed feelings. I greatly enjoyed Thaler's account of how his ideas had originated and evolved, but I was appalled by the way that his book gave the impression that he had created behavioural economics pretty much from scratch. To be sure, he had done a wonderful job in garnering interest in the 'new' behavioural economics to which he had made seminal contributions, but his scholarship was mostly woeful in terms of giving due credit to 'old' behavioural economics. It was not that he was unaware of Herbert Simon, for he noted that Simon had coined the term 'bounded rationality'. But Thaler (2015, loc. 527) had then made the extraordinary claim that Simon 'had not done much to flesh out how boundedly rational people differ from fully rational ones.' He had then portrayed Simon as merely one of a number of economists who had tried unsuccessfully to take economics in a somewhat different direction. Specifically, he pointed to Baumol's (1962) contribution to the literature on 'new theories of the firm', oblivious to the fact that Baumol's model is, as Loasby (1989) had emphasised, a conventional deterministic model of optimising behaviour, except that it uses imperfections in product and capital markets as the pretext for modelling managers as maximising the growth of turnover rather than profits.

Some Simon scholars might wonder whether this way of brushing aside Simon's contributions – the basis for Simon receiving the 1978 Nobel Memorial Prise in Economic Sciences – was a wilful act, designed to deter his readers from exploring Simon's contributions, rather than merely a reflection of poor scholarship. Whatever it was, it made me want to write a book in which I presented where I had got to as a behavioural economist not merely in relation to consumer behaviour but also in relation to firms and other organisations – territory on which the 'old' behavioural economists had mainly focused but which the 'new' behavioural economists mostly ignored.

Such a book would be much bigger than the one that I had been discussing with Edward Elgar; in effect, it would be my magnum opus, a legacy volume setting out where I had got to as a behavioural economist with a much wider range of influences than were deployed by those like Thaler who were getting so much attention while those that had inspired me were being left unappreciated. The final impetus for me to write it came in January 2017 when Sanjit Dhami sent me an email to draw my attention to his recently published book *The Foundations of Behavioral Economics* and an online video of his book-launch presentation about it.

Dhami's (2016) book is a remarkable contribution that runs to 1764 pages. Yet it is essentially an encyclopaedia only of 'new' behavioural economics. Someone needed to set the record straight in a constructive manner, so in July 2017 I began writing the book that was published five years later as *Principles of Behavioral Economics: Bringing Together Old, New and Evolutionary Approaches* (Earl, 2022).

With Oxford University Press having published Dhami's book, and the long road to my book having started in Cambridge, it seemed appropriate to see whether Cambridge University Press would be interested in being its publisher. To limit its risks of being ignored by US scholars, I wrote it in US English. The typesetting process was handled by Cambridge's New York operation.

After the book had gone to press, I noticed that I had written it oblivious to the potential for an acronym that lay in its subtitle: I could have called the synthesis that I had written the 'ONE behavioural' approach. I was able to use the acronym in an invited paper for a special issue of the *Journal of Consumer Behavior* (Earl, 2023a) in which I set out where I had arrived at in methodological terms as a behavioural economist.

8.5   CONFERENCE PARTICIPATION

Between 2001 and 2013, I presented papers at six conferences in the UK and three in Australia, as well as sharing with Bruce Littleboy the task of organising the 2007 Conference of the History of Economic Thought Society of Australia, held at UQ. In my time living Down Under, I was mostly lucky that the imperfect alignment between university timetables in the northern and southern hemisphere did not prevent me from attending conferences that I felt obliged to attend. However, this was not the case with a conference organised by Marina Bianchi and her colleagues at the University of Cassino on 'How to bring joy into economics: Revisiting Tibor Scitovsky'. It was scheduled for 27 and 28 June 2012 and I was to be a keynote speaker (along with Robert Frank and George Lowenstein). I got as far as writing my paper, which was published in revised form after the conference (Earl, 2014). However, when the time came to make the travel arrangements, I decided to withdraw due to uncertainty about the timing of the exams for the subjects that I was teaching. The problem was that the conference was scheduled to occur in the small window between the end of UQ's first semester examination period and the date that results had to be submitted. Bailing out proved to be a wise decision, for the examination for one of my subjects did indeed get scheduled for the very end of the examination period.

The conferences that I attended during my time at UQ did have a few academic payoffs as well as being pleasant social events. It should be evident from the previous section that the 2007 HETSA conference played an important role in the evolution of my thinking as a behavioural economist. The 2008 conference of the Association for Heterodox Economics (AHE) enabled me to solve the puzzle of what kind of diet Shackle was on in his later years: my partner Annabelle and I were talking with Vicky Chick about the challenges that conferences and overseas travel bring for those on special diets, and it suddenly occurred to me, and was confirmed by Vicky, that George Shackle, like Annabelle, was gluten-intolerant. Annabelle, too, enjoyed the social events at the conferences I attended from 2006 onwards. She usually found interesting things to do while I attended conference sessions: for example, on the final day of the 2006 AHE conference, she went 'mud-larking' on the banks of the Thames and arrived back at the LSE with archaeological trophies that included early seventeenth-century tobacco pipes and a Roman pottery fragment.

However, after attending the 2013 AHE conference, I decided that I was not going to attend any further international conferences. It was a decision that I had pretty much reached after the 2008 AHE conference. But I had felt obliged to accept Marina Bianchi's invitation to the 2012 conference in Italy that I ultimately was unable to attend, and in 2013 I felt that I might as well attend the AHE conference as it could be tacked on to the end of a six-week, long-service leave trip to the UK and Ireland that Annabelle and I had been planning for a long while. This time, I stuck to my decision; indeed, I also stopped going to interstate domestic conferences. This would be viewed disapprovingly by the promotion committees of most universities, but the misgivings that I had started to have in the 1990s about conference attendance (see Section 7.5) had grown and had been augmented by my concerns about the ethics of conference travel.

The latter particularly hit me following the 2006 AHE conference at the LSE/UCL, when my paper (later published as Earl and Wakeley, 2010a) was scheduled in the final set of parallel sessions. It drew a tiny audience and generated little useful feedback. If I had come half-way around the world purely for the conference, I would have been very uncomfortable in environmental terms, given what I knew of the per-passenger greenhouse gas emissions of even the most fuel-efficient of modern jet airliners. The fact that the conference was only a small part of a month-long trip made the environmental downside seem somewhat easier to justify, but it raised the issue of how conference travel is often little more than a means of getting subsidised travel for a vacation and obtaining additional days of leave, some of which are more honestly to be viewed as additions to one's recreation leave.

Extra days of leave were welcome on any conference trip that I made to the UK up to 2008, for significant parts of each trip would entail spending time in Cornwall to see how my parents were faring. This limited the time available for taking a care-free vacation. Being able to augment recreation leave with a few days of conference leave to recover from the long flight before attending the conference became more important when I moved to UQ: I needed to visit my parents more frequently, but I ran into the constraint that Australian universities only offered four weeks of normal recreation leave, compared with the six that Lincoln University offered. Long-service leave did accrue to give the equivalent of a couple of extra weeks of recreation leave per year, but one had to work for ten years before one could take long-service leave (and I thus never got to take any long-service leave when I worked at the University of Tasmania, due to leaving after only seven years). Both my parents died before I had completed my first decade at UQ. My participation at the 2005, 2006 and 2008 AHE conferences was thus mostly driven by concerns about the wellbeing of my parents as they aged into their eighties.

But family ties may not be the only obligational driver of conference travel. Over many years, I have felt bad about not attending the annual conferences of the Society for Heterodox Economics, Australia's equivalent of the AHE. A key reason why I did not bother to go to these events was that their programmes seemed to be dominated by papers on radical and feminist political economy. But of course, in not attending, I helped to ensure that the programmes lacked papers based on the more eclectic kind of heterodoxy that I practise. The fact that I started going to AHE conferences rather than other UK conferences was a result of Fred Lee telling me that those who did not participate in AHE conferences did not seem sufficiently devoted to the cause to deserve the 'heterodox economist' label. But the AHE conferences likewise failed to attract a very pluralistic representation of heterodox approaches to economics. Economic psychologists, socio-economists, evolutionary, institutionalist and Austrian economists seem to prefer to have their own conferences. By applying Simon's travel theorem and not going to conferences, one avoids the problems of choosing and the sense of not really fitting in due to being too eclectic, as well as avoiding jet-lag, difficulties in meeting special dietary requirements, and environment-related guilt.

8.6   RESEARCH AUDIT

Australia's Federal Government took far longer than I expected to emulate the UK's Research Assessment Exercise (RAE) process. Over two decades after the first research audit of UK universities, as the 2008 Australian General Election approached, the Howard Coalition Government was preparing its Research Quality Framework (RQF), but this was promptly replaced after the election of the Rudd Labor Government by the Excellence in Research Australia (ERA) research audit process. When this was put in place, the quality of academic conversation collapsed: instead of talking about the research they were doing, my colleagues seemed to become mainly interested in talking about where they were publishing their research, and especially about whether they were succeeding, or hoping to succeed, in getting their papers accepted by journals that the Australian Business Deans' Council had ranked as being of A* quality.

This was not an environment conducive to the kinds of conversations at the water-cooler that result in fresh research ideas. But UQ proved to be a great environment for producing research output, especially when the SOE adopted the policy of timetabling each teaching and research academic's annual teaching into a single semester. If one had three subjects to teach, as I did in some years, the teaching semester could be very gruelling, but there was always the teaching-free semester to look forward to at the other end. If one only had two subjects, research could be kept going during the teaching semester. Table 8.1, which spreads across two pages, summarises, from the ABDC standpoint the output that I produced in my time at UQ.

Table 8.1 (Part 1): A Dean's View of My University of Queensland Research Output

Output Type	2001 to 2005	2006 to 2010	2011 to 2015	2016 to 2020	Reference Tag (and Name of Journal) in Reference List Order
A*-Ranked Articles (3)	0	1	1	1	Earl, Friesen and Shadforth (2019) *J.Ec.Be.Org.* Friesen and Earl (2015) *J.Ec.Be.Org.* Earl and Wakeley (2010a) *Res.Pol.*
A-Ranked Articles (8)	2	2	3	1	Earl (2005a) *Cam.J.Ec* Earl (2012a) *J.Bus.Res.* Earl (2013a) *Cam.J.Ec* Earl, Peng and Potts (2007) *J.Ec.Psy..* Earl and Potts (2004) *Cam.J.Ec* Earl and Potts (2013) *J.Cult.Ec* Earl and Wakeley (2010b) *J.Evol.Ec.* Friesen and Earl (2020) *South,Ec.J.*
B-Ranked Articles (10)	0	4	3	3	Earl (2009, 2010a) *Prometheus* Earl (2011a) *N.Z.Ec.Papers* Earl (2018a) *Rev.Pol.Ec.* Earl, Friesen and Shadforth (2017) *J. Inst.Ec.* Earl and Mandeville (2009) *Prometheus* Earl and Peng (2012) *Rev.Pol.Ec.* Earl and Potts (2011a) *Rev.Pol.Ec.* Earl and Potts (2016) *Man.Dec.Ec.* Foster, Earl, Haines and Mitchell (2010) *Health Policy*
C-Ranked Articles (1)	0	0	0	1	Earl (2017a) *J.Bioeconomics*

Table 8.1 (Part 2): A Dean's View of My University of Queensland Research Output

Output Type	2001 to 2005	2006 to 2010	2011 to 2015	2016 to 2020	Reference Tag (and Name of Journal) in Reference List Order
Unranked Articles (5)	0	2	2	1	Earl (2008a) *On the Horizon* Earl (2014a) *Int.J.Pl.Ec.Ed.* Earl (2015a) *Ec.e-J.* Earl (2018b) *J.Be.Ec.Pol.* Earl and Wakeley (2007) *Int.J.T.P.*
Refereed Conference Papers (1)	0	1	0	0	Earl and Wakeley (2006)
Research Monographs (1)	0	0	1	0	Earl and Littleboy (2014)
Other Books (2)	2	1	0	0	Earl (2002) Earl and Wakely (2005)
Parts of Edited Books (17)	4	4	5	4	Chai, Earl and Potts (2007) Earl (2003a, 2003b, 2004a, 2007, 2010b, 2011b, 2012b, 2013b, 2016a, 2016b, 2017b, 2019a) Earl and Peng, 2011) Earl and Potts (2005b, 2011b) Earl and Wakeley (2009)
Edited Conference Proceedings (1)	0	1	0	0	Earl and Littleboy (2008)
Review Articles (1)	0	0	1	0	Earl (2012c) *Prometheus*
Book Reviews (10)	2	4	3	1	Earl (2004b, 2005b, 2006a, 2006b, 2006c, 2008b, 2012d, 2014b, 2015b, 2019b)
Other	1	0	0	0	Earl (2005c)

The contrast between Table 8.1 and its counterparts in earlier chapters is striking, for my research output involved a much greater proportion of joint work, and there were many journal articles. This contrast became increasingly marked as the research audit process loomed, but that was mainly due to the lack of material 'in the pipeline' when I arrived at UQ (which consisted merely of the 'market for preferences' paper that eventually appeared as Earl and Potts, 2004), coupled with my involvement with editing the *Journal of Economic Psychology* and working on the Earl and Wakeley (2005) business economics textbook. From 2005, Tim Wakeley and I moved on to writing joint articles and conference papers, and the pipeline proceeded from there – albeit with some long lags. However, the composition of my research output remained abnormal compared with that of my orthodox colleagues who rarely published sections of books or wrote book reviews and instead concentrated on winning places for their work in the top two journal categories.

The two books that chewed up time in my first five years at UQ were failures in two senses: they did not constitute 'research monographs', and their impacts were poor. I would have made better use of my time if I had immersed myself in catching up with recent literature in my areas of interest. The first of these books (Earl, 2002) was based on a dozen previously published papers, though quite a few of them were reworked somewhat and in some cases I moved material between them to make the book flow more like an integrated work. Aside from my *Journal of Post Keynesian Economics* paper on normal cost pricing (Earl, 1991a), they all came from my time at Lincoln University. The idea of putting this volume together came after I received an email from Stephen Dunn in which he commented on having unexpectedly come across one of the papers (Earl, 1998a) from that period, which had led him to wonder what others I had published in places that might not normally be browsed by economists who were interested in my work.[19] However, except for the Earl and Potts (2000) paper on the economics of shopping mall configurations, none of the papers in this volume went on to have

---

[19] In hindsight, I regret that I did not include the unpublished paper on coordination problems in tertiary education and research that I had presented at the G. B. Richardson Colloquium (Earl, 1995d), rather than the one that I subsequently wrote (Earl, 1998c) on Richardson's neglected place in the literature of economics for the Richardson festschrift. It would have been of wider interest and would have complemented the chapter based on my Coase-inspired examination of the organization of the tertiary education industry (Earl, 1994a).

significant citations. This was not due to the versions in this book being cited instead of the originals. Despite the effort I had invested in enhancing and integrating the papers as I turned them into chapters, the book had the same fate, rather than proving to be an effective way of relaunching them. Nowadays, of course, sharing one's work via ResearchGate and/or Academia provides a much easier way of making one's work readily available if one has misbehaved by publishing papers in the wrong kinds of places.

The Earl and Wakeley (2005) business economics textbook fared a bit better in its citation score, but it had very disappointing sales. Indeed, we have probably earned bigger royalties (collected via an Australian organisation, Copyright Agency Limited) from the copying of individual chapters than from sales of the book. It was as if, when commissioning our book, McGraw-Hill had misjudged the openness of university teachers of business economics to new perspectives as badly as they had judged potential for a new kind of introductory text three decades previously when they commissioned Robinson and Eatwell's (1973) *Introduction to Modern Economics* (for the story of the latter, see King and Millmow, 2003). In our case, it is possible that our publisher had got a good idea of the potential size of the market for a heterodox business economics text but did not realise that a pluralistic text that contrasted orthodox ideas with a behavioural/evolutionary/Post Keynesian approach was the wrong kind of heterodox approach to offer. What we wrote focused on the challenges of building a successful firm and growing it into a large corporation. This probably would not have appealed to those who take a hard-left political economy view of the world of business and who probably also are not familiar with the heterodox approaches to microeconomics that Tim and I employed in the book. The book failed despite including, ahead of the Global Financial Crisis, a Minsky-inspired view of the impact of speculation on the macroeconomy.

From a dean's perspective, I should not have sacrificed any of my research time writing any C-ranked or unranked articles, for they could have a counterproductive impact on departmental performance in external audits. From my personal standpoint, these papers could be damaging, too, since they might be construed as implying that I did not know how to play the modern research game and/or was not capable of producing enough 'quality' output. As can be seen via Tables 8.1 and 8.2, only one of these five papers (Earl, 2014a) was an unsolicited article, and this one was a conscious experiment in going against the rule that 'thou shalt concentrate on achieving high-ranking publications.' It was a reworked version of the paper that I had written for the 2012 Scitovsky conference at the University of Cassino that I decided not to attend. In terms of its content, the journal whose name fitted it best was the recently established *International Journal of Pluralism and Economic Education*, for which I had recently done some refereeing. It is difficult to see how such journals can get ranked and go on to improve their rankings if they are viewed as outlets in which no one from a top-100 university would dream of stooping to publish. One question, therefore, was whether the refereeing process would be lax; another was whether my paper would sink without trace if it were published there or would actually get picked up by those who preach pluralism. Although even UQ's wonderful library did not take this journal, anyone whose library likewise did not subscribe to it could readily contact me to get a copy if they discovered the paper.

So, what did I discover by submitting it – in effect, as a gift – to this journal? As far as refereeing was concerned, the process was just like that of dealing with an established, well-ranked journal: as I expected from my own experience as a referee for the journal, the editor, Jack Reardon, did not choose referees who would merely rubber-stamp my submission, and he required me to deal thoroughly with the referee reports. However, by December 2025, my paper had achieved no citations and there had been no requests for it, even after I joined ResearchGate.

As can be seen from Table 8.2, only about half of the articles that I wrote or co-authored in my time at UQ were regular submissions to journals. The average rank for these articles is significantly higher than those that I was invited to submit or that were written for special issues and symposia. But one of the papers for a special issue in a B-ranked journal (Earl, 2011a) was a reworked version of a paper that several years earlier I had decided not to revise and resubmit for the A*-ranked *Journal of Economic Behavior and Organization*. From a dean's perspective, my failure to pursue the invitation to revise and resubmit the paper to this A*-ranked journal would be seen as an act of misbehaving, but for me, it was a matter of principle.

Table 8.2: Origins and Refereeing of My University of Queensland Research Articles

Type of Article	N	Reference Tag and [ABDC Ranking Category] (in Reference List Order)	% of Total N
Journal articles that were unsolicited submissions and were fully refereed	13	Earl (2013a [A], 2014a [Unranked]) Earl, Friesen and Shadforth (2017 [B], 2019 [A*]) Earl, Peng and Potts (2007 [A]) Earl and Potts (2004a [A], 2013 [A], 2016 [B]) Earl and Wakeley (2010a, [A*], 2010b [A]) Foster, Earl, Haines and Mitchell (2010 [B]) Friesen and Earl (2015 [A*], 2020 [A])	21.67
Invited submissions accepted after being revised in response to referee comments	4	Earl (2005a [A], 2010a [B], 2018a [B]) Earl and Potts (2011a [B])	6.67
Articles written for 'special issues', or as invited contributions to symposium sections	8	Earl (2008a [Unranked], 2009 [B], 2011a [B], 2012a [A], 2015a [Unranked], 2017a [C]) Earl and Peng (2012 [B]) Earl and Wakeley (2007 [Unranked])	13.33
Articles that were invited submissions and/or were accepted by journal editor without referee reports being supplied or revisions being requested	2	Earl (2018 [Unranked]) Earl and Mandeville (2009 [B])	3.33

The paper had started out as one of two pluralistic papers that Tim Wakeley and I wrote for the 2005 AHE conferences at City University in London. I wrote most of it, and Tim wrote most of the other one (which later became Earl and Wakeley, 2006). The title of the original paper was 'The role of introspection, text and anecdotes in pluralistic approaches to economics.' Later that year, we sent a shorter version of the paper to the *Journal of Economic Behaviour and Organization*. Eventually, we received a letter from the editor, J. Barclay Rosser, who invited us to revise and resubmit it. It was clear that he found it interesting, though he stressed that it was very 'left field' and hence it might be a challenge to get it accepted. However, one of the things that he wanted us to do was remove the section that examined economic content in two novels by David Lodge. Rosser said that we should remove the section because he had never heard of Lodge, and neither had his assistant, who had studied English literature. In other words, the problem was not how we had used Lodge's novels in the paper; rather, it seemed a parochial US-centric view of what was an acceptable source of text to illustrate the paper's argument that novels can sometimes offer economic insights that economic theorists miss when they engage in deductive theorising.

Rosser's attitude really bugged me. It wasn't that the two novels that I had employed were unknown. Lodge was Professor of English Literature at the University of Birmingham, and his campus-based novels were widely read by academics in the UK. One of the novels that I had used was *Nice Work* (Lodge, 1989), which had been written after Lodge had done some research by talking with businesspeople in Birmingham. It had been shortlisted for the Booker Prise and its success had led to it being turned into a four-part BBC drama mini-series starring Warren Clarke and Haydn Gwynne. But even if it had been an obscure novel, I did not see why I needed instead to show that one could get economic insights via novels from US writers. This was why I decided not to revise and resubmit it along the lines that Rosser had set out. Soon after that, we sent the paper to the *Journal of Economic Methodology*. However, despite its subject area seeming to Tim and me to be in economic method, it was rejected as not fitting the area of the journal. At that point, we decided to focus on the other papers that we were writing, as we had trouble thinking where next to send it.

I gave no further attention to the paper until 2011, when Simon Kemp sent me the call for papers on experimental economics and economic psychology for a special issue that he was co-editing for *New Zealand Economic Papers*. By this point, Tim had decided to take time out from academia, so I decided to rework the 2005 paper into a solo article, making extensive changes as well as removing Tim's contributions. That way, I eliminated the risk of the paper being held up by Tim finding it difficult to get time to participate further. This time around, the referees raised no objections to the use that I had made of David Lodge's novels, but the journal in which it was published was not one that was likely to catch the attention of North American (or even European) behavioural economists. The special issue was also released as a book (Kemp and Wall, 2013) but, so far, despite this, and despite *New Zealand Economics Papers* being published via the global Taylor and Francis online journals platform, my attempt radically to augment Thaler's well-known use of anecdotes has not garnered much interest.

Research and Promotion

It is not hard to understand, from a research audit-focused perspective, why the two promotion applications that I submitted while working at UQ were rejected. The first was for promotion from senior lecturer to associate professor (the modern term in Australia for what used to be called the 'reader' level). I submitted it in the 2003 round, after I had been at UQ for slightly less than two years. To apply after less than two years' service required approval from the Dean of Faculty, and I had no difficulty in obtaining it. However, the Promotions Committee decided that I had not yet got my research back on track to a sufficient degree to demonstrate that I could offer a sustained research performance at the required level. This was a disappointment to me, but it was entirely understandable, given that the Promotions Committee was unlikely to have had much knowledge of why I had failed to perform in line with the promise I had shown prior to my decade at Lincoln University.

John Foster was not happy with the outcome and promised that he would see what could be done. Things then went quiet on this matter for a while, but then, with no forewarning, I found an envelope in my SOE mailbox that contained the offer of a contract for a continuing position as an associate professor of economics. In other words, I did not get promoted from senior lecturer to associate professor; rather, a new associate professor position was created for me, and I duly accepted it. It implied that the Dean of Faculty, Ian Zimmer, was as keen as John Foster to ensure that I would not start looking elsewhere for a better job, and that they were confident about how I was going to perform.

I waited until the 2011 promotion round to submit an application to be promoted to full professor. By that point, as is evident from Table 8.1, my research output had started to look more like what was expected, and Lana Friesen and I had won our large ARC Discovery Grant. Yet, in terms of what really counted, i.e., recent A*- and A-ranked journal articles, my application was premature, for the tally was simply too small. Given this, it was no surprise that my application only received lukewarm support from the SOE's professoriate. My application was then rejected by UQ's Promotions Committee without external references being sought. This was despite a very supportive reference from John Foster, in his role as my supervisor. He had emphasised my standing within heterodox economics. When I mentioned to Geoff Harcourt what had happened, he sent an email expressing his surprise and disappointment to UQ's then-Vice-Chancellor, Professor Paul Greenfield. Really, though, all that UQ had done was align its reward system with the incentive structure imposed by external pressures. These pressures just happened not to favour those who misbehaved by pursuing the wrong kind of economics thereby limiting their opportunities to publish in journals of the highest status.

Despite fully understanding this, I decided to take up the opportunity that was offered for a feedback meeting with Professor Michael Keniger, the Deputy Vice-Chancellor. It proved to be a very useful meeting. Professor Keniger explained that the committee had not taken up references because they suspected (rightly, I think) that if they followed the procedure of selecting one of the referees that I had nominated, plus an independent referee, they would just get another pair of sharply contrasting reports, which is never a good situation for a promotions committee to be in when it is trying to avoid making a mistake. He therefore advised me that I should wait until I could reapply with reference to impact metrics that showed I was clearly on an upward curve. Such metrics were the best way of trumping disagreements between economists about what kinds of contributions to economics are valuable. I had included a screenshot of my Google Scholar metrics in my application, noting that my scores were on a par with some of UQ's existing economics professors. Unfortunately, it did not have an obvious upward trajectory. A decade later, it still did not do so: behavioural economics may have become mainstream, but not my kind of behavioural economics. My annual Google Scholar citation rate failed to go beyond the figure of 200 that it clocked up in 2011.

I asked Professor Keniger whether, if I reapplied four or five years later, I would also need to have had another success by that point with an ARC Discovery Grant application. His answer was again instructive. He said that he did not think that this would be decisive; rather, the key thing was to demonstrate that I could get highly ranked papers out of the one that Lana and I had already won, which would signal that I could have a good chance of winning funding again. In other words, if a grant recipient succeeds in achieving (fails to achieve) well-ranked publications from a past grant in a timely manner, it will signal to referees of subsequent grant applications that, if the application is approved, it is not likely (could be likely) to result in a waste of scarce research resources.

In the end, Lana and I did get some well-ranked publications out of our study, but the process took much longer than we imagined, with the penultimate and final papers not being accepted for publication until 2019. By that stage, as can be seen from Table 8.1, it would have been clear to any promotions committee that I was failing to deliver A*-ranked articles with the frequency that my orthodox colleagues could achieve, and even my output of A-ranked articles was tailing off. Work on the Shackle book in the period 2012–2014, and work on my behavioural magnum opus from mid-2017, left little time for new research papers aside from those from the mobile phone service contracts project. It had long been clear to me that there was no point in reapplying for promotion to full professor.

8.7   EXIT

For much of my time at UQ, I engaged in routine scanning for professorial positions at other institutions even though I doubted that I could get better pay, better students, and a better resourced research environment than I had at UQ. Indeed, from 2011 to 2013, I actively explored what my options might be in heterodox economics departments in the UK, even though I suspected that I had not got my recent publications record into good enough shape to be a serious contender there. I got as far as applying for a few positions after the unsurprising failure of my application for internal promotion and I was interviewed for chairs at Goldsmiths, University of London (remotely, via a rather disrupted Skype video) and (in marketing) at the University of Plymouth (while I was in the UK on long-service leave). These would be my last formal applications: head-hunters approached me about senior positions at City University in London and the University of Otago in New Zealand, but they then confirmed my suspicion that I was not enough of a catch in terms of recent publications. It was clear that, in the research audit-driven academic labour market, the deal I had at UQ was rather generous, as I probably would not have been able to win even an associate professor position there if I had been an external applicant around that time.

Even when chairs were advertised by lower-tier institutions (for example, Nottingham Trent University, which had some appeal in terms of heterodox economics), it was evident that I would have to think up topics for potentially successful research grant applications to talk about with insincere enthusiasm if I were shortlisted. It was not in my nature to try to get a position by promising things that I did not really intend to try to deliver. The work that I was then doing with Lana Friesen on the mobile phone connection service confusopoly project allowed me to tick my personal box of experiencing an interesting project funded via a large competitive grant, so I did not plan to apply for funding again unless I happened to come up with an idea that seemed more important to pursue than projects on my 'to do' list that merely required access to a very good library.

The process of exploring chairs elsewhere led me to realise that I was not really determined to get back to that level before I retired and that there was a lot to be said for staying at the UQ SOE even as pluralism withered there: if I moved to a second-tier university in the UK, I would probably end up with poorer library facilities, students of lower average ability, at least one extra subject to teach each year, and more expensive housing. This seemed too big a price to pay to be among more colleagues who had an open-minded view of how economics might be practised or who operated in inter-disciplinary settings, and to be closer to old friends. My partner Annabelle was happy to stay in Brisbane, too, despite it not offering opportunities to pursue her interest in archaeology or try her hand at being a detectorist. Moreover, there was also the big problem of what would happen regarding Annabelle's mother, who lived a short distance from us, was then in her early 80s, and was not very mobile. If I stayed at UQ, I might end up as the last non-mainstream economist in the SOE, but I could probably undertake more of the writing that was on my 'to do' list. I find it hard to imagine that, if I had a chair in a small heterodox department, I would have embarked on my behavioural economics magnum opus, given its opportunity cost in terms of articles that could more rapidly have enhanced the research standing of such a department.

Although most of my colleagues busily focused on enhancing their career prospects by chasing research grants and publishing articles in A*-

ranked journals, my failure to do this never resulted in any attempt to induce me to change my ways. My final supervisor, Professor Chris O'Donnell, seemed perfectly happy that I was being productive in my own way, rather than trying to cruise toward retirement. So, why did I decide to retire at age 65 rather than follow the examples set by quite a few colleagues who carried on working at UQ until they were almost, or even beyond 70? In brief, it was to escape from administration and, more importantly, from aspects of teaching that seemed part of how things were going in tertiary education generally rather than that were peculiar to UQ.

It was early 2019 when I began seriously to consider retiring: at that point, if I had given the required six months' notice and used some of my long-service leave to complete the notice period, I could have handed in my office keys in the middle of the year, exactly 40 years after I had started my lectureship at the University of Stirling. That rounded number seemed big enough, and it looked like there was enough in my superannuation account to make retirement financially viable. But if I did that, I would be throwing away the research semester that I would get in the second half of 2019, for all my teaching took place in the first semester. I would also give up the chance to see how things went in the process of revamping the PhD programme in a pluralistic way, and the chance to participate in whatever other processes of change that the SOE's new head, Daniel Zizzo, intended to bring about. I therefore decided to keep going. Once I had passed the middle of the year and that 40th anniversary, my decision focus seemed to be mid 2021, when I would reach the end of 20 years of my employment at UQ. However, by mid-2020, I had decided that I wanted to be retired by the time that teaching began in 2021.

Earlier in 2020, my focus had been on what I could do to get work on my magnum opus happening again. The writing of the book had been going well up to the start of teaching in 2019, but it then stalled due to the demands of my HDR coordinator role. In my 'research semester', I struggled even to find time to finish the chapter that I had been working on at the start of the year. To prevent that from happening again, I decided in March 2020 to give the required six months' notice of my desired to use my ten-week balance of long-service leave from the start of October. That would buy me research time in what I knew from my 2019 experience would be the worst time of the year in terms of postgraduate administration (due to the need to shortlist and interview applicants for the Master of Advanced Economics and rank applicants for PhD scholarships). Yet it was obvious to me that even if I made good progress during the second half of 2020, the book would still require quite a few months of work. There seemed to be a very real risk that, if I did not retire before teaching started in 2021, the book might not be completed until early 2022, or even, if it were not quite complete before that year's teaching started, until about July 2022, with the production process taking a further year.[20] I did not want my preoccupation with finishing the book, and the stress that this entailed, to go on for that long.

Much would depend upon whether the HDR coordinator role came back to me in December 2020, and what teaching came my way. There seemed to be a major risk that I would be given the task of teaching the new Ethics in Economics subject or Economics of Innovation and Entrepreneurship. Either of these subjects would require me to do a lot of reading if I were to stick to my operating principle of basing my lectures on a view of the subject that I had assembled by doing my own research rather than operating merely as a franchisee-like conduit for the view that someone else had assembled and embodied in a textbook whose chapters were to be presented week by week. The fact that a colleague and I had been able to assemble an indicative subject outline did not mean that we had the knowledge required to teach Ethics in Economics. I thought it likely that the colleague in question might retire at the end of 2020 (as indeed he did), leaving me as the obvious contender to run the subject, In the end, in mid-2020, without knowing what my 2021 workload might be, I decided that I simply did not want to do coursework teaching ever again.

Getting to that conclusion was not the result of the unforeseen COVID-19 pandemic and the sudden switch to online teaching. Many of the shifts that this entailed seemed to me to be highly desirable. Long before screen-capture recording facilities were available for my subjects, I had been recording my lectures, first only in audio form and then, via a tripod-mounted video camera, more in the style of a TED talk with my slides visible on the screen next to me. The great majority of the class were already relying on recordings rather than attending the live lectures,

---

[20] By working on the book as a full-time retirement job, I was able to complete it by the end of June 2021, with its length resulting in a further three weeks being required merely to compile the index. Later, there would be a couple of months' work checking the copy-edited typescript and proofs, and the book (Earl, 2022) was eventually published on 28 July 2022.

adding further weight to Simon's travel theorem. Pre-recording lectures at home did not have the dispiriting effect that lecturing in a largely empty lecture theatre had. Better still, it freed me from having to fit lectures to the two-hour timeslots; some could be longer or shorter in pre-recorded form and I could slice them into multiple attention span-friendly modules if I wished, instead of having to reclaim attention after a typical mid-lecture break. It also seemed a very good idea to supplement these recordings with online Q&A sessions running via Zoom, just a click away from the subject website, in the timetabled lecture slots, and then post the Q&A recordings there, too.

Having Zoom-based office hours resulted in more students being willing to approach me for advice than I was used to seeing at my office in normal times. However, I preferred face-to-face tutorials, as attendance and participation were far worse at Zoom tutorials. If attendance at the latter had been better, I would have used Zoom's 'break out room' facility to alternate between small-group and full-group mode, but because I also posted Zoom recordings of tutorials on the subject's websites, many students operated as if Simon's travel theorem applied for tutorials, too.

I was glad to have had this online teaching experience in my final semester of lecturing. But regardless of the pandemic-induced changes and the extent to which teaching would return to pre-pandemic modes of delivery, I had lost the will to teach.

My conclusion that I did not want to teach courses anymore was not the result of any UQ-specific factors. Rather, it came from reflecting on what had happened to the business of teaching due to education policies in Australia and overseas, and the associated commodification of tertiary education. In Australia, the progressive squeeze on university funding had produced a system in which fees from international students were a vital source of revenue for funding research even in top-tier universities. Although UQ required its international students to meet demanding English language proficiency scores, a significant fraction of the international students in my classes did not really possess the reading skills needed to operate in the way that I knew domestic students could operate. Indeed, in some cases one could be left wondering whether the international students who struggled had employed others to achieve their IELTS scores. On top of this, the cost of being an international student, and the desire or necessity that domestic students felt to avoid accumulating massive debts while studying, meant that many 'full-time' students from both groups could only operate as part-timers due to the hours they were working elsewhere to pay their fees and/or living expenses. I had a growing sense that this situation had a bigger impact on academics who tried, as I did, to cling to the idea of 'reading for a degree' than on colleagues who taught in the modern orthodox way.

It was clear that my students *did* read energetically when undertaking assessment tasks that were designed to be research-based. Otherwise, however, they seemed mostly to rely upon lecture slides unless there were clear signals of where they would need to read to score well, such as when I gave them long menus of questions from which final exam questions would be taken, or when I replaced the final exam with three 1000–1200-word essays to be chosen from a relatively short menu. However, neither of the latter ensured they read widely. A long menu of potential questions tended to result in teams of students dividing reading among their members and pretty much parrot-learning their team-mates' mock answers to such an extent that it was often obvious who had been in the same team. This was not what I wanted: the idea was to leave enough room for reading other than that needed for assignments, but in most cases, it seemed not to be happening because no marks were attached to it unless an annotated bibliography was one of the submission tasks. (I tried the latter one year, but it was not well received by the class and proved very problematic to mark.)

In contrast to the 1970s Cambridge system, where one read a lot for weekly essays that counted for nothing, the modern students typically seemed to allocate time with a view to where the marks pay-offs lay. Hence, if short of time, they would do weekly tests and exercises set by orthodox colleagues, for these assignments had marks attached, and they would mainly attend tutorials if these were where the weekly tests occurred or if there were rewards for attending. But few would do the required few hours of preparatory reading that was intended to provide the basis for tutorial discussions. Even when I merely required preparation in the form of watching a one-hour TV documentary, I would find that many of those who showed up to get their tutorial participation mark had done no preparation.

In my Behavioural and Evolutionary Economics class, I set out to circumvent this issue by designing a tutorial programme that simply tried to employ lecture material to address real-world issues, and I set Thaler's (2015) *Misbehaving* as the required reading. But for other courses where I wanted pre-tutorial reading to be done, it seemed that the only way to motivate the class would have been to have weekly tests or written tasks attached to it, which would chew up tutorial time from discussions and/or greatly increase the time needed for the tutorial team to read and grade assessable work. I had had enough of trying to design and implement tutorial systems to induce the level of participation that it had once been possible to expect from most students in classes of high average ability. With the tightened time budgets that students had come to face, members of my classes increasingly showed little shame or embarrassment when they confessed their lack of preparation. Policies of economic rationalism had ensured they operated like incentive-driven economic agents rather than young adults with a sense of responsibility derived from the privilege of having won a place to study at university.

Another key concern for me was that students did not appreciate the effort I put into providing them with written feedback on their work. If anything, they seemed to find the idea of feedback on open-ended assignment tasks puzzling as more and more of their other subjects did not contain writing-based assignments and instead had answers that could be marked objectively as right or wrong. I was also troubled to see my domestic students increasingly finding it difficult to cope with any criticism of their work: it was as if these 'snowflakes' were products of high-school environments in which the ethos had been to give awards and commendations for even the slightest achievement and never to risk harming the self-esteem of pupils by saying anything negative about their work. I always tried to extract something positive from contributions that students made in my classes, but I provided them with detailed written comments about the shortcomings of their written work so that they could see how to do better in future.

The penny dropped for me in this respect when the feedback that I provided was described as 'brutal' by a student in one of my final course evaluations. Others said that they did not want feedback on what they had done, since they would not be doing those specific assignments again; rather, they wanted generic 'how to' advice. I started to infer that today's students believe that, since they are fee-paying customers, their university teachers should always be nice to them, just like the provider of any other service for which they pay.

Related to this is the sense of 'entitlement' displayed by some students who have been used to getting high scores and who therefore think that, regardless of reasons given in the feedback, an unexpectedly low grade is not one that they should tolerate. To the extent that such students set out to use appeals processes in a litigious way and succeed in getting the grades raised by a different marker who may not be aware of the system under which the original marks were awarded, it is possible to end up with injustices to students to whom the original marking criteria have been consistently applied but who accept their marks. I wonder what William Perry would have made of the 'ethical and intellectual development' of students who harass university staff to get the marks to which they feel entitled: should they be placed at the 'anything goes' fourth stage of the five-stage version of the Perry Progression?

The stresses that I experienced from having to deal with 'entitled' students were compounded by those I faced from trying to teach in a pluralistic way and with open-ended assignments if my classes had significant percentages of international students from countries whose education systems are based on 'parrot learning' and whose political systems do not permit debate or tolerate dissent. Such students may cope with non-pluralistic courses whose assignments involve objective tests and technical exercises. However, they are very difficult to teach if one is running what is perhaps the sole pluralistic subject in their programme. This was the case at UQ with the master's level version of Evolution of Economic Systems, where local students or international students from, say, Malawi or Germany performed very well but many from China seemed to flounder. I started to realise that some of the latter were attempting to tackle my 'authentic' role-play assignments by putting phrases from the assignment remits into Google, without trying to connect the material from class with the situation they were supposed to analyse. The result of this was that I could be faced with assignments that seemed to be incoherent collages of tenuously related points, with no use of material from the subject.

This was happening despite me having segments of the tutorial programme devoted to considering where material from my lectures might be used in tackling the upcoming assignment. One of the tasks that I assigned to what turned out to be my final cohort of Evolution of Economic Systems students was to write a briefing document that critically assessed a proposed project called 'Iron Boomerang'. The central idea of the project (the brainchild of Brisbane entrepreneur Shane Condon, one of my first MBA students) entails the construction of a 3,300km railway to ship coking coal from mines in Queensland, all the way to Western Australia's iron ore mining district, with iron ore then being sent to Queensland on the return journey. Large-capacity steel production precincts would be built at each end, with steel slabs then being exported, in contrast to the existing situation in which the coking coal and iron ore are exported on ships that return empty. One of the assignments included a paragraph of poorly paraphrased material from a book called *Spinning Flight: Dynamics of Frisbees, Boomerangs, Samaras, and Skipping Stones* (Lorenz, 2006), but there was nothing from my lectures being employed as a basis for analysis, nor any use of material that I had put in the assignment folder on the subject's website as strong hints about possible issues to raise (such as the proposed system's vulnerability to disruptions to the long rail link across outback Australia, and the significance of attempts to devise methods of smelting steel via green hydrogen rather than coal). Here I was, doing my best to help students move beyond the first stage of the Perry Progression in a way that would help them learn how to participate effectively in real-world business decision-making, and this was what I was up against. It was time to give up going against the stream – not by abandoning pluralism and open-ended assignments, but by retiring.

9 Career Lessons

9.1   INTRODUCTION

The account presented in the previous eight chapters began as a tale of someone with great potential, but it then morphed into a tale about failure to live up to that potential. In the first three chapters, the ingredients were there for a career that achieved a significant impact in economics. My childhood and teenage years primed me to have an interest in contributing to an evolutionary approach to behavioural economics. I went on to achieve a double-first in Cambridge that should have been a springboard to becoming a 'big fish' in the world of behavioural economics. But my career did not turn out that way.

It was not a terrible career by any means, but I should have done better. Sometimes, I was my own worst enemy, but time and place mattered, too. My career was able to unfold as it did because, in my first decade and a half in academia, universities in the UK and Australasia operated according to very different rules and systems from the more US-style ones that began to be imposed thereafter. In the absence of modern rules and systems, I operated in a way that earned me rapid promotion. But it was not a modus operandi that was conducive to the production of research outputs that would have anything like the impact that Thaler and others achieved despite their work being based on more ad hoc thinking than I was trying to employ.

What I was able to achieve was also significantly limited by the career-stalling choice that I made to take up the position of Professor of Economics at Lincoln University in New Zealand and how I dealt with the situation in which I then found myself. For eight years, my flow of original research largely dried up. After that, I started performing more like I should have done at the outset, for I was able to escape and spend the rest of my career in a well-paid position in a well-resourced university ranked around 50th globally. However, my impact in terms of citations failed to display an upward curve and merely continued at a respectable annual level that generated a total of around 4200 hits on Google Scholar by early 2026, though with a declining trend in recent years. I did not retire as a full professor, but at least I managed to get to retirement without compromising my key academic principles as a researcher and teacher. I did it my way, not the way that today's deans, heads of department and student customers prefer their staff to perform.

Such a career has been conducive to arriving at many 'do' and 'don't' lessons after reflecting on how I ended up failing to realise my potential, and on the significance of the ways that universities have changed during my career. These lessons are set out in this concluding chapter. I have not attempted to construct a comprehensive 'how to' career guide, but I hope what follows will be worth reading and help those who are contemplating trying to have academic careers in economics, or who have already embarked on such careers, to fulfil their potential more fully than they otherwise might have done, especially if they do not wish to adhere to the rules of the dominant economics research programme. Naturally, as a pluralist, I do not claim that what I say in this final chapter is definitive, and I hope that readers will also seek alternative perspectives, such as those offered by Hay (2017) and in other sources that I recommend as the chapter proceeds.

9.2   FOR PLURALISTIC TEACHERS OF ECONOMICS

Pluralistic teaching ideally entails providing students with rival theoretical perspectives, rival empirical methods, and opportunities to become experienced in making judgments about which tools to use for dealing with a succession of both closed and open-ended problem-solving tasks that take a variety of forms. Students can receive a pluralistic economics education in a variety of ways, some of which may be feasible even in departments in which almost all staff simply teach the dominant view of economics:

- Multiple lecturers presenting different personal perspectives, within a single subject.
- One lecturer teaching multiple perspectives on a particular area via primary sources and/or a pluralistic textbook, or several single-perspective textbooks that collectively cover rival perspectives, with a mixture of styles of tasks.
- Within-programme pluralism via some subjects offering heterodox theoretical perspectives (e.g., behavioural, evolutionary, feminist, institutionalist, Marxian) within a subject menu that is predominantly

mainstream, or offering alternative empirical methods (e.g., experimental, qualitative) rather than merely covering econometrics.

- Scope for students to study alternative approaches, despite being enrolled within a very mainstream programme, by taking electives on alternative approaches that are offered by other departments (e.g., via politics, psychology, economic history, or business studies).
- Combinations of the above.

The key problem with the third and fourth variants is for students to be aware of the benefits of having a pluralistic education and of their options for achieving it by constructing a suitable mix of subjects.

Those who try to stick to pluralistic principles in an environment in which fewer and fewer colleagues are doing likewise will find it increasingly challenging to do this. For example, suppose you work in a department whose students are used only to multiple choice questions, technical problem sets and short-answer questions. If you are the only lecturer who still uses writing-based assessment tasks (such as essays, case studies, and role-play report-writing), you will need to invest time in training your students how to cope with the latter kinds of assignments. This may be especially challenging if the tutors assigned to work with you lack experience with such assignments as well as with the content of the subject.

To reduce the risk that your use of pluralistic teaching methods will cause you to run into resistance from your head of department, you should:

- Take care not to cause difficulties for your colleagues. Your colleagues are unlikely to feel threatened if they know that you teach alternative approaches to economics, for they will normally expect to be able to deal with any challenges that come from your students, and they will view such challenges as rather unlikely. What *will* annoy them is the removal of content that they used to be able to presume students had covered in upstream subjects that you have been assigned. It will be a wise move to consult with them to find out what they expect students to bring into the subjects to which your subjects serve as prerequisites. Try at least to cover the essence of this material in your pluralistic expositions, and document that you have done so.
- Be mindful that although you may think pluralism is a good thing, students may be very uncomfortable when there is ambiguity about

'the right way' to address a particular economic issue and about the lack of definite answers to tasks that you set. You will need to be proactive to get your students on your side by demonstrating at the outset that you have anticipated their concerns and have a strategy for dealing with them.

- A pluralistic textbook is key for reducing student anxiety if your students are used to learning from textbooks rather than via primary sources. If a suitable book does not exist, you may need to provide detailed lecture notes to your students and explain that their feedback will be helpful for turning these notes into a textbook.

- Emphasise that although it may be pretty obvious which theoretical approach you favour, you do not want your class to submit work that panders to you by ignoring other approaches, and that it will be possible to score well by defending the use of such approaches and making a case against the one that you often favour: what matters is how well they argue their case in relation to the context in question.

- Emphasise that displays of critical and creative thinking about ideas covered in the subject are what you particularly want to see, and that you will also reward those who demonstrate the capacity to do this by bringing in perspectives that have not been covered in class.

- Devote some of your first lecture to introducing your class to the ideas of the educational psychologist William G. Perry (1970) about how students change their views of the teaching and learning process as they develop their intellectual maturity. Emphasise that you appreciate that members of your class will differ in which of Perry's stages they are at. Those who are not yet comfortable with moving on from dualistic, black-or-white ways of thinking may be able to get some confidence to try to make the move if you can show them that they probably are already beyond that stage in other areas of their lives, such as in sport and entertainment where they can critically reflect on the quality of performances.

9.3   FOR UNDERGRADUATES, MASTER'S, AND FUTURE RESEARCH STUDENTS

A key lesson from my undergraduate experience, as set out in Chapter 3, is that ambitious, able undergraduates can approach their studies in a research-oriented way rather than viewing the learning process simply as being about mastering the contents of textbooks. A research-based approach to learning can be especially fruitful if you study with an interest in the evolution of ideas and different ways of thinking about how the economy works. The following suggestions may also be worth keeping in mind:

- Do not presume that you know best when it comes to choosing the subjects that you need to study to become a capable economist, even if your university advertises that it gives you a lot of choice because it is 'student-centred'. Be mindful that elite universities limit choice despite admitting the smartest students: Cambridge requires economics students to study economic history and politics; students at Oxford take economics with politics and philosophy.
- Take seriously the reading suggestions that your lecturers and tutors make, based on their experience; do not assume that online searches will give you better results.
- If your lecturers and tutors do not introduce you to the work of educational psychologist William G. Perry (1970) on the different learning stages that students go through as they develop intellectually, take a little time to find out about it by yourself and see if you can relate to what he argues. The Wikipedia entry on Perry is a good place to start. Explore Perry's work in your second undergraduate year and revisit it in your third year.
- If you are attempting an essay-based question, do not spend your introduction repeating/paraphrasing the question. Instead, use it to identify what is the underlying point of the question. Consider beginning your answer with, for example, 'This question raises the following important analytical issues...' or 'The wording of this question is an allusion to (or appears to be inspired by) ...' if you think you have decoded the point of the question. Then list the issues that you think you need to address to answer it successfully.
- Do not simply report what you have read; think critically and creatively about it and share your thoughts in your written work and in class.
- If you are presented with a practical problem, try to see what light you can shed on it by using material from previous lectures and tutorials; do not construct your answer based simply on material that you discover by putting key phrases into an online search engine while ignoring material from class. Your lecturers and/or tutors will have set

the assignment as a means of seeing what you can do with tools provided in class, and these tools should provide a framework for deciding which additional information you should try to find to check arguments or address additional questions that you raise in trying to deal with the task at hand.

- When you write assignments, put your sources and notes aside after revising them. Then assemble your arguments based on memories of what you have read. Only look at your sources if you need to quote directly from them. This way, you will write in your own words and your work will not end up merely as a set of sentences paraphrased from your sources in a way that differs little from plagiarising them. You should also end up with a better sense of where to refer to sources instead of making the mistake of believing that you must have a source at the end of virtually every sentence. You will be writing in a way that is not far from how you will need to write in examinations, and you will therefore be getting good practice for this, too.

- If you are an able student and have been studying seriously for an examination, you may be wise not to try to work out what is the best set of questions to attempt if the examination paper gives you a lot of choice. Uncertainty about which is the best set of questions will delay your commencement of writing and may prove distracting when you are writing. It may be better simply to start by scrolling down the paper and attempting the first question that you feel confident you can do well, and only look for your second question, in the same way, after completing the first, and so on.

If You Are Considering Applying to Study for a PhD

Getting a PhD involves a major investment of time, both in chasing scholarships in an effective way and then in completing a research project to a satisfactory standard. Modern systems for managing the progress of graduate students are designed to ensure that PhDs are completed in a timely manner, but they cannot guarantee that everyone who is admitted has what it takes to complete a PhD. So, before applying to study for a PhD, ask yourself the following questions to see whether you should go ahead:

1. Do you have a passion for doing economics because you hope to contribute, or enable others to contribute better, to human and environmental wellbeing?

2. Are you primarily interested in playing with economic models or econometric tools because of the technical challenges and opportunities they present?
3. Do you want to complete a PhD as a means to start a career as an academic or research economist?
4. Are you thinking of applying to do a PhD because you cannot think of anything else to do when you graduate, or simply because you like the idea of 'having a PhD'?
5. Are you the sort of person who gets engrossed in tasks and can handle working for long periods under uncertainty about how well and how soon you will be able to solve problems and without frequent rewards for your efforts?
6. Are you the sort of person who prefers to take life on a transaction-by-transaction basis, working to tight, short-term deadlines with immediate feedback on how well you have done, frequent rewards for successes, and a 'You win some, you lose some; it's the overall trajectory that matters' way of dealing with tasks that do not go so well?

You are probably better suited to doing a PhD if you answer 'yes' to the odd-numbered questions, for you appear to have the intrinsic motivation to contribute to knowledge in the long term and the resilience to keep going when the going gets tough rather than switching to something else. If you answer 'yes' to question 6, you might be wiser to consider aiming for a career in economic/management consulting, investment banking or in public service advisory roles in, say, a treasury department. However, if you answer 'yes' to question 3 because you hope to teach economics to university students, then you may be wise to reflect very seriously on whether you would enjoy what university teaching has become, compared with how your life might be if you decide instead to aim to become a high-school teacher of economics, with no pressure to keep producing research output that ticks the right boxes and without the challenges of dealing with dumbing-down pressures, international students with poor skills in the language of instruction, and students who have a sense of entitlement about the grades they deserve. A university job may offer better pay than you will get as a high-school teacher, but it will not necessarily be more enjoyable. If you become an academic, you will most likely find that, even if they have been to university, your neighbours will be under the misapprehension that you are on vacation for all the weeks that you do not spend lecturing or marking examinations. The key thing that an academic career offers, if you are not confined to a 'teaching-focused' position, is scope for engaging in research and getting the buzz that comes from discovering new things about your field of interest and sharing them with others, as opposed to being merely a conduit for knowledge that others have generated.

If you do decide to apply for a place in a PhD programme, you will need to attract interest from potential thesis advisors. In attempting to do this,

- Do not send untargeted email messages to all the academic staff in the departments in which you are interested: such messages are generally viewed as 'spam' and simply get deleted, even if the sender claims to be familiar with, and inspired by, the addressee's work.
- Only send inquiries to academics whose research appears to be in the area in which you hope to work. Be direct about which of their publications has led you to believe they will be interested, and why, in the research proposal that you attach to your expression of interest.
- Your research proposal should be a document of 6–10 pages and should include details of the issue you hope to study, how you hope to study it, and the key references. You probably will not end up doing exactly what you propose, but the point of sending the proposal is to indicate your research potential and provide the basis for starting a dialogue with the potential advisor to whom you are writing.
- The PhD supervision track records of academic staff may be available from their research profile webpages. Only seek to enlist as a principal advisor someone whose track-record as an advisor (preferably, in at least one case, as a principal advisor) includes some completed PhD projects. This is not merely likely to reduce your risk of receiving poor-quality advice; enlisting experienced advisors may also enhance your ranking in the processes whereby scholarships are awarded. Your ability to attract an experienced advisor will be a good signal to the scholarship ranking committee about your research potential. It will also signal, in conjunction with the advisor's track record, a high probability that a successful candidacy will result if a scholarship is awarded to you. For associate advisors, a track record in PhD supervision is less important, for it will be expected that they will learn the art of PhD supervision by working with an experienced principal.

- Be mindful of the risk that members of your prospective advisory team could decide to switch to another university before you have finished your PhD. It is not always possible to follow an advisor who moves. Nor should you count on an advisor who moves being willing to switch to serving in an external role. Given this, ask yourself whether other academic staff in the department might be able to fill a gap in your advisory team if one were to arise.
- Be mindful that the department may need to provide staff from outside your advisory team to assess your progress at PhD milestones. If there are no staff in your research area who are not in your advisory team, this could prove problematic – for example, if you were doing a macroeconomics project from a heterodox standpoint and all the heterodox macroeconomists were in your team, you could end up running into opposition from a mainstream macroeconomist who did not view your methods as valid. So, when applying, this is another reason for trying to ensure the department has more staff in your area than you need for your advisory team.

9.4   FOR RESEARCH STUDENTS

Research students differ greatly in how ready they are to undertake research and produce research-based publications, so there are no sure-fire sets of rules about how they and their advisors should interact to ensure that a research thesis is produced on time and to an adequate standard. At the outset, some students will already have inferred what an original research project needs to entail and how academics go about writing up their research findings. Such research students may mainly need mentoring about authors and publications to explore and feedback about the quality of what they produce. These students are likely to be able to produce theses that contain no work that has been jointly authored with members of their advisory teams. But some research students may struggle to get started unless they work initially more as if they are their advisors' apprentices, for example, by initially working on small projects jointly with their advisors, gradually doing more and more themselves until they can, so to speak, 'fly solo'. Clearly, the latter may need to have advisors that are extremely prolific as producers of research papers, so that the process of turning ideas into research activities can be fast enough for them to get enough experience of how to do it in time to develop a viable project plan for their confirmation milestone. Then, while implementing their own planned research, such research students may continue apprentice-style work on joint projects that were already underway, moving on to the stage of learning how to write up research. In these kinds of cases, the finished theses may include some jointly authored work from the apprenticeship stage. It is important for research students and their advisory teams to discuss which of these cases, or a case somewhere between them, applies to their own situation.

Keeping on Track

- Have a 'plan B' in case what you are trying to do proves impossible to do in the time available to you.
- Ensure that you have regular meetings with members of your advisory team at which you discuss what you have done in following up on objectives set at the previous meeting and set objectives for the next meeting. If your advisors do not try to develop such a routine with you, you will benefit from initiating it with them.
- You should expect to receive critical feedback about the work that you do, and you should view critical comments not as a personal afront but as offered with your best interests in mind. This may take some adjusting to if, as a high achiever, you have previously been used only to being praised.
- Act upon the advice that you are given, unless you can demonstrate to your advisors that it is not appropriate advice. This is what you are going to need to get into the habit of doing not just to get a PhD but also for getting your work published in high-quality outlets that use rigorous peer-reviewing processes.
- Seek to develop a capacity to 'gut' the articles and books that you read so that you neither waste time reading every word nor fail to discriminate between works that require very careful, in-depth and possibly repeated reading and works that have only a few points of relevance to your research project.
- Expect to work on your research beyond regular office hours, and do not allow teaching and other activities to take up more than a day-and-a-half of your time per week.
- Attend departmental seminars and the progress review presentations given by your peers. This will not merely widen your knowledge of

economics; it will also give you food for thought about the process of doing and presenting your own research.

- Avoid social isolation: being part of a social group will help give you the gumption to keep going when you run into challenges with your work. You may also benefit from exchanging ideas with your peers.
- If you run into difficulties of a personal nature, or in your relationship with your advisory team, that seem to be jeopardizing your chances of passing your next progress review milestone, discuss them with your PhD programme coordinator sooner rather than later.
- Read Creedy (2007, 2008) and Townsend (ed.) (2020).

Your Contribution to Knowledge
You are likely to experience difficulties with progress reviews, thesis examiners, and in turning your PhD research into publications, if you cannot demonstrate the following with clarity:

- That you (are going to) offer an original contribution to knowledge and what it consists of in terms of filling, to some degree, a knowledge gap that you can demonstrate to exist in the existomg literature..
- How you (plan to) achieve your results, and the strengths and limitations of your method versus those of other methods that others have advocated for use in the area in question and/or that you considered and rejected. Do not simply 'follow standard practice'.
- Why your contribution is significant, both in terms of the issues that it addresses and the issues that it reveals as needing to be addressed and/or capable of being addressed by building on what you have done.

If you are writing a traditional monograph-style PhD thesis, you also need to be mindful that you are writing for an academic audience, rather than for the public in general: achieving clarity should not get in the way of being relentlessly analytical and stylistically formal in your writing. If you identify relationships between variables or patterns in the way that events unfold through time, you need to try to establish the causal mechanisms that have a high probability of underpinning them.

Just as with capacity creation and innovation by firms, research students face the risk that the value of their investment will be less than they hoped due to their failure to discover that others have already done something similar or that their work is similar to what others are doing.

The latter may launch it first or launch it at the same time in a better-executed form. You may reduce this risk if you do the following:

- View a 'leave no stone unturned' mentality as a key aspect of being a good scholar.
- Search for existing contributions using as many synonyms and related terms as possible.
- Always check primary sources in your area of interest; relying merely on what others have said about them (for example, in book reviews) puts you at risk of not knowing about things secondary sources have failed to mention or misrepresented.
- Always seek to uncover the genealogy of contributions that you find especially interesting: their authors may have raised similar ideas to yours in precursor or successor works to those that you have read (and they may have noted good reasons for not taking them further).
- Be mindful that searching via library catalogues may fail to indicate works that the library does not hold, such as the latest working papers produced by scholars at other institutions. Library catalogues may at least reveal the existence of books that are not held insofar as reviews of books appear in journals that are in the catalogue.
- Do collect and compare reviews of books that you view as significant for your research area, but do not let them serve as substitutes for your own reading of the books in question. If possible, read potentially significant books *before* you read any reviews of them; this way, you may have a bigger chance of arriving at original insights.
- Avoid research topics that seem to you and/or your advisors to be obvious opportunities and straightforward to undertake – especially if they have already figured as 'suggestions for further research' in previous PhDs and publications.
- Pursue research projects that arise because you can see a problem that has long been unrecognised by academic researchers (even if it might seem to be something that would not surprise people who are not used to thinking as the academics have become accustomed to think), or because you can see a highly original way of trying to deal with a significant problem that has long bedevilled a particular area of knowledge and research.
- Stake your claims to originality by publishing them in departmental working papers as soon as you can; do not wait until you can get them accepted in journals.

- Take careful account of the work of those that you nominate as potential examiners.

In Relation to the Limitations of Advisory Inputs

- Ask to have PhD advisors removed from your list of advisors if your work diverges from their area of expertise to such an extent that you do not seek advice from them. If you do not do this, they are likely to take a share in a 'completion reward' that they do not deserve and be able to use you completion as a means of attracting more PhD students.
- Do not hold back from registering complaints to your PhD programme coordinator if any members of your advisory team repeatedly fail to provide you with feedback about the quality of your work. Doing this is not merely in your own interest; if, as a result, you switch to a better advisor, your action may help other students by preventing your PhD from being listed on the research profile of your former advisor.

Publishing Your Contributions to Knowledge

- Do not delay the process of trying to get your research published, for others may be working on similar lines and may receive more attention if they get published first, even if their work has less to offer.
- Even if your PhD research is submitted in the traditional 'monograph' format, you should seek to publish your findings in well-ranked journals rather than as a book. This will serve you better for signalling the quality of your work to potential employers. It is also likely to result in more publications. This is not to say that you should not seek to publish your work in book form several years after your articles have been published, by which time you may be in a stronger position to know how to revise your thesis for publication and take your contributions beyond the articles.
- The exception to the 'articles first' rule is where your thesis examiners and others who have seen your work are convinced that you have made a significant contribution whose significance can only be properly appreciated if it is published as a book. The higher the standing of those who urge you to publish it as a book, the more

seriously you should take their advice. It will be especially helpful if they are prepared to write a foreword for your book.

Three PhD-based books illustrate the need to be careful here. The fate of Duncan Ironmonger's (1972) belated PhD-based book provides a cautionary lesson about the first-mover advantages that go to those who publish articles ahead of those who publish more extensive complementary work in books (see further, Earl *et al.*, 2022). Jason Potts's (2000) PhD-based book is an example of a career-launching monograph: his PhD was right for this format, especially given its instant success with the J. A. Schumpeter Prise. My own PhD-based book (Earl, 1986b) was far less successful than Potts (2000), despite being reasonably successful for a heterodox economics monograph; my PhD could have yielded worthwhile articles even though the material in the book was presented in an integrated manner. If the book had been released later, the articles could have helped to market it by developing interest in my wider contribution.

Advisors as Co-authors
There are ethical and reputational issues to be mindful of here, and research students should be aware of the risk that their advisors may act in a predatory manner. For example, a research student who is well beyond the stage of needing an 'apprentice-style' relationship with his or her principal advisor is potentially at risk of being used by the advisor as someone who can generate joint publications for which the advisor has done rather little and yet tries to claim lead author status. (Note that if the advisor's family name comes after the student's, an alphabetical list of authors can also give the impression that work has been shared equally even if the truth is that the advisor has done virtually none of it.) Those who feel uncomfortable about pressure to engage in joint publications should discuss such matters with their PhD programme coordinators. Consider applying the following operating principles:

- Defer joint publications with PhD advisors until your PhD is complete unless they are based upon work that is not part of your PhD research. In respect of the latter, do not let 'side projects' divert you from doing what is expected of you at your next progress review milestone.
- Avoid agreeing to have any of your PhD advisors listed as co-authors of publications based on work that you have done for your PhD. Co-

authored PhD chapters and/or publications create ambiguity about your capacity to do original work on your own.

- Be mindful that some PhD advisors may be mainly interested in working with you as a means of enhancing their publications records. You may test to see whether your prospective advisors fall into this category by establishing at an early stage (preferably in writing, in email interactions) what their policy is in relation to joint publications with PhD students. Except in cases where joint papers emerge via an initial 'apprenticeship' process, advisors of integrity should view their roles as limited to the provision of advice, much in the way that they advise journal editors when serving as referees of papers. Referees do not become co-authors by virtue of the suggestions that they make.

- It is unlikely to be ethically acceptable to publish papers from an initial 'apprentice' phase as anything other than jointly authored. However, if your thesis advisors feel entitled to claim joint authorship of later work from your PhD because it is essentially based on original ideas that they have supplied, they have been spoon-feeding you and co-authorship does indeed signal limits to your capacity to do original research. Your credibility as a researcher will be in doubt unless at least some of your PhD-based publications are solely in your name. Ideally, your job-market paper should be one of the latter.

- To ensure that you can establish the extent of your original contributions, routinely record meetings with your advisors (with their permission, of course: they should appreciate that it is good to have such recordings due to the challenges of taking good written notes during meetings) and keep records of email interactions with them.

9.5   CONFERENCE PARTICIPATION

All too often, attendance at an international conference is little more than a means of achieving subsidised access to opportunities for touristic experiences or visiting friends and family. Much of the networking that goes on at conferences amounts to a collective 'whinge-fest' about the state of the university system. Those who have non-standard dietary requirements are often catered for poorly. Those who travel long distances may find that the size of the audience at their presentation makes the ordeal and environmental impact of the journey hard to justify, and they have to contend with a significant risk of picking up a nasty bug during the flights. Hence, my general conclusion is that wise and environmentally responsible academics should take note of Herbert Simon's (1991) travel theorem and adopt his practice of desisting from attending conferences. It is usually possible to learn more by spending an equivalent amount of time downloading and reading recent articles and working papers in the field in question, and networking can be done more efficiently by email and Zoom interactions with those in one's field.

You may find yourself under pressure to attend conferences from PhD advisors, or from promotion and tenure processes that expect you to use conferences as venues for publicising your research and for networking, or because you have been invited to be a speaker at a conference organised by academics you know and/or whose work you respect (as opposed to a commercial conferences, which generally should be avoided). In such situations, the following rules may be worth applying:

- Avoid large general conferences unless: (a) you need to attend job market interviews being held adjacent to them, or (b) there will be multiple sessions (i.e., not merely a single session of you plus a couple of other speakers in the same broad area) in your field of interest.
- Favour small, specialised conferences, or better still, workshops on well-defined topics relevant to your research area.
- Recognise that the main career benefits of conference attendance will go to: (a) research students who may get feedback on their work from a wider range of scholars, as a check on the quality of feedback provided by their advisory teams, and who may be able to enlist as referees eminent figures that they succeed in impressing; or (b) those who are invited to give plenary presentations, for such invitations will be viewed favourably by promotion committees looking for signs of reputation and impact.
- If you are a heterodox economist and attend sessions of papers by mainstream economists, or if your paper is included in a session at which the other papers are by mainstream economists, be prepared to experience difficulties in getting the other participants to see where you 'are coming from' when you raise questions or give your presentation.

If you decide, as I eventually did, that you are no longer going to attend conferences, do keep in mind the potential benefits of instead spending time on (a) identifying those who may be interested in your work, and (b) writing emails to them in which you send your recent work to them and explain why you think they may find it complementary with their own work. At the very least, use time that you might have spent on attending a conference to set up, and load your work to, a ResearchGate account and create 'following' links with like-minded scholars, as a prelude to sending your papers to them. This kind of virtual networking can be much more effective than face-to-face networking at conferences as a means for marketing your contributions to knowledge.

9.6   'DO' AND 'DON'T' PUBLICATION RULES

The Publications Pipeline and Your Promotion Prospects
It is vital to get enough of a stream of publications whose quality is high enough to enable you to go beyond probationary employment and into a continuing position. Failure to do this will condemn you to positions in lower-status institutions with less scope for research, or to a teaching-only position. But after surviving probation, you should not feel you have to avoid periods when you have no publications. During my career, I felt that I should keep delivering two or three publications on average per year, with very few years in which there were none. I met this objective, but it was not an objective that I should have set. It came about because that was the publication rate that I established early in my career, and it seemed to serve me well in terms of advancement. This led me to fear that if I ceased to sustain at least the same rate of output, I might harm my career prospects by giving the impression that I had lost my urge and/or capacity to keep delivering output. But what I should have been doing, once the research audit system arrived, was to concentrate on trying to demonstrate that I was determined to produce only research output of the highest quality and that I could achieve an average of at least one publication of such quality per year.

Academics in research audit-driven systems are only as valuable as the quality of their output in the upcoming audit. This means that it is possible to be 'hot property' in the academic market and in internal promotion processes even if there are noticeable gaps in one's publication list. Those gaps might seem, to lay observers, to signify periods in which one has been taking it easy. But the key thing is what follows such periods, for the gaps may signify years during which one has been beavering away trying to crack difficult problems or gathering and analysing data, followed by years in which some papers were held up in refereeing processes that, in economics, can take up to a year to deliver even an initial verdict on work that is not desk-rejected.

Of course, one is not 'hot property' when such a publications drought has been going on for many years and there are not even 'revise and resubmit' verdicts to report. But once the drought is over and one can point to a bunch of valuable outputs, it can be time to make one's next career move. With half a dozen A*-rank journal articles in the past five years, a chair may be attainable even after a publication drought of similar duration. There is no need to plug potential gaps in one's publications list with works of lower quality to demonstrate that one never takes it easy. Indeed, such works send the wrong signal: they suggest that you do not know how to play the publications game, for you are not resolutely focusing on original research of the highest standing.

A related area to bear in mind when considering when to apply for promotion is your capacity to demonstrate that your work is having an impact that is on an upward trajectory. Screen shots from your Google Scholar profile provide a vivid way to demonstrate the uptake of your research as a whole and of individual publications. If there is evidence of an exponential uptake of your work in the years since your appointment or most recent promotion, your chances of winning promotion will be enhanced, whereas if your annual citation rates have not reached stellar levels and seem to have plateaued, you may be viewed as having got as far as you deserve to go up the career ladder.

Aiming for Impact
It is important to know how to play the publications game even if you are not promotion-obsessed and merely want to leave a legacy of publications whose collective impact is not needlessly lower than you might have generated from the effort you put into producing them. Most of what most academics write garners very few readers and citations. Instead, as with the market for popular music, the market for academic contributions is dominated by a very small proportion of superstars who manage to write multiple works that are spectacularly successful. Richard Thaler's Google Scholar profile illustrates this: by April 2023, he had a dozen works whose citation scores each exceed the total citation count that I had been able to achieve for *all* my (slightly more than 100) publications. Indeed, Thaler had 106 publications that had been cited at

least 106 times. However, by behaving in a suitably strategic manner, you can advance a long way up the tail of the publishing distribution even if your ideas do not have superstar potential.

The first step in doing this is to recognise that, if you do not reflect on how you use your time, you run the risk of ending up with a publications list that includes items that, if you were being realistic, you should have expected to have no significant impact. If you are an early-career researcher or are hoping to achieve promotion or win a position in a better university, it is vital that you set out to reduce the risk that this will happen.

Time spent producing research outputs that hardly anyone reads, and which have negligible impact on practice and/or the knowledge-generation process, is time that has not been well spent. For example, if we judge impact purely in terms of citation counts, it is far better to devote 500 hours to producing a paper that yields 150 citations than to use the same amount of time to produce ten papers of lower quality that can only be published in little-read outlets and which each have trouble garnering even ten citations.

Of course, it is important to recognise that some publications have significant impacts despite receiving very few citations, but you need to be able to judge whether what you are thinking of writing comes into this category and how you would document its impact. A possible example of such a contribution is a chapter written for a book aimed at undergraduates that introduces a heterodox field and inspires someone who reads it to pursue a successful academic career in that field. But how would you expect to be able to document this impact if you were the author of the chapter? Moreover, note that, even that kind of prospect does not imply that you should accept an invitation to write such a work: in terms of comparative advantage, it might be better if a teaching-focused academic wrote it and you remained focused on a research article for a well-ranked journal. The exception might be where you had a distinctive perspective to offer on the field in question and believed it to be important that undergraduates and their lecturers were exposed to it: this was why I accepted two invitations of this kind (Earl, 2004a, 2011b). It is OK sometimes to go against what you know your dean would prefer you to be doing, but your career will stall if you do this frequently, for you will end up with a list of publications whose impact is hard to demonstrate as being significant.

So, you should aim to publish the bulk of your work in well-ranked journals and concentrate on quality rather than on the quantity of publications that you achieve. If you play the research audit game as if you crave promotion, you will delight your dean while also giving yourself your best chance of not squandering your potential to have a significant legacy of impact. In the past, research audits may not have been as focused on impact as they should have been, but the situation will improve during your career as education ministries and research funding bodies seek to ensure better social payoffs from resources invested in research. It is vital to recognise that the ways that the audits typically view types of publications are roughly right in terms of the citation probability of an average paper published in a particular category.

The following rules may help you to limit the investments you make in publications that have very little chance of making an impact:

Articles

- Attempt to find out whether your institution's library has any agreements with journal publishers or individual journals whereby articles by members of staff will automatically qualify for open access. (I had no idea that such arrangements sometimes existed until I wrote Earl, 2023a.)
- Do not aim unduly low when you first submit a paper for a journal due to presuming that the demands from referees and editors of top-ranked journals will be tougher. You might indeed have a bigger probability of a 'desk rejection' from a top-ranked journal, but if your paper gets as far as being sent for refereeing, the refereeing process might even be less challenging than with journals of lower rank. The lower-tier journals aspire to be promoted to a higher tier, so they may try harder to ensure that the papers that they accept have been through a very thorough polishing process to ensure a strong impact. The key thing is to be submitting a paper that looks potentially original and significant enough not to be 'desk-rejected' by the editor and instead goes on to achieve at least a 'revise and resubmit' initial verdict.
- Do not publish any of your work in C-ranked journals, as papers published in them are unlikely to achieve more than a handful or two of citations and will be viewed as of insufficient quality to have been published elsewhere.

- If you cannot get a paper published in at least a B-rank journal, simply leave it as a departmental working paper: your work will be more readily accessible, and hence more likely to be cited, as a working paper than as an article in an obscure journal to which very few libraries subscribe.

- It is a mistake to make an exception to the above rules based on the assumption that, if you publish a paper in an obscure journal whose field seems best aligned with the subject of the paper, online search tools will ensure that it will get discovered and read. In reality, search engine algorithms may favour publications in journals whose articles are frequently cited. Moreover, even if a contribution in an obscure journal does get listed early in the search results, this does not guarantee that those who ought to read it will do so, for they may not go far enough down the list of search results or may opt only to read works by familiar experts in the area and/or that are published in well-ranked outlets. Availability will also be an issue: if the publication is not part of one of the major academic publishing platforms, it may be unwise to assume that potential readers will bother to incur the small cost in time and effort of checking whether it is available from the author via ResearchGate or Academia and then applying for a copy via such portals.

- Do not publish in unranked journals unless they are too new to have become ranked and have editors, editorial boards and publishers whose standing signals that they will soon become B-ranked or better.

- Do not seek to publish in journals whose names include a country adjective unless your paper is about research specific to that country. If you publish other kinds of work in them, it will usually have a far smaller chance of being cited than if you had published it in a journal that specialises in the field to which it contributes. There are a few exceptions to this rule, such as where the journal name includes the word 'American'.

- Be mindful of the risk that parochialism could affect whether your work is read by some US scholars: other things equal, seek to publish in US journals.

- Do not seek to publish short 'comment-style' papers about shortcomings of papers in the journals in which the latter were published. Journal editors are likely to prefer not to publish them, as doing so indicates that they were culpable in not spotting the issue earlier, and the original author typically will get an opportunity to whitewash over the problem via a rejoinder. It will usually be better to save the critical perspective for inclusion in a full-length stand-alone article in the same area.

- Always attempt to deal with all the referee requests that you receive unless you can demonstrate a good reason exists for not acceding to them. Lazy waffling justifications for not attending to some requests will be seen for what they are, and they may increase the risk that the referees will retaliate by raising additional issues to be addressed.

Books

- Do not seek to publish a book until you have achieved more than a handful of articles in well-ranked journals, even if your first book does not include sections reprinted from your articles. This rule ensures that you can demonstrate that you can play the article publication game and can produce work of a high enough standard to be accepted via thorough, double-blind peer review processes. If you begin by writing books, the quality of your work and your willingness and capacity to produce high-ranking research articles to help your department score highly in research audits will be in doubt, as books are typically much more lightly refereed than journal articles. Although books may be reviewed in journals, the reaction there may be far more lukewarm than in pre-publication reviews, thereby making it difficult to demonstrate the quality of your book by using extracts from reviews in the portfolio you use when applying for tenure and promotion.

- If you have an idea for a book that is not built primarily on papers that you have previously published, map out a detailed draft contents page and then ask yourself which original chapters or sections of chapters have potential to be developed into high-quality journal articles. If some of them have this potential, work on them instead of the book in the first instance. In other words, a draft detailed contents can signify the basis for a much bigger research programme than you have realised.

- Beware of writing a scholarly book that will be consigned to 'other books' in a research audit even though you view it as an original contribution. Any such book that is based on a subject that you have been teaching is unlikely to look like a research-based monograph when viewed by a research auditor unless you have chosen a suitably 'dry' title and have had it published in a respected monograph series.

- Do not seek to publish a book that is a collection of related, previously published papers unless the papers have already had a significant impact and unless their impact will be enhanced by being packaged together with a substantial reflective introduction. Such books are likely to be viewed as 'other books' in research audits because the research in them is not new. If the papers did not have an impact when first published, collecting them in a book may fail to relaunch them even if you invest time in improving them.

- Do not set out to write a pluralistic textbook to fill what seems to be a gap in the market. The gap may be smaller than you think due to many heterodox economists who preach pluralism not favouring the approach(es) that you cover alongside dominant thinking. If you write such a book and do the job well, it may win you respect from your heterodox peers and achieve reasonable citation scores, but it will not enhance your career prospects: it will come at considerable cost in terms of foregone original research papers and it will signal that you cannot be relied upon to concentrate on helping your department to maximise its research ranking. Consider instead making your teaching resources freely available via your personal website.

- Be mindful that publishers differ considerably in how they operate, so try to find out what recent authors' experiences have been like with publishers that you are thinking of approaching. Working with a well-established private company that looks after its employees and handles copyediting and typesetting inhouse or locally can be a much less stressful experience than working with part of a large multinational that has very rapid staff turnover and outsources copyediting and typesetting to low-wage economies. Also, think carefully about how potential publishers differ in how they market and price their books, and how user-friendly their eBook platforms are.

Edited Books

- Only accept the role of book editor for handbooks and 'companion'-style books or for anthologies where you have an opportunity to write a substantial introduction to the field in question. Such works have a reasonable chance of being cited and the editorial role signifies your standing in the field. The same cannot be said of conference proceedings or festschrift volumes.

- Editing a book will be more time-consuming than it needs to be if you do not set a template for your authors to follow and do not provide regular progress updates as a source of social nudging to laggard contributors.
- Be very careful about whom you invite to contribute to any book that you edit. Rejecting disappointing chapters is problematic because they are invited works, unlike regular articles submitted to journals. If you are very disappointed with a chapter, get a couple of referee reports on it and use them as grounds for rejecting it or insisting on major revisions. The author will be impressed by your use of external referees and may not realise that not all chapters have been given the same treatment.
- If you have an idea for an edited book of complementary chapters, pitch the concept instead to the editors of a related journal as a potential 'special issue' of the journal that you would be prepared to edit.
- If you wish to honour someone who has been a great mentor to you, do not do this by editing a festschrift in their honour. With such books there is a big risk that contributors will dig into their filing cabinets and submit a paper that they have not been able to place elsewhere but which has a title that aligns with the proposed title of the book. A significant festschrift is unlikely to result unless contributors are willing to write original papers that genuinely pick up themes raised by the person being honoured. You can show your appreciation more effectively via a retrospective journal article about the scholar in question that marks a particular milestone in his or her life. This is more likely to be read than a festschrift volume, for it will be readily noticed by subscribers to the journal and by those searching for a paper in the issue in which it appears.
- If you do edit a book, do not consolidate references from individual chapters into a single bibliography at the end of the book: those who wish to photocopy (or, in the case of an eBook, download) individual chapters will want the references, too.

Chapters or Sections of Edited Books

- Be very wary about accepting an invitation to contribute a chapter to an edited book unless the editor is a major figure in the field in question and has taken note of your work before it has become widely noticed.
- There is a possible exception to the rule above: entries for handbooks or chapters for 'companion'-style books that would not be suitable for submitting to journals may yield positive impacts for your reputation as an authority in the area and will have a better chance of being cited than a typical edited book chapter.
- Before accepting an invitation to contribute to an edited volume, check other edited books by the publisher in question to see how well they are designed to ensure that individual chapters can be discovered by search engines (for example, are individual chapters listed at the publisher's website and in library catalogues and, if the book is available online, are chapters listed for individual downloading?). These factors will affect a chapter's chances of being read and cited.
- Be mindful that having a significant proportion of your published outputs consisting of chapters in edited books is likely to have a negative impact on how your research capabilities are perceived, as edited books are generally seen as only lightly refereed (if at all) and likely to have very poor citations scores.
- Being asked to write a book chapter can play a useful role by leading you to think of a paper that you otherwise would not have thought of writing. However, ask yourself whether the paper you are considering offering as a chapter for an edited book appears to have potential to be developed into a journal article of B-rank or better. If it does, save the paper or the idea for the paper for a journal unless there is a compelling reason for allowing it to appear in the book. (Be careful here regarding 'obligational' reasons. You can earn respect by declining and referring to you existing commitments to high-quality work.) If it seems to be suitable only for a C-rank or an obscured journal, do not agree to write it up it to become part of a book: few will read it and your time is better spent working on a better paper for a more highly ranked journal.
- Do not assume that, if you contribute a chapter to an edited book whose other contributors are well-known in the field in question, the other contributors will enhance your reputation by reading your paper

and then citing it in their subsequent work. What is likely is that when the other contributors receive their personal copies of the book, they will note the details of their contribution on their publications list, shelve the book and move on to other projects without ever bothering to read the other chapters.

In sum, if you doubt that the work you are considering doing is going to be viewed favourably in a research audit, do not go ahead with it. Invest your time in raising the quality of work that does seem to have potential to be viewed favourably (for example, if you think the planned research could be published in a B-rank journal, consider what you will need to do to get it into an A-rank journal), or in devising better projects and/or developing your research capabilities. If you do not see potential payoffs to such investments, you should consider using the time to do a better job as a teacher or in your administration and service contributions.

Two Caveats
I acknowledge that there is scope for taking a pluralistic view about what constitutes a wise academic publishing strategy. Those who are already well established and have no aspiration to move upward or onward to other jobs may feel comfortable about not sticking to the strategy of publishing fewer works and restricting their publications to research audit-friendly output categories. With no concerns about establishing their reputations, they may accept frequent invitations to provide papers for obscure journals and for edited books in areas closely related to their previous output. Such papers may only make incremental advances on their existing contributions, but their authors may view them as means by which they can get their latest thoughts into shape and stake their claims to them. Authors of such papers may expect that they will eventually pull together sets of their fresh ideas from such papers into much more significant papers that can be published in well-ranked outlets and may end up getting cited frequently. The extent of overlap with previous work, and the authors' experience in putting papers together quickly, may mean that producing these staging-post contributions has negligible opportunity costs: the time spent on them is essentially part of the product development time for the significant later works that they envisage. Insofar as such publications lead to work by less established authors getting noticed in the same journal issue or book volume, established authors who pursue this strategy are also operating

in a collegial manner. But this is not a strategy that early-career researchers should try to follow.

Secondly, I want to stress that, if word gets around that a paper is a key source in a particular area, it will attract readers even if it is not published in a high-status journal so long as would-be readers can get access to it. This was the case long before the advent of modern information and communication technologies: in the 1950s and 1960s, despite the absence of modern photocopiers, email and pdfs, determined scholars would manage to get hold of 'mimeographed' working papers that they had heard were must-read contributions. Indeed, the authors of such papers could leave them unpublished because their career advancement depended on their reputations rather than on publication metrics. (Gorman, 1956, is a classic example of a paper that was well known and influential long before its belated formal publication in 1980; for further discussion of attitudes at that time toward publishing, see the tribute to Gorman's contemporary, J. A. C. Brown, by Creedy, 2023.) Today, the combination of a hot topic and open access can generate a huge audience even if a paper is not in a top-tier journal. For example, consider the access statistics for the article that I wrote about Richard Thaler for the series of articles on Nobel Laureates that is published by the B-ranked *Review of Political Economy*. The editors and publisher decided to publish my paper with open access (Earl, 2018a) and by 24 January 2026 it had been viewed 42,330 times. Clearly, I did not waste my time writing that paper even though it delayed progress on my *Principles of Behavioral Economics* by several months. Moreover, writing the paper also helped me clarify my plans for writing that book.

9.7   THE PRODUCTION AND MARKETING OF RESEARCH
       OUTPUT

Heterodox economists will probably react to the suggestions set out in Section 9.7 by arguing that it is very difficult for them to achieve publications in high-status journals because there are so few of these journals that are open to papers that do not conform to the standard modern template whereby a mathematical model is expected. They will probably also be concerned that many well-ranked economics journals are run by people who conflate orthodox economics with the discipline of economics and view anything that does not fit the orthodox template as being something other than economics (such as sociologoy). That may indeed apply to economic theory journals, but I have come to believe it is a needlessly defeatist view of the state of economics. A brighter future awaits those who design and market the products of their research mindful of what is needed for competitive success in the market for contributions to knowledge.

Conceptual/Theoretical Contributions versus Empirical Contributions
There is little hope for those who go against the grain in economics if the dominant way of doing economics is little more than a religion whose adherents construct and worship abstract mathematical models that are disconnected from reality. But if, deep down, those who operate in the dominant way view themselves as scientists, the way ahead for those who believe economics should be practised differently lies in applied research and the pursuit of implications from evidence-based models. Unlike priests, scientists will change how they see the world if they are presented with an empirically based case for doing so. They may resist initially but, sooner or later, they will accept such alternative points of view – even if only into the 'protective' belt of their research programme because they can find a way of doing this while adhering to their 'hard core' notions (cf. Lakatos, 1970).

It is only in the latter way that 'new' behavioural economics has been admitted to the mainstream. But at least it is a foot in the door that might eventually enable more radical empirically based challenges to be admitted that further diminish the domain of the orthodox theoretical core. In the meantime, mainstream behavioural economics has been, and continues to be, extended via the construction of what Berg and Gigerenzer (2010) call 'as if' behavioural models – i.e., models that are every bit as mathematically abstract as conventional constrained optimisation models. But Thaler's career success show that the mainstream will, sooner or later seek to accommodate evidence-based views of decision-making that clash with orthodox theory, especially if these contibutions are marketed in relation to anecdotes that ring true in terms of everyday experience.

So, if you seek to make an impact with work that goes against the grain, do not concentrate on producing papers on economic method and conceptual aspects of your approach to economics; instead, concentrate on producing high-quality empirical work that demonstrates the power of your conceptual perspective. If you need to employ a non-standard empirical method, be mindful that even if it proves problematic with well-ranked economic journals, it may be perfectly possible to find well-ranked journals that mainly publish research from, say, marketing scholars but which are open to the method that you have used. Producing this empirical work may take much longer, per paper, than the conceptual papers that many of your heterodox peers keep producing, but if done well it should open the door to higher-impact journals.

Grant-Funded Research
Operationalising your ideas in a timely manner via empirical work may require a large research grant so that you can pay others to gather and process data for you. It may take several attempts to learn how to play the grant-chasing game successfully, even if your institution provides support such as 'grant-writing workshops'. Be mindful of the following:

- If you are not successful in winning funding but need the funds primarily to buy research time rather than to pay for equipment or to reward subjects in experiments, consider trying to implement the project by assembling a larger team to contribute some of their own research time to it and share in the authorship of output from it. As was evident with the swift completion of the map of the human genome, many hands make light work. Moreover, we might expect journal editors to be less likely to 'desk reject' submissions from a large team of authors: the size of the team should signal a credible project.
- If you only make available enough time to 'throw together' a major research grant application, you will be wasting that small investment of time. To have a good chance of success, such a grant application needs to be approached with the thoroughness that is necessary when writing a PhD confirmation document or a paper for a top-tier journal. You will need several months to review the literature and establish why your project deserves to be funded.
- If you have no previous experience of grant-funded research, try to recruit a colleague with a track record of success in grant-funded research to be a co-chief investigator: project management expertise may be just as valuable as project-specific knowledge of the area in question.
- If your application is successful, do not presume that your research plan will run smoothly. The referees may be as oblivious as you are

to issues that you will encounter. If things start to get problematic, consider at an early stage what alternative methods there might be and be mindful that you could suffer from sunk-cost bias and escalate your commitment to something that cannot be made to work. See also Townsend and Saunders (eds) (2018).

- Be very careful about whom you hire as researchers to assist you: if you hire a lazy researcher or one who turns out to lack the skills you thought they had, you may have great trouble doing what you promised. If none of those who apply for your research position inspire confidence, do not hire the least unsatisfactory applicant so that you can get the project running: unspent funds from your first year's allocation can usually be rolled over, whereas wasted funds are non-recoverable. A couple of very bright students, whose capabilities you know well and who can work on a part-time basis, may be far more productive than a full-time applicant for an externally advertised position who has more advanced credentials but seems not entirely convincing when interviewed.

- Be mindful that how swiftly you extract publication outputs from a major grant-funded project is likely to affect your promotion prospects and ability to win further grants. As far as promotion is concerned, demonstrating that you can complete a project successfully and in a timely manner may be more important than demonstrating that you are trying to get funding for your next project even while completing the current one. If it looks like there are going to be delays in achieving publications from the project, it may be wise to apply for promotion before you get close to the end of the funding period, which will leave you in a position to talk, if you are interviewed, about the publications you anticipate, without it being evident that the project has definitely fallen behind schedule.

- To minimise the risk of damaging your reputation by failing to complete grant-funded research in a timely manner, consider delaying your grant application until you have completed front-end and 'proof of concept' work for the project, even though this work is listed as part of the project and you do not mention in the application that you have already done it. If your time budget for the project is right, you will finish the project ahead of time and have funds left over to invest in equivalent work for your next project, and so on for a succession of projects. Applying for funds to do work that, in part, has already been done might seem ethically questionable to some, but operating in this way reduces the risk of project failures and overruns.

- If your research project involves using a large questionnaire to gather data from a large sample of subjects for statistical analysis, ensure that, when you test your questionnaire with a small sample of subjects, you attempt to ascertain not merely whether these subjects can understand the questions and complete it in the time you expect without appearing to get fatigued and/or flustered but also whether the answers that they provide are consistent with each other and seem plausible.

If the project on mobile phone connection service plan choices that was discussed in Section 8.4 had been conducted in line with the final two points above, funds and time could have been much better spent as the first phase of the project would have been rethought before the application was submitted: it would have been perfectly possible to get as far as designing and testing the questionnaire before applying for funding, and we could have checked to see whether our test subjects' usage rate responses were consistent with their responses for their monthly spending on mobile phone services and the plans they said they used.

Positioning Research

If you take care with how you seek to position your work relative to the existing literature, you may be able to increase your chances of getting it accepted by higher-tier outlets and even place heterodox contributions in journals that you normally view as mainstream. Consider using the following strategies:

- Do not try to align your work with a particular school of thought unless the outlet in question is aligned with the school of thought whose principles you are employing. (For example, consider the work of Brian Loasby. He drew on a very similar range of sources to me and his output could readily be described in the ways that I have characterised my contributions. However, he never aligned himself with a single school of thought and achieved a wider readership across many schools: see further, Cañibano *et al.*, 2025.) If you signal attachment to a particular school of thought, you risk losing readers who are partial to other schools of thought and are not open to pluralistic ways of thinking. This applies even within heterodox economics, for although heterodox economists may often argue that students should be taught in a pluralistic manner, what they may really mean is that the approach to which they are partial is what students should be taught in parallel with the mainstream approach. In other words, they may not be keen on pluralism within heterodox economics and may be suspicious of heterodox approaches other than their own. Anyone who explicitly pursues (as I have done) an eclectic approach that weaves together elements from multiple research programmes may raise hackles across a wide front rather than motivating scholars from diverse research programmes to explore how elements from seemingly incompatible research programmes can be integrated.

- Present your contributions as means of expanding the realm of economics by taking account of things that economists have hitherto had to exclude when working in the area in question, but first note the achievements of those who have made contributions subject to those limitations. In other words, demonstrate that you are not trying to trash previous contributions and that you seek to augment them by revealing new opportunities for those who research in the area in question. Try to get a foot in the door by this strategy even when you can see that your approach can also deal with the areas in which the established approach has been applied and can accommodate the latter's findings.

- Implicitly use a pluralistic method as a Trojan horse for opening the minds of readers to your favoured approach (see also Earl and Peng, 2012). For example, first show the results of modelling the situation of interest in terms of conventional variables, and then show the difference it makes to include variables (for example, from psychology) that are not normally used.

- Do not allow yourself to get diverted from potential for a constructive synthesis or a context-focused pluralistic approach because you feel a need to demonstrate difference to establish that you have something new and important to offer. (This is where I made a key mistake when writing *The Economic Imagination*, which I sought to correct when writing *Lifestyle Economics*.)

Do You Have an Appropriate Research Programme?
A scientific research programme is the academic equivalent of the corporate strategy of a firm. Like a firm (cf. Kay, 1982, 1984), you need to consider the following:

- What are the common threads between research that you have done previously and research that you plan to do? If your research lacks common threads, your research essentially entails a shotgun approach in which you seise opportunities wherever you spot problems in the existing literature; you do not really have a research programme that directs your research based on a dynamic view of your comparative advantage in each field. You would be wise to consider potential for achieving synergies between your investment in new project and investments that you have previously made in acquiring and being able to contribute to knowledge in particular areas.
- Are you placing your research bets in too few areas? There are risks of not having 'several threads to one's research bow': although you may be more readily able to be an expert in a single focal area, your output may dry up due to you being unable to see opportunities that you would notice if you also worked in other fields and were mindful of scope for cross-fertilisation. With 'all your eggs in one basket', you will be especially vulnerable to the impact of your work being truncated and to having trouble achieving publications of high standing if interest in the field wanes as more exciting opportunities are noticed elsewhere with scope for bigger marginal contributions.
- How crowded are your research fields with other researchers and how easy is it for others to enter these fields?
- Are your research goals feasible in terms of their scale, even if they seem promising in terms of synergy links between them? The answer to this question may depend greatly on how much time you expect to get for research and the quality of your research facilities. In my own case, the idea of building an integrated behavioural/Post Keynesian approach to economics by successively returning to consumer behaviour, corporate behaviour, and monetary economics/ macroeconomics over rolling ten-year cycles might have been feasible in the long run if I had moved much earlier to a top-100 university instead of having a lost decade in one that left me with little time for research and lacked adequate library facilities. After my lost decade at Lincoln University, it was not realistic to try to get back on

that track, as there was too much new literature to catch up with. Hence, a strategic rethink was necessary when I escaped to the excellent research environment at the University of Queensland.

- What capabilities do you need to develop or access as prerequisites for doing high-quality research in the fields in which you hope to contribute?

Working with Co-authors

Co-authored contributions to knowledge are the academic equivalent of joint ventures between corporations, with multiple contributions by a particular set of authors being the academic equivalent of strategic alliances between corporations. Such arrangements have grown in popularity in academia (as in business) in the past half century. There are good career reasons to consider making such arrangements part of your research strategy and for not trying to work mainly as a solo researcher:

- Although you may generate a higher overall RePEc ranking, other things equal, if your work is not co-authored, you will likely produce more output if you work with others, and it is likely to be better in quality due to the creativity boost that comes from bouncing ideas around with co-authors and due to scope for overcoming individual capability limitations by working with those who have different skill sets. This can apply even with skills as a writer (which, say, econometricians may welcome) or in using graphics software (which may mean that you become more inclined to put graphical analysis into your papers rather than avoiding doing so because you lack the capacity to turn handwritten sketches into high-quality digital diagrams).
- Promotion and job search committees typically do not count co-authored works on a fractional basis per author; rather, they seem mainly to look at the total number of papers an applicant has in each ranking category. Indeed, co-authoring seems to be generally favoured as indicative of potential for work of high quality, as well as a sign that one is easy to work with and a team player.

Given this, you might want to consider the following strategies:

- A 'Lennon and McCartney' approach to authorship may prove productive if you can find a research partner who is 'on your wavelength' and is at least as capable and industrious as you are. It involves agreeing to write a joint paper on each occasion that one of the pair has an idea for a paper. The person who has the idea writes the original version of the paper largely single-handedly after initially discussing it with the research partner. When the revision requests arrive, the other person attends to them. Thus, although all the papers produced in this way are listed as being jointly written, like Lennon and McCartney songs, over the long term about half will be mainly 'Lennon' and the remainder mainly 'McCartney'. This way of writing should not be at odds with ethical codes of conduct, for the second author adds value at the revision stage, and the revision process may proceed more smoothly insofar as the revising author is more flexible when it comes to making changes and can see creative ways of addressing issues that the referees have raised. For this strategy to work effectively, the research partners need to have similar amounts of time for research. If this is not the case – for example, if one author is in an elite research-focused institution and the other is in a more teaching-focused institution – a backlog of revisions will build up for papers first written by the author who has more time and/or the author with less time will have trouble contributing enough papers on which he or she is the initial author.

- If you supervise colleagues who keep failing to produce research output of the quality and quantity that they should be capable of delivering, consider working with them as a co-author. This may be a more hands-on means by which you can steer them into developing good research habits and it is a potential way to achieve success in your administrative role while increasing your own output. If your supervisee's main problem is procrastination, he or she may be much more productive when working with you than working alone so long as you are firm in setting goals and monitoring your supervisee's progress on a project of mutual interest. But do not try this strategy with underperforming supervisees who are simply not putting in the hours that they should be working and are, for example, simply 'cruising towards retirement'.

The creative side of joint research is an area where virtual methods of communication are not so productive as face-to-face communication between researchers. Highly creative ideas for joint work tend to emerge unexpectedly in the flow of conversation between academics rather than from scheduled meetings specifically set up for brainstorming purposes.

Obligational Issues

You should be mindful that some of those who seem to be impressed by your work and seem to be trying to help your career by serving as your patrons may be imposing net costs on you. For example, they may divert you from doing original research of greater value by offering you opportunities to edit books or to contribute book chapters or articles for special issues of journals. Instead of mentoring you about how to get your papers published in well-ranked journals, they may ask you to let them publish your work in journals that they edit but which are not of high status. You need to be assertive enough to decline these kinds of invitations. The patrons that are worth having are those who offer constructive criticism and advice, as well as encouragement and praise. When a worthwhile patron offers you an opportunity that serves his or her interest, it will be one that results in you doing more valuable work than you might otherwise have done.

Conference Papers and Self-Control

Given the shortcomings of conference travel that were noted in Section 9.6, the main reason for presenting a paper at a conference instead of sending it straight to a journal may seem to be that you suspect you will not get around to writing the paper unless you commit to writing it for presentation at a conference. Beware of using this basis for making conference submissions: if your self-control is so poor that you feel you have to write papers under the pressure of external deadlines, you are likely to end up producing a thrown-together paper at the last moment. Such a paper will be nowhere near ready for submitting to a journal. You need to consider alternative strategies for coping with your weakness of will, such as working with a co-author whom you would not want to let down and whom you know will keep prodding you to make your contributions.

9.8   EXTERNAL SERVICE

Book Reviews

- When you receive invitations to review books. be mindful that orthodox economists who focus on publishing journal articles rarely write book reviews. So, if you decline invitations to review books, you should not view your behaviour as at odds with professional norms.
- Be mindful of the extent of your reciprocal collegial duties to be a reviewer if you are a writer or editor of books that others review.
- Limit your book reviewing to books that you believe you need to read and have readily available in the long term for your own research. Your career will benefit little from having a significant list of book reviews except insofar as they get listed in the RePEc database and affect the ranking scores that you include in your applications for tenure and promotion.
- If you want to read a newly published book as part of your own research, consider volunteering to serve as a reviewer of the book in an appropriate journal. Generally, a review can be written in a day or less, whereas the main demand on the reviewer's time is reading the book ahead of writing the review. Making a commitment to review a work that you think you ought to read is a good self-control strategy for ensuring that you do find the time to read it.
- If you are reviewing a book that seems significant and you have a lot to say about it, consider asking the review editor if you can write a review article instead of merely writing a review. If this is approved, choose a title that does not signal 'review article' yet is still appropriate for what you write and may grab the attention of those who browse the journal.

Journal Refereeing
This is an essential area in which one must make collegial contributions but doing the job properly will have significant opportunity costs. Logging your refereeing contributions via your ORCID record is a way of getting evidence of the role you are playing in this area. Some journals (such as the *Journal of Institutional Economics*) even offer annual 'best referee' awards with significant cash prises, as part of their efforts to maintain the quality of the articles that they publish and ensure timely

delivery of referee reports. But as you become better known and more heavily cited, you will be wise to set yourself a set of rules for managing your commitments as a referee. Consider, for example, the following:

- Decline any invitation that you do not have time to attend to properly in the very near future and explain why: editors prefer honesty here (with suggestions for other scholars to approach) rather than having to chase reports that are overdue, especially as late reports in response to such prompts are prone to be prepared in haste and thus to be of low quality.
- Decline all requests from journals of less than B-rank unless they are new, yet-to-be-ranked journals with a clear focus that relates to your work and with well-known editors and editorial board members. The latter kinds of journal could rapidly become well-ranked and potential outlets for your own work and/or potential venues for you to serve as an associate editor in the long run if you establish refereeing relationships with them.
- Try to limit your refereeing tasks to those for journals in which you aspire regularly to publish your own work. Quite apart from any reciprocal relationship you might establish with the editor(s) for getting your work over the line, your refereeing activities will help you keep abreast of the fate of the kinds of submissions received by these journals and increase your knowledge of the latest work in the field.
- If you are an early-career researcher, you should not expect to referee more than about half a dozen papers per year.
- If, as an experienced referee, you start receiving an inordinate number of refereeing requests from a particular journal, you probably should inquire with the managing editor about whether you should be given an associate editor role (perhaps multiple associate editors are inviting you to referee for them, without realizing the total load you are getting).
- Always address the authors of the papers that you referee in as civil and constructive a way as you hope you will be addressed by those who referee your work.

Many of these points should also be kept in mind if you receive invitations to referee book proposals and research grant applications. In relation to the latter of these, the last point is especially important. I have been told that economists are prone to referee research grant applications in the hyper-critical way that they tend to referee journal articles, and to fail to be really clear about whether they believe the project that they are refereeing should be funded. This can result in grant applications by economists having disproportionately low success rates when they are considered within a pool of applications that includes submissions from disciplines such as psychology and sociology whose referees give clear signals about whether projects should be funded. Even without being hobbled in this way, grant applications by economists will often struggle in such pools because the rigours of refereeing processes and the more technically challenging nature of writing applied papers in economics result in economists tending to accumulate publications at a slower rates than scholars at similar career stages in the other disciplines in the pool.

Journal Editing

Depending on the quality of the journal, an associate or managing editor role can send valuable signals about your academic standing, with positive effects for the standing of your department. In some cases, you may find that your head of department is willing to take account of such a role when making departmental 'service' allocations via a fair workload formula. Before you agree to take on such a role, check whether this applies. However, you should also:

- Be mindful that, if you agree to be a journal editor, it will chew up more time than you think, even after you have allowed for it to chew up more time than you initially estimate of what it will consume.
- Before you accept a journal editing role, engage in due diligence regarding the statistics for submissions, acceptance rates, refereeing times, and the number of accepted papers in the publication queue. The last of these is especially important for limiting the stress of the role: if there is 'nothing in the bank' in terms of accepted papers, maintaining quality standards while meeting publisher deadlines may become a nightmare.
- Do not accept even an associate editor role if you have not yet reached the mid-career stage.
- Ideally, only become a journal's main editor if you can do so in a co-editing role with someone who is not likely to exploit your collegiality and whom you know you can rely on to help keep things running if you are indisposed or when you take a vacation. It may be useful to

work with a co-editor whose skills complement yours rather than duplicating them – for example, if you are a 'big picture' thinker, work with someone who has an eye for detail-related quality, or vice versa.
- Do not agree to become an editor of an existing journal of less than B-rank.

External Examination of PhDs

The consequences of making an unwarranted assessment in either direction in this role could be much more significant than with a refereeing task, so:

- Do not accept a PhD examination task if you think it could be tricky to complete with due reflection on the thesis in the time allowed, even if you are keen to accept because this will help you establish your professional standing. Late submission of a report may cause major problems for the candidate in the job market.
- Never accept a PhD examiner role if you have any kind of obligational link with anyone in the candidate's advisory team.
- Be mindful of the challenges of assessing whether work submitted for a PhD represents a sufficient contribution to knowledge to justify the award of a PhD. Hence, it is probably wise not to start accepting invitations to be a PhD examiner unless you have (a) read more than a handful of PhD-based books, (b) a good sense of the quantity and quality of journal articles that past PhD students from the institution in question have been able to extract from their PhDs, (c) received an external examiner invitation that includes detailed criteria by which you are expected to assess the thesis, or (d) some experience of seeing how the examination process has worked for students in whose advisory teams you have served.
- If a thesis that you are examining seems to have major flaws, be mindful that this may reflect poor supervision and a poor progress review system rather than being purely due to the student's shortcomings. In such a case, if you can suggest how it might at least be brought up to master's standard, opt for a 'revise and resubmit' verdict rather than a 'fail' verdict. Then indicate in your covering letter your uncertainty about how the thesis came to have such shortcomings. If the student has a record of ignoring advice, the revision will probably be denied, but otherwise you may be throwing a much-needed lifeline to the student and attempts will probably be

made to find a new advisor to help the student see how to achieve a major improvement.

9.9   THE PURSUIT OF PROMOTION

Not all academics are well-suited for enjoying senior academic positions in the modern university environment. So, before you set your heart on attaining such a position, you should reflect carefully on why you want one and what such jobs are really like. In the past, when academics were trusted to get on with their jobs and there were minimal top-down managerial pressures, professors could reasonably expect that their roles would not entail a reduction in their research opportunities except in years when it was their turn to be the head of department, though even then research time might not be reduced if a reduced teaching load provided time for the extra administrative tasks. But now that universities are being run on managerialist lines, a full professorship typically entails administrative tasks that lower-tier staff are spared.

The only kinds of professors who seem to be able to avoid major administrative tasks are: (a) those who hold research chairs, and (b) those whose research is of the kind that enables them to keep moving between universities every few years, before they are assigned major administrative roles, or who can use the threat that they will move, with a significant negative impact on the departmental research rating, as a means of deterring anyone from increasing their administrative duties. The latter category appears to be the preserve of orthodox theorists who maintain a steady output (not necessarily a huge quantity) of papers in the highest-status journals – especially if they can demonstrate administrative ineptitude if they are ever assigned administrative tasks. They are unlikely to be readers of this book.

So, my message to readers is that it may not be a good idea to focus on trying to obtain a full professorship if the aspects of academic work that you most enjoy are research and teaching. If you cannot resist the temptation to chase a professorship, you should be very careful about which ones you pursue. As I discovered the hard way, positions at the senior lecturer and associate professor levels in well-resourced universities can be much more enjoyable than a full professor position in a poorly resourced university with predominantly weak students and where one has both little time for research and no power to change departmental modes of operation in ways that one views as desirable.

The prospect of higher pay that a senior position brings should not be allowed to conceal the importance of being able to enjoy the job itself, given the hours that the job will consume – including sleepless nights and distracted leisure hours if it does not go well. If you crave a professorial position, it is vital to be clear about why you crave it in non-pecuniary terms and whether your expectations about such a position are realistic. In some cases, the prospect of losing research time that you have been used to being able to enjoy may indeed not seem to be problematic because you are genuinely keen to immerse yourself in rather different roles from those of a sub-professorial academic, such as:

- Building or transforming a department into an entity with a specific set of characteristics that you value (for example, a thoroughly pluralistic approach to teaching and research).
- Taking on administrative roles such as head of department or as a deputy dean that would set you on track toward the role of a dean or even higher in university management.
- Creating a centre of excellence in your field, in which you spend more of your time in a leadership or managerial role, getting others to do research and doing rather less yourself.

However, if you are telling interview panels and yourself that you crave such roles, you need to ask yourself whether you *really* crave them, given that they are likely to limit your time to enjoy teaching and do your own research. It is very important to ask yourself if your real reasons are more narcissistic in the sense that what really appeals to you is the title, which you believe you deserve based on your achievements so far. If so, be mindful that the position may not turn out to entail 'life as before but with more pay and status' and that you may not enjoy the loss of control that you are likely to experience even if you gain a bit more control in some areas.

Better pay may be welcome to those who otherwise will struggle to meet expensive family commitments if they have children and are living in countries where public health and public education systems have been so run down that recourse to the private sector seems necessary if one can afford it. But those who find themselves in such a situation may be wise to consider whether a sideways move that entails emigration to an economy with a less ravaged public sector might be better than a domestic move to a full professor position to meet their family-related goals.

Finally, take happiness economics seriously when considering the pursuit of promotion. If you desire a higher-status position because the extra pay that it brings will enable you to buy, say, a larger house, a more up-market car and other consumer durables, more expensive holidays, and so on, you would be wise to recognise that you are likely rapidly to habituate to any elevation in material standards that you achieve once you go beyond the real income level at which you cease having to worry about meeting your basic needs and start to have resources left over to enable you to engage in self-actualisation. My first job did not enable me to enjoy that kind of situation, but it would have done had I stayed in it and continued to rise up the incremental pay scale. Moving from Stirling to Tasmania took me into the comfortable zone with time and resources to pursue self-actualising leisure activities. Moving to the chair in New Zealand greatly increased my access to such resources but reduced the time that I had for enjoying them, and frustrations at work overshadowed everything to a far greater degree than my PhD saga had overshadowed my time at Stirling. My professorial experience was a lesson about the importance of being careful about what you wish for, as your wish may be granted.

9.10   AVOIDING BAD JOBS

In the academic environment of the 2020s, it is crucial to avoid jobs that leave insufficient time to make original research contributions, for it is the quality of one's research that determines potential for moving to better positions or achieving promotion. In Chapter 7, I showed how research can be problematic to do in a bad professorial position. But it is clear that early-career academics, too, are vulnerable to this kind of problem if they allow themselves to become casual academic staff to support their families. Despite not being paid to work as many hours per week as colleagues who have the luxury of continuing positions, casual academic staff may find themselves putting in additional hours that are unpaid; this may be the only way that they feel they can do their jobs properly. They are especially at risk of doing this if they inherit subjects that badly need to be revamped. In the academic part of the 'gig economy', these types of casual teaching staff are at risk of being exploited by the employers that they hope will one day hire them for continuing positions. Having been hired as teachers, they throw their energy into showing how well they can perform as teachers, and they find themselves unable to extract publications from their PhDs or establish post-PhD research programmes.

The key to avoiding ending up in such dispiriting, dead-end roles is to be aware that they exist and then gather intelligence to determine the realities of jobs that one has been, or might be, offered.

If you aspire eventually to be offered a continuing role but are only being offered a casual position, you must get an answer to the following question: 'What is the track record of the institution in question for hiring its casual staff into continuing positions?' This needs to be answered not merely with reference to instances of staff who have managed to make such transitions but also with reference to the ratio between such staff and those who fail to get continuing positions despite serving as casual staff for more than a couple of semesters. If the odds look poor, look for jobs elsewhere; do not kid yourself that you will get lucky and be offered a continuing position sooner or later.

If you are competing for a continuing, salaried position, you should use informal meetings with prospective colleagues more as occasions for gathering intelligence than for creating favourable impressions of yourself. But such intelligence can be sought in ways that may create favourable impressions of the standards that you hope to meet in research and teaching. You should not be shy about asking questions such as:

- What is the workplace culture like here?
- Is this the kind of department where interactions between colleagues mainly consist of whingeing behind closed doors about the state of things, rather than collegial cooperation, team-based research, and so on?
- What is the operating style of the head of department? For example, does he or she practise 'micro-management', 'management by walking about', delegate a lot to committees, or simply trust you to get on with your job as you see fit?
- How frequent are departmental meetings?
- How bureaucratic is this institution's operating system?
- How much 'working from home' is common here?

- How many contact hours for lectures and tutorials do you have in a typical teaching week?
- Is there a formula-based system for allocating workloads, and do you think it works fairly?
- Which administrative roles would have the biggest cost in lost research time?
- How does the timetable system work, and does it give you any teaching-free days during the teaching period?
- How easy is it to get the library to add books to its collection?
- What is the process for getting study leave, and what financial support
- is available for study leave travel?

Not everyone will answer truthfully, but if you ask many prospective colleagues the same questions you may eventually be able to discern, say, whether you are looking at a toxic workplace that offers little scope for research and is blighted by favouritism, in-group and out-group divisions, and so on. Your best chance of discovering unpleasant truths will come from meeting with someone who has decided to exit and would feel guilty about encouraging you to take a job that will probably result in you experiencing similar pain to what he or she has been experiencing.

If you don't ask directly, there is no guarantee that anyone will volunteer the key things you need to know. This is especially the case where the job in question is a senior role and those in more junior positions are keen not to deter someone who, if they take the job, might make a serious effort to derail dysfunctional practices of an established in-group whose existence they were not aware of at the time they accepted their own jobs.

If you end up with a bad academic job, bail out as soon as you can, even if it means that you will need to move to a city that appeals to you less than the one to which the bad job brought you; do not spend, as I did (as set out in Chapter 7), nearly a decade trying to make the bad job come good.

The key to being able to get a job in which you will have good long-run prospects for doing original research is to lower your academic sights in the short run, in ways that enable you to buy time to get your research sufficiently on track to demonstrate that you are hungry to do research and have the capacity to flourish in a good research environment. In my case, I was able to do this by being willing to abandon the title 'professor' and take a lower-status job at a different institution where my head of department appreciated my capabilities and understood why I had been failing to deliver original research contributions in my previous position. Casual academics have to think more laterally than I had to if they are to get their research happening. First, they need to recognise that they are unlikely to obtain continuing academic appointments unless they cease being casual academics and switch to jobs that pay more per hour but provide them with opportunities to shift to part-time work or buy extended periods of leave during which they can work on research projects. Casual academics who are economists can do this more readily than their counterparts in many other disciplines.

One strategy for buying time to do research is to find a job working for an economics consultancy. After you have established your capabilities, you may then be able to have your billable hours limited to say, 70 percent of what they have been. If you can get such an arrangement and get your research happening again, you would be wise to try to arrive at a clear sense of whether you want to do such research because you see a good academic job as being of higher status than a well-paid consulting position and/or because you miss teaching, or because you enjoy doing research per se. You might find that such an arrangement is a long-term way for avoiding the drudgery of university teaching and administrative duties, and therefore not even feel it necessary to go on to chase academic positions.

Another possibility, suggested by Mark Casson (near the end of an interview by Gokh, n.d.), is to obtain employment as a university administrator. Even if such a job cannot be negotiated into a part-time role, it may leave the would-be academic with enough time and energy to work on research as a hobby, rather in the way that a part-time PhD student might do. Such roles may not necessarily come with access to a good research library but that is no longer the problem it might have been, thanks to the emergence of research-sharing websites such as Academia, ResearchGate and, better still, DeepDyve. The last of these is a legal means for independent academics to download journal articles on payment of a small monthly subscription – this is the academic equivalent of Spotify, the audio streaming service that displaced the illegal music file-sharing service Napster, whose journal paywall-subverting counterpart has been Sci-Hub. Academic appointment committees seem likely to respect those who end up with high-quality research publications via determined efforts of these kinds.

9.11   MOVING 'DOWN UNDER'

There is much to like about life in Australia and New Zealand. However, even in the age of jet airliners, those who moves there are likely to experience a chronic sense of being a very long way from Europe and North America. For me, moving 'Down Under' worked well as a route to a higher material standard of living but there were fewer opportunities to spend time with researchers whose ways of looking at economics had major areas of intersection with mine. Research audits arrived slightly later but then seemed largely to copy, with an ongoing lag, the evolution of the UK system. My overall verdict is that, even though the cheaper housing costs that I enjoyed would not apply for new migrants in the 2020s, it is worth considering the possibility of moving to Australia or New Zealand if you do not think you can make you next career move without relocating. So long as you do not choose a 'bad job', such a move is unlikely to wreck your career.

Those who consider moving to Australia or New Zealand should not view such a move as irreversible in the way that it would have seemed to, say, Irish famine orphans, Scottish miners or German peasant farmers in the mid-nineteenth century. Video conferencing makes it possible for Australasian academics to be interviewed remotely by northern hemisphere universities that are less used than those in Australasia to investing in fly-out visits by candidates. If your research record is appealing and your referees are scholars of standing, you should not fear being disadvantaged against domestic applicants. Being able to move 'back home' is important even if you find you like living Down Under, for you may one day feel duty-bound to return to handle 'aged parent' problems, either because you are an only child or because you would otherwise feel guilty about not sharing carer roles with your siblings. However, if you are very close to your family, long-term migration to Australia or New Zealand may not be a good idea.

If you are tempted by the idea of moving to Australia or New Zealand, you will be wise to consider how psychological factors may affect your experience and whether you become a long-term resident there. The psychology of making such a move goes well beyond issues relating to family ties. It can relate to your identity, especially if you get as far as becoming a dual-national and notice changes in what you think of the country that you left behind. The fact that there is scope for reversing such a long-distance migration brings scope for psychological complications, especially for those who have successfully dealt with the challenges of making an international relocation and do not view another one with great trepidation. Scope for returning 'home' without undue drama can result in migration being associated with what I think of as the cost of being 'torn', i.e., a chronically unsettled state where one feels pulled in conflicting directions. However, this chronic condition will not apply where migrants bail out and return 'home' after only a few years away. The likelihood of an early bail-out seems to depend on how migrants construe what their new lives are going to be like.

When I moved from Stirling to Hobart, I did not do any research on Tasmania, despite knowing virtually nothing beyond what I could infer from applying my knowledge of A-Level Geography to the island's location and from my general knowledge of Australia. But I did not make the mistake of expecting Australia to be like the UK except for having bigger distances between major urban centres, better weather and different wildlife. Such a view would have been akin to viewing it in institutional and cultural terms as a colonial branch office of the UK. Instead, I tried to arrive with an open mind and then see what I made of it. This was conducive to ensuring that any downsides that I noticed did not get in the way of noticing and appreciating positive differences from how things were in the UK.

This way of dealing with new environments helps to promote trading off the pros and cons that experience reveals or, if one thinks in terms of templates and checklists, being open to considering whether one has an appropriate ranking for pertinent characteristics and/or needs to slot new characteristics into one's list of priorities. It was conducive to doing a lot of exploration in my leisure time and in vacations, first in Hobart and around Tasmania, then on the Australian mainland and to New Zealand. The fact that, when I left the UK, I did not know whether I was going to live Down Under in the long run led me to want to ensure that I did not move on without having used my opportunities to be an explorer.

Clearly, if there is a lot to explore, the explorer mentality is conducive to becoming a long-term resident. By contrast, an early bail-out is likely in cases where migrants arrive with a point of view that centres on expecting to live largely as before but with new friends and colleagues and better material opportunities. As an example, suppose one's social life in the UK had been built around the ritual of 'going to the pub' on a Friday night. Despite Australia's reputation as a nation of beer drinkers and wine producers, things will prove problematic when it comes to

Friday nights except for those who live in small country towns or inner-city areas. Australia does not offer a pub-based culture since most of its population live amid vast suburban sprawl and there are very strict drink-driving rules; city centre bars tend to be a long way from most campuses and from where academic staff live. Insofar as there are bars out in suburbia, they are normally within large, returned services league or sporting clubs that focus on sitting down for a meal or gaming activities. Without the explorer mindset, such social disappointment is conducive to focusing on what one is missing, not on building a new kind of social life and getting out and about to get a bigger picture.

The social disappointment may be enhanced if the migrant has also assumed that the move will entail moving into a social setting with a similar socio-demographic profile: for example, if the migrant is an early-career academic who expects to continue with something like a student lifestyle, this may prove impossible if the new social circle consists mainly of couples who are preoccupied with raising children. A change in that direction may be underway within the set of social connections that was left behind in the UK, but, oblivious of this, the migrant may attribute this type of social disappointment to the place rather than to the passage of personal lifecycles. If the migrant came from a relatively small university town but has moved to a large, multi-campus university in a very large city, surprise at the demands of commuting to the various campuses will promote further concentration on the downsides of having left the UK. The idea of bailing out and moving 'home' will look especially attractive if, in the few years since leaving, the Australian dollar has risen significantly against the UK pound: the Australian experiment can then be abandoned with a profit.

In saying that an explorer perspective is less conducive to bailing out and returning 'home', I am not claiming that adopting an explorer mindset when moving Down Under will rapidly make one feel settled. My contention is merely that, with a lot to explore and reflect upon, one is more likely to stay longer than someone with misplaced expectations who hankers for what turns out to be missing.

In my own case, the explorer approach left me unsettled for many years as I developed a better appreciation of the pros and cons of the life that I had left behind and the range of antipodean lifestyles that were now available to me, especially as I ran out of new local exploration opportunities in Tasmania. The idea of moving to New Zealand seemed worth exploring because of its potential for a 'best of both worlds' lifestyle that offered a less extreme climate and (Auckland aside) smaller, less sprawling cities, without foregoing spacious, interesting housing and limited congestion. My then-partner was willing to try this lifestyle, too, but she ended up preferring a subtropical Australian lifestyle in Brisbane despite its downsides. After being a Down Under explorer for fifteen years, she settled. At that time, I had concluded that I preferred Christchurch in New Zealand as a better place to live than Brisbane but there were aspects of the UK that I missed. Yet, a few years later, I, too, moved to Brisbane, not to explore or settle but purely to try to get my career on to a better track.

Even after more than twenty years in Brisbane, I would not claim to feel settled as opposed to being unable to move elsewhere due to my partner Annabelle's obligational family ties. We both hanker after aspects of life in the UK, Ireland and New Zealand, yet we know that if we were to move to one of these three locations, we would hanker after aspects of life in the other two and in various parts of Australia.

Uncertainty about where one will end up settling is not conducive to investing heavily in embedding oneself socially where one currently lives. This can result in social ties to 'home' continuing to exert a bigger pull than those Down Under, with more attention given to maintaining the former than developing the latter. Yet, it is important to be aware of the entropic forces that migrants face in maintaining their social networks 'back home'. Although there may be a sense of 'picking up where one left off' when visiting friends on a trip 'home', it is not the same kind of friendship that one might have enjoyed if the migration opportunity had not been taken up. In time, friends disperse from the location where one originally knew them, so trying to catch up with them on flying visits every two or three years becomes increasingly challenging in logistical terms, forcing choices about whom to see as often as possible, sometimes, or possibly never again.

There is a seemingly obvious solution to being torn between rival places in which to live if you are not tied to any particular location by a job or family obligations: divide your time between the rival locations. Having homes in both the British Isles and Australasia is possible without being super-rich and can be done without anxiety via appropriate choices of 'lock-up-and-leave' kinds of residences such as apartments. But is such a lifestyle morally right, even if one can comfortably deal with its income tax implications? Guilt about leaving properties unoccupied while some people are homeless can be addressed by renting one home while away at the other, but we might have reasons to doubt that the use of carbon offset markets by airlines will genuinely eliminate the carbon footprint associated with each trip between the two residences.

Such environmental concerns should be addressed by anyone who entertains the idea of moving Down Under without eliminating all except for virtual ties to the rest of the world. In a world of environmental challenges, such a move may be something that you can do without feeling guilty so long as you accept Simon's travel theorem and feel comfortable with using services such as Zoom or WhasApp to keep in touch, and using online resources (including podcasts, Wikipedia and Google Earth) and television documentaries as means of seeing what other places are like. In my experience, having 90-minute Zoom catchups with old friends several times a year is much more enjoyable and authentic than visiting them in person once every few years for a day or two as part of a hectic schedule within what is supposedly a vacation. Simon's travel theorem also holds up well in relation to using travel documentaries as a substitute for 'being there': they often provide far superior information-gathering opportunities (for example in relation to views captured by drones and in ideal weather), though virtual tourism clearly does not offer the sense of achievement that comes from 'getting there' (for example to the top of a Scottish mountain) under one's own steam. But the same logic may be used to argue the case against moving Down Under as an exploration exercise as opposed to a means of getting a better quality of life: documentaries and online resources provide remote means of getting to know what antipodean life is like without foregoing attractive aspects of life that you already enjoy and without adding significantly to your environmental footprint.

9.12   RETIREMENT-RELATED ISSUES

It is wise to be mindful, throughout your career, of the implications of your career choices for when and where you will be able to afford to retire. The superannuation savings that you accumulate as an early-career researcher will grow far more by compound interest than your larger, late-career superannuation savings will grow. Hence, you need to be careful not to lose the potential retirement benefits from your early-career jobs if your career moves entail moving between different superannuation systems. This is especially so if your career involves moving between countries. Such moves may entail not merely switching to a new superannuation scheme but also may affect your entitlements to state pensions and medical services and may carry tax implications. Furthermore, the total value of a disparate set of pension rights accumulated in different countries will be affected by changes in relative rates of inflation and changes in exchange rates between currencies.

These are issues that I only became aware of rather belatedly, by experience. If I had delayed by one month my first international move, from Scotland to Tasmania, I would now enjoy a fractional UK pension from my years at Stirling. Instead, I was forced out of the UK universities' pension system and forfeited my employer contributions. On moving from Tasmania to New Zealand, I was again forced out of the tertiary education sector's superannuation fund, but this time my employer contributions were parked in another fund. Here, taking the default fund paid off as it was with an organisation that demutualised while I lived in New Zealand and it paid a significant bonus into the account when the demutualisation occurred. On returning to Australia, I was able to roll that balance back into the tertiary-sector fund that I re-joined. However, having a relatively small starting balance after 22 years as an academic had implications in relation to the choice that I was required to make between a defined benefit fund or a much less predictable accumulation account, pushing me toward the latter. Fortunately, the Australian pay and associated superannuation benefits enabled me to build up my balance to a far better position than I would have faced had I stayed in the New Zealand system – except that the latter was inflation indexed and built on a defined benefit; it also entailed a non-means-tested state pension, whereas the Australian state pension is means-tested. Finally, as retirement approached, the issue of taxation of retirement income came into focus, with the realisation that Australian retirement income would be taxable in the UK but untaxed (beyond the eligible age) in Australia or (as far as I can ascertain) if one is an Australian retiree living in New Zealand. Considerations of where to live in retirement may be further complicated by changes in relative real estate values.

So, be warned: if you move around a lot during your career, you can run into these kinds of issues. Moreover, if a career move is accompanied by an opportunity to withdraw and spend money from your retirement fund as you make an international move, you should ask yourself serious questions about your willpower in relation to whether you will be able to restore what you have spent, plus interest, so that your increase in current spending is not going to come at the cost of having to work significantly longer before you can retire. Be mindful that you are at risk of your cognitive processes driving you to overestimate your willpower as you contemplate drawing on your retirement savings to fund, say, a better car or house in the country to which you have moved. Perhaps the return on buying the better house will exceed the rate by which the savings would have grown if they were put straight into the fund that you now need to join, but this certainly could not be used to justify buying a better car. In such situations, it is important to do the financial calculations and be mindful of scope for present bias.

If your desire to retire comes from hoping to be free to get on with research without the pressures of having to teach and contribute to administration and service tasks, you need to be aware that it is easy to underestimate the benefits of retirement until one has retired. Suddenly, it becomes possible to operate as a no-stone-left-unturned kind of scholar and produce research output at one's preferred pace and without concerns about how it will fare in a research audit. If you wish to continue research but do not qualify for, or receive, an emeritus or honorary position, do not be fearful that research will become problematic because you will lose access to a university library. Such fears used to be justified, but they hardly apply in the era of DeepDyve, ResearchGate, Academia and scope for contacting authors directly by email to request their papers.

Given the challenges of working in a university, there is only one good reason not to retire on arriving at the point at which a financially comfortable retirement has become feasible, namely, an imminent credible possibility that your employer will shortly offer generous voluntary severance packages as part of a strategy of downsizing or infusing new blood into the ranks of its staff. Here, potential for incurring the pain of regret (and an associated sense of having foolishly misjudged the situation) will be hard to ignore (cf. Loomes and Sugden, 1982): if you resign just ahead of such a scheme being announced, you may experience regret about missing the opportunity to receive, say, a couple of years' post-tax salary as a reward for volunteering to leave via the scheme, but holding out for such a deal may bring regret about putting up with the job's downsides while waiting for a scheme that fails to eventuate. Would-be retirees should recognise here the risk of unduly delaying the start of an enjoyable retirement unless they set a firm rule about the maximum duration of the bets that they are prepared to make about the eventuation of voluntary severance packages. Otherwise, they will keep finding themselves with the same conundrum each time a deadline for giving their resignation notice approaches, and the more rounds they have kept working, the more likely it may seem that 'this time' the severance deals will get offered. It may be wise to remind yourself that 'money isn't everything' and then resolve only to make a single bet on voluntary severance packages being offered if they seem likely to be announced within the notice period following the point at which you think you have achieved enough savings for a comfortable retirement.

10 A Wider Vision of Behavioural Economics

10.1   INTRODUCTION

I have long been puzzled by the failure of most heterodox economists to embrace ideas from the kind of behavioural economics that I practised throughout my career. These ideas seemed to have enormous potential to be used in a co-evolutionary micro–macro synthesis with Post Keynesian economics, as well as complementing other heterodox approaches. Early in my career, before Thaler-style behavioural economics became widely known, there were signs that other heterodox economists of my generation were open to taking up behavioural ideas and using them in place of orthodox microeconomic theory. For example, I had no trouble sharing my behavioural enthusiasm for the normal cost approach to pricing with Fred Lee over many years, and I have admired how Marc Lavoie has (beginning with Lavoie, 1992) been weaving what I regard as behavioural ideas into his vision of Post Keynesian economics. However, despite the success of Lavoie's work, Therese Jefferson and John King (2010–11) found it necessary to reflect on the potential for bringing behavioural and Post Keynesian economics closer. Nearly a decade later, Geoff Hodgson (2019) made a further attempt to signal the potential role for behavioural economics in giving heterodox economics a brighter future. So, what is deterring younger generations of heterodox economists from enhancing their careers by embracing behavioural ideas of the kind that I habitually use?

Perhaps they find daunting the idea that they should get to grips with unfamiliar literature and concepts. That possibility was on my mind when I wrote my pluralistic textbook *Microeconomics for Business and Marketing* (Earl, 1995a), my first attempt to show how one could start bringing behavioural ideas into the classroom. Making it easy for others to adopt my kind of behavioural approach was again on my mind more recently when, when I wrote my *Principles of Behavioral Economics* (Earl, 2022) magnum opus and did my best to package it as a textbook and made a substantial investment in providing accompanying online teaching resources.

However, I have long suspected that resistance of most heterodox economists to adopting any kind of behavioural approach may also be due to them *not* being completely unfamiliar with behavioural economics but being unaware that not all behavioural economics aligns with their vision of it and with objections that they have arrived at based on their limited knowledge. If heterodox economists equate behavioural economics with the 'new' approach that centres on heuristics, biases, nudges and 'predictably irrational' behaviour, they may be hostile to *anything* tagged as 'behavioural economics' because they see it as being used in the following two ways:

(a) to prop up orthodox microeconomics (since it provides tools for addressing situations in which people seem to behave in ways that clash with orthodox notions of rationality, while it leaves other areas firmly in the purview of rational choice theory), and
(b) for devising policies to manipulate consumer behaviour in ways that serve governments and corporations rather than those whose behaviour is being manipulated.

But even if some people are indeed using 'new' behavioural economics in these ways, neither use provides a logical basis for shunning a wider, heterodox view of behavioural economics.

Regarding (a), it is important to understand that my approach to behavioural economics is an attempt to construct a methodologically coherent *alternative* to orthodox microeconomics by integrating ideas from 'old/evolutionary' behavioural approaches with *compatible* elements from the 'new' approach.

Regarding (b), I wholeheartedly agree that we should be concerned that knowledge of consumer psychology and decision-making processes may be employed to manipulate people against their best interests. However, the way towards a socially responsible economics lies not in blaming behavioural economics for the possibility of such manipulations but in acquiring knowledge of the forms that they take and then designing and advocating policies to counter them (see further the major papers by Hanson and Kysar, 1999a, 1999b). In other words, heterodox economists may find opportunities for taking what might be called a 'critical behavioural economics' approach to consumer protection. We should probably also recognise that although much of conventional modern behavioural economics appears to pander to libertarian sentiments by focusing mainly on nudge-based policies rather than on trying to enhance wellbeing via education and regulation, such work at least represents a 'foot in the door' in terms of steering mainstream economists away from the idea that wellbeing is maximised by taking a non-interventionist stance and leaving people free to choose.

Mindful of all this, I attempt in this final chapter to ensure that readers of this book end up with a sense that heterodox economists have much to gain by practising the kind of behavioural methods that I have worked with, without compromising core heterodox principles, over the past five decades. Here, I set out the essence of my vision of how behavioural economics should be practised and the areas to which it has potential to contribute, and I highlight the key differences between my heterodox approach and the approach of mainstream behavioural economists. It is useful to begin by bringing out the non-reductionist nature of my approach by highlighting the co-evolutionary nature of human agents, economic and social institutions, and the wider economic environment. What follows in Section 10.2 should be kept in mind when reading subsequent sections.

10.2   ECONOMIC AGENTS AND THE SOCIO-ECONOMIC SYSTEM

In the popular narrow vision of behavioural economics, the focus is on behaviour in situations where stimuli from the external environment are not employed in the way that a fully rational 'econ' would employ them; unlike an 'econ', real-world economic agents use repertoires of heuristics to simplify the process of forming expectations and selecting actions. Accepting that starting point should not be a problem for heterodox economist, for it is a statement of fact. However, although modern behavioural economists have shown considerable interest in social behaviour, in areas such as behavioural game theory and 'in-group' and 'out-group' behaviour, they cast economic agents in cognitively complex situations as self-sufficient users of heuristics. The analytical focus is on the use of heuristics that people in general are prone to use, as if these heuristics are part of human nature, and it seems to be assumed that the only way that others impact on the choices that individuals make is by shaping the flow of stimuli with which they are presented (such as when corporations and governments seek to shape the architecture of choice to nudge people to behave in a particular way). Otherwise, rather like Robinson Crusoe before he encounters Friday on his desert island, people are presented as if they choose alone and as if their environment is something that they simply take as given.

This simple vision has yielded powerful results, but richer research opportunities and potential for new findings are to be found via the more complex perspective at which I gradually arrived. It was not until the 2020s that I discovered that the ways that I had come to view human action implicitly embodied what cognitive scientists call 'enactivism' (see Frolov, 2024; Viale, 2024). This entails not merely accepting John Donne's famous 1624 poetic line that 'No man is an island, entire of itself.' It also entails a co-evolutionary view of humans and their socio-economic environment: we affect each other's ways of thinking and behaviour, while the ways in which we think and behave are affected by the contexts in which we operate, with our own behaviour potentially also affecting the nature of the choice environment in which we and others operate.

The following are among the implicitly enactivist ingredients that I picked up from my environment over the decades and which became part of my way of thinking, or that I have been involved in contributing:

- Market coordination processes are enhanced to the extent that disaffected customers 'voice' their concerns to suppliers rather than simply making an 'exit' without explaining why, though even better outcomes may eventuate if the provision of feedback is combined with a display of 'loyalty' that helps suppliers stay in business and effect changes (Hirschman, 1970). Those who meekly 'put up with' mediocre products and accept 'rip-off' prices will help to ensure that such deals continued to be offered.

- In dealing with uncertainty about what levels of attainment they should aim to achieve, people commonly use the behaviour and/or achievements of others as reference points (Loasby, 1976). Hence, their attainments will depend on whether they use local or more global (for example, 'world-class') reference points. External reference standards also have vital roles to play when figuring out how bold to be when taking financial risks (Minsky, 1975, 1982) or engaging in creative/innovative behaviour (Earl and Potts, 2013, 2016), and tidal shifts in boldness can result from competitive responses to what others are doing. This can result in the ratcheting up of boldness to the point of over-reach.

- Innovative ways in which consumers use or combine products sometimes run ahead of, and inform, the behaviour of established entrepreneurs. (A classic example of demand-side innovation is the mountain bike: see Buenstorf, 2003.)
- A significant amount of spending is fashion-related rather than based on personal preferences (Foley, 1893; Fullbrook, 1998; Andreozzi and Bianchi, 2007). People who view themselves as fashion leaders have to keep experimenting with different ways of consuming to maintain their differentiation from those who imitate their behaviour (Chai, Earl and Potts, 2007).
- The uptake trajectories of new products resemble how contagious diseases spread (Ironmonger, 1972).
- To a significant degree, expectations and behaviour are based on norms that are socially acquired through repeated exposure to patterns of stimuli that get increasingly memorised (without necessarily even being consciously processed) as probable features of particular contexts (Hodgson, 2003). However, changes in the relative frequency of exposure to rival patterns of behaviour can affect what a person views as normal, leading to changes in that person's behaviour that, in turn, affect the norms of other people (Hayek, 1952; Earl, 2017a).
- Some of the decision rules in a person's repertoire are acquired socially, though they may be incompletely acquired or improved upon by the recipient (Earl, Peng and Potts, 2007).
- People may develop knowledge about effective ways of allocating resources in a particular environment as a result of their preferred strategies being blocked by institutional factors, for such contexts are conducive to more extensive searching for solutions to problems (Loasby, 1967).
- Most of our wants arise via cultural processes rather than purely from in-built preferences; moreover, although firms may intend their advertising to serve as a tool for manipulating choices, it can also provide 'food for thought', i.e., ideas for consumers to consider in areas where they do not have well defined preferences (Hayek, 1961).
- Individuals commonly form their cognitions about the relative efficacy of rival products and/or suppliers as means toward particular ends, and about which ends they should attempt to pursue, not on their own but with the aid of other individuals and institutions that comprise the 'market for preferences' (Earl and Potts, 2004). In such

situations, their choices are 'market-assisted' rather than 'self-reliant' (Earl, Friesen and Shadforth, 2017). However, the possibilities to which they are exposed, and which ones are presented as credible (or 'thinkable'), will depend on the social contexts and networks within which their lives are embedded (Granovetter, 1985) and the extent to which 'their hands are tied' by prior lifestyle choices (Earl, 1986b, 2017a; Thompson, 1996).

• Decision-makers' attitudes towards a potential course of action are not based purely on how they see the possible consequences of selecting it but also on how they imagine their social referents would view such a choice, and how willing they are to comply with the views of their social referents (Fishbein and Ajzen, 1975).

This way of viewing decision-makers in relation to their economic and social surroundings intersects to some degree with Dekker and Remic's (2024) 'extended mind' characterisation of Hayek's approach to rationality, and with institutionalist perspectives that Frolov (2024) sees, with behavioural and Austrian thinking, as ingredients of an enactivist approach to economics. It offers ingredients for analysing whether and when the social side of cognition facilitates much better decisions than we might expect from a heuristics and biases standpoint, or whether it merely drives 'echo-chamber' processes that feed conspiracy theories and foster dysfunctional behaviour.

10.3   RESEARCH METHODS

At its core, behavioural economics involves analysis that is informed by studying how people behave, rather than analysis that is arrived at by making assumptions based on a view of how resource allocation decisions should ideally be made. Much of the knowledge that behavioural economists have hitherto deployed or have sought to generate has used experiments as means of studying behaviour. This method is commonly employed in computer laboratories that enable researchers to isolate the drivers of behaviour by setting the experiment in a stripped-down environment and running alternative treatments and a control group. However, the experimental method typically creates closed problems that research subjects are prevented from trying (or have no need to try) to address by using some of the means they would employ when trying to solve supposedly similar problems in real-world counterparts of the kinds of contexts on which the experiments focus. Economics experiments also require research funds for paying performance-based rewards to subjects. Other ways of studying behaviour may be less costly and may at least yield ideas that can be fed into the design of experiments even if they point to plural modes of behaviour rather than attesting to the truth or lack of truth of a specific hypothesis. Hence, I hope that readers will consider the following research methods:

- *Using research tools from personal construct psychology* – such as repertory grid technique (Kelly, 1955), construct laddering, implication grids and resistance to change grids (Hinkle, [1965] 2010) – to uncover (a) how people view their options as bundles of characteristics, (b) the deeper ends that these characteristics serve or compromise (Gutman, 1982; Reynolds and Gutman, 1984), (c) ideal and tolerable options, and (d) determinants of responsiveness to changes in incentives (Earl, 1986a, 2022, chapter 7).

- *Asking people how they behave in the context of interest, or (if observations are already available) why they behaved as they did.* Questionnaires and focus groups may not be completely reliable, but researchers can reflect on what the incentive might be not to tell the truth or how answers might be affected by how research subjects manage cognitive dissonance, and whether more reliable answers can be achieved by having more open-ended questions and/or asking subjects about how they believe people (rather than themselves) make decisions in the context in question. These kinds of research methods have advanced greatly since the days when Austin Robinson (1939) and Fritz Machlup (1946) reacted with hostility towards, respectively, behavioural research conducted by the Oxford Economists' Research Group in the 1930s and Lester's (1946) study of whether employers based their use of labour on marginalist principles.

- *Conducting ethnographic research by embedding oneself among decision-makers in the area of interest.* Even during the Lester– Machlup debate, Machlup was prepared to consider whether embedded researchers might get deeper insights into behaviour than a brief interaction with research subjects might reveal (see Lavoie, D., 1990). Moreover, it should not be forgotten that the use of embedded researchers can pay dividends when research subjects know much more about the research context than the researchers do (as with the study of New York bond traders by Abolafia, 1996, 1998) or by having more general implications, as with the embedded research that led psychologist Robert Cialdini (1984, 2009) to his influential analysis of the process of persuasion.

- *Using published text* – such as product reviews by lay consumers and professionals, case studies of business history, passages from novels, plays and screenplays, and transcripts of parliamentary proceedings and public inquiries (cf. Mosley, 1981), minutes of board meetings, and so on, as sources of information about behaviour or lay theories of behaviour (see further, Earl, 2011). At the very least, you can be confident that (except for the case of Crick, 2025) such sources will not have been authored wholly or partly with a view to impressing or helping behavioural economists. Even if you cannot create a statistical sample by such means, you may find anomalies or ideas from which to build testable hypotheses. Introspection may serve a similar role (Earl, 2001a, 2012a).

- *Using computerised simulation models* to explore whether observed behaviour is consistent with what is predicted by building and calibrating models based on simple decision rules. This method was pioneered by Cyert and March (1963) in the early days of computers and has been widely used by researchers in the 'old/evolutionary' behavioural tradition.

Those who intend to conduct economic experiments should consider incorporating verbal protocol analysis (Ericsson and Simon, 1993), supplemented with screen capture movies (Earl, Friesen and Shadforth, 2017, 2019), as means for analysing how subjects arrive at their decisions in naturalistic on-screen decision-making settings.

10.4   HUMAN OBJECTIVES AND THE IMPLICATIONS OF CHOICES AND CHANGES IN CIRCUMSTRANCES

If we want to know what people are trying to achieve and how they see their options in a particular context, we can readily find out by using repertory grid technique (Kelly, 1955) and construct laddering (Hinkle, [1965] 2010) to undertake 'means–end chain' analysis (Gutman, 1982). This makes it possible to peel back from how people view the surface-level characteristics of their options to the psychological connotations of having or not having these characteristics. This does not of itself explain how decision-makers rank their options based on such psychological connotations, but it certainly signals potential for behavioural economists to move beyond the conventional economists' practice of modelling economic agents 'as if' they maximise utility.

This opportunity has not been seized by 'new' behavioural economists. Although they emphasise that humans are not 'econs', they still model people essentially as utility maximisers – utility-maximisers whose choices are systematically – and therefore predictably – different from those that an 'econ' would make. We have Kahneman and Tversky's (1979) prospect theory to blame for this: knowledge of bias-inducing heuristics is used to infer that probabilities are not incorporated in the way that a skilled statistician would take account of them, while the utility function is reference-dependent and S-shaped, with its inflexion point at the reference point and displays loss aversion. It is essentially a modified version of the orthodox expected utility maximisation model: the heuristics that it embodies only play the role of generating predictable biases relative to what an 'econ' would do; they are not procedures or simple decision rules that play the role of ranking the options at hand. This is rather ironic, for one example of the latter type of heuristic is 'elimination by aspects', an earlier contribution by Tversky (1972) himself. (Another example of the latter kind of heuristic, which addresses uncertainty, too, is what I labelled 'characteristic filtering' in Earl, 1983a, 1986b.)

Prospect theory may indeed be the best tool available for explaining how financial gambles are taken (see Barberis, 2013), and it might deal even more plausibly with bounded rationality if behavioural economists follow my suggestion (in Earl, 2023b) that Shackle's (1949, 1969) 'ascendancy function' view of focus gains and focus losses could be bolted on to it to show how investors might remove the complexities of distributions of (adjusted) probabilities. However, in ultimately reducing choice to a form of utility maximisation, it sits rather uneasily alongside 'old' behavioural thinking in terms of satisficing with respect to multiple objectives (where conflicts are dodged by giving sequential attention to goals, as in Cyert and March, 1963, or via ranking goals hierarchically, as in Ironmonger, 1972). Unlike Tversky's (1972) analysis, prospect theory does not even serve implicitly as a behavioural reworking of Lancaster's (1966) characteristics-space model of consumer behaviour, which is constructed using orthodox tools except for abandoning the Hicksian goods-space view of preferences. Kahneman and Tversky's theory readily accommodates prospective financial gains and losses of rival ventures, for these are all expressed in monetary terms. However, when rival options are seen in terms of multiple dimensions, it seems to require that the decision-maker reduces gains and losses on these dimensions to a single scale of measurement. Clearly, that scale cannot pertain to the utility/disutility of the various types of gains/losses, for this would result in a circular argument: the S-shaped value function is supposed to show how utility/disutility is a function of gain/loss.

My wider view of behavioural economics offers a way of escaping from that looming circularity, namely, the 'implications-based' approach that I proposed (in Earl, 1986a, 2022, chapter 7), based on work by Hinkle ([1965] 2010) in personal construct psychology. It takes means–end chain analysis further and its practical implementation similarly involves one-on-one sessions with research subjects to elicit the multilayer networks of positive and negative implications that they see as being associated with particular changes in their behaviour or arising from changes in their external environment. Scores for the sum of positive implications can then be tallied, and likewise for negative implications. Some changes, even from pole to pole, on a characteristic scale will carry very few implications of either kind, so we are 'indifferent' between facing them or their reference point counterparts. But other changes may seem to have many subsidiary implications fanning out from them and, in some cases, they may be skewed in a negative or positive direction. If so, the changes 'matter' to us and we are in what marketers call a 'high involvement' situation (see the Hinkle-inspired work of Laaksonen, 1994). If this perspective is bolted on to prospect theory, non-financial gains and losses can be quantified in terms of numbers of positive and negative implications rather than numbers of dollars gained or lost.

I hope that behavioural economists will share my sense of the empirical relevance of cascading webs of implications for understanding how people feel as they think about alternative prospects from those they were using as their reference points: to me, it captures well the sinking feeling we get as we identify the wider consequences of giving up something that we already have, or the excitement that comes as we perceive the opportunities that will come from getting something we do not have right now, whether the 'something' is a good or a feature of a good. But I think there is much more for behavioural economists to take from this perspective if they do not focus purely on employing it as a complement to utility-maximisation perspectives.

For one thing, it makes very clear the demands that are placed on short-term memory capacity if people attempt to compute the overall implications of selecting rival options that have many dimensions, differ from each other in many ways, and have complex webs of perceived implications. In such situations, computational overload is likely to lead to ranking errors, so it will be wise to simplify the decision-making process by using a decision rule that does not entail the computation of relative overall values for the options under consideration. Overall values seem likely only to be computed, if they are computed at all, after non-compensatory, checklist-style rules have been used to arrive at shortlists of options that are deemed acceptable.

Where the absence of (enough of) a particular feature is viewed broadly (i.e., without formally counting implications while one mentally scrolls through them) as having, on balance, the greatest excess of negative implications, one might simply make the presence of (enough of) that feature a high priority and reject any option that seems unlikely to meet it, before then examining the remaining options in terms of the characteristic whose absence broadly seems likely, on balance, to have the next-biggest excess of undesirable implications, and so on. If only one option, or none of the options 'ticks all the boxes', a verdict can be arrived at without weighing together all the positive and negative implications for any of the options: in other words, the choice is arrived at in a procedural manner without reference to a utility function, *S*-shaped or otherwise.

Such considerations favour taking a pluralistic, context-focused view of how decision-makers operate, rather than assuming that any individual approaches each occasion for choice in the same way. Sometimes, people may be open to making trade-offs and can usefully be viewed as assessing prospects in terms of total scores for desirable and undesirable implications, with these prospective pairings of gains and losses being ranked along the lines envisaged in prospect theory. But we need to recognise that, in other situations, people will approach choices in a less open manner: for example, they may simply have in mind a set of templates that specify what they 'ideally' would like to get, and a set templates for what 'acceptable' options should offer if ideal ones are not available, with priority rankings or rules for further search being called upon if nothing fully conforms to their 'acceptable' specification. In my wider vision, then, behaviour can be viewed as resulting from the application of repertoires of rules for selecting actions, with these repertoires including procedures that determine which rules are selected as decision-making aids as particular contingencies arise. Hence, for decades, I have not felt any need to think of behaviour as consequent on the desire to maximise utility.

This is not to say that I advocate viewing humans as doing nothing more than applying rules, for seeing them as applying rules – whether compensatory or non-compensatory – to patterns of implications that they infer by applying cognitive rules begs an important question: in relation to *what* are implications being deemed as good or bad, or as representing gains or losses in the decision-maker's wellbeing? Here, the view that I arrived came via George Kelly's (1955) psychology of personal constructs and the similar view of human action in Adam Smith's ([1795] 1980) study of the history of astronomy. My contention is that we can learn more about why people do what they do if we view them as if they are, like scientists, trying to predict and control the world in which they find themselves, than if we view them as utility maximisers. So, a perceived implication of an event or choice is viewed positively (negatively) because it is seen as enhancing (reducing) the capacity of the person in question to predict and control events. This capacity is central to the role of the mind as a device for enhancing the fitness of a person to survive in challenging environments and not be at the mercy of events. Where possible, people avoid situations that they do not expect to be able to fathom and/or where damage to their predictive systems seems likely, whereas they become fascinated with aspects of the world that they do not yet fully understand but which they believe they will be able to fathom by using, and thereby enhancing, their predictive system. In short, what motivates people is potential to enhance (or, at least, limit any withering of) the capacities of their predictive systems.

On this view of human motivation, a person's predictive system, like a scientific paradigm or research program, is itself rule-based. The sets of implications that a person sees as associated with a choice or change in the external environment are arrived at by applying a personal set of rules for theorising and determining what constitutes knowledge and when a conjecture has been refuted or supported. Depending on the system's rules, the abandonment of one hypothesis may have wider implications due to the hypothesis in question having been used as a foundation for other expectations, without which the person may have little or no idea of how to be in control in the areas in question. Those whose personal predictive systems are resilient will typically have built systems that resist changing core constructs that are used as foundations for many other expectations about the world, with this resistance being upheld by twisting more peripheral aspects of their systems (including denial of evidence that conflicts with core ideas) to remove cognitive dissonance.

In other words, in this wider vision of behavioural economics, economic agents are viewed fundamentally as slaves of their predictive systems rather than as utility seekers. Their predictive systems are organised systems of rules and heuristics. However, their heuristics include not merely those that 'new' behavioural economists presume all humans tend to use, but also those that they have worked out for themselves or picked up from others. People thus have some freedom to use their imaginative capacities and successively modify their personal predictive systems during their lives, rather in the way that purveyors of operating systems for computers design system upgrades. However, people can only assess potential changes to what they do, and to their predictive systems, from the standpoint of their existing predictive systems. Some actions and potential new ways of trying to predict and control events may be ruled out because their existing systems deem them to be unthinkable/inadmissible.

Even if behavioural economists do not employ research methods from personal construct psychology that were developed by Kelly (1955) and Hinkle ([1965] 2010), they have great potential for forming conjectures about the kinds of events that people with well-functioning predictive systems will find appealing or be keen to avoid. (Note that people may avoid some activities not because these activities seem beyond the scope of their predictive systems but for the opposite reason, namely. because they construe them as offering nothing new and/or unexpected to make sense of and hence no prospect of enhancing their predictive capacities.) This view of motivation also opens opportunities to make sense of dysfunctional, emotional behaviour, such as hoarding, compulsive shopping, getting into personal debt crises, domestic violence, reclusive lifestyles, and aversions to technologies that most of the population use to get more out of their lives.

From this Kelly-inspired standpoint, it seems likely that dysfunctional behaviour patterns are manifestations of at least one of the following:

(a) *Anxiety*, i.e., people attempt to avoid any situation that has potential for unpredictability (including uncertainty about how one might cope with it);

(b) *Guilt,* i.e., people try to avoid forms of behaviour that they see as being at odds with how they see themselves, with departures from their self-construct having major implications for the capacity of their predictive systems.

(c) *Threat,* i.e., behaviour is a means of heading off a change in social standing, a position that the threatened person uses as an assumptive foundation for how they see themselves and try to cope with life.

(d) *Hostility*, i.e., efforts to extort evidence consistent with what is predicted by the person's system when other people appear to be challenging their core predictions.

As with many new ways of looking at the world, this Smith- and Kelly-inspired way of viewing human motivation may initially seem daunting to those who have not practised trying to use it. The good news is that there is a simple way to avoid anxiety that taking it up will bring a period in which one suffers diminished capacity to make sense of economic behaviour: try it initially as if it signifies a switch into a pluralistic way of understanding motivation, in which it can be tried as an alternative to utility-based thinking without requiring that one immediately jettisons any model based on utility maximisation.

10.5   FINDING AND ADDRESSING PROBLEMS

One of the payoffs to thinking about people in general as scientists is awareness of the impact of their predictive systems on which problems they notice and deem worthy of attention, as well as on how they seek to address them. Problems do not speak for themselves, and what I see as a problem may not be something you even notice, let alone deem worthy of attention, and vice versa. The problem identification issue is not centre-stage in 'new' behavioural economics. Moreover, because of the centrality of cognitive shortcomings to that way of thinking, instances in which problem recognition is addressed are prone to focus on how such shortcomings affect whether a problem is identified: an obvious example here is Thaler's (2015, p. 32) reference to how, due to threshold effects in the processing of stimuli, a person may mistakenly believe that both headlights on his or her car have failed together when what has really happened is that the person in question has been driving around previously with no awareness that one headlight has failed and then notices there is a problem when the second one fails, causing the road to become too hard to see and prompting a check of the headlights.

Behavioural economists need to be alert to the possibility that *their* methods may affect which problems *they* notice. Because prospect theory emerged via research on lottery-style choices, its focus on gains and losses has resulted in the theory not being conducive to recognising the lack of attention that economists have traditionally given to the information-processing challenges posed by a perceived need to choose between products that have many different characteristics, especially if there are many products between which to choose. But because the classic studies on which prospect theory was based presented the research subjects with pre-specified problems and payoff matrices, they were also not conducive to noticing that real-world decision problems are often open-ended: having identified a problem (not necessarily the best problem to work on given the goal(s) being pursued), the decision-maker then needs to identify and assess potential solutions in order to arrive at a payoff matrix.

Issues associated with identifying problems and solutions became a key part of my wider vision of behavioural economics via the work of Loasby (1967, 1973, 1976), who became aware of them by studying behaviour in the real world, not in psychology laboratories. These issues are important elements of a wider view of behavioural economics, not merely in relation to policy design but also in relation to the need to take seriously work on decision-making from 'old' behavioural economics rather than focusing primarily on the impacts of bias-inducing heuristics on utility-maximisation. If people have to choose how to allocate their attention and are dealing with open-ended problems, behavioural economists need to view decision-making as a process that in some contexts may be protracted but may be brief in other contexts; either way, it ultimately must be underpinned by rules that enable the decision-maker to circumvent several problems of infinite regress.

Such problems arise because the process of dealing with an open-ended problem entails a set of problems, each of which raises their own problems, and so on, such as the following (see also Earl, 2022, 2023c):

1. The problem of knowing where problems lie and which of them deserve attention.
2. The potential to discover better solutions to problems if one can find better ways of searching for them.
3. The problem of knowing what might happen that could facilitate or prevent other things from happening, including things that might be possible and which might play facilitating or blocking roles in relation to desired events.
4. The normative question about which preferences one should prefer in the context in question, or how to decide which decision rule or heuristic to apply to make a choice and proceed to try to implement it.

Choices that entail these kinds of issues cannot be addressed as optimisation problems until they have been turned into closed problems by using rules or heuristics to stop the infinite regress spiral, and the rules or heuristics that people use to close problems-within-problems may in some cases be ones that proceed directly to solutions without first applying optimisation techniques to closed-off versions of open-ended problems. So, for example, after using rules to define where problems exist and which ones are worthy of attention, and after using rules to limit search for solutions and conduct appraisals of them, the set of remaining options may be ranked via a simple rule (for example, a non-compensatory checklist-based rule) rather than their overall performance in terms of a utility function.

Ultimately, then, in the wider vision of behavioural economics, all choices are wholly or partly arrived at by applying rules-based procedures, which may include satisficing processes (as argued by Simon, 1947, 1957, 1959) and 'fast and frugal' heuristics that may perform even better than attempts to apply optimising procedures (Gigerenzer *et al.*, 1999). In saying this, I am not attempting to claim that prospect theory should be discarded as an analytical tool within a wider vision of behavioural economics; on the contrary, it may, as Thaler and others have demonstrated, be a powerful source of insight for understanding how people behave once they have arrived at closed problems that are computationally simple enough to address in a manner akin to that envisaged in the theory. Indeed, prospect theory could be relevant to some of the earlier sub-problems within a decision cycle (e.g., when choosing between alternative search strategies) even if it seems implausible at the ultimate ranking stage. What I *am* saying is that, if one adopts the wider vision of behavioural economics, the 'ways' by which people identify and go about closing open-ended problems become research problems that are themselves worthy of attention from those who regard themselves as behavioural economists.

10.6 EVOLUTIONARY PROCESSES VERSUS EQUILIBRIUM STATES

Instead of studying how people find and attempt to deal with problems, economists usually engage in comparative static equilibrium analysis, focusing on how people change their behaviour to adapt optimally to changes in their external environment. Analysis begins with the representative agent in a state of equilibrium, which is then disturbed by a change in the agent's external environment. The representative agent adapts to the new external environment as an 'econ' would and settles at a new equilibrium, pending any further shock.

This is such an ingrained part of a typical economist's predictive system that it prevents economists from considering the possibility that life is an ongoing process of trying to cope with problems and challenges rather than a succession of equilibrium states. Disequilibrium analysis therefore comes to entail studying what happens when transactions are made at prices that are out of line with what they ought to be, given the underlying fundamentals of supply and demand. This mindset has predictable consequences when behavioural economics is practised by using knowledge of heuristics and biases to address the predictive shortcomings of conventional economics: the act of making a choice in the context being analysed will be viewed as an endpoint, a form of equilibrium but not the equilibrium at which an 'econ' would arrive.

This truncated approach to thinking about behaviour can generate useful results and is convenient for those who want to stick as far as possible with conventional formal modelling tools and pursue what Berg and Gigerenzer (2010) call '"as if" behavioural economics.' However, 'old/evolutionary behavioural economics' opens a wide range of additional analytical opportunities by taking account of aspects of real life that are at odds with the equilibrium-focused way of thinking. They include the following:

- The capacities of the systems that people use to predict and control events are finite: they may employ false assumptions and mistaken inferences; they may fail to include relevant dimensions in terms of which possibilities could usefully be construed; and limitations of imagination, memory and computational capacity may prevent appropriate consideration of relevant issues. So, even if there are no disturbances in the external environment, choices tend to result in the generation and/or identification of further problems, rather than the attainment of full control.

- People who acknowledge the limitations of their predictive systems will make their choices in a tentative manner and will expect to adjust what they do after seeing what happens because of their choices. Those who do not acknowledge the limitations of their predictive systems will be prone to encounter surprises. Insofar as the latter's predictive systems are at least partly permeable to these surprises, they will rethink their behaviour to improve their control over their lives. Those whose predictive systems are dysfunctional to such a degree that they cannot see the need to change how they think are also likely not to behave as if they are settled after they have made choices: things that most people would view as minor surprises can be viewed with alarm by those with obsessive–compulsive disorders, while new purchases may fail to set compulsive shoppers' minds sufficiently at ease to result in them exploring fully what they can get from what they have just purchased; instead, the latter are likely to start to dwell on what they might buy next. (Musicians frequently exhibit this behaviour, which Steely Dan bandmember Walter Becker famously called 'gear acquisition syndrome.' For many guitarists, the answer to the question, 'How many guitars are enough?' is always, 'One more.') And those who cannot control their spending will sooner or later be forced by their creditors to change their behaviour.

- As Schumpeter (1943) recognised, we live in a world of 'creative destruction' in which established order is continually being disrupted due to entrepreneurs experimenting with new sets of connections, such as new products, new production processes, new sources of supply and new methods of organizing and managing how they do business. These entrepreneurial experiments have the potential both to render some existing systems obsolete and to provide a basis from which better systems can be developed. The innovation and adjustment processes play out through time, reflecting the fact that the creative capacities of the human imagination are finite at any point in time and they work by creating new combinations based on extending or hybridising existing concepts,

So, within a wider view of behavioural economics, the processes by which knowledge grows take centre-stage and the process of problem solving is viewed as entailing the ongoing development or (for, say, ageing consumers who feel they are being left behind as the world around them changes) the shoring up of personal predictive systems. Therefore, these systems at any point should be viewed as works in progress rather than as in temporary equilibrium. Sometimes, these processes may entail revolutionary shifts in how people view the world and in how they behave, but for much of the time what we need to be studying is the relentless evolution of people's predictive systems and the consequent gradual changes in their lifestyles as they incorporate new ways of meeting their goals and abandon older ways as they do so. The 'micro–meso–macro' analytical framework proposed by Dopfer, Foster and Potts (2004) provides a very good means for viewing such evolutionary processes, with the 'meso' level pertaining to the changing popularity of a generic way of doing things (e.g. the smartphone meso, as distinct from a micro-level aspect of it, such as the product lifecycle of a particular model of an Apple iPhone). I have provided an extended behavioural discussion of the micro–meso–macro perspective on structural change in Earl (2022, pp. 355–75).

10.7 HUMAN PRACTICES AND PROCEDURAL RATIONALITY

The wide range of research methods available to behavioural economists is fortuitous, given the challenges of assessing the quality of behaviour outside experimental laboratory settings and the hopes that we might have of designing effective policies for improving wellbeing. To design such policies, it is necessary to understand where organisations and consumers could be doing better than they are and what is causing them to do less well than they should be able to do, given their resources. Here, we run into the question of what the reference point should be against which we measure under-achievement. To a 'new' behavioural economist, the automatic answer is that it should be what an idealised 'econ' would achieve. This may be reasonable if the goals of decision-makers and optimal means of reaching them can readily be identified. In such situations, we can specify what Herbert Simon (1976) called 'substantively rational' solutions to the choice problems in question. However, there are many situations in which optimal strategies cannot readily be identified, even if we can ascertain what the decision-makers are trying to do. In such situations, we need to look at rationality in a different way to assess the quality of decision-making.

Behavioural economists (and economists in general) should be open to taking a practice-based view of the extent (if any) to which decision-makers should be characterised as under-achieving and how they might do better. In other words, we need to devote more attention to studying practices and the outcomes they yield among research entities or individuals whose situations are rather similar but whose practices and attainments differ – for example, how practices and productivity levels differ between firms who produce the same, or similar, products, or between households with similar compositions who live in similar geographical areas but differ in their spending on, say, public utilities or meeting nutritional needs. Then, even if we cannot specify substantively rational choices for the subjects of our research, we can at least take best-practice behaviour as our reference point and analyse what it is about best-practice ways of operating that contributes to superior outcomes. We might also use our skills as economists to suggest practices that could beat observed best-practice ways of choosing, without any need to spend significantly more time on addressing the choice in question, or which could serve as 'fast and frugal' heuristics that could deliver best-practice outcomes more rapidly. (For example, Lana Friesen and I were correct to predict that the research subjects in the naturalistic experiment in the third phase of our mobile phone service contract study could in many cases have achieved far better rewards by applying the heuristic 'First, examine plans offered by providers whose websites mention that they are "award-winning" providers.')

In the past, behavioural economists have left practice-focused research to sociologists and social anthropologists. (A good place to start to get a sense of such work is via the Google Scholar profile page of Professor Elizabeth Shove, a University of Lancaster sociologist who is one of the foremost practitioners of practice-focused research. Much of her work has a dynamic aspect, seeking to address the processes by which practices change, as in transitions to more sustainable lifestyles.) If we catalogue the habits, heuristics, and rules that different people use, and the results that these ways of operating deliver, we can then take a statistical view of the ingredients of good practice in the context of interest (see, for the case of mobile phone connection service plans, Earl, Friesen and Shadforth, 2019). In other words, by studying the behaviour of people who differ in the quality of their ways of making decisions, we can arrive at a context-specific view of what Herbert Simon (1976) called 'procedural rationality', which he defined in terms of 'appropriate deliberation'.

A practice-based approach to the quality of behaviour would make behavioural economics less susceptible to the claim that Mehta (2013) has levelled at 'new' behavioural economics, namely, that the heuristics and biases-based perspective 'pathologizes' consumers in general. The approach may put us in a position to do something akin to what schoolteachers routinely do in respect of their students, namely, categorise users of different operating systems as 'High achievers,' or 'In the normal range' or 'Having special needs for improving their ways of operating'.

10.8   UNDERPINNINGS OF UNDER-ACHIEVEMENT

From the standpoint of 'new' behavioural economics, under-achievement by organisations and individuals is viewed as resulting essentially from decisions being made with the aid of heuristics that generate biased probability judgments and/or behaviour such as procrastination and giving weight to sunk costs and other 'supposedly irrelevant factors' that a 'fully rational "econ"' would ignore. I do not dispute the potential value of viewing these factors as contributing to under-achievement by human decision-makers, but I think that it can be useful for behavioural economists also to have other perspectives at their disposal. For example, if we observe consumers seemingly paying the so-called 'lazy tax' due to not bothering to shop around, we might be wise to consider whether they do this because they have set their aspirations needlessly low and are not searching because the prices that they can already see are acceptable (an 'old' behavioural satisficing perspective) rather than inferring that their behaviour is a manifestation of, say, the default bias.

As part of a wider view of why attainments fall short of the best that can be identified as feasible, or, at least, what current best-practice ways of operating can deliver, behavioural economists could profit by adopting Leibenstein's (1966, 1976) notion of X-inefficiency and his 'old' behavioural perspective on why it arises. He introduced the *X*-inefficiency term to denote the extent to which an organisation incurs needlessly high costs for reasons other than some of the prices of factors of production being kept above those that would prevail in markets that were not afflicted by monopolistic behaviour (such as wage costs that trade unions have inflated) or policy-driven distortions (such as tariffs on imported machinery). But we can also apply the *X*-inefficiency term to the extent to which consumers pay more than they need to pay for reasons that pertain to the choices they make rather than because some market prices are higher than those that would prevail in a competitive market. I think we are likely to arrive at a better understanding, and better policies for improving attainments, if we undertake analysis in this area mindful of the consumption *X*-inefficiency equivalents of the four causes that Leibenstein identified for organisational *X*-inefficiency (see also Earl, 2005, 2007):

- *Organisations and consumers may lack knowledge of best-practice methods for minimising the costs of achieving what they are trying to achieve.*
  Such knowledge will be hard to keep pace with when technological change is rapid, but it may also be problematic in relatively slow-changing markets for products that are only sought infrequently, or where products are complex to use, offer multiple outputs and there is a wide range of choice. This knowledge pertains to organisational and household production functions, both in engineering terms (i.e., the feasible outputs of products or production systems or characteristics that can be obtained from alternative combinations of inputs) and the cheapest ways of sourcing alternative sets of inputs. In other words, compared with those who achieve best-practice performance, some people may purchase inferior combinations of inputs and/or pay too much for their inputs and/or use ineptly the inputs that they purchase.
- *The deals that organisations and households make with those who supply products and services to them commonly do not completely specify what is going to be supplied.*
  In the case of employment contracts, this fuzziness is key to enabling adaptation in light of new information and changed circumstances (Coase, 1937); it is a potential issue for purchasers of anything that is not a 'search good' in the purest sense of one whose qualities can be

fully ascertained before a purchase agreement is made, and in reality most purchases involve 'experience good' and/or 'credence good' aspects. When labour services are contracted at an hourly rate, the quality and quantity of work undertaken will depend on the skills that workers have and how industriously they apply them. Payment-by-results contracts may guard to some degree against opportunistic behaviour by workers, but it is often problematic (a) to specify fully what is to be produced and (b) to obtain redress in the event of a dispute about the quality of what is delivered. Where physical products are purchased, their specifications may be incomplete or misleading. So, organisations and households can end up with needlessly high costs due to their suppliers behaving opportunistically in respect of vague aspects of contracts. Supplier opportunism may arise even in respect of what the contracts have specified if they believe that their clients will face significant enforcement costs and cannot inflict reputational damage on them. However, poor value for money spent on experience goods and credence goods is not always the result of supplier opportunism; it may also arise when dealing with suppliers who act in good faith but are not as competent as they believe themselves to be.

- *Organisations and consumers may face barriers to elevating their achievements towards best-practice levels by developing or efficiently outsourcing the requisite capabilities.*

  In principle, it may be possible and worthwhile to invest in obtaining knowledge of the relevant production function and associated know-how for (a) extracting output from well-chosen sets of inputs, (b) shopping for supplies and negotiating deals, (c) motivating and managing suppliers of labour inputs, and (d) obtaining redress on occasions where there are shortfalls in the standard of what is supplied. However, those who need to develop or outsource such capabilities must first recognise their need for them and then have the capacity to source them efficiently. It is possible that personal pride, self-reliance ethics and/or lack of awareness of the potential relevance of the 'it takes one to know one' problem will result in such needs being denied rather than admitted. Clearly, there is also scope for failures in markets for such capabilities due to difficulties in judging which of those who profess to have the desired capabilities actually possess them and will not behave in an opportunistic manner. A further complication (emphasised in the work of Nelson and

Winter, 1982) is that some of the knowledge that is sought may be of the 'tacit' variety that cannot be fully articulated in words and can only be acquired (if at all) by experimenting, armed only with incomplete instructions, until one stumbles upon the necessary knack.

- *If organisations and consumers operate in environments where competitive pressures are weak, they are less likely to seek to find ways of reducing the costs of what they do or improving its quality.* This may seem obvious enough for firms in which internal competition is limited due to social pressures among workers not to break productivity norms. It may likewise apply with firms that operate in markets where there are significant entry barriers, trade policies that provide protection from imports, and customers whose demands are not challenging due to them not habitually being careful to search for lower prices and having modest non-price aspirations. But consumers, in varying degrees, may likewise feel they are under pressure to shop and use purchased items efficiently. Households differ in the extent of internal competition for resources – for example, because of the size of the household relative to its budget or because members of households differ in how adept they are at bargaining for resources. (There are parallels here with the underpinnings of organisational slack in the behavioural theory of the firm proposed by Cyert and March, 1963.) External competitive pressures will be present to the extent that consumers are status seekers who set out to demonstrate their place in society via conspicuous consumption. If one is not a status seeker, there is less to be gained from, say, getting one's weekly groceries more cheaply than there is for a status seeker. The latter will be able to finance more daring acts of conspicuous consumption if it is possible to find ways of economising when buying less discretionary products that are not chosen for their status signalling capacities.

The last of these four factors aligns well with a demand-side laziness-based perspective on under-achievement (or even one formally based on search for cost savings being repeatedly postponed due to present-bias/quasi-hyperbolic discounting). That perspective encourages behavioural economists to focus on failures to gather information about cheaper supply sources, or failures to switch to cheaper sources so long as old habits deliver adequate outcomes. However, the X-inefficiency perspective is otherwise conducive to taking account of shortfalls in capabilities for making the most of one's budget. Note, too, that knowledge deficiencies in relation to household production functions may not relate merely to areas such as how to make tasty, nutritious meals more cheaply but also to combinations of activities that can make people happy. There may be plenty of sources of information about what these combinations might be, but many of the activities in question may yield payoffs only to those who are prepared to persist with them until they develop the requisite capabilities. People who underestimate their capacity to learn and who expect that failure to acquire new capabilities will result in losses in their self- and/or social-esteem will be prone to waste funds if they get as far as experimenting with such activities – instead of ramping up their commitment to any of them when things start to prove challenging, they are likely merely to dabble with them in succession before abandoning them. If they were more susceptible to sunk-cost bias, they might be able to do rather better.

10.9 POLICIES FOR IMPROVING PRODUCTIVITY AND WELLBEING

One year before Thaler and Sunstein's (2008) book *Nudge* appeared, nudge-style policies were used successfully by my local water services utility to ensure that a severe drought in Queensland did not result in the water levels in local dams becoming dangerously low. Instead of raising unit prices for water, the utility sent out water bills that compared the addressee's water usage with usage rates in their suburb as well as in previous periods and made it known that those with abnormally high usage rates would be sent 'please explain' letters. Those who thereby felt that they ought to try to reduce their water consumption could readily find ideas on how to do this via a newsletter that accompanied the water bills. The strategy achieved its goal in a very equitable manner, whereas following the conventional economic wisdom would have made it harder for Brisbane's poorer residents to meet their basic needs while the rich would have been without non-price pressure to reduce the extent to which they continued watering their lawns.

What my local utility did went beyond the nudge concept, for its policy for reducing the demand for water did not merely try to induce change by getting customers to think about their use relative to others and by imposing what are sometimes called 'frown costs' on heavy users; it also tried to educate water users about how they might be wasting water. It was thus better aligned with the wider policy philosophy that is implied by the wider, knowledge-focused view of behavioural economics that I practise, and which is central to the extended X-inefficiency perspective offered in the previous section.

In contexts where under-achievement results from poor knowledge and inadequately developed capabilities, it is important for designers of economic policies to understand the extent to which these shortfalls result from limited opportunities to acquire knowledge and develop capabilities, or from people using predictive systems that are not conducive to them taking up opportunities to learn and develop their capabilities. Insofar as the latter is the issue, policy designers need to focus on bringing about changes in how people view the process of acquiring the relevant knowledge or capabilities.

Suppose, for example, that the barrier to people learning how to do better is that the very thought that they need to develop their decision-making capacity in the area in question conflicts with their self-images as capable people, and they do not want to show others how little they know about the area in question. They may in any case not want to present themselves as people who need to find out how little they really need to spend on a product that would suit their requirements (if only they knew what these should be). The result of such thinking may be that they make uninformed purchases of 'default option' products. In such a case, the use of an attainment-limiting heuristic has more complex foundations than the 'heuristics and biases' approach to behavioural economics considers, and policies for improving attainments may fail unless they take account of these issues.

So, members of 'behavioural insights teams' should not merely view themselves as working for 'nudge units.' Rather, they should recognise that they will be able to contribute more to policy design if they keep the following issues and possibilities in mind:

Boosting Decision-Making Capabilities
In essence, nudge-based policies apply knowledge of commonly used heuristics to steer people to make choices that will enhance their wellbeing or to help the policy instigators (government agencies, not-for-profit organisations, and firms) towards meeting their objectives. The policy measures entail changing the choice architecture – i.e., how options are presented to the target audience

– rather than changing prices and/or product characteristics. An alternative, potentially complementary approach is to supply people with better heuristics and knowledge about decision-making to 'boost' their capabilities (see Gigerenzer, 2015; Grüne-Yanoff and Hertwig, 2016; Hertwig, 2017). This is essentially what management education programmes in business schools aim to achieve, but behavioural insights teams have roles to play in advocating and helping to design programs that will enable consumers to limit the extent to which they are susceptible to using dysfunctional heuristics. Such programs could be particularly effective as parts of school curricula – for example, to develop better generic statistical thinking to apply to the problems of everyday life, or more context-specific knowledge such as in matters of financial literacy. To reduce risks that people will succumb to nudge-based policies and persuasive techniques that run counter to their own interests, education can be provided in how these techniques work, while assertiveness training is a way towards ensuring that people can get treated fairly and obtain outcomes to which they are entitled.

Those on the political right who have warmed to the libertarian side of Thaler and Sunstein's 'libertarian paternalism' will doubtless object to 'boost' programmes that aim to change the repertoires of heuristics that people use, on the basis that such programs could be the start of a slippery slope from 'nanny state' interventions to more sinister attempts to brainwash people to think in particular ways. They might question the need for such policies by pointing to the ready availability of helpful websites and moderately priced self-help books – such as Cialdini (1984, 2009) on techniques of persuasion, Alberti and Emmors (2008) on assertiveness training, and Belsky and Gilovich (1999) on financial decision-making – that have sold in huge quantities. From an enactivist view of cognition, there is clearly something in this market-based perspective. However, it has a key limitation, namely, that shortcomings in people's predictive systems and/or decision-making processes may prevent them from acknowledging that they would be wise to invest in aids to improving their decision-making (an 'old/evolutionary' behavioural perspective). Moreover, even if people recognise that they have such shortcomings, they may repeatedly defer any action in that direction because they are susceptible to present-bias and/or quasi-hyperbolic discounting (a 'new' behavioural perspective).

Making it Easier to Gather Information and Switch to New Providers and Practices

The wider view of behavioural economics acknowledges that there is also a role for policies that aim to foster higher attainments by making it easier for people engaged in problem-solving activities to gather relevant information, draw reliable inferences from it, and, if they wish, change their behaviour. This vision of what needs to be made easy is wider than what is often observed in 'new' behavioural contributions because it includes a role for policies that make it easy to find options and evaluate them, rather than merely for policies that make it easy to implement a change of behaviour.

For example, we might indeed anticipate that consumers will be more likely to fail to switch to cheaper providers of electricity if they face a system in which they are required to contact both their existing and their new providers to initiate the handover. This hurdle can be removed by a policy intervention that requires the new provider to liaise with the old one once the consumer has clicked acceptance of the new offer. But first the consumer needs to be able to ascertain which provider and plan to select. Making it easy in this area could require a government-sponsored website that pulls together all the necessary information about how each plan works, along with the customer's past bills that detail usage history and solar-generated feed-in (or even, if required by regulations, fine-grained time-of-day-and-month consumption and feed-in information from smart-meters), and which can calculate prospective costs for all the plans and thereby rank them. A policy that addresses consumers' cognitive needs by creating such an institution is what naturally comes to mind if one takes an enactivist view of cognition, though it would, of course, need to be complemented by one that made it easy to implement changes of provider. The cognitive institution that this policy example entails would require a much greater investment in programming and would no doubt be met with much more resistance from providers, than half-baked state-provided websites that only go as far as making comparisons against typical usage patterns and fail properly to adjust for the effects of solar systems on electricity bills. However, it would remove the need to 'boost' customer expertise in respect of complex tariffs with time- and grid usage-dependent pricing.

Consumer and Worker Protection
Regulation- and tribunals-based consumer and worker protection and arbitration policies warrant consideration in contexts where:

- There is good reason to believe, or evidence that, appropriate decision-making capabilities and knowledge are uncommon and hence consumers and workers are at risk of being nudged or otherwise persuaded to accept offers that serve them far less well than offers they could have discovered if they had such capabilities – including capabilities required for obtaining redress if suppliers or employers engage in unethical behaviour towards them.
- Effective 'boost' policies prove impossible to design or are precluded by political opposition, or if they end up entailing programmes in which participation is (like buying and reading self-help books) not compulsory.
- Competitive pressures are neither strong enough to promote ethically appropriate behaviour by suppliers, nor so strong (for example, due to extremely low entry barriers – cf. Richardson, 1960) as to put suppliers in a position in which they are so desperate to survive that they resort to unethical practices.

The third point implies that market deregulation may be unhelpful if it goes as far as some libertarians wish (as was recognised at an early stage by Etzioni, 1988). However, it is also important to recognise that there are two reasons why it may not take a particularly high proportion of skilled and diligent shoppers to deter suppliers from engaging in 'rip-off' pricing and other forms of ethically questionable behaviour that come under Akerlof and Shiller's (2015) umbrella term of 'phishing for phools.' One reason comes via the enactivist view of cognition: canny shoppers may play an active role as sources of knowledge for those who lack shopping expertise or time to engage in gathering information in the market in question. Secondly, there is what is known as the 'Ward-Perkins point' by those who, like Loasby and I, have been influenced by the work of Andrews (1964, p. 102). Neville Ward-Perkins, one of Andrews's students at Oxford, argued that it may only require a small percentage of customers to be canny shoppers for incumbent players to be concerned about deterring new entry. What concerns potential entrants to a market will be whether there are enough canny shoppers who would switch to a new player that offered a better deal than the incumbent suppliers. If the minimum efficient scale of production in a market is small relative to the total volume of goods sold in the market, and if canny shoppers can be expected to give their goodwill to an entrant who offers a better deal even if the deal is later matched by the incumbents, the incumbent suppliers may take the threat of entry very seriously and seek to deter it by neither engaging in greedy pricing nor trimming quality.

Promoting Constructive Criticism to Facilitate Experimentation and Learning

In situations where other people's predictive systems enable them to see actual or potential problems that have not been noticed by a decision-maker, scope for the latter to avoid under-achievement will be reduced if the former are reluctant to raise the issues in question, even in a constructive manner, because they fear that this will be seen as a personal affront and elicit a hostile reaction. The 'shooting the messenger' reactions that whistle-blowers commonly face are but one indication of the need to design systems for drawing attention to problems and ensuring that what is said will be taken seriously. Such systems could, in the case of households, play significant roles in reducing domestic violence, while they could have a major role to play in helping organisations to terminate or rethink projects that are heading for disaster and likely to lead to sunk-cost bias and escalation of commitment. There is enormous potential for behavioural insights teams to offer consultancy services in this area if they can uncover effective operating principles for making fearlessly offered and gratefully received constructive criticism a routine feature of how organisations function.

If we are viewing people in general as if they are scientists, an obvious starting point in thinking about what these kinds of principles might look like is to reflect on academic best-practice methods for promoting the growth of knowledge and avoiding misallocation of research resources. However, given the application of modern divide-and-rule methods to universities in recent decades, current practice seems less conducive to a healthy, constructively critical work environment than the kinds of operating principles that Ed Catmull (2014) and his colleagues developed to ensure the success of the Pixar animated movie firm.

Pixar's operating system is very much in line with enactivist views of cognition rather than the individual-centred perspective that dominates in mainstream and 'new behavioural' economics. If applied in academia, it implies that staff should be discouraged from taking pride in operating alone (which they may otherwise do to make their originating roles clear in what they publish), and they should not seek to maximise their promotion prospects by contributing nothing to their colleagues. Those who recognise the benefits of social inputs in cognition and who therefore operate in a collegial, collaborative manner will facilitate each other's intellectual growth in a cumulative manner. They will appreciate being expected to air their latest thinking at least once a year at departmental workshops, share drafts with each other and provide feedback, and work collaboratively. By such means, their research outputs should be closer to being publication-ready by the time they submit them than otherwise would have been the case.

When it comes to hiring new colleagues, such academics will strive to secure people whose potential to contribute to collegial knowledge-generation exceeds their own by the widest margin; existing staff should not be fearful that brilliant new colleagues who are highly collegial and therefore pleasant to work with could make them look less valuable than hitherto. The academics to avoid are those who are arrogant, self-absorbed and who have prima-donna tendencies, however capable they are of writing papers for top-tier journals single-handedly or as part of a narrow clique; those who fancy themselves are likely to contribute as little as possible in collegial terms and to focus instead on moving onward and upward to higher-status organisations before their deficiencies become elements of their international reputations.

Secondly, it is vital that research grant allocations and research outputs are peer-reviewed in a civil and constructive manner, in which referees write their reports on the work of others in the way that they would like to see others report on their own work. The current norm is to use double-blind refereeing to promote frank criticism of submissions and ensure that grant proposals and submitted works are assessed based on their scholarly merits rather than who submitted them. However, the anonymity of referees is not as conducive to civil and diligent conduct as would be a system in which referees were not anonymous (see also, Holbrook, 1995a). If referee reports were signed by referees, with dates of when the reports were invited and received, and if they were published as supplements to the works in question, authors could be more confident of getting worthwhile reports, written in a civil style, and delivered in a timely manner. This would have the added benefit of providing an incentive for authors to address referee comments assiduously rather than trying to grind down the resolve of referees and journal editors by merely paying lip-service to what the reports say. Indeed, the knowledge generation process might be improved further if it became standard practice for journals to signal the quality of their processes by requiring authors to allow them to post rejected submissions and accompanying referee reports on the journal websites. Such a transparent process would surely concentrate wonderfully the minds of researchers on getting collegial feedback on their works before submitting them for publication.

Providing Role-Models of Ambition and Practice

Insofar as under-achievement results from people setting their aspirations needlessly low and therefore not searching as far as they might have done before choosing, an obvious policy remedy is to provide role-models of what can be achieved and of the practices that can make it possible. I first came across this kind of policy as a second-year undergraduate when studying the development of Japan in the late 19th century: efforts to raise agricultural productivity were built around demonstrating what was being achieved by best-practice 'model farms' that farmers from the surrounding areas could visit. Other elements of what I later discovered was called 'agricultural extension' include farmer-focused newspapers, magazines and, more recently, radio and television programkes, as well as visits from roving farm advisors to spread awareness about innovations and improvements in practice. Such initiatives need not come from governments; they may also be market institutions and benchmarking services that result from entrepreneurial activities or trade associations. These include bodies such as the UK-based Centre For Inter-Firm Comparisons that are set up to collect performance data of rival firms on an anonymous basis and which then provide their members with details of their rankings and the productivity levels of the best and median firm attainments.

Using Regulatory Constraints to Induce Search and Learning

Where policies based on nudges, boosts and exemplars are impractical or prove ineffectual as means to trigger search and learning about ways of raising achievements, those who have a wider vision of behavioural economics should consider how regulatory constraints may be used to generate search activities that will result in better choices. Clearly, one can attempt to ensure that people and organisations perform better than they otherwise would have done by imposing regulations that, in effect, force them to meet required levels of performance, as with making it illegal to drive a car without supervision if one has not passed a driving test, or reducing vehicle emissions by requiring carmakers to comply with combined average fuel economy (CAFE) standards that are progressively tightened.

We might even envisage regulations that prevent consumers from purchasing products if they have not first engaged in due diligence in terms of developing a basic appreciation of how the charges they will incur are calculated – for example, requiring them to take a financial literacy test before they are allowed to sign a loan contract, or to demonstrate that they can do a multi-tier pricing calculation before they sign up for, say, electricity supply or mobile phone service products that involve such pricing systems. Internet technology makes it feasible to require that prospective customers are diverted to official websites that provide training material and test whether the concepts have been understood, before purchasing decisions can be actioned. The imposition of such requirements might also prod service providers to offer products whose price structures are simpler, more transparent, and easier to compare with those of rivals.

However, policy designers should also be mindful of potential for efficiency enhancing consequences of attempts to circumvent regulations. This is a lesson that comes from Loasby's study of the impact of UK location policies in the late 1950s and early 1960s that made it difficult for firms to meet their growth objectives by moving to larger premises unless these were in new towns or depressed areas (see Loasby, 1967, 1973, and Cañibano *et al,*, 2025). Loasby emphasises that when firms did expand their operations by moving to areas where Industrial Development Certificates could readily be obtained, they searched for ways of overcoming the disadvantages of these locations and were often successful in finding solutions – often, things they could have done long ago in their original locations. However, in some cases, managers thought creatively about ways in which they might grow in their present area without needing to obtain Industrial Development Certificates - i.e., they sought to find a way of getting round the regulations. An example (though not one mentioned by Loasby) concerns the Jaguar car company: it solved its need for more capacity in the Birmingham area by taking over Daimler, its ailing local rival, which enabled it to get Daimler's factory and to get economies of scope by creating a new, smaller Daimler sedan by putting Daimler's small V8 engine into a Daimler-badged variant of the Jaguar Mark II.

Reducing Human Environmental Impacts

Behavioural economics who start to view consumers as if they are scientist rather than compromised utility maximisers will have a wider range of opportunities to contribute to policies aimed at reducing human impacts on the natural environment. Implied in the Adam Smith/George Kelly view of human action is a view of human wellbeing that only depends on consuming more and more insofar as people view this as their preferred way of enhancing their abilities to predict and control events. So, behavioural economists should be mindful of how they might contribute to the design of policies that present acceptable cases for people to rethink, in environmentally more sustainable ways, how they should go about trying to improve, or prevent reductions in, their capacities to predict and control events.

Such policies can take many forms. For example, if people prefer private cars to public transport because they view the latter as having high probabilities of not adhering to their timetables, then policies could focus on making public transport journey times more predictable (for example, via the introduction of bus lanes) and/or making journey times in private cars more unpredictable (for example, by reducing the availability of parking spaces, thereby making it hard to find somewhere to park, or by limiting road space for cars via creating bus lanes). If cars are seen as devices for upholding how people see themselves relative to others, the policy role could be in promoting different ways of viewing social standing or in dealing with issues that contribute to the use of alternative means of transport being viewed as signifying low status. Attention could also be given to promoting greener views of which kinds of people and behaviour are to be valued in society.

10.10 WIDER OPPORTUNITIES FOR BEHAVIOURAL ECONOMISTS

Behavioural economists would be wise not to view themselves as confined to analysing the behaviour of consumers and how firms and government agencies can seek to manipulate consumers. They should be mindful that, before Thaler came along, behavioural economics focused mainly on firms and other organisations. Much of that work in the early post-World War II decades paid rather little attention to the potential for external pressures to deter employees from pursuing personal sub-goals, and this may have left economists with the impression that satisficing behaviour, organisational slack, and X-inefficiency were only of interest where competitive pressures were limited. Internal competitive pressures increased from the mid-1960s in large firms that switched to profit-centres-based (M-form) organisational structures. Then, from around 1980, competitive pressures both inside and outside organisations were cranked up following the political success of neo-conservatives/neo-liberals that drove the transition to the modern world of managerialism, deregulation, privatisation, and globalisation. But despite today's pressures for members of firms and other organisations to raise their productivity, optimal choices remain elusive. Understanding differences in the 'ways' that organisations work and how they deal with changing situations is not something that economists should view as the preserve of management scholars; it should be part of behavioural economics, just as it used to be.

Behavioural labour economics (surveyed by Berg, 2015) is arguably the main area in which modern behavioural economics has embraced issues relating to firms and other organisations, such as the effort that workers put into their jobs and the impact of social norms on productivity. Yet it is also a good example of a field in which 'old/evolutionary' ideas are under-applied. This is evident in areas related to labour supply behaviour, such as educational choices, career orientation and management, choosing when to quit or which jobs to apply for, willingness to move geographically and the extent to which this is affected by non-price and emotional factors, and so on. On the demand side of the labour market, the processes by which workers get matched with jobs is one that seems to align perfectly with the use of non-compensatory decision rules for shortlisting, even if final choices are made in terms of trade-offs in a compensatory manner. From an 'old/evolutionary' behavioural standpoint, the 'even if' condition seems rather unlikely to apply where the capabilities of workers are key to getting a competitive edge. A case in point appears to be how academic positions are filled in today's world of research audits and university league table rankings, where it appears that disjunctive or lexicographic decision rules are used to rank shortlisted applicants: so long as applicants are viewed as adequate in research and teaching, their research potential may be the dominant criterion, with teaching capabilities only referred to if there is a tie for the best researcher.

But labour economics is just one area in which it helps to think with a wider vision of behavioural economics. Here, I will list just four others within economics. First, consider development economics, which captured my attention at an early stage via the attempts of Bauer (1971) to argue that economic development depended on attitudes and motivation rather than ready access to natural resources. Information overload associated with a surfeit of options may be less of a driver to the use of simplifying decision rules in less developed countries than in advanced industrial economies, but that does not mean there are few gains to be had from understanding the operating systems that people in developing countries develop for surviving or trying to get ahead amid challenges posed by cultural traditions, corruption, and other institutional factors.

Secondly, consider potential for applying 'old/evolutionary' behavioural economics to the field of international trade – not merely in relation to the possible significance of non-compensatory decision rules for understanding non-price drivers of trade, but also the search strategies that exporters use to solve problems caused by external changes that reduce their access to established markets, the pricing strategies that exporters use for dealing with currency fluctuations, how would-be exporters develop the knowledge they need to become credible competitors in foreign markets, and how customers go about judging the quality of unfamiliar foreign products.

Thirdly, consider ecological economics and the transition to a sustainable future. For me, when writing an entry (Earl, 2017b) on the theory of the firm for a handbook on ecological economics, it was natural to consider how the behavioural theory of the firm might be useful for understanding how firms can end up behaving in ways that damage both the environment and their reputations (as with Volkswagen's 'dieselgate scandal'). If I were studying, say, the uptake of electric cars, I would certainly find Thaler's (1985) work on mental accounting relevant: insofar as buyer resistance comes from such vehicles being much more expensive than what people are used to paying, then a potential solution is to offer cars on a 'battery not included' basis and then lease the battery separately, especially if this can be done for a monthly fee less than what people budget for fuel and servicing. But I would also consider non-price dimensions that may be deal-breakers, as where, say, vehicles have inadequate range, touch-screen controls that require menu-diving operations, batteries that contain nickel and cobalt mined by questionable means and/or that cannot be charged at home from rooftop solar due to the would-be buyer living in an apartment or having other lifestyle constraints, are made in politically repressive countries such as China and/or by a firm in which Elon Musk has a major interest, and so on.

Finally, consider the history of economic thought. Here, there are many more opportunities if one does not accept Thaler's portrait of behavioural economics as beginning with the work of himself, Kahneman and Tversky in the late 1970s. My vision of behavioural economics begins with work from the 1930s onwards, plus some inspiration from earlier work by Marshall, Smith, and Veblen. Some of those who were major influences on my work have already been studied in depth, but excellent opportunities remain in respect of others – Brian Loasby is an obvious case of the latter, and I have tried to facilitate research on his contributions by preparing a comprehensive bibliography of his publications (see Earl, 2023d). However, as Bondo Hansen and Presskorn-Thygesen (2022) and Jefferson (2025) have demonstrated, there are many scholars from before the 1930s who took a psychological view of human action, in a line that stretches back as far as Aristotle. Some of their contributions, too, may warrant further attention.

Taking a wider view of behavioural economics also has potential to enable behavioural economists to contribute more readily to other disciplines, especially if they work with co-authors from these areas. These disciplines include not merely marketing and finance, both of which were early adopters of Thaler's work, but also fields such as:

- Business history.
- Corporate culture.
- Criminology (for food for thought, see the Google Scholar profile of Professor Mandeep Dhami).
- Entrepreneurial studies.
- Health policy (cf. Foster, Earl, Haines and Mitchell, 2010).
- International business.
- Organisational behaviour.
- Project management.
- Strategic management.

Indeed, rather than merely making contributions to such fields, those who have wide-ranging behavioural economics expertise may even find it relatively easy to advance their careers by defecting from departments of economics to positions in these areas. I explored such possibilities during my career and had no trouble getting shortlisted up to full professor level in marketing or strategic management. What limited my determination to pursue such opportunities and ultimately kept me in economics were concerns that I had about being able to continue doing work that would be recognised as economics and, in doing so, would help to promote behavioural economics (as I saw it) as an alternative to conventional economics. I was probably mistaken in having these concerns, especially given the mistakes I was making in trying, as an economist, to generate interest in the behavioural alternative that I was pursuing.

10.11 CONCLUDING REFLECTIONS

For almost five decades, I have been trying to build on behavioural contributions that existed before Thaler's (1980) seminal article was published, and on extensions of those contributions on which I was then working at the time Thaler's article appeared. But even in 1980, I could see that interest in what I viewed as behavioural economics was waning. I sought to understand what was going on by applying behavioural ideas to the behaviour of economists (Earl, 1983b). Given what was happening, I did not entertain thoughts that my work would enable me to become an academic superstar; I merely hoped that it would win some converts and enable me to work among congenial colleagues and enjoy a comfortable lifestyle. I similarly did not imagine that Thaler would become an academic superstar and have a profound effect on what behavioural economics was viewed as constituting. I enjoyed his 1980 paper and was among the first to cite it, even though it seemed a bit odd relative to the behavioural contributions that inspired me: although it began by referring to the notion of bounded rationality, I was unable to find any way in which it claimed to offer a satisficing analysis of consumer behaviour, whereas that was what I was busily engaged in trying to develop. It did not occur to me that what I found odd about Thaler's paper might ultimately help it to win (by February 18, 2026) well over twice the number of citations that my entire output had achieved (10313 on Google Scholar, from Thaler's 230,786 total, versus my far from terrible total of 4212).

But despite the misgivings that I came to have about Thaler's way of doing behavioural economics, I was delighted when he won the 2017 Nobel Memorial Prize in Economic Sciences (see Earl, 2018): the sight of so many economists working with a Thaler-inspired way of doing behavioural economics is, to me, far better than would have been the sight of just a few scholars such as myself claiming to be doing behavioural economics and winning very few converts to the field. Because of what Thaler kickstarted, there are now vastly more scholars than there would have been who might be open to stepping from the narrow view of behavioural economics to the wider one that I have been canvassing here.

I do not regard the difference between the spectacularly greater interest that there has been in 'new' behavioural economics than in work in 'old/evolutionary' behavioural economics as a sign that my wider vision of the field is based on flawed thinking and/or a deluded sense of its potential to be applied. Rather, I probably have myself largely to blame for my behavioural perspective not being widely known and/or adopted. In essence, the problem was that I operated as if it would be impossible to interest most economists in the ideas that excited me, because these ideas clashed with the core axioms and operating rules of the conventional research programme in economics. Hence, I mainly consorted with historians of economic thought, economic psychologists, and self-styled 'heterodox' economists whose core ways of thinking and doing research should have made them open to the kind of behavioural approach that I was pursuing.

With hindsight, I believe that I should have treated mainstream economists as being true to their words when they preached the methodology of positive economics. This was what Thaler did in his seminal 1980 paper, and his strategy thereafter was to emphasise phenomena that were anomalous for conventional economics but which he could explain with his behavioural analysis. My mistake was to view positivistic preaching as a disingenuous smokescreen and to think that the reality was that mainstream economic theorists were not open, no matter what empirical claims were being made, to contributions that did not seek to conduct analysis with the aid of formal mathematical models and did not seek to do economic analysis as if choices were always acts of constrained optimisation. Hence, I mostly did not focus on making systematic empirical contributions. Instead, I sought to build a better theoretical picture of the economic system by drawing on behavioural principles. I illustrated it with reference to real-world examples, instead of testing it, one hypothesis after another, by applying statistical methods.

My cynicism about how open economists really were to empirical critiques of their core ideas had been considerably reinforced when I noticed how Rabin and Thaler (2001, p. 230) seemed to be exasperated by attempts to cling to expected utility theory despite evidence that risk aversion was widespread: they conveyed how they felt by likening the behaviour of those who would not face up to this evidence to the behaviour of the pet-shop manager in the legendary 'Dead Parrot Sketch' from the television comedy series *Monty Python's Flying Circus* – except that they noted how, after making farcical attempts to deny that the parrot he had sold was dead, the manager of the pet-shop did eventually concede that it was indeed dead. But, despite their exasperation, Rabin and Thaler did not abandon their attempts to win over the mainstream and (perhaps partly because of what they had said) the tide soon turned in their favour: their 2001 paper appeared in the same winter as the *New York Times* articles on behavioural economics by Lowenstein (2001) and Uchitelle (2001).[21] I had never even started trying to do what they were doing.

In a sense, what I did was perhaps an unfortunate result of being blessed at an early stage with an economics education that gave me an unusually good sense of the existence of alternatives to the mainstream approach to economics and how they were faring: if I had been unaware of all this, I might have viewed my only hope as being to play the long game via a systematic Thaler-like evidence-based strategy.

My way of operating was by no means a complete failure, but it ensured that almost all interest in my behavioural approach came from outside the mainstream and not from 'new' behavioural economists. It led to a stream of invitations for me to produce works whose forms (for example, book chapters and papers in lower-tier journals) often guaranteed that they would have less impact than it might have been possible for me to achieve if I had instead concentrated on producing fewer outputs but ones that concentrated on providing proof-of-concept demonstrations of how my ideas could be implemented and/or demonstrations of why the ideas were important for policy design.

---

[21] It is possible that Rabin's impact had much to do with his demonstrations that psychological factors can be incorporated in formal models, for this may have led growing numbers of technically skilled mainstream economists to engage in what Berg and Gigerenzer (2010) call 'as-if behavioural economics.' By contrast, the uptake of Thaler's heuristics and biases-driven approach is consistent with mainstream economics being what Lakatos (1970) calls a 'degenerating research program.' Thaler-style behavioural economics could be accepted as a way of dealing with anomalies in areas where they were identified, while enabling conventional economics to continue to be practiced, with no change to its hard-core axioms and operating heuristics, in the areas that remained unscathed.

References

Abolafia, M. Y. (1996). *Making Markets: Opportunism and Restraint on Wall Street*. Cambridge, MA: Harvard University Press.

Abolafia, M. Y. (1998). Markets as cultures: An ethnographic approach. *Sociological Review, 46*(May), 69–85.

Ackley, G. (1961). *Macroeconomic Theory*. New York: Collier Macmillan.

Adams, T. F. N., & Kobayashi, N. (1969). *The World of Japanese Business*. London: Ward Lock.

Akerlof, G. A., & Shiller, R. J. (2015). *Phishing for Phools: The Economics of Manipulation and Deception*. Princeton, NJ and Oxford: Princeton University Press.

Akerlof, G. A., & Yellen, J. L. (eds) (1986). *Efficiency Wage Models of the Labor Market*. Cambridge: Cambridge University Press.

Alberti, R. E,, & Emmors, M. L. (2008). *Your Perfect Right: Assertiveness and Equality in Life and Relationships* (9th edn). St Luis Obispo, CA: Impact Publishers.

Alexander, S. S. (1952). Effects of a devaluation on a trade balance. *IMF Staff Papers, 2*(2): 263–278.

Allen, G. C. ([1939] 1970). *British Industries and Their Organization*. London: George Allen & Unwin (5th edition, 1970, London: Longman).

Allen, G. C. (1968). *Monopoly and Restrictive Practices*. London: George Allen & Unwin (reprinted 2003, London: Routledge).

Andreozzi, L., & Bianchi, M. (2007). Fashion: Why people like it and theorists do not. In M. Bianchi (ed.), *The Evolution of Consumption: Theories and Practices. Advances in Austrian Economics, Volume10* (pp. 209–229). Oxford: Elsevier.

Andrews, P. W. S. (1949). *Manufacturing Business*. London: Macmillan.

Andrews, P. W. S. (1958). Competition in the modern economy. In G. Sell, ed., *Competitive Aspects of Oil Operations*, London: Institute of Petroleum. Reprinted in F. S. Lee and P. E. Earl (eds) (1993), *The Economics of Competitive Enterprise* (pp. 323–362). Aldershot: Edward Elgar.

Andrews, P. W. S. (1964). *On Competition in Economic Theory*. London: Macmillan.

Andrews, P. W. S., & Brunner, E. (1951) *Capital Development in Steel*. Oxford: Basil Blackwell.

Andrews, P. W. S., & Brunner, E. (1975). *Studies in Pricing*. London: Macmillan.

Archibald, G. C. (ed.) (1971). *The Theory of the Firm*. Harmondsworth: Penguin.

Arrow, K. J. (1974). *The Limits of Organization*. New York: W. W. Norton.

Bain, A. D. (1964). *The Growth of Television Ownership in the United Kingdom since the War: A Lognormal Model (University of Cambridge, Department of Applied Economics Monographs, No. 12))*. Cambridge: Cambridge University Press.

Barberis, N. C. (2013). Thirty years of Prospect Theory in economic: A review and assessment. *Journal of Economic Perspectives, 27*(1): 173–196.

Barnard, C. I. (1938). *The Functions of the Executive*. Cambridge, MA: Harvard University Press.

Barro, R. J., & Grossman, H. I., (1976). *Money, Employment and Inflation*. Cambridge: Cambridge University Press.

Bator, F. M. (1957). The simple analytics of welfare maximization. *American Economic Review, 47* (1): 22–59.

Bauer, P. T. (1971). *Dissent on Development*. London: Weidenfeld & Nicolson.

Baumol, W. J. (1962). On the theory of the expansion of the firm. *American Economic Review, 52*(5): 1079–1087.

Baumol, W. J. (1972). *Economic Theory and Operations Analysis* (3rd edition). London: Prentice-Hall International.

Baumol, W. J., Panzar, J., & Willig, R. (1982). *Contestable Markets and the Theory of Industrial Structure*. New York: Harcourt Brace Jovanovich.

Belsky, G., & Gilovich, T. (1999). *Why Smart People Make Big Money Mistakes and How to Avoid Them*. New York: Simon and Schuster.

Berg, N. (2015). Behavioural labor economics. In M. Altman (ed.) *Handbook of Contemporary Behavioural Economics* (pp. 479–500). London and New York: Routledge.

Berg, N., & Gigerenzer, G. (2010). As-if behavioral economics: Neoclassical economics in disguise? *History of Economic Ideas, 18*(1), 133–166.

Bettman, J. R. (1979). *An Information-Processing Theory of Consumer Choice*. Reading, MA: Addison-Wesley.

Bondo Hansen, K., & Presskorn-Thygesen, T. (2022). On some antecedents of behavioural economics. *History of the Human Sciences, 35*(3/4), 58-83,

Bradbury, F. R. (1969). *Words and Numbers: A Student's Guide to Intellectual Method*. Edinburgh: Edinburgh University Press.

Brooks, M. A. (1988). Toward a behavioral analysis of public economics. In P. E. Earl (ed.), *Psychological Economics: Development, Tensions, Prospects* (pp. 169–188). Boston, MA: Kluwer Academic Publishing.

Brooks, M. A., & Earl, P. E. (1987). On the implications of jointness in a normative model of behavior based on an activity hierarchy. *Journal of Consumer Research, 14*(3): 445–448.

Buchanan, J. M., & Thirlby, G. (eds) (1973). *LSE Essays on Cost*. London: Weidenfeld and Nicolson.

Buckley, P. J., & Michie, J. (eds) (1996) *Firms, Organizations and Contracts: A Reader in Industrial Organization*. Oxford: Oxford University Press.

Buenstorf, G. (2003). Designing clunkers: Demand-side innovation and the early history of the mountain bike, In U. Cantner and J. S. Metcalfe (eds), *Change, Transformation and Development* (pp. 53–7,0) Heidelberg: Physica.

Cañibano, C., Earl, P. E., and Muñoz, F.-F. (2025), Career lessons from economists' life stories: Brian J. Loasby as an exemplar, *Journal of Institutional Economics, 21.* published online 25 February, https://doi.org/10.1017/S1744137425000013.

Casson, M. (2006). Collecting books on economics. In F. Kells (complier), *The Australian Book Auction Records, Series Three, Volume Three* (pp. xiii–xv). Carlton, VIC: Bread Street Press.

Catmull, E. (2014). *Creativity, Inc.* New York: Random House.

Chai, A., Earl, P. E., & Potts, J. (2007). Fashion, growth and welfare: An evolutionary approach. In M. Bianchi (ed.), *The Evolution of Consumption: Theories and Practice. Advances in Austrian Economics, Volume 10* (pp. 187–207). Oxford: JAI/Elsevier.

Challen, D. W., & Hagger, A. J. (1981). *Unemployment and Inflation: An Introduction to Macroeconomics*. Melbourne, VIC: Longman Cheshire.

Chamberlin, E. H. (1933). *The Theory of Monopolistic Competition*. Cambridge, MA: Harvard University Press.

Chandler, A. D. (1962). *Strategy and Structure: Chapters in the History of the American Industrial Enterprise.* Cambridge, MA: MIT Press.

Channon, D. F. (1973). *The Strategy and Structure of British Enterprise.* London: Macmillan.

Chick, V. (1973). *Theory of Monetary Policy.* London: Gray-Mills.

Chick, V. (1983). *Macroeconomics After Keynes.* Deddington: Philip Allan.

Christensen, C. (1997). *The Innovator's Dilemma: When New Technologies Cause Great Firms to Fail.* Boston, MA: Harvard Business Review Press.

Chrystal, K. A. (1979). *Controversies in British Macroeconomics.* Deddington: Philip Allan.

Cialdini, R. B. (1984). *Influence: The Psychology of Persuasion.* New York: William Morrow & Company.

Cialdini, R. B. (2009). *Influence: Science and Practice* (5th edn). Boston: Pearson Education.

Clark, J. (2007). Essays on Complexity, Choice and Competition in the Market for Retirement Funds. PhD dissertation, University of Queensland.

Clower, R. W. (1965). The Keynesian counter-revolution: A theoretical appraisal. In F. H. Hahn and F. P. R. Brechling (eds), *The Theory of Interest Rates.* London: Macmillan.

Clower, R. W. (1967). A reconsideration of the microfoundations of monetary theory. *Western Economic Journal* (now *Economic Inquiry*), 6(1): 1–8.

Clydesdale, G. (2006). Creativity and competition: The Beatles. *Creativity Research Journal, 18*(2): 129–139.

Clydesdale, G. (2015). Capabilities and industrial policy: Lesson from the New Zealand movie industry. *Industrial and Corporate Change, 24*(5): 1149–1171.

Clydesdale, G. (2016). *Waves of Prosperity: India, China and the West – How Global Trade Transformed the World.* London: Robinson.

Clydesdale, G. (2021). *Reducing Inter-generational Ethnic Poverty: Economics, Psychology and Culture.* Abingdon and New York: Routledge.

Coase, R. H. (1937). The nature of the firm. *Economica, 4 (new series)* (16): 386–405.

Coddington, A. (1976). Keynesian economics: The search for first principles. *Journal of Economics Literature, 14*(4): 1258– 1273.

Coddington, A. (1982). Deficient foresight: A troublesome theme in Keynesian economics. *American Economics Review, 72*(3): 480-487.

Cord, R. (ed.) (2017). *The Palgrave Companion to Cambridge Economics*. London: Palgrave Macmillan.

Coursey, D. K. (1985), A normative model of behavior based upon an activity hierarchy. *Journal of Consumer Research, 12*(1): 64–73.

Courvisanos, J. (2025). Book Review: *Beyond Misbehaving: Changing Universities, Pluralism, and the Evolution of a Heterodox Behavioural Economist* by Peter E. Earl. *History of Economics Review,* published online 31 Mar 2025, DOI: 10.1080/10370196.2025.2475531.

Creedy, J. (2007). A PhD Thesis Without Tears. Department of Economics Working Papers Series 987, University of Melbourne.

Creedy, J. (2008). *Research Without Tears: From the First Ideas to Published Output*. Cheltenham: Edward Elgar.

Creedy, J. (2022). Fifty Not Out: Reflections on Fifty Years of Publishing in Economics Journals. Working Papers in Public Finance 22/2022, Victoria University of Wellington, December. Downloadable at: https://www.wgtn.ac.nz/cpf/publications/working-papers/2022-working-papers/WP22-2022-Fifty-Not-Out-Reflections-on-Fifty-Years-of-Publishing-in-Economics-Journals.pdf.

Creedy, J. (2023). J. A. C. Brown: Early economic modelling and applied econometrics in the UK. *History of Economics Review*, published online 9 May 2023, DOI: 10.1080/10370196.2023.2195256.

Crick, D. (2025). *Dealbreakers: Sex, Quiz, and Rock 'n' Roll*. Brisbane: Darcy Crick.

Cripps, T. F., & Tarling, R. J. (1973). *Growth in Advanced Capitalist Economies, 1960–1970 (Department of Applied Economics Occasional Papers, No. 40)*. Cambridge: Cambridge University Press.

Cross, R. (1982). *Economic Theory and Policy in the UK*. Oxford: Martin Robertson.

Cross, R. (1984). Methodology in economics. *Scottish Journal of Political Economy, 31*(1): 100–110.

Csikszentmihalyi, M. (1990). *Flow: The Psychology of Optimal Experience*. New York: Harper & Row.

Cuthbertson, K. (1979). *Macroeconomic Policy: The New Cambridge, Keynesian and Monetarist Controversies*. London: Macmillan.

Cyert, R. M., & March, J. G. (1955). Organizational structure and pricing behavior in an oligopoly. *American Economic Review, 45*(1): 129–139.

Cyert, R. M., & March, J. G. (1963). *A Behavioral Theory of the Firm.* Englewood Cliffs, NJ Prentice-Hall.

Cyert, R. M., & March, J. G. (1992). *A Behavioral Theory of the Firm.* (2nd edition) Malden, MA and Oxford: Blackwell.

Darby, M. R., &. Karni, E. (1973). Free competition and the optimal amount of fraud. *Journal of Law & Economics, 16*(1): 67–**88**.

Davies. J. E., & Lee, F. S. (1988). A Post Keynesian appraisal of the contestability criterion. *Journal of Post Keynesian Economics, 11*(1): 3–25.

Deane, P. (1978). *The Evolution of Economic Ideas.* Cambridge: Cambridge University Press.

Dekker, E., & Remic, B. (2024). Hayek's extended mind: on the (im)possibility of Austrian behavioural economics. *Journal of Institutional Economics*, published online March 7, 2024, e19, 1–19 doi:10.1017/S1744137424000055.

Dempster, M., & Gatheral. J. (2022). In Memoriam Mardi Dungey. *Quantitative Finance, 22*(4): 631.

Denison, E. F. (1967). *Why Growth Rates Differ: Postwar Experience in Nine Western Countries.* Washington, DC: Brookings Institutions.

Dewey, J. (1910). *How We Think.* New York: D. C. Heath.

Dhami, S. (2016). *The Foundations of Behavioral Economics.* Oxford: Oxford University Press.

Doidge, N. (2007). *The Brain that Changes Itself: Stories of Personal Triumph from the Frontiers of Brain Science.* New York: Viking Penguin.

Dopfer, K., Foster, J., & Potts, J. (2004). Micro-meso-macro. *Journal of Evolutionary Economics, 14*(3), 263-279.

Douglas, E. J. (1987). *Managerial Economics: Analysis and Strategy* (3rd edition). Englewood Cliffs, NJ: Prentice-Hall.

Dow, S. C. (1985). *Macroeconomic Thought: A Methodological Approach.* Oxford: Basil Blackwell.

Dow, S. C., & Earl, P. E. (1982). *Money Matters: A Keynesian Approach to Monetary Economics.* Oxford: Martin Robertson.

Dow, S. C., & Earl, P. E. (1984). Methodology and orthodox monetary policy. *Économie Appliquée, 37*(1): 143–163.

Dow, S. C., & Earl, P. E. (eds) (1999a). *Economic Organization and Economic Knowledge: Essays in Honour of Brian J. Loasby, Volume I*. Cheltenham: Edward Elgar.

Dow, S. C., & Earl, P. E. (eds) (1999b). *Contingency, Complexity and the Theory of the Firm: Essays in Honour of Brian J. Loasby, Volume II*. Cheltenham: Edward Elgar.

Downie, J. (1958). *The Competitive Process*. London: Duckworth.

Drakopoulos, S. A. (1994). Hierarchical choice in economics. *Journal of Economic Surveys, 8*(2): 133–153.

Drakopoulos, S. A., & Karayiannis, A. D. (2004). The historical development of hierarchical behavior in economic thought. *Journal of the History of Economic Thought, 26*(3): 363–378.

Duesenberry, J. S. (1949). *Income, Saving and the Theory of Consumer Behavior*. Cambridge, MA: Harvard University Press.

Earl, P. E. (1980a). Characteristic Filtering: Towards a Behavioural Theory of Individual Choice. University of Stirling Discussion Papers in Economics, Finance, and Investment, No. 84, August.

Earl, P. E. (1980b). A Behavioural Theory of Economists' Behaviour and the Lack of Success of Behavioural Economics. University of Stirling Discussion Papers in Economics, Finance, and Investment, No. 85, August.

Earl, P. E. (1981). J. M. Keynes' *General Theory of Employment, Interest and Money*: A Guide for Readers. Department of Economics, University of Stirling. A scanned version is available to download at: https://shredecon.files.wordpress.com/2023/05/guide-to-keynes.pdf.

Earl, P. E. (1983a). T*he Economic Imagination: Towards a Behavioural Analysis of Choice*. Brighton: Wheatsheaf Books/Armonk, NY: M. E. Sharpe, Inc.

Earl, P. E. (1983b). A behavioral theory of economists 'behavior. In A. S. Eichner (ed.), *Why Economics is not yet a Science* (pp. 90–125). London: Macmillan/Armonk, NY: M.E. Sharpe, Inc.

Earl, P. E. (1983c). The consumer in his/her social setting: A subjectivist view. In J. Wiseman (ed.), *Beyond Positive Economics? (Papers presented to Section F of the British Association for the Advancement of Science, York, 1981)* (pp, 176–191). London: Macmillan.

Earl, P. E. (1984), *The Corporate Imagination: How Big Companies Make Mistakes*, Brighton: Wheatsheaf Books/Armonk, NY: M. E. Sharpe, Inc.

Earl, P. E. (1986a). A behavioural analysis of demand elasticities. *Journal of Economic Studies, 13*(3): 20–37.

Earl, P. E. (1986b). *Lifestyle Economics: Consumer Behaviour in a Turbulent World.* Brighton: Wheatsheaf Books/New York: St Martin's Press.

Earl, P. E. (1986c). Book review: *Methodology for a New Microeconomics*, by L. A. Boland. *Economic Journal, 96(*384): 1134–1135.

Earl, P. E. (1987a). Unexploited scope for quantitative work in the history of economic thought. *HETSA Bulletin* (now *History of Economics Review*), No. 8, Summer: 1–11.

Earl, P. E. (1987b). Entries on P. W. S. Andrews, A. G. Hart and G. L. S. Shackle. In J. Eatwell, M. Milgate, & P. Newman (eds), *The New Palgrave: A Dictionary of Economics*, pp. 94 (vol. 1), 604-5 (vol. 2), 315-6 (vol. 4). London: Macmillan.

Earl, P. E. (1987c). Book review: *Handbook of Behavioral Economics*, edited by B. Gilad & S. Kaish. *Journal of Economic Psychology, 8*(3): 385–388.

Earl, P. E. (1987d). Book review: *Handbook of Behavioral Economics*, edited by B. Gilad & S. Kaish. *Economic Journal* **97(388)**: 1012-1014. (This is a different review from the Earl (1987c) review, for a different audience.)

Earl. P. E. (1987e). Scientific Research Programmes, Corporate Strategies and the Theory of the Firms. Information Research Unit Occasional Paper, University of Queensland.

Earl, P. E. (ed.) (1988a). *Psychological Economics: Development, Tensions, Prospects.* Boston, MA: Kluwer Academic Publishers.

Earl, P. E. (ed.) (1988b). *Behavioural Economics.* Aldershot: Edward Elgar.

Earl, P. E. (1988c). Review article: *Economic Psychology: Intersections in Theory and Applications*, edited by A. J. MacFadyen & H. W. MacFadyen. *Prometheus, 6*(1): 142–149.

Earl, P. E. (1988d). Book review: *The Economics and Management of Financial Institutions*, edited by D. Juttner & T. Valentine. *Economic Analysis and Policy, 18*(2): 255–257.

Earl, P. E. (1988e). Book review: *How the West Grew Rich*, by N. Rosenberg & L. Birdzell. *Prometheus. 6*(1): 174–176.

Earl, P. E. (1988f). Information, Transaction Costs, and the Economic Analysis of Financial Firms. Information Research Unit Occasional Paper, University of Queensland.

Earl, P. E. (1989a). Bounded rationality, psychology and financial evolution: Some behavioural perspectives on Post Keynesian monetary analysis. In J. Pheby (ed.), *New Directions in Post Keynesian Economics* (165–189). Aldershot: Edward Elgar.

Earl, P. E. (1989b). Book review: *The Individual in the* Economy, by S. E. G. Lea, R. Tarpy & P. Webley. *Economic Analysis and Policy, 19*(1): 118–121.

Earl, P. E. (1989c). Book review: *Economic Choice Under Uncertainty,* by J. L. Ford. *Review of Political Economy, 1*(2): 238–240.

Earl, P. E. (1990a). Economics and psychology: A survey. *Economic Journal, 100*(402): 718–755.

Earl, P. E. (1990b). Coping with uncertainty in economics: Interview with G. L S. Shackle. *Review of Political Economy, 2*(1): 104–113.

Earl, P. E. (1990c). *Monetary Scenarios: A Modern Approach to Financial Systems.* Aldershot, Edward Elgar.

Earl, P. E. (1990d) Book review: *Decisions and Organizations*, by J. G. March, *Review of Political Economy, 2*(3): 368–369.

Earl, P. E. (1990e) Book review: *Psychological Foundations of Economic Behavior*, edited by P. Albanese. *Journal of Economic Literature, 28*(December): 1716–1717.

Earl, P. E. (1990f) Book review: *Understanding Economic Behaviour*, edited by K. Grunert & F. Olander. *Economic Journal, 100*(403): 1341–1342.

Earl, P. E. (1990g) Book review: *The Mind and Method of the Economist*, by B. J. Loasby. *Economic Journal, 100*(401): 642–644.

Earl, P. E. (1991a). Normal cost versus marginalist approaches to pricing: A behavioural perspective. *Journal of Post Keynesian Economics, 13*(2): 264–281.

Earl, P. E. (1991b). Principal–agent problems and structural change in the advertising industry. *Prometheus, 9*(2): 274–295.

Earl, P. E. (1991c) Book review: *Perspectives on the History of Economic Thought, Volume IV*, edited by D. Moggridge. *Manchester School, 59*(1): 107–108.

Earl, P. E. (1992a). The evolution of cooperative strategies: Three automotive industry case studies. *Human Systems Management, 11*(2): 89–100.

Earl, P. E. (1992b). Scientific research programmes and the prediction of corporate behaviour *Cyprus Journal of Economics*, 5(2): 75–95.

Earl, P. E. (1992c). On the complementarity of economic applications of cognitive dissonance theory and personal construct psychology. In S. E. G. Lea, P. Webley, & B. Young (eds), *New Directions in Economic Psychology* (pp. 49–65). Aldershot: Edward Elgar.

Earl, P.E. (1992d). Tibor Scitovsky. In W. J. Samuels (ed), *New Horizons in Economic Thought: An Appraisal of Ten Leading Economists* (pp. 265–293). Aldershot: Edward Elgar Publishing Ltd.

Earl, P. E. (1992e). Shearnur on subjectivism. In S. Boehm & B. Caldwell (eds), *Austrian Economics: Tensions and New Developments* (pp. 129–135). Boston, MA: Kluwer Academic Publishers.

Earl, P. E. (1992f). Book review: *The Market Experience*, by R. E. Lane. *Economic Journal, 102*(415): 1566–1568.

Earl, P. E. (1992g). Case study and instructors' notes: The Erebus air disaster. In G Hearn *et al. Organisational Behaviour: Australian Teaching Resources to Accompany R.P. Vecchio, G Hearn and G Southey: Organizational Behaviour: Life at Work in Australia* (pp. 190-202). Sydney: Harcourt Brace (instructors' notes jointly written with C. Fisher).

Earl, P. E. (1993a). The economics of G. L. S. Shackle in retrospect and prospect (triple review article). *Review of Political Economy, 5*(1): 245–261.

Earl, P. E. (1993b) Book review: *Artificial Intelligence and Economic Analysis*, edited by S. Moss & J. Rae. *Economic Journal, 103*(419): 1106–1107.

Earl, P. E. (1993c). Book review: *Models of My Life*, by H. A. Simon. *Eastern Economic Journal, 19* (2): 247-249.

Earl, P. E. (1994a). The economic rationale of universities: A reconsideration. *Prometheus, 12*(2): 131–151.

Earl, P. E. (1994b). Herbert Alexander Simon. In G. M. Hodgson. W. J. Samuels & M. R. Tool (eds), *The Elgar Companion to Institutional and Evolutionary Economics*, Vol. 2 (pp. 284–287). Aldershot: Edward Elgar.

Earl, P. E. (1994c). Book review: *Behavioural Foundations of Economics*, by J. L. Baxter. *Economic Journal* 104(425): 945–946.

Earl, P. E. (1995a). *Microeconomics for Business and Marketing: Lectures, Cases and Worked Essays*. Aldershot: Edward Elgar.

Earl, P. E. (1995b). Liquidity preference, marketability and pricing. In S. C. Dow & J. Hillard (eds), *Keynes, Knowledge and Uncertainty* (pp. 271–294). Aldershot: Edward Elgar.

Earl, P. E. (1995c). The dissenting economist (Book review: *G. L. S. Shackle: The Dissenting Economist's Economist*, by J. L. Ford,). *History of Economics Review*, 23(Winter): 135–138.

Earl, P. E. (1995d). Coordination problems in tertiary education and research. Paper presented at the G. B. Richardson Colloquium, St John's College, Oxford, 4–6 January. Available for downloading at: https://shredecon.files.wordpress.com/2010/12/cep-richardson-colloquium.pdf.

Earl, P. E. (ed.) (1996a). *Management, Marketing and the Competitive Process*. Cheltenham: Edward Elgar.

Earl, P. E. (1996b). Shackle, entrepreneurship and the theory of the firm. In S. Pressman (ed.), *Interactions in Political Economy: Malvern After Ten Years* (pp. 43–60). London: Routledge.

Earl, P. E. (1996c). Book review: *Paradigms and Convention*, by Y. B. Choi. *Journal of Economic Psychology, 17*(1): 145–148.

Earl, P. E. (1998a). Information, coordination and macroeconomics. *Information Economics and Policy, 10*(3): 331–342.

Earl, P. E. (1998b). Consumer goals as journeys into the unknown. In M. Bianchi (ed.), *The Active Consumer: Novelty and Surprise in Consumer Choice* (pp. 122–139). London: Routledge.

P. E. (1998c). George Richardson's career and the literature of economics. In N. J. Foss & B. J. Loasby (eds), *Economic Organization, Capabilities and Coordination: Essays in Honour of G. B. Richardson* (pp. 14–43). London: Routledge.

Earl, P. E. (1998d) Book review: *Pattern in Corporate Evolution*, by N. M. Kay. *Scottish Journal of Political Economy, 45*(3): 345–346.

Earl, P. E. (1999a). Marketing as information economics. In S. Macdonald & J. Nightingale (eds), *Information and Organization: A Tribute to the Work of Don Lamberton* (pp. 243–261). Amsterdam: Elsevier.

Earl, P. E. (1999b). Managerialism and the economics of the firm. In P. Werhane & A. E. Singer (eds), *Business Ethics in Theory and Practice: Contributions from Asia and New Zealand* (pp. 13–26). Dordrecht: Kluwer.

Earl, P. E. (1999c). Book review: *The Laws of the Markets*, edited by M. Callon. *International Journal of Social Economics,* 26(12):1505–1506.

Earl, P. E. (2000). Book review: *Alchemies of the Mind*, by J. Elster. *Economic Journal, 110*(464): 462–463.

Earl, P. E. (2001a). Simon's travel theorem and the demand for live music. *Journal of Economic Psychology*, 22(3): 335–358.

Earl, P. E. (ed.) (2001b). *The Legacy of Herbert A. Simon in Economic Analysis*. Cheltenham: Edward Elgar

Earl, P. E. (2001c). Book review: *The Psychology of Saving*, by K.-E. Wärneryd, *Journal of Economic Psychology* 22(2): 295–299.

Earl, P. E. (2002). *Information, Opportunism and Economic Coordination*. Cheltenham: Edward Elgar.

Earl, P. E. (2003a). The perils of pluralism in economics and how to reduce them. In E. Fullbrook (ed.), *The Crisis in Economics* (pp. 90–93). London: Routledge (originally in *Post-Autistic Economics Review*, issue no, 11, January 2002, article 1).

Earl, P. E. (2003b). The entrepreneur as a constructor of connections. In R. Koppl (ed.), *Austrian Economics and Entrepreneurial Studies – Advances in Austrian Economics, Volume* 6 (pp. 117–134). Oxford, JAI/Elsevier.

Earl, P. E. (2004a). How economists model choice, versus how we behave, and why it matters. In E. Fullbrook. (ed.), *A Guide to What's Wrong with Economics* (pp. 95–105). London: Anthem.

Earl, P. E. (2004b). Book Review: *The Personality Continuum and Consumer Behavior* by P. Albanese. *Journal of Economic Psychology, 25*(2): 293–296.

Earl, P. E. (2005a). Economics and psychology in the twenty-first century. *Cambridge Journal of Economics, 29*(6): 909-926.

Earl, P. E. (2005b). Book Review: *The Economics of Sin: Rational Choice or No Choice at All?* by Samuel Cameron. *Journal of Economic Psychology, 26*(1): 147–149.

Earl, P. E. (2005c) Behavioural Economics and the Economics of Regulation. Briefing Paper for the New Zealand Ministry of Economic Development and Ministry of Consumer Affairs. Available at: https://espace.library.uq.edu.au/view/UQ:8811.

Earl, P. E. (2006a). Book review: *Hollywood Economics*, by A. De Vany. *Review of Political Economy, 18(*4): 577–579.

Earl, P. E. (2006b). Book review: *The Elgar Companion of Post Keynesian Economics*, edited by J. E. King. *Journal of Economic Behavior and Organization*, 60(4): 608–611.

Earl, P. E. (2006c). Book review: *Schumpeter on the Economics of Innovation and the Development of Capitalism*, by A. Heertje. *History of Economics Review*, *44*(Summer): 120–122.

Earl, P. E. (2007). Consumption X-inefficiency and the problem of market regulation. In R. Frantz (ed.), *Renaissance in Behavioral Economics: Essays in Memory of Harvey Leibenstein* (pp. 176–193). London: Routledge.

Earl, P. E. (2008a). Heterodox economics and the future of academic publishing. *On the Horizon, 16*(4): 205–213.

Earl, P. E. (2008b). Book review: *The Emergence of Modern Marketing*, edited by R. Church & A. Godley. *Review of Political Economy, 20*(4): 630–632.

Earl, P. E. (2009). Information technology and the economics of storing, spreading and generating knowledge. *Prometheus, 27*(4): 389–401.

Earl, P. E. (2010a). Economics fit for the Queen: A pessimistic assessment of its prospects. *Prometheus, 28*(3.): 1–17.

Earl, P. E. (2010b). The sensory order, the economic imagination and the tacit dimension. In W. Butos (ed.), *The Social Science of The Sensory Order: Advances in Austrian Economics, Volume 13* (pp. 211–236). Bradford: Emerald.

Earl, P. E. (2010c). Remembrance of Cars Past: An Experiential Analysis of Automotive Consumption (The Much Too Long Version). Available at: https://shredecon.files.wordpress.com/2023/05/earl-motoring_much-too-long-version.docx.

Earl, P. E. (2011a). From anecdotes to novels: Reflective inputs for behavioural economics. *New Zealand Economic Papers, 45*(1/2): 5–27.

Earl, P. E. (2011b). Behavioural economics and economic policy. In G. Argyrous & F. Stilwell (eds), *Readings in Political Economy: Economics as a Social Science* (pp. 264–269). Prahran, VIC: Tilde University Press.

Earl, P. E. (2012a). Experiential analysis of automotive consumption. *Journal of Business Research, 65*(7): 1067–1072.

Earl, P. E (2012b). Behavioural Theory. In M. Dietrich & J. Krafft (eds), *Handbook of the Theory of the Firm* (pp. 96–101). Cheltenham: Edward Elgar.

Earl, P. E. (2012c). On Kahneman's *Thinking, Fast and Slow*: What you see is not all there is. *Prometheus, 30*(4): 449–455.

Earl, P. E. (2012d). Book review: *The Economics of Abundance*, by B. Sheehan. *Economic and Labour Relations Review. 22*(1): 173–184.

Earl, P.E. (2012e). Kahneman's *Thinking, Fast and Slow* from the standpoint of old behavioural economics. Paper presented to HETSA conference, Melbourne, July. Available at: https://shredecon.files.wordpress.com/2012/06/hetsa-2012-earl.pdf.

Earl, P. E. (2013a). The robot, the party animal and the philosopher: An evolutionary perspective on deliberation and preference. *Cambridge Journal of Economics, 37*(6): 1263–1282.

Earl, P. E. (2013b). Satisficing and cognition: Complementarities between Simon and Hayek. In R. Frantz & R. Leeson (eds), *Hayek and Behavioral* Economics (pp. 278–300). Basingstoke and New York: Palgrave.

Earl, P. E. (2014a). Bringing psychology and pluralism into the teaching of welfare economics. *International Journal of Pluralism and Economics Education, 5*(1): 58–77.

Earl, P. E. (2014b). Book review: *On Skidelsky's Keynes and Other Essays* and *The Making of a Post-Keynesian Economist: Cambridge Harvest*, by G. C. Harcourt. *Economic Record, 90*(291): 553–556.

Earl, P. E. (2015a). Anchoring in economics: On Frey and Gallus on the aggregation of behavioural anomalies. *Economics E-Journal*, 2015-21: 1–25, July 15. http://dx.doi.org/10.5018/economics-ejournal.ja.2015-21.

Earl, P. E. (2015b). Book review: *Alfred Marshall and Modern Economics: Equilibrium Theory and Evolutionary Economics*, by N. Hart. *History of Economics Review, 62*(Summer): 98–101.

Earl, P. E, (2016a). Bounded rationality in the digital age. In R. Frantz & L. Marsh (eds), *Minds, Markets and Milieux: Commemorating the Centenary of the Birth of Herbert Simon* (pp. 91–112). Basingstoke: Palgrave.

Earl, P. E. (2016b). The evolution of behavioural economics. In R. Frantz, S.-H. Chen, K. Dopfer, F. Heukelom, & S. Mousavi (eds), *Routledge Handbook of Behavioral Economics* (pp. 5–17). London: Routledge.

Earl, P. E. (2017a). Lifestyle changes and the lifestyle selection process. *Journal of Bioeconomics, 19*(1): 97–114.

Earl, P. E. (2017b). Theory of the firm. In C. L. Spash (ed.), *Routledge Handbook of Ecological Economics* (pp. 194–202). London and New York: Routledge.

Earl, P. E. (2018a). Richard H. Thaler: A Nobel Prise for behavioural economics. *Review of Political Economy, 30*(2): 107–125.

Earl, P. E. (2018b). G. L. S. Shackle's introspective behavioural economics. *Journal of Behavioral Economics for Policy*, 2(1): 19–25.

Earl, P. E. (2019a). The mortgage treadmill versus discretionary spending and enforced leisure. In A. Chai and C. M. Baum (eds), *Demand, Complexity and Long-Run Evolution* (pp. 51–68). Cham: Springer.

Earl, P. E. (2019b). Bool review: *Human Evolution, Economic Progress and Evolutionary Failure*, by B. Rao. *Economic Record 95*(311): 512–514.

Earl, P. E. (2022). *Principles of Behavioral Economics: Bringing Together Old, New and Evolutionary Approaches*. Cambridge: Cambridge University Press.

Earl, P. E. (2023a). Rules all the way down: Consumer behaviour from the standpoint of the 'ONE behavioural' research programme. *Journal of Consumer Behavior, 22*(3): 531–546.

Earl, P. E. (2023b). Shackle's analysis of choice under uncertainty: Its strengths, weaknesses and potential synergies with rival approaches. *Journal of Post Keynesian Economics, 46*(3): 400–419.

Earl, P. E. (2023c). Infinite regress problems and the methodologies of behavioural economics, In I. Negru & P. Hawkins (eds) *Economic Methodology, History and Pluralism* (pp. 94–107). London and New York: Routledge.

Earl, P. E. (2023d). A Comprehensive Bibliography of the Works of Brian J. Loasby. School of Economics, University of Queensland (available via ResearchGate, DOI: 10.13140/RG.2.2.35301.37608).

Earl, P. E., & Dow, S. C. (1984). Monetary policy in a speculative environment. In P. G. Hare & M. W. Kirby (eds), *An Introduction to British Economic Policy* (pp. 61–75). Brighton: Wheatsheaf

Earl, P. E., Friesen, L., & Shadforth, C. (2017). The efficiency of market-assisted choices: An experimental analysis of mobile phone connection service recommendations. *Journal of Institutional Economics, 13*(4): 849–873.

Earl, P. E., Friesen, L., & Shadforth, C. (2019). Elusive optima: A process-tracing analysis of procedural rationality in mobile phone connection plan choices. *Journal of Economic Behavior and Organization, 161*: 303–322.

Earl, P. E., & Frowen, S. F. (eds) (2000). *Economics as an Art of Thought: Essays in Memory of G. L. S. Shackle*. London, Routledge.

Earl, P. E., & Glaister, K. W. (1979). Wage Stickiness From the Demand Side. University of Stirling Discussion Papers in Economics, Finance, and Investment, No. 78, December.

Earl, P. E., & Kay, N. M. (1985). How economists can accept Shackle's critique of economic doctrines without arguing themselves out of their jobs. *Journal of Economic Studies, 12*(1/2), 34-48.

Earl, P. E., & Kemp, S. (eds) (1999). *The Elgar Companion to Consumer Research and Economic Psychology*. Cheltenham: Edward Elgar.

Earl, P. E., & Littleboy, B. (eds) (2008). *Regarding the Past: Proceedings of the 20th Conference of the History of Thought Society of Australia*. Brisbane, QLD: School of Economics, University of Queensland.

Earl, P. E., & Littleboy, B. (2014). *G.L.S. Shackle (Great Thinkers in Economics Series)*. Basingstoke and London: Palgrave.

Earl, P. E., & Mandeville, T. (2009). The competitive process in the age of the Internet. *Prometheus, 27*(3): 195–209.

Earl, P. E., Markey-Towler, B., & Coutts, K. (2022). 50 Years Ago: Duncan Ironmonger's *New Commodities and Consumer Behaviour* and its relationship with Lancaster's 'New Approach' to Consumer Behaviour. *History of Economics Review, 83*(1): 40–67.

Earl, P. E., & Peng, T.-C. (2011). Home improvements. In S. Cameron (ed.), *Handbook of the Economics of Leisure* (pp. 197–220). Cheltenham: Edward Elgar.

Earl, P. E., & Peng, T.-C. (2012). Brands of economics and the Trojan horse of pluralism. *Review of Political Economy, 24*(3): 451–467.

Earl, P. E., Peng, T. C., & Potts, J. (2007). Decision-rule cascades and the dynamics of speculative bubbles. *Journal of Economic Psychology, 28*(3): 351–364.

Earl, P. E., & Potts, J. (2000). Latent demand and the browsing shopper. *Managerial and Decision Economics, 21*(3–4): 11–22.

Earl, P. E., & Potts, J. (2004a). The market for preferences. *Cambridge Journal of Economics, 28*(4): 619–633.

Earl, P. E., & Potts, J. (2004b). Bounded rationality and decomposability: The basis for integrating cognitive and evolutionary economics. In M. Augier & J. G. March (eds), *Models of a Man: Essays in Memory of Herbert A. Simon* (pp. 317–333). Cambridge, MA, MIT Press.

Earl, P. E., & Potts, J. (2011a). A Nobel prise for governance and institutions: Oliver Williamson and Elinor Ostrom. *Review of Political Economy, 23*(1): 1–24.

Earl, P. E., & Potts, J. (2011b). Creativity under competition and the overshooting problem. Ch. 5 in J. Potts, *Creative Industries and Economic Evolution* (pp, 55–67). Cheltenham, Edward Elgar.

Earl, P. E., & Potts, J. (2013). The creative instability hypothesis. *Journal of Cultural Economics, 37*(2): 153–173.

Earl, P. E., & Potts, J. (2016). The management of creative vision and the economics of creative cycles. *Managerial and Decision Economics, 37*(7): 474–484.

Earl, P. E., & Wakeley, T. (2005). *Business Economics: A Contemporary Approach.* Maidenhead: McGraw-Hill.

Earl, P. E., & Wakeley, T. (2006) Entrepreneurship as a potential point of departure for a course in pluralist economics principles. In P. Kriesler, M. Johnson, & J. Lodewijks (eds), *Essays in Heterodox Economics: Proceeding of the Fifth Australian Society of Heterodox Economics Conference, 11-12 December 2006 (*pp 499-512). Sydney, NSW: University of New South Wales.

Earl, P. E., & Wakeley, T. (2007). Conjectures about future wants: Some insights from evolutionary economics with reference to digital photography. *International Journal of Technological Intelligence and Planning, 3*(1): 24–38. (Special issue on learning from failure.)

Earl, P. E., and Wakeley, T. (2009. Price-based versus standards-based approaches to reducing car addiction and other environmentally destructive activities. In R, P. Holt, S. Pressman, & C. L. Spash (eds), *Post Keynesian and Ecological Economics (*pp. 158–177). Cheltenham: Edward Elgar.

Earl, P. E., & Wakeley, T. (2010a). Economic perspectives on the development of complex products for increasingly demanding customers. *Research Policy, 39(8):* 1122–1132.

Earl, P. E., & Wakeley, T. (2010b). Alternative perspectives on connections in economic systems. *Journal of Evolutionary Economics, 20*(2)*:* 163-183.

Eichner, A. S. (ed.) (1979). *A Guie3 to Post-Keynesian Economics.* London: Macmillan/White Plains, NY: M.E. Sharpe, Inc.

Eichner, A. S. (ed.) (1983). *Why Economics is Not Yet a Science.* London: Macmillan/Armonk, NY: M.E. Sharpe, Inc.

Engel, J. F., Blackwell, R. D., & Kollat, D. T. (1978). *Consumer Behavior* (3rd edition). Hinsdale, IL: Dryden Press.

Engel, J. F., & Blackwell, R. D. (1982). *Consumer Behavior* (4th edition). Hinsdale, IL: Dryden Press.

Engel, J. F., Kollat, D. T., & Blackwell, R. D. (1968). *Consumer Behavior*. New York: Holt, Rinehart & Winston.

Ericsson, K. A., & Simon, H. A. (1993). *Protocol Analysis: Verbal Reports as Data* (2nd edition). Cambridge, MA: MIT Press.

Etzioni, A. (1988). *The Moral Dimension: Toward a New Economics*. New York: Free Press

Farrell, M. J. (1959). The new theories of the consumption function. *Economic Journal, 69*(276): 678–696.

Festinger, L. (1957). *A Theory of Cognitive Dissonance*. New York: Harper & Row.

Fishbein, M., & Ajzen, I. (1975). *Belief, Attitude, Intention, and Behavior*. Reading, MA: Addison-Wesley.

Fisher, D. (2000). The Socio-Economic Consequences of Tourism in Levuka, Fiji. PhD Dissertation, Lincoln University, New Zealand.

Foley, C. A. (1893). Fashion. *Economic Journal, 3*(11, September), 458–474.

Foss, N. J. (ed.) (1997). *Resources, Firms, and Strategies: A Reader in the Resource-Based Perspective*. Oxford: Oxford University Press.

Foster, J. (1987). *Evolutionary Macroeconomics*. London: Unwin Hyman.

Foster, M. M., Earl, P. E., Haines, T. P., & Mitchell, G. K. (2010). Unravelling the concept of consumer preference: Implications for health policy and optimal planning in primary care. *Health Policy, 97*(2–3): 105-112.

Friedman, M. (1968). The role of monetary policy. *American Economic Review, 58*(1): 1–17.

Friesen, L., & Earl, P. E. (2015). Multipart tariffs and bounded rationality: An experimental analysis of mobile phone plan choices. *Journal of Economic Behavior and Organization, 116*: 239–253.

Friesen, L., & Earl, P. E. (2020). An experimental analysis of regulatory interventions for complex pricing. *Southern Economic Journal, 86*(3): 1241–1266.

Frijters, P., & Foster, G. (2013). *An Economic Theory of Greed, Love, Groups and Networks*. Cambridge: Cambridge University Press.

Frolov, D. (2024). The economics of cognitive institutions: mapping debates, looking ahead. *Journal of Institutional Economics. 20*: e28. doi:10.1017/S174413742400016X.

Frowen, S. F. (ed.) (1990). *Unknowledge and Choices in Economics.* Basingstoke: Macmillan.

Fullbrook, E. (1998). Caroline Foley and the theory of intersubjective demand. *Journal of Economic Issues, 32*(3), 709–731.

Garfinkel, H. (1967). *Studies in Ethnomethodology.* Englewood Cliffs, NJ: Prentice-Hall.

Gigerenzer, G. (2015). On the supposed evidence for libertarian paternalism. *Review of Philosophy and Psychology, 6*(3): 361–383.

Gigerenzer, G., & Goldstein, D. G. (1996). Reasoning the fast and frugal way: Models of bounded rationality. *Psychological Review, 103*(4): 650–669.

Gigerenzer, G., Todd, P. M., & The ABC Research Group (1999). *Simple Heuristics that Make Us Smart.* New York: Oxford University Press.

Godley, W., & Cripps, F. (1983). *Macroeconomics.* London: Fontana.

Godley, W., & Lavoie, M. (2007). *Monetary Economics: An Integrated Approach to Credit, Money, Income, Production and Wealth.* Basingstoke: Palgrave.

Gokh, I. (n.d.). International business conversation with Professor Mark Casson. *YouTube,* https://www.youtube.com/watch?v=06st_oiMZ9U.

Goodhart, C. A. E. (1975). *Money, Information and Uncertainty.* London: Macmillan.

Gorman, W. M. (1956). A Possible Procedure for Analysing Quality Differentials in the Egg Market. Ames, IA: Iowa State College, mimeo. Reprinted (1980) *Review of Economic Studies* 47: 843–856.

Gouldner, A. W. (1954). *Patterns of Industrial Bureaucracy.* Glencoe, IL: Free Press.

Granovetter, M. (1985). Economic action and social structure: The problem of embeddedness. *American Journal of Sociology, 91*(3, November), 481–510.

Grüne-Yanoff, T., & Hertwig, R. (2016). Nudge versus Boost: How Coherence are policy and theory. *Minds and Machines, 26*(1–2). 149–183.

Grupp, H., & Maital, S. (2001). *Managing New Product Development and Innovation: A Microeconomic Toolbox.* Cheltenham: Edward Elgar.

Gutman, J. (1982). A means–end chain model based on consumer categorization processes. *Journal of Marketing, 46*(2): 60–72.

Hanson, J. D. & Kysar, D. A. (1999a). Taking behavioralism seriously: the problem of market manipulation. *New York University Law Review, 74*: 630–749.

Hanson, J. D. & Kysar, D.A. (1999b). Taking behavioralism seriously: Some evidence of market manipulation. *Harvard Law Review, 112*: 1420–1572.

Harcourt, G. C., Cosh, A., Hughes, A., Sen, S., Patnaik, P., Harris, D. J., Whittington, G., Meeks, G., Earl, P. E., Rowthorn, R., Sen, A., Ghosh, J., Nolan, P., & Scherer, F. M. (2016). The legacy of Ajit Singh (11 September 1940–23 June 2015). *Economic and Labour Relations Review 27* (3): 293–313.

Harrigan, K. R. (1980). *Strategies for Declining Businesses*. Lexington, MA; Lexington Books.

Harrigan, K. R. (1983). *Strategies for Vertical Integration*. Lexington, MA; Lexington Books.

Hay, I. (2017). *How to be an Academic Superhero: Establishing and Sustaining a Successful Career in the Social Sciences, Arts and Humanities*. Cheltenham: Edward Elgar.

Hayek, F. A. (1952). *The Sensory Order: An Inquiry into the Foundations of Theoretical Psychology*. Chicago, IL: University of Chicago Press.

Hayek, F. A. (1961). The non sequitur of the 'dependence effect.' *Southern Economic Journal, 27*(4): 346:348.

Hedges, M. R. (2010). Tertiary Education Choices in New Zealand: A Pluralistic Investigation. PhD dissertation, University of Queensland.

Henry, H. (!958). *Motivation Research: Its Practice and Uses for Advertising, Marketing and Other Business Purposes*. London: Crosby Lockwood.

Hertwig, R. (2017). When to consider boosting: Some rules for policy-makers. *Behavioural Public Policy, 1*(3): 143–162.

Hey, J. D. (1983). Unshackling economics. *Scottish Journal of Political Economy, 37*(2): 202–208.

Hey, J. D. (1987). Book review: *Lifestyle Economics*, by P. E. Earl. *Manchester School, 55*(1): 101–102.

Hicks, J. R. (1937). Mr Keynes and the 'Classics': A suggested interpretation. *Econometrica, 5*(2): 147–159/

Hicks, J. R. ([1939] 1946). *Value and Capital: An Inquiry into Some Fundamental Principles of Economic Theory* (2nd edition, 1946). Oxford: Clarendon Press.

Hicks, J. R. (1942). *The Social Framework: An Introduction to Economics*. Oxford: Clarendon Press.

Hicks, J. R. (1950). *A Contribution to the Theory of the Trade Cycle*. Oxford: Clarendon Press.

Hicks, J. R. (1976). Some questions of time in economics. In A. M. Tang, F. M Westfield and J. S. Worley (eds), *Evolution, Welfar and Time in Economics: Essays in Honor of Nicholas Georgescu-Roegen*. Lexington, MA: Lexington Books.

Hicks, J. R. (1981). *Are There Economic Cycles? The Robbins Lecture, 1981*. Stirling: University of Stirling.

Hinkle, D. N. ([1965] 2010). The change of personal constructs from the viewpoint of a theory of construct implications. [PhD dissertation, Ohio State University, 1965]. *Personal Construct Theory and Practice, 7*(Supp. No. 1), 1–61.

Hirschman, A. O. (1970). *Exit, Voice and Loyalty*. Cambridge, MA: Harvard University Press.

Hodgson, G. M. (1982). *Capitalism, Value and Exploitation*. Oxford: Martin Robertson.

Hodgson, G. M. (1988). *Economics and Institutions: A Manifesto for a Modern Institutional Economics*. Cambridge: Polity Press.

Hodgson, G. M. (1997). The ubiquity of habits and rules. *Cambridge Journal of Economics, 21*(6): 663–684.

Hodgson, G. M. (2003). The hidden persuaders: Institutions and individuals in economic theory. *Cambridge Journal of Economics, 27*(2), 159–175.

Hodgson, G. M. (2019). *Is There a Future for Heterodox Economics? Institutions, Ideology and a Scientific Community*. Cheltenham, Edward Elgar.

Hofstadter, D. R. (1979). *Gödel, Escher, Bach: An Eternal Golden Braid*. Hassocks, Sussex: Harvester Press.

Hogarth, R. M., & Makridakis, S. (1981). Planning and forecasting: An evaluation. *Management Science, 27*(2): 115–138.

Holbrook, M. B. (1995a). The four faces of commodification in the development of marketing knowledge. *Journal of Marketing Management, 11*(7): 641–654.

Holbrook, M. B. (1995b). *Consumer Research: Introspective Essays on the Study of Consumption.* Thousand Oaks, CA: Sage.

House of Commons (1974) *Ninth Report from the Expenditure Committee, Session 1974, HC328.* London: HMSO.

Houthakker, H. S., & Taylor, L. D. (1970). *Consumer Demand in the United States: Analysis and Projections.* Cambridge, MA: Harvard University Press.

Hutchison, T. W. (1938). *The Significance and Basic Postulates of Economic Theory.* London: Macmillan (reprinted 1965, New York: Augustus M. Kelley).

Hutchison, T. W. (1977). *Knowledge and Ignorance in Economics.* Oxford, Blackwell.

Ironmonger, D. S. (1972). *New Commodities and Consumer Behaviour.* Cambridge: Cambridge University Press.

Irving, J. (1978). P. W. S. Andrews and the Unsuccessful Revolution. Ph.D. dissertation, University of Wollongong, NSW.

Jackson, D., Turner, H. A., & Wilkinson, F. (1972). *Do Trade Unions Cause Inflation? (University of Cambridge Department of Applied Economics Occasional Paper 36).* Cambridge: Cambridge University Press.

Jangu, N. (1997). Decision-Processes of Adopters and Non-Adopters of an Innovation. PhD Dissertation, Lincoln University, New Zealand.

Jefferson, M. (1983). Economic uncertainty and business decision-making. In J. Wiseman (ed.), *Beyond Positive Economics? Proceedings of Section F (Economics) of the British Association for the Advancement of Science, York, 1981* (pp. 132–159). London: Macmillan.

Jefferson, M. (2025). A personal recollection of behavioural economics. *Economic Perspectives and Trends, 2*(2), published online 29 December. DOI : http://dx.doi.org/10.26855/ept.2025.12.007.

Jefferson, T., & King., J. E. (2010–11). Can Post Keynesians make better use of behavioral economics? *Journal of Post Keynesian Economics, 33*(2): 211–234.

Kahneman, D. (2011). *Thinking, Fast and Slow.* New York: Farrar, Strauss and Giroux.

Kahneman, D., Knetsch, J. L., & Thaler, R. H. (1986). Fairness as a constraint on profit seeking entitlements in the market. *American Economic Review, 76*(4): 728–741.

Kahneman, D., & Tversky, A. (1979). Prospect theory: An analysis of decision under risk. *Econometrica, 47*(2): 263–291.

Kaldor, N. (1970). The new monetarism. *Lloyds Bank Review*, No. 97 (July): 1–18.

Katona, G. A. (1960). *The Powerful Consumer: Psychological Studies of the American Economy*. New York: McGraw-Hill.

Kay, N. M. (1979). *The Innovating Firm: A Behavioural Theory of Corporate R&D*. London: Macmillan

Kay, N. M. (1982). *The Evolving Firm: Strategy and Structure in Industrial Organization*. London: Macmillan.

Kay, N. M. (1984). *The Emergent Firm: Knowledge, Ignorance and Surprise in Economic Organization*. London: Macmillan.

Kelly, G. A. (1955). T*he Psychology of Personal Constructs*. New York: W. W. Norton.

Kelly, G. A. (1963). *A Theory of Personality*. New York: W. W. Norton.

Keynes, J. M. (1921). *A Treatise on Probability*. London: Macmillan.

Keynes, J. M. (1936). *The General Theory of Employment, Interest and Money*. London: Macmillan

Keynes, J. M. (1937). The general theory of employment. *Quarterly Journal of Economics, 51*(2): 209–223.

Keynes, J. M. (1971). *The Collected Writings of John Maynard Keynes, Volume 5: A Treatise on Money, Volume 1: The Pure Theory ofd Money*. London: Macmillan/Royal Economic Society.

Keynes, J. M. (1979). *The Collected Writings of John Maynard Keynes, Volume 29: The General Theory and After: A Supplement*. London: Macmillan/Royal Economic Society.

King, J. E. (2008). *Nicholas Kaldor (Great Thinkers in Economics Series)*. Basingstoke: Palgrave.

King, J. E., & Millmow, A. (2003). Death of a revolutionary textbook. *History of Political Economy, 35*)1): 105–134.

Koestler, A., & Smythies, J. R (eds) (1969). *Beyond Reductionism: New Perspectives in the Life Sciences*. London: Hutchinson.

Kornai, J. (1971). *Anti-Equilibrium: On Economic Systems Theory and the Tasks of Research*. Amsterdam: North-Holland.

Kuhn, T. S. (1962). *The Structure of Scientific Revolutions*. Chicago, IL: University of Chicago Press.

Laaksonen, P. (1994). *Consumer Involvement: Concepts and Research. London: Routledge.*

Lafferty, G., and Fleming, J. (2000). The restructuring of academic work in Australia: Power, management and gender. *British Journal of Sociology of Education, 21*(2): 257–267.

Lakatos, I. (1970). Falsification and the methodology of scientific research programmes. In I. Lakatos & A. Musgrave (eds), *Criticism and the Growth of Knowledge* (pp. 91–196). London, Cambridge University Press.

Lamberton, D. M. (1965). *The Theory of Profit.* Oxford: Basil Blackwell.

Lamberton, D. M. (ed.) (1971). *Economics of Information and Knowledge.* Harmondsworth: Penguin.

Lancaster, K. J. (1966). A new approach to consumer theory. *Journal of Political Economy, 75*(2): 132–157.

Latsis, S. J. (1972). Situational determinism in economics. *British Journal for the Philosophy of Science, 23*(3): 207–245.

Latsis, S. J. (ed.) (1976). *Method and Appraisal in Economics.* Cambridge: Cambridge University Press.

Lavoie, D. (1990). Hermeneutics, subjectivity and the Lester/Machlup debate: Towards a more anthropological approach to empirical economics. In W. J. Samuels (ed.), *Economics as Discourse: An Analysis of the Language of Economics* (pp. 167–184). New York: Springer.

Lavoie, M. (1985). Credits and money: The dynamic circuit, overdraft economics, and Post-Keynesian economics. In M. Jarsulic (ed.), *Money and Macro Policy* (pp. 68–84). Dordrecht: Springer

Lavoie, M. (1992). *Foundations of Post-Keynesian Economic Analysis.* Aldershot: Edward Elgar.

Lavie, M. (2024). Book review of Earl, Peter E.: *Beyond Misbehaving: Changing Universities, Pluralism, and the Evolution of a Heterodox Behavioral Economist. European Journal of Economics and Economic Policies: Intervention,* published online: April 2024; doi: 10.4337/ejeep.2024.0133.

Lee., F. S., & Earl, P. E. (eds) (1993), *The Economics of Competitive Enterprise: Selected Essays of P. W. S. Andrews.* Aldershot: Edward Elgar.

Lee, F. S., Irving-Lessman, J., Davies, J., & Earl, P. E. (1986). P. W. S. Andrews' theory of competitive oligopoly: A new interpretation. *British Review of Economic Issues, 8*(Autumn): 13–40.

Leff, N. H. (1985). Optimal investment choice for developing countries: Rational theory and rational decision-making. *Journal of Development Economics, 18*(2–3): 335–360.

Leibenstein, H. (1966). Allocative efficiency vs. "X-efficiency." *American Economic Review, 56*(3): 392–414.

Leibenstein, H. (1976). *Beyond Economic Man: A New Foundation for Economics*. Cambridge, MA: Harvard University Press.

Leijonhufvud, A. (1968). *On Keynesian Economics and the Economics of Keynes*. New York: Oxford University Press.

Leijonhufvud, A. (1969). *Keynes and the Classics.* London: Institution of Economic Affairs.

Leijonhufvud, A. (1973). Effective demand failures. *Swedish Journal of Economics, 75*(1): 27–48.

Lenton, A. P., & Stewart, A. (2008). Changing her ways: The number of options and mate-standard strength impact mate choice strategy and satisfaction. *Judgment and Decision Making, 3*(7): 501–511.

Lester, R. A. (1946). Shortcomings of marginal analysis for wage-unemployment problems. *American Economic Review, 36*i(1): 63–82.

Loasby, B. J. (1967). Making location policy work. *Lloyds Bank Review*, No. 83, 34–47; reprinted in P. E. Earl (ed.) *Behavioural Economics, Volume II*, Aldershot, Edward Elgar, 1988: 264–277.

Loasby, B. J. (1973). *The Swindon Project*. Lonson: Pitman.

Loasby, B. J. (1976). *Choice, Complexity and Ignorance*. Cambridge: Cambridge University Press.

Loasby, B. J. (1977). On imperfections and adjustments, University of Stirling Discussion Papers in Economics, Finance, and Investment, No. 50.

Loasby, B. J. (1978). Whatever happened to Marshall's theory of value? *Scottish Journal of Political Economy, 25*(1): 1–12.

Loasby, B. J. (1983). Knowledge, learning and enterprise. In J. Wiseman (ed.), *Beyond Positive Economics? Proceedings of Section F (Economics) of the British Association for the Advancement of Science, York, 1981* (pp. 104–121). London: Macmillan.

Loasby, B. J. (1987). Book review: *Lifestyle Economics. Consumer-Behaviour in a Turbulent World*, by P. E. Earl. *Scottish Journal of Political Economy*, 34(4): 420.

Loasby, B. J. (1989). *The Mind and Method of the Economist*. Aldershot: Edward Elgar.

Loasby, B. J. (1996). The division of labour. *History of Economic Ideas*, 4(1–2), 299–323.

Loasby, B. J. (1999). *Knowledge, Institutions and Evolution in Economics*. London and New York: Routledge.

Loasby, B. J. (2004). Hayek's theory of the mind. In R. Koppl (ed.), *Evolutionary Psychology and Economic Theory:Advances in Austrian Economics, Volume 7* (pp. 101–134). Oxford: Elsevier.

Lodge, D. (1989). *Nice Work*. Harmondsworth: Penguin.

Loomes, G., & Sugden, R. (1982). Regret theory: An alternative theory of rational choice under uncertainty. *Economic Journal, 92*(368): 805–824.

Lorenz, R. D. (2006). *Spinning Flight: Dynamics of Frisbees, Boomerangs, Samaras, and Skipping Stones*. New York: Springer.

Lowenstein, R. (2001). Exuberance is rational. *New York Times Magazine*, 11 February.

Lutz, M. A., & Lux, K. (1979). *The Challenge of Humanistic Economics*. Menlo Park, CA: Benjamin–Cummings Publishing.

Lutz, V. (1969). *Central Planning for the Market Economy: An Analysis of the French Theory and Experience*. Harlow: Longman, for the Institute of Economic Affairs.

Machlup, F. (1946). Marginal analysis and empirical research. *American Economic Review, 36*(4): 519–554.

Machlup, F. (1967). Theories of the firm: Marginalist, behavioral, managerial. *American Economic Review, 57*(1): 1–33.

Mackinnon, L. A. K. (2006). The Social Construction of Economic Man: The Genesis, Spread, Impact and Institutionalisation of Economic Ideas. PhD dissertation, University of Queensland.

Macmillan, P. J. (2015). Thinking Like an Expert Lawyer: Measuring Specialist Legal Expertise Through Think-Aloud Problem Solving and Verbal Protocol Analysis. PhD dissertation, Bond University, QLD.

March, J. G., & Simon, H. A. (1958). *Organizations*. New York: Wiley.

Markey-Towler, B. (2017). Foundations for Economic Analysis: The Architecture of Socioeconomic Complexity. PhD dissertation, University of Queensland.

Marris, R. L. (1964). *The Economic Theory of 'Managerial' Capitalism*. London: Macmillan.

Marshall, A. (18900. *Principles of Economics*. London: Macmillan.

Maslow, A. H. (1943). A theory of human motivation. *Psychological Review, 50*(4): 370–396.

Maslow, A. H. ([1954] 1970). *Motivation and Personality* (2nd edition, 1970). New York: Harper & Row.

McKenney, D., Perrings, C., Dovers, S., & Perman, R. (2019). In memory of Mick Common (1940–2018). *Ecological Economics, 156*: 424–426.

Meeks, G. (1977). *Disappointing Marriage: A Study of the Gains from Merger*. Cambridge: Cambridge University Press.

Mehta, J. (2013). The discourse of bounded rationality in academic and policy arenas: Pathologizing the errant consumer. *Cambridge Journal of Economics, 37*(6): 1243–1261.

Miller, A. (1972). *The Price*. New York: Bantam Books.

Millmow, A. (2021). *The Gypsy Economist. The Life and Times of Colin Clark*. Singapore: Palgrave Macmillan.

Minsky, H. P. (1975). *John Maynard Keynes*. New York: Columbia University Press (London: Macmillan, 1976).

Minsky, H. P. (1982a). *Can "It" Happen Again? Essays on Instability and Finance*. Armonk, NY: M. E. Sharpe (Published in the UK *as Inflation, Recession and Economic Recovery*. Brighton: Wheatsheaf, 1982).

Minsky, H. P. (1982b). The financial instability hypothesis: A restatement. In P. Arestis & T. Skouras (eds.), *Post Keynesian Economic Theory* (pp. 24–55). Brighton: Wheatsheaf/Armonk, NY: M.E. Sharpe.

Minsky, H. P. (1986). *Stabilizing an Unstable Economy*. New Haven, CT: Yale University Press

Mirowski, P. (1989). The measurement without theory controversy: Defeating rival research programs by accusing them of naive empiricism. *Economies et Societes, Série Oeconomia-PE*, No.11: 65–87.

Moe, A. G., & Earl, P. E. (2009). Bandwagon and reputation effects in the popular music charts. Available for downloading at: https://shredecon.files.wordpress.com/2009/12/moe-and-earl-bandwagon-effects.pdf.

Moore, B. J. (1988). *Horizontalists and Verticalists: The Macroeconomics of Credit Money*. Cambridge: Cambridge University Press.

Mosley, P. (1981). The Treasury Committee and the making of economic policy. *Political Quarterly, 52*(3): 348–355.

Myrdal, G. (1957). *Economic Theory and Underdeveloped Areas.* London: Gerald Duckworth.

Nelson, R. R., & Winter, S. G. (1982). *An Evolutionary Theory of Economic Change.* Cambridge, MA, Belknap Press of Harvard University Press.

Nicosia, F. M. (1966). *Consumer Decision Processes: Marketing and Advertising Implications.* Englewood Cliffs, NJ: Prentice–Hall.

Nightingale, J. (1994). Situational determinism revisited: Scientific research programmes in economics twenty years on. *Journal of Economic Methodology, 1*(2): 233–252.

Nightingale, J. (1997). Anticipating Nelson and Winter: Jack Downie's theory of evolutionary economic change. *Journal of Evolutionary Economics, 7*(1): 147–167.

Nightingale, J. (1998). Jack Downie's Competitive Process: The first articulated population ecological model in economics. *History of Political Economy, 30*(3): 369–412.

Nisbett, R. E., & Ross, L. (1980). *Human Inference: Strategies and Shortcomings of Social Judgment.* Englewood Cliffs, NJ: Prentice-Hall.

Olshavsky, R. W., & Granbois, D. H. (1979). Consumer decision-making – Fact or fiction? *Journal of Consumer Research, 6*(2): 93–100.

Payne, J. W., Bettman, J. R., & Johnson, E. J. (1993). *The Adaptive Decision Maker.* Cambridge: Cambridge University Press.

Peng, T.-C. (2004). Mainstream versus Heterodox Perspectives on the Dynamics of the Brisbane Residential Property Market, 1998–2003. Master's thesis, University of Queensland.

Peng, T.-C. (2009). A Pluralistic Analysis of Housing Renovation Choices in Brisbane. PhD dissertation, University of Queensland.

Perry, W. G. (1970). *Forms of Intellectual and Ethical Development in the College Years: A Schema.* New York: Holt, Rinehart and Winston.

Phelps, C. (1990). Motivational determinate of occupational choice in Arthur Miller's 'The Price'. In S. Lea, P. Webley, & B. Young (eds), *Applied Economic Psychology in the 1990s: Papers Presented to the 15th Annual Colloquium of the International Association for Research in Economic Psychology* (pp. 411–427). Exeter: Washington Singer Press.

Pickering, J. F. (1976). Book review: *Studies in Pricing*, by P. W. S. Andrews and E. Brunner. *Economic Journal*, *86*(343): 621–622,

Pickering, J. F. (1977). *The Acquisition of Consumer Durables: A Cross Sectional Investigation*. London: Associated Business Programmes.

Porter, M. E. (1980). *Competitive Strategy: Techniques for Analyzing Industries and Competitors*. New York: Free Press.

Porter, M. E. (1985). *Competitive Advantage*. New York: Free Press.

Posner, M. V. (1978). Wages, prices and the exchange rate. In M. J. Artis & A. R. Nobay (eds), *Contemporary Economic Analysis*. London: Croom Helm.

Potts, J. (1999). Choice, complexity and connections. In S. C. Dow and P. E. Earl (eds), *Contingency, Complexity and the Theory of the Firm" Essays in Honour of Brian J. Loasby, Volume II* (pp. 287–305). Cheltenham: Edward Elgar.

Potts, J. (2000). *The New Evolutionary Microeconomics: Complexity, Competition and Adaptive Behaviour*. Cheltenham: Edward Elgar.

Prais, S. J. (1973). Book Review: *New Commodities and Consumer Behaviour*, by D. S. Ironmonger. *Economic Journal* 83 (330): 578–580.

Proust, M. (1913–1927). *À la Recherche du Temps Perdu*. Paris: Éditions Grasset

Quiggin, J. (2012). *Zombie Economics: How Dead Ideas Still Walk Among Us*. Princeton, NJ: Princeton University Press.

Rabin, M. (1998). Psychology and economics. *Journal of Economic Literature, 36*(1): 11–46.

Rabin, M., & Thaler, R. H. (2001): Anomalies: Risk aversion. *Journal of Economic Perspectives, 15*(1): 219–232.

Reid, G. C. (1981). *The Kinked Demand Curve Analysis of Oligopoly*. Edinburgh: Edinburgh University Press.

Remenyi, J. V. (1979). Core demi-core interactions: Toward a general theory of disciplinary and subdisciplinary growth. *History of Political Economy, 11*(1): 30–63

Reynolds, T. J., & Gutman, J. (1984). Laddering: extending the repertory grid methodology to attribute–consequence–value hierarchies. In R. E. Pitts & A. G. Woodside (eds.), *Personal Values and Consumer Psychology* (pp. 155–167). Lexington, MA: D. C. Heath.

Ricardo, D. (1951). *The Works and Correspondence of David Ricardo, Volume I: On the Principles of Political Economy and Taxation*(edited by P. Sraffa). Cambridge: Cambridge University Press.

Richardson, G. B. (1960). *Information and Investment*. Oxford: Oxford University Press.

Richardson, G. B. (1972). The organisation of industry. *Economic Journal, 82*(327): 883–896.

Robinson, E. A. G. (1939). Review article on *Oxford Economic Papers. Economic Journal, 49*(September): 538–543.

Robinson, J. (1937). *Introduction to the Theory of Employment*. London: Macmillan (2nd edition, 1969).

Robinson, J. (1964). *Economic Philosophy*. Harmondsworth: Penguin.

Robinson, J. (1977). What are the questions? *Journal of Economic Literature, 15*(4): 1318–1339.

Robinson, J., & Eatwell, J. (1973). *An Introduction to Modern Economics*. London: McGraw-Hill.

Rostow, W. W. (1960). *The Stages of Economic Growth" A Non-Communist Manifesto*. Cambridge: Cambridge University Press.

Rotheim, R. J. (1981). Keynes' monetary theory of value. *Journal of Post Keynesian Economics, 3*(4): 568–585.

Rothschild, Lord (1982). *An Inquiry into the Social Science Research Council*. London: HMSO

Rutherford, M. (1988). Learning and decision-making in economics and psychology: A methodological perspective. In P. E. Earl (ed.), *Psychological Economics: Development, Tensions, Prospects* (pp. 35–54). Boston, MA: Kluwer Academic Publishing.

Saith, A. (2019). *Ajit Singh of Cambridge and Chandigarh: An Intellectual Biography of the Radical Sikh Economist* (Palgrave Studies in the History of Economic Thought). Cham: Springer International Publishing.

Saith, A. (2022). *Cambridge Economics in the Post-Keynesian Era: The Eclipsing of Heterodox Traditions* (Palgrave Studies in the History of Economic Thought). Cham: Springer International Publishing.

Salter, W. E. G. (1966). *Productivity and Technical Change* (2nd edition). Cambridge: Cambridge University Press.

Scherer. F. M. (2017). Ajit Singh (1940–2015). In R. Cord (ed.) *The Palgrave Companion to Cambridge Economics* (Volume II, pp. 1113–1130). London: Palgrave Macmillan.

Schoenberger, E. (1997). *The Cultural Crisis of the Firm*. Oxford, Blackwell.

Schuetz, A. (1943). The problem of rationality in the social world. *Economica,10* (38): 130–149.

Schumacher, E. F. (1973). *Small is Beautiful: A Study of Economics as if People Mattered*. London: Blond and Briggs.

Schumpeter, J. A. (1943). *Capitalism, Socialism and Democracy*. London: George Allen & Unwin (new edition, 1992, London and New York, Routledge).

Scitovsky, T. ([1951] 1971). *Welfare and Competition*. (2nd edition, 1971). Chicago, IL: Richard D. Irwin.

Selznick, P. (1957). *Leadership in Administration*. Evanston, IL: Harper & Row.

Sen, A. K. (ed.). *Growth Theory*. Harmondsworth: Penguin.

Sent, E.-M. (2004). Behavioral economics: How psychology made its (limited) way back into economics. *History of Political Economy, 36*(4): 735–760.

Shackle, G. L. S. (1940). The nature of the inducement to invest. *Review of Economic Studies, 8* (1): 44–48.

Shackle, G. L. S. (1941). A means of promoting investment. *Economic Journal, 51* (202/203): 249–260.

Shackle, G. L. S. (1943). The expectational dynamics of the individual. *Economica, 10* (38): 99–129.

Shackle, G. L. S. (1949). *Expectation in* Economics. Cambridge: Cambridge University Press.

Shackle, G. L. S. (1953). *What Makes an Economist?* Liverpool: Liverpool University Press (reprinted in Shackle, G. L. S. (1990). *Time, Expectations and Uncertainty in Economics* (edited by J. L. Ford). Aldershot: Edward Elgar).

Shackle, G. L. S. (1958). *Tine in Economics*. Amsterdam: North-Holland.

Shackle, G. L. S. (1967). *The Years of High Theory: Invention & Tradition in Economic Thought, 1926–1939*. Cambridge: Cambridge University Press.

Shackle, G. L. S. (1969). *Decision, Order and Time in Human Affairs* (2nd edition). Cambridge: Cambridge University Press.

Shackle, G. L. S. (1974). *Keynesian Kaleidics*. Edinburgh: Edinburgh University Press.

Shackle, G. L. S. (1979). *Imagination and the Nature of Choice.* Edinburgh: Edinburgh University Press.

Shackle, G. L. S. (1982). Means and meaning in economic theory. *Scottish Journal of Political Economy 29*(3): 223–234.

Shipman, A. (2019). *Wynne Godley: A Biography*. Cham: Springer.

Shone, R. (1975). *Microeconomics: A Modern Treatment*. London: Macmillan.

Shone, R. (1981). *Applications in Intermediate Microeconomics*. Oxford: Martin Robertson.

Shone, R. (1983). *Autohypnosis: A Step-by-Step Guide to Self-Hypnosis*. London: Thorsons Publishing.

Silberston, A. (1970); Surveys of applied economics: Price behaviour of firms. *Economic Journal, 80*(319): 511–582.

Simon, H. A. (1947). *Administrative Behavior*. New York: Macmillan (3rd edition 1976. New York: Free Press).

Simon, H. A. (1951). A formal theory of the employment relationship. *Econometrica, 19*(3), 293–305.

Simon, H. A. (1955). A behavioral model of rational choice. *Quarterly Journal of Economics, 69*(1): 99–118.

Simon, H. A. (1957). *Models of Man*. New York: Wiley.

Simon, H. A. (1959). Theories of decision-making in economics and behavioral science. *American Economic Review, 49*(3): 253– 283.

Simon, H. A. (1962). The architecture of complexity. *Proceedings of the American Philosophical Society, 106*(6): 467–482.

Simon, H. A. (1969). *The Sciences of the Artificial*. Cambridge, MA: MIT Press.

Simon, H. A. (1976). From substantive to procedural rationality. In S. J. Latsis (ed.), *Method and Appraisal in Economics* (pp. 129–148). Cambridge: Cambridge University Press.

Simon, H. A. (1991). *Models of My Life*. New York, NY: Basic Books.

Singh, A. (1977). UK industry and the world economy: A case of de-industrialisation? *Cambridge Journal of Economics, 1*(2)): 113–136.

Skidelsky, R. (2013). *John Maynard Keynes 1883–1946* (Abridged paperback edition). New York: Penguin.

Skinner, A. S; (1979). Adam Smith: An aspect of modern economics? *Scottish Journal of Political Economy, 26*(2): 109–125.

Smith, A. ([1795] 1980). The principles which lead and direct philosophical enquiries; illustrated by the history of astronomy. In W. P. D. Wightman (ed.), *Essays on Philosophical Subjects* (pp. 33–105). Oxford: Oxford University Press.

Sraffa, P. (1960). *Production of Commodities by Means of Commodities*. Cambridge: Cambridge University Press.

Steer, P. S., & Cable, J. R. (1978). Internal organization and profit: An empirical analysis of large companies. *Journal of Industrial Economics, 27*(1): 13–30

Steinbruner, J. D. (1974). *The Cybernetic Theory of Decision: New Dimensions of Political Analysis*. Princeton, NJ: Princeton University Press.

Stewart, M. (1967). *Keynes and After*. Harmondsworth, Penguin.

Stoneman, P. (1976). *Technological Diffusion and the Computer Revolution: The UK Experience*. Cambridge: Cambridge University Press.

Stout, D. K. (1977). *International Price Competitiveness, Non-Price Factors and Export Performance*. London: National Economic Development Office.

Strotz, R. H. (1957). The empirical implications of a utility tree. *Econometrica, 25*(2)): 269–280.

Swinnerton-Dyer, P. (1982). *Report of the Working Party on Postgraduate Education*. London: HMSO.

Thaler, R. H. (1980). Toward a positive theory of consumer choice. *Journal of Economic Behavior and Organization*, 1(1): 39–60.

Thaler, R. H. (1985). Mental accounting and consumer choice. *Marketing Science, 4*(3): 199–214.

Thaler, R. H. (2015). *Misbehaving: The Making of Behavioral Economics*. New York: W. W. Norton.

Thaler, R. H., & Shefrin, H. M. (1981). An economic theory of self-control. *Journal of Political Economy, 89*(2): 392–406.

Thaler, R. H., & Sunstein, C. R. (2008). *Nudge: Improving Decisions About Health, Welfare and Happiness*. New Haven, CT: Yale University Press.

Thirlwall, A. (1987). *Nicholas Kaldor*. Brighton: Wheatsheaf Books.

Thompson, C. J. (1996). Caring consumers: Gendered consumption meanings and the juggling lifestyle. *Journal of Consumer Research, 22*(4): 388–407.

Townsend, K. (ed.) (2020). *How to Keep your Doctorate on Track: Insights from Students' and Supervisors' Experiences*. Cheltenham: Edward Elgar.

Townsend, K., & Saunders, M. N. K. (eds) (2018). *How to Keep Your Research Project on Track: Insights from When Things Go Wrong*. Cheltenham: Edward Elgar.

Townshend, H. (1937). Liquidity premium and the theory of value. *Economic Journal, 47*(185): 157–169.

Trevithick, J. (1978). Recent developments in the theory of employment. *Sottish Journal of Political Economy, 25*(1): 107–118.

Tribe, K. (2002). The Cambridge Economics Tripos 1903–1955 and the training of economists. *Manchester School, 68*(2): 222–248.

Tribe, K. (2022). *Constructing Economic Science: The Invention of a Discipline, 1850–1955*. Oxford: Oxford University Press.

Tuck, M. (1976). *How Do We Choose? A Study in Consumer Behaviour*. London: Methuen.

Tversky, A. (1972). Elimination by aspects: A theory of choice. *Psychological Review, 79*(4): 281–299.

Uchitelle, L. (2001). Some economists call behavior a key. *New York Times*, Business section, 11 February.

Varian. H. (2014). *Intermediate Microeconomics*. New York: Norton.

Wells, W. D. (1975). Psychographics: A critical review. *Journal of Marketing Research, 12*(2): 196–213.

Wheelen, T. L., & Hunger, J. D. (1986). *Strategic Management and Business Policy* (2nd edition). Reading, MA: Addison-Wesley.

Wheelen, T. L., & Hunger, J. D. (1990). *Strategic Management* (3rd edition). Reading, MA: Addison-Wesley.

Williamson, O. E. (1964). *The Economics of Discretionary Behavior: Managerial Objectives in a Theory of the Firm*. Englewood Cliffs, NJ: Prentice-Hall.

Williamson, O. E. (1975). *Markets and Hierarchies: Analysis and Anti-Trust Implications*. New York: Free Press.

Williamson, O. E. (1985). *The Economic Institutions of Capitalism: Firms, Markets and Relational Contracting*. New York; Free Press.

Williamson, O. E., Wachter, M. L., & Harris, J. E. (1975). Understanding the employment relation: The analysis of idiosyncratic exchange. *Bell Journal of Economics, 6*(1), 250–278.

Woodward, J. (1965). *Industrial Organization: Theory and Practice*. London: Oxford University Press.

Index

Harcourt, G. C., 44, 96, 120, 133, 199°200, 206, 374
Hare, P. G., 136, 139, 194
Harper, D. A., 304
Harrigan, K. R., 214–15
Harris, J. E., 194
Harsanyi. J., 314
Hart, A. G., 249
Hart, O. S. D., 78, 101, 233
Hay, I., 378
Hay, J., 314
Hayek, F. A., 24, 112, 156, 178, 180, 184, 228, 238, 292, 353–7, 443
Hedges, M. R., 333
hedonic pricing analysis, 149, 247
Heijdra, B. J., 230, 212, 257
Henry, H., 128
Hertwig, R., 463
heuristics, 38, 83, 162–3, 227, 234, 345–7, 440, 453
    bias-inducing, 235, 439, 443, 446, 452, 454, 458, 463–4, 477
    'do' and 'don't', 187, 344
    fast and frugal, 39, 357, 457
    inherited (part of human nature), 346, 450
    non-compensatory, 132, ,245
Hey, J. D., 119, 133, 189, 218, 227, 254–5, 260, 262
Hicks, J. R., 56–7, 67–8, 72–3, 152–3, 167, 446
Hicks, U., 152
hierarchical decision processes, 162, 167, 171–80, 196, 204, 222. 245, 355, 446
hierarchical systems, 154, 222
Hinkle, D. N., 222–5, 444–7, 450
Hocking, A., 199, 204–5
Hodgson, G. M., 3–4, 159, 165, 199, 246, 438, 442
Hofstadter, D. R., 167
Hogarth, R. M., 163, 230, 235
Holbrook, M. B., 272, 293–4, 468
House of Commons, 70
Houthakker, H., 57, 128
Hughes, A., 45, 55, 86, 100, 104
Hughes, G., 89
Hunger, J. D., 214

Hutchison, T. W., 114, 293–4

income effect, 57
inflation, 14, 19, 33, 67, 100, 175, 239, 435
institutional economics, xv, 4, 127, 246, 250, 255, 270, 334, 420
introspection, 293–4, 445
Ironmonger, D. S., 37, 172, 178–80, 184, 397, 442, 446
Irving, J., 126, 192, 196, 244–5
IS–LM model, 67, 209, 232, 275
Iyer, C., 357

Jackson, D., 67
James, C., 133
Jangu, N., 284
Jefferson, M., 188, 218, 359, 470
Jefferson, T., 432
Johnson, E. J., 186, 351
Joseph, K., 194

Kahn, R. F., 70
Kahneman, D., 22, 183–4, 227, 230, 232–5, 356–8, 446, 473
Kaldor, N., 44, 50, 67–8, 140, 235, 250–1
Karayiannis, A. D., 178
Karni, E., 20
Katona, G. A., 231
Kay, N. M., 119, 122, 129, 137, 154–9, 167, 204, 218–20, 223, 237, 244–5, 303, 324, 415
Kearley, G., 79
Kelly, G. A., 10, 16, 24, 130–3, 176–8, 195, 222–5, 292, 444–5, 449–51, 470
Kemp, S., 290, 299, 304–5, 372
Keynes, J. M., 4–5, 30–1, 39, 54, 64–74, 77–84, 96, 99–102, 108–18 *passim*, 141, 144, 153–5, 159, 168, 182, 189, 193–4, 204, 209–13, 232, 237, 275, 283, 316, 34, 3360
Kidd, S. W., 30, 73, 75
King, D. N., 136, 147
King, J. E., 140, 267, 369, 438
King, M., 77
Knetsch, J., 230